DEWIGGED, BOTHERED, AND BEWILDERED

British Colonial Judges on Trial, 1800–1900

AF608025

JOHN McLAREN

Published for The Osgoode Society for Canadian Legal History and
The Francis Forbes Society for Australian Legal History by
University of Toronto Press
Toronto Buffalo London

© Osgoode Society for Canadian Legal History 2011
www.utorontopress.com
www.osgoodesociety.ca

Reprinted in paperback 2022

ISBN 978-1-4426-4437-3 (cloth)
ISBN 978-1-4875-4888-9 (paper)

Publication cataloguing information is available from Library and Archives Canada.

University of Toronto Press acknowledges the financial support of the Government of Canada through the Canada Book Fund for its publishing activities.

We wish to acknowledge the land on which the University of Toronto Press operates. This land is the traditional territory of the Wendat, the Anishnaabeg, the Haudenosaunee, the Métis, and the Mississaugas of the Credit First Nation.

University of Toronto Press acknowledges the financial support of the Government of Canada, the Canada Council for the Arts, and the Ontario Arts Council, an agency of the Government of Ontario, for its publishing activities.

Canada Council for the Arts
Conseil des Arts du Canada

Funded by the Government of Canada
Financé par le gouvernement du Canada
Canada

DEWIGGED, BOTHERED, AND BEWILDERED

British Colonial Judges on Trial, 1800–1900

Throughout the British colonies in the nineteenth century, judges were expected not only to administer law and justice but also to play a significant role within the governance of their jurisdictions. British authorities were consequently concerned about judges' loyalty to the Crown and on occasion removed or suspended those who were found politically subversive or personally difficult. Even reasonable and well-balanced judges were sometimes threatened with removal.

Using the career histories of judges who challenged the system, *Dewigged, Bothered, and Bewildered* illuminates issues of judicial tenure, accountability, and independence throughout the British Empire. John McLaren closely examines cases of judges across a wide geographic spectrum – from Australia to the Caribbean, and from Canada to Sierra Leone – who faced disciplinary action. These riveting stories provide helpful insights into the tenuous position of the colonial judiciary and the precarious state of politics in a variety of British colonies.

(Osgoode Society for Canadian Legal History)

(Forbes Society for Australian Legal History)

JOHN McLAREN is a professor emeritus in the Faculty of Law at the University of Victoria.

PATRONS OF THE SOCIETY

Blake, Cassels & Graydon LLP

Gowlings

Lax O'Sullivan Scott Lisus LLP

McCarthy Tétrault LLP

Osler, Hoskin & Harcourt LLP

Paliare Roland Rosenberg Rothstein LLP

Torkin Manes LLP

Torys LLP

WeirFoulds LLP

The Osgoode Society is supported by a grant from
The Law Foundation of Ontario.

The Society also thanks The Law Society of Upper Canada
for its continuing support.

This volume is dedicated to the late A.W.B. 'Brian' Simpson (1931–2011) who epitomized the very best legal historical research and writing, was an inspiration to legal historians of the Common Law world, and was a most amusing lecturer and raconteur. He is sorely missed.

Contents

Foreword

THE OSGOODE SOCIETY FOR CANADIAN LEGAL HISTORY

Canada was but one part of a large and complex empire, and this book is a reminder of that fact and a fascinating exploration of one important aspect of the legal history of the empire – the role of superior court judges. Professor John McLaren gives us a series of case studies of nineteenth-century judges from across the empire, including, of course, the Canadian colonies, who found themselves the centre of political controversy and were either suspended or removed from office. Frequently they landed in another colony, despite their chequered pasts. The book also provides a very useful and informative survey of the process of judicial appointments and the developing rules on judicial independence within the empire.

The purpose of the Osgoode Society for Canadian Legal History is to encourage research and writing in the history of Canadian law. The Society, which was incorporated in 1979 and is registered as a charity, was founded at the initiative of the Honourable R. Roy McMurtry, formerly attorney general for Ontario and chief justice of the province, and officials of the Law Society of Upper Canada. The Society seeks to stimulate the study of legal history in Canada by supporting researchers, collecting oral histories, and publishing volumes that contribute to legal-historical scholarship in Canada. It has published eighty-four books on the courts, the judiciary, and the legal profession, as well as on the history of crime and punishment, women and law, law and economy, the legal treatment of ethnic minorities, and famous cases and significant trials in all areas of the law.

Current directors of the Osgoode Society for Canadian Legal History are Robert Armstrong, Christopher Bentley, Kenneth Binks, David Chernos, Kirby Chown, J. Douglas Ewart, Violet French, Martin Friedland, Philip Girard, John Honsberger, Horace Krever, C. Ian Kyer, Virginia MacLean, Patricia McMahon, R. Roy McMurtry, Laurie Pawlitza, Paul Perell, Jim Phillips, Paul Reinhardt, Joel Richler, William Ross, Paul Schabas, Robert Sharpe, Mary Stokes, and Michael Tulloch.

The annual report and information about membership may be obtained by writing to the Osgoode Society for Canadian Legal History, Osgoode Hall, 130 Queen Street West, Toronto, Ontario, M5H 2N6. Telephone: 416-947-3321. E-mail: mmacfarl@lsuc.on.ca. Website: www.osgoodesociety.ca

R. Roy McMurtry
President

Jim Phillips
Editor-in-Chief

Foreword

THE FRANCIS FORBES SOCIETY FOR AUSTRALIAN LEGAL HISTORY

John McLaren is an important figure in the study of Australian legal history. He visits Australia frequently and has delivered a number of public lectures and conference papers there. His significance lies in his comparative approach to the history of the British legal empire. He has published influential books and was the primary compiler of a brilliant comparative legal history course, which was taught simultaneously in Canadian and Australian law schools. Students in both countries studied the same materials in the same week.

Dewigged, Bothered, and Bewildered is the culmination of Professor McLaren's comparative approach. It shows how colonial judges were appointed, how they were disciplined, and how they took legal ideas from one colony to the next, developing colonial law that was sometimes as much influenced by other colonies as it was by the law of England.

The Francis Forbes Society for Australian Legal History (ABN 55 099 158 620) was established in 2002. Inspired by and partly modelled on the Osgoode Society, its principal object is to encourage the study of the history of Australian law and, to that end, to publish books and other publications and to promote continuing education and the compilation of records of Australian and Indigenous law. It has already published several books, and it cooperates with journals in the publication of articles and lectures. It conducts an annual Forbes lecture and an essay competition for students, and it publishes research papers on its website at www.forbessociety.org.au.

The current members of its Council are Bruce Kercher, The Hon. Keith Mason AC, QC, Wendy Robinson QC, Geoff Lindsay SC, Carol Webster, Michael Tidball, Laurie Glanfield AM, Michael Pelly, and Stephen Toomey. Its Honorary Executive Director is Philip Selth OAM, Executive Director of the New South Wales Bar Association. The Society's membership, which is open to the public, includes senior lawyers drawn from the ranks of the judiciary, barristers, solicitors, and academics.

Membership information may be obtained by writing to the Secretary, Geoff Lindsay SC, at secretary@forbessociety.org.au or at Francis Forbes Society for Australian Legal History, Basement, Selborne Chambers, 174 Phillip Street, Sydney, NSW 2000.

Bruce Kercher
President

Philip Selth
Honorary Executive Director

Preface

This book is the product of a developing interest in teaching and researching comparative British colonial history. Much of the inspiration came from a joint teaching learning venture (OZCAN) involving faculty and students at four Australian and Canadian law schools between 1997 and 2005. Tribute is due to both groups for exciting this interest and piquing my curiosity in colonial judicial cultures. The faculty included Simon Bronitt, Ian Holloway, and John Williams at ANU; Andrew Buck at Macquarie; and Lyndsay Campbell, Doug Harris, and Wes Pue at UBC.

The research for the book would not have been possible without the important financial support of the Social Sciences and Humanities Research Council of Canada, directly through a three-year research grant (2006–9), and indirectly, through an internal seed grant from my own university. My deep appreciation goes out to that body.

I was assisted in my research by Emily Boyle, Stefan Jensen, and Nicole O'Brien, each of whom did important archival work on segments of the book. Special plaudits are due to John McCurdy, who served as my overall research associate for the years of the grant and who embodies that combination of skills, enthusiasm, initiative, and insight that constitutes the inspired researcher. The output and quality of his research were phenomenal, and I appreciated his running commentary on what he was finding and enjoyed the conversations to which they gave rise.

The scope of the book involved travel and consultation with historians in several regions of the former British Empire. I owe them a deep debt of gratitude for their guidance and enthusiasm for the project, and, in several cases, for outstanding hospitality. Bruce Kercher in Sydney went way beyond the call of duty by reviewing an earlier version of the manuscript and lending both great encouragement and helpful commentary to my work. Stefan Petrow in Hobart and John Williams in Adelaide reviewed chapters and provided guidance with access to archival material in Tasmania and South Australia respectively, as well as acting as delightful hosts. Peter Moore of Crossing Press in Sydney helped me with editing the chapter on Judge Boothby and opened up for me a new dimension to this turbulent judge's career – his financial difficulties. Andrew Buck and Nancy Wright offered elegant shelter in both Sydney and the Blue Mountains, during which we spent many hours indulging our mutual interests in legal history, popular culture, jazz, and much more. Elizabeth Olsson in Adelaide was generous in making available her collection of research materials on Justice Boothby. Justice Paul Mullaly, Janine Rizzetti and Chris O'Brien in Melbourne and Ned Fletcher in Auckland helped me hone my insights on John Walpole Willis, whom they too have researched. Through the good offices of David Williams in Auckland I was able to share work in progress with New Zealand colleagues. In the Caribbean I was similarly welcomed and encouraged. Bridget Brereton was a great source of insights into the political and social, as well as the legal, history of Trinidad and Tobago, shared her extensive knowledge of the life and times of Sir John Gorrie, and assisted me in navigating the archives in Port-of-Spain. In Barbados, Anthony Phillips gave me the benefit of his broad grasp of the legal history of that island and the British West Indies more generally. Nathan Brun at the Hebrew University and Maria del Pilar Kaladeen at Royal Holloway College of the University of London shared important information on Chief Justice McDonnell's quarrel with the high commissioner of the Palestinian Mandated Territory, and on the trials and tribulations of Chief Justice Beaumont in British Guiana, respectively. Keith Smith and his family were excellent hosts at the British end of my research, and I benefited from Keith's expansive knowledge of nineteenth-century English legal history.

Jim Phillips, editor-in-chief of the Osgoode Society for Canadian Legal History book series, has been the consummate guide and counsellor, combining enthusiasm for my work and inspired suggestions for substantive enrichment, with a welcome firmness in reining in a propensity for verbosity on my part. Marilyn MacFarlane, the society's administrator, has, as always, provided helpful and genial guidance on the publication process. Michel Morin helped me with important leads on judicial accountability in Lower Canada (Quebec). I am also grateful to John Weaver and Barry Wright, who reviewed the manuscript anonymously for the Osgoode Society and who were both positive in their comments and had valuable suggestions for improving the quality of the text. The editorial staff at the University of Toronto Press, especially Len Husband and Wayne Herrington, have been a pleasure to work with. Closer to home I feel fortunate to have had the constant support of two colleagues and friends in this venture, Hamar Foster and Ben Berger, both of whom not only talk the talk but walk the walk in recognizing the value of history and historical research in understanding legal cultures. Rosemary Garton of the Faculty of Law was generous with her time and enormously efficient in helping with the administrative and secretarial dimensions of the project.

Given the geographic scope of this book, it is very gratifying that the Francis Forbes Society for Australian Legal History has agreed that it should be published under its banner as well as that of the Osgoode Society. My thanks to the Forbes Society's president, Bruce Kercher, and secretary, Geoff Lindsay, SC, for making this fruitful example of scholarly collaboration possible.

Last but not least, I appreciate the support and encouragement of Ann and our children, who have been so willing to indulge my flights into nineteenth-century colonial culture and the lives and times of some of the judges who served the empire in the colonies, and who were patient with me in the sometimes difficult process of my returning to the twenty-first century and the realities of this world.

DEWIGGED, BOTHERED, AND BEWILDERED

British Colonial Judges on Trial, 1800–1900

1

Colonial Judges in Trouble: Setting the Scene

A Man of Law's Tale

Lieutenant Governor Peregrine Maitland of Upper Canada ordered Justice John Walpole Willis, puisne judge of the province's Court of King's Bench, removed from office in June 1828. By challenging the legality of the actions of the conservative law officers of the Crown, by consorting with reformist politicians and questioning the constitutionality of the Court sitting with less than a full bench, this judge had driven the colonial executive to the point of exasperation.[1] But this was not to be the end of Willis's troubles as a colonial judge. Having persuaded the Colonial Office that he had been unjustly treated in Upper Canada, if not on the merits of his case then by virtue of faulty process in not allowing him to respond to the charges against him, London appointed him to the British Guiana bench. There he served by and large without legal complication, although he developed a chronic liver complaint associated with dysentery or malaria. In 1836 he accepted an invitation from the Colonial Office to transfer to the Australian colony of New South Wales as an associate justice of its Supreme Court. Six years later, in June 1843, Governor George Gipps removed Willis from office in that colony. As a judge in Sydney, Willis had by his actions and incautious comments antagonized his judicial colleagues and the Roman Catholic population of the colony. In 1839 Gipps sent him to become the new resident judge in Port Phillip (now Melbourne) to avoid the ongoing bad blood with his judicial brethren. In the new location, Willis's increasingly choleric disposition, his antipathy to those in authority in and the gentlemanly elite of the district, his perceived partiality in cases argued before him, and continued sniping at his colleagues in Sydney so severely tried the governor's patience that he gave the judge his marching orders in June 1843. Although Willis succeeded in an appeal to the Judicial Committee of the Privy Council over the failure of the governor to accord him a hearing, this proved a pyrrhic victory. In their terse advice to the monarch, their lordships added the gratuitous opinion that on the basis of what they had heard and read, Gipps had adequate substantive grounds for removing the judge in this instance. No further judicial preferment was forthcoming and Willis faded from history.[2]

The Tale and Its Relevance to the Tenure and Accountability of Colonial Judges

Although the disciplining of Willis not once but twice in different colonies provides a particularly dramatic tale of a colonial judge in trouble, that story, along with those of other judges who suffered or were threatened with discipline during the nineteenth century, have a deeper significance. These narratives provide intriguing insights into the administration of justice in the higher courts of the colonies; imperial and local colonial expectations about judicial loyalty to the mission of colonial governance and the role of the judge within the colonial system; the systems for disciplining recalcitrant colonial judges; and the perils associated with a colonial judge speaking out in opposition to a colonial executive or legislature on a matter of law or politics or both. More broadly, these tales speak to competing interpretations of the rule of law in imperial, colonial, and judicial circles in the British Empire during that century.

The Scope of the Study and Its Place in Judicial Historiography

In the core of this book I examine these issues of judicial tenure, accountability, and independence, or lack of it, through a set of histories of colonial judges disciplined for 'misbehaviour' or threatened with discipline.

The major focus, the nineteenth century, reflects my sense that it is in that time span that one sees most clearly both the mechanics and the legal and political impacts of judicial disciplining in a wide range of colonial possessions. After the shock of the American Revolution and the departure of the thirteen colonies, the British Empire grew significantly in size and global span through the nineteenth century, comprising settler, plantation, trading, penal, and strategic colonies. The imperial system's disciplining of judges took place across that world. I also argue that the attempts to remove or suspend several colonial judges related to the broader politics of empire. Accordingly, it is possible within this time span to trace important changes in imperial policy on – and priorities relating to – colonial governance, and how those played out in the careers and lives of 'troublous' justices.

It is important to emphasize that the scope of the study is selective and, therefore, limited in both geographic and biographical scope. In the multiracial empire (where non-Europeans outnumbered Europeans), India receives only passing mention. The focus is firmly on the Caribbean colonies and island possessions in the Indian Ocean and South Pacific.[3] The coverage of the white settler empire is more extensive, but even here the account is not exhaustive. In a biographical context, the study does not track the career and impact of every colonial judge who got into trouble in the colonies or region examined. My concern has been to concentrate on those individuals who were targets because they actively engaged in colonial politics, who otherwise found difficulty in navigating the uncertain line between law and politics, or whose views on law and justice became a political embarrassment. Only brief reference is made to those jurists who suffered discipline or criticism for their morals, were charged with criminal conduct, or received their marching orders for being indolent or incompetent. Finally, with one exception, the parts of the narrative that deal with white settler possessions do not cover the period after the grant of responsible government in the 1840s and 1850s.[4] The hope is that the present work will provide an impetus to other scholars to expand the scope of this type of investigation.

Issues of judicial accountability and tenure have attracted the attention of legal historians in England.[5] There is also a fast-developing literature on the lives and times of British colonial judges.[6] Several legal historians in Australia and Canada have examined closely the role and careers of the judges in individual colonial states, with special reference to issues of judicial independence (or lack of it).[7] This is the first work to engage in a comparative examination of the accountability and tenure of colonial judges within the British imperial system. It draws on the scholarship already mentioned and takes inspiration from a growing comparative imperial and colonial legal historiography on law and the administration of justice across the British colonial world.[8] In view of the fact that judges, as well as other imperial officials, moved within the empire to new postings, taking their views on law and justice with them, and were part of a web of contacts with both the metropolis and other colonies that influenced them, reference is made to the recent suggestive literature that investigates those peregrinations and networks.[9]

In a thoughtful reflection on judicial biography, Philip Girard points to the value of work that focuses on what we know about the professional careers of the judiciary, and uses the data to explore not only their role in constructing and working with legal institutions and developing doctrine, but also their interaction with the societies in which they served. He describes it as the 'the windows on the age' approach to judicial biography.[10] This is the approach I take in this book, in comparing and contrasting the careers of colonial judges in several regions of the British Empire through the nineteenth century. It is a calculated exercise in story telling that uses the empirical, qualitative study of the professional lives and experiences of a set of colonial jurists to demonstrate the challenges that the imperial constitution, the assumptions of both London and the local governments about the judicial role in colonial governance, and the often visceral politics of the colonies, presented to those administering justice in them. It also records how they reacted to and addressed those realities. The work benefits from a pattern of analysis and synthesis exemplified in recent studies by Anthony Musson on late medieval English judges and lawyers, Mary Jane Mossman's comparisons of the experiences of the first women lawyers in a range of jurisdictions, and Tony Earls in his examination of the careers of lawyers in nineteenth-century New South Wales and Victoria.[11]

A Narrative on the Disciplining of British Colonial Judges

None of the stories that I tell about defrocked judges or those threatened with discipline exist in isolation, but they reflect attitudes and ways of thinking about judicial tenure over previous centuries. They need, therefore, to be put into a broader context of judicial accountability tenure and independence, briefly in England, and then more extensively in the pre-1800 English and British imperial worlds.

Chapter 2 begins with a historical introduction to judicial accountability, and the struggle for judicial independence in England that led to its recognition in the Act of Settlement of 1701 with the acceptance of appointments 'during good behaviour.'[12] Most attention is paid to the seventeenth century and the attempts by the Stuart monarchs to have the Common Law judges do their political bidding, and both judicial and parliamentary resistance to those efforts. Those battles over judicial independence have both circumstantial and political resonance, as well as discursive similarities to the colonial conflicts at the core of this book. Reference is also made to what judicial independence in England actually meant in practice after 1701.

In seeking to understand why the tenure of colonial judges was generally more tenuous than that of their English colleagues, it is important to consider the status and supervision of judges in the English or first British Empire. This is also a focus of chapter 2. These appointments 'at the pleasure of the Crown' gave rise to several conflicts about who should hire and fire colonial judges – London or local legislatures – and where the jurists' loyalties should lie, most especially in the years just before the American Revolution. The imperial government's resistance to colonial attempts to extend local power in these matters, and colonial reaction to interference from the centre are traced, as well as the effects of this history on what remained of British rule in the Americas. The geographic scope is the thirteen American colonies and the possessions in the Caribbean, as well as the British North American colony of Nova Scotia, founded in the mid-eighteenth century.

In chapter 3 I examine the developing institutional and supervisory context of imperial supervision of the colonial judiciary, the general contours of judicial appointment, tenure and independence across the empire during the nineteenth century, and both the imperial and colonial authorities' expectations of judges. Consideration is also given to the latter's agency as the transmitters of English law and culture to the colonies, and the challenges they faced in applying English law, local law, or a combination of the two to the issues that came before them, during that era. I also consider the professional backgrounds, selection and conditions of appointment, and working circumstances of colonial jurists appointed during the nineteenth century, by comparison with their English counterparts.

Chapters 4 to 10 focus on the stories of particular colonial judges who were disciplined or threatened with discipline for conduct considered unbecoming, during the nineteenth century.

In chapter 4 the context is the fate of judges who preached reformist political and constitutional ideas in settler colonies in the period of counter-revolutionary imperial ideology and practice, that marked the first three decades of the nineteenth century. The focus shifts in chapter 5 to the different experience of colonial jurists who embodied overriding loyalty to the colonial state, during that same period of conservatism and backward-looking constitutionalism, and those of that ilk who in 1830s were faced with changing circumstances, as reformist, liberal understandings about the constitutional relationship between settler colonies and the metropolis began to take hold. The geographic setting of these chapters is British North America, especially Upper Canada, Lower Canada, and Newfoundland.

The subject of chapters 6, 7, and 6 is the tension between colonial executives and judges, or legislatures and judges over whether English law or locally generated law, reflecting colonial opinion about perceived social and economic needs of the community, should enjoy primacy. The Australian colonies are at the centre of this part of the study. In chapter 6 the battles between governors and professional judges in New South Wales over the introduction of English law between 1810 and 1830 are analysed. In chapter 7 the focus is the relative status of local statutory and regulatory law and its repugnancy to English law in the Australian colonies of Van Diemen's Land (Tasmania) and New South Wales between 1830 and 1850. Chapter 8 addresses the major *casus belli* over the doctrine of repugnancy, and its relationship to colonial self-government in South Australia, during the late 1850s and the 1860s.

Chapters 9 and 10 address the perilous nature of judicial service in Britain's West Indian colonies, where judges reacted unfavourably to the gross social and economic inequalities and racial tensions in those possessions, and sought to uphold the English notion of the rule of law in the system's dealings with non-European majorities. In chapter 9 the focus is the period before the abolition of slavery throughout the British Empire in 1834. It switches in chapter 10 to the remainder of the century, a period marked by the introduction of new and oppressive labour regimes in Britain's Caribbean and Indian Ocean possessions. I highlight imperial anxieties about civil unrest or outright rebellion in these territories after 1865, and its manifestation in moves towards closer political and legal control of these territories, including increased constraints on judicial independence.

In the final chapter, chapter 11, I set out my general conclusions on the role and challenges of the judiciary in the colonial state during the nineteenth century. Furthermore, as an earlier history of judicial accountability influenced judicial discipline during that period, it is relevant to consider briefly how it affected events after 1900. The issue of judicial independence or lack of it continued to be an irritant from time to time in the relations between the British Crown and its colonies during the twentieth century. Furthermore, even in the dominions and later the post-colonial states that emerged after independence, the seemingly timeless, enduring, and unresolved issue of the proper relationship of the judges to politics has continued to cause tension. Accordingly, soul-searching of where to set the balance between judicial independence and accountability remains in the former British colonial world. This afterlife of judicial tenure and accountability is touched on briefly in the final chapter.

2

Judicial Tenure, Accountability, and Independence in the Common Law World before 1800

To understand the histories of judicial tenure and accountability in the British Empire in the nineteenth century, it is important to have a sense of not only the struggle for judicial independence in England itself before 1701, but also of the status and exercise of control over colonial judges in the pre-1800 empire.

Judicial Tenure, Accountability, and Independence in Pre-Eighteenth-Century England

There is a long history of judicial discipline in England prior to 1701.[1] Before the seventeenth century, judges in the royal courts acted primarily as the servants of the monarch. First of all, the King or Queen sought to exercise control over their behaviour through the oath that judges took on assuming office, which, while enjoining them to exercise equal justice between other litigants, expected them to serve the royal interest where it was involved in suits before them.[2] The other key instrument of control was their appointment at pleasure, which meant that their tenure was subject to a ruler's distaste or even whim.[3] On accession every new monarch was entitled to review existing judicial appointments, providing a third opportunity for royal angst to be visited on those in disfavour.[4] During the fourteenth century, several royal justices suffered discipline and punishment for backing the wrong horse politically, and crossing the monarch, or his enemies.[5] One particular context in which judges were expected to do the ruler's bidding was in providing extrajudicial advice, typically to indicate their opinions on pending prosecution or litigation in which the royal interest was engaged. The classic examples involved treason charges.[6]

It was the seventeenth century, however, that was to provide a battleground over the terms of appointment of the royal judges, and who was endowed with the authority to remove them from office or otherwise punish them.[7] At the opening of the century, the traditional mechanisms of control over the judiciary continued – the oath, now expanded to ensure allegiance to the Anglican faith, appointments at pleasure, and a new monarch's review of judges' records.[8] In James I's reign, two opposing models of judicial responsibility emerged, reflecting very different ideologies of constitutional legitimacy and the role of the Common Law. The first, associated with Sir Edward Coke, argued that as the King, like other mortals, was under the law, most notably the Common Law, a system of great respectability and vintage, he and his officers were subject to the jurisdiction and the application and interpretation of the law by the stewards of that body of law, the judges of King's Bench, Common Pleas, and Exchequer (the 'Cokeian' model).[9] That view, supported by appeal to an Ancient Constitution and the 'rights of freeborn Englishmen' had strong support in Parliament among those committed to the subversion of any 'Divine Right of Kings' doctrine, an expansive understanding of the rule of law and to the ascendancy of the legislative branch within the constitution.[10] Parliamentary pressure that persuaded Charles I in 1642 to revise the terms of appointment of judges, granting them tenure during good behaviour, reflected that alternative conception of the judicial role.[11] The rival vision, propounded by Lord Francis Bacon, emphasized that, above all else, judges must be loyal servants of the monarch who was constitutionally at the apex of legal power and authority in the land, whose word was literally law, and to whom they owed allegiance through both the ruler's appointment of them and their oaths of office (the 'Baconian' model).[12] The latter view reflected that of the Stuarts, who expected the judges to practise loyalty and deference to them, provide supportive advice when it was sought, and promote the royal interest in constitutional challenges. Charles I's manipulation of the judges to support his exactions of the ship tax and other imposts to pay for rearming his navy and army provides a singular example of support for this model.[13]

Lord Protector Cromwell trod carefully in chastising his judges because he lacked confidence in his constitutional status. Neither Charles II nor James II, however, felt so constrained and sought to ensure a Baconian bench.[14] The terms of appointment reverted in 1678 to tenure during the King's pleasure during Charles II's reign, a practice maintained by his brother. The period up to 1688 was marked by an expanding number of judicial sackings, especially under James, as some on the bench resisted these executive pressures and sought to divine and apply the law impartially and independently of the royal will.

A new element in the equation was that Parliament periodically challenged the contention that only the monarch was empowered to discipline the judges. With the help of Coke – whom James I had removed from the bench for his opposition to the exercise of the royal prerogative and sat as a member of the Commons in opposition to the King – the legislature rediscovered the old institution of impeachment. It provided the means for the Commons and Lords to call royal officials before them to account for their actions, to level serious charges against them (the role of the Commons), and to try them for 'high crimes' (the task of the Lords). From the 1620s oppositionists used it to attack judges partial to the Crown and its policies. In one of the more dramatic examples of the process, Parliament found Justice Robert Berkeley of King's Bench guilty of high treason for siding with Charles I in John Hampden's challenge to the ship tax, fined him heavily, and disabled him from holding further office.[15]

Stuart judges, like it or not, were in a position of having to make choices between loyalty to the monarch, or to the Common Law and the will of Parliament. Even though, to their credit, a number of jurists stood up in a principled way to the Crown's badgering and threats, the fact that others proved both servile and vindictive – like Lord Chief Justice William Scroggs under Charles II and his counterpart, George Jeffreys, in James II's reign – caused a palpable decline in the reputation of the judiciary.[16] James's wholesale and opportunistic changing of the judicial guard during his reign was one factor in moves to rid the country of him.[17]

Under the new constitutional order associated with the Glorious Revolution of 1688, formal recognition was accorded to judicial independence in the Act of Settlement.[18] Although the monarch would appoint judges, tenure was henceforth to be during good behaviour, and authority for removing judges from office was vested in the two houses of Parliament through the device of a joint address. The reality was that English judicial appointments continued to reflect political loyalties, depending on which elite political grouping was in the ascendant in Westminster and was in a position to reward its supporters and parliamentary placemen.[19] However, it is also true that normally it was talented leaders at the bar with well-established reputations that secured preferment. Moreover, it seems undeniable that the new system protected jurists who challenged the Crown and the state from punitive action by the executive. Chief Justice Charles Pratt of the Court of Common Pleas (later Lord Camden) – in declaring illegal, arbitrary, and oppressive executive acts against the populist politician John Wilkes and his friends in the mid-eighteenth century – provides a notable example.[20]

Although the second British Empire dates effectively from the reaction of imperial politicians during and in the wake of the American War of Independence in the second half of the 1780s and early 1790s, the end date for this discussion is 1800. By that time several of the features of the new imperial order had begun to take shape, especially in the case of the new British North American colonies of Lower and Upper Canada. These possessions constituted 'flag ships' for how the British government intended to create and organize settler colonies, in order to avoid the mistakes made in the thirteen American colonies.[21] The end date also falls within the long period of warfare between Great Britain and France, in which the British acquired new colonial territories in the West Indies, southern Africa, and the Indian Ocean. These territories possessed either strategic military, or economic significance, or both. They also had racially segmented and ethnically diverse populations. For these reasons, London considered that they required even closer imperial control and more limited political and legal rights for their populations than existed in settler colonies.

The discussion also recognizes that the discontinuities with the pre-Revolutionary empire were not complete. The remaining colonies in the Americas, such as Nova Scotia, Barbados, and Jamaica, continued under systems of governance and law established earlier, although now with a propensity by the imperial authorities to try to control more closely those of strategic importance.[22]

The Colonial Judiciary in the English Empire of the Seventeenth Century

The development of the English Empire was not systematic. In the seventeenth century, colonies were established in a variety of ways: by commercial charters, by proprietary grants by the royal prerogative, and even by religious covenant.[23] Apart from specific directions in the various grants, patents, and instructions to named persons or bodies to run particular colonies, and the understanding that it was English law that settlers took with them, considerable discretion existed in local officials and the colonists themselves in constructing justice systems appropriate to colonial conditions.[24] Because of distance, and political and constitutional turmoil in England itself, imperial control was often weak, providing leeway to colonists to experiment.[25] As representative assemblies became the norm, there was a strong impulse among the locals to view the administration of justice and governance generally as self-determined and local in quality.[26] When courts were established in colonies, the sparseness of the settler populations, the straightforward nature of the legal issues, and the lack of professional lawyers all spoke in favour of simplicity in institutional structure, the use of lay justices, and avoidance of the complex procedures of the royal courts and of strict application of English law (if anyone could remember it clearly), in favour of relevant, home-grown solutions.[27]

In North America, despite variations in governance between the New England and Chesapeake colonies, there existed a 'relatively simple, layered system of courts.'[28] At the apex were the colonial legislative bodies, which followed the English Parliament's view of itself as a court, heard appeals. and in some instances took original jurisdiction (unlike Parliament). Below that level there were superior courts that had original jurisdiction and assize functions in a range of civil matters and capital crimes, comprising the governor of the colony assisted by an appointed council (for example, the Quarter Court in Virginia), or elected assessors (for instance, the Assistants' Court in Massachusetts). At the base, with a broad civil and criminal jurisdiction, stood the local courts, with single or multiple justices sitting as quarter sessions (as in Massachusetts and New York), or county courts (as in the Chesapeake colonies). These last institutions, like their counterparts in England, exercised wide legislative and administrative functions as well as judicial ones, constituting the core of local government.[29] There was a lack of any notion of the separation of powers in the court systems. The political, social, and legal dimensions of law and justice were indistinguishable. Lawrence Friedman notes, 'The same people made rules, enforced them, handled disputes and ran the colony.'[30] The absence of professionally trained judges and lawyers meant that the law that was applied relied on imperfect understandings or recollections of English law, laced with English customs and invented American solutions to problems that seemed to fit the circumstances.[31] The doctrine of precedent was not much in evidence, still less law reporting.[32]

The pattern of courts in the British West Indies was at once more variegated and more reflective of English models than was true of North American colonies. All the early Caribbean colonies shared the institutional reality that governors and councils were the final colonial courts of appeal.[33] Jamaica had the most advanced and uncomplicated system, with a single supreme court, supplemented by two courts of assize over which a single chief justice presided. This was in contrast to Barbados, in which civil and criminal jurisdictions were divided and which had separate courts of chancery, exchequer, common pleas, and probate, as well as a vice-admiralty court and courts of grand and quarter sessions.

Governors, superior court justices, and the justices of the peace were laymen. Moreover, the same individuals, all drawn from the planter elite or their friends, could and did occupy executive, legislative, and judicial roles contemporaneously.[34] Parallel legal systems law co-existed, the one applying to white settlers and residents administered by facsimiles of the Westminster courts and the magistracy, the other governing the slave population, embodied in slave codes or legislation formulated by colonial assemblies, and administered by separate slave courts or by the magistracy operating under special laws. Two magistrates, assisted by three freeholders, usually administered these courts without juries. The original model for a slave code was that of Barbados, devised in 1661 and revised in 1688.[35] Slave legislation was designed to underline both the status of slaves as the property of their masters and, most especially, the threat that they posed to public order.[36] Little, if any, reference was made to their protection from abuse.[37]

Recorded instances of dissatisfaction with judicial behaviour in the seventeenth-century North American colonies reflected tension between a social elite and the population-at-large in the colony. An example is the dispute at mid-century between the magistrates and freemen in Massachusetts because of the elitism of the former. This conflict led to the promulgation of the *Laws and Libertyes* of that colony, issued in 1648, specifically to make them broadly accessible and thus available 'to educate all citizens.'[38] George Haskins observes that a widely held view was that the leaders 'who sat as judges in every one of the courts of the colony, could not be trusted to decide fairly unless the rules which were to guide their decisions were public property.'[39]

Imperial Direction, Colonial Resistance, and the Colonial Judiciary, 1700–1760

In the wake of the Glorious Revolution of 1688 and the establishment of political stability in England, the imperial gaze descended more often and closely than before on the American and West Indian colonies.[40] Politically, despite the new constitutional order's domestic emphasis on Parliament's pre-eminence in law-making, London's attempts to superintend its colonies more systematically took take place almost exclusively under the royal prerogative. The Board of Trade and Plantations deployed various instruments of control, direction, and advice – commissions and instructions issued to colonial governors in royal colonies, and ongoing correspondence with those officials – to achieve greater control and consistency.[41] Moreover, the power of the Privy Council to review and disallow legislation from colonies and to take appeals from colonial courts was accentuated and invoked more often.[42] Central to imperial concerns about the concurrence of imperial and colonial law, and resistance in the colonies to that pressure, was the doctrine of repugnancy and its corollary, permissible divergence, both embedded in the unwritten imperial constitution. As early as 1663 the Rhode Island Charter articulated the two elements: 'The laws, ordinances and constitutions [of Rhode Island], so made, be not contrary and repugnant unto, but as near as may be, agreeable to the laws of our realm of England, considering the nature and constitution of the place and people there.'[43]

Enshrined later in Sir William Blackstone's writings, this instrument for balancing an imperial wish for control and consistency with a colonial desire for leeway to craft law and legal solutions that seemed appropriate to local circumstances would loom large in tensions between colonial judges, executives, and legislatures.[44] Greater sophistication in judicial analysis developed as superior courts with both trial and appellate jurisdiction and encouraged to apply English law replaced the conciliar or elected appeal courts of the seventeenth century, and distinctive legal professions emerged in the colonies.[45] Law and its articulation gradually became more formal, propelled by a desire for increased rationality, and the system became more demanding of legal knowledge and experience among the colonial judiciary.[46] However, this pattern of professionalization of the judiciary affected only its higher reaches, and, even then, it was by no means consistent across the empire.

London sought to extend and consolidate its control over judicial appointments, tenure, and judicial accountability in its colonies. That concern about the quality of judicial appointees was growing is evident in communications dispatched to the Board of Trade. Governors complained from time to time: 'The earl of Bellmont [governor of New York], writing from New York in 1698, drew a vivid picture of conditions in that province: "Colonel Smith, one of the council, is chief justice in that province, but is no sort of lawyer, having been bred a soldier. He is a man of sense and a more gentlemanlike man than any I have seen in this province, but that does not make him a lawyer ... As to the men that call themselves lawyers here and practice at the bar, they are almost all under such a scandalous character, that it would grieve a man to see our English laws so miserably mangled and profaned."'[47]

Members of colonial communities were also responsible for other letters that were critical of governors as the local sources of judicial appointments: 'An anonymous writer prepared a paper in 1700 describing the conditions of the courts in the colonies, with special reference to Barbados. The state of affairs was so bad, he declared, that even English merchants were unwilling to venture much in colonial trade, for they "find more security and better and more speedy justice in the most distant provinces of the Ottoman dominions from their bashaws, than they do in some of the American colonies, though under the dominion of their own prince."'[48]

The root of the problem, in this writer's opinion, was the power of governors to appoint judges, which he urged should be removed from them. Spurred on by these and other complaints, the Board of Trade initiated steps through instructions to governors to improve the quality and speed of justice in territories under their rule.

The British government's assertive role in supervising colonial justice became a bone of contention as its expectations that judges should work closely with the governor in administering justice and applying English law clashed with the notion that judges were accountable to the local legislative assembly.

From the seventeenth century, imperial practice had dictated that royal appointment of colonial judges, typically by governors, was at the pleasure of the Crown, although there was no explicit, formal instruction to that effect.[49] Two concerns prompted this claim of the royal prerogative. On the one hand, London wanted to make sure that judges should not suffer removal from office without 'good and sufficient cause,' which meant that governors had to justify their actions in disciplining jurists.[50] On the other, the imperial authorities wanted to exercise a power, if it proved necessary, to discipline colonial judges who became an embarrassment, not only because of personality and tendencies towards corruption, but also, more importantly, because they were politically suspect and unduly sympathetic to local interests. As Joseph Smith asserts, 'It was an obvious maxim of administration that the judiciary in the dominions should be kept in the same state of dependency as it had been in Stuart days.'[51] The provision in section 3 of the Act of Settlement proclaiming judicial independence in England had no application in the colonies, where the royal prerogative reigned supreme.[52]

London used disallowance to scotch legislative attempts to secure control over judicial appointments and to substitute service during good behaviour in several American and Caribbean colonies.[53] Events in Jamaica in the 1750s provided the catalyst for the imperial government to generalize the policy.[54] An Act of the Jamaican legislature in 1751 prescribed that all judges in the colony were to be appointed 'during good behaviour.' The Act included formal steps necessary in that process: the consent of the Legislative Council, notice to the judge, and an open trial with the hearing of evidence on both sides. However, on the advice of the English law officers, the imperial government disallowed the legislation as an interference with the royal prerogative.[55] The only authority, they stated, with the power to change the conditions of appointment was the King's. The imperial government set the seal on this policy stand through a 1760 Privy Council diktat that noted local legislative attempts to change the terms of appointment of colonial judges and 'decreed that no judicial commission was good unless it specifically stated that the holder served "at the pleasure of the Crown."'[56]

Conflict over the Loyalties of Colonial Judges in America, 1760–1775

The timing of this directive from the council is important in that it coincided with a growing frustration in the American colonies with the exercise of judicial power, seen increasingly by Patriots as subservient to the wishes of the British Crown. Judges, especially those upholding the royal prerogative and imperial legislation that was burdensome to colonists, became identified as the 'running dogs' of British tyranny.[57] The reputation of the royal colonial courts suffered as a consequence, and some assemblies in the thirteen colonies began to challenge the directive. They believed they had ample precedent for doing so.

Immediately in the wake of the directive, a conflict developed in New York.[58] Bridling at the Privy's Council's order, which assembly members claimed defied precedent and made the judiciary subservient to the governor, the legislature passed a bill providing that judges in the colony be appointed during good behaviour. Despite attempts by the lieutenant governor, Cadwallader Colden, to chart a conciliatory course, his insistence on preserving royal initiative as one option for removing a judge proved a sticking point. The situation was further complicated by the fact that the existing New York judges refused to take commissions under the new monarch, George III, unless they held them during good behaviour. The result was a stalemate only partially resolved by bringing in a Boston lawyer as chief justice, ready to serve at royal pleasure. The Board of Trade rejected out of hand attempts by New York legislators to draw parallels between the parlous state of the English judiciary under James II, and that of the American judiciary. In its view, the equation did not reflect the reality of justice in the colonies. Moreover, the board asserted, 'Tenure during good behaviour would prevent the governors from displacing [such] men as offered themselves with more capable men whenever the latter should be found.'[59] It revised instructions to governors to underline the point. The impasse was ultimately resolved by one of the existing judges changing his tune and agreeing to take the position of chief justice at pleasure.[60]

It was not only the issue of the conditions of employment of colonial judges that was to drive a growing wedge between reformist colonial politicians and the imperial authorities in North America. The conflict over control of the judges and judicial power was also played out in several attempts to impeach jurists in the years just before the War of Independence. It was these cases that proved to the imperial government the dangers associated with judicial tenure being subject to local control.

During the late seventeenth century, the Pennsylvania legislature had sought to invoke impeachment as an English institution that settlers carried with them as a right, in an attempt to rid the colony of an incompetent and avaricious judge, Nicholas More, a crony of the proprietor, William Penn.[61] Although London denied any such power in a colonial legislature, given the subordinate status of colonies, and would do so repeatedly thereafter, American legislatures viewed impeachment as a perfectly legitimate way of calling judges to account, whether appointed by the Crown in Britain or by the local governor.[62]

The new battle lines formed initially in the impeachment of William

Moore, chief judge of Chester County in Pennsylvania in 1758.[63] The tension reflected a popular backlash against proprietary government in the colony ruled by Moore's mentor, the Reverend William Smith. When complaints and petitions about the chief judge's behaviour reached the colonial assembly, it was unable to remove him, because his appointment was at pleasure. The assembly then impeached Moore. However, Lieutenant Governor Denny refused to remove him. Smith petitioned the King that the assembly lacked any right to impeach, and succeeded. Hoffer and Hull note, however, that the episode had a significant psychological effect, as 'the Moore impeachment broadened the assembly's own conception of its authority.'[64] The symbolism was noted elsewhere in British America.

A high-profile attempt at impeachment of a judge occurred in Massachusetts in 1774, illustrating the conflict about authority and legality in the American colonies as they drifted towards revolution.[65] Although the target was Chief Justice Peter Oliver, the attack was directed at royal control over the superior court of the colony.[66] Lieutenant Governor Thomas Hutchison deprecated the colonial courts' unresponsiveness to the governor's supremacy within the colonial constitution, and the failure of the local bench to emulate their English counterparts and follow English authority. For their part, Hutchison's opponents believed that he was attempting to corrupt the judiciary by craftily combining royal patronage (including royal salaries) and his own family's alliances. When the lieutenant governor became governor and appointed Peter Oliver, an in-law, as chief justice, the opposition stiffened. A rumour that British government would henceforth pay superior court justices made the assembly (the General Court) even unhappier, and it launched impeachment proceedings. The assembly issued articles of impeachment, and Hutchison faced the prospect of a trial of his appointee before him and the council. He saw dangers in putting the matter before that body, perhaps unsympathetic to his man. Instead he prorogued the assembly, and the impeachment initiative died. Despite the governor's manoeuvre, as Hoffer and Hull comment, 'the impeachment helped to doom royal government in Massachusetts.'[67]

In Britain's Caribbean colonies, where the majority of the settler population remained loyal to the British Crown during the Revolutionary War in America, judicial behaviour was not a major issue during this period. Although, as Andrew O'Shaughnessy wryly puts it, 'the colonists saw every governor as a potential reincarnation of Charles II and James II,' the preponderance of judges appointed from settler ranks in these possessions worked against conflict between them and the plantocracy.[68]

With the independence of the thirteen American colonies, the Constitution of 1789 enshrined the principle of appointment during good behaviour for American judges. The disciplining of errant jurists developed its own trajectory and peculiarities, with impeachment as its major mechanism. However, the fact that impeachment had been tried during the colonial period in America was not lost on reformers in colonies that remained British, especially in British North America.

The Challenges of the Nova Scotia Assembly to the Colonial Judges

Not all British colonial possessions in North America fell to revolution. Nova Scotia, in particular, stands out as the example of an older British colony that remained loyal and resisted the spread of the republican credo from the south. As that territory experienced an influx of American Loyalists and was divided into the colonies of Nova Scotia, New Brunswick, and Cape Breton, the region – together with Prince Edward Island (the former French possession of Ile Ste Jean) – developed as a new configuration of British presence and authority. Politically and legally, Nova Scotia represents the model of a more closely controlled colony than any of the former thirteen colonies to the south, or those in the Caribbean.[69] With its important strategic position in the North Atlantic, the British government sensed the need to establish a possession that, while it was allowed an elected legislative assembly, was also subject to the unambiguous authority of a governor with significant plenary and fiscal authority, and an appointed council.[70] Moreover, after a short dalliance with a superior court comprising the governor and council and a lay-administered court of common pleas, London concluded that a court with a professional judge at the helm was needed if English law and British justice were to be secured and to prosper.[71] The colony's Supreme Court was irrefutably a creation of the royal prerogative. Although it embodied a decisive step away from the old system of appeals to an executive body, the Governor in Council, this in no way resulted in diminution of the political engagement of the judiciary.[72] Under the new regime, the role of the chief justice was clear. Apart from his important judicial role in resolving disputes and supervising the criminal work of his court, he occupied a key role in governance – acting as a close confidante of the governor on both legal and political issues, and as a leading member of the council, who was expected both to advise on and draft legislation for the colony. The Baconian notion of the judicial role of loyal service to the Crown above all else was operative. Executive government dominated, and a separation of powers was only dimly perceived, if at all.

The raison d'être of colonial governance and law in the Maritime colonies, as David Bell notes, was to safeguard loyalty and preserve order.[73] In this view, leadership in colonial government flowed down from the 'sovereign's local viceroy, rather than upwards from the elected representatives of the governed.'[74] Bell adds, 'It was a system in which the rudimentary formal machinery of governance was enhanced by a pervasive ideology of deference and dependence, in which personal and dynastic influences were of fundamental importance, with no sharp distinction between public and private interests.'[75] The expectation was that judges knew where their duty lay. If they did not, they were readily dispensable, as they were appointed at pleasure. Moreover, as lawyers grew in numbers in colonial jurisdictions and those with professional knowledge and experience began to practise before the courts, expectations of judicial competence increased markedly.

This was the theory at least. David Bell has also argued that in the Maritime colonies judicial tenure proved remarkably secure, and that it was government that had to suffer the judges rather than vice versa.[76] To a significant extent that is true. There were, however, instances, in both Quebec and the Maritime provinces in which attempts at disciplining judges were made in the late eighteenth century, although they all proved abortive. However, those examples, especially a protracted battle in Nova Scotia that raised the issue of who had the authority to discipline judges and how, pointed to the potential for trouble when colonial judges courted criticism and fell out with powerful or vocal elements in the population who decided to press for their removal from office.[77]

The Supreme Court of Nova Scotia suffered in its early decades from a series of chief justices, imported from England or Ireland, who proved problematic or ineffectual – too involved in the political life of the colony, as with the first, the ultra-Tory Jonathan Belcher,[78] too detached from its life, like the second, the raffish Brian Finucane,[79] or present for too short a time, the experience of Jeremy Pemberton, the third appointee.[80] Both these problems and delays in appointments and arrivals[81] meant that the two local assistant (puisne) judges carried a heavy judicial load, especially on circuit.[82] Those men – James Brenton (a former attorney general) and Isaac Deschamps (a lay judge) – became the focus of increasing criticism in the late 1780s and early 1790s, involving allegations that they were incompetent and partial in their judgments.[83] Several seasoned Loyalist American lawyers, Thomas Barclay, Jonathan Sterns, and William Taylor, who had arrived in the colony in the mid-1780s and began appearing before these jurists, levelled the charges.[84] The conservative lieutenant governor John Parr, convinced that these men were 'tinctured with Republican spirit' and had insinuated faction and seditious tendencies into the colony, was deeply suspicious of them and their motives.[85]

In the wake of complaints about judicial incompetence from jury members and unsuccessful litigants, the House of Assembly in November 1787 resolved to establish a committee of inquiry into the judges' conduct.[86] On the basis of the inquiry, the assembly requested that Parr investigate the conduct of the two justices. Having consulted Brenton and Deschamps, who flatly denied all the allegations against them, branding the charges as the product of animus towards them by dissident lawyers, the lieutenant governor equivocated. Although acknowledging that such serious charges warranted investigation, Parr wondered whether the real issue involved differences of opinion on applicable law. He added that he could find no evidence of criminality, partiality, or corruption on the part of the jurists, and reserved final judgment. While the assembly was prorogued, in February 1788 Parr put the matter before the Legislative Council. It cleared the justices of charges of incompetence and partiality, branding the assembly's allegations as 'groundless and scandalous.'[87]

The conflict continued with mutual recrimination, during which the judges disbarred two of their adversaries, Jonathan Sterns and William Taylor, for contempt of court in publishing letters critical of the bench in the newspapers.[88] While the assembly was prorogued, there was no further discussion for the rest of 1788. With the recall of the assembly in March 1789, Parr finally responded to its address, stating tepidly that the charges were 'not supported by the Proofs which accompanied [the] Address.'[89]

Further instances of apparent partiality in criminal trials, and evidence that the judges had lied in their responses to the 1787 charges, provided the catalyst for renewed attempts to dislodge them. Early in 1790 the assembly drew up draft articles of impeachment, accusing Deschamps and Brenton of 'High Crimes and Misdemeanours.' That body passed seven articles of impeachment in April of the same year, after a full public hearing with counsel, witnesses, cross-examination, and both oral and documentary evidence being led.[90] The assembly forwarded the charges to London with the request that the King establish a court in Nova Scotia to try the judges. Meanwhile, Lieutenant Governor Parr refused to suspend Deschamps and Brenton. William Grenville, the secretary of state for home affairs and the colonies, declined to set up a special court and referred the address to the Committee of the Privy Council for Trade and Plantations. In the middle of 1792, after a four-day hearing, the Privy Council cleared the judges of all the charges against them and 'excoriated their detractors.'[91] The new chief justice, Thomas Strange was able to defuse the local tension by quietly supporting his colleagues and engineering the return of Sterns and Taylor to practise.[92] Despite the judges' victory in London, Loyalist lawyers began to make their mark, not only as advocates, but also in the political life of the province.[93]

The Nova Scotia case indicates haziness in the colony as to whether and how a colonial assembly might move against judges considered unfit for office. Colonial judges were appointed at pleasure, and governors could remove them from office, with good and sufficient cause.[94] If there was any doubt about a governor's authority over judges appointed by London rather than locally, British legislation in 1782 arguably had the effect of subjecting both groups of judges to gubernatorial authority to remove for cause.[95] Such an initiative was not in the cards for Deschamps and Brenton, because Parr and the Legislative Council were sympathetic to them and unwilling to do the bidding of the 'radical' forces in the assembly. That left the question of whether the assembly itself possessed an inherent power to move against the judges. Earlier instances in the American and Caribbean colonies pointed to a negative answer.[96] Furthermore, London disallowed a 1782 Nova Scotia statute that would have given the assistant judges tenure during good behaviour, because the lack of *any* method of removing them put them in a better position than the judges in Great Britain. This too indicates that the imperial government continued to deny colonial legislatures a power of impeachment or anything like it. A 1789 Act of the colony that provided alternative ways of moving against a delinquent puisne judge – at the pleasure of the Crown, or, like the Act of Settlement, by a joint address of the council and assembly to the lieutenant governor – and was not disallowed, provided no solace in this instance, because the council was strongly opposed to disciplining the judges.[97]

The managers of the campaign against the associate justices were forced by circumstance to fix upon a hybrid process, described as impeachment, in which the place of the upper chamber would be taken by a court appointed through the royal prerogative.[98] In the absence of any other viable way of dealing with the judges, impeachment appeared to have the virtue of flexibility. However, London was not about to fall for this ploy, instead referring the address to the Privy Council, which had for a long time claimed the right to hear petitions or addresses from colonial legislatures. Here, the Committee of the Privy Council in hearing the case was exercising an established original jurisdiction and thus conceding nothing regarding local assembly control over the process.[99]

The inspirations of those seeking a more assertive role for the assembly in the tenure of locally appointed judges are not hard to find. The British Parliament's ongoing impeachment of Warren Hastings for his activities in India was probably influential. If this was the way in which the 'mother of Parliaments' dealt with corrupt and partial officials, then why should the colonial counterparts of that body lack that authority?[100] It is likely too that the American experience of the Loyalist lawyers, intent on unseating the assistant judges, played a role here. Jonathan Sterns and Thomas Barclay were Harvard graduates and had experience in government or private practice in New York. William Taylor had practised in New Jersey and fled to New York during the War. It is probable that they were aware of the previous attempts of American colonial assemblies (or governors) to set the terms of appointment of colonial judges, as in New York, and of the attempted impeachment in Massachusetts. The stratagems of the Loyalist assemblymen came to naught in this instance. However, that attempt to invoke impeachment to unseat colonial judges in Nova Scotia would have resonance in a later campaign in Lower Canada to get rid of unpopular judges there.[101]

The Disciplining of Colonial Judges in the Late Eighteenth Century

There were then two avenues for dealing with complaints about judicial misbehaviour in the colonies and testing whether there was a sufficient basis for removal at pleasure. One involved the initiative of the governor, who was empowered to remove or suspend a judge for cause, subject to review by the imperial authorities and appeal to the Privy Council. The other was by petition by a colonial assembly that proceeded directly to the council exercising original jurisdiction.

The latter was effectively the process that London followed in the Nova Scotia case.

There were three instances of the former process at work between 1776 and the early 1790s in British North America. Governor Guy Carleton dismissed Peter Livius, the chief justice of Quebec, from office in 1778, 'for political rather than judicial failings.'[102] The jurist had offended the governor by pressing him to reveal the details of his powers under his commission, and questioning his practice of proceeding in council meetings with a small group of trusted supporters, thereby disenfranchising the rest. Livius successfully appealed his removal to the Plantations Committee of the Privy Council and was restored to office. The committee hinted that there was some substance in the judge's allegations and stressed the requirement of cause implicit in the governor's instructions. They concluded that there was no complaint against him in his judicial capacity, so that cause was lacking.[103]

In 1788, Lieutenant Governor Macarmick of Cape Breton suspended Chief Justice Richard Gibbons from his position.[104] In this backwater colony there had been bad blood between the previous chief executive, Joseph Desbarres, on the one hand, and the colony's attorney general, David Matthews, and registrar general, Abraham Cuyler, on the other. Gibbons, who owed his appointment to his friend Desbarres, took his side. Desbarres's antagonists brought pressure in London to recall the chief executive, and the British government dispatched Macarmick to reconcile the warring factions. As a conciliatory gesture he sought to work with the chief justice. However, Gibbons, resentful at the apparent increase in the power of his adversaries, Matthews and Cuyler, formed a quasi-military association, the Friendly Society, to protect him and others from Macarmick acting tyrannically. Gibbons rejected Macarmick's plan to set up a regular militia to prevent violence between the rival groups, whereupon the lieutenant governor outlawed the society. When the chief justice took to campaigning for a legislative assembly for the island and advocating the use of the grand jury as a temporary substitute, Marcarmick suspended him from office. In 1791, although the Privy Council's committee report disapproved of Gibbons's conduct 'as inconsistent with the Duty and Functions of a Judge and tending to disturb the Good Order [of the colony]' and found his suspension justified, it also advised that the judge be restored to office on the 'grounds of his generally good character.'[105]

The chief justice of Prince Edward Island, Peter Stewart, was also to face suspension by the colony's governor, only to have his position restored and later confirmed by the Privy Council.[106] The politics of the island colony were visceral, a product of the British government's unique form of settlement by lot to large proprietors, and the animus felt by tenants and others hungry to own their own land, especially towards those landlords who were absentees and neglected to settle and improve their holdings. At the same time institutions of government were underdeveloped. J.M. Bumsted has noted that the administration of justice in the colony 'was on the slow track to maturity.'[107] It was not until the early nineteenth century, for example, that the colony had a truly professional chief justice, and the earliest lawyers attracted to its shores were not notable for the depth of their experience or legal acumen. At the same time, the court infrastructure and legal procedures, which aped those of the mother country, were unnecessarily complex and demanding for a small jurisdiction with a scattered population.

Stewart lacked qualifications as a lawyer. He had been a mere law clerk in Edinburgh and was unversed in English law. However, the Scottish lord advocate, James Montgomery, a landowner on the island, was his patron. In 1775 he moved his large family to the island to assume his position and soon became enmeshed in its Byzantine politics. He had a falling out with the governor, William Patterson, who took exception to grants of land to Stewart and his family that an acting governor had made in his absence. The governor was also miffed that Stewart had opposed his legislative attempts to call to account absentee landlords, as illegally formulated. Patterson's 'compromising' of Stewart's wife exacerbated an already fraught relationship.[108] When the governor prorogued the Legislative Assembly after an election in which the Stewart clan had fared well, the chief justice complained to London that he was being set up for dismissal from office. After a further election the governor obliged by suspending Stewart, citing Stewart's political opposition to his government, and particularly for revealing a council secret on the hustings at polling time, by asserting that the governor intended to tax the colony heavily.[109] The chief justice succeeded in an appeal to the Privy Council in 1789, although this seems to have merely confirmed action already taken by a new governor, Edmund Fanning, on his arrival in the colony.

Stewart's troubles did not end there. Supporters of the former governor, outraged by his recall, initiated action in the Privy Council to unseat Fanning and several colonial officials, including the chief justice. Bumsted indicates that while the charges against Stewart 'of using his office for political purposes by perverting the law in his judgments, of disregarding and refusing evidence, of condoning the malpractice of [Attorney General] Aplund ... , of misdirecting and influencing juries were not always well documented,' the complainants had a far stronger case against him than any of the others accused of malfeasance.[110] He adds, 'They might have had more success with the chief justice had they not alleged a conspiracy they could not prove.' In the result the council exonerated Stewart and the others in 1792.[111] The chief justice's continuing judicial partiality and, in particular, a contretemps with his patron, James Montgomery, caused further embarrassment to the local government, and he was induced to retire in 1799, lest his actions provide an excuse for further investigation in London of the Fanning administration.[112]

These cases underline the existence of a practice, well established in British imperial practice from the seventeenth century, implicit in the instructions issued to governors, of removing, or at least suspending, troublesome jurists for cause.[113] In 1782 a legislative basis with potential for removing a colonial jurist was added – Burke's Act, a statute of the Westminster Parliament.[114] The legislation, directed primarily at prohibiting the practice of officials appointed to the colonies absenting themselves and appointing surrogates in their places, also made reference to 'misbehaviour' of colonial officials more generally. Section 2 provided that, where colonial office holders 'neglected the Duty of such Office or *otherwise misbehaved* [author's emphasis],' they might be amoved. In an implicit recognition of the Privy Council's directive of 1760 on judicial appointments, the statute also made it clear that nothing in its terms was considered to prevent the grant of offices at pleasure.[115] Having provided this basis for disciplining colonial officials, the framers, mindful of the injustices that could be done to innocent office holders in these communities, also provided a right of appeal. Once amoved, said section 3, the person, if aggrieved, was entitled to appeal, 'whereupon such Amotion shall be finally judged of and determined by His Majesty in Council.'[116]

Disciplining of Judges and Late-Eighteenth-Century Politics of Empire

Although attempts at unseating colonial judges met with no success in the latter decades of the eighteenth century, processes were irrefutably in existence for their removal. These instruments of control jibed with the philosophy of colonial government in settled possessions envisaged by William Pitt the Younger and his secretary of state for home affairs and the colonies, William Grenville, as they constructed the constitutional order for the colonies of Lower and Upper Canada in 1790 and 1791.

Despite Whiggish interpretations to the contrary, the new order, as John Manning Ward and Robert Fraser have argued persuasively, was counter-revolutionary.[117] The lesson to be learnt from the secession of the thirteen American colonies was that they had enjoyed too much political and legal freedom. If the stability of the remaining empire in North America was to be secure, it required the consolidation of imperial power in the colonies rather than its loosening. Admittedly the impression given by the political and legal structures devised and advertised of colonies enjoying the rights and blessings of 'free-born Englishmen' – such as an elective legislative assembly, trial by jury, and the application of English law – suggested a liberal touch and reference back to the earlier 'representative' system in the first empire.[118] However, the power of the governors, with their right to call and prorogue elective assemblies, appoint members of legislative councils, and enjoy partial control over colonies' purse strings – was designed to prescribe limits to colonial freedom of action and to underline the dependent status of those settler colonies vis-à-vis the imperial government.[119] Judges, especially chief justices, were expected to play a central political role in the colonial administration, as well as administering the law, serving as legislative councillors and as members of the executive (or inner) council of key advisers to the colonial executive.[120] The senior judge would also often draft legislation in the absence of law officers available or competent to do the job.[121] Some colonial judges of the period sat in elective legislative assemblies, expected to support the executive's initiatives and policies. From London's standpoint, it was vitally important that the judges, as important players in colonial administration, recognize fully the obligations of loyalty to monarch, empire, and the colonial state – that they represent a Baconian concept of justice. Appointing them 'at pleasure' was one way of impressing on them that they needed to behave themselves.

At the same time a system for the expeditious disciplining of colonial judges arguably grew in importance with the evolving formal attenuation of executive and judicial functions that attended the establishment of professionally led superior courts and the attendant pressure for colonies to adhere to English law. The establishment of a superior court of record in Nova Scotia in 1754 – embodying all or part of the jurisdictions of the royal courts in England, with original and appellate jurisdiction administered by a legally trained chief justice and puisne judges (whether legally qualified or not) – was subsequently copied in New Brunswick, and ultimately in Prince Edward Island, Cape Breton, and Newfoundland. The Constitutional Act for Lower and Upper Canada in 1791 opened the door for an even clearer commitment to the centrality of Common Law administered by a superior court in the North American colonies. Henry Dundas, the secretary of state for the home office and colonies from 1791 to 1794, developed a 'plan' for colonial judicatures in the Americas, to ensure a central superior court system administered by a professionally qualified chief justice.[122] Although quickly lost sight of in wartime conditions, Dundas had encouraged the legislative introduction into Lower Canada of a Court of King's Bench in 1794, replacing the older and simpler lay-run Court of Common Pleas.[123] Through the joint efforts of Lieutenant Governor John Simcoe and Chief Justice William Osgoode, Upper Canada quickly followed suit, with provincial legislation establishing a central court of superior jurisdiction later that year.[124] In both jurisdictions two puisne judges, both legally qualified, were appointed to share the bench with the chief, along with provision for the appointment of an attorney general.

Although it would be wrong to suggest that there was a master plan being forged here, by design or happenstance by 1800 the major British North American colonies had developed strong systems of superior court justice with judges largely dispensing English law. Ostensibly, the system was one in which the distinctive role of the judiciary in the administration of justice had been underlined. However, the realities of colonial governance and the political roles that judges were expected to play meant that judicial accountability and independence were closely controlled. The matter of control would become a live issue in several of these colonies in the new century. The assumptions about judicial loyalty were underlined by an imperial tendency to appoint chief justices from among the ranks of barristers at the English or Irish Bars. These men, it was thought, possessed better training, had more experience, and were less partial to local, sectional interest than local lawyers, whether trained in England, Ireland, or America.[125] There were exceptions, however, in New Brunswick and Quebec of appointing local Loyalist lawyers to the bench. The practice of drawing on local talent would become the norm in due course in these colonies.

Lower Canada presented a special challenge to London, because judges were expected to administer a mixed system of jurisprudence, reflecting both the territory's civilian legal heritage in private law, as well as the introduction of English criminal law.[126] By 1800 several civilian lawyers shared the bench with Common Law judges in that jurisdiction. However, the dominance of anglophone judges and their attempts to anglicize the law further would lead to tensions with both reformers in the Legislative Assembly and some of their colleagues.

Elsewhere in the empire, the pattern of governance and the administration of justice remained more diverse, reflecting the various histories of acquiring colonies. Royal colonies in the Caribbean dating from the seventeenth century had elected assemblies and justice systems similar to those that had existed in the thirteen American colonies. This was true of possessions 'discovered' by the English, such as Barbados, Bermuda, and several of the Windward and Leeward Islands, Jamaica ceded by Spain in the mid-seventeenth century, and several other islands, such as Grenada and Tobago ceded to the British Crown prior to 1790.[127] In time, several of these colonies (including Jamaica, the British Virgin Islands, and Bermuda) would have superior courts presided over by a legally trained chief justice, although he might be drawn from the West Indian legal fraternity, rather than from Britain itself.[128] As judicial business grew in volume, puisne or assistant judges might be added. There were still, however, established colonies, such as Barbados, where the judiciary, even the chief justice, whose salaries were paid for by the local assembly, were lacking in legal training.[129] Despite criticism, these lay-run systems survived well into the next century. In all of the colonies operating under the old representative system of government, formal or informal slave courts continued to operate.

From the late eighteenth century, imperial policy towards newly acquired colonies by conquest or cession changed. Britain's acquisition of colonies from other European powers with mixed-race populations including European settlers (a small minority), slaves, and growing freed slave and Creole populations (Cape Colony, Ceylon, Mauritius, Trinidad, and several other West Indian islands) presented imperial policymakers with a conundrum.[130] Leery about granting these new possessions representative bodies monopolized by planter elites, and yet unwilling and afraid to grant the franchise and representation to freemen of colour, the question was how these territories could be governed at all. The solution, based on the governance of Quebec after 1763, and of India, in the immediate aftermath of the impeachment of Governor Warren Hastings, was to repose exclusive political and constitutional powers in the colonial executive, and to govern either by imperial Orders in Council or gubernatorial decree. A colony might be granted an advisory legislative council, but this body would be firmly under the control of the governor and able only to respond to his request for advice. In these colonies, courts were established, reflecting the notion that English common law would apply in the territory, and that the administration of justice would follow the English system. In time, chief justices who had legal training were appointed, and associate justices (whether lay or legally qualified) were added. Even though these were mixed jurisdictions where English law existed alongside a pre-existing European colonial system of governance and justice and some indigenous judges were maintained in office – such as in the Cape Colony – it was normally assumed that English judges would be able to discern and apply the doctrine and principles of the older system, to the extent that they still obtained.[131] London appointed professionally trained chief justices of Crown colonies directly and paid them under parliamentary estimates, so that they were not in principle subservient to local interests. To what degree they identified with the values of the colonial elites varied, as it did with governors. Some fell afoul of those elites.[132]

There were exceptions to the patterns outlined above. Several conquered or settled colonies were run for very specific purposes and had organs of government and courts that reflected those objectives. Thus in Gibraltar, a possession of major strategic significance in the imperial mind, military governance and quasi-military law prevailed. In New South Wales, designed as a penal colony, a justice regime with similarities to that in Gibraltar was established.[133] It had a governor possessing great administrative discretion and punitive power, who acted very much as the warden of a vast outdoor prison, and a body of law reflecting local needs, as well as elements of English law, administered by military or naval, as well as lay civilian, officials.[134] Newfoundland, which London had treated for two centuries as a temporary, seasonal land base for visiting fishing fleets, had inevitably attracted settlement by merchants, fisherfolk, and service providers. The colony possessed a hybrid system of 'admiral's law' administered by fishing captains, and land-based law developed by lay magistrates.[135] Only in the 1790s was this beginning to change, with establishment of a superior court with both original and appellate jurisdiction in civil matters, but as a complement to the system of naval justice that continued.[136]

Lawyers' Reason and the Reality of British Colonial Rule

Despite William Blackstone's attempt, in the last half of the eighteenth century, to reduce the pattern of colonial governance and law and its administration across the empire to a system of rational explanation in terms of governance and the administration of justice, depending on how colonies had been acquired, the reality was more complex.[137] What can be said about the situation in the 1790s is that among these variegated colonies, institutions of government, and forms for administering justice in Britain's colonial possessions, there were emerging common understandings of how justice should be organized and supervised and what law would be applied. In the first third of the nineteenth century, these 'common understandings' – as they related to the professionalization of the courts, the role of judges within the colonial state, and the desired dominance of English law and both its ideological and pragmatic underpinnings – would become stronger. This process would be assisted by the development of institutional guidance and strategies designed to inject greater order and consistency into the governance and law of the empire. Such would be the institutional context in which the realities of judicial tenure and accountability and expectations about judicial independence would be played out. Also changing notions about imperialism and its imperatives in various parts of the globe and their reflection in divergent notions of governance across the empire, between 1830 and 1900, would also affect how the roles of colonial judges were viewed, as well as the outcomes of attempts to discipline particular colonial judges.

3

The Administration of Colonial Justice and Law in the Nineteenth-Century British Empire: General Contours

Managing the Empire: The Colonial Office and Judicial Committee

The year 1800 did not represent a clear divide in the character of the colonial judiciary and its administration. The trends noted at the close of the previous chapter – emphasis on judicial loyalty to the colonial administration, professionalization of the judiciary, and pressure for English law to predominate in the colonies – continued, albeit fitfully, as the British government dealt with the distractions of the Napoleonic Wars and their economic and social aftermath.

In one important respect, this was a period of institutional reorganization and reform in the way in which colonial policy was formulated, organized, and administered. In 1801 London transferred responsibility for the colonies previously under the supervision of a committee of the Privy Council since the 1780s to the new secretary of state for war and the colonies. This date marks the establishment of the Colonial Office as the organ of government with primary authority over the running of the empire (with the exception of India). However, only with the arrival in 1812 of Earl Bathurst as secretary of state and of Henry Goulburn as undersecretary did a true department of state emerge.[1] The process of overseeing the legal implications of colonial governance, including the administration of justice, took more tangible form with the appointment of James Stephen Jr as legal counsel to the office in

1814. This was a position he held until 1836, when he became permanent undersecretary. Stephen was a dominant figure in the Office in moulding its policies and administrative character for the better part of thirty-five years. It was he who breathed life into the Crown colony system. Moreover, as the person who vetted legislation from the colonies and advised on disallowance, he played a central role in the monitoring and amelioration of slave regimes, and later in the dismantling of slavery and slave laws, across the empire.[2]

As a consequence of this institutional initiative, London began to keep closer tabs on what was or seemed to be happening across the empire, to establish commissions of inquiry into colonial matters, to make comparisons and contrasts between colonies, to formulate proactive policies on colonial rule, and to develop a more effective institutional memory than was possible before.[3] The Colonial Office now became the effective organ for considering and making judicial appointments to colonies, for checking on the performance of colonial jurists when necessary, and for administering the system of judicial discipline, whether in reviewing removals and suspensions by colonial executive authorities, or by directly recalling troublesome jurists. In due course, the Office's priorities were sometimes influential when a judge, who had been removed or suspended from office, appealed to the Privy Council or appeared before the council on a petition from a colonial legislature for his removal. The Office also used the venerable practice of seeking legal opinions on colonial legal matters from the English law officers, including disputes that pitched judges against governors and their officials.[4]

A later important institutional development was the establishment of the Judicial Committee of the Privy Council as the final imperial court of appeal in 1833.[5] Until that change, ad hoc committees heard and adjudicated appeals from the colonies, which, while they would have at least one legally trained person on board, were not exclusively judicial bodies. A permanent committee comprising serving and retired judges now replaced that loose system. Its jurisdiction extended to appeals from colonial judges who had been suspended or removed from office. Moreover, the Judicial Committee inherited the original jurisdiction of the Privy Council to pass upon petitions from colonial legislatures seeking jurists' removal. The emergence of this new body was in time to lead to attempts to produce consistency in the English law applied across the empire. It would also provide direction on the process of judicial discipline in the colonies.[6]

Colonial Governance and the Administration of Justice in the Nineteenth-Century Empire: General Features and Contexts

Despite these bureaucratic and judicial improvements, the fate of Britain's imperial possessions was very much in the hands of the viceroys sent out to govern the pieces of this far-flung empire.[7] Consonant with the British view that firm control at the top was needed, and that a commander of men was the ideal type to govern a colony, these were originally individuals with military – or less frequently naval – experience. These 'proconsular regimes,' as Christopher Bayly has described them, largely mirrored and reinforced the conservative values of the imperial government during the first three decades of the century.[8] The possessions over which they held sway were variegated in their politics, law, economics, and social ordering, reflecting the time of founding, geographic and demographic realities, and imperial policy towards them.

Vice-regal appointments, in tune with those throughout the imperial system, were the result of patronage decisions. Success or failure in these men's missions depended on a set of variables – character, political and social values, leadership qualities, ability to interact effectively with and conciliate various interest groups often at odds with each other, capacity in taking decisive initiatives, when needed, without direction from London, and a commitment to hard work. Given the often fractious nature of the communities they were sent to govern, it was difficult for even the most reasonable and genial of characters to avoid offending someone in the governing elite or some vocal interest group in society. Within the colonial pecking order, relations between a governor and his chief justice or justice who ranked numbers one and two in the government, varied considerably, depending on personalities, ideologies, and attitudes to justice and the rule of law. As succeeding chapters demonstrate, differences of opinion on policy and the relative allocation of authority, as well as clashing competitive urges, sometimes got the better of them.

Proconsuls carried with them general and less frequently specific instructions on what the imperial government expected of them and what it was they were to achieve in guiding the colony in question, as well as information on the character of governance and of the administration of justice in their charges. Much was inevitably left to their discretion. Even with the later substitution of civilians as governors, the changing politics of the metropolis, and ultimately the development of faster means of communication, both the developing complexity of imperial rule and perceived instability in some colonial territories would mean that colonial executives continued to enjoy a measure of freedom in crafting solutions to local problems throughout the century. One difference was that the Colonial Office was readier to second-guess those seen as less reliable agents of the imperial purpose.

As the nineteenth century dawned, how justice and law were administered across the empire varied considerably, depending on the level of attention of the imperial government, the stability or otherwise of political, economic, and social conditions, and the extent to which there was an existing or developed legal infrastructure ready and able to take on the challenges. Significant differences existed between the situation in the major British North American colonies, Nova Scotia, New Brunswick, and Lower and Upper Canada on the one hand, and that of their poorer North American cousins and West Indian colonies on the other. The former group boasted professionally trained justices in their superior courts, chosen exclusively or primarily from the ranks of often experienced and talented Loyalist or locally trained lawyers, with relatively open access to the sources of English law, and more or less adequately funded resources. The North American 'poor cousins' comprised Cape Breton, Prince Edward Island, and Newfoundland. The chief justices of these colonies were mostly legally trained, recruited from the English and Irish bars, although often from the ranks of inexperienced counsel who were struggling financially. They worked with assistant judges (civilians in the case of Cape Breton and Prince Edward Island, and naval officers in the case of Newfoundland who were not legally trained). Finances to support the justice infrastructures were very limited, and access to the sources of law tenuous.[9]

The West Indian colonies with representative government had even more parlous justice systems.[10] A number of them possessed judiciaries entirely unlearned in the law. According to the commissions sent by the Colonial Office to review the administration of justice in the British Caribbean colonies in the 1820s, this was the norm in courts exercising chancery jurisdiction, and the rule rather than the exception in the common law courts.[11] Barbados, St Kitts, Monserrat, Nevis, and the Virgin Islands all had chief justices who were not lawyers, and, in the remainder, Grenada, St Vincent, and Tobago, as well as in Jamaica, where the chief justices were legally trained, they were the only lawyer-judges on the bench.[12] The reports noted that local lay assistant judges sought at times to undermine the authority of lawyer–chief justices.[13] Where lay chief justices presided in criminal trials, it was attorneys general – the only sources of legal knowledge in court – who typically called the shots in prescribing and explaining the law.[14] The commissioners also reported that governors, assisted by several councillors without legal training, continued to act as final courts of appeal.[15]

Legal records were often in a hopeless state. The commission reports singled out Barbados, Tobago, St Vincent, Monserrat, St Kitts, and the Virgin Islands as needing revision, and systems for their consolidation and amendment.[16] Grenada, where an energetic lawyer–chief justice, George Smith, had published the enacted laws, was one of the few bright spots in an otherwise dismal landscape.[17] The law applied, although theoretically based on English precedent and models, in reality reflected a legal culture that favoured local custom, especially when it came to slavery. Given these descriptions, it is not at all surprising that the commissioners concluded that the administration of justice in the islands was defective and required reform. Changes, they opined, should include a requirement that the leading judge presiding in any colonial superior court be legally trained, and, in the case of Jamaica, a general increase in the number of superior court judges learned in the law – recommendations gradually implemented.[18]

Even more remote from a replication of the English system of justice was the special-purpose convict colony of New South Wales, in which the courts selectively applied the principles and procedures of English law. Amateur judges constructed law and justice according to perceived local needs, without much, if anything, in the way of direct control or influence from the centre.[19] The stories in chapter 6 show that, as the British government sought to regularize justice in this possession to bring it closer to the structures, doctrines, and culture of English law, tensions developed in which several judges became embroiled.

The Political and Juristic Challenges of Conquered and Ceded Colonies

London directed more attention to the administration of justice in colonies newly acquired by conquest or cession as a result of hostilities between Britain on the one hand, and France, Holland, and Spain on the other. This was because the imperial authorities felt challenged by the existence of both pre-existing European systems of law governing property, commercial transactions, and human relationships within these territories, and multiracial populations severely segmented in economic, and therefore social, terms. In most of them slavery was an established institution.[20] Despite these factors and their common experience of Crown colony government, British policy towards these systems varied. It is true that there was a chauvinistic tendency among some imperial and colonial officials (strongly aided and abetted by British local elites) to press for English law and procedures to replace the inherited systems of law and justice.[21] However, these sentiments did not always prevail. Among the factors that affected the retention or replacement of the earlier law were the extent and tenacity of previous European settlement and the proportion of non-British European settlers in a colony; the difficulties of dismantling in their entirety complex institutional structures that had become imbedded culturally; the popularity or otherwise of the inherited law; and its treatment of indigenous, slave, and Creole populations, as well as imperial dictates. In one area of law there was no contest. The imperial government introduced English criminal law and procedures in all these territories – a reflection of the strong, and in some respects erroneous, belief that it was a system superior to that of its European rivals, and more humane. It was in the realm of civil or private law that pre-existing systems had more staying power, such as Roman-Dutch law in Cape Colony and British Guiana, and the French *Code Civil* in Mauritius.

Politics, Loyalty, Independence, and the Colonial Judiciary

The notion of a Baconian colonial judiciary that had taken root in the eighteenth-century empire lived on into the nineteenth century. Here again the story reveals inconsistencies, and there is evidence that the notion was the object of challenge by some judges.

In England the authorities took grudging steps in the early years of the nineteenth century to further divorce the judiciary from both the executive and legislative arms of government, and to underline judicial independence. After an outcry from both the legal profession and parliamentarians about the appointment of Lord Chief Justice Ellenborough in 1807 to the Cabinet, government policy – while refusing to yield in this case – quietly changed. No further such appointments were made, although the lord chancellor continued to straddle the awkward divide of judicial, executive, and legislative functions.[22] The English common law judges were barred from taking seats in the House of Commons, a practice entrenched by the end of the seventeenth century, although the master of the rolls, a chancery judge, continued to sit until the 1870s. The Scottish judges became ineligible to sit in that chamber by statute in 1733, and the Irish judges in 1821.[23]

With the exception of Lord Chancellor Westbury's forced resignation from office in 1865 after exposures of venality among members of his department, no English judges suffered formal discipline during the nineteenth century, although from time to time members raised questions in Parliament over the conduct of several jurists and sought to test the waters on their removal.[24] None of these other initiatives succeeded. The terms of their appointment during good behaviour insulated the English judiciary from attack.[25] The situation was initially different in Ireland – a part of the United Kingdom still ruled with a distinctly colonial mentality.

In 1805 petitions to Parliament called for the removal from office of Justice Luke Fox of the Irish Court of Common Pleas, for advocating in open court the recall of the lord lieutenant of Ireland, the Earl of Hardwicke, as well as seeking to persuade a senior army officer to follow suit.[26] Doubts about the way in which the parliamentary disciplinary process was initiated resulted in proceedings being abandoned, and the judge continued sitting.

For his part, also in 1805, Justice Robert Johnson of the same court variously attacked the lord lieutenant and other high officials, including the lord chancellor and a judge, in a series of articles published in England under a nom de plume. He described them as sheep feeders, wooden headed, devious, and corrupt.[27] In this instance the targets of the invective chose to pursue their detractor through the English criminal courts. The jury found the Irish jurist guilty of criminal libel. However, the English attorney general issued a stay of prosecution (*nolle prosequi*) before sentencing, saving Johnson from formal punishment, but only on the understanding that the jurist would forthwith resign from the bench with a pension, and he did.[28] As Irish judges were still appointed at pleasure at this time, these two cases provide some indication of the level of concern in London about judicial irresponsibility and its perceived dangers in a possession in which the stability of British rule could not be taken for granted.[29]

Unlike the situation in England, in the colonies election of judges to legislative assemblies, where they existed, continued to occur, although the practice was short-lived. Discomfort with the practice in British North American colonies led to the barring of judges from the lower chambers by 1812.[30] In the multiracial colonies, assistant judges continued to sit in legislative assemblies, where they existed, until much later in the century – a reality that caused problems when they happened to fall out with a chief justice, as happened in one of the stories canvassed in chapter 9.

Justices of the superior colonial courts continued longer as key players in the work of legislative and executive councils. This was especially true of chief justices who acted as close advisers to governors on political, legal, and cultural matters. In the North American colonies they often acted as speakers or presidents of legislative councils, in some circumstances assuming the mantle of prime minister.[31] The early appointment and longevity of some judges, contrasted with a frequent turnover of governors, added to their political power.[32] In both the Canadas, the tensions caused by judges exercising executive political power, playing reformist politics, or causing outrage among reformers, is evident in the stories in chapters 4 and 5.

In a practice that harkened back to seventeenth-century tensions, colonial executives called upon judges to render extrajudicial opinions in the expectation that they would receive favourable or helpful advice on legal matters and issues of state. In the two Canadas, in particular, the ghosts of seventeenth-century and even medieval practice in England still had matter on their bones, even though the practice was on the wane in the metropolis.[33] Requests were commonplace. Few, if any, judges considered providing this advice as inappropriate, nor did they reserve the right to change their minds in subsequent cases.

Under these conditions, the relationship between the law officers of the provincial Crown and the judges could also be close – close enough in Upper Canada, for instance, to warrant collusion in political trials for sedition.[34] The suspicions generated by extrajudicial opinions and the cosy relationship between judges and law officers again provided grist for the mill in the stories related in chapters 4 and 5.

After 1830 the British government revised its position on the involvement of judges in British North America in executive politics, progressively barring judges from serving in executive and legislative councils, and appointing them during good behaviour.[35] They were henceforward removable on addresses by colonial legislatures, although they had a right to appeal to the Privy Council against their dismissal.[36] Occasionally, in emergencies, such as the 1837–8 rebellion in Upper Canada, a chief justice might be called upon to exercise temporary executive function akin to that of a prime minister. In such circumstances the device of colonial executives seeking extrajudicial opinions from judges also occurred.[37] More generally, however, the developing conception of a separation of powers worked against a more generalized continuation of this practice. From 1850 this process of insulating the judges from active political involvement and providing them with firmer tenure spread to the Antipodean colonies. There chief justices had sat on executive and legislative councils, and in two colonies, New South Wales and Van Diemen's Land (Tasmania), judges of superior courts had possessed statutory powers to disallow or vet local statutes for repugnancy.[38] With the exception of Vancouver Island and British Columbia (newly established as proprietary and Crown colonies respectively),[39] and Western Australia (which was sloth-like in its political and legal development, and in which responsible government was delayed until 1890),[40] by 1860 the new system of appointment, tenure, and accountability operated in all North American and Australasian colonies.

These latter developments would not occur in West Indian colonies that continued with the old representative system of colonial governance. Nor was their influence felt in multiracial Crown colonies that at most possessed councils advisory to the colonial executive. Jurists, especially chief justices, advised the colonial executives and sat on executive and legislative councils, where they existed, and continued to play a supportive political role in addition to their strictly judicial functions. The imperial authorities continued to control chief justice appointments, on the one hand to prevent superior courts making common cause with powerful local interests, but on the other to be able to deal directly and promptly with judges who wandered too far from a Baconian line.[41] Judges appointed to these colonies continued to serve at the pleasure of the Crown for these reasons. That imperial concern to exercise firm control over the colonial judiciary in the non-white empire would strengthen in the last third of the nineteenth century, as anxieties about disaffection among the 'subject races' grew in intensity, is apparent in the narrative in chapter 9.

The Colonial Judiciary and Issues of Legal Culture

With the appointment of more judges with legal training and some professional experience to British colonies during the first half of the nineteenth century came at least a clearer understanding of the substance and procedures of that system.[42] The preferment of qualified and competent law officers with legal training and the growth of an indigenous bar often helped in that process. However, the introduction of

English law was not invariably seen as a blessing in colonial societies. The overall messy evolution of the Common Law and Equity and their procedural complexity did not necessarily fit well with the needs of societies in which people wanted simple, speedy, and comprehensible responses and solutions to their disputes and needs, in which they had some say.[43] Furthermore, in the older West Indian colonies there was confusion over how much of English common and statute law applied to them, planters in particular protesting that in the case of slavery local custom and legislation had replaced that parent legal system, if it had ever applied.[44] In colonies with unconventional and legal systems, such as those of New South Wales (a convict colony) and Newfoundland ('a nursery for fishermen'), in which local and authentic legal institutions and rules had developed in response to those communities' needs, the Common Law and Equity must have seemed like unnecessary excrescences on the local law, if not positively subversive of it.[45]

Judges who saw themselves as agents of English law and culture were on occasion caught between the demands of received law, and of the customs and practices, or novel legal predilections of the colonial societies that they served. English Law was, of course, not a system in stasis. It had evolved creatively under the leadership of Lord Chief Justices Sir John Holt and Lord Mansfield during the eighteenth century, especially in commercial matters. During the early nineteenth century it was transforming itself further to deal with the growth of trade and emergence of liberal economic theory, and the political, economic, and social impacts of and disruption wrought by the Industrial Revolution.[46] By 1830 a buzz was also in the air about rationalizing the received system of courts and simplifying civil procedure, although the pace of reform would be slow.[47] As well, reformist critics were assailing the traditional system of criminal justice, the first steps in response to those broadsides occurring after 1815. All these movements and mutterings had resonance in the colonies.

The introduction of the Common Law system into colonies with a pre-existing European legal system, or served by an 'advanced' indigenous system, was by no means smooth. Older systems were permitted to subsist, raising expectations in non-British populations about their preservation, while local colonial regimes and elites, sometimes with the verbal support of London, sought to have the Common Law supplant the previous system. Attempts at anglicization produced resistance, not to mention confusion, in several colonies including Lower Canada, Cape Colony, Trinidad, Mauritius, and Ceylon. Even where the pre-existing system seemed secure, it could undergo corruption if there were no judges trained in it on the bench or allowed to sit on cases, and judges trained in the Common Law applied its principles and procedures ineptly. As chapters 5 and 9 demonstrate, colonial judges were sometimes caught in the eye of the storm in these clashes of legal culture.

During the nineteenth century, Common Law colonial judges generally reacted negatively to the laws and customs of indigenous peoples that those groups wished to have govern them and their relationships.[48] In the main, these were men who had a monolithic view of sovereignty and its legal significance, assumed the superiority of English law to its 'savage' counterparts, and possessed little patience with the accommodation of custom and communal practices within the dominant legal system. Many shared the values of progress and improvement, held by the governments and communities that they served. Even the more humanitarian among them entertained no doubts about the value of inculcating in indigenous folk the values of European civilization, embodied in the notion of the trusteeship of the 'lesser races.'[49]

An underlying ideological construction of British justice and English law that produced different interpretations of law and justice in the colonies, as it did in the metropolis, was the slippery concept of the rule of law. Social historian Roy Porter, in his work on eighteenth-century Britain, describes it and the rhetoric supporting it most eloquently: 'In England … king and magistrates were beneath the law, which was the even-handed guardian of every Englishman's life, liberties, and property. Blindfolded Justice weighed all equitably in her scales. The courts were open, and worked by known and due process. Eupeptic fanfares such as those on the unique blessings of being a free-born Englishman under the Anglo-Saxon-derived common law were omnipresent background music. Anyone, from Lord Chancellors to rioters, could be heard piping them (though for very different purposes).'[50]

By the early nineteenth century, rule of law discourse and pride in its embodiment in institutions such as the right to judgment by one's peers, trial by jury, habeas corpus, right to petition the Crown, and a range of real or imagined 'rights of freeborn Englishmen' were ubiquitous among the British inhabitants of the empire.[51] As their new geography had nothing to offer them in the way of historical identity and connection, it was natural that they would look to political and legal culture of the metropolis that they believed they had carried with them.[52] The deployment of rule-of-law discourse reflected their strong sense of where they felt the balance between individual and state interests should lie in governance and the administration of justice. In a political sense it acted as a standard (or perhaps more correctly, a set of standards) by which to appraise the performance of those possessing governmental and judicial authority.

As I have argued elsewhere, interpretations of what the rule of law meant varied widely.[53] At one end of the spectrum was the conservative and legalistic view that the rule of law demanded that the actions of the state and its agents match a standard of legal validation. So if the action taken proceeded under the authority of a validly enacted statute, or according to the Common Law, then it was within the rule of law, even if the motives behind it and its effects were thoroughly arbitrary, illiberal, and discriminatory. Politically, this view operated on the assumption that liberty was achieved not by debate, disagreement, and dissension, least of all by the faction of parties and contesting ideologies, but by an ordered and deferential polity. At the other end of the spectrum, rule of law had a much more liberal, at times even radical, political meaning. Under this formulation the concept was a means of evaluating not only the formal legitimacy of the law, but also its substantive content and operation. Examining the latter allowed a determination of whether it accorded with the values of liberty, reflecting the belief that freedom meant protection of the individual from arbitrary, overweening, and corrupt action by the state. It followed that there was an obligation to challenge the policies of governments and their servants that undercut or threatened hallowed liberties. In multiracial colonies, such as those in the Caribbean, what appeared on the surface to be a liberal rendering of the concept was in fact an inversion of it, because its white (typically elite) champions confined its scope and protections exclusively to their own interests.[54] Those of colour were simply outside or barely within the pale.

The nature of rule-of-law engagement varied among the colonies. One feature of understanding of the rule of law in England, that was lacking in the colonies until the easing of executive control in the white settler colonies, was independence of the judiciary. Elsewhere in the empire this fundamental difference continued into the twentieth century. In some colonies trial by jury was a fact of life, while in others it was absent and a bone of contention. Several constitutional freedoms firmly established in Britain, such as no taxation without representation, proved contentious in various colonies, and others, like protection from arbitrary arrest and detention, were selectively and discriminatingly applied, such as in Caribbean possessions. Aspirations to freedoms, such as freedom of the press and of religion, were contested as they were in Britain, although constraints were removed or relaxed as the century progressed. In the case of developing rights, the colonies followed trends in the metropolis, except in those territories in which security considerations, reflecting the fault lines of racial discrimination and exploitation, made the process more fitful and tenuous.

Non-British European, non-European, and even indigenous inhabitants of these territories were ready to subscribe to the rule of law, insofar as it afforded rights, protection, dignity, and respect to them. They were not, however, impressed with attempts to deny its application to them on grounds of their assumed cultural inferiority. Moreover, non-Europeans and Aboriginal peoples were not at all happy when the rule of law and its underlying individualistic culture was used to submerge their traditional laws and cultural practices, especially those that reflected deeply held communal and spiritual values.

Conflicting interpretations of the rule of law and the rhetoric that supported them were as alive and well in the colonies of the second empire as they had been in the metropolitan power, the thirteen colonies, and Ireland in the eighteenth century.[55] The elusive argot of the rule of law was deployed, whether in the context of political debate in representative assemblies, on the hustings, in discussions in non-representative legislative and executive circles, arguments in court proceedings, in the columns of the colonial press, or, no doubt, in domestic parlours, taverns, and campsites. It should not be surprising, therefore, that within professional legal communities in imperial possessions, there were differing interpretations over what the rule of law meant in those societies. As chapters 4, 9, and 10 indicate, despite the imperial government's desire for a colonial judiciary that served primarily its interests and those of the colonial state, a minority of jurists, whether from conviction or for convenience, hewed to a more liberal interpretation of the rule of law than that of the executive or even their own colleagues. This brought several into conflict with colonial regimes they were expected to serve. By the same token, as chapter 5 demonstrates, there were instances in which ultraconservative jurists found themselves in conflict with legislative assemblies that represented predominantly reformist and liberal sentiments over the rule of law and its provenance.

If colonial judges were the primary agents of the translation of English legal culture to the empire, we need to know more about who these men were professionally as a group, what attracted them to the colonies, how they were appointed, the terms of their employment, and the sort of working and living conditions they encountered.

Colonial Judges: A Group Profile

How were colonial judges appointed, who were they in professional and personal terms, and what was the pool from which they were selected? Although political affiliation continued to play an important part in the selection of English judges during the nineteenth century as it had in the eighteenth, there is little doubt that it was leaders at the bar who secured judicial preferment.[56] These men were also wealthy, some as substantial landowners and an increasing number as a result of commercial investment. These were not people living in a state of 'genteel poverty.'

Closest to England and Ireland in a judiciary fashioned from a professional meritocracy were the British North American possessions. In several of these – Lower and Upper Canada, Nova Scotia, and New Brunswick – there were indigenous bars including men of considerable talent and success in practice who had prospered financially, such as William Smith of Quebec (who had practised and served briefly as a judge in New York), Jonathan Sewell of Lower Canada (who had practised in New York), John Beverley Robinson of Upper Canada (the scion of a Loyalist family from Virginia that had settled in Quebec and who was called to the English bar), Sampson Salter Blowers of Nova Scotia (yet another Loyalist lawyer from New York), and Ward Chipman of New Brunswick (who had been a junior lawyer in Massachusetts). Whether they would have made it to the top of the ladder in England or Ireland it is impossible to say.

By contrast to the English bench and the more celebrated members of the British North American judiciary, the colonial judicial service elsewhere attracted the 'also rans' among English, Irish, and Scottish barristers or advocates. Those attracted were drawn from the relatively large pool of men who would not make it to the dizzy heights as barristers in London or Dublin, or as advocates in Edinburgh. They came largely from the ranks of those struggling to make a name for themselves, or, at best, reaping the modest rewards of being journeymen counsel. A mark of their struggle to make ends meet is that they often had to supplement their incomes by court reporting or writing texts and annotations on areas of law with which they were acquainted.[57] Their situation did not necessarily reflect sloth or incompetence, although there were examples of both, but was a product of being in a profession that relied heavily on independent financial resources and the right contacts to bring in business. In John Bennett's pungent words, these men 'languished under the "closed shop" system that kept the Bar the wealthy domain of the anointed few.'[58] A certain proportion of them were also in debt, some to a chronic degree.[59] For those ready to try their hand at legal service overseas, either as judges or law officers of the Crown, the financial prospects, not to mention enhanced status as important fish in the small ponds of colonial societies, were undoubtedly tempting.

Salary and Pension Issues

The salaries and pensions finally set for the English bench in 1825 in a scheme that replaced the prior system of basic salaries supplemented by fees and the sale of lucrative jobs as court officials, were handsome, ranging from £10,000 for the lord chancellor down to £5,500 for puisne justices.[60] Fees were directed to the public purse to help cover the cost of running the courts. These figures, along with the sources of wealth derived from successful practices, family inheritance, successful land management, or investment (or all of these blessings), meant that these were well-heeled individuals.

Within the empire the only region where salaries came close to those in England was India, although not enough to attract the rising stars of the English and Irish bars.[61] Outside India, judicial salaries varied widely. Factors such as the importance of the colony in the imperial mind, a general policy of parsimony in paying colonial officials (whether the paymaster was in London or a colonial legislature), a judge's level of experience, access by judges to fees, judges' pressure for increases (although this worked only episodically), and possibly a felt need for 'danger pay' seem to have played into the calculations.

In British North America, salaries that ranged between £450 for a puisne judge to £850 for the senior judge (the figures for Nova Scotia by 1838) seem parsimonious in the extreme until fees are factored in.[62] The fact that when in the 1830s the Nova Scotia legislature sought to abolish access to fees there was consternation among the judges suggests that it was only a blending of salary and fees that provided a comfortable level of remuneration.[63]

In the Australian colonies there were great disparities. The first chief justice of New South Wales, Francis Forbes, received a salary of £2,000 in 1822 – the high end of Australian judicial rewards.[64] At the other end of the scale the original salary of the chief justice of South Australia, the first viable free settler colony in Australia established in 1836, was pegged at £500 (a sign of the stinginess of the colony's commercial founders).[65]

In Caribbean colonies, according to the commissions investigating the administration of justice in these possessions during the 1820s, the spectrum of rewards for judges in the first third of the nineteenth century was broad. Professionally trained chief justices received between £1,000 and £3,000 per annum, often with access to fees.[66] Lay chief justices, assistant or puisne judges, were salaried at lesser amounts, received a combination of stipend and fees, or survived solely on fees. These men were typically planters or merchants or professionals servicing them, and often independently wealthy.

The Appointment System for Colonial Judges

How did colonial judges secure their positions? In most instances through a combination of patronage and the impenetrable fashion in which the Colonial Office made appointments. John Bennett has wryly observed, 'In the appointment of judges, the [Office] moved in a mysterious way its wonders to perform.'[67] Patronage meant that there was someone of substance, an aristocrat, judge, academic, educator, or even a senior practitioner, who was willing to vouch for the talent, experience, and morals of an applicant for preferment to the colonial bench. Often left unstated, but nevertheless an important, possibly the dominant, ingredient in the menu of qualities was that the individual was a 'gentleman.'[68] With the occasional exception, the assumption would have been in most instances that the individual's status as a barrister or advocate meant that he was by definition a gentleman.

Serving as a law officer of the Crown, and especially as attorney general, was one route into the colonial judiciary, although, unlike the situation in England, this was not guaranteed. It was, moreover, an avenue that allowed for clearer assessment of an individual's experience in an office of state as a criterion for preferment. In the translation of law officers to the judiciary, the views of the governor or lieutenant governor were usually of considerable importance, although the final word always lay with London. There were duds elevated to the bench from the ranks of government lawyers, such as the unspeakable sot and wife-beater Alexander Baxter, appointed to the Van Diemen's Land bench after an inglorious term as attorney general in New South Wales.

However, there were also examples of former attorneys general and solicitors general serving with distinction, although not always without controversy, as colonial judges. They include Sampson Salter Blowers of Nova Scotia, Ward Chipman of New Brunswick, Jonathan Sewell of Lower Canada, John Beverley Robinson of Upper Canada, and Roger Therry of New South Wales.

In colonies such as the Canadas, Nova Scotia, and New Brunswick, with well-established legal communities, the practice of appointing members of local bars was well developed by the 1830s.[69] Although, as David Bell notes of New Brunswick, petitions for appointment as a law officer or judge, whether for the petitioner or a relative, between 1788 and the 1830s, depended on pulling strings in London, and thereafter to the grant of responsible government, 'factors such as professional eminence, especially status as attorney- or solicitor-general, and the favour of the lieutenant governor, played more of a role.'[70] The process of advocating both for and against the appointment and continued tenure of judges in the Caribbean lasted a great deal longer, on occasion affected by powerful lobbying groups representing West Indian planters in London.

And what of those appointed from the British Isles? Men uncertain of their future at a metropolitan bar and attracted to colonial service would variously apply to the Colonial Office on their own motion, follow the advice of a patron or mentor, or let the latter propose his name formally or informally.[71] Although the individual's politics was not necessarily a deciding factor, it no doubt helped, if it matched that of the government in power in Westminster. In this the political connections of patrons could also be important.

To demonstrate how the system worked in individual cases, it is sufficient to point to a few examples. Robert Thorpe, one of the subjects of this book, was able to parlay an association (maybe even a friendship) with Lord Castlereagh during their years as students at Trinity College Dublin into support by this rising star in the British government for his appointment as first chief justice of Prince Edward Island and then as puisne justice in Upper Canada.[72] Prior to his initial appointment, it appears that he had been a struggling barrister in Dublin. Remarkably, the ties that bound in this case were strong enough to survive Thorpe's removal from the Upper Canadian bench for misbehaviour. Castlereagh was ready to recommend the judge for appointment as the first professional judge in Sierra Leone.[73]

James Dowling, having surmised that his modest salary as an English barrister with a wife and six children, which he supplemented with income from law reporting, was inadequate, applied for the new position of puisne judge of the New South Wales.[74] After twelve years at the bar he was able to call in aid the patronage of Henry Brougham, 'then in his ascendancy,' and favourable testimonials from Justice Bayley, Solicitor General Tindal, and Serjeant Henry Stephen, elder brother of James Jr. Brougham remarked to Lord Goderich, the secretary of state, that he had 'known [Dowling] for some years – both professionally and personally' and that 'he would be a very excellent person for any such station and his name is well known in Westminster Hall.'[75]

Charles Cooper, second chief justice of South Australia, had rather blotted his copybook at the Colonial Office by earlier turning down the position of solicitor general of New South Wales.[76] His practice was modest and he had written a minor practice book on the regulation of municipal corporations, either to make money or while away the time left by the gaps in his briefs. He garnered support in his application from an array of legal heavy hitters, including Lord Denman, Justices Littledale and Patteson, the attorney general, and Serjeant Taulford. Crucial though in persuading the Colonial Office to overcome its doubts over Cooper's fitness was a letter from Dr Charles Mayo, an educational reformer and acquaintance of Cooper's. As John Bennett reports, 'Mayo could offer no opinion as to Cooper's standing as a lawyer and he was disarmingly frank in his general appraisal. "So far," he wrote, "as concerns high principle and solid rather than brilliant talents he is I conceive eminently qualified to fill a situation of high responsibility."'[77] This, together with Mayo's description of Cooper as a devout Anglican tending towards evangelical views but not entirely embracing them, and 'liberal in his view of those that differ' was sufficient, suggests Bennett, to persuade James Stephen Jr, by now permanent undersecretary for the colonies, that here was the man for the job.

Patronage continued to play an important role in colonial judicial appointments throughout the century. Matthew Baillie Begbie, the first chief justice of the mainland colony of British Columbia, appointed in 1858, was fortunate enough to have attracted the attention and support of Sir Hugh Cairns, the solicitor general of England in the Tory government of the Earl of Derby, and later lord chancellor.[78] Cairns was also a fellow member of the Lincoln's Inn. Cairns described Begbie, a chancery barrister of fourteen years' standing, who also added to his income by law reporting, 'personally, physically and mentally *well* qualified for the every [*sic*] peculiar office that is to be filled.'[79] He added that he knew 'of no other person (*who would accept* it) of whom the same could be said.'[80]

On occasion, chief justices were drawn from the ranks of the puisne justices. Clearly the governor or lieutenant governor would have a significant say in who should be appointed in such cases. In some instances there was heavy competition from among the puisnes for the *palm d'or* that produced a spirited, if not vicious, round of lobbying by patrons in London. This occurred on the retirement of Chief Justice Forbes from the New South Wales bench in 1837, when the advocates of both Justice James Dowling and Justice William Burton, who coveted the prize, moved into full gear.[81] In the face of pressure from Dowling's brother, Vincent, a London newspaper editor, and Lord Brougham on that judge's behalf, and from Governor Bourke, his son Richard, James Macarthur, the scion of a leading Tory family in the colony, and P.M. Stewart, an English MP, who supported Burton, the secretary of state, Lord Glenelg, prevaricated.[82] This was so, despite Undersecretary Stephen's inclination towards Dowling. Glenelg, having given the green light informally to first Dowling then Burton, changed his mind. He sought to 'placate' the rivals and save himself embarrassment by a plan to move Pedder from Van Diemen's Land to fill Forbes's shoes, replace him as chief justice there with Dowling, and leave Burton where he was.[83] On hearing of this plan, Vincent Dowling, whose paper supported the Whigs, unleashed his fury on the Colonial Office. The veiled threats of Vincent and his proprietors came through 'loud and clear.' Glenelg confirmed Dowling as the new chief.[84] He left Pedder where he was, and Burton, denied the prize, licked his wounds for a while in New South Wales but then moved on to an arguably more prestigious position, and higher salary as a judge in Madras.[85]

The Realities of Working in the 'Trenches' of Colonial Justice

If the English judges were both competent in the law and well heeled, they also benefited from the deference paid to them as the 'guardians of the Common Law,' symbolized, for instance, in the pomp and circumstance surrounding the opening of the county assizes, when the judges took the law to the provinces.[86] Also important was the experience of professional and class connections that they enjoyed, both as members of a small and close-knit judicial community to a man imbued with a profound sense of tradition, and their place within it, and of the broader community of barristers with whom they interacted at the Inns of Court and provincial bar messes. The tightness of the community, especially that of brother judges, meant that they were privy to the collective professional and personal values of that group, and to sources of counsel and advice in dealing with the challenges of interpreting and applying the law. It is likely too that the eccentricities an individual betrayed were often either hidden or regulated by that person's membership in this group. As public men, social contact with politicians and intellectuals was open to them and actively pursued by some.[87] The style of life that British high court judges enjoyed went with the privilege and high status accorded to them and was sophisticated, rich, and rewarding.

Some of these benefits existed in colonies, such as the major possessions in British North America, in which an indigenous bar had developed and a local lawyer joined the judiciary. In possessions with less mature legal and judicial institutions, they were lacking. This could be and was a shock to jurists appointed from Britain. When a colonial jurist, perhaps flush with the warm feeling of recognition and status, reached the colony to which he was appointed, he sometimes faced challenges that undercut that initial sense of success. Unlike his counterparts in Britain and British North America, he was seldom part of a tight-knit community of judges and lawyers as a source of professional and personal support. In some colonies he would be the sole judge, or at best blessed with one or two colleagues, and with a sparse bar, on whom he could rely for support and camaraderie.[88] At the same time, colonial societies were typically fractious, as individuals and groups vied openly and vigorously for power and influence. In consequence, one could not invariably take one's status or reputation for granted or assume goodwill, even from one's professional colleagues.[89] This reality proved to be a problem for judges who took positions on law and politics that were contrary to the views of the colonial executive, their own judicial colleagues, powerful elites, assemblymen, newspaper editors, or sizeable segments of colonial society.[90] Moreover, if a judge exhibited a cantankerous disposition, it could often reverberate to his detriment in these places. The 'living in a fish bowl' syndrome was a fact in these communities. A vigorous and none too respectful colonial press was invariably interested in the professional, political, and personal lives of judges, along with those of other colonial officials.[91] When a colonial judge proved to be controversial for one reason or another, different segments of the local press would line up for and against him. He was, like it or not, newsworthy.

If issues of professional status and respect were not potential irritants, the conditions of judicial service at a personal level could be. For gentlemen who took their professional status seriously, impressed by the salaries granted to them and the comfortable living that those emoluments promised, the actual conditions of colonial life were sometimes a bitter disappointment. In some territories, especially those far distant from the centre of empire, salaries were inadequate to meet local costs and the style of life to which these men and their families believed they were entitled.[92] There were frequent complaints from colonial judges about arrears in their salaries and the stinginess of the colonial authorities in approving expenses.[93] The complainers were not only the chronically indebted, but also those who were not independently wealthy and found it difficult to make ends meet. Some judges, especially in the earlier years of colonial settlement, benefited from grants or the purchase of land in the possessions in which they served and generated wealth as a consequence.[94] However, possession of tracts of land, as the experience of judges or their widows in several Australian colonies demonstrates, could itself become a burden if the productive use of that property was undercut by a period of economic depression.[95]

In addition to financial insecurity were some of the less pleasant features of life on the imperial 'fringes.' These included inadequate court facilities (including the judge's residence and a theatre)[96] and domestic accommodation (draughty and leaky residences),[97] diseases (a particular problem in colonies in the tropics),[98] the rigours and privations of life on circuit (in territory ranging from desert, through jungle, to mountainous terrain and sub-zero temperatures in ice and snow),[99] social ostracism if one fell out with the politically powerful or vocal, and what must have seemed to some a cultural wasteland (a concern for those who pined for the glittering life of London, Dublin, or Edinburgh).

Having made this point, it is important not to belabour it. The conditions of employment for colonial judges and the contexts in which they had to operate did not always match those in Britain, nor did they invariably live up to the expectations of ambitious professionals who as gentlemen and jurists anticipated both career success and personal comfort from their employment. However, there were some like Matthew Baillie Begbie of British Columbia who revelled in the challenges of doing justice in the remote fastnesses of the colonial world and prospered as a result (Begbie enjoyed doing circuits on horseback, was an itinerant polymath, hunter, and amateur cartographer, participated enthusiastically in local cultural initiatives, and died well heeled).[100] A significant majority of those appointed, once they had settled into life in the colonies they served, put their heads down and did what was expected of them in applying the law and administering justice. As a result, they kept their seats. For some of these men the perquisites of office and respect in which they were held were sufficient to maintain their interest and loyalty.

With a sense of the evolution of the administration of justice in Britain's overseas possessions in the nineteenth century and of the pedigree of and working conditions experienced by colonial justices, it is now time to consider the stories of colonial judges in trouble.

4

The Perils of the Colonial Judiciary: Courting Reform in a Counter-revolutionary Empire, 1800–1830

A By-election in East York

It was late December 1806. The excitement of a by-election was in the crisp winter air in the riding of East York in Upper Canada. Supporters of the two candidates were in the streets enthusiastically waving flags and banners. Across the banners of Robert Thorpe were emblazoned the words 'The King, the People, the Law, Thorpe and the Constitution,' and his flags displayed Irish harps without a crown above them. Thorpe was an unlikely candidate for an assembly seat, as he was a puisne justice of the Court of King's Bench.[1] Supporters of his rival, Thomas Gough, noted the lack of crowns, which suggested Thorpe sympathized with the United Irishmen who had rebelled against the British Crown in 1798.[2]

Thorpe prevailed, winning the seat left vacant by the untimely death in a duel of William Weekes, an excitable Irishman, lawyer, member of the House of Assembly, and close friend and confidante of the judge.[3] On taking his seat in the House, Thorpe made it clear that his mission was to act as leader of the opposition. It was not long before Lieutenant Governor Francis Gore moved to relieve him from office, a decision confirmed by the secretary of state for the colonies, Lord Castlereagh.[4]

What are we to make of this remarkable scenario's significance for an understanding of the tenure, accountability, and independence of colonial judges in the early-nineteenth-century British Empire? The answer lies in part in the counter-revolutionary system of colonial governance in place in British North America in the wake of the American War of Independence, and the resistance it inspired among those members of this colonial society who were committed to a more liberal and egalitarian notion of constitutionalism.

The assumptions of the imperial government about the establishment of peaceful, ordered, and compliant communities in Upper and Lower Canada soon proved to be misplaced, as both demonstrated a growing spirit of fractiousness from their founding in 1791.[5] In particular, there was a diversity of political ideology – both within the Loyalist population born of their experience as North Americans, and across the broader European societies in these territories – that belied the notion of automatic acceptance of Pitt and Grenville's constitutional vision and uncomplaining acceptance of British values.[6] For the moment, however, we need to look at Robert Thorpe and his introduction to life as a colonial judge.

Robert Thorpe as Chief Justice of Prince Edward Island

Thorpe was Irish. Born in Dublin a Protestant, he graduated from Trinity College in 1789 and was called to the Irish bar a year later.[7] We know nothing about his years as a young barrister in the Irish capital. However, he might well have been drawn to the growing concern among young members of the bar about Ireland's constitutional subservience and the emasculation of Whig attempts to achieve its self-determination within the empire.[8] Through preferment secured by his connections with Lord Castlereagh, a former colleague at Trinity and a member of Pitt the Younger's coterie, and later, government, Thorpe entered the colonial judicial service in 1802 as chief justice of Prince Edward Island.[9] He arrived in the colony in November of that year.

The unsatisfactory state of land tenure on the island was touched upon briefly in chapter 3 in referring to Peter Stewart's problems as chief justice.[10] The problem was London's decision to carve up the former French colony into large domains, offered by lottery to British landlords. The belief was that they would eagerly develop the land for settlement and productive use.[11] Many were not so moved, content instead to hold the land without improving it, playing the classic role of absentee landlords (the comparisons with Ireland are obvious). The imperial government had proven ineffective in ensuring that these grandees paid for their failure to carry out their obligations by enforcing the system of quit rents that were a condition of holding the land and designed to provide for the costs of administering the colony, and escheat whereby proprietors in breach would forfeit their land to the Crown (providing the Crown with the freedom to reallocate it). This 'feudal' system of land grants and lack of enforcement engendered a deep sense of injustice among those genuinely trying to develop and settle their land: small holders and landless tenants. As the new judge arrived, steps were underway to underline the obligations of large landholders by a statutorily sanctioned enforcement system of quit rents and escheat.

Thorpe's sojourn in the colony was not a happy one. His communications with the Colonial Office betray several characteristics symptomatic of his behaviour throughout most of his colonial service: the first, reporting to the Office on the political state of the colony, its players, and what was needed to improve things, much as one might expect a colonial governor to do; the second, bad mouthing those individuals whom he disliked; the third, whining about the personal circumstances in which he and his large family found themselves.

In terms of a political role for the chief justice, Thorpe made his intentions clear about a political role early in his tenure, pompously announcing that, in that position, he would play an important role in the law and politics of the island, while, of course, acting 'without any insinuation, or partiality.'[12] He discerned very quickly the problems the colony faced in attracting settlement, the reasons for its slow pace, and the resulting tensions within the community. His advice to the secretary of state on overall policy towards the island and several other maritime colonies in the region was that London needed to pay more attention to their defence, welfare, and economic potential.[13] Key to the success of that policy, he asserted, was the active encouragement of settlement.

Thorpe recognized that the legal tools for enforcing quit rents, and using escheat to penalize and divest ownership of those landholders who did little or nothing to improve and settle their land, were crucial to working economic and social change on the island. Moreover, he counselled London that vigorous enforcement of the quit rent legislation required imperial government pressure, because the colonial executive was so closely allied with the landed interests on the island.[14] However, as he reviewed the history of unsuccessful attempts to enforce earlier legislation, he concluded that local legislative initiatives were 'useless, inadequate and unjust.'[15] The only viable solution lay with the courts and the Crown's invocation of the writ of *scire facias* to induce owners to comply with the law or lose their land. This approach would provide the secretary of state with all the discretion needed to confirm or reallocate grants, impose conditions, balance interests, and, most importantly, encourage settlement.[16] Implicit in this advice was the strong feeling that the judiciary provided the only guarantee that justice would be done on the land issue.[17] London did not follow his advice on this matter, as the legislative scheme was proclaimed and enforcement proceedings began. True to form, Thorpe fought to ensure that lots released from their previous owners did not go 'to mercenary individuals or [were] bartered to enrich the few and disgust the many,' but were distributed 'amongst the Loyal and industrious to induce population, stimulate trade and promote prosperity.'[18]

It was not only the system of landholding that offended Thorpe. The attitudes and behaviour of the people in charge of the colony, the social and economic elite, and, for good measure, those of the general population also affronted him. The 'upper orders' he described as 'inert, irresolute and undignified'; the 'lower orders' as licentious, slothful, inebriated, and disaffected.[19] His distrust of the elites was matched by an undemocratic lack of faith in the wider community, particularly when it came to land holding: 'There is a levelling Republican spirit in the People, no respect for the Government or the officers of the Crown. All is equality, ignorance and inebriation ... [I]f [escheated lands] are divided among the lower orders here of a few hundred acres each I fear it will increase these dangerous principles.'[20]

This dyspeptic view of the masses was also evident in his even less charitable view of his own countrymen. Commenting on Ireland, he described it as 'radically rotten,' adding, 'how fortunate it would be if you could transport two million of the inhabitants to Santo Domingo.'[21]

Thorpe's enthusiasm for the politics of the colony did not serve him well in job satisfaction. A year after arriving in Prince Edward Island, he reported plaintively to his colonial masters that he had no support in the island for his efforts to build it up.[22] In the absence of a colonial government willing to provide 'dignified, intelligent, active vigorous' leadership, he feared that he could not be useful in the affairs of the islands and sought retirement or reassignment.[23]

Little is known of Thorpe's performance as a judge. However, one episode suggests a lack of impartiality where he felt an antagonist had unjustifiably eluded the law's jealous gaze. He and the attorney general of the colony, Peter Magowan, had a falling out over Magowan's refusal to indict the chief justice's leading nemesis, Magistrate John

Holland, for his imprisonment of a sailor.[24] Thorpe claimed the man had been the victim of 'tyranny, malice, oppression [or] wilful neglect,' or had been treated 'improperly from interest, favour or affection.'[25] Magowan concluded that Holland was justified in detaining the sailor. Passengers on the vessel on which he served had made allegations of assault and threats by him. Mr Attorney believed it legitimate to have imprisoned him so that he could dry out before being examined. The magistrate in error had overlooked the incarceration the next day, only remembering his oversight on his way to another community. The man had been duly released and had taken his leave. He had made no complaints about his treatment. The attorney general could find no basis for alleging malice. Holland had been guilty, at worst, of administrative neglect – not a sufficient basis for prosecuting him. He duly reported these conclusions to the chief justice.[26] Thorpe remained unrepentant in this matter, effectively accusing the law officer of showing favouritism to Holland as a witness.[27] Magowan, defending himself and the prosecutorial discretion of the attorney general in English practice to Lieutenant Governor Fanning, noted the maudlin and dyspeptic view that the judge entertained of the colony and its inhabitants.[28] Moreover, he indicated that there were other occasions on which the judge had proven dictatorial towards him, and impossible to budge from a preliminary assumption of guilt, unsupported by the available evidence.

The chief justice was not shy about criticizing and snitching on associates in the governance of the colony, in some instances in gossipy terms. In a thinly veiled swipe at Lieutenant Governor Fanning, he reported that Fanning had accompanied a dissenting preacher to the local place of worship, where this man had the gall to preach (this in the absence of the overworked Anglican minister).[29] The incident was, he felt, symptomatic of the subversive ways in which Protestant dissenters had insinuated themselves into the colonial power structure.[30] The implication was strong that the chief executive had allowed this distasteful episode to occur. More open and vitriolic, however, was Thorpe's attack on Holland, who was acting fort major and a member of the Legislative Assembly, as well as a magistrate, who the judge feared would be confirmed in his military post.[31] This man he described as 'the veriest [*sic*] reptile that could be placed in a New Country to destroy it by viciousness.'[32] He also referred to Holland's 'democratical exertions,' which, said the judge, he assured by being guilty of every conceivable 'wickedness that could be practiced in a little community.'[33] Along with this fusillade, Thorpe stressed Mrs Holland's friendship with Madame Ste

Le Rouge, the Duke of Kent's 'reported mistress.'[34] It was the duke, he added with a wink and a nod, who had given the acting fort major his military preferment.

The lifestyle that the Thorpe family encountered fell well below their expectations. Their house was in ill repair. This, together with the high cost of living, the rigours of the climate, and illness in the family weighed heavily on the judge's mind, as he was at pains to report to the Colonial Office.[35] Mrs Thorpe's health seems to have been most affected. However, according to Thorpe, the seven children (all under the age of ten) were also suffering from the privations of life on the island. They were, he said, 'enfeebled in both mind and body from want of education and exercise, neither of which they can obtain here.'[36] Arrears in salary are mentioned in the judge's correspondence from the island, although it is not clear whether these relate to him or other servants of the Crown, or, if to him, the exact time frame of the shortfall.[37] What is certain is that he was experiencing difficulties in making ends meet, and feeling the frustrations of failing to match the lifestyle to which he believed he and his family were entitled.[38]

Despite the self-important and self-serving content of Thorpe's letters to the Colonial Office, his plea for a leave to return to England was granted. He made the journey late in 1804.[39] He was anxious to have the issue of salary arrears resolved and to be allowed to retire from or to be reassigned in the colonial service.[40] He succeeded in a request to have his leave extended, because of the impracticality of returning to the island in winter.[41] The judge clearly used the time to good effect in testing the colonial job market, because by the end of April 1805 the Colonial Office appointed him second puisne judge of the Court of King's Bench of Upper Canada.[42] One suspects that his friend Lord Castlereagh once again went to bat for his protégé.

In his two short years in Prince Edward Island, Robert Thorpe appears as a complex, intelligent individual with a restless spirit, sharp tongue, and overdeveloped ego. Politically, he had a very good grasp of the unsatisfactory state of land settlement on the island, and of the perils of not dealing resolutely with it. His experience of Ireland's social and economic problems may well have been influential in this regard. Moreover, he had a good, if paternalistic, view of the need to advance the fortunes of the colony and region. His comments on both the colonial 'lower orders' and the majority of his countrymen betray an illiberal and anti-democratic streak in his political makeup. Thorpe's problem was not the fact that he had political views, but that politics was already an obsession with him. He could not resist expatiating on it and propagating his own remedies at the drop of a hat. The role of self-styled political guru was potentially perilous for any colonial judge, even though he was, as in Thorpe's case, formally involved in the governance of the colony as chair of the Legislative Council. What authority, if any, did he have to report to Westminster on the state of the island's politics? The records are silent on whether he had any special instructions from London. On occasion the Colonial Office requested that chief justices report on the state of affairs in the colonies in which they served.[43] The only hint in Thorpe's correspondence with the home government was in a May 1803 letter to Lord Hobart, in which he stated that on leaving England he 'was desired by friends accustomed to official etiquette to lay before your Lordship the best information [he] could obtain of this Island.'[44] These 'friends' might have included Castlereagh. Whatever the inspiration, this jurist had established a pattern of reporting to London on colonial politics. What did Lieutenant Governor Fanning make of all of this? In such a small settler community he cannot have been insensible of what his chief justice was up to. However, there are no extant records of complaints to London about Thorpe poking his nose into matters that should not have concerned him. However, Attorney General Magowan's comments on Thorpe's distempers may well have reflected Fanning's sentiments.[45] Fanning's career in Prince Edward Island seems to have been prompted by a desire to avoid the sharp lines and pace of change that the chief justice favoured on land policy and settlement.[46] He would likely have been relieved to hear that Thorpe would not be returning to the island, even though he himself retired in 1805.

Thorpe's excessive judgmentalism was evident in his capacity for treating those he disliked, or whom he saw as standing in his way, as untrustworthy, or worse still, subversive, and in his lack of scruple in reporting his sentiments. This side of his personality had the potential to get him into trouble with both those who were the targets of his barbs and imperial officialdom. Even if there was substance in his criticisms, their tone was unlikely to win him many friends or influence people. The same was true of his propensity to whine about his personal circumstances. Although the imperial authorities could be frustratingly insensitive to legitimate concerns about the salaries and working conditions of colonial officials, they were likely to tire of this sort of self-indulgent pleading.

The Misadventures of Robert Thorpe in Upper Canada

This was the man who arrived in Upper Canada in 1805. Carved out of the western reaches of Quebec, the colony was the product of pressure from English-speaking inhabitants of the area, predominantly Loyalist refugees from the United States. These people desired to live in a colony in which they would constitute the English-speaking majority, governed not only by English criminal law that applied in Quebec, but also by its private and commercial law, which did not.[47] Along with a powerful lieutenant governor, appointed Legislative and Executive Councils, and an elected representative assembly, a centralized court system with the Court of King's Bench at the apex had soon been added.[48] In the new colony the British constitution would be emulated as far as possible, subject to the indirect but nevertheless overarching authority of the imperial executive and Parliament. Furthermore, English law would normally be applicable. London ensured the subservient status of the colony by vesting considerable executive power in the lieutenant governor, allowing him to ignore local legislative advice, dismiss ministers at will, and prorogue the legislature whenever he considered it appropriate.[49] His powers to raise funds immune to scrutiny in the assembly meant he also enjoyed a degree of fiscal independence. Control over colonial judges was secured by their being appointed by the imperial government and serving at the pleasure of the Crown. Jurists were expected to be loyal servants of the empire.[50]

This vision of Upper Canada as an ordered and deferential polity was soon belied by tensions in political and social thought among the colonists. Within Loyalist ranks there were different interpretations of what it meant to be a British North American. True, some individuals clung to a conservative British Whig ideal of governance and law, and the political and social assumptions underlying it. However, others felt the influence of their American experience more strongly and brought with them egalitarian notions of government and localized traditions of law and law-making. The arrival of new American immigrants in the colony attracted by the liberal land policies of the first lieutenant governor, John Simcoe, resulted in a further watering down of the political homogeneity of the population, and greater indifference towards elitist notions of British constitutionalism and the replication of strictly British values.[51]

Within the first decade of Upper Canada's founding, signs of discontent with the colonial government emerged. Among irritants were executive favouritism in making land grants to the military brass and to its friends, and the award of monopoly franchises to commercial entrepreneurs close to the regime.[52] Another bone of contention was creditors' seizure of defaulting debtors' land. A majority of the Court of King's Bench determined in 1798 that they could, citing in support much earlier imperial legislation applicable to 'the plantations.'[53] Justice Henry Alcock, dissenting, contended that the majority's decision would be ruinous to small farmers – a position he made clear to Lieutenant Governor Peter Hunter in 1801 when Hunter was considering whether to enshrine the majority decision in legislation.[54] As in other frontier colonies, problems associated with mercantile credit and debt were never far from the surface.[55]

By the turn of the century, immigration added other flavours to the ideological stew. A group of Irish Whigs arrived in Upper Canada in the wake of the 1798 Irish Rebellion. Unlike United Irishmen seeking freedom from the British yoke who gravitated to the United States, those remaining loyal to the British Crown in that conflict sought a new and more peaceful life elsewhere under British rule.[56] They did so because of the turmoil in their native land and opposition to its absorption into the British state, wrought by Pitt's Act of Union of 1800.[57] Although republicanism was not part of their political credo, the American War of Independence had profoundly affected the thinking of these migrants or their immediate ancestors.[58] The war had provided evidence of a need to reconfigure the relations between Britain as the imperial power and its dependencies, by loosening imperial bonds. These individuals had a strong belief in a form of governance based on a constitutional compact between monarch and people, with a parliament responsible to its electors, and an executive responsible to the legislature. In theory the British Parliament's grant of constitutional independence to Ireland in 1782 had embodied this vision.[59] However, its potential had been subverted as the ink dried on the legislation. London failed to surrender its control over the Irish ministry, and the conservative ascendancy rejected or watered down reformist measures designed to reduce their control and that of absentee landlords over land, to liberalize trade and social relations, and to remove Roman Catholic religious and political disabilities on the island. The dream of an executive responsible to the Irish people through the parliament foundered. In the minds of its advocates, its betrayal was responsible for Ireland's slide into anarchy and rebellion in the late 1790s.[60] Given that bitter experience, it was natural enough that these men would favour a reformed conception of the relationship with the colonial power in their newfound home, in which colonists would have power to govern themselves.[61]

The new judge arrived in York during an administrative interregnum caused by the death of Lieutenant Governor Peter Hunter, a former army officer who had served in Ireland in 1798. The Executive Council chaired by Alexander Grant as president, himself a former army officer and office holder under Hunter, was governing the colony.[62] Another councillor, Peter Russell, had objected to Grant's appointment over him. Russell, an Irishman and veteran of the American War, had earlier administered the colony in the late 1790s, after John Simcoe, the colony's first lieutenant governor, left office, and he felt aggrieved at being passed over in favour of Hunter. He now expressed bitter disappointment at being sidetracked once again.[63] Grant, for his part, suspected that both Thorpe and his Irish lawyer friend William Weekes were encouraging Russell's latest bid to secure leadership of the government. Certainly there was a degree of animus between Scottish office holders, pejoratively described as 'Scotch pedlars,' and several Irish aspirants to colonial government posts. The latter believed that the Scots received unfair preferment and were autocratic in their approach to governance.

True to form, Thorpe quickly became embroiled in Upper Canadian politics. His hastily developed views on the state of politics and law in the colony reflected the sentiments of these disgruntled Irish immigrants, with Russell as their symbolic head. The group had already developed into an informal opposition to Hunter's regime, led by the capable, if mercurial and irascible, Weekes.[64]

Hunter, these men asserted, had treated the colony as he would a regiment. They criticized him for his policy on land grants, to which he justifiably tried to bring some order.[65] An increase in fees for land grants, needed to support the registration system, led to resentment by all new grantees. Furthermore, the group, although not themselves affected, attacked Hunter's attempts to clean up the system of free grants by putting pressure on those who had failed, often over a term of years, to take up their allotments. They dubbed the initiative a particularly egregious example of arbitrary rule, especially in contrast to the ease with which newcomers secured land. Weekes, who had represented clients with grievances against the government on the land issue, no doubt encouraged these jibes. Suspicions that Hunter had benefited financially from pushing through patents for land grants amplified the criticism directed at him.

Hunter's administration had also been in bad odour because it used money raised by duties to cover executive expenses, without the assembly's approval. Finally, it was during his rule that the legislature, fearful of both Bonapartist designs and the activities of United Irishmen, passed the Sedition Act,[66] to deal resolutely and harshly with dissent and faction within the colony. The statute endowed not only the courts but also the executive and the legislature with power to issue warrants against non-residents, or those failing to take the oath of allegiance to His Britannic Majesty, and who were suspected of having spread or being about to spread sedition in the colony. The procedure was summary, the accused subject to a reverse onus, and the penalties included banishment. Failure to leave in the face of such an order was considered a capital offence. Weekes had vigorously opposed this legislation, in particular during a successful by-election bid in 1804, describing it as an arbitrary and oppressive measure infringing on the ancient liberties of Englishmen and open to executive and judicial abuse.[67]

Alexander Grant's interim regime sustained Hunter's policies, relying heavily on John McGill, treasurer, and Thomas Scott, attorney general, whom Hunter had appointed.[68] Opposition forces viewed these Scots as incompetent and malevolent, a shopkeeping 'aristocracy,' controlled by and toadying to merchants in the province and in Montreal. On opening the legislature early in 1806, Grant, noting Weekes' and Thorpe's criticisms, described them as 'fomenters of all the disorder amongst the Commons.'[69] Nevertheless the president proved conciliatory on several contentious issues, removing the restrictions on existing land claimants and restoring the funds previously appropriated by Hunter without legislative approval.

Various interest groups looked back on the Hunter era as a period during which a haughty, uncaring administration had ignored or trampled on their rights. The gripes that people had tended to be regional, related to their experience of life in areas where they had settled, and the nature and composition of society in those parts of the colony. The fertile lands of the southwest where many late Loyalists and other American migrants had put down roots were a particular site of grievances, particularly among the farming communities. Here were people, often with experience of a more democratic system of governance, uncertain of their political status, subject to local rule by seemingly insensitive and corrupt magistrates, and of a central government that appeared distant and autocratic. Insofar as they had a voice by representation in the House of Assembly, they found it ineffective in the face of executive manipulation and manoeuvre.[70]

Thorpe wasted no time in taking stock of the province's political situation. His views reflected his friendship with Weekes, whom he saw often in court and socially, whether in York or on circuit. Weekes, as a practising lawyer, felt himself well in tune with the colony's sources of tension.[71] He introduced Thorpe to the unfortunate situation of debtors, especially small farmers, now subject to forfeiture of their land to their creditors. In a dissenting decision in January 1806, in *Gray v. Willcocks*, in which Weekes represented the debtor, Thorpe followed Alcock's earlier opinion, concluding that land could not be seized for debt.[72] He also used the opportunity as an assize judge addressing grand and petit juries to feel the pulse of communities through interaction with those people. In the process he expatiated on his own views of governance, law, and the constitution.[73] The authorities suspected, and it was likely true, that Weekes assisted in bringing the judge into contact with the people. Significantly, the one assize circuit that Thorpe took was in the southwest, in which grumbling about arbitrary and corrupt government was strongest.

As in his Prince Edward Island sojourn, Thorpe was not shy about reporting his views to the Colonial Office in London. The fact that his mentor, Lord Castlereagh, had become secretary of state for colonial affairs in 1805, shortly after the Upper Canadian appointment, may have encouraged him. The judge's communications to his colonial masters give the impression of 'Thorpe and his friends ... [as] a turbulent, half-crazed handful of discontented placemen given to violent but cliched rhetoric out of all proportion to known grievances.'[74] The judge, convinced that he had an official responsibility to report to London on the state of the colony, and provide advice on improvements to its condition, found plenty to criticize and did so injudiciously. He described Hunter variously as 'rapacious,' 'guilty of the plunder of Eastern princes,' 'unjust and arbitrary,' and reliant on 'a few Scotch instruments about him ... that he made subservient to his purposes.'[75] The province Thorpe described as in 'a wretched state' but still redeemable from revolution or American design, if only *his* suggestions for its welfare were followed, painting himself as the potential saviour of the colony.[76] He warned London against further preferment of John McGill and Thomas Scott – the 'reptiles' appointed by Hunter who were, he asserted, universally 'execrated.'[77] Thorpe pleaded incessantly with the Colonial Office to appoint him the next chief justice. If not, then he requested a transfer, with the Cape of Good Hope as his preferred destination. When Thorpe learnt that the 'despicable' Attorney General Scott has been appointed chief justice, these entreaties intensified.[78]

The judge had hoped that the new lieutenant governor, Francis Gore, would bring good government and justice to the colony but on first encounter, concluded that he was likely no better than his predecessor. As he reported to Undersecretary Sir George Shee, in undiplomatic terms, he found Gore 'imperious, self sufficient and ignorant, impressed with a high notion of the old system' and surrounded by the old gang of 'Scotch pedlars.'[79]

Thorpe's inflated ego and hazy sense of discretion and decorum got the better of him with his decision to forego the Cape and stand in a by-election for the seat formerly held by his friend William Weekes.[80] Ironically, Weekes died in a duel with another lawyer, William Dickson, who had objected to his describing Hunter in open court as 'a Gothic Barbarian whom the providence of God had removed from this world for his tyranny and Iniquity.'[81] Several observers noted that Thorpe from the bench had done nothing to chide Weekes for this outburst.[82]

Despite Thorpe's claim that his standing for the seat reflected the popular will, it seems clear that the impetus was his belief that from the floor of the House he could lead the opposition and eventually exercise leadership in that chamber. His political obsessions by this time were dictating his actions. Even before his election he had appeared at the bar of the assembly giving advice to members.[83] As a member, Thorpe made it clear that he saw his role as one of vigorous opposition to the executive, even if it left him in a minority of one.

Thorpe's career as both a judge and provincial politician came to an abrupt end. Gore, already aware of Thorpe's 'interference' and 'designs,' had formed the opinion that he was a 'dangerous demagogue.'[84] After failing to persuade the judge not to run for the assembly and finding him a thorn in the gubernatorial flesh, Gore made his move to unseat him.[85] He sought London's authority to remove Thorpe from office and in the interim dropped him from the 1807 Commission of Assize.[86] He also encouraged a libel suit against the judge for suggesting that his mail was being tampered with (it may well have been).[87] The chief executive listened intently to reports of indiscretion by one or more or all of the 'Irish faction' as confirming his belief that they were United Irishmen in spirit, if not in name.[88] Castlereagh officially pronounced the judge dismissed from office by a letter dated 19 June 1807.[89] When

Thorpe headed back to England to make his case against suspension, he quit the scene of Upper Canadian law and politics. His final appointment was not the craved Cape, but Sierra Leone, hardly a plumb. As chapter 9 reveals, he became a controversial figure in that colony too, and Secretary of State Lord Bathurst recalled him in 1815.[90]

The Ideological Significance and Legacy of Robert Thorpe

This opéra bouffe makes it tempting to dismiss Thorpe and those around him as ineffective, unbalanced bit players in the Upper Canadian story. However, another side to this tale suggests otherwise.[91] Thorpe's extreme rhetoric, while strange for a judge in his public communications, was commonplace in both British and colonial oppositionist circles and had gotten two members of the Irish bench into trouble at roughly the same time.[92] Moreover, beneath it lay a set of beliefs about law and governance that were influential in Canadian constitutional evolution.

Thorpe's constitutional position reflected the experience of the Irish Whig opposition in the Irish Parliament in the last two decades of the eighteenth century, and their advocacy of compact constitutionalism. Those of this political heritage who settled in Upper Canada thought that they recognized signs of this idea written into the legislation establishing the colony. As they imagined it, the colony was given the full range of governmental and legislative institutions, a superior court system and trial by jury, with the purpose of creating a British domain in which something like responsible government would exist.[93] Ultimate power would reside in the representative body, ministerial responsibility would obtain, there would be no taxation without representation, and dependence on Westminster would be limited to matters of genuine imperial concern.[94] John Graves Simcoe's overenthusiastic reflection that the Upper Canadian Constitutional Act was 'the Magna Carta of the Colony' and 'a Perfect Image and Transcript' of the British constitution lent rhetorical weight to this view.[95] These men believed that the representatives of the Crown and their colonial friends had corrupted that original vision.

Apart from Irish Whig ideology, men like Thorpe and Weekes were also well versed in the beliefs and rhetoric of reformist British Whig ideology. Right of petition, freedom of the press, redress of grievances, trial by jury, habeas corpus, and the unacceptability of suspension of rights, whether by the prerogative or legislation, were part of the political and legal argot of both Irish and British reformers. This form of

Whig discourse also had resonance among those Loyalists who, while wishing to preserve the links with the British Crown, were not willing to accept all the cultural baggage that was said by conservatives to go with it. Further, migrants from the United States, attracted by economic opportunity rather than ideological or emotional ties, provided further fertile ground for more liberal views of colonial governance.[96] It was this combination of ideas about governance and law that drove the reform agenda in Upper Canada during the first decade of the nineteenth century. When Robert Thorpe talked to the grand jury about the glories of the British constitution, when he fulminated in correspondence against executive corruption and arbitrariness, when, in the assembly, he cited the impeachment of Charles I's favourite, Lord Strafford, and when he warned his fellow assemblymen of the dangers of abdicating control over duties levied by imperial statutes, it was this larger constellation of ideas and values that inspired him. They also reflected a concern that the Canadian colonies might well be on the same road to perdition as Ireland. In his correspondence Thorpe recognized the looming presence of the United States in Canadian affairs, and the potential for disaffection among the populace, particularly those who had migrated voluntarily from the south. Contrary to Lieutenant Gore's view that Thorpe and his friends were closet republicans, the evidence is that they passionately adhered to the British constitution as they understood it and saw themselves in the vanguard of protecting it from those who would subvert it.[97]

The problems were, as so often in history, those of timing and personalities. Thorpe and his faction had seriously miscalculated the intentions and motives of Pitt the Younger and his successors. The establishment of Upper and Lower Canada did not augur a new and more liberal colonialism. Rather, while giving the impression that the colonies would enjoy a copy of the balanced British constitution, the intention was that significant power should repose in the colonial executive to ensure the dependency of these territories. Lieutenant Governors Hunter and Gore fit the part, although perhaps with less agility and intelligence than the imperial government might have wished. The tension between the Irish party and Gore and his supporters reveals the clash of two diametrically opposed visions of colonial rule and authority. The era was hardly felicitous for the official version of colonial constitutionalism to give way, to be replaced by more liberal understandings of the relative rights and obligations of the imperial power and its colonies. With the unbending and anti-democratic sentiments of Gore and the petulant ego, political meddling, and impatience of Thorpe, any positive chemistry between them was impossible. Thorpe's insistence on adding an activist career in politics to his judicial role could only produce fission. It was not unheard of for judges to sit in representative legislatures,[98] but Thorpe's problem was considering himself as a power in – rather than just a commentator on – provincial politics, while also acting as an official arbiter of disputes, some of which would have involved government action. It is not surprising that Gore moved to dismiss him, and that London acceded to the request.

Although this maverick judge left Upper Canada, never to return, and quickly faded from memory, his constitutional views made a more indelible impression. They provided the basis for the version of responsible government that William Warren Baldwin and his son Robert advocated after 1820. The former, a non-vocal member of the Irish opposition group between 1804 and 1812, inherited his father's Irish Whig ideology.[99] This was blended with a conservative view of the British constitution learnt from his study of Blackstone's *Commentaries.*[100] However, the seal was set on the lawyer's constitutional views by his association with Thorpe and Weekes. Baldwin's constitutional theory followed very closely the compact theory of the Irish Whigs and may well have originated in an anonymous tract under the name 'Canadiensis' thought to be Thorpe's work.[101] Embryonic notions of responsible government in Upper Canada were rooted in the heady events of 1804 to 1807, and the thought patterns of a group of impatient, excitable, and egotistical Irish men for whom the colonial world was moving too slowly. Baldwin's contribution was to recognize the value of patience and moderation in pressing the argument for responsible government. Robert Thorpe and his friends had set the scene for it in the vivid tones that hastened their professional burial, but which lived on as inspirations to later and more politically astute reformers.

The Conservative Instincts and Behaviour of the Upper Canadian Government and Its Impact on the Administration of Justice, after 1807

Robert Thorpe was not the only Upper Canadian judge to fall afoul of a conservative colonial executive. Twenty-one years later, John Walpole Willis, also a puisne judge of the Court of King's Bench, suffered the same fate.[102] Lieutenant Governor Peregrine Maitland dismissed him from office in June 1828, in a decision that Secretary of State William

Huskisson confirmed the following month. Much water had flowed under the legal and political bridge in Upper Canada since Thorpe's departure.

The fault line between the conservative colonial executive, its members, and supporters on the one hand, and those of a reforming bent on the other, was to harden in the years after 1807. Most notably the lieutenant governor and his legislative supporters managed to silence Sheriff Joseph Willcocks of the Home District, one of the former judge's close associates who, like Thorpe, favoured a liberal interpretation of the colonial constitution and the rule of law, and was the editor of the first opposition newspaper, the *Upper Canadian Guardian*. This they did by having him convicted for contempt of his parliamentary privileges.[103]

The War of 1812 caused serious rifts in Upper Canadian society, as some, including Willcocks, threw in their lot with the Americans. Others, perhaps a majority of the population, were disaffected to one degree or another in mind, if not in action. A third politically influential group remained firmly committed to preserving the British connection and imperial governance at all costs.[104] The colonial and military authorities deployed both the Sedition Act of 1804 and militia legislation to deport or hold in preventative custody those suspected of disloyalty during the conflict. The government also mounted treason trials of a number of individuals either actually or suspected of aiding the enemy.[105] The generally accepted view among historians is that the procedural conduct of these trials was beyond reproach.[106] However, a backwash of suspicion about the loyalty of a sizeable portion of the population, and a hardening of the conservative mentality of the colonial executive and its friends, produced serious ideological conflict within Upper Canadian society. The bones of contention extended to the place and meaning of loyalty, the colony's constitution and its reading, the motives of its governors and those who opposed them, and, not least, the state of justice in the province.[107]

By the late 1810s the conservative and unimaginative viceroys appointed by London to Upper Canada were finding support in a definable colonial elite committed to high Tory notions of government and possessing a strong animus towards not only republicanism, but also democracy. This loosely aligned group that included judges and lawyers earned the unflattering sobriquet, the 'Family Compact.' Its members possessed a 'garrison mentality' and were not averse to manipulating and even perverting both the political and legal systems to preserve their interests, and those of their minions.[108] For these men the dangers to the survival and welfare of the colony lay in the republic to the south and its ideological influence within the colony. Ranged against them were the makings of an increasingly active opposition (by the 1820s sometimes enjoying a majority in the House of Assembly) who developed a commitment to notions of responsible government and an impartial judiciary.[109] The group included a number of lawyers. Various radical spirits in the press and elsewhere were also nipping vigorously at the heels of the colonial government and the Family Compact.

In a thoroughly misplaced attempt in the 1810s, sponsored by the Colonial Office to secure the loyalty of American settlers in Upper Canada, the colonial authorities introduced legislation that put in doubt naturalization of immigrant settlers in the colony from south of the border, and, by extension, their rights to the land they occupied – the alien's land conflict.[110] This initiative, and the unconvincing attempts by the colonial executive and its officers to explain its effects, became running sores in relationships between that segment of the population and the authorities well into the 1820s. The jaundiced attitudes of the colonial executive and its elite supporters towards radicals and attempts to provide for a more open airing of political, social, and economic grievances was evident in the harassment of the Scottish radical Robert Gourlay, at the hands of the attorney general, John Beverley Robinson, and the solicitor general, Henry John Boulton, in 1818 and 1819.[111] Gourlay had criticized the government of the colony and suggested holding a colonial convention to discuss its problems. On his acquittal by two juries of sedition, the government invoked the Sedition Act against him and expelled from him from the province. The executive's action reflected a liberal interpretation of the legislation's scope, reached in a private conclave between the law officers and the members of the Court of King's Bench.[112]

During the 1820s, the partiality of the elite in the administration of justice intensified. On the one hand, the law officers pursued with obvious relish the most vocal critics of government and its elitist friends, the radical journalists, in prosecutions using the tensile offence of seditious libel.[113] On the other, seeking refuge in their prosecutorial discretion and the claim that victims of others' criminal conduct were able to launch their own criminal law actions, they were disinclined to go after their own supporters and minions for acts of violence committed against their political adversaries. Two notable examples were the case of young Tory hoods, including students at law in the chambers of both law officers, trashing the printing presses of radical newspaper owner and editor William Lyon Mackenzie, and that of hooded men including several magistrates and lawyers tarring and feathering George Rolph, clerk of the peace in Ancaster, and brother of a reform politician.[114] It was into this highly charged political and legal climate that John Walpole Willis sauntered in September 1827, blissfully ignorant of the social strains that would surround him. It was not long before he became enmeshed in them.

John Walpole Willis and His Misadventures in Upper Canada

As a child Walpole Willis seems to have had problems fitting in and getting on with his schoolmates, and was asked to leave both Rugby and Charterhouse.[115] Nevertheless, after graduating from Cambridge, he was called to the English bar in the 1810s and, it seems, quickly became a very capable Equity practitioner.[116] In addition to his practice, he published a number of practitioners' works in the field, one of which became a well-known and respected authoritative text. One might have thought that he was set for a successful career as a barrister in England. However, fate intervened when, in the course of legal work for the eleventh Earl of Strathmore, he met and fell in love with the earl's daughter, Mary Isabella Bowes-Lyon, nine years his junior. They married in 1824. This connection brought little in the way of material gain to one who, with a widowed mother and sister to support, was struggling financially. His desire to get ahead and that of his young wife to elevate his and their status and wealth led him to accept a judicial appointment in Upper Canada, for which his father-in-law had paved the way.

From 1825 the Colonial Office toyed with idea of establishing an Equity jurisdiction in the province. No explicit provision had been made for hearing equitable suits when the Court of King's Bench had been established in 1794.[117] As John Weaver has noted, without the clear existence of an equitable right of redemption in the local law, creditors had through the decisions in *Bliss* and *Gray* secured a dominant position because of their ability to seize the lands of defaulting debtors.[118] During the mid-1820s local reformers demonstrated interest in the addition of an equitable jurisdiction, in order to afford greater protection to debtors. However, they wanted this done without the expenditure associated with a new court. The grudging agent for pressing London on the issue was Attorney General John Beverley Robinson, who with his penchant for landed interests had no enthusiasm for introducing equitable principles into the colony. Secretary of State Lord Bathurst indicated that he favoured giving the jurisdiction to the Court of King's Bench, with one new justice exercising that part of its work, although he expressed uncertainty as to whether the Crown or a legislature should take the initiative.[119] In communications between Willis, who had been advised that he would be the equity judge, and the new secretary of state, Lord Goderich, the former was left with the understanding that a final decision was pending in London on a court of chancery, subject to the tying up of a few constitutional loose ends. In the meantime, his appointment would be that of an associate justice of the Court of King's Bench. He anticipated that he would soon become the chief judge of the Court of Chancery, with a salary commensurate with that position.[120]

The new judge, buoyant with anticipation of the expected preferment, arrived in Upper Canada on 11 September 1827, with his uneasy ménage of wife, mother, and sister in tow.[121] Initially York's charmed elite circle welcomed them warmly.[122] Willis threw himself into both his judicial responsibilities and community and charitable activities: advocating a savings bank, becoming a trustee of the local grammar school, re-establishing the Anglican Sunday school, and showing interest in the relief of 'strangers in distress.' However, various factors were soon to take the bloom off the rose. Willis reacted unfavourably to what he considered the vicious infighting among the Upper Canadian elite, and their absolutist obsession with loyalty, which he saw as subversive of the outcomes of the Glorious Revolution of 1688.[123] His criticisms of local legal practices and culture did not endear him to members of that elite, especially those in or beholden to government, nor would his perceived associations with reform elements in the community, under suspicion by its Tory leaders.[124] Professional jealousy of Family Compact lawyers, who resented this appointment of an outsider over one of their number, was a further irritant.[125] Domestic pressures from a wife who, prevented from commanding the Willis household and smarting from insufficient recognition of her status as an earl's daughter, also played a role in propelling the judge forward at a seemingly precipitous rate.[126]

It was, however, the derailing of the plan for a Chancery court, with him as its head, that was to cause most embarrassment to Willis. Shortly after his arrival in October 1827, he communicated an inflated and costly draft plan for such a court to Maitland.[127] However, since the judge had left England, the Colonial Office, now under a new minister, William Huskisson, was developing doubts about the need to establish a separate court, rather than extending the express jurisdiction of King's Bench to matters of Equity.[128] The English law officers had questioned whether the Crown could achieve this end by the use of the prerogative, without the initiative of Parliament or the local legislature, and floated the idea of bestowing the jurisdiction on the existing court.[129] Moreover, when Maitland, following instructions from Huskisson, canvassed the local judges and his legal advisers on the matter, there was a division of opinion. The judges were clearly at odds. Willis had proven coy in an initial letter to Maitland on the issue. He followed up with another, arguing that the joining of the Common Law and Equity functions in the one court was impossible.[130] Chief Justice William Campbell's and Associate Justice Levius Sherwood's joint report argued for integrating the two systems in the Court of King's bench, with the three judges participating in the Equity work – a solution not incompatible with the Common Law.[131] Solicitor General Boulton equivocated. He was on record as in favour of bestowing the jurisdiction on King's Bench, although ready to accept the alternative.[132] Attorney General Robinson, perhaps masking his true feelings, claimed that he was not averse to a new court, but conditioned his support on its powers being precisely laid out and limited in scope, rather than being a facsimile of the English Court of Chancery.[133] The dispatch from Huskisson also encouraged Maitland to consult the assembly.[134] Robinson was instructed to get the assembly to debate the matter.[135]

Frustrated at the slow pace of action from the colonial executive in furthering the court proposal, the judge had made contact with a reformist group in the assembly, including John Rolph, William Warren Baldwin and his son Robert, and Marshall Spring Bidwell, lawyers all. These men, increasingly disturbed by the partiality and arbitrariness of the administration of justice in the colony, had committed themselves to securing a more independent judiciary, and excluding the chief justice from the Executive Council.[136] Early in 1828, Willis had lent support to their concerns by testifying before a select committee of the assembly, considering William Forsyth's case.[137] Forsyth felt aggrieved, because in attempting to bring the military to book for trespassing on his land overlooking the falls at Niagara, the legal establishment had sided with the military. Maitland had ordered the militia to remove fences erected by the complainant, which, it was claimed, interfered with the adjacent military reserve. Robinson had acted for the military in the trespass action against them. Spurned in the courts, Forsyth appealed to the assembly to vindicate his civil rights against what he argued was military oppression. In his testimony to the committee controlled by the reformers, Willis testified that the monopoly of the law officers over prosecutions was detrimental to the administration of justice in the province.[138] When the committee sought to compel the attendance of two officials at their hearings and committed them for contempt for failing to appear, Maitland stepped in and prorogued the assembly on 23 March 1828.

In the meantime, Robinson had been considering how to induce the assembly to consider the introduction of an Equity jurisdiction. If Willis believed that reform-minded members would flock to his standard, he was to be disappointed.[139] Reform members pressured the attorney general, who was seeking to delay debate, to draft a bill establishing a new court.[140] Robinson referred a draft bill to reformer John Rolph for his information only, but Rolph made its terms public. This revelation engendered vigorous debate in the assembly resulting in a majority (including reformers) rejecting any further discussion of the matter. The result was the scotching of the plan for a Chancery court with Willis as its head. Robinson got the result he wanted, and the reformers opposed were content that a new avenue for the preferment of government placemen had been closed off.[141]

Early in April 1828, reformers in the assembly working with Willis in a piece of political theatre, sought to invoke the principles of Equity by the back door in dealing with a petition by one of their number, Robert Randal. Randal had a running dispute with Solicitor General Boulton who, he claimed, with some justice, had bilked him of his land by invoking dubious legal procedures.[142] Randal, having received no joy from the law officers or King's Bench, decided to plead the matter before the assembly, but the prorogation in March stopped the Randal petition in its tracks. Defiant members of a now-defunct body sought to pass a 'phantom' Equity bill that would empower Willis in his judicial capacity 'to act as chancellor and ... Investigate and retry' the Randal case.[143] Although the plan went no further, it is likely that this play acting raised further questions about the judge's affiliations in the minds of the executive and its advisers.

Although the demise of the Equity court plan hurt Willis's vanity, it was resilient enough for him to seek opportunity elsewhere in the judicial system. His wife's craving for status and his own desire to enjoy a higher salary, no doubt, propelled him. By early 1828, it was clear that Chief Justice William Campbell would be retiring because of illness. In the meantime, he would be going on health leave in England. Willis lost no time in letting the Colonial Office know that, both professionally and socially, he was the man to fill the position: 'As an English Barrister of more than ten years standing – the Son in law of one of the oldest Scottish peers – & the husband of the only Titled Female in the Province, with the exception of Lady Sarah Maitland I must confess that I feel it *rather irksome* under the Circumstances in which I came here, to remain in an inferior situation.'[144]

Remarkably, the judge ended his epistle by indicating that his Upper Canadian colleagues would speak to his character. Lieutenant Governor Maitland had other ideas, however. He had already recommended to Huskisson John Beverley Robinson's appointment as chief justice.[145] When he learned of Willis's bid, the chief executive let it be known in London that his appointment 'would be doing an incalculable injury to the Colony.'[146]

Whether out of a sense that he was on the cusp of a reformist moment in London's relationship with its North American possessions, or of an inflated sense of his own importance and destiny in the colony, or more likely both, Willis continued his relationship with the reformers in the assembly.[147] Moreover, he took the reformist agenda into the courtroom, to the great consternation of his judicial colleague Levius Sherwood, the Law Officers Robinson and Boulton (all members of the Family Compact), and, not least, the lieutenant governor. The judge seems to have determined that it was his role to root out injustice in the colony's criminal justice system. There was much to complain about.[148]

Willis called to account the law officers, especially Attorney General Robinson, for their administration of criminal justice. He was sitting on the trial of the radical Irish editor of the *Canadian Freeman*, Francis Collins, for libelling Samuel Jarvis and Henry John Boulton.[149] Jarvis, who had led the Types rioters in 1826 in the trashing of Mackenzie's printing press, had come into Collins's sights for his killing of John Ridout in a duel in 1817, in which Boulton had acted as one of his seconds. Collins decried both the acquittal of Jarvis and the failure of the law officers to prosecute Boulton and his colleague James Small as accessories.

When Collins appeared before Willis, the judge permitted him to make a long statement attacking Robinson for prosecuting him for libel, when he had chosen not to prosecute either the Types rioters, including Jarvis, or Boulton for his role in Ridout's death.[150] Despite Robinson's remonstrations at the propriety of this self-serving diversion, Willis allowed Collins to continue. Moreover, the judge suggested that, if Collins was right, the attorney general had neglected his duty, and advised the accused to present his charges to the grand jury and Crown officers.

An angry exchange ensued between Willis and Robinson in which Willis lectured Robinson on his sacred obligation to prosecute breaches of the peace, while Robonson rejoined that he knew his duty as well as any judge, which did not include charging suspects in a case like that of the rioters where no application had been made by the alleged victim.[151] Willis turned up the temperature by threatening to advise Her Majesty's government of the attorney's failure in his duty, and assuring Collins that he personally would see that the grand jury and Crown officers did theirs. In a letter to Maitland's secretary, Major Hillier, the judge stated ominously, 'The *crisis* has arrived at which it must be determined how criminal prosecutions here are to be conducted and how far the Law Officers of the Crown as practicing attorneys of the Court are accountable to the Judges of the Province.' To his mind, the law officers were obliged to prosecute 'of their own accord' all crimes 'they know to have been committed.'[152] The judge was also quick to complain to Maitland about Robinson's language towards him in court (apparently a clerk had overheard Robinson describe Willis as 'a damned rascal' for his leniency towards Collins).

When Collins presented his evidence to the grand jury, true bills were returned in both the Types Riot and Ridout cases.[153] The accused parties, including both Boulton and Small, the seconds to Jarvis the dueller, both of whom were lawyers, were arrested.[154] A further dispute emerged in the prosecution of both cases between Collins, who wanted Robert Baldwin to prosecute, and Robinson, who claimed it as his right. The attorney general conceded to Baldwin in the Ridout case but stood firm on the Types Riot incident. In the result, Boulton and Small secured acquittals at trial on the accessories charge, while Jarvis and his associates were found guilty in the Types Riot imbroglio and fined.[155]

The outcomes of the trials were less important than the issue of prosecutorial initiative and its deployment. On the one hand, Willis, who had little knowledge or experience of criminal law and procedure, believed that the law officers were bound to pursue miscreants seriously, including their own friends, when law and order demanded it. On this they had defaulted badly.[156] On the other hand, Robinson argued plausibly, if self-interestedly, that within the system of criminal justice inherited from England there was prosecutorial discretion applied in all cases, other than those affecting the Crown or its traditional wards, and that they had a monopoly of representation in those cases that they chose, but were not obligated to prosecute. For the rest, it was up to the victims of alleged crimes to launch prosecutions.[157] What Willis in an officious, bumbling, and insulting way had exposed was a tender nerve in the Upper Canadian body politic. A segment of the population believed that the administration of justice had fallen into disrepute because of partiality among judges, the law officers, and their minions, especially in the repression of political dissent.[158] As Collins had argued, even-handed justice had become a mockery in a jurisdiction when law officers rushed to launch libel suits and the courts to judgment against their detractors, while ignoring, and even condoning, the violent conduct of their own supporters against the property and persons of those who criticized them or merely associated with the opposition to them. That Boulton, the solicitor general, in defending the perpetrators of the tar-and-feather outrage in a civil suit brought by George Rolph, had urged that the plaintiff's witnesses not be sworn, and praised the accused in court for their moral motivation in talking action in this instance, was emblematic, in the minds of many, of corrupt motives.[159] Even the moderate William Warren Baldwin, former treasurer of the Law Society, in a letter to Robinson as attorney general that criticized him for his failure to prosecute and take disciplinary action against the perpetrators of the Types Riot, stated that Mr Attorney had brought discredit upon the society and the profession.[160]

Willis's astringent criticism of the conduct of the law officers voiced in the Collins case, repeated when George Rolph's application for a new hearing in the tar-and-feather case came before him and Judge Sherwood in May 1828, ensured him the bitter enmity of the leading members of the conservative elite and the colonial executive.[161] His announcement of a plan to produce a publication on the state of jurisprudence in the province, *Meliora Spera*, did nothing to calm their anxieties.[162] Johnson suggests that Maitland had been developing a strong animus towards Willis months earlier. In December 1827 he had written to Huskisson opposing any change in the tenure of colonial judges from 'at pleasure' to 'during good behaviour.'[163] He suggested that an alteration would attract the wrong men, those who were not going to make it to the top of the tree in Britain, and who would seek to court popular acclaim, citing Robert Thorpe as an example. Of course Thorpe, like almost all colonial judges, had been appointed 'at pleasure.' Likely his point was that it would be dangerous appointing a judge such as Willis 'during good behaviour,' because it would be so much more difficult to get rid of him.

The jurist's challenge to the way in which the Court of King's Bench operated sent new shivers up the Tory spines of the colony's governors, lost him support in London, and exposed him to drastic action by the lieutenant governor. At the end of May 1828 Willis wrote to James Stephen Jr, legal counsel at the Colonial Office, about the frustrations of adjudicating when he and his colleague Sherwood regularly differed on the disposition of the cases before them.[164] He also voiced fears that the Court of King's Bench was acting unconstitutionally when it sat with less than its complement of three judges.[165] Section 19 of the Judicature Act of 1794 prescribed that 'His Majesty's Chief Justice of this Province, together with two Puisne Justices, shall preside in said Court.'[166] This issue, Willis argued, required London's early consideration, in view of the excitement any confirmation of the problem would cause in the colony. He announced that he would raise the issue when the new sittings of the court opened. In addition to this potential bombshell, he asserted that Chief Justice Campbell's leave was illegal, because the lieutenant governor had granted it in the absence of Legislative Council approval. This move by Willis, unexceptional on its face, involved a gaff on his part, in that he made this overture directly to London rather than first advising Maitland of his misgivings.[167] The chief executive was quick to share with Huskisson his displeasure at Willis's breach of protocol. In his opinion, the judge's view of the court's workings ran counter to long-standing practice that he had previously accepted, and that, in raising the matter, caution should have been his watchword.[168] The lieutenant governor added that he would consult with his Executive Council and the law officers about what action to take, should the judge publicly challenge the propriety of the court sitting with fewer than three judges. Unbeknownst to Willis, his conduct in the Collins trial had lowered him in the Colonial Office's estimation. In a memo to his superiors, Stephen observed that the judge had 'irretrievably injured his reputation as a Man of calm and dispassionate demeanour as a judge,' which would adversely affect his chances of advancement.[169]

When Trinity term opened on 16 June 1828, Willis, true to his word, made a lengthy statement outlining his position on the unconstitutionality of the court sitting with fewer than three judges.[170] His objections, he asserted, flowed from the wording of the Judicature Act and accorded with English judicial wisdom on the need to follow statutory prescriptions to the letter.[171] The statute contemplated the court operating as a body, not as a collection of individual judges. He announced that as a consequence decisions of the court with any fewer than three judges, the chief justice presiding, were void, and that in the future he would discharge only those functions as a judge of the court that were lawful. While recognizing the public inconvenience this would cause and that he had been complicit in the illegal practice, he attributed his error to the apparent unconcern of his learned and more experienced colleagues.[172]

The consternation of Willis's judicial colleague Sherwood, the law officers, and the colonial executive was predictable and profound, and its effects were immediate. Willis had called into question the legitimacy of the court's previous decisions decided by fewer than a full bench since 1794.[173] Maitland consulted Justice Sherwood, Robinson, and Boulton. All reported that a more nuanced reading of the founding statute provided room for the practice that had developed.[174] For his part, Robinson noted that section 19 of the Act also stated that the chief justice, or in his absence, any other judge, had the power to validate writs or rule on points of law, clearly contemplating hearings with fewer than three judges. The court continued to be a court, even though the chief justice was dead or absent from the colony. To 'preside' was merely 'to be set over,' which did not imply presence of the subject.[175] Maitland forwarded the opinions to the Executive Council. The law officers in their reports contained advice on the process of removing a judge, stressing the necessity of finding sufficient cause.

The council was disturbed that with Willis refusing to sit, there was now a serious bottleneck for the decision of pending cases, particularly those from the circuits. However, they had qualms about moving against the judge, because of doubts about their authority to appoint a replacement. Seeing no easy way around it, on 25 June the council requested that Willis reveal which of his judicial duties he was willing to discharge.[176]

During the time Willis took in replying, Maitland – clearly impatient with Willis, pressure from Lady Mary to do right by her man, and criticisms in the reform press – signed and registered a commission for the removal of the judge on 26 June.[177] This was before the receipt by the council of the jurist's response and their determination of what to do about him.[178] On 27 June the council hastily passed a resolution that Willis 'be forthwith removed from office of one of the justices of His Majesty's Court of King's Bench ... until His Majesty's pleasure be known.'[179] They advised Maitland that he appoint a person to fill the vacancy left by Willis's amoval. Major Hillier advised the jurist of his fate, noting that he could, if he wished, exercise a right of 'appeal to the King in Council as to the sufficiency of the Cause.'[180] Willis protested what he described as his 'suspension' and sought a leave of absence to plead his case in London.[181] Maitland denied the leave, taking the view that the former judge was now free to leave the province at any time.[182] The lieutenant governor sent a dispatch to Huskisson, outlining the reasons for removing Judge Willis, stressing that Willis had forgotten his loyalty to the Crown and immersed himself in opposition politics, all in the cause of self-aggrandizement.[183]

The Motivations and Legacy of John Walpole Willis in Upper Canada

The judicial career of John Walpole Willis in Upper Canada had come to a screeching halt. He hastily decamped to London to press his case, leaving his family, except for his mother, in Toronto.[184] The Willis affair, however, had immediate repercussions in the colony's politics. The reformers were quick to use this latest example of executive perfidy as a rallying call for a public meeting and a petition to His Majesty. In the petition they set out a list of grievances about the administration of the colony and called for a form of responsible government for the province, similar to Judge Thorpe's earlier reflections on the matter and a manifesto of the *parti Canadien* in Lower Canada during that same era.[185] The document also complained of the all-too-cosy relationship between the judges and the executive, and their partiality, advocating their future appointment 'during good behaviour,' and exclusion from both the Executive and Legislative Councils.

The reformers secured a majority in the House of Assembly in the late July elections, a result in part of their ability to play on the arbitrary and oppressive actions of their opponents in the Willis case.[186] This inspired them to believe that they might be on the cusp of dramatic change in the constitutional relationship between the province and the metropolis. However, their ascendancy proved short lived.[187] More importantly, the British government was not close in its thinking at this time to introducing responsible government in its North American colonies.[188] However, the issue was, thanks to the Willis dismissal, now firmly on the public agenda. Where the petition proved in tune with growing concern in the Colonial Office was on the independence, or lack of it, of the colonial judiciary. By 1830 the chief justice, now Robinson, was vexed to learn that on London's orders he was to be excluded from membership on the Executive Council. In 1834 the legislature substituted tenure during good behaviour for that at pleasure, and introduced the process of removal by a joint address of the legislature, conditioned by a right of appeal by the judge to the Privy Council.[189] The imperial government, however, was not willing to bend to the reformers' suggestion that future appointments to King's Bench should be drawn from the English bar, to liberate the Bench from 'the entanglements of family connexions [*sic*], the influence of local jealousies and the contamination of Provincial Politics.'[190]

Fate was not to prove kind to the reformers' hero at this stage in his career. Willis argued vigorously that he had been most unjustly treated and that his removal was illegal. He also implied that the local government had framed him, because his appointment was in preference to a local boy, James Macaulay, and that he was not pliant to the wishes of its legal advisers.[191] Moreover, he stressed that Maitland had acted illegally in registering his removal before the Executive Council had met to deal with his case. He also noted that the House of Assembly in its petition had pressed vigorously for his reinstatement. But Willis's earlier conduct, especially in the Collins case, had not endeared him to the Colonial Office, and there was no impulse there to take his part in his dispute over his removal from office.[192] It is likely too that his advocacy of the authorities calling Maitland before the English courts to answer for his acts of oppression in the colony, and his description of his Upper Canadian opponents as 'little insects,' merely confirmed the view that he was sadly lacking in judgment.[193]

The Privy Council to which Willis appealed his dismissal dashed his hopes of professional rehabilitation. In his brief, the judge reaffirmed his view that he was correct in his position on the constitutionality of the court sitting with fewer than three judges, and that in this matter and on the irregularities in granting leaves of absence the colonial executive proved oblivious to the demands of the law, employing arguments based on mere usage and tradition. He reiterated his contention that Maitland had jumped the gun on dismissing him. As a consequence, the executive's action was 'illegal and void.'[194] The council in its characteristically terse way reported that, having considered Mr Willis's memorial and hearing from him, his counsel, and the English law officers, 'the Amoval of John Walpole Willis by Lieutenant Governor Sir Peregrine Maitland was not Unwarranted, Illegal or Void' – in other words, appeal dismissed.[195]

Willis had meanwhile suffered the personal indignity and hurt of his wife, Lady Mary, who had planned to rejoin him in England, cuckolding him in favour of Lieutenant Barnard of the 38th Light Infantry with whom she eloped.[196] The reformers' white knight's fall from grace professionally had tarnished his reputation on the domestic front as well.

What are we to make of the stormy sojourn of John Walpole Willis in Upper Canada? In making an assessment, it is important to divorce issues of personality from those of the politico-legal climate in both Britain and Upper Canada at the time. Although Willis may have been a highly competent Equity lawyer, on the rise professionally in England, he suffered from evident character flaws. Paul Romney is correct in describing Willis 'as a self-seeking, insensitive snob, who was as much to blame as his official enemies for the rift between them.'[197] 'Vanity gleams in his efforts before leaving England to get the colonial secretary to present him to the king ('Answer *No*' Goderich jotted tersely on his second plea) and in a dozen snubs offered in Upper Canada to his colleagues and York society in general.'[198]

The evidence is perhaps circumstantial, but his 'dream marriage' to an impatient and demanding young aristocrat likely inflated his propensity to social climbing. For whatever reason, he was a man in a hurry. Willis's professional moves as a judge in the colony suggest that his vainglory and difficulty in dealing with those in authority over him were both factors in his actions in challenging the system of governance and justice that he found. Disappointed in his bid to create an Equity empire, he immediately turned his covetous gaze to the position of chief justice and started slamming the administration of justice in the colony, oblivious to the colony's political and legal culture and the claims of the local legal elite to preferment. In fact, it may be that his bid to become chief justice, his attacks on the law officers, and his challenge to the executive on the constitutionality of the work of King's Bench represented for him a calculated campaign to convince politicians in the Westminster Parliament, particularly of a reformist bent, that his claims to become senior judge was both just and unassailable.[199] In short, compared with the incompetent provincial dolts responsible for the parlous justice system, he was a shining example of judicial propriety and impartiality.

There is, however, another side to all of this. We have no clear evidence that Willis had any developed tendency towards reform politics in England before he landed in Upper Canada. As a barrister on the Northern Circuit, he had rubbed shoulders with Henry Brougham, the Whig reformer, and radical and reform discourse was being heard in the late 1810s and the 1820s from among young lawyers. Whether Willis was among them we do not know. But that does not close the issue of ideological predilection. Being a lawyer, with a keen sense of the traditions and culture of the English bar and judiciary, he could be expected to recoil at what he found in the way of judges being hand-in-glove with the colonial executive, and in the political partisanship of the law officers. In his introductory chapter to *Meliora Spera,* Willis indicated that loyalty to the executive depended on its protection of the liberties of the individual, and he argued that how those protections were embodied in the law and statutes reflected the 'Spirit of the Age.'[200]

A person did not have to be a committed reformer to discern that the local authorities were manipulating and corrupting English law and procedures to serve local, elitist, and political ends. Viewed in this light, it may very well have been that a principled juristic heart was beating in the breast of John Walpole Willis, and that he felt genuinely uncomfortable with how English law was being abused and the administration of justice perverted in the colony.

Whatever his motivations, the presence of Willis in Upper Canada at that time was to prove significant in the arduous struggle by moderate reformers for change in the constitutional relationship between Great Britain and the colony, and especially in how justice was administered there. He clearly earned the reputation among not only moderates, but also radicals, as someone of independent mind who was not afraid of standing up to the ruling colonial elite. Those individuals seem to have thought the time was auspicious, as it was not in Judge Thorpe's time, for an impartial judge to help shake the Tory foundations of colonial governance and assist in producing a new political and legal order. Despite the dashing of the reformers' broader political agenda, they were able, in part through the advocacy of John Walpole Willis and his demise, to highlight the very real problems with the justice system in Upper Canada. Both the former judge and they had exposed publicly the partiality and corruptness that infected it, and this assisted in persuading London that a degree of separation and formal judicial independence should replace the existing symbiotic political relationship between the judges and the executive. These changes took time to realize and were, it can be argued, briefly compromised by the close involvement of the Upper Canadian judges, especially Robinson, in advising the colonial executive during the 1837–8 rebellions.[201] However, the Willis affair, as Peter Oliver has argued, serves as an important watershed in both imperial and colonial perceptions about the judicial function in the North American colonies.[202] In due course those changes in understanding about judicial roles would have an impact in Australasia. Unlike in the empire in Thorpe's day, discernible murmurings about reform in the constitutional relationship between Britain and its settler colonies were beginning to be heard, reaching a crescendo in the 1840s and 1850s.

Remarkably, Willis proved to be a survivor, serving in British Guiana and New South Wales before his eccentricities caught up with him once again. However, the fate of conservative colonial judges in British North America who wore their politics on their sleeves, and the extent to which they dodged the barbs of outrageous fortune or fell to the swords of their opponents between 1800 and 1840 is now what beckons.

5

The Perils of the Colonial Judiciary: Ultra-Conservative Judges in an Era of Developing Reformist Sentiment in the British Empire, 1810–1840

Governance, Justice, and Constitutionalism in Quebec, 1763–1791

If the case of Robert Thorpe illustrates the limits set to the independence of reform-minded colonial jurists during the first third of the nineteenth century, that of Jonathan Sewell, chief justice of Lower Canada, and James Monk, chief justice of Montreal, threatened with impeachment in 1814, demonstrates the extent to which the imperial system would protect Baconian judges politically involved in the conservative cause, during the same period.

Quebec, seized by the British from the French in the early 1760s, had gone through several stages of colonial rule prior to 1791.[1] Originally governed by British military authorities, it had in time become what later would be classified as a Crown colony, with a governor possessing extensive plenary powers.[2] Even in this latter stage, the military presence and influence remained strong, especially during the years of the American War of Independence, when concerns about the loyalty of the *Canadiens* induced the British authorities to apply draconian security measures.[3] The acquisition of a colony in which a majority population possessed a strong attachment to their land, organized in a seigneurial system that placed traditional limits on alienability, owed allegiance to a religious tradition that the British considered heretical, and were suspicious of the economic, social, and religious motives of their colonial masters, presented the British with challenges.[4] The presence of a minority English-speaking population whose priorities lay in encouraging and building up Atlantic and continental trade links, valued land in terms of its wealth-producing capacity, and felt the need to appeal to English law to frame and mediate their transactions, deepened these challenges.

At the apex of the political system were the colonial administrators, drawn from both Britain itself and, after the loss of the thirteen colonies, Loyalist refugees, committed to preserving order and stability, and demanding deference from the ruled. Some of these men (including the judges appointed to administer Quebec law) shared the values of the anglophone merchant population and sympathized with their arguments on the need to adopt English common law.[5] Imperial policy on Quebec's political, social, and legal destiny reflected the geopolitical context, calculations on how to preserve the loyalty of the populace, and the personal views of the imperial politicians or officials in question. Much to the consternation of that commercial class, as British authority in the American colonies came under challenge, London extended recognition to the Roman Catholic religion and agreed to preserve French civil law in the colony, under the terms of the Quebec Act of 1774.[6] The use of imperial legislation to achieve these ends led, under newly accepted principles of public law, to the necessity of replacing governance under the royal prerogative with an imperially or locally legislated system of governance.[7] The distractions of the conflict in the thirteen colonies and of dealing with the patriot victory delayed a decision on this, despite an uneasy alliance of English-speaking merchants and *Canadien* leaders pressing for representative government.

The Counter-revolutionary Constitution of Lower Canada and Its Impact on Governance and Law

Faced with pressures to resolve the constitutional status of Quebec, to provide an elective, legislative forum, and to carve out of its western regions a new English-speaking colony, the British government pushed through the Constitutional Act for the new colonies of Lower and Upper Canada in 1791. The counter-revolutionary character and assumptions of this imperial move were outlined in chapter 2.[8] Prior to 1800, a social equilibrium made for accommodation or, at least, non-engagement between the major economic and social interest groups. A buoyant economy and fears among both anglophones (officials and merchants alike) and francophones (especially, but not exclusively, the

Roman Catholic hierarchy and clergy, and the seigneurial class) about the excesses of the French Revolution led to a degree of understanding and common cause. For most of the decade the English party and its elite *Canadien* allies dominated the assembly. However, there were tensions and mutual suspicions. The fear generated by revolutionary France and its conflict with Britain led to a garrison mentality among officials, including the law officers and the judges.[9] These men were Baconian in their adherence to the colonial state and to a conservative vision of the British constitution. Suspicions about the loyalty of the *Canadien* population were rife, exacerbated by both rioting among *habitants* over militia and road taxes, and evidence of agents provocateurs active in the province.

Fears about insurrection were, in fact, completely overblown and misplaced. However, the judiciary, as fearful as the rest of the administration, manipulated the justice system to ensure a favourable outcome for the state in cases against spies and rioters hauled before them. This was apparent, for example, in Chief Justice William Osgoode's advice to Governor John Prescott on a special trial for accused American provocateur David McLane, charged with treason in 1797. The judge's counsel included rewarding Crown witnesses with promises of land, advising that charges of high treason be laid against the accused, and advocating that he be tried on a special commission by the Executive Council. In his address to the grand jury and in his summing up to the trial jury, the chief justice was careful to give a broad substantive and geographic interpretation to treason, as compassing the King's death.[10] Not surprisingly the trial jury convicted McLane and he was hanged.

The political understandings of the 1790s partly evaporated during the first decade of the nineteenth century.[11] Stagnation in agriculture and decline of the fur trade meant harder times for the colony's predominantly francophone population. At the same time, anglophone merchants, especially in the emerging lumber industry, were becoming a more wealthy elite and ever more influential in the economic sphere, as they worked their international trade connections and markets. English-speaking settlers, not least from the United States, continued to come into the province and secure land. Anglo interests owned an increasing number of seigneuries. These factors were causing anxiety among the *Canadien* professional and small-business operators, especially among the attorneys and notaries, about both discrimination against the majority population and the fate of French civil law. As Greenwood has suggested, these fears increased as the colonial government, egged on by its supporters, pressed for 'anglification' of education, land tenure, and church–state relations.[12] As a consequence, it was the bourgeoisie who became more politically involved, replacing older elite groups in the francophone community, and organized as the *parti Canadien*. Their talk was increasingly of injustices against the majority and the need for constitutional reform. In English-speaking circles a garrison mentality continued to operate, marked by a resolve to ensure a conservative and ordered system of governance and law, and to assimilate further the majority population's political and legal culture. Suspicions of the disloyalty of the whole *Canadien* population and angst towards those promoting a more democratic vision of the province's future fuelled the anxieties.[13] The wiles of Napoleon Bonaparte, and strained relations between Britain and the United States, exacerbated tensions in the colony.

The conflict between the assertive *Canadien* bourgeoisie and the colonial administration, dubbed pejoratively the 'Chateau Clique,' played out in the strained relations between the assembly, which the *parti Canadien* had effectively controlled since 1797, on the one hand, and the governor, his councillors, and the judges in their advisory and judicial roles, on the other.[14] The *parti*, led by lawyer Pierre-Stanislas Bédard, interpreted the constitution of the colony in much the same way that Robert Thorpe did in Upper Canada.[15] As they saw themselves as representatives of the majority of the colonial population, they advocated the constitutional and fiscal dominance of the elected body. They pressed for a system of ministerial responsibility like that in Westminster, in which the governor (responsible to the monarch) would seek and take the advice of the ministers enjoying the majority support in the House. As a necessary corollary, he would dismiss and replace them, or call an election when they lost that support. It followed that the assembly would be entitled to censure and even move for the impeachment of a minister for abuses of power. This interpretation of the Constitutional Act would replace the existing system, in which the governor acted on the advice of ministers without popular support, and against the *Canadien* interest. The founding of the reformist newspaper *Le Canadien* in 1806, a development noted with apprehension in the jumpy Anglo community, enhanced the *parti*'s ability to disseminate its message.[16] Such a manifesto lacked appeal to the British government, the colonial executive, and its judicial advisers (not to mention the English party in general). The Lower Canadian judges were active in the political life of the province in support of the executive and the existing structure of government, as members of the assembly, but most importantly in the Executive and Legislative Councils. Episodically, the chief justice acted as a de facto chief minister. These two conflicting conceptions of colonial governance and the role of the judges within it produced a major political crisis in 1810 and 1811, during the governorship of Sir James Craig – a period often described in radical and reformist circles as Governor Craig's 'Reign of Terror.'

Governor Craig's 'Reign of Terror' and Its Outcome

Craig was a stiff-necked army officer who had been involved in the capture of Dutch South Africa in 1795. Fecteau and his colleagues describe him as 'aristocratic, paternalistic and autocratic,' someone unlikely to warm to the democratic and increasingly strident demands of reformist assembly members.[17] Although originally believing that the *Canadiens* were loyal, he changed his mind during the first part of 1808. Vituperative rhetoric directed against Judge Pierre-Amable De Bonne, who held an assembly seat, along with other 'placeholders,' began to prey on Craig's mind as he reflected on the dangers of Bonaparte's quest for worldwide conquest.[18] He concluded that, if the French attacked, the *Canadien* population would support it by open rebellion. He persuaded himself that the *parti Canadien* was working for Napoleon and that the Roman Catholic hierarchy very likely was. If the French did not intervene directly, he surmised that they might induce the Americans to invade with some token help on their part.

Using the analogy of the fate of Charles I at the hands of his parliamentary opponents, Craig read the leadership of the *parti Canadien*'s claims as threatening a takeover of the government.[19] The governor found particularly troubling its attempt to establish a lobbyist in London, 'offering' to appropriate all government revenues, and expelling Judge De Bonne from the House. A decrease in sympathetic members in the wake of the 1809 election led the governor to prorogue the assembly in February, and a further election was called. Extreme, accusatory rhetoric on both sides marked this new campaign, with rumours of French intervention rife among government supporters. *Le Canadien* stepped up the anti-establishment rhetoric, publishing an electoral song recommending that the people wipe out as 'scum' officials who, it alleged, Craig meant to reward out of land taxes. The governor could contain himself no longer.[20] He put the military on alert. He moved against the newspaper, first arresting its publisher and then, as an ownership group came to light, all those who were members of the assembly, including Bédard. 'Treasonable practices' was the offence charged against them and they were held in jail. Craig averred that he had acted out of the purest motives to forestall a rebellion.

The governor did not act alone. Chief Justice Jonathan Sewell served as his close adviser, as he prepared his strategy to deal with his misplaced fears of insurrection.[21] Sewell, a Loyalist refugee from the United States, had served as attorney general of the province before his elevation to the chief justice's post in 1808.[22] A more complex character than Craig, the judge adhered strongly to a vision of the British constitution that emphasized order, stability, and deference. Although fluent in French and sympathetic to French culture, he possessed 'a visceral fear' of the masses, stemming perhaps from his boyhood memories of a patriot mob sacking the family mansion in Massachusetts and his reflections on the French Revolution.[23] Sewell was convinced that the way to avoid this spectre in Lower Canada was to strengthen the institutions that could 'regulate the masses,' while curbing those, such as a free press, that could excite their passions. He was equally concerned that the absence of sufficient power in the executive helped to strengthen disaffection. Fearing disorder fomented by journalists, he naturally advised Craig to arrest Bédard and his colleagues. In so doing, he expatiated on the steps needed to reduce the hold of French institutions on the minds of the masses, or to change them outright into British institutions. Sewell in his advice rehearsed what he had advocated for some time: control of the Roman Catholic clergy, substituting English freehold tenure for the seigneurial system, government-controlled education, and encouraging immigration from the United States. He was, in short, a leading apostle of the 'anglification' of the colony.

Both Sewell and Chief Justice of Montreal James Monk, who shared his colleague's views on the need to decrease the influence of French law and procedure, had been engaged in attempts during the first decade of the nineteenth century to issue rules of court that they and some reformers felt were necessary to improve, clarify, and expedite court procedures.[24] The judges did not doubt that these changes lay exclusively within their jurisdiction.

Sewell's judicial role in supporting Craig's actions was to add to his reputation in reformist circles of his role as the governor's chief henchman. The members of assembly who were detained continued to be held on charges of 'treasonable practices.' When the Spring Assizes opened in March 1810, the chief justice's delivered a 'Burkean' address to the grand jury, called in the hope of their indicting the accused for sedition,[25] proceeding to define seditious libel in broad terms, lecturing the jurors on the responsibility of the press to aid in the preservation of order, and to desist from encouraging the masses' 'discontents' against rulers. Government could not tolerate such behaviour. The jury, comprising government sympathizers, seemed unconvinced and failed to issue indictments or recommend prosecutions for libel.[26] The government, now worried that prosecutions might well fail, decided on another tack. It determined to hold the accused in prison, if necessary indefinitely, while their printing equipment remained sequestered. Not surprisingly, Bédard and his colleagues treated this as an invitation to apply for a writ of habeas corpus.

Predictably the Court of King's Bench, led by Chief Justice Sewell, gave short shrift to the application.[27] All three justices concluded that as a prisoner and a member of a dissolved assembly, Bédard was not covered by parliamentary privilege. The fact that he was an electoral candidate did not assist him. Sewell went further, concluding that the privilege did not extend to the indictable offences alleged against the *Canadien* leader, seditious acts and treasonable practices. Soon after these events, several of the prisoners were released on bail, two having confessed to wrongdoing, and others because of ill-health. Bédard, who remained obdurate, remained in prison for over a year before his release in April 1811.

Later that year, the conciliatory George Prevost replaced Craig as governor.[28] The new man accommodated the Roman Catholic hierarchy, so distrusted by his predecessor, and moved to placate the leaders of the *parti Canadien*. Moreover, he distanced himself from the more assertive members of the English party. Prevost restored the militia commissions of the leaders of the *parti*, and, in a controversial move, appointed Bédard a judge in Trois Rivières.[29] The new governor's policies were beneficial to the colony's peace and harmony, as the *Canadien* elite moved to ensure the people's loyalty during the War of 1812 with the Americans.[30] Despite the outbreak of a riot in Lachine by men objecting to service in the militia, and the inclination of Prevost to invoke martial law in the event of a threatened invasion or rebellion, there was no question about the *Canadien* leaders' commitment to the war effort. Still smarting from the treatment by Governor Craig and his judicial cronies of some of its members, the assembly moved to ensure that in the event of a decision to intern members of that body, the warrants would issue from the executive and not the judges, for it would be they who would be responsible for trying the resulting prosecutions, or deciding on habeas corpus applications. Quebec City and London both accepted these reservations about judicial independence, although they balked at tying their hands on the issue of martial law.

The Abortive Attempt to Impeach Chief Justices Sewell and Monk

By 1814 the assembly, with a *parti Canadien* majority led by anglophone lawyer Andrew Stuart, felt that it was time to rein in the judges and have its revenge for the events of Craig's 'reign of terror.'[31] Personal as well as political animosities drove Stuart, who had been frustrated in his bid to rise in government legal service by the preferment of members of Sewell's family.[32] In 1808 the assembly had moved to enact legislation to deny judges the right to sit in the chamber.[33] When Craig had prorogued the assembly in 1809 in response to this and other actions by the *parti Canadien*, the British government rebuked him, and he had to accept a second bill on the judges to the same effect, in 1810. In 1814 the assembly's focus shifted to the involvement of the judges, and especially Sewell and Monk, in the work of the Executive and Legislative Councils and as advisers to the executive.

On 26 February 1814 Stuart rose in the assembly to read out twenty-five charges warranting impeachment against Sewell and Monk. The charges of political corruption were confined largely to Sewell, who, it was alleged, 'traitorously and wickedly endeavoured to subvert the constitution and established Government' of Lower Canada, and to introduce 'an arbitrary, tyrannical Government against Law, which he had declared by traitorous and wicked opinions, counsel, conduct, judgments, practices and actions.'[34] The charges also accused the chief justice of aiding the cause of American influence in the colony, to the detriment of the *Canadiens.* It was Sewell whom the *parti Canadien,* intent on reducing the judges' political power, viewed as the éminence grise of the administration, the one who had poisoned Craig's mind and directed his arbitrary actions.

In Monk's case, a few of the political influence charges against his colleague were repeated. However, his greater sin was that, along with Sewell, he had endeavoured to undermine the law and constitution by promulgating rules and orders of practice.[35] The position of the *parti Canadien* from 1807 onwards had been that the Anglo judges who dominated the bench were using procedural law to introduce English to replace Quebec civil law.[36] Considerable confusion surrounded the practice of the civil law in the colony, flowing from English-style courts seeking to administer uncodified French law. The situation demanded some degree of rationalization of procedures. A succession of statutes had given the power to the judiciary to issue rules of order and practice. The position of the two judges on the retention of French civil law was ambivalent, both harbouring the feeling that the law of Quebec should progressively be assimilated with that of England.[37] The place to start was replacing the old French rules with those attuned to English court procedures. With Sewell, this attitude had a distinctive political dimension, because his experience and instincts told him that the colony would never be safe for Britain until thoroughly anglicized institutionally and culturally.[38]

The heads of impeachment on practice related more to the assembly's position that these were matters for legislative and not judicial direction, and less to any substantial critique of particular reformative steps taken by the judges. However, some of the changes in procedure, particularly those penalizing lawyers for failure to pay court fees, demonstrated to its enemies the bench's authoritarian impulses.

The two justices proved to be more than a match for Stuart and his colleagues, who fastened upon impeachment as a venerable and helpful device for attacking the arbitrary and corrupt conduct of royal servants whom a legislature wanted removed from office.[39] As in the case of the Nova Scotia Assembly's initiative of the early 1790s, there were structural obstacles to its use in a colony in which the executive and Legislative Council were implacably opposed to such an initiative. As in that earlier instance, it was necessary for the impeachers to rely on a favourable British response to the articles of impeachment and hope that the governor would suspend the justices, pending a decision in the metropolis. Prevost refused to do so.

The judges' strategy, which Monk devised, was to go on the attack and paint the impeachment of the judiciary as a thinly disguised attempt to disturb the peace and tranquillity of the colony.[40] The central issue became one of protecting the colonial constitution and order, and its protectors, from those who were of dubious loyalty, whom the existing governor had encouraged by his appeasement policies.[41] The first line of defence was to induce the Legislative Council to reject out of hand the impeachment charges and to use its control of the public purse to deny financial support to the assembly's representative, wishing to make its case in Westminster.[42] The second line of response was to accuse the assembly of seeking to take control of the entire legislature of the colony, and to interfere drastically with the constitutional responsibilities of other sectors of the colonial state, most especially the executive.[43] The third argument focused on the explicit subversion of the colonial judicial role contained in the impeachment initiative. To allow this ploy to succeed would be to undermine the judiciary's responsibilities.[44] The imperial government needed to protect the judges from the calumny directed towards them.[45] The chief justice of Montreal was also quick to argue that the efforts of the judges to bring order to procedure by marrying French and English practices had helped consolidate British rule, by producing a more efficient court system.[46] On the rules and orders of practice charges, the agreement of the other judges of King's Bench and of executive councillors to join them as targets of the charges strengthened the hands of the two justices, as the former had been consulted about and approved those rules.[47]

Sewell translated these strategic points into a sophisticated defence for use before the imperial authorities.[48] He went off to London to argue the judges' case, armed with petitions of support from the colony. Prevost provided the financial support and introductions needed to make the journey worthwhile. Despite this assistance, Sewell did not spare Prevost in his argument that the governor's conciliatory policies had compromised and subverted the respect that Craig had drawn from the *Canadiens* by his tough policies.

On the chief justice's arrival in London, Secretary of State Lord Bathurst quickly assured him that he had no intention of allowing the case to proceed to the Privy Council on the political charges, as 'it would be to admit that a councillor was responsible for the acts of a Governor contrary to every principle.'[49] Undersecretary Henry Goulburn also expressed the view that the council would quash the charges related to the rules of practice,[50] and this is exactly what happened. The Investigating Committee of the Privy Council relied heavily on an opinion from the English law officers that there was a vital distinction 'between an alteration of the general rules of law by which Justice is to be administered, and an alteration of mere rules of practice for regulating the mode of proceeding in the Courts.'[51] Effective administration of the courts meant that the judges had to have the power of alteration of the rules of procedure. Although some of the impugned rules, said the law officers, were unnecessary in their opinion, none exceeded the judges' jurisdiction. In June 1815 the committee advised that the chief justices had not acted independently in proclaiming the rules but in consultation with the other judges, their actions were clearly within their jurisdiction, they had not exceeded their authority, and they had not usurped the power of the legislature.[52] The council uncharacteristically published the names of the blue ribbon investigating committee to impress upon the assembly the importance and solemnity of this inquiry.[53] The assembly was not impressed with this exercise in noblesse oblige.

The Failure of Legislative Impeachment of Colonial Judges in British North America

Monk's strategy and Sewell's advocacy had worked brilliantly. They had turned the tables on the assembly, converting the issue from one of judicial misconduct to the loyalty of the *parti Canadien*. Even though the British government may have felt discomfort at some of the ways in which ultra-conservative ideology in the colony translated into action, when push came to shove on security there was no doubt where their public support would lie. Prevost's successor, Sir Gordon Drummond, whom Lord Bathhurst instructed to express London's position to the assembly, summed it up nicely in his comment that the purely political nature of the impeachment process was regrettable, because of its 'tendency to disparage in the Eyes of the inconsiderate and ignorant their [the chief justices'] Character and Service' and diminish their influence.[54]

Despite the rejoicing among the English party at the result, this conflict between the judges and the assembly and its outcome undermined their authority among the *Canadiens*.[55] Monk soon retired, only to suffer the indignity of receiving a half-pay pension from the assembly. For the rest of his career, Sewell proved more conciliatory towards the *Canadiens*, likely because, on reflection, he concluded that his fears about their loyalty were belied by their conduct during the War of 1812. He also appears to have had a change of heart on anglicizing the colony's private law. Brian Young asserts that the chief justice was a key influence for the maintenance of French civil law in the province and so could be said to have laid some of the groundwork for the Quebec *Code Civil* of 1866.[56] The major antagonist of the two jurists, Andrew Stuart, showing again his opportunistic motivations, joined the ranks of government supporters in the 1830s, became an office holder, and ultimately a puisne judge and chief justice.[57] The defeat of the assembly's stratagem of using impeachment, confirmed in two subsequent unsuccessful attempts to get rid of superior court judges, was to induce that body to change its tactics in questioning and attacking judges' political involvement in Lower Canada.[58] It continued to investigate the record of 'anglicizing' judges, who in the 1820s and 1830s came to monopolize the bench and to advocate their dismissal.[59] At the same time they directed their energies to securing legislation to guarantee the independence of the colonial judiciary. It was not, however, until the 1840s that the dream of judicial independence was fully realized. Indeed, during the 1837–9 emergencies the old garrison mentality re-emerged, as military justice and courts martial replaced the civil courts as forums in dealing with actual or imagined rebels and, under Lord Durham, the Special Council replaced the legislature. Three francophone judges, Phillippe Panet, Elzéar Bédard, and Joseph-Remi Vallières de Saint-Réal, who had the temerity to contest the validity of broad executive interpretations of these special powers by reference to the British constitution and issued writs of habeas corpus, were suspended from office.[60] In 1843, the legislature of the new Province of Canada passed legislation for Lower Canada that both barred judges from sitting on executive and legislative bodies and made their tenure subject to good behaviour. Removal was on an address of the council and assembly, although, as in the case of Upper Canada, subject to an appeal by the jurist to London.[61] By this time the winds of colonial governmental reform had begun to blow through the corridors of Westminster, and the imperial government was drawn, albeit grudgingly, into recognizing the need to revise the constitutional relationship between Britain and its North American colonies.[62]

Chief Justice Henry John Boulton of Newfoundland: A Man of High Tory Pedigree

With reform underway in British institutions of government and in the air in imperial–colonial relations, the assurance that Baconian judges would receive imperial protection was no longer guaranteed. Henry John Boulton, a member of Upper Canada's Family Compact, who had demonstrated a perverse degree of loyalty to the colonial government in that province, was to discover this to his cost.[63] Edward George Geoffrey Smith Stanley, the second secretary of state for the colonies in Earl Grey's Whig government, appointed Boulton chief justice of Newfoundland in 1833.[64] This was a odd decision because Stanley's predecessor, Lord Goderich, had recently sacked him from the position of attorney general in Upper Canada for his harassment of the radical newspaperman and member of the House of Assembly, William Lyon Mackenzie. Boulton's actions had contravened instructions from London.[65] Whatever the motives of the colonial secretary, it proved to be a disastrous choice, and, after a stormy tenure, Boulton was removed from office in 1838. Before investigating the circumstances of the demise of his judicial career, we need to know more about the man and the colony he was appointed to serve.

Henry John was born in England in 1790, the second son of D'Arcy Boulton from a family of Lincolnshire gentry.[66] After migrating to the United States in the late 1790s, the family moved to Upper Canada in 1802 and were granted land. The young Bolton followed in his father's footsteps and pursued a legal career.[67] During his childhood years he sat at the feet of the conservative Anglican cleric, the Reverend (later Bishop) John Strachan. Strachan's Cornwall Grammar School was something of a nursery for those who became members of the Family Compact in later decades.[68] Equipped both academically and ideologically, the young man emulated his father by travelling to England to qualify for the bar there, and was called to the Middle Temple in 1815.[69] Returning to Upper Canada, he received his admission to the province's bar in 1816. D'Arcy Boulton, who had been appointed attorney general, coveted a position on King's Bench that was due to open up, hopefully in an arrangement in which his appointment would be tied to Henry John's as solicitor general.[70] While the colonial executive mulled over the options, the younger Boulton became embroiled in the first of a series of controversies that were to dog his professional career as lawyer and judge, and to cast doubts on his sense of personal and professional judgment – acting as a second to Samuel Jarvis in a duel between him and John Ridout, in which Ridout was mortally wounded.[71] Henry survived the potential ignominy of prosecution as an accessory on Jarvis's acquittal for murder, but doubts about his character among the colonial elite delayed a decision on his preferment.[72] Likely through the lobbying of his former teacher, Strachan, Henry John was appointed acting solicitor general in March 1818, and was confirmed in that post two years later.

Boulton's Record as a Law Officer in Upper Canada

As a law officer, working closely with Attorney General John Beverley Robinson, Boulton exhibited a mixture of partiality and arrogance that cast serious doubts on his professionalism and made him the butt of criticism from reformers and radicals alike, and, on occasion, principled conservatives.[73] Boulton's reputation suffered first because he was not averse to manipulating the legal system to serve his private interests. The most ignoble example was the abuse of King's Bench procedures to bilk a debtor of his, Robert Randal, out of his sizeable landholding – a move aided and abetted by the judges.[74] However, it was his conduct in hunting down political opponents that earned him the most intense and damning criticism.

As acting solicitor general, Boulton was implicated in hounding Robert Gourlay out of Upper Canada in 1819, conducting two unsuccessful prosecutions of the Scottish dissenter for libel that ultimately led to the invocation of the Sedition Act and Gourlay's banishment.[75] More damning to his reputation, however, was his performance in several cases involving depredations against reformers and radicals by conservative yahoos. His inbred bias was reflected in a casual but telling remark during the civil action brought by W.L. Mackenzie against the perpetrators of the Types Riot who had acted in part to avenge the calumny poured on Boulton by the newspaper man in the columns of the *Colonial Advocate*. The solicitor general followed up on an observation by one of the defendants that Mackenzie was barren of character. To widespread laughter, the law officer claimed that he 'valued character much more than property and would rather that a person rob him of a horse or other property than take away his character.'[76] Tellingly, the solicitor general, like Robinson, had desisted from prosecuting, or at least upbraiding, the young men who had engaged in this vigilante action, some of whom came from his office. Boulton's partiality could also be disingenuous, as when he and Robinson argued vigorously in the Collins libel trial that the law officers had an effective monopoly in prosecuting criminal offences, and discretion in refusing to prosecute. True, victims of crime could retain private counsel, but even this was at the discretion of the law officers. The reason, Boulton claimed, was that without this monopoly a law officer would not 'have enough work to make a living.'[77] Here he was invoking prosecutorial discretion and financial need to shroud the two men's wilful and partial administration of justice. The ruse did not deter reformers in the assembly, or, as we have seen, Francis Collins and Justice Willis in court, from publicly challenging the monopoly.

It was Boulton's conduct in the aftermath of the tar-and-feather outrage against George Rolph that was to prove the most despicable example of how the law officers confounded their public duty and their private beliefs and sentiments.[78] A gang of men with blackened faces and garbed in sheets, gagged, blindfolded, and stripped Rolph naked and daubed him with tar and feathers. On discovering the identity of three of his attackers, including magistrates and lawyers, Rolph sued them civilly for damages. The law officers chose not to prosecute on their own account. Boulton acted for the defendants, arguing that the defendants were entitled to thanks for acting to protect public morals, although in error, counselled plaintiffs' witnesses not to appear, and influenced the judge, James Macaulay, his former student, not to commit the delinquent witnesses for contempt.[79] Rolph succeeded against two of the defendants but was justifiably dissatisfied with the fines of £20 and the way in which defence counsel and trial judge had acted. He sought an order for a new trial from the superior court. When Willis and Sherwood heard the case, Boulton reversed his stance on the contempt issue. On a subsequent rehearing, Boulton argued against retrial because, he averred, doing so on procedural grounds could open up numerous earlier trials, clogging the courts and leading to instability in the system.[80] Boulton's aggressive championing of the vigilantes as defence counsel made a mockery of justice in this case. A leading reformer, lawyer Marshall Spring Bidwell, wrote to William Warren Baldwin, 'The present period seems to me to be a crisis in the affairs of this province.'[81]

This record was not only to incense the opposition, but also to raise doubts about his character in the colonial government. The new lieutenant governor, Sir John Coleborne, considering Boulton for the position of attorney general when John Beverley Robinson became chief justice in 1829, had deep reservations. He complained to London of the candidate's blameful conduct, lack of professionalism, and unpopularity. 'The local Government will [thus] be rather embarrassed,' he asserted, 'by his promotion.'[82] Boulton nevertheless received the prize. Sitting now as the member for the 'rotten borough' of Niagara, he demonstrated his enthusiasm for corporate and civic initiative, while continuing to follow an irredentist line on issues of governance and loyalty.[83]

It was Boulton's unremitting desire to see the vociferous critic of the executive, William Lyon Mackenzie, hounded from his membership in the House of Assembly that demonstrated that his ultra-conservative instincts and arrogance were still very much in play. On three occasions between late 1831 and 1832 Boulton, with Solicitor General Christopher Hagerman in tow, orchestrated Mackenzie's expulsion from the House.[84] This was despite contrary instructions from Secretary of State

Lord Goderich to Coleborne. On the second occasion, injury was added to insult because Mackenzie was the victim of a gang beating led by a local magistrate. When Mackenzie travelled to London to plead his case, Goderich and the undersecretary, Viscount Howick, a son of the prime minister, received him. He persuaded Howick that problems in achieving reconciliation in the colony lay with the law officers.[85] When, in spite of a further warning from Goderich to Coleborne to ensure that no further expulsion occurred, the assembly expelled Mackenzie a third time, and the assembly and law officers – through a protest penned by Chief Justice Robinson – snubbed London's directive, the Whig government lost patience. Goderich was furious and advised Coleborne that he was dismissing both Boulton and Hagerman from office forthwith.[86]

Boulton resented his sacking, and when advised that the minister had assumed that the lieutenant governor had shared the instructions with the law officers, hastened to London to deny the transmission of the communications.[87] He successfully argued his case to the new and more conservative Secretary of State E.G. Smith Stanley. In due course, Stanley approved Boulton's appointment as chief justice of Newfoundland.[88]

Newfoundland's Distinctive Legal History

Newfoundland had a long and unique history as an English, later a British, possession.[89] At the end of the seventeenth century, London's policy towards it, embodied in 'King William's Act,' dictated that the island's only purpose was as a base for the summer fishery, and that permanent settlement was to be discouraged, by force of arms, if necessary. The legislation also confirmed an existing justice regime operating during the fishing season. The captain of the first fishing vessel on the scene (the fishing admiral) was authorized to resolve disputes and mete out punishment for all but the most serious crimes. By the Act this authority was now subject to a right of appeal to the captain in charge of the naval station in the neighbourhood.[90] The policy against settlement, although formally maintained, proved unavailing as wintering over – and the more permanent sojourning of merchants and fisherfolk – increased.[91] By exercising the prerogative, the Crown established a complementary system of land-based justice during the first half of the eighteenth century, with magistrates exercising criminal and informal civil jurisdiction. They administered justice in the long winter season, deferring to or collaborating with naval captains, who acted as justices during the fishing season. The British government gave some institutional cohesion in 1729 by appointing a visiting governor (the naval commodore) while the fishery was in operation, but whose authority had more permanent effects. The governor appointed resident civilian justices of the peace and delegated judicial powers to naval officers to act as surrogates. In 1750 London added a Court of Oyer and Terminer.[92] The law in Newfoundland was an amalgam of English law, locally developed custom, naval law, and informal dispute resolution. Gerry Bannister has argued vigorously that, given the time and circumstances, the system worked reasonably well and served the simple legal needs of this nascent colonial community.[93]

The court system received a jolt in 1787, when a court in Devon, hearing an appeal against a fine that a Newfoundland court had levied, raised questions about the legality of the jurisdiction of the local courts, causing a backlog of stalled cases (many involving actions for debt).[94] In response, Parliament – acting on the advice of Chief Judge John Reeves, sent out to review the situation – passed legislation setting up a Supreme Court with both civil and criminal jurisdiction administered by a chief justice.[95] The court had the authority to apply English law 'so far as the same can be applied to suits and complaints arising in the islands.'[96] The system of surrogate courts was maintained.

The history of the Supreme Court between its founding and the mid-1840s was a chequered one. Following Reeves, who served as chief justice from 1792 to 1794, there were several lay justices appointed. One of these, Thomas Tremlett, 1803–13, so antagonized the merchants of St John's that they petitioned the governor for his removal.[97] The judge's sin was to favour the wage and lien system that protected the wages of fishermen, in preference to the claims of the merchants who bankrolled fishing expeditions, and the 'planters' or vessel operators who hired them.[98] Although the Privy Council found no legal grounds to remove him, the British government, recognizing his unpopularity and lack of judgment, devised the remarkable expedient of switching him with the chief justice of Prince Edward Island, Caesar Colclough, a former Irish barrister.[99] Colclough had fallen out with the former lieutenant governor of that colony, Joseph Desbarres, and his political supporters. Buffeted by unfair charges from his PEI opponents, less than happy with his new environment and salary, overworked, and increasingly paranoid about disaffection among Irish 'rowdies,' the new man suffered a breakdown in his health. Allowed to take leave, he ultimately decided to throw in the towel and retire on half pay.

The one exception to this sequence of contrarian or incompetent jurists was Francis Forbes, a barrister hailing from Bermuda, who replaced Colclough in 1817. A man of considerable legal ability with a liberal view of empire, the new chief justice applied himself in a series of decisions balancing a concern to enshrine local customs in the law of the colony where they served stability in its law and social relations, with recognizing the value of English law as the embodiment of more liberal economic principles applying in the appropriate circumstances.[100] Much to the chagrin of the naval governor, Sir Charles Hamilton, Forbes recognized individual property rights against the claims of the Crown to ownership, while asserting an appellate jurisdiction over the surrogate courts and challenging gubernatorial authority on the grounds that its exercise was outside the power granted.[101] Despite later attempts by reformers to argue otherwise, Forbes had reservations about the continuation of the wage and lien system, which, he felt, protected fishery workers, in the event of planter insolvency (with a first call for the wages), from discipline for laggardly work.[102] However, recognizing that legislative change was required to achieve that end, he sought to redefine the relationship between planter and workers as a co-adventure, in which they shared in the losses as well as in the gains of the enterprise.

When Forbes left the island, to the general regret of the population, because of ill health, Richard Tucker, an English-trained lawyer, also born in Bermuda, replaced him.[103] In his jurisprudence he followed very much in the footsteps of his predecessor. In 1825 two associate justices joined the Court as result of reforms to the colonial government the previous year.[104] One of these, John Molloy, 'a reckless, gay, squandering, squireen,' was in serious debt and was soon forced to resign.[105] By the early 1830s Tucker faced problems as chief justice. His tenure coincided with a vigorous reform campaign for representative government, which was appropriate, the reformers argued, for a colony that had experienced significant population growth and expanding trade.[106] Overlaying this campaign and combining with it was the struggle of the majority Roman Catholic – mainly Irish – population for recognition of their civil and political rights. This campaign, led by the vigorous and feisty Bishop Michael Fleming, intensified when their co-religionists in Ireland and elsewhere in the British Isles achieved emancipation, and some were admitted to the franchise and to Parliament in 1829.[107]

Lord Grey's Whig government, committed to political reform in the metropolis, convinced that Newfoundland's claim to representa tive government was justified, piloted legislation through Parliament granting the colony an assembly with a franchise broader than that of Britain or any other British colony at the time.[108] It disregarded the advice of the governor, Thomas Cochrane, a naval man and Tory, who argued that the island was simply not ready for it, given its leading men's business distractions and the lack of sophistication among the lower orders, especially the Irish.[109]

None of the reforms sat well with the conservative Tucker. To the annoyance of the governor, Thomas Cochrane, the chief justice proved obstructionist in challenging the power of the assembly to enact revenue legislation, and using his role as president of the Legislative Council to derail such statutes. Tucker argued that local legislation that imposed duties on wines and spirits from British and foreign sources amounted to double taxation, because these products were already subject to tax by imperial legislation, and was therefore illegal. For good measure he asserted that the island was close to a state of 'primitive barbarity,' its people illiterate and without the means to advance education and religion.[110] He stubbornly stuck to his guns, vowing to overturn revenue legislation from the assembly should it come before the court, while bizarrely suggesting that the legislation might be reintroduced and passed while he went to England to state his case in London.[111] When Cochrane refused his request for leave, Tucker sailed for England anyway, and the secretary of state accepted his resignation.[112]

Although an unashamed conservative in constitutional matters, Tucker betrayed liberal economic proclivities. In 1831, along with his associate justices, he penned a report that advocated legislative changes to the merchant–planter–worker relationship, arguing on grounds of economic efficiency that that system placed too great a burden on merchants and encouraged sloth and inertia among workers in the fishery.[113]

Chief Justice Boulton as the Lightning Rod for Reformist and Catholic Angst

This, then, was the general state of affairs in the colony when Henry John Boulton arrived in St John's in November 1833. His selection for the post may well have reflected the priorities of E.G. Smith Stanley, the secretary of state, more conservative than his predecessor, Goderich, no fan of representative government and, as former chief secretary for Ireland, tough on concessions to Roman Catholics. For Stanley, Boulton combined the pedigree and experience of a no-nonsense colonial conservative and enemy of demagogues, with seasoned political and legal skills.[114] As fate would have it, Boulton would be thrust directly into the politics of the colony. Ironically, Governor Cochrane had argued vigorously to Goderich that the chief justice should not be a member of the Legislative Council, because his political duties might well conflict with his judicial ones, and those who opposed him politically might attribute political motives to his conduct of his judicial role.[115] The suggestion fell on deaf ears.

The first assembly had a majority of merchants in its ranks, ostensibly a supportive forum for both Governor Cochrane and his new chief justice. Within its ranks, however, were a vocal group of reformers – the Roman Catholics Patrick Morris, Peter Brown, and John Kent, and the Protestant, William Carson, who would be ardent critics of both, and particularly Boulton. These men too had the support of Bishop Fleming and his priests, who had no compunction about announcing from the pulpit where the loyalties of good Catholics should lie.[116] They did so in supporting Carson for a seat in the assembly in a by-election over his rival, Thomas Hogan, 'a rather independent Roman Catholic, not amenable to clerical pressure in the political field.'[117]

To Boulton, whose wife Eliza was a Roman Catholic, but used to the well-ordered and deferential behaviour of the hierarchy and faithful in Upper Canada under the loyalist Bishop Macdonnell, the alliance of the Newfoundland church with liberal reformers and its vocal activism was both a revelation and profoundly irritating.[118] Eliza Boulton went further and wrote to the cardinal prefect of propaganda in Rome to complain about Bishop Fleming, under whose prelacy, she claimed, every educated priest had left the town.[119] More generally, as Sean Cadigan has observed, Boulton, who was used to appealing to the 'producing classes' in Upper Canada, ready to rally support for the Crown and its representatives when the tocsin of loyalty was sounded, simply 'did not understand the new political ground on which he had to fight' in the island.[120] Unfortunately for him, too, the judge arrived at a time when relations between the governor and both the reformers and the Catholic clerics were strained, not least by Cochrane's calling out the troops to break up a hostile crowd outside Henry Winton's home. Winton edited the *Ledger* (the organ of the Protestant merchant elite) and had been a vocal critic of the influence of the Catholic clergy over their flock during the by-election.[121] Moreover, the reformers and the Catholic hierarchy now had an important public mouthpiece with the

Protestant reformers, Robert Parsons and William Carson, establishing the weekly *Newfoundland Patriot*.

Soon Boulton's actions in carrying out what he perceived to be his mandate to rationalize the colony's law and its procedures, and to take a tough stand against lawlessness and insubordination on the island, brought him into conflict with the reformers.[122] The first bones of contention were the changes to the jury selection system that the chief justice and his colleagues adopted.[123] Although Roman Catholics previously constituted a small minority on the grand jury, the reformed rules that provided for peremptory challenges by the parties, could be and were interpreted as meaning the exclusion of the majority of the population from service. The provision for special juries in the new rules vexed the reformers, because it made their use more frequent. With the petit juries, the new rules provided for a general pool of jurors, some of the members of which could be recycled, depending on the number of trials, instead of juries with different memberships being selected each day. Again the suspicion was strong that the judges had designed this system to exclude Catholics.

When the Chief Justice, working with the new juries, cleared a backlog of twelve accused awaiting trial for capital felonies (all Roman Catholics), and sentenced six to death, reformers viewed this as the chickens coming home to roost. Boulton fell further in their estimation when he piloted substantive criminal law legislation through the council and assembly that gave the judges wide discretionary power over punishment, including banishment, whipping, hard labour in iron clogs and shackles, and solitary confinement, and, in their role as prison administrators, inquisitorial powers before and after conviction.[124] Reformers and most Roman Catholics now viewed Boulton as public enemy number one.

His reputation was already receiving attention on the other side of the Atlantic. Daniel O'Connell, the architect of Catholic emancipation in Great Britain in the 1820s, paid keen attention to the lot of his co-religionists in British colonies. He forwarded a remonstrance from Newfoundland to the Colonial Office in January 1834, complaining about the changes in the jury selection rules and a petition seeking the remission of two of the six death sentences pronounced by Boulton.[125] It was not to be the last time that the Irish reformer would show interest in the chief justice's career.

The negative halo that the reformers had placed round the head of Henry John Boulton as one who rigged the justice system and revelled in imposing harsh penalties, especially against Catholics, was perhaps an understandable response to the judge's political credentials and perceived insensitivity to his new surroundings. His judgments in capital cases, however, do not invariably match the dark picture that his adversaries painted. Two early cases, for example, *R. v. Downing and Malone* and *R. v. Hackett*, demonstrate that the chief justice was ready to advocate remission of the death penalty when he felt it just to do so, and that it was the attorney general, James Simms, who was inclined to play the institutional pit bull.[126] However, given the different ideological worlds in which Boulton and the reformers operated, none of this was to make any difference, so the bad chemistry continued.

Boulton's policies on who was fitted for practice as lawyers on the island became another source of reformist angst. At a personal level, his refusal to admit John V. Nugent, newly arrived on the island from Ireland, where he had studied law, incensed them and produced another enthusiastic recruit to their ranks.[127] When the chief justice drew up an Act incorporating a law society and sought to limit admission to those called to a bar in Great Britain, or with five years' service with a Newfoundland practitioner, this was seen as a more general stratagem to close the bar to aspirants from the local community who lacked those qualifications, and to deny legal representation to those without the resources to retain the qualified few.[128]

In the realm of politics and religion, Boulton crossed swords with the bishop on the matter of education.[129] The chief justice, in somewhat inconsistent statements, first pronounced uncharitably that trying to amalgamate Protestant and Catholic children was as impossible as trying 'to blend oil and vinegar or bring the two poles together.'[130] He then proposed doing exactly that, amalgamating the Charity and Catholic Schools. Fleming, who feared 'Protestant proselytism and cultural assimilation,' made it clear to Boulton that he 'would compel all Catholics to withdraw their children' from such a school.[131]

In mid-1834 an earlier criminal law decision came back to haunt Boulton and generated further caustic criticism in the Roman Catholic community. He had tried Catherine Snow in February of that year for the capital offence of petit treason in arranging for the death of her husband by two men, Arthur Spring and Tobias Mandeville. Mandeville was her lover and she was pregnant by him.[132] On the basis of the confessions of both men, they were convicted of murder and petit treason respectively. The jury found Catherine Snow guilty of petit treason, largely on the basis of circumstantial evidence. Boulton sentenced her to death, but respited the execution until she delivered the child. In August 1834 the execution was carried out. The Catholic population were outraged, prompting Bishop Fleming in later communications with O'Connell and the Colonial Office to brand the chief justice as biased, bigoted, and sadistic.[133]

The reformers also attacked Boulton for his attempts to reform the substantive civil law of Newfoundland to bring it much more closely in line with English law. He strove to work fundamental changes to the law of property on the island by an abortive attempt to promote legislation that land would hereafter be considered real property, not, as previously under local law, real chattels.[134] Among its effects, this alteration would have made inheritance subject to primogeniture, rather than partibility.

In several judicial decisions the chief justice sought to demolish the customary law of Newfoundland concerning the fishery. Here he sought to radically alter the credit arrangements traditionally applicable.[135] First, he displaced the planters' suppliers in favour of the more distant merchant creditors in terms of who had preferential claims on planters' fish, oil, and gear. Along with this dramatic amendment he changed the terms of the writ of attachment, so that a planter's boat and gear could be attached for debt during the fishing season, and he denied the fishing servants (fishery workers) their customary right to follow and enjoy priority over the fish caught and oil rendered on a particular voyage.[136]

The changes to the law of the fishery, presaged by Chief Justice Forbes's reservations about the wage-lien system, and the 1830 judges' report advocating similar changes on grounds of economic efficiency,[137] affronted the planters and the fishery workers, because of what they feared were the greater uncertainties and lack of confidence that it would produce in a highly risky industry.

All this provided grist for the reformers' mill of criticism of Boulton at demonstrations and in the columns of the *Patriot*, and their identification of him as the mouthpiece of the merchants. In the calumny poured on the judge for seeking to change what they claimed was irrefutably customary law, the reformers were in fact inventing a history of the fishery convenient to their political agenda, which compared him unfavourably with his predecessors, Forbes and Tucker, despite evidence that neither had been happy with the old system.[138]

Despite, and perhaps because of, the reformers' campaign against him, Boulton was not without his supporters. The merchants were delighted with his attempts to change the law in ways that benefited them. His efforts to reform the law and stand up against the opposition also made him a hero in the eyes of newspaper editor Henry Winton and his friends.[139] Governor Cochrane, who left office in mid-1834, also encouraged the chief justice in his endeavours, advising the jurist to continue to act with a scorn for 'spurious popularity' and with 'a steady indifference to public opinion.'[140]

There was hope that the more conciliatory new governor, Thomas Prescott, would remove heat from the ongoing conflict between the reformers and the Catholic hierarchy on the one hand, and more conservative interests, including those of Boulton and his supporters, on the other. He certainly lent his best efforts to that end.[141] However, the political, legal, and cultural divide between the chief justice and his detractors was too wide. By January 1835 the reformist party and Roman Catholics aligned with Bishop Fleming were moving to bring charges against Boulton.[142] Disguised assailants attacked and mutilated Henry Winton, editor of the *Ledger*, who continued his sniping at the political and religious opposition, near Carbonear, in April of that year.[143]

For his part, the chief justice, who in capital cases continued to approach issues of mercy with some sensitivity, showed little of that sensibility in dealing with press criticism of the court.[144] In May 1835 Robert Parsons, editor of the *Patriot*, published a lampoon of the judge's address to the grand jury, under the heading 'Stick a Pin here: the beneficial effects of hanging illustrated.'[145] The chief summoned the newspaperman before Court and cited him for contempt, fined him £50, and imprisoned him for three months for striking 'at the very independence of the seat of Justice.'[146] The sentence once again outraged the reformers and inspired the formation of a constitutional society dedicated to liberating the editor and removing Boulton from office. In the face of a petition from 5,000 Parsons' supporters, the Colonial Office ordered Prescott to remit the fine and release the editor from jail.[147] The English law officers had determined that, while the judge was strictly correct in law, he should have followed the accepted English practice in such cases of securing an indictment or information, and proceeding by jury trial.

When Boulton heard of this rebuff, and in light of the attack on Winton, he sought a transfer from the colony to one in the West Indies, on the ground of personal danger to himself and his family.[148] His request was not granted, although Governor Prescott had indicated to the secretary of state that in view of tensions on the island a move for the chief justice would be desirable.[149] Colonial Office sources suggest that the chief justice was the subject of criticism for his imperious attitude towards his role on the Executive Council, and for bypassing the governor in communications with London.[150] Governor Prescott granted Boulton four months' leave of absence in May 1835, ostensibly to see to his family's affairs. His objective was to clear the air with the Colonial Office and ideally to secure a post in another colony.[151]

The chief justice's leave did nothing to relieve pressure from the island to have him removed. Earlier, Bishop Fleming had, through Daniel O'Connell, forwarded a petition to the British government seeking support for Catherine Snow's children.[152] In sending the Irish MP a further petition bearing 30,000 signatures seeking Boulton's removal, Fleming continued his vituperation of the chief justice, describing him in the same breath as 'a violent Tory … in the Legislature a coercionist [and] on the Bench a Jeffries [*sic*].'[153] Meanwhile, the Constitutional Society forwarded its own petition (signed by 5,000 citizens) accusing the jurist of flagrant violation of the Charter of the Supreme Court, ignorance of the customs of the colony, manipulation of the jury system, attempting to interfere with Catholic education through amalgamation of schools, trampling on freedom of the press, perverting the customary law of the fishery, and denying clemency to Catherine Snow.[154]

Boulton returned to Newfoundland in September 1835, having satisfied the Colonial Office of the propriety of his actions. Both Prescott, disillusioned at failing to bring peace to the warring factions on the island, and London's growing annoyance at Bishop Fleming's crass involvement in its politics, encouraged attempts by the British government to put pressure on the Catholic hierarchy in Britain itself and on Rome, to bring to heel the troublesome prelate.[155] Neither initiative achieved the desired results, the bishop recoiling at what he considered Prescott's perfidy, and Rome employing the mildest of strictures.[156]

It was not long before tension between Boulton and his detractors revived. Reformers and Roman Catholic activists roundly criticized him for his alleged mistreatment of Father Michael Duffy, the priest in St Mary's charged with provoking a riot, trespassing on private property, and demolishing fish flakes and other facilities belonging to a local merchant in that community.[157] Blame was attached to Boulton (it seems unfairly) for moving the case to St John's and the frequent delays in bringing the priest to trial – a process that went on for a further eighteen months.[158] His own refusal to allow an unlicensed Catholic lawyer to represent Duffy added to his negative halo.

The conflict between Boulton and the reformers grew worse, and doubts in London about his performance re-emerged the following year.[159] The chief justice continued to show sensitivity in his advice on the respiting of capital sentences, and was praised by the secretary of state for the colonies for his humane reform of the colony's jails.[160] However, his association with the Duffy case and, in particular, the imposition of what were viewed as inhuman burdens on the priest in travel to and from the capital, continued to rankle with reformers and the Roman Catholic population. Prescott was exercised by the continuing unrest in St Mary's, the inability of the local authorities to arrest Duffy's co-accused, and plans to send a naval detachment and troops to the area to restore order.[161]

Despite the fact that the Colonial Office sided with Boulton during the previous year, there was now evidence that both it and the governor were annoyed with him. London criticized him and his associate justices for responding directly to pressure by two justices of the peace seeking to persuade the court to allow representation of Duffy and his associates by Catholic lawyers, rather than communicating through the governor's office.[162] Prescott reported in May that Boulton's removal was desirable, because his association with the merchants 'made for the strongest party feelings.'[163] The Colonial Office continued to receive petitions calling for his dismissal from office, not least from John Nugent, that rehearsed the range of charges levelled against the chief justice for his partial administration of justice.[164] London's view was that the charges related exclusively to his exercise of his judicial office and that there was no basis for any joinder of the issue raised by these documents, in the absence of a petition to the Privy Council, which could be referred to the Judicial Committee. The secretary of state for the colonies wrote to Governor Prescott to that effect.[165]

By the summer of 1836 the St Mary's Harbour standoff had been resolved without the dispatch of troops, largely because Bishop Fleming ordered the accused to give themselves up and obey the laws.[166] After considerable discussion with London about the life of the House of Assembly, Prescott prorogued the assembly in September, and the writs for a new election were dropped.[167] The governor had severe doubts about the wisdom of this move because he feared that the result would be a reformist, Roman Catholic majority.[168]

The election and outbreaks of violence surrounding it was to provide new sources of grievance against Boulton. During October, riotous assemblies took place in Harbour Grace and St John's. There seems little doubt that there was intimidation by some involved, including several priests, against men running for office or taking their seats, because candidates were unsympathetic to the reform agenda.[169] When Boulton, on reviewing charges pending against rioters at Harbour Grace, discovered that the election writ lacked the Great Seal, he advised both the governor and the Executive Council that this oversight invalidated the election and voided the results.[170] The remaining elections were held, but the same default had occurred with all of the writs issued.[171]

Ironically, given his much more flexible stance against Justice Willis in Upper Canada on the constitution of its Court of King's Bench, the chief justice proved stubborn in upholding his position in this instance.[172] This was despite the fact that the defect in the writs extended back to the previous election in 1832, and invalidation of the recent election on that ground would raise questions about the status of legislation passed since that earlier date. Prescott requested London's direction.[173] When the Colonial Office grudgingly determined that a new election was required,[174] some of Boulton's adversaries were quick to attribute to him a malevolent plan to overturn the results of the election, which had produced a sizeable reformist, Roman Catholic majority in the assembly.[175] To these men it was also in character that he would have imposed heavy penalties on those convicted of electoral violence and intimidation, after trials in which the juries lacked any Catholic presence.

The year 1837 was to prove even more tumultuous in the relations between Henry John Boulton and his enemies. The chief justice was subjected to more intensive attacks as his opposition pressed again for his removal. In his own actions and statements he proved as vigorous as ever in justifying his own conduct and laying responsibility for unrest in the colony at the feet of a malign alliance of reform politicians, the Roman Catholic hierarchy, and, to his mind, its gullible flock.[176] Moreover, the Colonial Office now viewed him as the main lightning rod within colonial administration.[177] If Boulton had plotted to invalidate the results of the previous election for political reasons, the result of the new election was a bitter disappointment, as an even larger plurality of reformers and Roman Catholic representatives was the outcome in June of that year.[178]

Officials in London now began second-guessing the chief justice and his colleagues. Among the petitions seeking redress against him was one seeking remission of fines and other punishments exacted against various men for election assaults.[179] After reviewing several of these cases the secretary of state for the colonies, Lord Glenelg, pronounced several of the penalties unnecessarily harsh, recommending mercy for three of the petitioners. He further authorized the governor to use his discretion in remitting the other sentences in whole or part.[180]

As a judge Boulton crossed swords with reformer William Carson over the assault action launched against Carson's son, Samuel. This related to allegations of medical malpractice against the younger Carson in delivering the child of a poor pregnant woman. The action was brought at the chief justice's behest. Boulton had been heard to remark that, if the woman had died, he would have seen Carson and a medical colleague 'hanged.'[181] The elder Carson had added to the confusion surrounding this case by examining the woman, arguably without her consent, some weeks after the delivery, making him as well as his son a target for judicial spleen.

That the chief justice was again seriously reviewing his situation is evident in a letter to James Stephen Jr in which he reiterated a desire to fill a judicial vacancy in Upper Canada, especially if, as rumoured, a court of equity was to be established in the province.[182] Alas for him, the Colonial Office denied the rumour.[183] It was not, however, only Boulton who felt under pressure. Attorney General James Simms sought transfer to another colony, a result, according to Prescott, of increasingly strained relations with the judiciary.[184] The governor reminded the secretary of state that he had earlier advocated the removal of Boulton as chief justice. This and the departure of Bishop Fleming were essential to the colony's peace.[185] The Colonial Office, while agreeing with some of Boulton's strictures about the administration of inferior justice and policing on the island, now regretted his draconian prescriptions, expressing the naive hope that a new and more balanced assembly might provide legislative solutions to these problems.[186] Officials in London were beginning to recognize that the chief justice's strict and unrelenting approach to the application of English law and procedure might have been misplaced and counterproductive.[187]

The new legislative session was marked by conflict between the assembly and the Legislative Council with Boulton firmly at the helm as president of the council, over legislation proposed by the assembly, especially that relating to changes in the administration of justice, and revenue matters.[188] The result was an embarrassing legislative stalemate and a toxic environment in which principled argument was interpreted as malevolence. The struggle between Boulton on the one hand, and reformers and the Roman Catholic hierarchy on the other, moved towards its denouement when Patrick Morris delivered a speech in the House of Assembly on 25 August 1867 that was highly critical of the chief justice in his judicial capacity (ironically, comparing him unfavourably with his predecessor, Tucker). He called for an inquiry by a committee of the House into the charges against the jurist of partiality as a judge. The committee was quickly established with John Nugent as its chair and proceeded to hold hearings.[189] Meanwhile, as if intent on proving his ability to rile the reformers, Boulton made it clear that council would reject any bill from the House on the fishery that sought to re-establish the 'customary' protection of workers under the wage and lien system, because there was no agreement in the assembly on the character of the customs that the members sought to codify.[190]

The Report of the Committee of the Legislature was laid before the assembly on 10 October 1837. It listed a series of findings on Boulton's alleged perversion of the administration of justice in the colony in unfairly revising the jury selection system, seeking to change the substantive law of Newfoundland to the detriment of the fishing population, effectively excluding Catholics from the bar, and imposing harsh punishments and prison conditions.[191] The assembly moved quickly to appoint delegates to lay a prayer before Her Majesty for the removal from office of Boulton, who was, the members argued, guilty of party prejudice, injustice, and illegality.[192] The chief justice added fuel to the fire by taking out writs of libel against the three delegates from the assembly – Morris, Nugent, and John Kent – for speeches made in the assembly, a move seen as yet another attack on the privileges of the House.[193] The litigation took on an air of opéra bouffe when Boulton, vacating his seat on the bench, appeared as his own counsel and the jurors declined to attend. The assistant judges concluded that the court, as constituted, was incompetent to try the case and declined jurisdiction.[194]

With this, the effective action moved to Westminster, to which the three delegates from the assembly repaired to make their case to the Privy Council. There they were joined by Bishop Fleming, in Great Britain on church business, but anxious to provide what spiritual and moral support he could to the cause. Meanwhile, Boulton travelled to England to prepare and present his case.[195] That this conflict had taken on a life of its own in London is apparent in the background preparation for the hearing. Howell, one of the historians of the Judicial Committee, asserts that the contretemps between the chief justice and his antagonists had become primarily a political one in the sense that for the Colonial Office the issues were not Boulton's judicial decisions or reading of the law, but his controversial involvement in the political life of the colony.[196] This characterization had two consequences. In the first place, the Judicial Committee expressed serious reservations about its jurisdiction in the case, because of its political dimensions, resulting in a decision to refer the matter to a special ad hoc committee of the council itself.[197] Unless the Judicial Committee was genuinely feeling its way at this early point in its history, this seems a highly suspect characterization of a petition that was littered with complaints about Boulton's administering of justice and judicial decisions. Second, the Colonial Office arranged for the secretary of state, Lord Glenelg, to sit with the committee throughout its deliberations. This strongly suggests that the Colonial Office wished to directly influence the outcome of the committee's deliberations.[198]

The petition of the assembly, with Stephen Lushington, the liberal MP, and Daniel O'Connell MP, the Irish reformer, as counsel of record, set out at length the now familiar litany of charges against Boulton, most of which related to the way in which he had administered justice and attempted to reform the law of the island.[199] Reference was made to his partiality in reforming the jury system and partisanship in charging juries; his callousness in the sentences passed on those convicted of criminal offences; his insensitivity in seeking to abrogate the customs of the fishery that protected the fishers and the planters or supplying merchants, confirmed by his predecessors; his venomous treatment of a libel claim by reformer William Carson against the editor of the *St John's Times*; his unduly tough treatment of those prosecuted for allegedly fomenting election riots; his harshness in revising prison regulations to the detriment of Roman Catholic prisoners; and, finally, his bizarre attempt to punish leading assembly members by personally launching libel suits against them. The chief justice responded vigorously that he had acted as a judge and officer of the Crown at all times with integrity, within the parameters of the law as he understood them, and with the objective of improving the legal system of the island.[200] He also noted that his colleagues on the bench supported him and deprecated the scurrilous charges to which he had been subjected.

Ultimately all the forensic evidence proved to be largely irrelevant when the advice of the council to Her Majesty was pronounced.[201] The council slapped the petitioners' wrists for having heaped calumny on Boulton's administration of justice and asserting the need to 'purify' the system by his removal. The council found 'no corrupt motive or intentional deviation from his duty as a judge' and expressed 'disapprobation at the language of conduct adopted towards the chief justice as being unjust to him personally and inconsistent with the respect due to the High Office he was filling.'[202] However, their lordships also concluded that in some matters Boulton had been indiscreet in his conduct and 'that he had permitted himself so much to participate in the strong feelings which appear unfortunately to have to have influenced different parties in the Colony.' They concluded, 'Although we do not find that his judicial decisions have been affected thereby, we feel it our duty to state that we think that it will be inexpedient that he should continued in the office of Chief Justice of Newfoundland.'[203]

And so it was to be. Henry John Boulton was removed from office and replaced by a barrister from England, John Bourne.[204] The former's request to be reassigned fell on deaf ears in the Colonial Office, and, denied a pension, he was forced to return to the life of a practising lawyer in Upper Canada. In due course he was to again involve himself in the politics in that province, this time as an advocate of responsible government and reformer.[205]

Explaining Boulton's Demise: A High Tory in a Reformist Age

The wrong man in the wrong place at the wrong time would have been a fitting epitaph for Henry John Boulton's short-lived career as a colonial judge. With political reform in Britain on the political agenda in the early 1830s under a Whig administration, which had followed in the wake of Catholic emancipation, the appointment of Boulton seems entirely counter-intuitive. It is true that the Colonial Office viewed the law of Newfoundland as anomalous and favoured the more decisive introduction of English law as well as curbs on lawlessness, as it had in the previous decade in New South Wales. However, the appointment of a chief justice with less ideological baggage and a more balanced temperament than Boulton was surely possible. Even before he arrived in the colony, the Newfoundland reformers would have been well aware of the jurist's record in Upper Canada. In other words, his reputation would have preceded him. A chance change in the person of the secretary of state for the colonies from the liberal-minded Lord Goderich to the conservative E. Smith Stanley may account for Boulton's preferment, and it suggests that his appointment was the accidental result of portfolio shifting. It is nevertheless puzzling that the usually astute senior officials in the Colonial Office seem to have taken an indifferent position on this appointment and its political implications in the colony. Governor Cochrane's sage advice that Boulton, as the new chief justice, not be appointed to the Legislative Council was ignored, even though the Colonial Office had already taken steps to reduce the executive connection of his counterpart in Upper Canada.[206] Those officials were also well aware of the activist stands of legislative assemblies and the growth and impact of reformist sentiment within them. Although tending towards a *via media* that contemplated a legislative body in Newfoundland blending appointed and elected members, Whig politicians and Colonial Office officials dropped the ball on this, in the naive hope that the local interests might in due course move congenially in that direction.[207] Moreover, having appointed Boulton, the Office seems to have done little if anything to try to rein in the chief justice on his political stances, until the conflict with the reformers and the Roman Catholic population had become so fraught that the only feasible solution was to sack him.[208]

Although Boulton had much to answer for in his insensitivity to and stubbornness in the face of the political and religious culture of the island, which he did not or did not want to understand, his antagonists were not without blemish. Perhaps because of the negative halo already surrounding the chief justice when he arrived in Newfoundland, his actions in court or as a member of the Legislative Council were immediately the subject of sharp and even virulent criticism by reformers and the Roman Catholic hierarchy and priests. There is very little sense that anyone on the opposition side was willing to consider that Boulton was a more complex figure than any of them assumed. He was certainly not the unmitigated tyrant that they tried to paint, as his overall position on the remission of capital sentences suggests. Moreover, they seem to have been quite happy to treat him as the lightning rod for the ills of British colonial governance of the island, as if he were entirely a free agent. Moreover, his opponents were adept at fabricating a 'history' for the colony, especially in relation to the fishery, that provided them with a basis for criticizing and seeking to undermine his attempts a law reform.[209] As the invention of the 'Ancient Constitution' by the opponents of royal autocracy in seventeenth-century England demonstrates, this was a well-accepted practice in constitutional confrontation. The supreme irony of the story is, of course, that in the scheme of things Boulton was the reformer and his opposition the conservatives. Moreover, in taking the stance he did, he was to a significant degree following his instructions from London in improving the state of Newfoundland's law, substantively and procedurally, to bring it more into line with that of England and imposing order on its 'turbulent' society.

Given the nature of Boulton's remit from London and his attempts to reform the law, it was difficult for the Colonial Office and, in turn, the Privy Council to fault him in any public way for his handling of the law. However, there is no doubt that the Office had decided well before the hearing by the Privy Council that Boulton had to go. This explains why Lord Glenelg sat with the special committee hearing the case, to provide the decisive input that would paint the chief justice as a political rather than as a legal embarrassment. Both the Colonial Office and the Privy Council were also undoubtedly affected in their thinking by the recent outbreak of rebellion in both Lower and Upper Canada. They would have been aware of contacts between reformers in Newfoundland and reformers and radicals in these two mainland colonies, and sympathy of the former for the latter.[210] London would have wanted to nip in the bud any source of disaffection in its other North American possessions, notably one with a majority Roman Catholic population of predominantly Irish heritage. Boyd Hilton has noted that the Canadian rebellions were viewed with the utmost concern and anxiety in Westminster, because of the power of suggestion in them for dissidents in other parts of the empire, most especially Ireland.[211] Given such considerations, there was no question who was dispensable in the circumstances.

The stories of Chief Justice Sewell and Monk on the one hand and Chief Justice Boulton on the other are instructive at a number of levels. In the first place, they illustrate most clearly in the context of the British North American colonies the tension that existed in some instances between the colonial judiciary, particularly judges who took a Baconian stance in their relations with the state, and representative legislative assemblies containing persons of a reformist bent. Their provenance is thus different from the cases of Robert Thorpe and John Walpole Willis, men of reformist instincts or tendencies whose squabbles were primarily with the agents of strong executive government. Although the latter episodes had precedents in the first empire, as we have seen in chapter 2, and during the nineteenth century would have parallels in the Caribbean colonies with assemblies that dated from that earlier era, the stories in this chapter have a particular significance in the imperial legal history of the latter century. They are important because they demonstrate how the pendulum in imperial thinking about the North American colonies was beginning to swing from an ideology of close executive control towards legislative self-determination and self-government. The process would take another decade or two to work itself out fully with the grant of responsible government, first in the Canadian colonies and then in Australia and New Zealand. The separation of powers and the ability of legislative bodies to call uncooperative jurists to account would experience blips along the way, as the case of Benjamin Boothby in South Australia (discussed in chapter 8) would prove. However, the pattern already well established and understood in Britain itself of judicial independence and formal accountability to the legislative branch was spreading to the white empire.

The stories in chapter 5 are also suggestive in illustrating how colonial judges became enmeshed in tensions over the adoption of English law and procedures and the retention of existing legal or customary systems that local interests strongly supported as better suiting domestic circumstances. Not surprisingly, those tensions existed elsewhere in the empire, not least in the Australian colonies, and it is to the experience of activist judges, of different ideological persuasions, in those possessions that I now turn.

6

The Perils of the Colonial Judiciary: Guarding the Sanctity of the Common Law from Local 'Deviations' in a Convict Colony, 1800–1830

Barron Field's Shocker: A Challenge to Amateur Justice and Local Legal Culture in Australia

In 1820 two judgments of Justice Barron Field of the New South Wales Supreme Court of Civil Jurisdiction sent shock waves reverberating through the colony. In actions brought by emancipist (former convict) attorney Edward Eagar, one of which named Field himself as the defendant, the judge proclaimed that the English law of felony attaint applied in the colony.[1] The effect was to rob the plaintiff of any legal status as a litigant, maker of contracts, or seller, purchaser, or owner of property. Under the doctrine he was civilly dead. As the assumption since 1789 was that felony attaint had no place in this strange colony, this was a bombshell indeed. The judgment put into question a whole range of previous 'legal' transactions under the customary laws of the possession, to which convicts or emancipists had been parties.

It should already be evident from this study that early in the history of British colonial expansion amateur justice was the order of the day, and the law and procedure devised, while not entirely dismissive of English law, were moulded to the political, social, and economic realities of time and place.[2] This was so in the American colonies of the first empire.[3] It remained true in several British Caribbean colonies and Newfoundland into the nineteenth century.[4] New South Wales and Tasmania provide examples from the early decades of the second empire of this phenomenon. Amateur justice and local legal expedients were to remain important during the nineteenth century when the British government laid claim to new colonial territories on the imperial frontier that lacked professional infrastructures, as the early histories of Western Australia, Rupert's Land, Vancouver Island, and British Columbia all reveal.[5] Also at play in the politics of these possessions was imperial doubt over whether populations were considered mature enough, and whose circumstances were stable enough to warrant a fuller 'image and transcript of the British constitution.' As the mid-century constitutional history of South Australia demonstrates, the issue took a new twist when developed settler colonies became largely self-governing, and judges were faced with the question of whether they should sacrifice English law and procedure to the demands and priorities of local legislatures.[6]

Several judges whose careers have already been traced were at the centre and found themselves on one side or the other of conflicts between local law and English law and which system should prevail. This chapter considers several judicial careers that were marked in whole or in part by preoccupation with this tension.

The Distinctive Character of Law and Justice in Early New South Wales

Not surprisingly, the Australian colonies provide some of the most dramatic and instructive examples of this phenomenon of the struggles of the colonial judiciary in dealing with the clash of legal cultures. New South Wales was not a conventional colony. Established by the British government as an open prison for criminals who had escaped the death penalty by the grant of a conditional pardon, for whom transportation to the Americas was no longer an option, and who were warehoused in temporary quarters, its initial governance and law reflected a combination of the priorities of both an eighteenth-century carceral institution and a military encampment.[7] Although the governor was vested with ostensible autocratic power and authority, the realities were such that flexibility in dealing with local conditions, and discretion in handling the convicts became important. He had to exercise some care, too, in giving orders and directives, as he was not vested with formal legislative power. That reposed in Parliament in Westminster. As time went on and some people challenged the autocratic power of the governor, transgressing the line between an order and a legislative act, especially an edict seen as inconsistent with English law, became problematic. The precise objectives of the British government in establishing this colony were hazy. However, as Alan Atkinson has argued, there was some recognition in the mind of Thomas Townshend, Lord Sydney, the minister with responsibility for the colonies at its foundation, that, if the settlement was to succeed in the long term, the governors and their advisors would need to direct their attention to creating a civil society out of this unpromising mass of vicious and failed human beings.[8]

It took little or no time for the first governor, Arthur Phillip, and his successors to recognize that some English legal doctrines, such as felony attaint, were not feasible if the colony was to move beyond incarceration and punishment. Application of the criminal law of England in a quasi-military context, by the Court of Criminal Jurisdiction, comprising the judge advocate and six military or naval officers (and by justices of the peace),[9] was often unrelenting in its harshness with hangings, flogging, and the introduction of secondary punishment, involving further transportation to one of a number of Antipodean hellholes.[10] However, governors by their orders balanced that harsh stick applied to malefactors not inclined to change their ways, with the carrots of tickets-of-leave and pardons for those who proved themselves potentially responsible settlers by records of good behaviour.[11] The ticket-of-leave, first issued in 1801 during the governorship of Phillip Gidley King (similar to modern parole), enabled convicts to work for themselves and live in their own accommodation, while still under formal sentence. A pardon provided the governor with the power to terminate sentences before the expiry of their normal terms and to provide grants of land, so that the emancipists (the former convict population) would join a growing cadre of small farmers and artisans and be induced to settle in the colony. A major condition was that the pardoned individual stay in the colony until the term of his sentence had expired. Both expedients provided a way for the former convict to make the transition to civil society, and a responsible and productive life. There were many who did, and some became wealthy members of colonial society.

Not only in the field of criminal justice were things different. The Court of Civil Jurisdiction operated by the judge advocate with two lay assessors, while possessing most powers of the royal courts in Westminster, could not and did not slavishly follow English law and precedents.[12] As the First Fleet arrived in Botany Bay, the first judge advocate, David Collins, heard a suit by convicts Henry and Suzannah Kable against the captain of the vessel they had sailed in, Duncan Sinclair, claiming damages for the loss of their effects.[13] The judge found in their favour and awarded them £15. By this decision the door was open to suits by and against convicts, and the recognition of their commercial and land transactions, and felony attaint ignored. As Bruce Kercher observes, 'In practical terms, the Judge Advocates [who were with one exception not legally trained until 1811] and two lay members of the Court ... were free to make the common law however they wished.'[14] He continues, 'The main restraint on the creativity of the Judge Advocates was their own attitude to and knowledge of English Law ... The only guidance available to the amateur judges came from a few emancipist attorneys who practised in the court, and from whatever they could understand from their reading in the volumes of Blackstone and the few other law books in the colony.'[15]

Among the legal changes worked by these amateurs was the recognition of the power of wives to enter into contracts, as they often engaged in commerce, while their husbands were under assignment as convicts. Wives and children deserted by husbands, or cohabiters who returned to England, were permitted to share in property left in New South Wales, and magistrates ordered defaulting spouses still in the jurisdiction to make maintenance payments to their dependents. The limitations of a married woman's status in English law were either ignored or reduced in scope and effect. Collins and one of his successors, Richard Atkins, in their judgments mitigated the harsher aspects of the law relating to debt. Instead of forcing debtors into prison for failure to pay off their debts, a devastating blow to small farmers, the judges allowed payment in kind by crops or livestock, with extended periods to pay. Debtors could thus remain in gainful employment, while responding actively to their indebtedness.

The governance and administration of justice of this strange colony were not without vigorous critics in Great Britain.[16] The seemingly disorganized character of punishment and reward was offensive to the philosophical radical thinking of Jeremy Bentham and his utilitarian colleagues. Moreover, the perceived immorality of convict and free society in the possession were an anathema to William Wilberforce and the evangelical movement at home. Both groups sought to bring pressure to bear on the imperial government to change things.

The First Moves towards Normalizing the Legal System by Introducing English Law: Ellis Bent and His Discomforts

The government of New South Wales, a colony on the other side of the globe and neglected during the French Wars, had been creative in its development of local law. That situation continued into the 1810s. However, the so-called Rum Rebellion of 1808 sparked by the dissatisfaction with the administration of Governor William Bligh, by the venal New South Wales Corps, forced London to focus more clearly on the colony and its administrative and legal future.[17] First, it determined that strong, effective rule, unassociated with local interests, should replace that rebellious military clique. The man selected as governor was Lachlan Macquarie, a senior army officer with an impressive military record in several parts of empire, but with no connections to the corps, which was disbanded.[18] A second step was to appoint a lawyer, Ellis Bent, to the position of judge advocate, the senior judicial position in the territory.[19] His lay predecessor, Richard Atkins, haunted by his reputation as an alcoholic and incompetent, and by his spinelessness in the face of authority, had compromised himself during the rebellion.[20] As he had helped to trigger the uprising by his trial and conviction of the corps leader, John Macarthur, on Bligh's orders, the junta removed him from office. However, they later restored him to office to serve their interest in preserving 'legalities,' and to have the court continue its work.

Ellis Bent and his elder brother, Jeffery, were the sons of Robert Bent, a descendant of an old Lancashire family.[21] The father had been an associate of the influential Whig politician Charles James Fox. Interestingly, given that connection with a member of the anti-slavery movement, Robert, operating as merchant out of Liverpool, had slave interests in the West Indies.[22] He had been the member of Parliament for Aylesbury between 1800 and 1802 and, according to C.H. Currey, 'did not hesitate to invoke ministerial indulgence for his sons.'[23] Both the Bent brothers took a BA/MA degree at Cambridge: Ellis from Peterhouse and Jeffery from Trinity. Ellis went into practice in 1805. In granting Bent preferment to New South Wales, Secretary of State Castlereagh referred to him in formulaic terms as a 'barrister of eminence.'[24]

Relations between Ellis and Macquarie started out well. Ellis proved to be a hard worker and applied himself with skill and ability to the onerous job of judge advocate.[25] He seems to have had no qualms about approving a governor's proclamation insulating magistrates, constables, and jailers from prosecution, or action for acts done under rebel authority, in the wake of Bligh's removal from office. He received a grant of land and a building that combined a residence and a courtroom constructed for his use.[26]

Bent served as the senior judge in the Court of Civil Jurisdiction with a large caseload, as well as in the Court of Criminal Jurisdiction, where he ran the process of prosecution (absent law officers), advised the accused where necessary, and sought to secure a verdict from the panel of six army or navy officers. Although not part of his job description, he also sat with the Sydney magistrates in their deliberations, serving alongside at least one emancipist businessman, Simeon Lord.[27] The Criminal Court gave rise to a particular frustration for a conscientious professional judge like Bent – that the panel could overrule him, even on points of law. After his arrival in the colony, Ellis wrote to the Colonial Office in 1810 and 1811, complaining about the conflict that the multiplicity of functions on the criminal law side created for the judge, the less-than-influential role accorded to the judge advocate, and the tribunal's uncanny similarity to a court martial.[28] In the letter of 7 May 1810 the judge advocated that this court be administered by a judge sitting with a jury of twelve drawn from free settlers, those enjoying pardons for a considerable time or 'whose sentences had expired and were respectable in their conduct and situation.'[29] He was also in favour of the appointment of a person combining the functions of an attorney general and King's advocate to prepare and pilot criminal prosecutions. On the civil side he drew attention to the increased and complex caseload, as the population and the sophistication of its transactions expanded, as did the need for trained attorneys to act as agents for those litigating. He confessed that he had departed from the strict terms of his letters patent in order to facilitate court business, especially in the issuing of writs.

In an 1811 report to Secretary of State Lord Liverpool, Ellis Bent went further, recommending the establishment of a single Supreme Court of Judicature for the colony, serviced by a professional judge and two magistrates, with jurisdiction over civil, criminal, and ecclesiastical matters.[30] The judge, he asserted, unlike the situation of judge advocate, who acted under the control of the governor, should be appointed at His Majesty's pleasure. This would make the judge less dependent on the executive. Bent also advocated the abolition of civil appeals from this court to the Governor in Council, and an appeal to the Privy Council only in cases where the claim exceeded £6,000. In this missive he extended his advocacy of jury trial in criminal cases to include a grand jury comprising twenty-four men 'having lands or houses in the Territory,' while limiting the jurisdiction of the court to 'cases of a capital nature or of great enormity.' On the civil side, where he had early expressed doubts about the practicability of jury trial, he now thought that they might work in cases of relative simplicity. Bent adopted a *via media* on emancipist attorneys appearing in court (the only legally trained persons, other than himself, in town), between an outright ban and according them full rights of audience. Opposed to ignoring their crimes, while recognizing their value in expediting court business, he allowed them to appear before him not 'as attorneys, but as specially appointed agents of such suitors as might choose them to conduct their causes.'[31] He was careful to inform the three men in this category, George Crossley, George Chartres, and Edward Eagar, that permission was provisional and would be withdrawn if the imperial government managed to induce 'respectable solicitors' to settle in the colony.

Despite these recommendations and those of the Eden Committee on Transportation of the House of Commons, reporting in 1812, that jury trial should be introduced in New South Wales in criminal cases, the reforms of the new secretary of state, Lord Bathurst, were considerably more modest.[32] On the criminal side nothing changed. The judge advocate continued to act in that forum as before, although with an enhanced salary. On the civil side, jurisdiction was split between a new Supreme Court of Civil Jurisdiction with its own judge assisted by two magistrates, for cases of more than £50 value, and a Governor's Court administered by the judge advocate and two magistrates for those under that figure. An appeal from the Supreme Court lay to the Governor in Council, now to be assisted by the judge advocate. Earl Bathurst rejected the Eden Committee's recommendation that a council advisory to the governor be established in the colony. London's view was that the peculiar military and authoritarian cast of the possession needed to be preserved, for the maintenance of order and stability.

Bent was naturally disappointed by these less-than-half-measures, the complications created by the split in civil jurisdiction, and the odd role assigned to the judge advocate in appeals to the Governor in Council. He made his views known to the Colonial Office, where they were predictably dismissed as 'spilt milk,' inappropriate to the current state of the colony.[33] If there was to be any consolation, it was Governor Macquarie's support for his vision of a new order of justice for the colony. The governor expressed enthusiasm about the prospect of having Ellis Bent as the judge of a Supreme Court, a man 'in whose sound sense and professional knowledge' he placed 'the fullest confidence' and whose views on the administration of justice coincided with his own.[34] Macquarie also enthused at the prospect of Jeffery Hart Bent, Ellis's elder brother, being appointed to the new Supreme Court as a puisne judge to sit with his brother. In what was to prove an observation that would haunt him, the governor indicated that he understood that Jeffery was 'a man of considerable eminence as a lawyer, good sense and conciliatory manners, and as such, would be a great acquisition to the Colony.' Joined with 'the mild and conciliatory manners of this brother,' the twain would ensure, Macquarie predicted, that unanimity would prevail in the superior courts of the territory.

As fate would have it, under the revised Colonial Office plan, Macquarie's advice on personnel was taken and Jeffery Hart Bent was appointed as judge to the Supreme Court. In Currey's wry observation, 'When Macquarie realized how scourging could be the rod that he had put in the pickle for his own back ... he regretfully acknowledged, that he had "no control over Mr Justice Bent."'[35] Relations between the governor and Ellis had become distinctly strained before Ellis's elder brother arrived on Australia's shores. The already overworked judge advocate was increasingly beset by ill-health (described as dropsy – congestive heart disease). Ellis Bent's assertion that his problems reflected a failure to provide him with a comfortable courthouse did not sit at all well with Macquarie,[36] who viewed this statement as both uncharitable and a personal affront, especially galling because he had been pressing London hard for a new courthouse for the judge advocate and Supreme Court.

Far more substantive and important as an issue because it related directly to the relative status of the laws of England and local law in the colony was the conflict between the two men over the governor's desire to revise the port regulations, originally issued in 1810.[37] The executive's concern in promulgating the orders was to prevent the landing of undesirable characters from ships in the harbour, smuggling, and the escape of convicts. They were directed to masters of vessels coming into Port Jackson and 'all importers, consignees and other residents in the territory.'

Macquarie asked Bent to recast the revisions in the appropriate legal language. After a significant delay, the judge advocate responded with suggestions to the draft that he believed were in conformity with English law.[38] Apart from describing most of the provisions as unnecessary, because already contained in British legislation related to the plantations, Bent concluded that other sections were broader in their scope than they needed to be in order to deal with escaped convicts and in the process interfered with the freedom of perfectly innocent people. They were, he reported, illegal, contrary to the statutory plantations laws, and repugnant to the laws of England.

When the governor, disappointed at this response, sought to induce Bent to do what had been requested, Bent dug his heels in, at which point Macquarie ordered the judge to revise and frame the regulations. Assuming a Cokeian stance, Ellis followed his duty and conscience, in the process couching 'a lance for the rule of law, the independence of the judiciary, and, as a logical consequence, the circumscription of the power of the executive':[39] 'I cannot, in the due discharge of my duty to my sovereign or to my own conscience, consent to an attempt to give legal form to that which is illegal, or to frame or draw regulations, many of which in the due exercise of my functions as a judge, and with proper regard to administer justice according to law, I cannot enforce in my judicial capacity.'[40]

This exercise of judicial independence did not impress the conservative secretary of state. When he received news of the contretemps late in 1815 and responded early in 1816, he said so.[41] Bathurst emphasized the importance of cooperation between the judge advocate and the governor, especially in this instance where many of the regulations had earlier been approved in London, even if he had misgivings about some amendments. The colony still required strong government with an element of military discipline. However, the secretary of state was quick to advise Macquarie that, except where local conditions demanded a departure from normal practice, all regulations should be assimilated with British statutes.[42] In his view, the laws regulating trade would merit such treatment, except where the management of convicts or the preservation of public peace required special consideration.

Jeffrey Hart Bent: A Judicial Thorn in Governor Macquarie's Side

With the arrival of Ellis's brother Jeffery on 28 July 1814, the story of the tension between the former and Governor Macquarie was subsumed in the increasingly vitriolic conflict between the new judge and the viceroy. Jeffrey Hart Bent had, after his call to the Middle Temple in 1806, practised for seven years at the English bar. He received his commission as judge of the new Supreme Court of Civil Jurisdiction on 7 February 1814. Unlike his brother, he was to serve 'during good behaviour,' and so not under the exclusive control of the colonial executive.[43] His annual salary was set at £800 plus fees. Even before he ever set foot on Australian soil, J.H. Bent demonstrated an inflated sense of his own destiny and prickliness at not getting his way. He wrote to Bathurst on 21 February requesting that he be presented to the prince regent before his departure and that he 'receive the Honour usually conferred upon Professional Gentlemen filling similar offices to the one I now hold,' in other words a knighthood.[44] Presumably he thought an honour proffered to English judges on their appointments after highly successful careers at the bar or as law officers was his for the asking, with just a few years of practice under his belt. When the request was predictably ignored, he had the temerity to complain to Undersecretary Goulburn that these honours would have 'raised the character of the Colony, and added as much respectability as possible to the situation' he was to hold.[45]

Before he left England, Bent Senior did recommend two solicitors, William Moore and Frederick Garling, to the Colonial Office as good, respectable choices to go out to New South Wales, as the nucleus of a legitimate legal profession.[46] These men were duly commissioned. Jeffery Hart's penchant for vainglory were demonstrated again when on his arrival in Sydney Harbour he refused to land without recognition as a public official of great standing, and the governor hurriedly arranged a thirteen-gun salute and dispatched an aide-de-camp to welcome him.[47]

If the governor had not read this behaviour as raising questions about the 'good sense and conciliatory manners' of the new judge, he was to be quickly disabused of any illusions to that effect. Relations between the two began on a sour note on the lack of a residence for Jeffrey, for which the governor was blameworthy. Macquarie uncharitably denied the judge a house paid for by the colonial government, because, he said, it was a benefit not approved in his commission. The judge would be more than well compensated by his salary and court fees, and, drawing on his memory of service in India, this was not a benefit available to judges there.[48] Noting that his brother and every other high official in the colony had a home paid for by the state, Bent resented this rebuff, as he was forced to move in with Ellis and his family.[49]

It was, however, on the matter of courthouse accommodation that the first public and venomous spat occurred. Before he left England, Jeffery, perhaps on the advice of Ellis, had impressed upon Undersecretary Henry Goulburn the need for a new and separate courthouse in Sydney.[50] Macquarie did not disagree, but other priorities and fiscal constraints did not make that prospect feasible in the short term. What the governor proposed to the judges was that the court be housed in space developed for the purpose in the so-called Rum Hospital that was in construction and close to completion.[51] Under Macquarie's plan, the court would be located in the main building, with chambers for Jeffery and Ellis in one of the wings, which was a detached structure. Jeffery's position, in essence not unreasonable, but pressed with the increasing impertinence that marked his communications with government house, was that the court facilities and the judges' chambers should be housed together in the wing in question.

Macquarie, alas, had promised the rest of the wing to the principal surgeon, D'Arcy Wentworth, for his residence, and he was not willing to renege on a promise already made to another important official.[52] Jeffery's predictable reaction was to argue that in the colonial pecking order His Majesty's justices were a distinct cut above a principal surgeon. Moreover, the latter's convenience was insignificant compared with 'the proper, due and solemn administration of Justice,' and preferring his needs constituted 'an unnecessary degradation on the Office, the character and the Persons of [the judges] in the Colony.'[53] The letter stressed the dangers and inconvenience in the courtroom's proximity to the hospital wards. The judge's tone was not calculated to inspire sympathy in the mind of Lachlan Macquarie, who characterized the barrage from Jeffery as selfish and reflecting private convenience over the public interest. He dug in his heels over the courthouse location.[54] Jeffery, for his part, wrote to the Colonial Office to record his disapproval of the governor's actions, in the face of his own desire to improve the profile of His Majesty's court.[55]

Jeffery Hart Bent was not, however, one to relent and found a new casus belli on which to challenge gubernatorial power, one in which he could appeal to the authority and, for him, the irrefutable demands of English law. Governor Macquarie was in many ways the epitome of autocratic, paternalistic authority that the imperial government believed was essential to the welfare and future of this colony. He was also a realist. On the basis of his understanding of the vision of those who founded the colony, as well as his assessment of the present state of the possession, he had developed the belief that, if the colony was to progress, members of the former convict population who had kept their noses clean, proved their industriousness, and were contributing to the life of the colony, particularly in the economic sphere, should be progressively accepted into its political and legal mainstream.[56] None of this was to the liking of free settlers, whose vision of a future colonial society was one in which they would have social and political control – the 'exclusives,' to whose views J.H. Bent subscribed. Following his instincts, Macquarie had appointed several successful businessmen emancipists to the position of magistrate and was happy to welcome emancipists who met his criteria for respectability at Government House.[57] Like several previous governors, he also approved the appearance of former convict attorneys in court representing clients.[58] Macquarie, following the lead set by his judge advocate, had also argued for emancipist membership on juries in a superior court exercising criminal jurisdiction, which the two had unsuccessfully advocated in their recommendations to London.[59]

After his rebuff on the courthouse issue, Jeffery Hart Bent made the operation of his court contingent on the availability of non-convict lawyers to plead on behalf of clients. By the beginning of 1815 the courthouse facilities promised by the governor were completed and ready for use. Furthermore, one of the two English lawyers commissioned to plead in the court, William Moore, had arrived in the colony. The second, Frederick Garling, had been delayed and would not arrive in the colony until August of that year. In one of his earlier letters on the courthouse issue, Jeffery had ominously stated to Macquarie that he would not open the court until both lawyers were ready to appear before him.[60] True to his word, he refused to hold court in Garling's absence, to Macquarie's increasing consternation, but Macquarie believed that he had no control over what Bent did within his own institution.[61]

The judge made it clear that he would not entertain emancipist attorneys in his court, even in the role of agents for clients.[62] In this stand he appealed first to a statute of George I,[63] which proclaimed that anyone convicted of perjury or forgery who acted or practised as an attorney or solicitor or agent in any suit brought or to be brought in any court of law or equity in England was subject to transportation for seven years. This wording was, Bent claimed, proof positive that Parliament had a clear sense of the unfitness of such a person to practise law in His Majesty's dominions. Secondly, he cited a 1778 decision of all the English judges, *Ex Parte Bounsell*, involving an attorney struck off the rolls for stealing a guinea.[64] No less an authority than Chief Justice Lord Mansfield, supported by a unanimous full bench, had ruled that the exclusion of convicts and ex-convicts from the practice of law was absolute. In Bent's view, this authority was binding on all British judges throughout the empire. There was, the jurist added, no necessity now for the former convicts to appear, as two attorneys had been authorized to practise in the colony. The appearance of the former would, moreover, 'introduce a precedent, which would give rise to numerous other applications from person similarly circumstanced, and expose the Court to endless embarrassment.'[65] When Macquarie sought to suggest that allowing them to act as agents would allow for the disposition of cases in process, the judge discourteously told him he was attempting to bias the court and to mind his own business. Bent was unalterably opposed to former convicts practising in colonial courts.[66]

William Broughton and Alexander Riley, the two magistrates the governor appointed to sit with Bent on the Supreme Court of Civil Jurisdiction, entered the fray at this point. During the absence of Governor Macquarie up country, Jeffery Bent opened court without explanation on 1 May 1815, with Attorney Garling still nowhere in sight.[67] During a conference among the three judges, Bent made it clear to his colleagues that he would not entertain emancipist lawyers in any shape or form.[68] The two magistrates had already opined that the statute Bent cited was explicitly limited in its operation to England. They were also quick to note that Ellis Bent had previously allowed such men to appear as agents, and that even the presence of two commissioned attorneys would not completely solve the problem of lack of representation of clients. Jeffery reacted vituperatively to this advice from mere laymen, and the lack of deference to him on matters of law and process that it betrayed. He announced that he would report them to His Majesty's government. For Macquarie's benefit and with no hint of irony, the judge made it clear that if anyone tried to force him to hear former convict attorneys in his court he would close it down.[69] When the magistrates accused him of insulting them and threatened to refuse to sit with him, he lectured them on their role, likening it to that of jurors limited to determination of facts, and on the need to accept the decision of the professional judge on matters of law.[70] He also made sure that proceedings did not reach a point where the twain could outvote him on the issue of representation of litigants.[71]

Throughout this protracted period of sparring, no cases were being heard in the court. It had now been closed to business for ten months.[72] The sessions of the Governor's Court with jurisdiction over the less costly civil suits were becoming more infrequent, because of the decline in Ellis Bent's health. The two Bents were seemingly working in harmony, according to a script written by Jeffery, on court accommodation, emancipist attorneys, and port regulations. Beside himself with anger, Macquarie, who had already advised Lord Bathurst how frivolous and ridiculous J.H. Bent's stand on the attorneys issue was, informed the jurist that he was reporting him to the British government for his illiberal views and conduct.[73] In June 1815 the governor sent a long, at times irate, but overall thoughtful statement to the secretary of state.[74] He observed how Bent's position not only subverted the administration of civil justice in the colony but also the benign, humane, and forward-looking policy of introducing former convicts who had paid their dues, leading honest and productive lives, into the civic mainstream of the society 'where they would enjoy the privileges of free British subjects.'[75] Moreover, the governor complained, the judge had acted offensively and with unbecoming passion towards his fellow magistrates, and in one of his letters treated the chief executive with 'arrogance, insolence and intolerable ... insubordination.'[76] Shortly after, in a private missive to Lord Bathurst, the Governor concluded disconsolately that London should remove either the brothers or him from office.[77]

Frederick Garling's arrival in August 1815 did nothing to resolve the standoff between the judges and governor. This was now a bitter battle about the character of law in the colony and the sort of society that New South Wales should be, as well as who had authority over the administration of justice. Was it local law or the dictates of English law that should predominate? Would emancipists enjoy the same rights as free settlers, or would exclusive policies shut them out of full participation in the political and social life of the community?

That same month was to mark the beginning of new conflict, this time about the legitimacy and application of the Turnpike Regulations Macquarie had issued. Jeffery Hart Bent announced that the governor had no power or authority to levy taxes on the subject and complained that the money raised was going into a general account rather than to turnpike maintenance, as was the rule in England.[78] Since the same statement suggested that judges enjoyed 'equal civil powers' to the chief executive and his deputy, and therefore should be exempt from this impost, Macquarie might have been forgiven for concluding that the real reasons for Bent's opposition were his personal convenience and contempt for the executive. Informed by his nemesis 'that no Judge in any part of His Majesty's dominions was ever before treated with so much indignity, and that your Excellency appears in the ebullitions of your violence to have lost sight of your own high station and to have totally forgotten the rank and office' did nothing to reduce the viceroy's blood pressure.[79] Jeffery was to add insult to injury by refusing to pay tolls at turnpikes, forcing his way through gates, and, when summoned before the police magistrate and fined, declaring himself as judge of the Supreme Court to be in no way amenable to the criminal jurisdiction of the colony.[80] After the governor sought to issue a public order directing the payment of tolls, targeting the recalcitrant jurist, Bent responded by alleging that Macquarie was treating him as an officer under his command, 'not as a Judge holding a Commission from His Majesty.'[81]

During 1815 Ellis Bent's health deteriorated to the point where there was talk that he might need to leave the colony. Jeffery reported this to the governor and had no qualms about offering to stand in as judge advocate, an offer which Macquarie was quick to decline.[82] He cited Bent's offensive conduct towards him, as well as the legal problems associated with the same judge serving on both courts. Jeffery then wrote to Earl Bathurst, rehearsing the reasons for his resistance to admit former convicts to his court and to the turnpike regulations, as well as suggesting the consolidation of the institutions of superior justice in one court much along the lines that his brother had advocated earlier.[83] He saw no problem in his holding both judicial positions in the interim. He expressed annoyance that Macquarie had offered the position of judge advocate to Frederick Garling.

In November 1815 Ellis Bent died and Garling replaced him pro tem. Garling now earned more than Jeffery and had become his professional superior.[84] Bent had intended to open court in the autumn of 1815, as there were now two respectable lawyers in the colony. With the elevation of Garling, the problem of adequate representation of clients reemerged, and the doors of the Supreme Court remained firmly shut.

London's responses to the distempers of Macquarie and the Bents indicated a lack of patience with both judges' carping about and disrespect towards the governor on port regulations, the location of courthouses, and the process of civil justice. The message was simple: You are in a colony with a quasi-military regime. It is incumbent upon you to work closely and cordially with the governor and to uphold and be obedient to his authority.[85] In the case of Jeffery, it was made clear that he should have been aware of the particular political and social conditions obtaining in New South Wales when he went there, and adjusted his claims to consideration and convenience accordingly.[86] Earl Bathurst had decided that the only antidote to the poisonous relationship between Macquarie and the Bents was to recall both judges.

In January 1816 Jonathan Wylde was commissioned as judge advocate to replace Ellis.[87] News of the Colonial Office's action soon reached the ears of Robert Bent, the father of the two jurists, who was quick to rush to the aid of his boys. If they had erred 'in resisting the Will of [the governor] ... they did it ... from the purest of motives, the Wish to uphold the Honor of the Crown and the purity of British Justice,' he said.[88] Bent Senior added that he could vouch for his sons 'that to the decision of His Majesty's Government on every and any particular point, they will pay *prompt* and implicit attentions and obedience.' The hint was that they should be granted preferment elsewhere in the empire. Interestingly, Undersecretary Goulburn, in responding, indicated that it was impossible to overlook the brothers' indiscretions in New South Wales, and so the offices they had filled were being offered to other gentlemen. However, the letter concluded, Ellis would 'not be disqualified from holding a Judicial Situation in any other Colony.'[89] Jeffery, about whose future no comment was made, was undoubtedly seen in London as the natural provocateur of the pair.

Recall of the Brothers Bent: J.H. Bent's Campaign to Unseat Macquarie

Lord Bathurst recalled the brothers Bent by letters dated 12 April 1816. In Ellis's case his failure to cooperate with the governor on the port regulations issue, and his objections to serving in such a colony as New South Wales were cited as the reasons for his recall.[90] The matter was academic for the deceased younger brother.[91] Jeffery's errancy related to his suspension of civil justice in the colony between his arrival and the issuing of further instructions on the issue from the Colonial Office, this in the face of an existing practice of having emancipist attorneys appear in the judge advocate's court.[92] Barron Field replaced him in the Supreme Court of Civil Jurisdiction. In his letter to Macquarie announcing the recalls, Bathurst was careful to stress that it was not their concerns nor even protests about the executive acting illegally or improperly that had landed them in trouble, but their actions in withholding from the governor the legal assistance that he required, or holding up judicial proceedings on the basis of differences of opinion about the law.[93] In short, Bathurst did not object to the actual opinions of the Bents, but rather to the way they had expressed and acted upon them.

During the time it took for these communications to reach the Antipodes, the nastiness between Governor Macquarie and Justice Bent continued unabated. Justifiably, the governor saw the judge at the centre of dissent in the colony against his rule, 'the root of every faction and cabal that takes place in the colony.'[94] The latter was not alone. The Reverend Samuel Marsden used his homily at Ellis Bent's funeral to engage in thinly veiled criticism of Macquarie. The cleric invoked the Old Testament story of the early death of King Hezekiah, who 'did that which was right in the sight of the Lord,' to paint the former judge advocate as the young and virtuous victim of tyranny.[95] The governor, who had been sitting in the pews listening, was apoplectic and subjected the cleric to a gubernatorial dressing down. This controversial minister, disliked by the viceroy, had become a close friend and confidante of Bent. Macquarie, who let his sense of pride and stubbornness and a certain degree of vindictiveness get the better of him, played into the hands of his critics, not least the judge. Already the focus of opposition among free settler exclusionists for his attempts to make colonial society more inclusive, when he took actions that were autocratic in style and substance he offended both those people and others who saw the rule of law and 'the rights of freeborn English men' as compromised.

The governor also attracted criticism in the Colonial Office for his cavalier attitude to rights, as when he ordered the court martial of an assistant chaplain, Benjamin Vale.[96] During a Macquarie absence from Sydney, Vale had ordered the seizure of a visiting American vessel as prize, a response to complaints from the masters of an English merchantman and of East Indian commercial vessels at anchor in the harbour. The action contravened the governor's policy of attracting American trade. There was no legal warrant, said Bathurst, for treating Vale's actions as a matter of military justice.[97] Unfortunately, the viceroy added to others' perception of him as a sore loser by stopping the salary and revoking other perquisites of lawyer William Moore, who had represented Vale.[98] The injustice of this step was an issue that Bent pursued with vigour with London, a diversion that increasingly occupied the time that he would otherwise have spent sitting in court.[99] The secretary of state responded to this news testily and ordered Macquarie to reinstate Moore.[100] When Macquarie received this rebuff, he submitted his resignation. This Bathurst was not willing to accept.[101]

The governor provided further grist for Jeffery Hart Bent's complaints in the former's refusal to grant a marriage licence to – and decision to deport – former army officer Philip Connor.[102] These executive acts, which reflected the viceroy's opinion that Connor had been lucky at an earlier point to dodge a murder conviction while in military service in the colony, drew the judge's criticism. The judge characterized this as a denial of the right of a British subject to travel where he wished, and to enjoy full legal status in His Majesty's dominions.[103] Macquarie rejected the advice, and Bent advised London of this latest example of a governor seemingly out of control.[104] Macquarie's order that three men climbing the walls of the Domain in Sydney to take a short cut should be summarily flogged produced a similar reaction. A gubernatorial order had proscribed the practice of cutting across the property. In this case the governor, while admitting that his action might be considered 'somewhat illegal,' had gone ahead anyway with this extrajudicial process. The men swore affidavits before Bent, which were dispatched to the secretary of state, so that he would be 'able to gather of how little consideration and how powerless the law is in this Colony.'[105]

If Macquarie was guilty of acting outside the parameters of English law and the rule of law, Bent himself was not beyond acting deviously and even illegally. The evidence is clear that the judge lent his drafting skills to a petition being drawn up by disaffected colonists seeking relief from the oppressive rule of the governor.[106] More serious was Bent's manipulating the administration of justice to satisfy personal or family convenience, as he did in the case of John Harvey.[107] Mrs Ellis Bent had discharged Harvey, a convict assigned to her, and a cook in her household. Harvey then entered the employ of an official, William Hutchinson, but Mrs Bent changed her mind, demanding Harvey's return. Judge Bent issued a warrant for his return. William Broughton, the magistrate who had earlier drawn the judge's ire, considered the warrant invalid. He offered Harvey refuge at his house. Jeffery then ordered Broughton brought before him for contempt. Bent found him guilty and committed him to jail. Macquarie reacted by granting a warrant for Broughton's release, and the Sydney Bench of Magistrates pronounced the judge's actions unconstitutional. In this case it was the governor who wrote to Lord Bathurst complaining about the irresponsible extrajudicial conduct of the judge.[108] At the end of the missive he wistfully stated his regret at ever having recommended Jeffery Hart Bent for his post.

The arrival of Judge Advocate Wylde, carrying Bathurst's letter recalling the Bents, added to the tension between Macquarie and J.H. Bent.[109] There were squabbles over whether the judge was *functus officio* or not, pending the arrival of Justice Field; who had the authority to discharge magistrates from the Supreme Court Bench; the timing of Mrs Ellis Bent's departure from the house she occupied, to accommodate Wylde; and where Ellis's remains should be laid to rest.[110] The relationship between the two men descended into a toxic quagmire of mutual recrimination.

For Macquarie, temporary relief came with arrival of the new judge of the Supreme Court of Civil Jurisdiction, Barron Field, in February 1817, and the departure of the Bent clan from New South Wales early the following May. Jeffery Hart Bent had already written to Earl Bathurst complaining about his recall and the premises on which it had been made, and asserting that he would not have accepted the position had he known of the state of the colony.[111] In London, Bent made it his business to clear his name. In his correspondence with the Colonial Office, he stressed how he had stood as a beacon for English law and its values against the tyrannical instincts of the governor.[112] In alarmist rhetoric he referred to convicts and emancipists alike as vile and vicious creatures unworthy of any place of power and influence in a civilized society – all to make the point that he had been the victim of injustice. At the same time, together with the governor's enemies in the colony such as Marsden, and in England, like Benjamin Vale, he pressed vigorously for Macquarie's recall and disciplining.[113]

Whether the personal touch had a positive impact on officials in the Colonial Office, or that they wanted to be free from another broadside from the former judge, Bent's pleas of injustice were answered by a cautious concession that the secretary of state might grant him further preferment.[114] How such a stormy petrel – who had preached the virtues of English law and justice while doggedly avoiding their application from day to day – was seen as a promising prospect for a responsible position elsewhere in the empire is hard to fathom. Although Bent's campaign against Macquarie was not primarily responsible for the calling to account and ultimate removal of the viceroy, it did add to a climate of doubt in British government circles about Macquarie's administration of the colony. It was these misgivings that induced Whitehall in 1819 to establish a royal commission into the governance in New South Wales, under John Thomas Bigge.[115]

Explaining the Bent–Macquarie Conflict

Governor Macquarie's battle with the brothers Bent was the opening round in tension between executive and judiciary extending into the late 1820s. A clash between the values of quasi-military governance and of English law and justice was inevitable as free settlement and commerce expanded, the community as a whole moved closer to being a civil society, and social institutions took root. The 1810s were a difficult decade for those at the centre of the political and legal life of the colony. The imperial government, goaded into greater interest in the state and future of this possession by the revolt against Governor Bligh, recognized a need for the administration of justice to be placed in the hands of professional lawyers who would carry with them the values of English law and advise the governor accordingly. However, that same government, still distracted by the struggle with Napoleon, was anxious to maintain an autocratic, military style of governance in the colony. In this system, the concentration of power at the centre in a viceroy with military experience, and, in criminal matters, a system of justice that was military in its inspiration and form, continued. Only in civil justice did modest reforms take place. No provision was made for a legislative council advisory to the governor or trial by jury. London provided no new direction to guide either executive or judicial officers during these first halting steps towards more conventional colonial status. Together with the great difficulties of communication with such a geographically remote territory, this meant that both the executive and the judicial branch of government could be playing quite honestly and with integrity to different tunes and librettos.

There was room, of course, for negotiating a mutually satisfactory and appropriate path through the murky world of law and politics in New South Wales during that period. The early positive working relationship between Ellis Bent and Macquarie provide some hint of how this might have worked more generally.[116] Personality clashes, however, got in the way of calmly mediated solutions to problems in which the worlds of politics and law collided. On the one side was a governor, hypersensitive, imperious, and full of pride, convinced that he was doing right and using wisdom in his blend of policies for commanding a colony that continued to be a prison, while reflecting the economics and social life of a settler colony that, in his view, should be more inclusive in its make-up. On the other was a judge, stiff-necked and prickly, unwavering in his commitment to the primacy of English law and the rule of law in the colony, impatient to promote that system of law and justice, even at the expense of cooperation with executive authority, and wedded to a vision of colonial society in which free men alone would hold the political and social power. As is sadly evident, the chemistry between the two was explosive. However, despite the fact that it was the judges who paid the immediate price for the conflict by being recalled, the genie of English law and justice was now out of the bottle, and tension between the cultures of quasi-military governance and the law in New South Wales would intensify.

The Bigge Report and the Administration of Justice in New South Wales: The Rise and Fall of Barron Field

If Governor Macquarie breathed more calmly after the removal of the albatross of Jeffery Hart Bent from around his neck, his relief was short lived. Two factors explain a pattern of increasing criticism of his administration and management of the colony. From 1815 and the final conclusion to the Napoleonic Wars at Waterloo, London focused more closely on the state of its Antipodean colony.[117] Several government departments had become critical of the administration of New South Wales and were putting pressure on the Colonial Office to take the colony more firmly in hand. The Home Office, responsible for carrying out the penalties inflicted on criminals sentenced by the courts, considered that transportation to New South Wales had lost its earlier and undoubted punitive and deterrent edge, and seemed no longer an object of terror in the minds of convicts.[118] This change in attitude reflected criticism of Macquarie and his policies, not least his professed desire to incorporate emancipists into the mainstream of the colony's life. For its part, the British Treasury voiced its concern over 'extravagant' expenditure by the governor, at a time when fiscal retrenchment was paramount in Britain itself. The English law officers were distressed over Macquarie's tendency to take initiatives and assume powers that were outside the bounds of his authority and the law. The Colonial Office was well aware of the controversy swirling around the viceroy. Lord Bathurst, not one to rush to judgment over attacks on colonial governors without a careful canvassing of the facts, but well aware of the need to respond to the concerns of his ministerial colleagues, determined that the time for a commission of inquiry into the state of the colony, including its justice system, had come.

The man chosen to conduct the inquiry seemed well-suited for the job, politically and professionally. John Thomas Bigge came from a Northumberland family of landed gentry with developed commercial interests.[119] Although drawn to Whig politics, he came with the full and enthusiastic support of the Tory governor of Trinidad, Sir Ralph Woodford, where he had served as the chief justice in succession to the controversial George Smith, whom we shall meet in chapter 9. By his patron's account, Bigge was a skilled judge and lawyer, an able administrator, and a thoroughly reliable adviser on both legal and non-legal matters.[120] From London's perspective, the two men had brought effective government and thus stability to the island colony. In his instructions to Bigge, Bathurst directed the commissioner to consider, inter alia, the administration of criminal and civil justice and the conduct of persons in authority in New South Wales about whom there had been complaints, regardless of their position.[121]

It was with some surprise that Macquarie received Bigge on his arrival in New South Wales in September 1819. He had not received Bathurst's rejection of his letter of resignation dispatched late in 1817 (for it had gone astray), and only belated word arrived of London's intention to appoint the commission.[122] The initial enthusiasm that the governor evinced for an inquiry – which he was confident would vindicate him – soon faded. As Bigge was opposed to Macquarie's attempts to liberalize social relations, and in particular the elevation of emancipists to positions of authority in the colony, and not afraid to make his views known, the relationship between the two became quickly strained.[123] In the face of Bigge's inquiries into his actions, the viceroy became defensive and secretive in support of his record. The commissioner, whose approach to the gathering of evidence John Bennett has described as relaxed rather than demanding, found plenty of opposition, as well as outright hostility, against Macquarie and his approach to governance, especially among the exclusives.[124]

Bigge's inquiry into the administration of justice was to further expose the tensions between autocratic government and the law – difficulties with the existing court structure and the personalities and performance of the two senior judicial officers. The judge who was the more problematic of the two was Barron Field. A Tory by instinct and association, he had been called to the bar in 1814. He had written *An Analysis of Blackstone's Commentaries*, presumably during his pupilage. A friend of the writer Charles Lamb, he had become known in London as a literary and theatrical critic.[125] It was John Wylde, the man appointed judge advocate as successor to Ellis Bent, who strongly recommended Field for the position as chief judge of the Supreme Court of Civil Jurisdiction.

Field immersed himself enthusiastically in the colony's cultural life.[126] He produced one of the earliest book of poems in Australia and was active in the cause of Christianizing the Aborigines and in establishing public schools and a reading room in Sydney. His commitment to good works and devotion to the Church of England brought him into contact and an abiding friendship with the Reverend Samuel Marsden, the controversial Anglican minister, magistrate, landowner, and businessman – Macquarie's foe.

Barron Field's record as a judge could best be described as mercurial, a reflection of his conservative belief system, a commitment to the culture of English law, and an opportunistic streak in his character. Appointed to his judicial post in May 1816 (less than two years after his call), his salary of £800, plus fees, was the same as that previously offered to J.H. Bent.[127] Unlike his predecessor, however, the colony provided him with a house and a grant of land (2,000 acres at Cabramatta).[128] In the early years of his posting the judge proved to be a willing and helpful adviser to Macquarie, who in turn was generous in his praise for the advice he received.[129] On the matter of fiscal duties he was quick to advise the governor, as the Bents had done, that he no authority to proclaim and impose these imposts.[130] Unlike them, however, he was ready to reason calmly with the governor and press London to provide the necessary legislative authorization. Field willingly undertook to travel to Van Diemen's Land (later Tasmania) to conduct the first Supreme Court circuit there in 1819.[131]

Field's counsel was not invariably sound or in keeping with the Colonial Office's understanding of the legal proprieties. For example, Field's advice to Macquarie that Lieutenant Governor James Erskine was covered by the governor's commission when he issued orders during Macquarrie's absence in Van Diemen's Land was characterized by Downing Street as erroneous.[132] His views on legal matters, moreover, were not always in tune with those of his colleague, Wylde. The judge advocate concluded early that his colleague tended to be dictatorial in his pronouncements on legal issues and was too keen to introduce the complex processes of English law into the colony, for they were ill-suited to local conditions.[133] The two jurists collided, most dramatically, in their advice to Macquarie on the fate of soldiers on a convict ship, the *Chapman*, who shot and killed or injured a number of convicts on board. The troops argued that they had so acted because they were facing a mutiny. While Field pressed for both instigators and abettors to be sent home to face murder charges (a position favoured by Macquarie), the judge advocate counselled caution, as manslaughter or misadventure might better describe what had occurred, and he recommended bail.[134] London upheld Wylde's position.

However, it was not these legal gaffes and differences of opinion that provided the basis for doubts about Field's standing as a judge in New South Wales. The problem was his heavy-handed and manipulative use of substantive English law and the lack of judiciousness that it exposed, as well as his close association with certain exclusives in the colony. The state of colonial society in the early 1820s (the waning years of Macquarie and those of his successor, Thomas Brisbane) was tumultuous and complex. Wealthy emancipists and exclusives were at each other's throats over the core issue of who should have power over the future development of the possession.[135] Voices from the emancipist side and their supporters, such as those of emancipist lawyer Edward Eagar, and sympathizer William Charles Wentworth, that called for representative government, including freedmen as well as free men, and trial by jury, were engendering spirited resistance from exclusives, led by the landowning and sheep-running clan of the Macarthurs (John Macarthur Senior and his brood).[136] However, within exclusives' ranks there were tensions too. Sir John Jamison, a wealthy free settler accused the Macarthurs of, as Manning Clarke put it, 'disturbing the peace of the colonies for thirty years and of diabolical and self-interested intrigues.'[137] For his part, Barron Field, who had enjoyed an early friendship with the Macarthurs, earned the hostility of John Macarthur for opposing his appointment to the magistracy, because of 'the rebellion that he almost alone caused in the year 1808.'[138]

Field originally raised eyebrows in some quarters by his self-interested and vindictive treatment of attorney Thomas Sterrup Amos.[139] A London merchant had given the judge a power of attorney to recover £424 owed to him by Joseph Underwood, resident in New South Wales. Field instructed Amos to take action to recover the money, and he did, but was dilatory in handing it over. The judge then sued Amos for the debt, using lawyer William Moore as his frontman. The judge insisted that he had the right to consider that suit in his court and was prepared to order Amos struck off the rolls for his tardiness. Amos hurriedly made arrangements for Moore to be paid to Field's account.[140] Nevertheless, the judge ordered the attorney's name removed from the rolls, without giving Amos an opportunity to show cause and explain himself.[141] In reviewing this episode, Commissioner Bigge was of the opinion that the judge 'ought not to have pursued the course he did.'[142]

Given his conservative mien, it was strange that Field should have thrown the book at Amos, while supporting the efforts of emancipist attorney George Crossley for admission to practice. Although the judge's actions in the Amos case could, with a stretch, be explained by a desire to root out unprofessional conduct, this explanation hardly holds up alongside his relations with this devious, albeit talented, character. Crossley had entered into an agreement with Amos under which Crossley became a full partner of Amos, so that he could work de facto, if not de jure, as an attorney. With his partner's expulsion from the profession, Crossley attended court to secure a right of audience to carry on litigation in which Amos had been involved. Field, far from laying any blame on Crossley, painted Amos as the villain of the piece in encouraging the partnership arrangement and then sought to admit the emancipist attorney to practice.[143] Only the refusal of the magistrates sitting with Field to follow suit undermined this ploy. As John Bigge observed in his report, 'But for this fortunate difference of opinion Crossley, with all his disqualifications of perjury and subsequent bad character would have been admitted in violation of your Lordships [Bathurst's] recommendation.'[144] Crossley was admitted as an agent. Field in his evidence to Bigge described Crossley as the best barrister in the colony, meriting admission to a bar short of such talent.

A propensity of Field, as a judge, to read the law in his favour when his interests were at stake was also revealed in his treatment of Edward Eagar, the Irish emancipist attorney.[145] Eagar had made comments critical of the amounts the judge received as fees. For his part, Field had publicly accused Eagar of making seditious speeches, sowing the seeds of disaffection, being a revolutionist, and committing common barratry while pressing the cause of several people imprisoned at Parramatta against the keeper of the gaol, John Beale.[146] The magistrate, Hannibal Macarthur, accused Eagar of fomenting rebellion and turned the matter over to Field, who let fly a verbal broadside at the Irishman, indicating that, if the lawyer could not be convicted on a barratry charge, then he personally would recommend that the governor ship him out of the colony. It was when Eagar launched a slander action against the judge that Field, sitting on the matter without any apparent discomfort over a conflict of interest, dropped his jurisprudential bombshell by invoking the law of felony attaint and denying his adversary's right to sue. The jurist appealed to a ruling of the English Court of King's Bench in *Bullock v. Dodds*, which had laid down that in England pardons were not effective until issued under the Great Seal. Because of an oversight, successive governors of New South Wales had failed to follow that procedure in granting clemency.[147] Their pardons, said Field, did not have the effect of removing the attaint. The fact that, as Eagar argued, local law had allowed suits by other emancipists was of no consequence.

That emancipists and freed convicts had no right to sue created jitters among the freed populace. Field added insult to injury six months later when in a real property action launched by the former Irish attorney, *Eagar v. De Mestre*, he proclaimed that emancipists were incapacitated from receiving property by grant or purchase, holding or conveying property, whether real or personal, and giving any evidence in a court of justice.[148] These decisions had the potential to undermine a whole series of property and contract transactions involving both emancipists and free settlers. Both Macquarie and Eager protested strongly to the secretary of state and sought legislation overturning the judgments. The governor's initially favourable attitude towards the judge changed abruptly as Field made his sympathies for the exclusives' cause more patent.

Commissioner Bigge, no supporter of the emancipist cause, considered that Field was in error in his characterization of pardons granted in New South Wales and their legal status, and that the consequences of this mistake were serious and required intervention by London.[149] In his report on the administration of justice in the colony, the commissioner elaborated on Field's divisive attitudes and lack of judiciousness. He began by praising Field for 'his cultivated mind and quickness of perception,' but added, 'His professional experience is not equal to his other attainments.'[150] Although he had sought to cure his deficiencies by study, his articulation of the facts in cases left much to be desired. His lack of judicial discretion was evident in his expressed contempt for emancipists, like Edward Eagar, and the undesirability 'of bringing them forward into Society.'[151] Bigge concluded, 'The convict part of the population of New South Wales view Mr Justice Field's administration of the law with sentiments of dissatisfaction and alarm. The Free classes of the Population do justice of his Impartiality, but they equally apprehend the effects of his violent and unforgiving temper, as well as of his personal prejudices, upon his future decisions ... In my opinion Mr Justice Field does not possess that degree of temper and deliberation necessary to conduct the Judicial business of such a Colony.'[152]

Attempts by Field in his reaction to Bigge's report to dissociate himself from personal interest in whether or not felony attaint applied in New South Wales, and seeking to show how easily it could be solved in favour of emancipists suing, did not cut any ice in the Colonial Office.[153] The jurist, moreover, earned no points by his support of the extrajudicial actions of the Parramatta magistrates in excluding fellow magistrate and surgeon Henry Grattan Douglass from their deliberations. Their action followed Surgeon Superintendent James Hall's allegation that Douglass has seduced Ann Rumsby, a convict servant girl working in his household.[154] When the girl appeared before the bench and denied that Douglass was guilty of such conduct, the magistrates charged her with and convicted her of perjury and sentenced her to secondary transportation.[155] The new governor, Sir Thomas Brisbane, who enjoyed Douglass's company, deeply concerned at this course of events, gave Ann a free pardon, threatened to remove the offending magistrates from office, and complained to the Colonial Office of a conspiracy against the man.[156]

Field's Departure and Legacy: An Assessment

Earl Bathurst was spared the decision of recalling Field for misconduct in office, because, following Bigge's recommendations, Parliament in the New South Wales Act of 1823 established a new Supreme Court with both civil and criminal jurisdiction replacing the two previous courts.[157] It was, therefore, possible to engineer a changing of the judicial guard and to appoint a new chief justice to take the place of both Field and Judge Advocate Wylde.[158]

Field, who committed himself to advocacy on behalf of exclusive friends such as Samuel Marsden and Hannibal Macarthur, received a pension of £400 per annum for his services.[159] The former judge also made it his business to add to the growing chorus of criticism of exclusives of Brisbane as governor of New South Wales, in a campaign launched before he left Australia's shores.[160] After returning to practice, he accepted preferment in 1828 as the first chief justice of Gibraltar. There he weathered tensions with Governor Sir William Houston, which resulted in the two men refusing to talk to each other, and Houston recommending to London the judge's removal from office, 'a situation where, with his disposition to thwart and throw difficulties in the way of measures of Government he has the power to cause much embarrassment.'[161] A significant casus belli was the chief justice's refusal to go soft on Spanish smugglers captured by British vessels, which Field read, with justification, as interference with the administration of justice and was forthright in saying so. He survived this contretemps and enjoyed good relations with Houston's successor, Sir Alexander Woodford. He retired on a pension in 1841 because of ill health, and died in 1846.

Field was an enigmatic character. Like his predecessor, Jeffery Hart Bent, he was conservative by instinct, which explains his developing identification with the exclusives. As to his professional qualities, the evidence, supported by Bigge's observations, is that Field was to a degree lacking in legal knowledge and judicial finesse (perhaps unsurprising, given his inexperience) and capable, therefore, of giving faulty judgments and proffering unsound advice. At times, he indicated a belief in the superiority of English law and the necessity that it predominate in the colony, although his advice to the governor did not always reflect that position. Moreover, his most dramatic action in espousing that body of law, the introduction of the doctrine felony attaint, was so entwined with his own personal interests that it is difficult, if not impossible, to treat it as principled. Finally, as his colleague John Wylde indicated, his hauteur made him appear dictatorial in his relations with others in the justice system. But whatever one can say about him, Field had kept alive the issue of the superiority of English law in the affairs of New South Wales. It was the successor of Field and Wylde, Chief Justice Francis Forbes, who would deal with the issue head on, especially its implications for the administration of justice and the exercise of executive power.[162]

Reform of the Justice System and the New Judicial Presence: Chief Justice Francis Forbes

John Thomas Bigge, in his report, had rejected the arguments of the emancipists and their supporters for representative government with a legislative assembly and trial by jury. The commissioner argued that, given the composition of its population and the tenor of politics in the possession, it was quite unready for such reforms. London's 'compromise' was to establish an appointed legislative council, which would, inter alia, receive and decide upon proposals for legislation by the governor – a recommendation embodied in the New South Wales Act of 1823.[163] The chief justice would serve as president of that body – a sign that the judges of this colony, like those elsewhere in the empire at the time, were expected to straddle the legal and political spheres in the cause of stable governance.

As an indicator of the concerns in Westminster about this concession to local legislative initiative, the statute vested in the chief justice a power of review of and veto over proposed legislation that he determined was repugnant to the laws of England – a form of pre-emptive disallowance.[164] At this time repugnancy was clearly deemed to mean local law that offended imperial legislation applying to a colony by express reference (e.g., a colony's constitution), or because of its general reach, by implication (e.g., the Navigation Acts limiting colonial trade). It extended beyond this limited meaning to English law more generally, although it was uncertain whether that meant the whole body of Common Law or certain 'fundamental principles' of the system. It was understood that the principle of repugnancy was subject to the much earlier caveat that English law was in the circumstances appropriate to local conditions in the colony.[165]

The tradition in other colonies of a governor relying on the senior judge for political advice was embodied in the establishment of a small Executive Council, comprising ex officio members, including the chief justice.[166] A further recommendation, the provenance of which went back to Ellis Bent's representations to London in 1811 that a single court of superior jurisdiction should be established, exercising both criminal and civil jurisdiction, was also accepted.[167] The heavy hand of the early history of the administration in this colony was to remain, however, in that as a criminal court the judge continued to sit with military assessors (although their power was now limited to matters of fact), and in the trial of civil matters with lay assessors, drawn from the magistracy or a jury by mutual consent of the parties.[168]

After the Colonial Office's less than stellar selection of earlier professional judges in New South Wales, the fifth senior judge to be appointed, Francis Forbes, was an inspired choice. Unlike his predecessors, he had already served in the administration of justice in two other colonies. After a posting as attorney general of Bermuda, his birthplace, he had served as chief justice of Newfoundland from 1816 to 1822,[169] where he brought a thoroughly professional attitude to his judicial role. He balanced his respect for English law with recognition of long-standing customs of the fishing industry, especially in the characterization of property rights, and he stood up to the naval governor over the errors of naval surrogate justices exercising jurisdiction in the outports.[170] Even at that early stage in his career, he demonstrated that he was a man of liberal sentiments and instincts in matters of empire.[171] During the gap between his leaving Newfoundland and arriving in Sydney, the Colonial Office retained Forbes to work with James Stephen Jr on the drafting of the New South Wales Act.[172] He was, as a result, intimately acquainted with the reforms and their significance.

His position on the present and future of New South Wales was that it was important for the colony to leave behind the autocratic form of governance and notions of justice that had applied (necessarily) in its early decades. English law should apply, except where to do so would produce nonsensical results, given valid differences in social and economic circumstances and conditions in the colony.[173] The arcane procedures of English law, he thought, were not pertinent to litigation in New South Wales and he sought to simplify them. He also considered it important to elevate the rule of law in the possession's political and legal affairs and was willing to give the concept a liberal interpretation in the appropriate setting. Trial by jury, Forbes believed, should not be delayed too long, while representative government lay further into the future as an important step in creating a truly civil society.[174] Although he was critical of Macquarie's policies on hastening the inclusion of emancipists in key roles in governance and law, he did not share the view of the exclusives that they were the only ones born or called to rule. One biographer, C.H. Currey, tends to the view that Forbes was influenced by Benthamite thinking, which explains his 'hostile attitude' to the concentration of central state authority in the colonies in which he served as judge, and a desire to assist in the realization of the civil society anticipated by the founders of New South Wales.[175]

Forbes's propensity to emphasize impartial justice was evident early in his tenure, in his advice to Governor Brisbane on the actions of the Parramatta magistrates, led by Hannibal Macarthur, in excluding Henry Grattan Douglass from their counsel during the *Ann Rumsby* affair. Despite the manoeuvring of Macarthur, Samuel Marsden, and their colleagues, apparently committed to denigrating their former colleague on any pretext they could find and seeking to influence British politicians in their favour, the chief justice steadfastly stood by his contention that the conduct of the magistrates was indefensible.[176] When Lord Bathurst censured Hannibal Macarthur for his conduct, Forbes had no illusions that, as a result, he personally had earned the enmity of a powerful group in New South Wales and their henchmen in London. As he wrote, 'I have been a marked man and no efforts have been spared to get me out of the colony.'[177] This same clique had already assisted in sealing the fate of Sir Thomas Brisbane by unfairly attacking him for his alleged weakness and laziness, essentially code for not kowtowing to their vision of the colony and its future.[178] London recalled the governor, with whom Forbes had worked closely and amiably, and replaced him with Ralph Darling, like his predecessor a veteran of the Peninsular Wars.

It was Darling whom Forbes and his colleagues on the Supreme Court felt compelled to educate in a principled way about the limits of executive power, and the demands of the rule of law in the administration of justice in the colony. By the mid-1820s New South Wales was a cockpit of political infighting as exclusives and emancipists pressed vigorously and vocally for acceptance of their ideals of governance and justice. The high level of vituperation reflected the fact that political power continued to reside in a strong executive. There was, however, a new ingredient in the overheated political stew. A boost to the emancipist cause was the launching of reformist newspapers: William Charles Wentworth and Robert Wardell's *Australian*, and Edward Hall's *Monitor*. Wentworth and Wardell were also barristers and thus interested in and knowledgeable about the law.[179] The tendency of these men in this newly constructed public space to press the emancipist agenda with enthusiasm, and to criticize harshly those officials and exclusive supporters whom they saw as wilfully subverting progress, was in the course of time to infuriate their targets.[180] Some were ready to make them pay, whether within or outside the boundaries of legality. On Brisbane's watch, the governor's office had resisted the call to bring the editors to account under the law of criminal defamation. This was a position Forbes approved and influenced. While Forbes was clear that gratuitous slurs on the character of another individual deserved punishment, he distinguished strong oppositionist criticism, such as that emanating from the columns of the *Australian*. In a society where the executive had 'such a mass of influence,' he considered a free press an important counterweight.[181]

The relationship between the chief justice, with his liberal sensibilities, and the stiff-necked, authoritarian, and blinkered Darling started cordially enough, with Forbes ready and willing to be helpful and provide his considered and sound advice readily and calmly.[182] Unfortunately, reliable counsel was not something the governor could expect from other members of the colonial government, particularly the eccentric and inexperienced attorney general, Saxe Bannister.[183] Forbes soon found that Darling had a limited understanding of the law and what it might require of him as chief executive, as well as an impatience that caused to him to charge into action and to see legal curbs on his authority as unnecessary nit-picking. Tension developed between the two men when the chief justice advised the governor, on the governor's request, that he did not possess the power to vary the sentences passed on two military deserters.[184] Darling went ahead nevertheless, and Forbes and his two colleagues, John Stephen and James Dowling, called him to account in the Supreme Court.[185] Darling's apoplexy at this rebuff grew because the reformist press launched broadsides against the governor that increased in intensity when one of the soldiers, Sudds, died in jail.

Governor Darling was to experience other challenges to his use of executive power by Forbes and his judicial colleagues that caused him to view Forbes as a calculating enemy out to embarrass him, and he had no compunction about advising the Colonial Office to that effect.[186] For his part, the chief justice was quick to defend himself from a standpoint of legality, while pointing to the skewed notions of government, disrespect for the law, and nepotism of which, in his mind, the governor was guilty.[187]

The most charged issue between the two was that of press freedom.[188] Unlike Brisbane, who had let sleeping dogs lie in the face of press criticism, Darling rose to the bait as he and his officers became targets of often withering editorial comment, although initially he dithered. His initial move was to instruct the attorney general, Saxe Bannister, to launch a seditious defamation prosecution against Edward Hall for libel of several members of administration in the *Monitor*, only to reverse himself during the action, on the ground that the newspaper was altering its tone.[189] Bannister had so disappointed Darling in his position that relations between the two men had become impossible, and Bannister resigned. Before he quit the colony he failed in two private prosecutions for criminal defamation against Wardell of the *Australian* and Robert Howe of the *Gazette* for their less than charitable references to his resignation.[190]

In his frustration at these apparent failures of the court system to curb the press, Darling tried a new tack, which seemed to him to have already received the imprimatur of the Colonial Office. In his instructions, Lord Bathurst had advised Darling that it was agreeable to for him to introduce legislation requiring newspapers to secure a licence from the executive that could be revoked by the governor.[191] Lieutenant Governor George Arthur of Van Diemen's Land had submitted such a proposal to Brisbane before that possession had become a colony in its own right. Brisbane had denied the initiative on Forbes's advice.[192] As lieutenant governor of the new colony, Arthur put through legislation establishing a licensing system and imposing a stamp duty on newspapers, which Chief Justice John Pedder certified as non-repugnant.[193]

As Darling's blood pressure increased at his supposed inability to bring the errant newspapermen to book through the courts, he followed suit and placed draft legislation before his councils.[194] Exercising his statutory power of review, Forbes refused to certify the clauses in the proposed licensing legislation that gave the governor apparently untrammelled power over certification and its cancellation.[195] These provisions, he asserted, were repugnant to English law, which treated freedom of the press as a constitutional value. Initially, he had no problems with the bill to impose a newspaper tax in which the rate of stamp duty had been left blank, and duly certified the bill. However, when he received a final version of the Act, meanwhile proclaimed, that included an excessive figure for the tax (suggesting a punitive intent), he communicated his doubts about its validity to Darling. When Darling then grudgingly had his councils reconsider the Act and sent it to the chief justice in its original form, Forbes refused to certify it. The governor, clearly seething, suspended the operation of the Act. The exclusives, led by the irascible John Macarthur Sr, were convinced that not only was Forbes the 'idol' of the press, he also was committed to protecting it.[196]

Conservative historians have criticized Forbes for his conduct during this episode in resorting to technical objections in the law and remaining aloof from rather than providing proactive advice to the governor.[197] This was period during which the chief justice was suffering from the chronic illness to which he was prone. However, that apart, it can be argued that he did his duty as he was required by the New South Wales Act in the case of a chief executive who had already proved himself deaf to what he considered to be the unreasonable cavils of lawyers. What is more intriguing in Forbes's approach is his liberal reading of English law on press freedom. Given that the six acts of 1819 severely limiting the powers of criticism of government by the newspapers in England was still in force at this time, his appeal to constitutional verities was, as Bruce Kercher has pointed out, a political rather a legal decision.[198] The chief justice had lobbed the ball back into the courts, where it rightfully belonged, on whether political comment was defamatory or not. In later prosecutions that were more capably conducted, the court, showing perhaps less patience with the press, found Hall guilty of criminal defamation and sentenced him to prison terms for his pains.[199] These results suggest clearly that the judges, including Forbes, were willing and able to place limits on freedom of speech, but only when the case had been made convincingly to them.

When Darling sought by statute to regulate auctioneers and operators of places of entertainment, reserving unlimited powers of control to himself, Forbes again registered objections.[200] The governor seemed to have learnt his lesson from the press issue, because amendments were made and certification was issued. But Darling was not so compliant on the matter of regulations he issued on the assignment of convicts and the granting of tickets-of-leave.[201] The chief justice remonstrated at the extent of the powers claimed by the executive, in a stand that London approved. Apparently unmoved, Darling attempted to use the regulations to remove a convict assigned to a newspaper editor, to punish the editor for his temerity in attacking the executive. In a challenge launched by Edward Hall against the governor on this ground, the Supreme Court in a judgment of Justice Dowling, concurred in by his senior colleague, made it clear that the chief executive did not have unlimited discretion in these matters.[202] The law compelled him to act within his assigned powers and not to abuse them by exercising them for illegitimate purposes.

Forbes and Darling crossed swords on a number of other issues, ranging from whether or not progressive reforms to English criminal law should be adopted in New South Wales (which Forbes, but not his adversary, favoured), to attempts by the governor to rid himself of officials he did not like, such as Robert Robinson, nephew of Forbes's colleague John Stephen.[203] Darling, supported by a Greek chorus of angry exclusives, including members of the Macarthur clan and the dyspeptic Samuel Marsden, pleaded with the Colonial Office to relieve him of the 'troublesome' jurist.[204] John Macarthur Sr would refer to his judicial nemesis as a 'dangerous, detestable, unprincipled, immoral, base and artful man.'[205] Things came to head in 1828 when, on the advice of James Stephen Jr, Secretary of State George Murray, tiring at the seemingly intractable bad relations between the governor and chief justice, warned both 'that if dissensions similar in spirit continue to agitate the colony, I shall feel myself called upon to advise His Majesty to recall the Judges [Forbes and Stephen] and to relieve you [Darling] from our command.'[206] He charged Forbes with using 'the tone of asperity and coldness' in his official letters. Murray criticized both men for their failure to 'conciliate by courtesy and kindness,' and for 'the mutual jealousy and ill-will' that had been permitted 'to take possession of their minds.'

Forbes, the Liberal, and His Juridical Legacy

It is instructive that ultimately, after a period in which Forbes sought to reach out to and help the chief executive, and Darling continued his battles with the reformist press, it was the governor who was dropped from the ship by Lord Goderich, the new Whig secretary of state, in 1830.[207] The jurist remained chief justice of New South Wales until he retired because of ill-health in 1837. While his efforts were not fully appreciated by a parsimonious Colonial Office and deprecated by a majority in the Legislative Council, it was under his inspired guidance that the Supreme Court brought the rule of law to bear in its decisions and firmly established the basis of and framework for judicial review of executive action in Australia.[208] In that sense his stewardship of justice in the colony represented a watershed in the relationship between law and politics, even though for some decades to come the chief justice continued to sit in the Legislative Council, and judicial independence was not formally proclaimed until the 1850s.[209] The Australian Courts Act of 1828 removed the chief justice's power of certification of legislation and replaced it with a privilege accorded all the superior courts justices of commenting on the validity or otherwise of proposed ordinances, to be considered by the imperial authorities.[210] Although Forbes upheld the position of Field on the impact of felony attaint in New South Wales on convicts with tickets of leave (at the same time subscribing to a fiction that removed its sting), he was willing to depart from English law openly when his view was that local conditions demanded local solutions. This would explain his illiberal, although pragmatic, stance on the validity of anti-bushranging legislation with its harsh reverse onuses, and his liberal economic views reflected in his approval of higher rates of interest than those allowed by the law of usury in England.[211] His major legacy, however, was to elevate the application of English law and a liberal view of the rule of law in the colony, a move enshrined legislatively in the official reception date in the 1828 legislation,[212] to lay the basis for the Australian law of the judicial review of executive action, to press for the adoption of jury trial, and to envisage movement towards a more representative form of government.[213] Given his liberal propensities, it is perhaps not surprising that after the stresses of the Darling years his relations with Darling's liberally minded successor, Richard Bourke, were both cordial and co-operative.[214]

As long as the Australian colonies were subject to strong executive power and moved out into new frontier areas, issues of repugnancy, and judicial frustration at dubious government action and 'outback' law practice, were episodically to surface. The resulting spats were capable of disrupting the relations between judges and governors, and between judges, the legal profession, and the community at large. The next chapter (chapter 7) addresses two such examples from the 1830s and 1840s.

7

The Perils of the Colonial Judiciary: English Legal Culture and the Repugnancy Card in the Australian Colonies, 1830–1850

'I am a lieutenant governor and a good one too': Of Dogs, Taxes, and Repugnancy

In 1847 in Hobart, Van Diemen's Land (later Tasmania), a spat developed between the colonial executive and judiciary with a storyline reminiscent of a Gilbert and Sullivan operetta. The casus belli was the Dog Tax Act that the no-nonsense civilian lieutenant governor of the colony, William Thomas Denison, had recently enacted with the approval of his Executive Council.[1] The statute imposed a requirement on dog owners to secure a dog licence, for which they had to pay a fee. One of its purposes, alongside more money for the treasury, was to reduce the number of canines roaming at large in the colony. John Morgan, a journal editor and a dog owner, refused to pay and was prosecuted. Although Chief Justice John Pedder had voiced no objection to the legislation during its consideration in the council, both he and Puisne Justice Algernon Sidney Montagu threw out the prosecution on the grounds that the Act was repugnant to the Australian Courts Act of 1828.[2] Their reasoning, reflecting Montagu's pressure on his colleague, was that the local legislation imposed a tax, and that, under the imperial statute, it was necessary that the purpose of the tax be made explicit in the enactment.[3] That had not been done here.

Denison faced a dilemma. The two judges of the Supreme Court had already decided that his Legislative Council was improperly constituted.[4] The declared repugnancy of the legislation put in doubt previous revenue legislation on the island.[5] None of this, he thought, could be cured immediately by retroactive exculpatory legislation. Also worrying was Chief Justice Pedder's contention in his judgment that the council was subordinate to the Supreme Court in the colony's constitution. However, instead of discussing the problem with the judges to seek a resolution, he sought ways and means to rid himself and the colony of them.

The ill-defined doctrine of repugnancy that had been at the centre of spats between the New South Wales executive and judiciary in the 1810s and 1820s was to continue to cause episodic conflict between those branches of colonial government in the next two decades. Van Diemen's Land shared with New South Wales the provision of the Australian Courts Act of 1828, that when the executive and Legislative Council proposed legislation, the judges of the Supreme Court had the privilege of considering the statute and giving their opinion on whether or not it met the repugnancy test, within fourteen days.[6] In the event that the executive and judiciary disagreed and the former dug in its heels, the enactment was dispatched to London, along with the judicial critiques, so that the Colonial Office could determine whether to recommend to the Crown approval or disallowance of the legislation. The judicial role in reviewing legislation changed from one of pre-emptive disallowance to non-binding commentary. As Swinfen has noted, during the period after 1830, Colonial Office officials entertained doubts about the wisdom of maintaining a broad conception of repugnancy, as well as a desire not to compromise the status of the courts in exercising a power of judicial review over colonial legislation. It was a difficult, transitional period in the Office's policy.[7]

The Legal History of Van Diemen's Land to 1827

Van Diemen's Land, originally established as two separate settlements in the early years of the nineteenth century, was even more of a rough, tough place than the mainland territory of which it was constitutionally a part until 1825.[8] Lieutenant Colonel David Collins settled Hobart and the area around it in 1804 on instructions from London to secure British control over the island, while a second group dispatched by Governor Phillip Gidley King from Sydney put down roots near Port Dalrymple on the north coast.[9] The two settlements joined together as a single dependency of New South Wales in 1815.

A combination of the aggressive frontier mentality of settlers, tension and violence between them and the Aboriginal inhabitants of the island in rural areas, difficulties of establishing law and order, especially over escaped or rogue emancipated convicts, and periods of incompetent governance made for a turbulent society.[10] The prosecution of serious crimes could be removed to Sydney, but this happened inconsistently, and when it did, the results were sometimes less than satisfactory.[11] Moreover, the circuit of the Supreme Court of Civil Jurisdiction to the island to hear civil suits began only in 1819, and that of the Court of Criminal Jurisdiction in 1821, and both operated perfunctorily thereafter.[12] Local magistrates who had no compunction about doling out sentences for serious crimes that were not strictly within their powers effectively administered the criminal law. Penalties matched or exceeded in cruelty those in the parent colony. In the early days, magistrates dispensed what civil law existed until the establishment of the lieutenant governor's court in 1816, with jurisdiction in suits under £50. Headed by a military officer, the local court, in the absence of the Supreme Court on circuit, proved flexible in its interpretation of the monetary limit. Moreover, it acted much in the same way as the Court of Civil Jurisdiction had done on the mainland under Judge Advocate Richard Atkins, providing creative solutions to problems such as debt and the legal disabilities of married women.[13]

Van Diemen's Land, like its parent, came under the baleful eye of Commissioner John Thomas Bigge early in the 1820s and drew similar conservative recommendations for reform of its governance of and administration of justice. Under the New South Wales Act of 1823, provision was made for the dependency to become a separate colony with its own executive, led by a lieutenant governor sharing legislative power with an ex officio or appointed Legislative Council.[14] A court system similar to that in New South Wales was contemplated with a Supreme Court at the apex, headed by a professional chief justice.[15] Echoing earlier practice, the court would administer criminal justice with a judge and a military panel hearing cases, and civil justice with judge and two lay assessors, or a jury if both parties agreed.

Separation from New South Wales occurred in 1825. Two key figures arrived in Hobart that year to take on the administration of the colony: Lieutenant Colonel George Arthur, the lieutenant governor, and John Pedder, the first chief justice. They could not have been more different in experience or character. Arthur, after active military service, had been superintendent of British Honduras since 1815, with experience of ruling over subject peoples, both slaves and indigenous folk.[16] Believing in progress and reform (including abolition of the slave trade), he was a convinced evangelical in religion and entertained no doubts about his own capacity to rule, or his sense of what was right and beneficial for his charges. Pedder, just five years beyond his call to the English bar, was simply wet behind the ears, with little in the way of legal experience.[17] Retiring in personality, he necessarily had to learn on the job not only the law, but also the realities of colonial life. Unsurprisingly, the jurist who had been appointed to both the Executive and Legislative Councils tended to bend to the will of the lieutenant governor, especially in the early years. He did, for example, on the question of the introduction of juries and the enactment of restrictive legislation against the press (unlike Forbes). He also approved Arthur's stratagems to rid himself of his attorney general, Joseph Gellibrand, who was too ready to challenge the viceroy's exercise of his gubernatorial authority on certain issues, as beyond his authority, and so illegal.[18] As a judge, Pedder had a reputation as a traditionalist, one wedded to the intricacies of English substantive law and its arcane procedures.[19] For the rest he earned respect for being quiet and unassuming, and for his judicious behaviour. He had never invested or borrowed in the colony and was in every way the epitome of the loyal, journeyman judge doing what was expected of him. The same could not be said of his colleague on the bench for fifteen years, Algernon Sydney Montagu.

The 'Eccentric' Justice: Algernon Montagu

Montagu was the grandson through the natural line of the notorious fourth Earl of Sandwich, of culinary fame.[20] His mother had died while he was a young child, and his father, Basil, a lawyer, legal writer, and Benthamite reformer, consigned the young boy to the care of William and Dorothy Wordsworth, who saw him educated in a local private school in Ambleside in the Lake District.[21] Admitted to Gray's Inn in 1817, he was called to the bar in 1826, at the age of twenty-four. He had thus served for an even shorter period than Pedder as an English barrister, before arriving in Hobart to assume the post of attorney general of Van Dieman's Land in 1828.[22] As a law officer he was entitled to engage in private practice, although he declined to do so. Lieutenant General Arthur appreciated his work and efforts and had no hesitation in recommending him in 1832 as the second judge on the court, in place of the sot and wife-beater Alexander Macduff Baxter.[23] Unlike Pedder, Montagu invested heavily in land on which he grew crops and ran livestock.[24]

In his fifteen years on the bench Montagu had a remarkable love-hate relationship with opinion makers in the colony, including a burgeoning colonial press. His early billing was positive. Several editors opined that, on the basis of his record, he was an independent, humane jurist who would temper justice with mercy. It was not long, however, before he became the butt of press criticism, for as Stefan Petrow puts it, 'his odd behaviour and severe sentences.'[25] On several occasions in libel cases against journalists during the 1830s and early 1840s Montagu vented his spleen against them as licentious, degraded, and contemptuous of the court. Predictably they reacted angrily. For example, one of them, Gilbert Robertson of the *Hobart Town Courier*, accused the judge of sacrificing the court to 'personal feeling and animosity' and of committing 'illegal and capricious acts' that were 'nothing short of an arbitrary and tyrannous exercise of power.'[26]

The judge's eccentric behaviour at times persuaded the Colonial Office to raise its eyebrows and the press to call for his removal from office. One such case was that of Thomas Lewis, whom Arthur ordered prosecuted for disturbing the peace by allegedly taking steps to incite a duel.[27] William Bryan, an enemy of the lieutenant governor, had, it was charged, directed the accused to present a challenge to magistrate Thomas Lyttleton, who, Bryan claimed, had slandered him at trial. Montagu found Lewis guilty as charged and sentenced him to eighteen months in jail and a £150 fine. Lewis's friends likened the jurist to Judge Jeffreys. For its part, the Colonial Office criticized the judge for harassing Lewis, who was conducting his own defence, as well as for the harshness of the penalties.[28] On the advice of the English law officers, the Office asserted that Lewis had done what was his right in conducting his own case and seeking to elicit the facts, had been 'unfairly tried,' and 'sentenced to a punishment of almost unexampled rigour.'[29] London ordered Arthur to release Lewis from jail and remit the fine. When Lewis later sought compensation, the Legislative Council grudgingly agreed to a generous sum, which the Colonial Office approved.[30] The press predictably had a field day at the jurist's expense, variously describing him as 'rash and impetuous' and ignorant of rules of pleading and defence, urging his recall, and labelling him 'Mad Montagu.'[31]

It was the Privy Council's turn in 1847 to criticize Montagu for his intemperate comments from the bench when, together with Chief Justice

Pedder, the judges struck Sidney Stephen off the rolls of the colonial bar for professional misconduct.[32] The lawyer had accepted a bill of exchange in payment for his professional services and communicated with the client directly instead of through his attorney. On Stephen's attempting to obtain his fees in court, both judges condemned him for unprofessional conduct. Montagu, in full rhetorical flight, described the lawyer guilty of 'trickery, deception and falsehood,' whom he would consign to a 'moral tomb,' challenging Stephen to 'lift the lid if he can.'[33] Stephen appealed to the Privy Council against his removal, which allowed the appeal, declaring his professional reputation unsullied, and reprimanded Montagu for his language.[34]

Although agreeing on the result in the Stephen case, there were episodic complaints that the two Supreme Court justices were invariably in disagreement on results, to the chagrin of civil litigants and of prosecutors and defence counsel.[35] There is little doubt that the two men differed in their approaches to the administration of justice. Pedder was indecisive, loquacious, mild in his sentences, and wedded to traditional forms and procedures. By contrast Montagu, said to be Benthamite in his thinking, made quick decisions, was succinct, handed down sentences that were severe, and favoured newer, simpler procedures.[36] However, despite several entreaties from lawyers, merchants, and landowners, London, unconvinced, refused to appoint a third judge who would break the stalemate in cases where the twosome disagreed.[37]

Montagu was openly critical of juries and their verdicts. The judge viewed them as too prone to taking political stands rather than observing the dictates of the law. This too brought him into bad odour in the press, who read this attitude as reflecting Arthur's lust for power and antipathy to the public's involvement in the administration of justice.[38] If, however, the press expected a consistent pattern of Montagu supporting the executive power in the colony, they were to be disappointed. He was quite capable of letting intemperance get the better of him in his relations with public officers, as he did in a vicious spat with the attorney general, another member of the vast Stephen clan, Alfred, beginning in mid-1836.[39] Montagu asserted in court, during an application by the attorney general for a criminal information, that 'he cared no more' for Stephen than for 'the meanest person in the Colony.'[40] He accused Mr Attorney of slandering him in the press. The judge was unwilling to grant the application. Stephen then sought to proceed in a private prosecution, at which Montagu barked that the law officer deserved 'no more compliance or courtesy from him,' and that he deserved to be treated 'like a Cur and a Dog.'[41] When the judge added that the attorney general had given inadequate consideration to the cases of convicts awaiting trial, Stephen complained to Arthur, requesting him to take action to preserve the integrity of the administration of justice.[42] Montagu followed up with several new charges – that the lawyer had insulted the judges by treating the courtroom like 'a Chop house,' eating and drinking at the bar, and had insinuated that he, the jurist, was corrupt and insane.[43] After another round of courtroom antics from both men, in which Montagu sought to explain his earlier intemperate outburst, he demanded that his nemesis be punished for insulting and slighting the judges.[44]

Arthur, expressing disapproval of the conduct of both men, but uncertain about what to do as he respected both and was about to leave Van Diemen's Land for Upper Canada, deftly referred the dispute to London.[45] In a dispatch to the new lieutenant governor, Sir John Franklin, the secretary of state, Lord Glenelg, spread the odium between both parties, assigning a greater share to Montagu for his intemperance and immoderation, which, he said, was 'unbecoming' and 'reprehensible' in a judge.[46] He criticized Stephen for lack of respect for the judges by engaging in conduct that gave them cause for complaint and lessened them in the public's estimation. In the end, as Arthur had expressed a high opinion of both men, Glenelg chose not to discipline them but warned both against any further nonsense of this kind.[47] The simmering hatred felt by both men continued until 1839, when Stephen moved to New South Wales.

If Montagu's eccentricities and biases were to excite negative comment, as they did, especially in the colonial press, his stand on other issues was to earn him plaudits from the newspapers. Among the differences between him and Pedder was his tendency to find fault with proposed legislation and to label it as repugnant to English law, while Pedder adhered mainly to a policy of upholding the legislative initiatives of the lieutenant governor and council.[48] Montagu's activist stance was perhaps a reflection of his philosophical radicalism, which on the one hand was ready to accept that statutes were necessary to create circumstances that contributed to a rational and comprehensible system of justice and facilitated economic initiative and the free market, but on the other deprecated those ordinances that allowed the state to interfere with people's freedom.[49] This attitude was appreciated by elements of the press concerned that legislation designed to increase executive power or curb public rights would be rammed through without adequate consultation.[50] The jurist drew particular praise for his public stand against the proposed Road Act that empowered the road commissioners to put through new roads, which, as a landowner, he feared would force him to forfeit segments of his property without his consent.[51] When the colonial government ignored the objections of Montagu and others voiced at a public meeting, he used his official right of comment to argue that the legislation was repugnant.[52] This was sufficient to induce the promoters of the statute to amend it, and it was passed. Ironically, Montagu's vigorous stand in the cause of repugnancy was not appreciated by the Colonial Office, 'wearied' by his objections.[53] At one point, in 1842, Secretary of State Lord Stanley, noting that none of Montagu's objections had stood up to scrutiny by the English law officers, and undercut the respect due to the Legislative Council, directed Lieutenant Governor Eardley-Wilmot to lean on the jurist to be more circumspect in his assessments, but the advice went unheeded.[54]

Eardley-Wilmot inspired little respect in Montagu, in particular his decisions to reprieve incorrigible criminals sentenced to death.[55] Indeed, so upset was the judge at what he described as the lieutenant governor's incompetence in exercising the royal prerogative of mercy, that he made a public issue of it by refusing to impose capital punishment, even on a gang of armed 'desperadoes,' because the executive would exercise clemency. This stand was to resonate with the press and a public frustrated at what was perceived to be a suspension of the supreme penalty, even in cases of 'the worst die.'[56]

If Montagu's public life was notable for his quirks of character, the same was true of his private life. The judge proceeded on the belief that his judicial role and domestic life should be insulated from each other, and he lacked the congenial spirit that would have allowed some connection between the two. As a jurist he was a loner.[57] His private affairs centred on his management of his land and livestock.[58] Colonial land ownership and husbandry could be a rewarding pastime while economies were buoyant. However, they could also become a serious drain on a family's wealth during slumps. Montagu experienced such a change of fortune when the provincial economy bottomed out in the early 1840s, and crop and livestock prices took a dive.[59] Indeed, recognizing that he and his family were living beyond their means, he sought to persuade Lieutenant Governor John Franklin to let him switch positions with Attorney General Edward McDowell, who was permitted to engage in private practice.[60] The chief executive's advisers would have favoured Montagu's return as senior law officer, because of the incumbent's incompetence. Franklin, not surprisingly, was unimpressed with McDowell's judicial potential. Accordingly, he demurred to the judge's self-interested request. But the reality of Montagu's indebtedness was not his only problem.

A Confusion of Debt, Repugnancy, and Colonial Constitutionalism

Following the eccentric lead of his father, the judge was prone to letting his debts pile up, before paying them off on the last date allowed by the law, even though in some instances he had had the resources to satisfy them earlier.[61] This was foolhardy, not only in and of itself, but also because it failed to take account of changing economic conditions that made it difficult to rely on the survival of assets to cover his debts into the future. The jurist's indebtedness was notorious, and was the subject of complaints to both the colonial executive and the Colonial Office that his creditors, on whose resources he planned to rely in satisfy his debts, were able to exercise influence over his judgments.[62] When Eardley-Wilmot advised Secretary of State Stanley that Montagu's position was that a Supreme Court judge could not be sued for his debts, predictably the minister reacted negatively. In 1843, he directed the jurist to pay his debts or take a leave of absence during any lawsuit directed against him.[63] Although Montagu paid off the particular debt, there were others lurking in the background.[64] In due course the judge's indebtedness was to become confused with the exercise of the repugnancy power by the judiciary, to his professional cost.

Late in 1847, through his solicitor, Thomas Young, an old adversary of Montagu, a creditor of the judge, Anthony MacMekan, brought a suit against the jurist before the Supreme Court, seeking repayment of the debt owing. Chief Justice Pedder effectively barred the claim, arguing that constitutionally the court of two judges was indivisible and required both to constitute it, and that therefore neither of them could be sued in it individually.[65] When Lieutenant Governor Denison questioned Montagu about the debt, the judge indicated that there was an agreement with MacMekan that he would pay the debt when certain property had been sold off. Moreover, he claimed that when he had offered to settle the debts, but without incurring the costs of the court case, the creditor had declined the offer. A suspension, while the matter was pursued in Equity, would, he argued, cause him great financial loss. Denison seemed satisfied with this explanation. However, shortly afterwards the two judge handed down their decision in the case involving the challenge to the Dog Tax Act, *R. v. Morgan*, in which they declared the legislation unconstitutional.[66] The lieutenant governor, aware of Montagu's influence on Pedder in determining the case, renewed his interest in the charges against the associate justice. Further allegations by Thomas Young that cast doubts on the veracity of the judge's earlier explanation sharpened his focus.[67] Young also produced hearsay evidence that the judge, who had earlier sat on a case brought by a bank against debtors, one of whom was pressing the jurist for a debt owed to him, sided with the debtors when the matter was in litigation. The lieutenant governor concluded that Montagu's conduct was 'neither wise nor proper.'[68]

Denison reviewed the matter with his Executive Council. He concluded that the judge's conduct was 'highly discreditable' and detrimental to the administration of justice in the colony.[69] He ordered Montagu to show cause why he should not be suspended. The judge's response emphasized the judgment of Chief Justice Pedder that he was legally shielded from suit, the self-interested and vicious motives of his adversaries, and the point that only the Queen had the authority to amove or suspend a judge. He categorically denied that he had demonstrated any bias in the case mentioned by Young, stressing his reputation for 'integrity ... independence, and honourable conduct.'[70] Denison, unimpressed with Montagu's defence, concluded that he had acted in a way unbecoming to his position as a judge. Although conceding that it would be impossible to determine whether the judge had been influenced by his conflicts of interest, his actions raised 'doubt and suspicions' against him and jeopardized his efficiency on the bench. Acting on the advice of his law officers, with the support of the majority of his Executive Council, the lieutenant governor substituted amoval of the jurist for the previously announced threat of suspension,[71] justifying his actions by appealing to section 2 of Burke's Act, 1772.[72] In later correspondence he pointed to a pattern of misbehaviour and 'a want of temper and discretion and uprightness of conduct.'[73]

Herman Merivale, undersecretary at the Colonial Office and Montagu's friend, doubted whether Denison had sufficient cause to amove the judge and desired the issue of his conduct referred to the English law officers. Denison's action in amoving Montagu had, however, forced the Office's hand. Merivale considered that the lieutenant governor's order of amoval was related to a desire to get him out of the way because of the constitutional embarrassment surrounding the striking down of the Dog Tax Act.[74] Elements of the colonial press shared this sentiment. The *Hobart Town Courier* led the charge, accusing Denison of 'destroying the independence of the Bench' and making it a vehicle for collecting 'illegal taxes.'[75] The paper had no doubt that Denison's removal of Montagu for seeking to shield himself from his creditors was a smokescreen to shroud his real reason – the judge's challenge to the executive. The *Examiner* added that the lieutenant governor's actions raised the serious question of whether Tasmanians lived 'in the nineteenth century, or ... [had] been thrown back on the sixteenth.'[76]

These acerbic comments and a large public protest meeting that reiterated the charges against Denison of interfering with judicial independence, a bulwark against the abuse of power by the local government, failed to redeem the judge. Montagu sailed for England to appeal the lieutenant governor's action, with the best wishes of many of his fellow colonists.[77]

In his appeal to the Judicial Committee of the Privy Council, Montagu stressed the correctness of his colleague's decision to bar the debt claim against him, the dubious motives of those complaining about him, and the illegality of Denison's action against him.[78] The argument was that Burke's Act did not apply to a judge appointed under letters patent. Even if the lieutenant governor had the power, he had abused it by amoving instead of suspending him, without giving him a right of reply.[79] The appellant also asserted that the real reason for his removal was his involvement in striking down the Dog Tax Act.[80] But none of this was to any avail. The Judicial Committee of the Privy Council upheld Montague's removal from office for cause.[81] In the first place, as a matter of law, Denison had the clear power to amove the judge from office.[82] The evidence the Judicial Committee accepted was that Montagu had sought to block attempts by creditors to bring him to court for non-payment of his debts, and may have used his office to protect defendants from debt default to whom he owed money. It was for these transgressions that the lieutenant governor had amoved him.[83] The committee tersely stated that 'there were sufficient grounds for the amotion of Mr Montagu.'[84] No reference was made to the dog taxation farrago. Though their lordships said there had been a minor defect in the process, by the substitution of amoval for the earlier threat of suspension, without calling on Montagu for further explanation, they felt that there had been no prejudice to the judge in this irregularity.[85]

Montagu's Demise and Gubernatorial and Imperial Motivations

It is likely that Denison's removal of Montagu was dictated by the constitutional embarrassment caused to the administration by the decision of the judges in *R. v. Morgan*. They had presented him with a serious constitutional challenge, with ramifications, as he saw it, stretching well beyond the facts of that case. Given their earlier opinion about the membership of the Legislative Council, not to mention Montagu's penchant for invoking the repugnancy power, Denison worried about paralysis in government caused by an overactive court. For him, the solution was to find or manufacture excuses for getting rid of them and replacing them with more compliant jurists.[86] That this was his motive is evident, less in the case of Montagu, who had made himself a sitting duck with his arrogant reaction to the use of court processes against him and failing to keep in mind Lord Stanley's earlier warning.[87] No, it was Denison's harassment of the retiring, judicious John Lewes Pedder that underlines the point.

Having removed Montagu from office, Denison replaced him with Attorney General Horne, a man more indebted than his predecessor, who had advised the amoval. He then engaged in a ham-fisted exercise to get rid of his chief justice.[88] First, he pressured the judge to take an extended leave of absence.[89] When Pedder refused, Denison had his Executive Council cite the jurist for 'neglect of duty' and demanded that he show cause why he should not be suspended for failing to register the repugnant character of the Dog Tax Act within the statutory time period. The council acquitted the chief of that charge, and the lieutenant governor, having received authority from London to revive the Legislative Council and secure remedial legislation, relented. This was not before the Colonial Office had firmly rapped Denison's knuckles over his actions. Lord Grey was of the opinion that Denison's conduct towards Pedder 'menaced' the independence of the judiciary and created a loss of confidence in that institution. To seek to suspend a judge for a previous 'error' after Pedder had canvassed the matter in litigation was, he asserted, an abuse of power.[90]

The Judicial Committee's motivation is harder to divine, not least because of its enigmatic report to the monarch. What is beyond debate is that they accepted that the evidence discussed in the written and oral arguments before them about Montagu's indebtedness, and his attempts to block consideration of actions by creditors, was sufficient cause for the judge's removal. It is odd that if judicial indebtedness concerned them so much, they did not take the opportunity to say so more openly and didactically for a broader audience. Montagu was not by any means alone in his financial problems as a colonial judge, and for others, as well as him, there was strong temptation to wrap themselves in some argument based on judicial immunity from suit. On the natural justice issue too, the elliptical nature of their report gives no hint of how they felt they could distinguish their report in *Willis v. Gipps* two years earlier.[91] In that case, lack of fairness in not allowing the plaintiff notice, and a right to be heard in his defence before amoval, was considered sufficient grounds for advising his restoration to office. This was so, even though, as in this case, the substantive evidence was felt to warrant the action taken against that judge.

The committee's dodging of the constitutional issue that Montagu raised may well have reflected a desire not to make the situation in Tasmania politically any more difficult than it already was. The political and economic state of the island colony during the late 1830s and early 1840s, under Sir John Franklin and John Eardley-Wilmot, had been unsettled, a matter of concern to the Colonial Office.[92] These anxieties in London increased in relation to a colony in which a growing vocal element was demanding responsible government of the sort being granted to Canadian possessions.[93] This, together with the less than happy experience with Montagu's mercurial character as a jurist may have proven conclusive in his case. Protecting the careful and judicious Pedder from executive punishment for following his 'conscience' on a constitutional matter was one thing. To extend the same consideration to a judge who, however bright he may have been, was increasingly viewed in imperial circles as a 'loose cannon' and had been warned earlier about possible problems with his exercising the judicial function, because of his indebtedness, was another.

Perhaps the last word on Montagu's stormy career as a judge should go to the press, which had viewed him with both antagonism and respect, and in reflecting on his departure summed up well the contradictions in the man. On his amoval, the *Courier* described him as 'moving in an eccentric orbit,' on occasion terrifying 'by those motions' but 'occasionally [delighting] us by the brilliant light he cast around his path.'[94] The paper went on to describe him as 'fresh, vigorous, and original,' with an 'intellect that drew respect, and, not infrequently admiration,' and as one not given to checking the 'luxuriance' of a wild and lively mind. Several years earlier, the *Launceston Examiner* had stated that Montagu's eccentricity related to 'a clear perception of right and ... a most powerful deep and prevailing love of justice.'[95] The writer added that, as a disciple of Bentham and Lord Campbell, he was 'a zealous reformer of the law's abuses – independent *almost* to a fault – no respecter of persons – and … no worshipper of those … in high places.'

The denial of Montagu's appeal was not the end of his association with the Colonial Office. In what Peter Howell has described as a 'genial policy of looking after its own,' the Office, undoubtedly influenced by the former judge's friendship with Herman Merivale, appointed him stipendiary magistrate for the Falkland Islands.[96] Having been demoted by any standards, Montagu soon tired of life on the wind-blasted British holding in the South Atlantic and of his wife, Maria, and his family. In 1854 he applied for and received a posting in Sierra Leone as register of deeds at £400 per annum, a portion of which was withheld to support his family, who returned to England from the Falklands. His professional exertions in the West African colony were well received, including an upgrading of his position in 1857 to registrar general, and spells at acting chief justice (premature mortality continuing to be a problem in the colony). However, true to form, he engaged in spats with at least two of the ten governors who came and went during the twenty-five years of his sojourn there.[97] He was long remembered in Sierra Leone for compiling, editing, and updating the laws of the territory, including historical documents that helped clarify the evolving political and constitutional status of the possession and the original allotments of land in it.[98] He died of a stroke suffered on arriving in England on a leave, at the venerable age of seventy-eight.

John Walpole Willis Regenerate: From Shame to New South Wales

If the career of Algernon Montagu bespeaks a lack of patience with conditions in the colony in which he found himself, a propensity to favour English legal ideology and solutions over those locally directed by executive power, and a mercurial disposition, that of his contemporary, John Walpole Willis, as a puisne judge in New South Wales could be said to track, if not to match it. Willis met a fate similar to that of his Vandemonian counterpart.

When last we met Willis, his fortunes were at a low ebb. He had failed in his appeal to the Privy Council in February 1829, and his aristocratic wife had cuckolded him.[99] However, the former judge was not going to take his amoval and its confirmation lying down. In a stream of letters to the Colonial Office, he argued that Lieutenant Governor Maitland in Upper Canada had unjustly treated him by denying him the right of being heard in his own defence and answering the charges against him. While Sir George Murray was secretary of state for the colonies in the Duke of Wellington's Tory government, these pleas fell on deaf ears.[100] The minister even stonewalled a question in Parliament, his view being that the Privy Council had spoken and that was that.[101] Willis's unrelenting pressure finally bore fruit when the new Whig secretary of state, Lord Goderich, reviewed his file and determined to give the jurist a second chance. In a letter of March 1831, he offered the jurist the position of vice-president of the Court of Civil and Criminal Justice of British Guiana at an annual salary of £1,500. Goderich was quick to add, however, that, given the difficulties he had encountered in Upper Canada, Willis was to keep strictly to his judicial functions in the South American colony.[102] Willis quickly accepted the offer and vowed to be guided by the advice tendered.[103]

Willis seems to have taken seriously Goderich's stricture against poking his nose into local politics. He carried out his responsibilities as a judge competently and effectively and advised Governor Benjamin D'Urban on revisions to the system of law and justice in the colony.[104] However, he had reservations about remaining in the colony too long, citing his concern about the education of his son, Robert, and expressing a desire to be closer to England.[105] At a social level, his sister's diary reveals that he enjoyed close and cordial relations with a number of influential people in the colony.[106] In 1833 he secured a parliamentary divorce from Lady Mary.[107]

Two events changed the fortunes of the judge once again. In the first place, on being appointed acting chief justice of the colony on the retirement of Charles Wray, Willis had a falling out with Lieutenant Governor James Carmichael Smyth.[108] This disagreement was over the question of the superior court's power to reverse a decision of a lower court on sentencing.[109] The English law officers concluded that Smyth's position, which was that under the laws of the colony the senior court lacked this power, was correct.[110] In the Colonial Office, officials, aware that Willis was anxious to be confirmed as chief justice, raised doubts about his fitness for that position, and instead it went to Jeffery Hart Bent, chief justice of St Lucia.[111] Secondly, Willis had contracted a tropical disease, in all likelihood malaria or amoebic dysentery, which had a lasting effect on his health.[112] Palpably disappointed by his failure to gain the prize of senior judge, he sought a leave on health grounds and requested a transfer to a colony with a more congenial climate.[113] London granted the leave, and Willis and his family sailed for England in mid-1836.

London extended the leave into 1837 because of the health issues. During this period, Willis met and married Ann Susanna Kent.[114] The judge continued to press the Colonial Office for a posting elsewhere, without success. However, just as he had resigned himself to returning to British Guiana, Lord Glenelg, the Whig secretary of state, offered him the vacant seat as puisne judge on the Supreme Court of New South Wales.[115] Willis jumped at the chance to relocate in what he considered to be a more hospitable physical climate.

New South Wales in the 1830s: Willis in Sydney

By the late 1830s New South Wales was a more vibrant and complex place than it had been ten years before. Although transportation of convicts continued, the proportion of free settlers had increased, and pastoral squatters were pushing out the frontier of settlement beyond the official boundaries.[116] Roman Catholics and Presbyterians were resisting elite Anglican attempts at dominance of the religious life of the colony.[117] Sentiment for political reform had increased, with both emancipists and some free colonists pressing for further concessions on representative government, which ran up against the exclusivist view that only men of respectability were capable of governing.[118] The growing battle over the political and constitutional future of the colony was in part fought out in the columns of a vigorous, and at times irreverent colonial press. In the administration of justice, juries had become more common in both civil and criminal trials, although resistance among the exclusives made a decisive move to jury trial in criminal cases difficult.[119] With the arrival of more liberally minded Governors Richard Bourke and George Gipps, and the retirement of Chief Justice Forbes, serious tension between the executive and the judges over the conduct of government became largely a past memory. The right of the judges to review proposed legislation by the governor and the nominated Legislative Council continued. The Aborigines had become or were becoming thoroughly marginalized. The sheer velocity of white settlement pushed them off their ancestral lands and they experienced death, if they resisted or, if they did not, corralling in mission stations, or eking out a miserable existence on the fringes of white settlements.[120] What one historian has described as the war against the Aborigines began in earnest during this period.[121]

Willis arrived in Sydney with his family on 3 November 1837. His relations with the new chief justice, James Dowling, began cordially enough, as Dowling hosted them as house guests. The professional climate quickly changed, however. As John Bennett reports, Dowling wrote to his son in April 1838 in less than glowing terms about his experiences on the bench with his new colleague: 'Neither of my colleagues particularly love me, but of the two Burton is the least disagreeable. Willis is a fidgety restless conceited fellow and it requires a good deal of forbearance and caution on my part to go on smoothly with him. Some people have the opinion that he is cracked. However, I hope to get on without quarrelling. Anything for the quiet life.'[122]

The latter hope proved unavailing and the relationship was to sour further. Willis directed sarcastic remarks to the chief justice while they were sitting together in the full court.[123] Moreover, as a trial judge, he went out of his way to ridicule Dowling's quirky sense of humour, with its overuse of the pun, while censoriously advising judicial dignity as a guiding rule of behaviour in the courtroom.

Willis's lack of judgment also landed him in trouble in the strained context of religious relations in the colony. The Anglican hierarchy, led by Bishop W.G. Broughton, believed that the Church of England should be the established church in the colony. They were not at all happy with the former governor, the tolerant Richard Bourke, whose legislation provided funding to the Roman Catholic and Presbyterian schools, as well as those run by the Anglicans.[124] Justice Burton, a dyed-in-the-wool member of the Church of England supported Broughton publicly.[125] Willis was invited to be a guest speaker at a public gathering organized by Broughton and supported by Burton. In the course of his speech Willis declared 'the Church of Rome' guilty of 'idolatrous worship.'[126] Not surprisingly, this did not go down well in the Catholic community in Sydney, which publicly declared its outrage. When Roman Catholic Bishop Polding pursued the matter with Willis with less than satisfactory results, and accused the jurist of injustice in his remarks, the judge and his supporters strained at the leash to have the prelate prosecuted for libel.[127] However, Governor George Gipps was not about to be drawn into this contretemps, privately remarking to Attorney General John Hubert Plunkett, himself a Roman Catholic, that the jurist had outdone himself on this occasion. The *Australian* criticized Willis for his lack of judgment in furthering the cause that he championed.[128] Bennett suggests that the judge, 'stung by the reaction,' was unusually quiescent for a year afterwards.[129]

Just as Dowling, suffering the effects of overwork and the strain of interpersonal relations on his health, thought that peace reigned, Willis again began attacking him. First he challenged the chief's sitting as a judge in the Vice-Admiralty Court, arguing that by doing so he was compromising his position in contravention of section 7 of the Third Charter of Justice, by accepting another 'office or place of profit.'[130] That he was serious in this move is evident in his threat to complain to the Colonial Office if Dowling did not resign the post, and his seeking the opinion of his friend Serjeant Henry Mereweather in London on the matter.[131] Having got nowhere with this complaint – the English law officers opining that the Vice-Admiralty appointment was 'incident' to the role of chief justice, not a separate office – Willis tried another tack in what looks like a calculated campaign to undermine Dowling's position.[132] In complaining to Governor Gipps about his own impecuniosity, he began harping on the fact that, unlike his judicial colleagues, he had received no land grants in the colony.[133] Then in a breach of contract case involving the transfer of land heard by the Full Court, *Walker v. Hughes*, Willis delivered a dissenting judgment that contained a gratuitous attack on Dowling. The dissenter held the contract void on grounds of public policy, because it involved the transfer of the services of a convict shepherd, a form of slavery in his opinion. Not content with taking that position, he noted the assignment of convicts to Dowling, which, he argued, contravened an imperial Order in Council of 1831 prohibiting judges from owning slaves. He insinuated that Dowling had put private interest before his judicial duty in using convict labour.[134] In a third incident Willis flew into a rage at Dowling in the robing room of the Sydney courthouse, when Dowling, after hearing additional evidence, changed his opinion, which Willis had shared, favouring the confirmation of the right of an attorney, George Nicholls, to appear before the Sessions courts.[135]

After a short truce, the accidental publication by Gipps of correspondence drawing attention to the tension between Willis and Dowling over the assignment of convicts to judges caused Willis's ire to rise. Gipps's attempts to placate the judge by admitting to his mistake in publishing the letters produced only a temporary thaw, as Willis was soon on the warpath again. In part, the jurist's renewed distemper related to the fact that he found himself isolated in approving a bill authorizing a colonial census.[136] Dowling and Stephen considered provisions requiring information on whether people had been transported, which Willis approved, offensive and invasive of privacy. Furthermore, he felt embittered when he was passed over for the position of Equity judge recently established in the colony under the Administration of Justice Act.[137] Willis, with his Equity experience in Chancery in England, viewed himself as the only possible candidate (indeed, he would have preferred a separate court with himself at the helm), but by a tactical error gave the impression that he did not covet it.[138] It was added to the responsibilities of the chief justice.

In his explosive reaction at being out-manoeuvred, Willis pressed Gipps to undertake a review of the system of justice in the colony. When Gipps demurred, the judge's attempts to use a patron, Viscount Morpeth, to get the ear of Secretary of State Lord John Russell and have the correspondence relating to his running conflict with Dowling tabled in Parliament, backfired. The viscount forwarded his self-serving letter to the Colonial Office, where the correct inference was drawn about the problems with the administration of justice in the colony. A note appended to Willis's letter in answer to the question 'What do we know of this?' minuted, 'We know nothing of this, but we know a great deal of the writer. He is one of the weakest men I ever knew so far as want of sense and a considerable amount of ability are compatible with each other. He has within my knowledge been ruined three or four times over by sheer vanity and an absurd self-importance, and I have no doubt that he is in a fair way to do the same again.'[139]

Dowling, whose health was once more compromised, completely lost patience and complained to Gipps that Willis's behaviour risked adversely affecting both the stature of the Court and the administration of justice in the colony. He pressed Gipps to lay the problem before the secretary of state.[140] Not sure of his ground in taking disciplinary action against the troublesome judge, the governor found an apparent way out of the dilemma by invoking the recently passed Administration of Justice Act and appointing Willis the sole resident judge in the District of Port Phillip in the south of the colony – the frontier community that would become Melbourne in time.[141]

A 'Knight' Errant on the Frontier: Willis in Port Phillip

Willis moved from Sydney, leaving a legacy of bitterness among his colleagues and elements of the population, because of his thoroughly self-centred and injudicious conduct with those whose authority he resented, whom he looked down upon or despised, or who dared to cross him. Some of the venom directed against Dowling may have reflected a covetousness, which he exhibited in both Upper Canada and British Guiana, to win the supreme prize – the chief justiceship. It is also not fanciful to suggest that his ill-temper, vindictiveness, and obsession with status may have been aggravated by his medical condition, even though his illness tended to be ignored by those whom he excoriated or criticized, or, perhaps, that they treated as a crutch which he hauled out, when convenient, to secure sympathy. The charges laid against him reflected more frustration with his narcissistic personality than any doubt about his professional ability. If there was a degree of doubt about his understanding of the law, it related to several instances in which he seemed unduly keen to invoke the repugnancy critique, although he was induced to relent in his opposition in some cases.[142] Willis liked to think of himself as a bastion of the principles and values of English law in the colony: 'I prefer the elucidation of the law by the Sages of Westminster to anything that can be obtained elsewhere, even from the profound philosophy of another Minos, or from the righteous rigour of another Rhadamanthus.'[143]

Gipps's motives in shifting him to Port Phillip, rather than suspending or amoving him, were likely associated with doubts about making the case against Willis in his professional capacity. Certainly in his correspondence with London at this time, the governor disingenuously stressed that the difficulties with the jurist existed at the personal rather than the professional level.[144] It is also true that Gipps had consulted Willis on the matter of native title as it related to New Zealand, which was governed from New South Wales until 1840, suggesting that he sought out and valued Willis's professional advice.[145] Gipps may have also wanted to avoid any suggestion in London that he was ineffective in managing the colony, and he did worry about whether he had the full range of talent to fill the seats on the Supreme Court and the law officers' positions. Whatever his motives in moving Willis on to the frontier community of Port Phillip, the decision seems to have been unwise, given the man's unsatisfactory record in interpersonal relations, not to mention his health problems. Perhaps Gipps assumed that Willis as the sole judge in his own domain, without competition, might put past squabbles behind him and get down to the important work of stabilizing and advancing the administration of justice in the community.[146]

If this was the governor's strategy, his naivety and that of Lord John Russell were to be amply rewarded.[147]

Port Phillip, as a political and economic unit, was the product of movement of settlers from both New South Wales itself and Van Diemen's Land (free settlers and emancipists alike), joined by some directly from the British Isles or elsewhere in the empire (whether merchants or assisted or independent migrants).[148] By 1840 there was sufficient settlement for the New South Wales government to have established at least the rudiments of an administration and legal institutions in the territory. A superintendent of the district responsible to the governor of the colony was appointed, assisted by a small, embryonic bureaucracy, and magistrates' courts were established.[149] The Supreme Court came intermittently on circuit, and a small number of cases proceeded to Sydney. As in the two existing Australian possessions, pressure from land-hungry settlers, especially those anxious to pasture their livestock, created tensions and violence with the local Aboriginal peoples, who were displaced, killed if they put up a fight, or left to survive in missions or at the edge of white communities.[150] A protector of Aborigines, who, as the name implies, was to act in the interests of the indigenous peoples, took office in 1838.[151]

The district, with what seemed like an extensive expanses of wasteland, attracted a diverse group of settlers – gentlemen (or those who considered themselves such) anxious to tame the land, make money, and live in conditions befitting their status, professionals anxious to reap rewards in a new landed society, missionaries ready to save souls and convert the Aborigines, former convicts looking for a new start and anxious to ascend the ladder of respectability, artisans and labourers looking for employment opportunities, and a proportion of cheats and swindlers on the make from each of the previous groupings.[152]

During the late 1830s the economy, propelled by the land rush, buoyant commercial enterprise, and the inevitable speculation that attended them, was in apparent good shape. However, by the early 1840s, with the effects of overheated activity and a decline in trade and prices for staples, the bloom came off the rose. The lines of credit, stretching from banks or merchants to other businessmen and settlers and supported by wide use of bills of exchange, often with multiple endorsements, predictably crumbled.[153] Harbingers of this period of economic decline were evident as the resident judge arrived in the district early in 1841, although the full flood of insolvencies occurred during 1843.[154]

As is normal in such periods, bankruptcies, insolvencies, and the disputes associated with them increased almost exponentially. In some instances roguery was exposed, and the less scrupulous sought to dodge their obligations by whatever means. At that period, governments were not viewed as having any central role to play in seeking solutions to economic crises, as the problems of the market were, presumably, self-correcting.[155]

Superintendent La Trobe and other leading citizens welcomed Willis, hopeful that he would bring stability and propriety to the administration of justice, and wisdom and clarity to law in the district. The judge's handling of the law in court was, according to both contemporaneous and modern commentators, learned and able. Justice Roger Therry, attorney general while Willis was on the bench, referred in his memoirs to the Willis's sound command of 'the practice and principles' of Equity and 'a quickness of parts which he possessed.'[156] Paul Mullaly observes that the judge conducted himself well in criminal trials, taking time to inform himself of the law reports and texts (he knew and in most instances correctly applied the law).[157] Moreover, he proved sensitive to the needs of accused who could not afford a lawyer, by assigning counsel to them. It was in the context of civil actions that Willis's actions were to prove much more controversial, although the evidence is that, in the main, his understanding of the law was not the problem, but his demeanour and behaviour.

Justice Willis correctly saw himself charged with the task of clarifying and rationalizing the law applicable in the district, and of bringing order and ethical standards to the process of litigation. When he realized the dismal state of the local economy, the adverse effects of rampant speculation, and the collapse of the overstretched credit system, he also concluded, with less justification, that it was up to him to repair the economic relations of the district.[158] It is important, as Bruce Kercher reminds us, to recognize that attitudes in Anglo-American society towards debt were changing during this period, from its characterization as a problem of moral deficiency in the debtor, towards the liberal view that debtors were not sinners, but risk takers who, with a help up, could well again become productive members of a capitalist society. Willis counted himself among the supporters of the old order in the matter and was resolute in pressing it.[159]

In his application of the law Willis tended to hew to a policy of strict application of English precedent.[160] He was fonder than his colleagues, who saw themselves as more attuned to what they considered the needs of the community, of invoking the repugnancy card. In several instances he took a lone position in dissent when asked to comment on the validity of colonial legislation, such as that providing for the incorporation of Melbourne.[161] At the same time, he could read into statutes broader purposes than their framers had imagined when pursuing his financial order agenda. For example, he sought to exact penalties from a third-party witness owing money to debtors who were involved in insolvency proceedings before him. On appeal to Sydney, his judicial brethren firmly rejected his opinion, as contrary to and an illegitimate extension of the powers granted by the colony's Insolvency Act, an enactment drafted by his colleague William Burton.[162] Willis also sought to strike out on a different course on the issue of whether Aboriginals were British subjects and thus governed by English law. He delivered an opinion in *R v. Bon Jon* that they were not.[163] This position accorded with decisions of the Supreme Court before 1836, and, as Bruce Kercher suggests, tied in with the judge's view that indigenous peoples retained rights to their land.[164] However, the Full Court had earlier rejected Willis's position in their decision in *Murrell*, as both Gipps and ultimately the Colonial Office asserted.[165]

It appears evident that Willis was a judge of independent spirit calling the decisions and advice he rendered, as he saw them, with a keen eye to English law and its demands. In that capacity he appears as a custodian of English law, the rule of law and their importance in colonial governance.[166] None of this would have rendered him unique or unduly eccentric.

In terms of court practice, Willis found a legal profession of five or six barristers and a larger number of attorneys or solicitors of varying competence, who were lax, as he saw it, in their professional relations and demeanour when they appeared in court.[167] A document addressed to the attorneys setting out the judge's higher expectations in this regard points to his belief that he had an important educative function to introduce legal practitioners to the values and practices of the English bar.[168]

The problem with this tempestuous jurist was that in Port Phillip, true to form, he exhibited all of the personality flaws and vindictive propensities identified earlier. He demonstrated his great difficulty in getting on with those in authority. Moreover, where he had legitimate cause for concern, his tactics in making his reservations known were often impetuous, proving offensive and therefore counterproductive. He developed contempt for Superintendent Charles La Trobe, whom he considered an incompetent administrator, evidenced by the economic mess and the deceit and unethical behaviour that had in some cases helped the financial bubble to burst. The judge, moreover, had no compunction about alleging gratuitously that when certain members of the colonial government engaged in land transactions they had been guilty of sharp, or at least dubious, practices.[169] In the case of one individual, Willis had genuine cause for voicing concern about that person's actions. Colonel Lonsdale, sub-treasurer of the district, while acting as executor of John Batman's estate, had bought bank shares that were assets of the estate. These were shares in an institution in which Lonsdale had an interest. To the judge's mind, as one knowledgeable of Equity, this appeared to be a breach of trust. In a letter to La Trobe, Willis raised questions about Lonsdale's purchase of the shares, as well as his more general dealings in land.[170] However, rather than leaving it to the superintendent to investigate the matter, Willis used the episode in court to defend himself publicly from doubts expressed about his own conduct in providing a mortgage at a high rate of interest to the owner of the *Port Phillip Patriot*, whose editor had become the judge's fast friend.[171] Unfortunately, La Trobe was not willing to take an early firm stand against this sort of public and generalized slur that dropped all too easily from Willis's lips.[172]

Executive complicity in or blindness to sharp dealing was not Willis's only gripe with the colonial government. In a spirit that does not jibe well with other views he expressed about Aboriginal Australians, he fulminated against government officials for what he claimed was its inconsistent stand in pursuing the alleged white killers of natives, even where the evidence was flimsy, while demonstrating a lack of enthusiasm for chasing down the suspected Aboriginal killers of whites.[173] Although couched in the language of equality of treatment, this attitude reflected a belief that the word of a 'black' could not stand up to that of a white, especially a supposedly respectable settler, and reflected little sensitivity to what was happening to Aboriginal communities, while he sat on the bench.[174] The protector's office vigorously denied Willis's charge that the government was racially biased in its policies.[175]

The jurist was no more charitable than before to his Supreme Court colleagues in Sydney. While hearing a case of insolvency, he moved to penalize Horatio Nelson Carrington, a lawyer and witness to the transaction between the parties, as a third-party debtor of a defendant litigant. In Willis's mind, the man was at fault for failing to produce documents relating to his own indebtedness. The judge reacted by striking the lawyer off the rolls, ordering his property attached, and imprisoning him.[176] The Full Court in Sydney reviewed and reversed that decision, on the ground that actions under the Insolvency Act had no application to third-party debtors.[177] Willis, unbowed, in the course of another case, turned to the Supreme Court's decision and, citing English authorities, insisted that he was right and that his colleagues were wrong at law.[178] To add insult to injury, in the case of John Batman's will, Willis criticized his colleagues for insisting that probate be processed in Sydney. This was, he asserted, 'a grievous irregularity' as they lacked jurisdiction, given the location of the testator when he died and of his assets. He also chided them for subsequently requiring security for the safe return of the will, as a condition of its release. Their action betrayed, he added, 'their ignorance of Chancery practice.'[179] Although Willis may have had genuine concerns about Batman's surviving children and their possible destitution, as he professed, this was not the way to treat his professional colleagues.[180] They were predictably outraged at his swipe at their judicial integrity and unimpressed by his backhanded response that he 'meant no disrespect,' but did not consider himself 'responsible for any expressions I may think fit to use, in the conscientious discharge of my legal duty, whether palatable or impalatable [*sic*] to others.'[181]

Several lawyers experienced bullying by and ridicule from Willis when they appeared before him. One young lawyer, Redmond Barry, who lived in fear of Willis and his outbursts, managed to avoid the embarrassments suffered by others by maintaining a respectful and cooperative air about him in his communications with the jurist.[182] The judge's relations with the crown prosecutor, James Croke, who, like Willis, was unduly temperamental, were less cordial, reaching a particularly low ebb when the judge dressed down the lawyer representing Lonsdale in the *Batman* case for having purchased land from the defendant using a bill of exchange (an 'accommodation bill,' he labelled it). The jurist considered that, although these notes were an acceptable mode of payment for businessmen, they were inappropriate for lawyers. At this barrage, Croke bowed and left the court in protest, joined by all the other barristers present, including Barry. Croke complained bitterly to La Trobe about the judge's publicizing his private transactions, not to mention implicitly attacking his integrity.[183]

Willis's strong views on professional conduct also tended to make him rush to judgment. He barred Sidney Stephen, disciplined unfairly by the Vandemonian Supreme Court and struck off the rolls there, from practice in the district, to the consternation of Stephen and members of the New South Wales bar.

Not surprisingly, witnesses who got on the wrong side of the jurist also felt the full force of his disapproval, and, on occasion, suffered imprisonment for contempt. A remarkable example was the experience of a prominent merchant and magistrate, J.B. Were, who in the course of trial was being examined in the witness box. When, in Willis's opinion, the witness proved reluctant to answer questions, the judge charged him with contempt for prevarication. He then inflicted and increased a term of imprisonment from two months to six months when Were, through counsel, sought a record of what had transpired and protested his mistreatment.[184]

Willis's behaviour on the bench initially received mixed reviews in the press. The jurist did not impress the young, headstrong George Arden, editor of the *Port Phillip Gazette,* who was sympathetic to the government and the gentlemen of the colony.[185] The editor published a letter that attacked Willis for his infuriating conduct in court, attacking people on often trumped up accusations of impropriety, injuring characters, and creating social confusion, while not being free himself of reproach for 'crimes' that he was alleged to have committed in married life, and while single.[186] Predictably, the judge reacted angrily, citing Arden for criminal libel, finding him in contempt, and ordering him imprisoned for twelve months with a stiff fine of £300. On the advice of the local law officers that Arden's publication was a 'gross libel' and warranted prosecution at Quarter Sessions, but did not constitute contempt of court, Governor Gipps remitted the sentence, much to Willis's annoyance.[187]

It was not only Willis's animus towards certain press men who had the temerity to attack him that was a problem. He also ran into increasing criticism for what was perceived as his too cosy relationship with the editor of the *Port Phillip Patriot,* the feisty Orangeman, William Kerr, who was quite as given to publishing libellous material as Arden. Moreover, the news man flew the flag of radicalism in the colony, purporting to represent honest and hard-working colonists, and to challenge the possessors of privilege and unearned wealth.[188] The view of Willis's targets and detractors, including his judical colleagues in Sydney, was that the judge used his relationship with Kerr to leak material, including confidential correspondence, to the paper.[189] The judges went further, suggesting that Willis himself had written articles disparaging their decisions for the paper.[190] When it was learned that, soon after his arrival in the district, Willis had given a mortgage to John Pascoe Fawkner, the owner of the paper, at an interest rate of 20 per cent, the tongues wagged even more.[191] Both men's claims that this was a regular transaction and had no influence on the editorial policy of the paper were received with scepticism.[192] Willis's attempts to portray himself as above the political fray, rather than, as his detractors viewed him, an irksome tribune of the people, took a further battering when he remained in studied isolation and repose in his home in rural Heidelberg while Kerr and his other supporters organized a public meeting to protest the judge's mistreatment at the hands of an uncaring and oppressive government.[193]

By the latter part of 1842, Gipps had serious doubts about Willis and what he saw as his attempts at subversion of both the administration of justice and the government of La Trobe.[194] The judges of the Supreme Court, furious at their former colleague's unprofessional behaviour towards them, strongly pressured him to bite the bullet and discipline Willis or at least recommend that the secretary of state censure him. Leading citizens who deprecated attacks on La Trobe in the columns of the *Patriot*, and the unrest generated by and surrounding the judge and his supporters, made their concerns known to the superintendent in a formal address.[195] The governor prevaricated for a while longer, hoping that Willis would follow through with a request for health leave in England and that the bad blood he had caused would vanish with him.[196]

When Gipps finally brought what was by now a litany of complaints against the jurist from the judiciary, legal profession, magistrates, government officials, attorney general, and superintendent to his Executive Council early in 1843, the executive took the peculiar step of reporting Willis and his misbehaviour to the Colonial Office, requesting that Stanley remove him. At the same time, they advised Willis of the charges against him, effectively putting him on probation by asserting that, if he transgressed again, he faced suspension.[197] However, a further build-up of opposition to the judge that now included gentlemen anxious to protect their economic and social reputations, and related to concerns about undue partisanship during the campaigns for forthcoming local elections in Melbourne, forced the governor's hand. [198] This was exactly the period when the direst effects of the financial meltdown were being felt throughout the district and across the European community.[199] The governor concluded that it was finally time to take drastic action and unseat the resident judge.[200] With council's support, he invoked Burke's Act and amoved Willis from office on 17 June 1843, without calling on the judge to defend himself.[201]

Despite the rejoicing in official circles in the district at Willis's demise, there was an even greater outpouring of support for the jurist, reflected in a series of petitions, with impressive numbers of signatures pointing to his sense of justice, impartiality, and fearlessness that demanded his reinstatement.[202] However, the die was cast and, with the weight of those in the government, judiciary, the professions, and the gentlemanly class against him, Willis left the colony, to the cheers of his supporters on the Yarra River quay, to fight the next phase of the battle in London.

The Colonial Office referred Willis's complaint of mistreatment to the Judicial Committee as an appeal under Burke's Act. Gipps had set out the litany of complaints against the judge from those he had attacked verbally and insulted, while careful to stress that his actions as governor had been necessary to respond to a pattern of misbehaviour that seriously compromised the administration of justice in the district.[203] He seemed intent on adding doubts about Willis's legal acumen to the challenges his insulting behaviour posed for the colonial government. Reference was made, for instance, to his excessive sentence in the *Arden* case, a clearly erroneous (but uncharacteristic) death sentence in the case of *Manuel*, his faulty interpretation of the law relating to intra-Aboriginal violence in *Bonjon*, and his challenge to Melbourne's incorporation.[204]

The jurist's appeal focused on a denial of the legality of his removal under the Act of 1782, which he argued had no application to judges appointed by the Crown, and the defective process of amoving him without granting him the opportunity to answer the charges at a hearing.[205] In defending himself against the barbs of injudicious and partial behaviour, and that he was in error in certain of his legal decisions and opinions, the judge's responses ranged from detailed justifications to dismissive comments.[206] In true Willis style he conceded nothing to his detractors – they were wrong and he was right, vindicated by English law and its values. For his part, Gipps argued that his actions were perfectly legal and that the charges were sufficiently clear and well known so that inviting Willis to comment on them would have been pointless.[207]

Clearly the authorities in London were of the view that this was a case with serious political dimensions. However, unlike Boulton's case in 1838, the Judicial Committee accepted it, perhaps because Willis's impugned behaviour related in large part to his conduct of his judicial responsibilities. The political significance of the case lies in the fact that the new secretary of state, William Gladstone, provided counsel to their lordships when considering their opinion.[208] Peter Howell has noted that, even before the case was heard, 'the Colonial Office staff had strong grounds for concluding that [Willis] had become so involved in personal and political squabbles, which deeply divided the leading citizens of the colon[y] in which [he] served, that it would be inexpedient for him to remain on the bench.'[209]

The Judicial Committee released its advice on 1 August 1846.[210] In its infuriatingly terse style, the committee concluded that Gipps was blameworthy in breaching the rules of natural justice by not allowing Willis to be heard in his own defence. That was sufficient, they opined, to warrant reversal of the amotion order.[211] However, they undermined the strength of that finding by also stating that, on the basis of what they heard in evidence about the case, the governor had possessed ample grounds for the jurist's amoval.

Unsurprisingly, the Colonial Office determined that Willis would not return to New South Wales, nor would it offer him any further preferment. He had tried their patience to the limit and beyond, and had become a liability as a judge. He was allowed his salary for the period between the date of his amoval and that of the announcement of the Judicial Committee's opinion. Secretary of State Lord Grey declined to allow Willis to resign, as this would have implied that his behaviour was unproblematic, and Gipps's and the council's action against him made without sufficient grounds.[212] By the same token, he was advised that he had no right to a pension. Perhaps as a means of getting the former jurist off his list of supplicants, the minister conceded that none of this reflected on the former jurist's integrity and honour.[213] Apart from a tendentious, self-published tract dedicated to Lord John Russell in 1850, giving his views on reform of colonial governance in the empire, Willis retired to Wick Episcopi in Worcestershire.[214] There he lived the life of a country gentleman and settled for the positions of a justice of the peace and deputy lieutenant of the county.[215] He died of old age in 1877.

The Final Demise of Willis: Assessing a Troubled and Troublesome Jurist

In assessing Willis's misadventures in Port Phillip, it is important to stress the less than ideal conditions in which he found himself. His position was that of sole professional judge, so that he had no resident colleague or colleagues to consult with at short notice. Admittedly, he had burnt his bridges with his colleagues in Sydney, so communing with them would have been difficult. His only source of professional advice was Chief Justice Pedder in Van Diemen's Land.[216] The district was a frontier colonial community that was unstable, competitive, fractious, and given to frantic financial speculation. The legal profession was diminutive, of variable competency, lacking in cohesion, and bereft of the standards of practice that the judge expected. As Edmund Finn, the famous commentator on nineteenth-century Melbourne life, put it some decades later in commenting on Willis, 'Even a man of much more equable temperament and a more judicial turn of mind, would have had an arduous task to give satisfaction in the exceptional state of things then prevalent.'[217]

The settler community was also small enough that rivals and ill-wishers, not least the more irreverent segments of an excitable and overly candid press, subjected everyone in government and law to close and critical scrutiny. As Roger Therry pointed out in his memoirs, the resident judge was expected to afford protection 'to all other persons in the community, and was himself the only person unprotected by it.'[218] When the press made him the butt of libel, he had the choice of either ignoring it, however scurrilous, or hauling the miscreant before him and acting as prosecutor and judge, 'a union which the policy of the law deprecates.' In Therry's opinion, provision should have been made for the reference of such a case to one of the Sydney judges.

There was also a serious flaw in how the system of justice administered by the resident judge in Melbourne related to that of the Supreme Court in Sydney. Superintendent La Trobe complained that under the Administration of Justice Act the position of the resident judge in Port Phillip in relation to the Supreme Court had not been clearly spelt out. As a result, Willis considered himself unanswerable for his actions to anyone but himself.[219] The consequences of this oversight had been detrimental to the social order.

There is also the question of Willis's health and whether it explains his bouts of temper and vindictiveness. Chief Justice Dowling, who initially was inclined to make allowances for his colleague's behaviour because of his health problems, remarked on his colleague's fidgety disposition and tendency to start shaking in court.[220] The *Sydney Herald*, in a column making fun of the jurist also made reference to evident physical afflictions:[221] 'We citizens of Sydney have not to learn Mr

WILLIS'S unenviable peculiarities. We are familiar of old with his grimaces on the bench; his fantastic tricks of wriggling upon his seat as if its cushion were stuffed with needles; starting upon his feet; twisting his gown as if he would tear it to a thousand shreds; twitching his wig as if he were going to fling it among the barristers; and altogether conducting himself like an unhappy victim of St Vitus's dance.'

Leaving aside the rhetorical strokes, the symptoms described may well have been reflective of quite serious personal discomfort. The judge certainly claimed as much, complaining of frequent pains in his side that rendered him 'feeble and debilitated,' the pain increasing when he sat for long periods in 'a crowded court' under the stress of adjudicating both criminal and civil hearings.[222] Keon-Cohen is certain that Willis's health problems contributed to 'his abrasive, judicial demeanour.'[223]

Apart from Sir George Gipps in framing his argument to the Colonial Office, no one, not even his most vigorous critics, seems to have doubted Willis's legal acumen.[224] Apart from the cases mentioned in which his colleagues demurred from his understanding of the law or interpretation of a statute – the sort of difference of opinion that was and is commonplace among the judiciary – his knowledge of the law was not in doubt, nor the correctness of the majority of his decisions. His concern to see that destitute accused parties were represented by counsel has already been noted. In civil cases he allowed impoverished suitors to appear *in forma pauperis* before him, requesting lawyers to act for them.[225] Willis was said to lean towards the poor rather than to the wealthy in his application of the law. To the extent that he dealt firmly and fairly with accused parties within the criminal justice system, and used the civil justice system to resolve disputes equitably, and sought to bring honesty and integrity to the colony's business dealings, it would be difficult to fault him. The fact that he hewed to English law and its values, at times in the face of local conditions that made its application of doubtful wisdom, would not in and of itself have damned him. It did not harm the long career of William Burton.

Willis's problem was the arrogant, vainglorious, and intemperate way in which he conducted himself, in particular in his relations with those in authority and those for whom he developed a strong dislike.[226] These personality traits were not new or a sudden symptom of his health problems, but were identifiable much earlier during his sojourn in Upper Canada – a period when perhaps he had more to complain about than in Australia.[227] With the exception of his time in British

Guiana, where he was on probation, Willis was one who tended to rush to judgment about the political and legal conditions in the colonies in which he served. Once he had made up his mind about something or someone, he stuck doggedly to his initial opinion, never doubting that he was right in his assessment, whatever others might say. They were simply wrongheaded. Given his inflated sense of his own importance and destiny, he held a dim opinion of those who he felt were his intellectual inferiors, especially when subject to their authority. This explains his contempt for both Dowling and La Trobe, who he assumed had no effective means of fighting back, and in the case of the former, might indeed be dislodged to Willis's benefit. Where he divined that his targets were hardier and not easily intimidated, such as his colleagues William Burton and Alfred Stephen, he sniped at them as unreliable and even dishonest professionals. At the same time he could demonstrate a rather sickening tendency to seek to ingratiate himself with those whom he saw as having the real power, such as Gipps.

John Walpole Willis shared Robert Thorpe's problem of an inability to divine where the line between law and politics should be drawn, and a failure to recognize the need to navigate it carefully and judiciously.[228] This is evident in his association with newspaperman William Kerr and the so-called radical element in Port Phillip politics. He also suffered from the delusion that somehow, single-handedly, he could mould the law to fit his own values and priorities and in the process change the politico-legal cultures of the colonies in which he served. Whether he held or developed well-defined ideological or political commitments is difficult to say on the available evidence. His view of law and legal development, tied as it was to the values and traditions of English law, seems to have been conservative rather than progressive, however much he might associate with would-be political reformers or radicals. He was certainly not impressed with the changes to the law of debt – the substitution of economic expediency and efficiency for moral judgment. In his bigoted views on the supremacy of the Anglican church in the colony, he ran against the growing movement towards religious tolerance. At the same time, one can read some of his moves as reflecting simply a resistance to authority, a trait that Leo Johnson noted during the judge's time in Upper Canada. However, the quirks of his personality so confounded his attitudes that it is difficult, if not impossible, to label him as anything other than a self-centred, even narcissistic, anti-authoritarian, except where his own authority was in question. It did not do his reputation any good in official circles that some in the Port Phillip community saw his court as one of the chief centres of entertainment, in the absence of a theatre or music hall – less the palladium of justice that either the local government or Westminster would have wished, and more an absurdist legal theatre.

In summing up the misadventures of John Walpole Willis, it is important to identify fully the primary reasons for his removal. It is tempting to assert that he was dumped from office a second time simply because he brought the administration of justice in New South Wales into disrepute. Gipps was certainly concerned to stress that motivation in his justifications to the Colonial Office, and there is no doubt that the jurist's venomous relationship with his judicial colleagues in Sydney, and his belief that it was quite legitimate to bad mouth in court those who got in the way or disapproved of his highly personal sense of justice, constituted one major reason for getting rid of him. There was, in short, a credible argument that he had brought administration of justice into disrepute, at least in a symbolic sense. However, as Janine Rizzetti has persuasively argued, equally important was the threat that Willis and his scattergun approach to exposing dishonesty and deceit in the governmental, business, and commercial communities presented to an increasing number of gentlemen in the district. These were men worried about exposure and damnation for the conduct of their economic transactions and their associations.[229] Even if he was not a serious political force in the community, with his thoroughly ungentlemanly manners he could do enough damage to the reputations of government officials and substantial settlers to cause disquiet in the broader society. This must have seemed particularly menacing during the parlous economic conditions that prevailed in 1843 when nobody could be sure quite what the future might hold for this European outpost, and the first election campaign in Melbourne was underway.

If Montagu and Willis, albeit from somewhat different points on the legal compass, were to demonstrate the problems associated with the formal or informal exercise of the repugnancy power, as a means of testing local legislative initiatives against the demands of British justice and English law in the Australian colonies before 1850, they were not to be the last champions of this challenge to locally developed legal solutions. Indeed, if they were the 'bad boys' of the Australian judiciary during the 1830s and 1840s, their activities were to pale into insignificance alongside Benjamin Boothby's use of repugnancy as a weapon against responsible government and colonial lawmakers in South Australia in the 1850s and 1860s. His story consumes the next chapter.

8

Repugnancy in Australia after 1850: Shoot-out in Adelaide, 1854–1868

Limiting Repugnancy in the Empire

In 1865 the British Parliament passed the Colonial Laws Validity Act, signed by Victoria Regina and duly proclaimed.[1] This crucial legislation recognized the lawmaking autonomy of colonial legislatures throughout most of the British Empire. Repugnancy was to be limited to just two categories of statutes: those imperial acts related to a specific colony, and those of general application throughout the empire.[2] The black letter of the statute shrouded an ongoing battle royal between one of the judges of the South Australia Supreme Court, Benjamin Boothby, and the colony's legislators about the relative powers of the legislative branch and the judiciary over what constituted the law of the colony.[3] Although comments on repugnancy had lain within the privilege of the judges of the New South Wales and Van Diemen's Land courts, that privilege was to disappear with the move towards the grant of responsible government in Australia.[4] This privilege had not been extended to the Supreme Court of South Australia founded in 1837.

There was a reference in the South Australia Act of 1834 to what had been standard imperial practice, the governor's duty to transmit legislation to the King in Council for approval or disallowance, and it directed that any legislation in the colony 'shall not in anywise be contrary or repugnant to any Provisions of this Act.'[5] The assumption would have been that, in addition to the formal power of disallowance in the imperial executive, the superior court judges in the colony had the power to determine whether or not local law was repugnant to the law of England, subject to appeal to the Governor in Council (the colonial Court of Appeal), and beyond to the Judicial Committee of the Privy Council. With the grant of responsible government to South Australia in 1855–6 by the South Australia Constitution Act, the judges of the Supreme Court henceforth held their appointments during good behaviour – judicial independence was formally pronounced. Moreover, the Act allowed for the removal of a judge on a joint address of both houses of the local Parliament.[6] The repugnancy questions left hanging were what residual power lay with the judges of the colonial Supreme Court in the exercise of their reading of local statutes, to determine that local law offended the laws of England, and how broad that power was. The legislators of the bicameral system of Parliament prescribed for South Australia, a House of Assembly (the lower house) and the Legislative Council (the upper house) and the governments, elected by a local franchise, believed that they had, if not a free hand, a relatively wide area of freedom to develop domestic legal solutions to the challenges they faced.[7] The Colonial Office, sympathetic to that position while sensitive to the need to protect judicial independence, seemed poised to try to limit the use of repugnancy doctrine by the courts to the ambit of clashes between local statutes and imperial legislation applicable to colonies.[8] Justice Boothby had other ideas.

South Australia: A Free Colony

South Australia was designed as a colony of free settlers, the second Australian colony based on this vision, after Western Australia. It was to be primarily a haven for middle-class religious dissenters dissatisfied with their lot in Britain. These were people whose civic disabilities the 1832 Reform Act had not relieved.[9] The South Australia Act of 1834 contemplated a possession in which a colonization commission would promote colonization, with power initially shared between the governor responsible for the political administration and the colonization commissioners for settlement and economic development.[10] The colony was to be a model of Edward Gibbon Wakefield's colonial system by which the prospect of securing significant land holdings (for which they would pay a moderate price per acre) would attract settlers 'of considerable property.'[11] Trusty, working-class settlers would supply the labour. Although not able to afford to buy land initially, these people might earn and save enough to buy their own farms in the future. The belief was that, as a free settler colony comprising respectable immigrants, the colony would move quickly to self-sufficiency. The new possession was originally described as a 'province,' perhaps, as Castles and Harris have suggested, as a reflection of what was meant to be a self-supporting 'paradise of dissent,' not a convict colony.[12] Relations within the settler population of the colony in its early years were to subvert the confident economic and political visions proposed.

The dream of an ordered settlement organized on rational principles was to fail in the face of widespread speculation.[13] The founding governor, John Hindmarsh, lacked the capacity to control events and to exercise firmness with the Colonization Commission, his partner in governance, and he was soon recalled.[14] The attempts of his successor, George Gawler, to place the colony on a firm footing were considered too costly in London and he suffered the same fate. It was only with appointment of Sir George Grey in 1841, his tough fiscal policies, and dismantling of the dual system of governance a year later, that the political and economic situation stabilized and the colony began to prosper.[15] It was on his watch in 1842 that a nominated Legislative Council replaced the Council of Government, the body that had combined political and economic functions. At the same time an Executive Council was formed to advise the chief executive.[16]

The administration of justice also got off to a shaky start.[17] The first justice of the Supreme Court, the rakish, insolvent Irishman, John Jeffcott, was more intent on repairing to Hobart in the hopes of wooing an heiress than in nurturing the development of South Australia's law and placing his imprint on its justice system.[18] When he died by drowning in 1837, the well-intentioned but eccentric and unduly timorous Henry Jickling replaced him temporarily. It was the third judge, the stolid and retiring Charles Cooper, appointed in 1838, who was to place the administration of justice finally on an even keel.[19]

Under 1837 legislation, the Supreme Court of South Australia had the combined jurisdiction of the royal courts in London, including that of the Court of Chancery.[20] A conservative in legal matters, Justice Cooper generally adhered to English precedents, although he did propose a voluntary registration scheme for deeds to simplify land transfers, which the colony adopted in 1841. He also firmly maintained the unified legal profession already in place.[21] His developing health problems led to the addition of a second judge in 1849. George Crawford, also appointed from England, died in office in 1852. It was Benjamin Boothby who replaced Crawford in 1853.

Judge Benjamin Boothby and His Early Ruminations on Law and Justice in South Australia

Unlike most men appointed to the colonial judiciary, Boothby, born in Doncaster, Yorkshire, was not of gentlemanly birth. As a young man he worked with his father, an iron-master by trade, in manufacturing in Nottingham.[22] In 1827 he married Maria Bradbury Robinson, with whom he was to have no fewer than fifteen children, a reality that would always strain the family resources to the limit and beyond. Attracted by politics, he managed the campaign of Thomas Wilde (later Lord Chancellor Truro) for election to Parliament. While reading for the bar, in Wilde's chambers, Boothby wrote briefs on the conflict between the judges and the House of Commons over the extent of parliamentary privilege, played out in the memorable case of *Stockdale v. Hansard*.[23] His principal was an extreme advocate of that privilege.

Boothby, called to the bar in 1841, served on the crowded Northern Circuit.[24] Like other aspiring struggling barristers, he put his writing talents to work authoring *A Synopsis of Law Relating to Indictable Offences*. He was not a fan of the new County Courts, arguing in a pamphlet that the extra demands on the court system could be adequately served by creating greater capacity within the existing order.[25] In the early 1850s his prospects took a turn for the better, as he came to the attention of the Duke of Newcastle, Henry Pelham Clinton. The duke became secretary of state for the colonies in the government of Lord Aberdeen in 1852.[26] This liberal-minded politician was convinced, in part because of the apparent success of responsible government in Canada, that it should be granted to the Australian colonies. When the need to fill the position of second judge in South Australia faced him, he had no qualms about appointing Boothby, at a salary of £1,200 per annum.[27] One of the new judge's friends described him as a 'dauntless advocate for high and liberal principles' and 'a stern defender of truth and impartial justice.'[28] Queen Victoria asked somewhat uncharitably why he would want the job. When the duke advised her that he had nine sons to provide for, Her Majesty's puzzlement seems to have faded.[29] As Boothby and his family sailed for Adelaide, the duke wrote to the governor general of Australia, Sir Charles Fitzroy, requiring that new constitutions for the Antipodean colonies contain provisions for responsible government.

The jurist's arrival in the colony in August 1853 was to cause him some initial angst. Apart from the refusal of the South Australian government to pay him a full salary from the date of his appointment, his first attempt to buy a house went sour. When he sued for specific performance of the contract, Justice Cooper found against him on the basis of faulty proceedings, inadequate evidential support for his claim, and a failure to disclose a case for relief.[30] In 1855 he subsequently took a lease of an estate, known as 'Urrbrae,' and the surrounding land that he assigned in part to Edward Stirling, a partner in Elder, Stirling & Co., financiers.[31]

In his first two years on the bench, Boothby's performance drew praise for the promptness that he demanded of litigants and their lawyers from the *Adelaide Times*, a paper that wavered between support for the establishment and the 'lesser orders.' However, the *South Australian Register*, a paper radical in its commitments, doubted the wisdom of this policy of 'celerity.'[32] Boothby was not impressed by the earlier abolition of the grand jury in the province.[33] He considered that the disappearance of this 'most admirable institution' justified him in directing the attorney general on the criminal charges brought before the Court.[34]

Between 1855 and 1856 South Australia achieved responsible government, boasting a bicameral elected legislature, with a relatively broad franchise for the lower house, and a limited property-based one for the upper chamber.[35] Boothby objected to two features of the constitutional settlement: first that it suggested a decrease in judicial salaries, and second that the legislation barred judges from election to Parliament.[36]

By 1855 Boothby's comments and views in court were beginning to attract negative comment in the press. For instance, the *Times* took him to task for stereotyping the Irish in *Purser v. Kelly* as violent, 'addicted to the use of the shillelagh,' and chiding him for shaking 'his awful wig at the whole race.'[37] At the close of 1855 Boothby became acting chief justice, during the absence of his colleague Cooper on health leave in England.[38] In his new role, Boothby soon incurred the *Register*'s wrath for his handling of *R. v. Popham*.[39] In this prosecution of a respectable doctor for having sexually assaulted Ann Mara, a counterclaim of perjury was laid by the accused. Boothby ordered that the perjury accusation be heard first. Despite his summing up against Mara on that charge, the jury acquitted her. The following day when the sexual assault prosecution was about to proceed, the judge put an ambiguous question to the jury about whether they wished to hear the case. When the question received the negative reply he seems to have wanted, he treated this 'as a formal verdict of not guilty.' Proclaiming Ms Mara 'a perjured woman' and Dr Popham an 'unstained character,' Boothby adjourned the court and left the bench.[40] A public meeting of 1,500 persons protested the jurist's actions, and a petition circulated calling for his suspension or removal. However, enthusiasm waned. Whatever Boothby's motivations for his actions, class bias or empathy with Popham, a fellow mason, he was a marked man as far as the *Register* was concerned.

The furore among some residents of Adelaide about the *Popham* decision, spurred on by the *Register*, revived when Boothby, citing the lead taken by eminent English judges, began redefining the relative functions of judge and jury at trial. He invoked section 182 of the Supreme Court Act, 1852, that allowed a judge to direct a jury, upon the trial of any cause, to find the facts specially and, upon those findings, to give judgment, or make such order 'as the right and justice of the case seemed to require.'[41] The effect was to limit the jury's role to providing answers to specific questions on the facts put by the judge, leaving it to him to both discern and apply the law to the facts, as found. The move was, he thought, necessary to protect the opinions of the judges from contemptuous juries.

This line of judicial reasoning did not go down at all well with those who saw the jury as an institution that embodied the 'rights of freeborn Englishmen,' nor with counsel who resented the judge's interference with their communicating their arguments to jurors, and suspected that he used this process to produce the results he desired.[42] The *Register* thundered, 'We feel that our liberties are at stake ... [With] Mr Justice Boothby on the Bench, jurymen are ciphers and barristers are schoolboys.'[43] Further, the paper asserted, 'He dictates to the Bar the line of remark which they must adopt in their addresses to the jury ... and [gives] the verdict himself instead of allowing the jury to give it ... We will be no party to the overthrow of trial by jury.'

Boothby was reported as reacting to the salvo by asserting that he knew where his duty lay and that he would discharge it according to his conscience.[44] He went on to suggest that, until the decent members of society did something to silence the segment of the press attacking him, the administration of justice was in jeopardy. The judge's disdain for juries who, to his mind, prevaricated unnecessarily in reaching verdicts, or took issue with him on directed verdicts, was evident in his having them locked way, without refreshments, except perhaps water, until they agreed or did his bidding.[45] Boothby's behaviour in court sufficiently ruffled feathers that when Chief Justice Cooper returned from his furlough in England in 1858, he found 'Adelaide in tumult over [his colleague's] legal interpretations.'[46]

While this climate of mistrust between Boothby and his detractors developed, the South Australia Parliament passed the Real Property Act, the brainchild of Robert Richard Torrens, registrar general of the colony, coming into force on 1 July 1858.[47] This radical legislative change to the system of conveyancing substituted an incontrovertible written record of registration to validate land transfers for the messy and often convoluted process of tracing title in English law.[48] Cooper's reforms in 1841 had only marginally improved the situation. Torrens's reform appealed to land purchasers, including speculators, and those who feared the legal costs associated with the old system. It also seemed entirely rational to administrators and liberal politicians, but was not invariably popular among lawyers practising as conveyancers. The latter, it was argued in some quarters, had a vested interest in preserving the complexity of the old and profitable system of searching title.[49] At about the same time a third judge was added to the Supreme Court bench, possibly to provide a counterbalance to Boothby. The man chosen was Edward Gwynne, a seasoned solicitor who had crossed swords with the jurist over his attempts, as the lawyer saw it, to unduly direct proceedings in jury trials and to bully counsel.[50] The new judge was, however, a conservative who distrusted elected legislative bodies, and not at all a fan of the Constitution Act or the Real Property Act.[51]

Until this juncture, Boothby's record as a judge was marked by some eccentricity and intemperate language against those he determined were subverting what he considered an ordered justice system. Moreover, he was capable on occasion of partiality to one side or the other in suits. However, it would be difficult to describe him as one who erred consistently in law (in the case of his approach to jury trials, he was directly appealing to it), or that he stood out from the crowd enough to warrant his disciplining, as the *Register* and its supporters demanded. Crusty and conservative he may have been, but so were judges elsewhere in the imperial firmament, including England.

It was Boothby's developing antipathy to local legislation that earned him the enmity of a large segment of the propertied class and politicians of various stripes, annoyed by his bid to undermine the autonomy of the province's legislature and executive. Initially, it was not evident that the jurist was on a frolic of his own in taking on the legislature. In three early cases interpreting the Real Property Act, Boothby and both his colleagues (Cooper and Gwynne) agreed that in certain circumstances a party to a land transaction should be allowed to avoid the statutory registration and go behind it to investigate earlier documents of title. In the first two cases they allowed the plaintiffs writs of mandamus, directed to Registrar Torrens, for this purpose, and, in the third, they declared an ejectment action against the holder of the registered title successful.[52] A sign that Boothby was laying the basis for a fundamental challenge to local legislation occurred in the last of the three cases, where he mused, without deciding the issue, that the Act might be in excess of the powers enjoyed by the colonial legislature, and thus repugnant to the laws of England. In discussing a bill to consolidate the Real Property Act and amendments to it, to deal with these judicial decisions, the majority of the House of Assembly noted Boothby's dictum but disregarded it.[53] The revised Act was passed in October 1860.[54] If the legislators had thought that this was the last word on the matter, they were soon disabused of that assumption.

The validity of the Real Property Act, even as amended, became entwined with another contentious issue, whether the Court of Appeal (the governor and Executive Council), which the Supreme Court Act of 1837 established, had survived the grant of responsible government.[55] In *Payne v. Dench*, an action on a contract of sale and purchase of land, the Full Court, in addition to concluding that registration under the RPA could not in and of itself ensure transfer of title, where no evidence existed that previous deeds had been given up and cancelled, also determined that the old Court of Appeals no longer existed.[56] Chief Justice Cooper, however, opined that the legislature had the power to revive the Court, or an equivalent. Boothby's tack, however, was that the Constitution Act of 1856 had so changed the composition of the Executive Council that the Court of Appeal could no longer exist. Moreover, if judges were ineligible for election to the council, executive councillors must surely be barred from acting as judges. The matter was referred to the English law officers, who reported that the Court of Appeal still existed and was therefore capable of functioning. However, to be sure, the Adelaide Parliament passed an act making it clear that the Court of Appeal continued to exist and had the power of review of the Supreme Court's judgments that would be binding on all judicial officers.[57]

In the middle of 1861, in the case of *McEllister v. Fenn*, an action for slander relating to alleged fraud under the revised Real Property Act, a rift developed between Cooper and Gwynne on the one hand, and

Boothby on the other, over the validity of the statute.[58] Cooper and Gwynne considered the legislation in force, while Boothby, dissenting, objected that it was invalid because the governor had, contrary to instructions, assented to the Act, rather than reserving it for royal assent.[59] In a later hearing in the same case, Boothby ignored the issue of the Act's validity but argued an earlier decision of the Full Court, in which he had dissented, did not bind him. In *Liebelt v. Hunt*, a defamation suit, Boothby argued with plaintiff's counsel about the coroner's procedures under colonial legislation that did not accord with English practice, asserting that 'the Parliament of this Province has no power to override the common law of England.'[60] In *Cleve v. Dashwood* there was a further division of opinion, this time between Cooper and Boothby on the validity of the Customs Act. Boothby rehearsed his objections to the governor assenting to a bill, rather than reserving it, while Cooper was willing to defer to the governor's discretion in such matters.[61] When Boothby pronounced that the Constitution Act itself was invalid, because of the governor's failure to reserve for royal assent the Electoral Act of 1855 under which members of Parliament had been elected, a palpable chill enveloped the governing elite of the colony.[62]

In June 1861 Boothby, in a statement from the bench, headlined in the *Register* as 'Accident to His Honour,' asserted that the legislature had been delinquent in not raising his salary. His remuneration, he claimed, was only £100 more than the chief justice had earned ten years before. He also noted that the governor's salary had doubled to £4,000 during the same period.[63] The truth was that the judge's finances were in disorder. South Australia Banking Company records for 1858 and 1859 reveal its local board's concerns about the judge's chronic indebtedness and his apparent inability, despite assistance from his adult sons, to discharge it.[64] A member of the bank's board was Edward Stirling, to whose company Boothby had assigned his lease in 1855. During 1859 the jurist had purchased an estate called 'The Glen,' with an additional tract of land, using funds provided by three mortgages, including one in the name of George Young as co-partner in the firm of Younghusband & Company that had held an equitable mortgage on the judge's residence since 1855.

In 1860 a shepherd, Patrick Ryan, found copper under the Moonta-Wallaroo property owned in part by Walter Watson Hughes, who, despite challenges by rival claimants, successfully resisted initiatives to dislodge him.[65] The Moonta Mine was immensely successful, paying over £1 million in dividends. Hughes had obtained development capital from Elder, Stirling & Co., in effect a joint venture. George Boothby, one of the judge' sons and a clerk in that company, facilitated the Hughes claim when it reached Adelaide after a furious race from the property, tipping off Hughes about Ryan's babbling about the find in the city's bars.[66] For this service he was allocated five of the first hundred shares in the mining company. In 1863 George, having received a further unspecified number of shares in Moonta, sold ten shares. He allocated several to George Young, his father's mortgagor. Young, who held a power of attorney for Hughes, attended board meetings in his principal's absence and was also involved with Thomas Elder and George Boothby in the floating of the Matta Mining Company in the same general location as Moonta.[67]

In July 1861, in the midst of a growing chorus of cries of concern from influential people about Boothby's challenges to the colony's lawmaking power, both the assembly and the council set up select committees to investigate his conduct.[68] Boothby refused a request to appear before the council's select committee, bridling at a demand for explanations of various statements and decisions he rendered. He lectured its members that judges' erroneous decisions were appealable to the Judicial Committee of the Privy Council, the only legitimate constitutional route for questioning judicial opinions.[69] He added that for him to concede Parliament's authority over him would be a violation of his oath, subversive of the courts' role in assessing the validity of legislation, and a denial of judicial independence and the role of the judge in protecting individuals.

When the council committee examined leading members of the bar, the general sentiment was that expressed by Richard Hanson, formerly attorney general, that a judge was entitled to determine the law as it appeared to him to be, noting that Boothby's more aberrant ideas had been expressed as obiter dicta.[70] He did add that 'a mistake by the Governor could not invalidate an Act … [and] [w]ith regard to repugnancy, … the South Australian Parliament could alter the common law, provided that it did not abrogate fundamental principles.'[71] He noted several local statutes that did depart from the common law, and that 'no objection had been hitherto raised to them.' The council committee's report was anticlimactic,[72] asserting that colonial judges were subordinate to and dependent on the local legislature, as, it claimed, was true in England of the relationship of the Royal Courts to Parliament. Moreover, it was important for effective government that the local legislature's enactments, on the assent of the governor, should be considered valid and operative, until disallowed by Her Majesty. However, the committee drew back from requesting the judge's removal, accepting that Boothby's views might not portend an active campaign by the judge to cripple the executive and legislature. However, they did warn that any judge who ignored a decision of the Full Court would be at risk of a recommendation for removal.

Boothby did agree to appear before the assembly's committee. There he asserted that a string of enactments, beginning with the Constitution Act of 1855, and including subsequent statutes relating to the administration of justice in criminal matters, abolition of grand juries, trial of petty felonies, customs, real property, and elections were all invalid.[73] The judges, he said, were entitled to take judicial notice of the Royal Instructions to the Governor, and to refuse to recognize any Acts to which he had given his assent in violation of those instructions. On this he was at odds with his judicial colleagues. In the face of this bold statement, the assembly committee took a weaker line than its council counterpart.[74] It noted that, following Boothby's contention, a valid Act of the South Australian Parliament would be the exception rather than the rule, a subversion of the supposed boon of self-government. However, the committee recommended that the English law officers be requested for an opinion about the status of legislation in the province, and that, if necessary, the imperial Parliament should pass curative legislation to validate existing statutes.

Governor R.G. MacDonnell forwarded these reports to the Colonial Office for its consideration, along with expressions of exasperation at Boothby's tactics. He also mused about the possibility of inducing the jurist to retire early.[75] These half-measures did nothing to salve public opinion outside the walls of Parliament in Adelaide. When a mass meeting of two thousand people took place in August 1862, calling for the judge's removal from office and condemning the assembly for its inaction, the reverberations were felt in the Cabinet.[76] The Reynolds ministry was split over whether to support the judge or not, and the premier resigned. His replacement was George Waterhouse, ready to form a ministry for the exclusive purpose of moving addresses in both chambers for Boothby's removal. The premier followed through with his undertaking, and both houses produced addresses to that end, that the governor forwarded to the Duke of Newcastle.[77] The assembly's address now asserted that, as a consequence of Boothby's position, 'public confidence in the administration of justice is destroyed – the validity of titles thrown into doubt – ruinous litigation threatened – and the whole system of legislation in the Province involved in confusion, contradiction and contempt.'[78]

While the government was awaiting London's response, Governor MacDonnell delivered a serious slap in the face to Justice Boothby. He appointed the former attorney general, Richard Hanson, to replace Charles Cooper, who had announced his retirement as chief justice. The chief executive expressed himself as confident in Hanson's talents and his ability to restore confidence in the administration of justice in the province.[79] The senior serving judge had no doubts that *he* was entitled to the position. The fact that Hanson was an attorney by training was an added source of resentment. In a tense encounter in the judges' chambers Boothby refused to recognize Hanson as chief justice and disputed his colleague's status in open court on several occasions, inducing Hanson to table his commission.[80] He was also quick to write to the secretary of state requesting that Hanson not be appointed.[81] On hearing of the addresses for his removal from office, Boothby expressed his objections to the initiatives taken against him and refused outright to take a leave of absence offered by MacDonnell.[82] He continued to raise objections to the validity of the Real Property Act and found inoperative the Convict Prevention Act of 1857 that made it an offence for any convict to enter the colony.[83]

London's response to the addresses proved a shock to Boothby's adversaries. The Duke of Newcastle had earlier informed the new governor, Dominic Daly, that a validating act was being rushed through Parliament at Westminster to revive all the South Australian legislation that the judge had put in doubt.[84] He had referred the addresses to the law officers, W. Atherton and Roundell Palmer. Their careful opinion sought to set both a conclusory and didactic path between the two sides.[85] They noted that the Supreme Court had the power (certainly the liberty) 'to satisfy itself of the legal validity of any Act of the Colonial Legislature, to provisions which it is called upon to administer.' The letter also indicated that the fact that an Act assented to by the governor was 'left to its operation by Her Majesty would not affect the question of its validity.' On repugnancy the law officers pointed to difficulty in drawing a line between 'fundamental and non-fundamental English law,' warning that judges 'should not ... be astute to discover repugnancy,' but only in cases that admitted of 'no reasonable doubt.' They were not impressed with Boothby's argument that governors had no right to judge the 'urgent necessity' of applying statutes immediately on vice-regal assent. There was, the lawyers maintained, no reason to doubt the validity of the South Australian Constitution Act per se, but noted that fresh imperial validating legislation would cure any lingering problems. It was their opinion that the local Parliament had an undoubted power to establish courts of justice, and that a single judge was bound to 'conform his own judgment to the decision, on the same point of the Supreme Court of which he is a member.' On the central question of Boothby's removal, they counselled against disciplining him:

> We have to observe, that, although Mr Boothby has in some instances, as it appears to us, mistaken the law (as for example, with reference to the Real Property Act, which we think not invalid, on the ground which he rests its invalidity, the Governor's assent being contrary to the Royal Instructions) yet, in some other respects he has been right; and the fault has been with the Governor in not 'reserving' Acts for the Royal assent which were expressly required by Statute to be so reserved. Moreover, the 'Houses of Parliament' in the addresses by which her Majesty is prayed to remove the Judge were not in strictness, when they so addressed the Crown, a lawful Parliament, although they either have been, or shortly will be, legalized from the beginning; and under these circumstances, we think that the Crown would not be well-advised to accede to the Addresses.[86]

Atherton and Palmer did add an important postscript that they had no doubt that 'the Crown might properly remove a Judge on the Address of both Houses, if satisfied that, owing to his perversity or habitual disregard of judicial propriety, the administration might be practically obstructed by his continuance in office.' In short, the advice urged judicial caution in the use of the repugnancy power, indicated to Boothby that a number of his objections to local legislation were specious, and warned of the possible adverse consequences of a pattern of judicial obstructionism, but concluded that mistakes at law were not sufficient by themselves to warrant a judge's removal, and that he had justifiably exposed a degree of slovenliness in executive administration of the colony.

The noble duke accepted the law officers' report and informed the governor that the past errors in the process of approving legislation, especially the Electoral Act, and their adverse effects on subsequent legislation would be cured by remedial imperial legislation.[87] On the matter of the status of colonial supreme courts in relation to local legislatures he was blunt: '[The] courts should exercise their functions in entire independence ... the principal guarantee of this independence is to be found in the assurance that a Judge once appointed will not be displaced without the reasonable concurrence of an authority wholly removed from all local and temporary influences.' Then, in a confusing passage, Newcastle indicated that under the law of South Australia the power of removal was entrusted to 'Her Majesty acting on the advice of Her Ministers in Great Britain,' while also musing that both Houses of the South Australian Parliament might petition the Queen to remove a judge, 'if satisfied that owing to his perversity, or habitual disregard of judicial propriety, the administration of justice might be practically obstructed by his continuance in office.' The latter might include 'undue rigidity in a Judge's rulings.' He provided no direction on how these two ideas were to be reconciled in particular cases.[88] His missive concluded that it was not appropriate to remove Justice Boothby from office. 'The Queen would not adopt this "grave responsibility" ... without satisfactory evidence that dismissal is proper.'

Boothby's Direct Challenge to Responsible Government

If the Colonial Office and its legal advisers believed this decision would be treated seriously by the man at the centre of the storm, they and the South Australian government and settler population were to be sorely disappointed. For someone who could be as picayune as Judge Boothby in his examination of legislation when it served his purpose, he had a developed a capacity for ignoring or selectively reading official communications. This was true of those from London containing legal advice the Colonial Office might be expected to follow. It is perhaps not idle to suggest that he may have felt that his patron's letter to the governor was a sufficient shield for further interrogation by him of local legislation. In one particular, he was 'hoist on his own petard.' In response to his continued griping about Hanson's appointment, London informed him that he would have to appeal his unsuccessful challenge to the governor's actions to the Judicial Committee, bearing the costs himself. At that point he changed tack.[89]

Boothby found another embarrassing example of the government's failure to respect the Constitution Act, this time in the matter of deficient signatures confirming public appointments. The South Australian Parliament again had to bring in remedial legislation to cure the defect.[90] Aided by his colleague Gwynne, whose conservative proclivities the Torrens system continued to offend, the Court placed a roadblock in the way of Parliament's attempt to repeal the 1841 Registration of Deeds Act. In *Driffield v. Torrens* they accepted the convoluted argument that the repeal of the Act amounted to an amendment to the Constitution Act, because it denied those whose land was registered under the old system a vote under the Electoral Act.[91] Property ownership was a condition of the franchise at that time. Any amendment to the Constitution required an absolute majority in Parliament in favour, which the new Deeds Registration Act lacked. Newcastle, in ordering yet another validating act to cure this problem, showed his impatience with the South Australian administration's shortcomings in adhering to proper procedures.[92] He wrote, 'It is not proper or desirable that the statute book of this country should be encumbered with enactments which are only required to extricate colonial governments and legislatures from the consequences of their own irregularity or inadvertence, especially when this irregularity consists in an omission on the part of the legislature to conform to rules of its own making. Your Government must therefore clearly understand that it is their province to see that the rules required by law in the process of legislation are constantly kept in view and carefully observed, and, if those rules are to be productive of inconvenience, to submit to the legislature measures for their amendment.'[93]

Although Boothby's cavils with local legislation were becoming more and more contrived, he outdid himself in *Auld v. Murray*, yet another title registration case. While Hanson and now even Gwynne were of the view that the imperial validating legislation had achieved its purpose in reviving the amended Real Property Act, their colleague dissented. He argued that not only was this Act invalid, but also all other South Australian legislation, because the Parliament had never existed in law as a duly constituted body.[94] Both Houses of Parliament in Adelaide, frustrated at both past judicial obstructionism and its future threat, and mindful of the secretary of state's recent strictures, prepared new addresses to Westminster. These, while avoiding the issue of Boothby's removal from office, set out their grievances against the Supreme Court. The House of Assembly's petition put it poignantly in praying that Her Majesty 'will relieve us of this enormous evil unknown to England's law, to wit, the power claimed by our judges to declare laws passed by Parliament of this Province illegal.'[95]

The parlous state of the judge's finances continued. South Australia Banking Company records reveal that, despite pressure from local officials of the institution, he had not cleared his indebtedness. By early

1863 the bank's Adelaide manager was writing to its London board that he was determined to get tough with the judge by demanding that he pay down his debt, with payments every month. The board's reply praised the manager for his arrangement with the jurist for 'closing the discreditable and long outstanding debts to the Bank.' Later that spring when the judge craved an overdraft that the acting manager had refused, the latter reported that things had not improved, noting that Boothby's monthly salary cheque could not cover payments on his existing debt. In October 1864, the manager, prefacing his remarks by mentioning the 'vagaries' of the judge's finances before he left England, reported pessimistically that he doubted that his accumulated debt could be satisfactorily adjusted in his lifetime. The board once again encouraged its local employee to continue with 'judicious and temperate measures' to press for periodical reduction of Boothby's debt, while refusing further loans and acceptance of 'any family accommodation paper.' That the bank probably had the measure of this particular debtor is evident in the fact that the board added, 'There can be no wish to feed the love of personal scandal by reducing a Judge to extremities or placing him in any humiliating position.'[96]

In May 1864 the case of *The Queen at the Instance of Samuel Mills v. Hughes and Stirling* (the *Moonta Mines* case) reached the Supreme Court. In this action between competing claimants to the mining property, and Hughes and Stirling whose find was the one registered, the defendants argued that the writ of scire facias, which the plaintiff was seeking in order to compel them to release the leases as records relating to the claim, could not issue. This was because the attorney general had not approved it. Boothby took this point one step further by opining that the writ could not issue because there was no attorney general in the province (as there was no chief justice), legislation establishing both office being invalid. In the result Boothby and Gwynne ruled against the plaintiff, on the much narrower ground that the leases were not records of the court and thus fell outside the reach of the writ sought.[97] Hague asserts that Boothby was delighted at the case being appealed to the Privy Council, because he could take the opportunity to transmit his own views to that body at someone else's cost.[98] He did this by appending to his judgment in the case 'a resume of his opinions upon the invalidity of the Constitution Act and of all subsequent legislation, and upon the "non-existence" of the Attorney General and the Chief Justice.'

There were suspicions at the time that Boothby favoured the de fendants in the *Moonta Mines* case in a partial way. Peter Moore's ongoing research reveals that, shortly after that decision was rendered, in September 1864, Boothby's son, George, approached the South Australian Bank and sought to renew a bill covering the judge's old debts. He pleaded for time until the payment of the new Moonta dividend took place. This might suggest that income from the shares that he owned was being used to pay off what Boothby owed to his creditors, and that the jurist had an interest in the fortunes of the mine and its sponsors.[99]

Meanwhile in London the Colonial Office referred the matter of judicial subversion of the South Australian Parliament's lawmaking authority to the law officers. Attorney General Roundell Palmer and Solicitor General Richard Collier reported back that the time had come for the imperial Parliament to intervene to provide further explicit power to colonial legislatures to determine their legislative agendas. They advised, 'It will be very expedient to pass an Imperial Act for the purpose of empowering the Legislature of that colony (and of any other colonies or colony which may be in like circumstances) to alter its own Constitution; and, at the same time, to confirm absolutely all South Australian Acts which down to this time have received the assent of Her Majesty, or of the Governor in her Majesty's behalf.'[100] A draft of the Colonial Laws Validity Act was sent to Adelaide for comment, which drew the support of both Governor Daly and Chief Justice Hanson, although the former prophetically commented that he doubted whether Justice Boothby would be satisfied.[101]

The viceroy was all too correct. Boothby and Gwynne had been cutting a swathe through the criminal justice system. In the first place, they invalidated the Local Court system, which operated without juries, as repugnant to the laws of England in cases of felony convictions.[102] The judges then added insult to injury and undermined the system completely by concluding that there was no Local Court at all, putting into suspense all the summonses issued by that body over the previous six years.[103] It was considered doubtful whether local legislation amending the Court of Appeals Act so that appeals could be taken from the Supreme Court on these matters would survive the two jurists' attack. It was into what Williams has described as 'the general legal mayhem which the *Dawes* decision had caused' that the Colonial Laws Validity Act dropped.[104] The enactment sought to narrow the exercise of a repugnancy power in colonial courts to imperial statutes applicable to that colony or British colonies in general. Section 5 of the Act put beyond doubt the validity of colonial legislation assented to locally contrary to instructions, and section 5 the power of local legislatures to establish, abolish, or reconstitute courts of judicature. With South Australia, section 7 of the Act sought to put beyond doubt the validity of all legislation from that province, past and present, that had received royal or the governor's assent.

Boothby Takes on the Empire

True to form, Boothby, joined by Gwynne, concluded in *Walsh v. Goodall* that section 7 of the Colonial Laws Validity Act that purported to protect all local legislation, validly made, did not save the Registration of Deeds Act (1862), which had been found invalid, because it had not passed by an absolute majority required under the Constitution Act of 1855–6.[105] The Court of Appeals decided otherwise. The *Register*, with calculated irony, announced, 'On Saturday Mr Justice Boothby commenced operations against the new Validating Act. Let not legislators, Imperial or colonial, think they are going to escape the clutches of this astute judge.'[106]

In what seemed now like an exercise in sheer obstructionism, Boothby began firing in all directions. In May 1866 when Randolph Stowe, a leading Queen's counsel, appeared before him, Boothby demanded to see his licence to prosecute and evidence that he had taken silk.[107] More menacingly, that same month he asserted that all indictments presented before him must be quashed, because there was no legally appointed attorney general in the province.[108] This move effectively scotched the Court's criminal session as the judge would dismiss every indictment in his courtroom, and cases collapsed in consequence.

Attorney General James Boucaut had represented the challengers in the *Moonta Mines* case in his private capacity and had no love for Boothby. He and William Wearing, the Crown solicitor, sent lengthy reports to the governor pointing to the judge's 'extraordinary behaviour.' They rehearsed the litany of complaints from legislators and members of the profession whom, in their opinion, the judge had treated with everything from condescension to contempt. Both the Legislative Council and the assembly passed motions praying for his removal on various grounds, including the fact that 'he obstructs the course of justice by perversity and an habitual disregard of judicial propriety, and has delivered judgments and dicta not in accordance with the law.'[109] Governor Daly transmitted the addresses to the Colonial Office, point ing to the near unanimity of feeling of members of both houses against the judge.[110]

The South Australian Parliament's actions did not satisfy the requirement of a joint address in the sense used in the Constitution Act of 1855. This would surely have required a hearing with Boothby present. The judge certainly thought so in his correspondence with the Colonial Office.[111] However, given the earlier confusing musings of the Duke of Newcastle, they may have assumed that the matter would be dealt with by the imperial Cabinet. Lord Carnarvon, secretary of state for the colonies in the new Tory government prevaricated, indicating that there were several legal questions relating to the case that needed reference to the Privy Council.[112] Mr Secretary also chided the governor about the less than precise way in which the charges against the judge had been formulated. He added that, if the local concern about Boothby's behaviour made his removal an urgent matter, then section 2 of Burke's Act could be invoked to deal with him, recognizing, of course, that under that same legislation the judge would have a right of appeal to the council. If that was the route taken, then the government of South Australia would be expected to have made their charges 'adequate and precise.' The Colonial Office wrote the Privy Council seeking its advice. The document set out the elements of the problem in Adelaide, pointing to the novelty and importance of this case concerning the proposed removal of a judge holding his position 'during good behaviour in a Colony possessing what is called Responsible Government – and in virtue of an enactment framed in terms of the Imperial Act of Parliament relating to the removal of Judges in this country' (the Act of Settlement).[113]

In Adelaide, meanwhile, relations within the Court were going from bad to worse. Boothby launched fresh attacks on the status of the attorney general and then the chief justice appearing in Equity trials, effectively holding himself out as the only legitimate personification of the Court.[114] The press had a field day, with the *Advertiser* joining the fray and pointing to the surreal muddle in the administration of justice that the judge's antics was causing: 'His Honor, under the plea of legal obligation is now literally at war with every institution in the colony. In rejecting the recently-passed Equity Act he pours contempt upon the enlarged authorities given to us by special imperial enactment. In declaring that there is no Attorney General, he again seeks to undermine the Constitution, fortified as it is by Imperial validation, and he practically gives free license to crime, which – in many of its forms – can only be punished through the intervention of a State officer, whose appointment the judge denies.'[115]

When Boothby continued his attacks on his brother judges, alleging that their appointments were invalid, Chief Justice Hanson concluded that the time had come to make a public statement regarding Boothby's tactics. He described them as designed to obstruct 'the course of business here, to compel the Government of this colony to try the question [in the Privy Council] of the Constitution of the Court not at his own expense – as the Imperial Government said he was bound to do – but at the expense of the colony.'[116] Hanson, with Gwynne's support, adjourned the Court until the next term, leaving Boothby trying stubbornly but unsuccessfully to continue proceedings before an assemblage of journalists. The two jurists wrote to the governor on 24 April 1867 letting him know that Boothby's attacks on them were not only 'personally offensive and insulting to ourselves,' but also 'inconsistent with the equal administration of justice.'[117]

As the Colonial Office promised no speedy resolution to the growing chaos in the justice system, and because of Boothby's blatant ignoring of the Colonial Laws Validity Act, Governor Daly and his Executive Council determined to take the judicial bull by the horns. They decided to invoke Burke's Act of 1782, as Carnarvon had suggested, and amove the judge under section 2 of that statute for misbehaviour. Attorney General Boucaut drafted charges against Boothby. They asserted that the judge was guilty of conduct and language disrespectful and obstructive of the Court of Appeals; refusal to recognize the Parliament's authority to make and administer law for the colony; language from the bench insulting the legislature, government, and institutions of the province; verbal attacks on his judicial colleagues and denial of their authority; and permitting his private and personal feelings to compromise the fair and impartial administration of justice.[118] Governor Daly announced an inquiry by the Executive Council and informed Boothby of the charges against him.[119]

When the hearing opened on 24 June 1867, Boothby, who attended with his son, Josiah Boothby, objected to the hearing proceeding with attorneys present, indicated that he did not recognize the charges levelled at him, and demanded that all correspondence between the governor and secretary of state be produced to him.[120] Over Boothby's protest, after the production of the documents requested and a short adjournment, the hearing proceeded. The judge withdrew after two days to prepare an argument on the jurisdictional issue.[121] The inquiry heard from leading counsel, Randolph Stowe and William Wearing, and from Hanson and Gwynne on the reasons for their letter to Governor Daly on their dispute with Boothby.

Ironically, it was Gwynne, Boothby's erstwhile ally, who came over as the most depressed by the experience: 'I got sick of it, and I did seriously think of sending in my resignation, but I determined not to sit with him any longer. I found that I was doing no good to the Colony, that the Court was being degraded, and business arrested: and that while in one view it was absurd, that it yet acted very seriously. I felt that I was compromising myself in submitting to it – not that I personally cared, but because the interests of the Colony and of the suitors, and the dignity of the Judicial Office were suffering, and I determined to make a stand.'[122]

Boothby reappeared on the final day of the inquiry with a brief addressed to Governor Daly in which he challenged Daly's jurisdiction under the Burke's Act.[123] First, he argued disingenuously that that process for removal had become inoperative because the South Australia Constitution Act had replaced 'Governor and Council' with a 'representative Parliament.' Second, he claimed that he had been denied natural justice, because the tribunal hearing the charges and applying the Act had previously 'given judgment and opinions on accusations substantially the same as those now before them.' Last, he complained that there was no provision for his expenses at the inquiry, while the government funded inquiry counsel. Boothby was not left long to speculate on his fate, as he was called back into the inquiry and advised that Daly and the council had no doubts about their jurisdiction and intended to proceed with the charges. Boothby gave notice of appeal and left the hearing, warning that he would have to be removed physically from the bench 'by the Tipstaff of the Court, or someone else.'[124] That same day the governor and council ordered the amoval of 'Benjamin Boothby from his said office of Second Judge of the said Supreme Court of the said Province and Colony' and formally advised the judge of the decision.[125]

In the result Boothby did not require physical carrying out of court, and calm descended on the colony, as the sides prepared for the next round in the Privy Council. As was true throughout his career, Boothby had his supporters who criticized the action of the executive as oppressive and based on 'more gossip and hearsay.'[126] However, any further proceedings were precluded by Boothby's death on 21 June 1868, at the age of sixty-five. The *Advertiser* noted in an obituary that Boothby had been sick for months, although not house bound. He suffered, the paper reported, from heart affection 'on which dropsy supervened.'[127] The paper, while asserting that the removal from office had been justified, predicted that 'the old aspersions will die and that our readers will endeavour only to remember what was favourable in his character and disposition. Death ought to heal all strifes and to settle all misunderstandings.' And so the remarkable shoot-out between Boothby and the South Australian executive and Parliament ended, without any final determination of the merits of each side's arguments on the substance or process of the judge's amoval.

Making Sense of the Boothby Saga

What are we to make of this remarkable convoluted saga, which John Williams has observed 'reads more like a colonial farce than a chapter in State legal history'?[128] Does it betoken, as Peter Howell suggests, attempts by 'Whiggish historians' to shroud the achievements of a principled colonial conservative?[129] Howell believes that Boothby would have won his appeal to the Judicial Committee. Alternatively, is the view of Castles and Harris closer to the truth, that Boothby received his just desserts for his obstructionism of the administration of justice and what amounted 'to a fundamental attack on the powers of the colonial government' under the new constitutional order?[130]

There were several factors at work during the early period of Boothby's tenure that might be said to support his scepticism (if that is what motivated him) on the exact extent of repugnancy. Comment was made earlier on the fluid limitations of the repugnancy power insofar as it was used by the colonial judiciary during this period. Earlier, the repugnancy power, as authorized in the Australian colonies, clearly reflected British sentiment that colonial law should accord with that of England as far as possible, although, as is evident in the Montagu and Willis cases, London grew weary of judges who used the power too liberally. The grant of responsible government, with the shift in responsibility for the development of local law to the colonial legislatures, promised to provide greater leeway for crafting local laws to fit domestic conditions. If, as suggested earlier, repugnancy in these possessions related to conflict with imperial statutes dealing with the particular colony or the empire in general, then the only question in most cases left hanging was whether the law in question offended fundamental principles of English law. This was the English law officers' view in their advice to the Duke of Newcastle in 1862.[131]

Before that authoritative statement, it might be argued in Boothby's favour that the matter was open to interpretation. Where the judge was on the strongest ground before the early 1860s was his musings about the effects of the less than careful processes for the initiation and implementation of colonial legislation in South Australia. Despite the angst of legislators over his dark ruminations, usually cast in the form of obiter dicta, about the invalidity of local legislation, he had a point. Indeed, so fundamental was the institutional error – the invalidity of the Electoral Act upon which the legitimacy of the Constitution Act and by extension every enactment passed by Parliament depended – that Westminster took remedial action to cure the problem in 1862, and again in 1865. Furthermore, one could make a case that some pieces of legislation, the provenance of which he doubted, were repugnant in the sense of offending fundamental principles of English Law – such as the Coroners Act, with its looser approach to the taking and recording of evidence. It is worth pointing out too, as Castles has noted, that Boothby's developed nose for sniffing out errors and miscues in the legislative history of the colony 'brought him into direct conflict with strongly entrenched political and economic interests.'[132] To the extent that he refused to bow to pressures to overlook such foibles, he could be said to exemplify the values of judicial independence.

After 1862, it is far more difficult to describe Boothby's tactics as anything other than purposely obstructionist, even malevolent. No less an institution than the imperial Parliament, which enjoyed insulation from direct challenges by the judiciary to its lawmaking capacity in Britain, clearly intended to cure and assumed that it had remedied South Australia's legislative stalemate. Not so the judge, who concluded that he could ignore London's actions to put the constitution on an even keel and attack any legislation of which he disapproved. Moreover, he continued a campaign of sniping at his two colleagues, who he alleged were not entitled to sit as judges, and in the result destabilized the administration of justice. What was increasingly viewed as a calculated campaign to have his own way, whatever the cost, became a scandal after the enactment of the Colonial Laws Validity Act, which not only clearly limited the scope of repugnancy, confining its area of application to direct conflict with imperial legislation applicable to the colony, but also endeavoured to put paid to any residual judicial concern about the legitimacy of the South Australian constitution. Boothby continued on his merry way, declaring local legislation invalid and taking every opportunity to silence judicial and legal officers whose appointment he refused to recognize. Even among the judicial stormy petrels that fill the pages of this book, Benjamin Boothby stands out as an intensely vainglorious and perverse individual.

The fact that Gwynne, the third judge, whom Boothby demeaned because of his qualification as a solicitor, concurred with Boothby in his reaction to colonial legislation, even after 1865, requires comment. Did this alliance reflect similar personal idiosyncrasies of his colleague, or of a more principled stance? Gwynne was a colonial conservative who was on record as opposing representative democracy, and thus not impressed with the new constitutional order, or reformative legislation after 1855.[133] In this he was not different from lawyers and judges in several other colonies of the British Empire during that era. Moreover, he strongly opposed the Torrens system of land registration, which, in tune with Boothby, he seemed set on scuppering. This stand may have reflected nostalgia and an animus towards new non-judicial administrative regimes that sometimes afflicted nineteenth-century, conservative jurists.[134] As one who had been an active buyer and seller of land, as well as a developer, his interest in preserving a complex system may also have had a self-interested slant. Gwynne's stand on local courts and the abolition of juries in felony prosecutions may have stemmed from principled attachment to the claimed protection of the individual traditionally associated with jury trials (by contrast, Boothby had no love for juries in Supreme Court trials). Gwynne's brief record of opposition to local legislation after the enactment of the Colonial Laws Validity Act can be explained, if at all, only on the tortuous ground that some of the Torrens legislation had already been declared invalid and could not be revived by that Act of the Westminster Parliament. The fact that he ultimately broke ranks with Boothby indicates that he concluded that his colleague was being wilfully obstructive and subversive in his decisions. It is noticeable that Gywnne avoided being a target of personal attacks for his judgments by his more liberal opponents (even though they undoubtedly disagreed with him at law), and remained a judge until 1881, when he retired.

There are enough other examples across the empire of conservative judges enjoying long and praiseworthy tenures, even during reformative eras, that 'Boothby as principled colonial conservative' does not ring true.[135] The more credible conclusion about this judge is that he was or became so convinced of the superiority of his own judgment on the constitution, law, and justice in the colony that he was incapable of entertaining any views other than his own, and impervious to advice about his conduct from even the highest imperial officials. As Castles has suggested, these attitudes may have fed on a basic disdain for the colonials with whom he was 'forced' to live and work – an attitude that, as we have seen, afflicted other problem jurists in the Antipodes and elsewhere.[136]

If this assessment is correct, what, if any, might have been the motivations for his increasingly bizarre behaviour? We do not know sufficient detail of his professional, personal, and family life before his departure for Australia to know whether any of the later traits of character were present. From the sketchy information we possess, he seems to have attracted favourable comment for his work as a barrister, was recognized as having Whig reformist sensibilities and a strong commitment to impartial justice, and impressed several men of consequence in law and government in England. He took pride in his family, by repute a close-knit group.[137] We are aware that his large family was a significant drain on his modest financial resources, which meant that he started his sojourn in Adelaide seriously indebted. Apart from concluding from the South Australian evidence that he was by nature pigheaded and unduly self-centred, the possibility arises that he had developed health problems that at least partially explain his behaviour. Castles notes that Boothby suffered from bouts of rheumatic gout, which, if it afflicted him regularly, might explain an advanced degree of tetchiness on his part.[138] The heart condition that felled him might also have been a factor if longstanding, and helped create ongoing anxieties. Other possibilities include undiagnosed neurotic or psychological conditions. Alas, we will probably never know whether physical or mental ailments, or both, were at the root of his problems.

Peter Moore has raised the interesting issue of whether Boothby's shaky financial state contributed to his discontents. He was in debt before he arrived in the colony and never got out of it before his death. As we have seen, there is also evidence that he found in favour of a party (the Hughes-Stirling group) in which business he or his close-knit family had a share interest, the dividends from which were being used to deal with his indebtedness. Was he perhaps using his campaign of threat and bluster to shroud his impecunious state? By some strange logic, did he believe that his patrons, such as Newcastle, would protect him, or that his bid for the chief justiceship, if successful, would add to his income while shielding him from his indebtedness and possible conflict of interest complaints? The answers to these questions must remain speculative until this field is tilled further, and require research on the state of judicial ethics during this period. However, this line of inquiry may provide a suggestive new dimension to the Boothby story.

So the motivations of Benjamin Boothby as a judge remain something of an enigma. The other issue is the institutional one of the processes employed to remove Boothby from office. Elizabeth Olsson has argued that the three attempts by the colonial executive and the Parliament of South Australia to get rid of him were unfair or improperly carried out, and that denial of natural justice might have worked in his favour before the Privy Council.[139] My own guess is that, with the cases of *Montagu* and *Willis* within recent memory, the Judicial Committee had ample precedent for finding against him.

Whoever is right, in the course of the Boothby saga the Colonial Office had muddied the waters over the process for dismissing a judge in a colony enjoying responsible government. By 1860 it was clear that Burke's Act could be invoked legitimately to remove a troublesome jurist from a colony where the judge was appointed and continued his tenure at pleasure. The Judicial Committee's opinion in *Willis* and *Montagu* put that beyond doubt.[140] The British colonies that were granted responsible government all opted for addresses of local legislatures to Her Majesty as the mechanism for moving against judges now appointed during good behaviour. This was the colonial equivalent of the process in the Act of Settlement of 1701 for English judges. Alas, there was uncertainty in English practice about how that process worked in a jurisdiction with a bicameral legislature.[141] As the Boothby case shows, there was also confusion in the Colonial Office on how the provision for removal in the new colonial constitutions related to section 3 of the English statute.

Colonial Office responses in Boothby's case point to residual concerns in London about leaving colonial judges entirely exposed to the vagaries of colonial politics, even in the era of responsible government. This explains why the Duke of Newcastle introduced some confusion into the mix by arguing that final authority in such cases lay with the Queen advised by her British ministers, but that in the appropriate case the two colonial Houses of Parliament might act to remove a judge. There was no clear indication that these were complementary parts of the same process.

Lord Carnarvon added a further element of complication in 1867 by indicating that there was a third process for getting rid of a judge, where a quick local decision was needed – the invocation of Burke's Act. If Parliament in Adelaide got it wrong, they did so in part for lack of any integrated policy on the matter in Westminster. What is certain is that Burke's Act survived the advent of responsible government in settler colonies. Strangely, there seems to have been reticence about mentioning the much older expedient of a colony with a legislature petitioning the Privy Council to rid it of a troublesome judge, the process used in the *Boulton* case. The Judicial Committee was to make clear in 1870 that it did not favour taking cases at first instance like this, which may reflect more general reservations about using the process at the time, even though it provided the imperial authorities with the final say in the fate of a colonial judge.[142]

The detailed stories so far reflect the experience of judges in territories that, whatever their earlier demographic make-up, in the course of the nineteenth century experienced increasing European immigration that eventually resulted in a majority settler population.[143] As the move towards responsible government in these possessions demonstrates, London treated them as worthy of an increasing degree of self-government. Political and legal realities were different in multiracial colonies in which Europeans remained a minority (often a small minority) of the population. We now turn to the experience of activist judges in several of those jurisdictions between 1800 and 1900.

9

The Perils of the Colonial Judiciary: The Incubus of Slavery in the West Indian Colonies and West Africa, 1800–1834

Slavery and the Administration of Justice in the British Empire

In the early spring of 1809 George Smith, formerly chief justice of Grenada, full of enthusiasm and good intentions, set sail from England for a new judicial assignment in Trinidad. Just over two years later, in March 1811, stripped of several of his judicial functions in the administration of justice on the island by Governor Thomas Hislop, Smith left the colony under cover of night, to sail back to England. His objective was to reach London before his nemesis and to argue his case to the imperial authorities.[1]

Judicial appointment from Britain to its Caribbean colonies was particularly risky for individuals who found difficulty with the deeply imbedded culture of slavery, and who were ready to hew to an independent line in their administration and application of the law. In these jurisdictions it was not simply the terms of their appointment at pleasure that jurists of this ilk had to fear. There was also a self-serving and suspicious local power structure, wedded for two centuries to the necessity of slave or slave-like labour to work the plantations that were the economic lifeblood of the several colonial economies, and the source of the plantation owners' and local merchants' personal wealth. Planters in these territories trumpeted the rule of law from time to time in disputes with London over *their* 'rights as freeborn Englishmen.' As

Andrew O'Shaughnessy has wryly remarked, 'the colonists saw every governor as a potential reincarnation of Charles I and James II.'[2] However, that vision of legality and justice had no purchase at all for the slave population, and very little for the small 'freed slave' and 'free coloured' populations of these territories. It was an inversion of the rule of law in any liberal sense. Slaves were subject to largely uninhibited disciplinary discretion of their owners, and the parodies of justice represented by the slave codes and slave courts.[3] In Richard Dunn's succinct and pungent comment, 'The slave laws legitimized a state of war between blacks and whites, sanctified rigid segregation, and institutionalized an early warning system against slave revolts. After all, the price of tyranny is eternal vigilance.'[4]

'Free coloureds,' the term applied to freed slaves, as well as the free offspring of mixed-race parents, were not free in a civic sense, subject, as they were, to discrimination in terms of the franchise, the giving of evidence, jury service, and educational and economic opportunity.[5]

The institution of slavery and its demands permeated the whole pattern of life and the institutions of these territories – from colonial governors who wanted to keep on the right side of the planter elite, to colonial officials subject to their legislative whim, to magistrates dependent on their patronage, and a local legal profession reliant for its bread and butter on the colonial government or the commercial needs of the wealthy, white population. This made for a set of overlapping and incestuous political and social relationships in close-knit communities that lived in mortal fear of the majority population that they exploited, and bridled at any sort of criticism of how they governed themselves and went about their lives. Even sworn enemies on other issues were only too ready to 'bury the hatchet' when the slave systems were under attack from within or outside these possessions.

As we have seen in chapter 3, reports commissioned by the Colonial Office in the 1820s noted that in half the jurisdictions in the West Indies, chief justices had not been professionally trained as lawyers, and that in colonies where they did have such training, the associate justices lacked it.[6] The latter, said the commissioners, were capable at times of undermining the authority of a lawyer chief justice. In time, when appointments of legally trained associates were made, if their experience at the bar was in the colony, partiality to local elite interests could become a source of friction between them and a senior judge appointed from a British bar. Moreover, a jurist dispatched from Britain, over the claims of a local aspirant to preferment, could expect hostility from the local profession. Finally, because slavery had existed for so long in the British Caribbean, its advocates had developed a powerful lobbying machine to ensure that its voice was heard in the halls of power in London. The formal abolition of the slave trade, and later of slavery throughout the British Empire, while it reflected a diminution of planters' influence in London, did not remove lobbying as an episodic powerful force in law and politics in the West Indies.[7]

There were, it is true, cases in which judges appointed to West Indian colonies suffered discipline for prosaic reasons, or on grounds that had nothing to do with race. Chief Justice Musson of St Lucia was removed from office in 1832 for failing to hold court for eight months after his appointment.[8] During the mid-1840s, one of his successors, Chief Justice Reddie, was terminated and found guilty by a judicial inquiry of writing anonymous letters to the local newspaper, signed 'The Sign of Polycarp.' These missives libelled the lieutenant governor, Arthur Torrens, and the Anglican bishop.[9] Richard Temple, the long-serving chief justice of British Honduras, was fired in 1861 for hearing a case involving a bankrupt development company to which he was indebted, and having provided paid advice to that company and several others seeking to engage in resource extraction in the colony.[10] Far more interesting and instructive, however, are those instances in which jurists were penalized for seeking to mitigate the effects of slavery or indenture.

The British Capture and Early Administration of Trinidad

British forces captured Trinidad, traditionally a neglected and underdeveloped outpost of the Spanish Empire in the Americas, in 1797.[11] The British government vacillated for the next fourteen years over the form of government and the legal system for this new possession. In the meantime, some institutions of the previous Spanish regime and Spanish law continued on the island.[12] The hiatus reflected both the distractions of the French wars and British reservations about granting representative assemblies in newly won territories, based on its less than happy experience with Quebec and Grenada.[13] Also, humanitarian reformers in Britain, not least the influential lawyer-activist James Stephen Sr, subjected the imperial government to increasing pressure to curb the extension of slavery on the island and to substitute a system of free labour.[14] The first British governor, Thomas Picton, had ruled as a tyrant, imposing harsh penalties on malefactors, both slaves and British soldiers. Moreover, he had encouraged the extension of slavery on the island by British planters and Royalist French refugees from Haiti with their inbred fears of slave insurrection and slave 'magic.'[15] A short period of commission government between 1802 and 1803 followed, reflecting anti-slavery criticism in Britain, but ended in dismal failure and recriminations (both Picton and his major antagonist, the humanitarian William Fullarton, were commissioners). For the next seven years, under the governorship of Thomas Hislop, the constitutional hiatus continued, as the distractions of warfare with Napoleon exercised the energies of British ministers. Hislop recommended a nominated legislative council in 1804 when asked by London to advise on a constitution for the island, but his counsel had fallen on deaf ears.[16]

The Tumultuous Tenure of George Smith as Chief *Oidor*

In 1808, the chief justice of Grenada, George Smith, arrived in London to look for advancement and a better paying position. Smith had built up some credits for himself by his consolidation and publishing of the statutes of the island.[17] He had written to his patron, Lord Castlereagh, secretary of state for the colonies, in March of that year, arguing strongly for the appointment of professional judges in the West Indies and the consolidation of smaller colonies under a single chief justice with an annual salary of £4,000, reflecting the demands of the job, as he saw it. He envisioned Trinidad as the judicial centre of a cluster of islands.[18] The government shelved this idea, but after months of procrastination over what to do about the island's constitution, Smith persuaded Secretary Castlereagh to allow him to write his own job description as chief *oidor* (chief justice) of Trinidad.[19] The description did not stop with the chief justice's mantle. He advocated that Spanish law should continue to govern in the possession, and that Spanish legal institutions that had fallen into abeyance after the conquest be revived. He divined that under Spanish rule in the Americas a considerable degree of power was vested in the *Audiencia,* the final court of appeal in the colonies, but with other significant functions in the administration, including advisory and legislative roles.[20] That body comprised representatives of the *oidors* (civil justices), *alcades* (criminal law magistrates), and *fiscales* (legal officers representing the state's interest, especially in financial litigation). Smith also noted that, although the viceroy (the senior representative of the Spanish Crown) was president of the *Audiencia*, this role had more recently in Spanish colonial practice devolved on the regent, a judicial figure who was the effective head of the court and manager of its business. The holder of that position could attend any chamber of the courts he desired and serve as judge in both civil and criminal cases. He also acted as viceroy in the absence or on the death of the incumbent. Smith's job description vested in him the functions of the former *Audiencia* (combining the roles of chief *oidor*, chief *alcade*, and *fiscale*) as well as the powers of regent.[21] His remit gave him both original and appellate jurisdiction. In the absence of Spanish judges and lawyers who had departed the territory after 1797, Smith had obviously concluded that the resurrection of Spanish judicial institutions required a firm and exclusive hand, namely his. At the apex of a revised system and subject only to an appeal to the Privy Council in London (ruling out an intermediate appeal to the governor, common in other British colonies), he would control and mould the administration of justice on the island. On receiving the general blessing of the English law officers for these blended responsibilities, Castlereagh approved Smith's commission, and the jurist hastened to the colony full of vim and vigour.[22]

Smith's potentially regal tenure as chief justice was to be an unhappy one. As James Millette notes, 'The new Chief Justice carried with him an aura of controversy. A man of undoubted ability he was unconnected to any local interest and he had the confidence of Government ministers who felt assured of his impartiality. He was a good observer and a good writer. He saw everything, missed nothing, and ... was an indefatigable correspondent. He had a lucid and penetrating style, and his lawyer's training enabled him to get directly to the heart of the most complicated problem. But he lacked finesse. He had the uncanny ability of being able to unite the most implacable enemies in opposition to himself on the very briefest acquaintance.'[23]

Governor Hislop greeted the chief justice with initial enthusiasm, craving a professional judge to advise him and take firm control of the justice system.[24] Smith reciprocated with plaudits of his own. Moreover, in his first year in office Smith went out of his way to emphasize his subordination to the governor. However, the aura of harmony dissipated quickly, as the terms and consequences of Smith's appointment began to sink in among the colonial elite. Millette suggests that, despite the chief justice's protestations, Hislop considered him a competitor, and by emphasizing the governor's administrative primacy the jurist wanted to make it clear that 'he would himself be left in the undisputed enjoyment of his awesome judicial prerogatives.'[25] Moreover, the fact that Smith's job description dislodged several existing office holders meant that his arrival generated hostility among members of the co lonial bureaucracy. John Nihell, a Roman Catholic Irishman who had settled in Trinidad under the Spanish regime and, as a lay person, Governor Picton had appointed chief judge, felt aggrieved that he was dislodged from office to make way for Smith, especially as initially he was not offered any other office in substitution.[26] For his part, Archibald Gloster found that as attorney general he had been largely divested of his functions by Smith's multifaceted appointment. The offer of chief justiceship of Grenada did not placate him for losing a well-paying position on his home turf. Nor did Smith's introduction of several Spanish lawyers from Caracas, to assist in the work of the courts, salve Gloster's distempers or those of other members of the bar.[27]

In due course the chief justice incurred the enmity of the British planter and merchant groupings on the island. By the latter part of 1809, Smith, strongly asserting his intention to insulate himself from any 'intimacy' with the community, was applying Spanish law with enthusiasm, especially in allowing creditors to recover debts.[28] Although merchants often brought these actions against planters, the line between the two was breaking down as merchants invested in land and bought on credit. The efficacy of Spanish law in the chief justice's hands in pursuing debtors was a shock to those who had assumed previously that they could hide behind it.[29] In his correspondence with London, he also made clear his opposition to the grant of a representative assembly and the introduction of English law on the island. The British Party, a well-organized group of British planters and merchants in the colony, and their agents in London were advocating these reforms, under the claim of the benefits of the British Constitution.[30] Smith, disdainful of the British members of the local community, believed such reforms would offend the political and legal sensibilities of the French and Spanish elite, and prove detrimental to the interests of the slave population.[31] For the moment he contented himself with the comforting but naive thought that the campaign was the work of an insignificant element in the community that was split in its aims. He reported, however, that he had reservations about the fortitude of the governor. Although the chief justice indicated that he admired Hislop, he harboured a concern that the governor lacked the stuff for standing up to the power elite.[32] One of Smith's major gripes in this missive was the laxity of the court officials with whom he had to work, a sign, in Milette's view, that 'the alienation of legal and judicial officers and [his] own isolation were already beginning to affect the administration of justice.'[33]

Early in 1810 the gulf between the chief justice and his enemies widened, and in the process he forfeited the governor's support. With an acting governor, Lieutenant General Henry Tolley, in place, while Hislop was on military service on Guadeloupe, Smith sought to consolidate his position within the colony and stifle the campaign for a British constitution.[34] The two men took measures to tighten up policing in the colony, issuing a diktat that made it an offence to discuss constitutional changes in public. When Matthew Gallagher, editor of the *Trinidad Weekly Courant*, a supporter of the campaign for British law and an assembly, continued to publish letters and comment on the issue, Smith summoned him to court and convicted him of publishing his paper without a licence under the relevant Spanish law.[35] When the editor refused to comply with an order to desist from printing, the judge imprisoned him. Smith continued his reforms by limiting the *alcades'* jurisdiction to Port of Spain and one other community, effectively turning rural justice over to the local commandants whom he expected to dispense it more efficiently.[36]

These measures reflected a belief in 'firmer government' that Smith felt was lacking and that he could supply even more effectively, if only he were given the reins of acting governor during what he describes as Hislop's 'proposed leave of absence.'[37] The chief justice reported the steps taken to the Colonial Office in lengthy and sometimes pungent correspondence in which he carefully elaborated his reasons for his antipathy to representative government and enthusiasm for Spanish law.[38] Representative government, he argued, was ill-suited to societies marked by the inequality of slavery, and ruled by small, unsophisticated, and paranoid white elites. In a multiracial colony it would also undercut the rights and privileges under Spanish law of the free coloured population, a larger segment of the population than in neighbouring British colonies. It was his view, too, that a government controlled by British settlers and merchants and a system of law that was alien to non-English-speaking settlers and their interests in both linguistic and cultural terms would compromise their interests. Spanish law administered by reformed and streamlined institutions of justice and firmly applied was, Smith argued, preferable to the alternative.[39]

The chief justice's actions early in 1810 played into the hands of the British Party, pressing hard their campaign for a British constitution. They now had a convenient lightning rod of 'judicial oppression' to strengthen the case for granting self-determination and freedom to the colonists.[40] Smith had miscalculated the effectiveness of this new cam paign for representative government under English law. His view that Governor Hislop was too accommodating to potential troublemakers among the colonists also proved to be misconceived. In March 1810 the chief executive returned to rapturous, self-serving plaudits by the colony's economic and social elite, claiming to be relieved from hardships under the interim regime and clamouring for representative government. Hislop, who had almost certainly been moving in this direction privately, now took the plunge, declaring himself publicly supportive of the introduction of a representative assembly and English law. In consequence the fur started to fly between him and Smith.[41]

The judge's opposition to representative government, his spirited attempt to adjudicate land law and debt cases using Spanish law, and his propensity to slam those who he felt were subverting his attempts to control and systematize the justice system made him increasingly unpopular within the British colonial community. The same was also true of some non-British settlers tiring of the never-ending debate on the political and legal future of the possession. For his part, Hislop became increasingly frustrated by what he saw as Smith's obstructionism on constitutional issues and heavy-handed treatment of critics, whether newspaper editors or litigants. The governor released Gallagher from prison and intervened in the case of the garrulous litigant William Lockhead, whom Smith had cited for contemptuous behaviour towards him personally.[42] Hislop and the council also called the chief justice to account for his handling of the debt case against Anthony Sablich, who had contested in a public notice an order authorized by Smith, without, he claimed, his consent, concerning other debts owed to him. The judge found Sablich in contempt of court and consigned him to the common jail. The Governor in Council, claiming ultimate authority in the justice system, concluded that Sablich had suffered an injustice and released him.[43] The majority of his council and the planter and merchant lobby in Trinidad and London firmly supported Hislop's approach.[44] The lobbyists were encouraging petitions in Trinidad in favour of a British constitution, as well as having members attend on British politicians to press their case.[45] Smith's actions became even a matter for comment in the British House of Commons through the efforts of Joseph Marryat, a member of Parliament who acted as agent for the colony in London.[46]

Not surprisingly the chief justice viewed these actions as playing into the hands of his enemies and undercutting his judicial authority.[47] In a letter to Undersecretary Jenkinson he described these events as 'the extraordinary rebellion which had broke out in this Colony against my authority with the Governor at the head of it.'[48] He was not alone in expressing these sentiments. James Stephen Senior, ad hoc legal adviser to the Colonial Office, who had no doubts that Smith had at all times acted in accordance with the laws of the colony, as well as with moderation and leniency, concluded in a report to the secretary of state that Hislop had treated the chief justice shabbily. The governor had sided with the jurist's detractors and as a result seriously compromised Smith's judicial authority and independence.[49] In hearing in council what was effectively an appeal from Sablich, the governor, said Stephen, had acted contrary to his revised instructions and thus extrajudicially.

By early 1811, Smith was effectively isolated in the colony with little or no power to affect events, except perhaps through his court judgments. He continued to be the target of complaints to the governor and council. The Cabildo (the governing body of Port of Spain) remonstrated over his insulting attitudes towards public officials, including several *alcades* (magistrates).[50] As a group the *alcades* complained about the conflict of interest that his position as both chief *oidor* (on appeal) and *alcade* (at first instance) created for the lower level of courts.[51] Hislop, for his part, countermanded the chief justice's appointment of Spanish lawyers and sent them packing, asserting that they were not British subjects and thus not considered loyal members of the community.[52] Smith also became involved in a battle royal with John Sanderson, the attorney general, when the judge suspended the lawyer for seemingly representing conflicting interests in a lawsuit. Sanderson, a leading member of the British Party, lambasted the chief justice and all his works in a letter to the *Courant* for which he was cited and committed to prison for contempt.[53] By March 1811 Hislop and the council had lost patience with the troublesome jurist. They divested him of any original jurisdiction that he had and confined him to a strictly appellate role.[54] Rather than continue the fight on colonial turf, Smith disappeared and decamped at night to a waiting ship, to reach London and explain himself to his imperial masters before Hislop could do so.[55]

Smith's Vindication and Subsequent Career

Despite all the bad blood and the colonial elite's pillorying of him, Smith's instincts and attitudes about governance and law on the island ultimately won the day in London. Because he took a position adverse to representative government, his detractors considered him the ally of James Stephen Sr – the anti-slavery advocate and 'evil genius of the

Colonial Office,' as John Sanderson dubbed him.[56] Although undoubtedly influenced by Stephen, whom he knew and admired, Smith was, in fact, also reflecting anxieties among British ministers about devolving political and economic power on local planters and merchants, of which he was well aware.[57] Vacillation in London continued during 1810. The imperial government's renewed request to Hislop for his views on a desirable colonial constitution, seemed to the governor, the British party, and their agents to be the harbinger of a move towards representative government and the introduction of English law.[58] The petitions from that quarter intensified and Hislop conducted a suspect survey of elite colonist opinion on the matter. But ultimately all of this pressure was to little or no avail.

The government constituted Trinidad a Crown colony (effectively controlled by London), governed in large part by Spanish law. A representative assembly was denied, in part because of the concerns of the free coloured population that the rights and respect accorded to them by both Spanish law and the British government would be at risk.[59] Hislop had treated these concerns cavalierly and even dismissively when representatives of that community submitted them to him late in 1810. Fortunately, the petitioners shrewdly copied the documents and sent them directly to the Colonial Office. Under the new policy, Trinidad became the major British Caribbean colony in which the policy of amelioration of slavery proceeded, under the guidance of James Stephen Jr, legal counsel to the Office, and, like his father, an anti-slavery advocate.[60] However, despite the fact that the Colonial Office's immediate response to curbing of Smith's powers had been to order their reinstatement, the former judge's egotistical and injudicious behaviour resulted in a decision not restore him to office in Trinidad.[61] The Privy Council rejected his appeal against his disciplining in 1813.[62] But as a sign that he had not completely burnt his bridges, London appointed Smith as chief justice of Mauritius in 1814. There he unsuccessfully argued a second time for a concentration of judicial power in his hands, a proposition the Colonial Office rejected.[63] Sadly, like his august patron, Lord Castlereagh, he died by his own hand.

Smith – sympathetic to the anti-slavery movement, a talented lawyer, and an astute observer of planter and merchant politics – suffered from a major flaw: advanced egotism. This clouded his vision about what it was possible for one person to achieve in legal reforms, not to mention the realpolitik of life in the closed and inherently suspicious elite community that called the shots, and made it difficult for him to work constructively with those around him.

Sierra Leone and Its Chequered History as a Colony

While Smith was using his creative powers in 1808 to compose his job description as chief justice of Trinidad, another Castlereagh protégé, Robert Thorpe, dismissed from office in Upper Canada the previous year, was cooling his heels in London. Undersecretary Edward Cooke had sent a letter chastising him soundly for his involvement in provincial politics in opposition to the colonial executive, and his thoroughly injudicious and unwarranted comments in his letters to the Colonial Office about Lieutenant Governor Gore and other colonial officials.[64] Yet, after this fusillade, the letter ended with a statement that the secretary of state 'is disposed to recommend you for some other professional situation when an opportunity shall arise.'[65]

Further judicial preferment was not long in materializing, as his patron appointed him the first chief justice of the newly minted West African Crown colony of Sierra Leone, early in 1808. In a letter to Castlereagh indicating his acceptance of the position, Thorpe sought to set his lordship's mind at rest about his commitment to observing the appropriate boundaries between his judicial role and politics. Despite his professional resurrection, in his familiar supplicatory style he was hopeful that, given his large family, he could be transferred to 'as beneficial an appointment in a more favourable climate.'[66] Sierra Leone for now, but please, not for long!

Sierra Leone already had a unique and rocky history as a British possession.[67] Originally established in the late 1780s at the behest of anti-slavery advocates in Britain, according to the utopian design of Granville Sharpe, to accommodate the black poor of London and freed slaves, it had barely survived a dire combination of tropical climate and diseases. The colony revived in the early 1790s under the auspices of the Sierra Leone Company representing the anti-slavery interest, adding as settlers Nova Scotian blacks who had fought with the British in the American War of Independence, and Maroons from Jamaica.[68] The company appointed the governors, including the zealous anti-slavery activist and close associate of William Wilberforce, Zachary Macaulay.[69] Relations between the company and settlers were strained, because of the settlers' annoyance at the company's failure to provide them with adequate plots of land the British government had promised, and a more general perception that their political role was being sidetracked.[70] Under a revised charter in 1799, formal political power shifted from Sharpe's Anglo-Saxon system of tythings and hundreds in which settlers were represented in government, to the governor and a council that was appointed and controlled by the company.[71] The new charter also conferred judicial and administrative powers on the council. This executive established a court of civil justice, as well as a court of requests. In frustration at their treatment, a group of Nova Scotian settlers rebelled in 1800. Although the initial uprising was put down, the situation remained unstable for much longer, as former rebels joined with a local chief in an attack on Freetown, the capital, in 1801, and the authorities only gradually cleared insurgents out of the countryside. Throughout the early period the economic potential of the colony to export crops and resources proved difficult to realize, under the British imperial trading system's constraints and the uncertain conditions created by the French Wars. By the middle of the first decade of the nineteenth century, a worsening economic situation caused the British government to answer the pleas of the company to take over political and fiscal responsibility for the territory. The imperial authorities did so in 1807, thereafter administering Sierra Leone as a Crown colony.[72]

Despite the change in colonial regime, the impetus for economic development remained sluggish at best. The year 1807 had also marked the legislated end to the British slave trade.[73] It was anticipated that liberated slaves would join the population of Sierra Leone as productive members of the community. Several of the leading anti-slavery advocates became members of a new organization called the African Institution, one of whose aims was to raise awareness of and provide financial and moral support for the colony.[74] Thomas Perronet Thompson, recommended as governor by William Wilberforce, fell out with the Institution and its anti-slavery sponsors, including his patron. Although he believed generally in the objectives of the Institution, he was increasingly critical of its support of a form of apprenticeship or indenture for the colony.[75] London devised this system as a transitory employment regime to accommodate the new sources of labour – freed slaves – in the territory. Thompson's outspoken criticism of it as a new form of slavery lost him support in the Institution and by extension in the imperial government, which quickly recalled him in 1809.[76] His successors proved more pliant, directing their energies to fostering agricultural development, trade, and the suppression of the slave trade in the region whether carried on by British interests or by those of other European nations that had not abolished that form of commerce.[77]

Thorpe Resurrected as Chief Justice of Sierra Leone

This was the tenuous outpost of empire to which Thorpe was appointed, on the assumption that he has learned his lesson in Upper Canada. Intriguingly, the Colonial Office delayed his departure for the colony for three years – a period during which his correspondence with the Colonial Office related largely to his growing impatience with not being able to begin his tenure, familiar anxieties about salary during this hiatus, and concern about money being paid as fees to a lay surrogate who was carrying out his judicial functions in his absence.[78]

The delay requires explanation. Although there is a lack of direct archival evidence on the matter, there are enough hints from later documents that the reasons are not difficult to discern. Zachary Macaulay's statements – while engaged in a pamphlet war launched by Thorpe in 1815 against the Institution and its leaders – suggest that he (and one assumes other anti-slavery activists) had not been pleased by the Thorpe's appointment.[79] Thorpe's performance as a judge in Upper Canada, and his disciplining for his uncooperative attitude and poking his nose into local politics, troubled them. In expressing his unease, Macaulay indicated that he had shared his reservations with former governor Ludlam of Sierra Leone, in letters in which he had stressed Thorpe's record of hot-headedness, lack of moderation, and ill-temper.[80] It is not fanciful to suppose that the Colonial Office shared some of the reservations from within the African Institution. London's caution took the form of an expressed desire to have in place a new Charter of Justice for the colony, before the chief justice took up office.

Thorpe received the charter, approved by Lord Chancellor Eldon, in March 1811 and sailed for West Africa.[81] It established the Supreme Court as a court of record with wide jurisdiction. As chief justice, Thorpe was the senior member of the Governor's Council, but in the event of the death or absence of the chief executive, the next senior member of that body took on the acting position, in order to separate executive and judicial functions. Thorpe's remit included the position of Vice-Admiralty judge. While he had waited in London, the Vice-Admiralty court in the colony had been active, as prosecutions under the slave-trade abolition legislation proceeded against the masters of slave vessels. In Thorpe's absence, Alexander Smith, a layman, acted as judge of that court disposing of cases brought before him. Although not paid a salary, he received fees.[82] Thorpe, with an eye to ensuring he received what he considered to be his full worth, demanded that Smith hand the fees over to him. When Smith refused, the chief justice, claiming that Smith was in contempt of his jurisdiction, brought an action against the surrogate in his own court, won, and awarded himself £300 damages. The secretary of state later forced him to disgorge the fees and damages.

Under the governorship of Lieutenant Colonel Charles Maxwell, Thorpe applied himself to his judicial duties and provided advice to the executive. Under the Slave Felony Act of 1811, the brainchild of the liberal Whig lawyer Henry Brougham, it was possible to launch prosecutions against British slave traders, wherever they operated, and foreigners trading slaves on British soil.[83] The legislation directed the release and settlement of slaves in their control. During Thorpe's only full year in the colony, 1812, he was active in enforcing the legislation, with more than two thousand slaves liberated on his watch.[84] The jurist was, however, wary about the extent of his court's jurisdiction in these matters. In the case of *R. v. Samo* the accused slave master was Dutch, and the place at which he was seized, the Iles Des Los, and the settlement where he resided, Rio Pongas, were in Thorpe's view outside British jurisdiction.[85] Maxwell, however, persuaded Thorpe that they should send an agent to the local chiefs in those locations to agree that they were living under the protection of British law, and thus within British jurisdiction. Armed with the consent of the chiefs, the chief justice exercised his tenuous jurisdiction, tried Samo, and found him guilty. However, the judge, still racked by doubts, especially on the matter of an appropriate sentence, dispatched another agent to the chiefs asking them to petition that Samo be pardoned. In Fyfe's words, 'they duly petitioned, and the pardon was graciously granted.'[86]

In his official correspondence Governor Maxwell betrayed no serious reservations about Thorpe, except concerns about the judge's claiming power over the appointment of Vice-Admiralty court officials, and the propriety of the judge's orders on security for costs.[87] He was refusing to issue writs of execution because security had not been given for the fees, which he was claiming as due to him. For his part, Thorpe advised the Colonial Office about his reservations over Maxwell's application of British law to foreign slavers.[88]

The governor granted Thorpe health leave in 1813.[89] On arriving in England, Thorpe began writing to the Colonial Office complaining about the payment of fees that he felt were *his* due, to surrogates – Alexander Smith in 1811 and during a health absence in 1812, and Dr Muncie, the new substitute appointed to cover his latest leave.[90] The chief justice's problem was that the Colonial Office had directed him to pay over these sums to the surrogates. Thorpe, claiming continued physical frailty, managed to spin out his leave until early 1815.[91] In the meantime, Maxwell had written to the Colonial Office requesting that Thorpe not be returned to Sierra Leone, describing him as 'a liability.'[92] Thorpe, now showing more clearly his facility for acerbic attacks on those he treated as his enemies, wrote to the Office claiming that Maxwell had defrauded the British Treasury, made illegal exactions of the possession's inhabitants, instituted other arbitrary measures, and otherwise committed 'heinous crimes.'[93] At this point Secretary of State Bathurst lost patience with the jurist. By letter from Undersecretary Henry Goulburn, the minister directed that Thorpe be advised definitively that he had no claim to payment for work not done by him, but done by others. Moreover, Bathurst intimated that he was distressed by the judge's charges against Maxwell. He noted that they had never been raised by the judge in any previous communication (indeed, Thorpe had praised the governor in a personal interview and by letter, emphasizing 'his judgement and integrity').[94] If the charges were, in his opinion, true, then Thorpe owed a duty to report them formally to the imperial government. If they were not, his conduct was 'indefensible.' The letter concluded, 'Under the circumstances therefore Lord Bathurst has thought it his duty to submit to His Royal Highness the Prince Regent the necessity of removing you from the situation of Chief Justice of the Colony of Sierra Leone.'[95]

The prince regent was pleased to accept the advice.

Thorpe's Final Salvos and an Assessment of This Turbulent Jurist

So this judicial stormy petrel was removed from office a second time. On this occasion there was no mention of the opportunity of further preferment, and no pension was forthcoming. The Colonial Office had tired of this jurist, and wanted nothing further to do with him. Thorpe, however, was not willing to go quietly. With *A Letter to William Wilberforce*, which may have been issued before the boom was lowered on his career, he launched a pamphlet war against the anti-slavery elite and especially the African Institution.[96] Under both its influence and that of the Sierra Leone Company, he claimed, serious mismanagement of the colony had occurred. Echoing several of the criticisms of former governor Thompson, the letter asserted that none of the objectives of viable settlement, exploiting trade opportunities, introducing a workable education system, constructing a moral community, and establishing a Church of England presence had been achieved.[97] The first target of ad hominem criticism was Wilberforce, who, said the former jurist, lacked the necessary leadership qualities (and in any event was something of a latecomer to the movement).[98] Moreover, the anti-slavery activists had missed the boat by failing to bring pressure on the Congress of Vienna to issue an anti-slavery declaration. The second target was Zachary Macaulay, who, Thorpe asserted, had used his leadership role to feather his own and his family's commercial nest.[99] His own experience in the colony had convinced him that the options for liberated slaves of apprenticeship under indenture or lifelong military service was the antithesis of responsible development of a viable and hospitable colony.[100] The abolition legislation he pronounced a failure, as it had merely transferred the slave trade to Spain and Portugal.[101] Complete abolition was the only practical policy, in his view. While applauding his own efforts at releasing slaves under the Slave Felony Act, he criticized Maxwell for duping the British Navy into illegal acts of violence against slavers and property in Portuguese territory.[102]

The anti-slavery movement was not ready to take this abuse lying down. In a personal rejoinder, Macaulay took issue with the detractor's scattergun criticism.[103] In this pamphlet Macaulay revealed his earlier doubts about the appointment of Thorpe as chief justice and dismissed his charges as so many sour grapes by a vindictive and unreliable individual.[104] For their part, the directors of the Institution, while candidly admitting that they had failed in some of their objectives in Sierra Leone, discredited their antagonist as malign and uninformed.[105] The disgruntled jurist replied in a no-holds-barred response to Macaulay's pamphlet by trumpeting in extravagant terms his record of judicial service,[106] which was marked, he said without a hint of irony, by an upward trajectory of promotion and salary increases – his 'own escritoire' containing 'public testimonials from every colony in which I have served, to prove that I have not only discharged my duty with the most assiduous attention and impartiality, but also with the highest public and general satisfactions.'[107] He concluded that Macaulay and others had worked to unseat him.[108] The delusional tone of that broadside continued in a response to the directors who alleged a conspiracy against him.[109] In this document Thorpe sought to justify his claims for fees from surrogates and argued that the denial of one of the payments, for work done by a surrogate while he was on health furlough in 1812, reflected 'the little select party's pressure on Lord Bathurst.'[110]

None of the former judge's criticism of the African Institution, its sponsors, and officers was lost on the West Indian planter lobby. They were fighting hard to derail the campaign for a slave registry that was designed to expose and limit the level of smuggling of slaves into British colonies.[111] Thorpe's attacks made him a partial hero in the minds of the resisters to the developing policy in London of amelioration.[112] As Fyfe put it, 'Once the flail of the slave traders: Thorpe became their prop.'[113] His publications also raised doubts about the performance of the African Institution and its sponsors in the minds of some members of the anti-slavery movement, such as the Quaker William Allen, who felt there was exploitation of settlers.[114] Thorpe's criticisms of the African Institution and British policy on the slave trade continued well after 1815.[115] Fyfe believes that Thorpe's criticisms, excessive though they were, weakened the reputation and resolve of the Institution.[116] But none of this benefited or helped him redeem his career. Unpensioned and unemployable in the colonial service, he faded into the obscurity of the life of a retired gentleman. London heard from him from time to time, as he continued to badger the Colonial Office about the injustices done to him and his right to compensation. The only joy in his life after Sierra Leone was a belated but successful defamation suit against the retired Francis Gore, his nemesis as lieutenant governor of Upper Canada.[117]

Once again the restless career of Robert Thorpe, who combined sound political observation and undoubted legal acumen, had foundered on the reefs of his remarkable capacity for self-delusion that only *he* could solve the problems in the colonies in which he served, on his unerring ability to lose sight of the boundaries between politics and law, and on his inability to control a loose and acerbic tongue. In this his last hurrah, his criticisms of the running of Sierra Leone and prescriptions for an end to slavery, stripped of the gratuitous negative rhetoric and ad hominem attacks, were legitimate, as had been the core of his concerns about the land issue in Prince Edward Island, and his remonstrations against counter-revolutionary government in Upper Canada. His mistake, like that of his contemporary, George Smith, was to believe that he was somehow specially predestined to work reformative magic and change things, and that, as a judge, he was well placed to lead what was essentially a political campaign. In this respect the record of judicial service of both men was flawed. And yet both Thorpe and Smith, unduly self-centred though they were, had visionary elements to their make-up that pointed to the need for more sensitive approaches to the British imperialism and colonialism during their time.

Ironically, the judge might have congratulated himself for being recalled from Sierra Leone when he was, and thus able to enjoy a long retirement. The next four successors as chief justice of the West African colony died in office, and the fifth was saved from the same fate only by being charged with murder.[118]

Grenada as a British Colony: The Amelioration Project

In the 1820s Grenada was a slave colony with a variegated plantation economy producing coffee, cocoa, cotton, and sugar. Ceded by France to Great Britain in 1763, it had a very small white population who effectively ruled the island. A hybrid system of French and English law governed their affairs and relationships. London granted the colony the form of representative government already in place in earlier British possessions in the region. The subject population included both black slaves and a sizeable 'free' mixed-race or Creole population, who traced their ancestry to the French period. Europeans controlled the slaves by harsh regulation on the estates and an oppressive slave code. A slave rebellion in the mid-1790s led by a French-speaking free coloured man, Julien Fedon, and inspired in part by the ideals of the French Revolution, had left an indelible mark on the white planter psyche, and a lingering suspicion of the disloyalty of those with a French and/or Roman Catholic identity.[119] Moreover, it put a damper on the grant of rights to the free coloured population of the island until the late 1820s, when they secured a degree of political representation in the Legislative Assembly. During that decade the colonial legislature on which the planters had an iron grip had made some concessions to the Colonial Office's desire to mitigate the legal oppression of the slave population of the island – the amelioration project.[120] This local legislation responded to instructions by the secretary of state, Lord Bathurst, in 1823 to colonial legislatures to alleviate the circumstances and extend the rights of slaves in their jurisdictions, following models in Crown colonies, such as Trinidad. The Grenadan legislation, although not viewed in London as entirely satisfactory, did provide, for example, that slaves could be baptized and instructed in Christian principles; workers must be given breaks for breakfast and lunch; and time must be given for female slaves with large families to cultivate their grounds. Limitations were put on the number of lashes meted out as punishment, and their infliction was to be more closely controlled.[121] The legislation also directed that the members of slave families could no longer be separated. Amendments to the Slave Code in 1828 made the evidence of slaves admissible in all civil and criminal trials.[122] At the same time, the planters, well aware of the momentum towards complete abolition of slavery and desperate to keep control of their 'assets,' did not always adhere to the letter, let alone the spirit, of their own amelioration enactments.[123]

Chief Justice Jeffery Hart Bent Takes on the Plantocracy

It was into this fragmented society that Chief Justice Jeffrey Hart Bent had come in 1820. A stiff-necked, hypersensitive individual with a rigid commitment to English law, Bent, as we saw in chapter 6, had already experienced the Colonial Office's discipline as the chief judge of the Supreme Court of Civil Jurisdiction of New South Wales in 1816.[124] Lord Bathurst had recalled him from that position for his intransigence in refusing to hold court in the colony while only former convict attorneys were available to plead before him. His stand on this matter reflected a more general attitude of non-cooperation with and carping against the allegedly 'tyrannical' Governor Macquarie. After a period in London campaigning for Macquarie's recall and lobbying for a judicial appointment to India, Jeffrey Hart Bent assumed the position of chief justice of Grenada in 1819.[125]

Bent's affinities in Australia had been conservative and pro-exclusionist, and thus at odds with the emancipist and convict populations. We lack firm evidence of how easily Bent fit into his new appointment and life in this slave colony. No data indicate that he engendered animosity among the planter elite, or that he adopted a vigorous position in opposition to slavery for most of the 1820s. The peace and quiet of his first eight years in office may be explained by the fact that the practice had developed (against the wishes of the British government, and out of tune with the reality in other colonies) of excluding the chief justice of the colony from its Legislative Council. Thus Bent was not involved in its deliberations, including those on legislative reform of the law relating to slavery.[126] But the seemingly equable climate surrounding the senior judge changed dramatically in 1829.

The chief justice fell afoul of the planter elite in the colony in taking a strong stand in protecting a Roman Catholic priest, Father Anthony O'Hannan, from what he saw as both ecclesiastical and secular oppression.[127] Despite the fact that many who professed Christianity on Grenada were Roman Catholics, for many decades the only support for religious activity and education was directed to the Church of England and its institutions.[128] Roman Catholic priests were allowed only to operate under a gubernatorial licence, and they felt constrained in their ability to minister to their congregations in anything other than the spiritual realm. The situation was to change in 1828 with the passage of local legislation requiring the colonial government to pay the Roman Catholic incumbent on the island a salary. O'Hannan, trained as a priest in Ireland, arrived to take up that charge.[129] He was popular among his slave and free 'coloured' parishioners. Edward Cox notes that the newcomer was both radical in his theology and activist in his educational and social agenda.[130] Well aware of the oppression to which the members of his congregation and other slaves and free coloureds were subject, he saw that both 'the Bible and Christianity were important vehicles for promoting not only the religious and moral improvement of members of those classes, but also their socio-political status. His was a true liberation theology.' Brizan claims that the priest and the chief justice became close friends, although he provides no evidence to support the assertion.[131] What we do know is that the jurist used the law assertively to shield O'Hannan from his powerful detractors, which suggests a degree of empathy, if not close association, with the radical pastor.

O'Hannan's attempts to elevate the education and spiritual and social aspirations of his flock caused concerns among the more well-heeled members of the Roman Catholic community, who complained to the ecclesiastical authorities. His superior, Bishop Macdonnell of the West Indian district, resident in Trinidad, was anxious to remove the troublesome priest from his charge. This was an initiative silently applauded by the planter elite in the colony, ever perturbed about those who they feared would whip up the passions of the slaves and free coloureds. O'Hannan initially agreed to resign but changed his mind when he realized the breadth of support among his flock for him and his ministry.[132] Macdonnell, in an attempt to carry through his plan to remove the priest, dispatched to Grenada Monsignor Le Goff, his personal representative, and two other priests appointed to replace O'Hannan and his associate, Father Power.[133] The acting governor and president of the Legislative Council, Andrew Houstoun, approved the move and consented to the delegation's presence in the colony.[134]

When the resident priest refused to vacate his charge and the parsonage house to Le Goff, the latter referred the matter to the president, requesting that he strip O'Hannan of his licence and develop new ones for his successors, Fathers Sanchez and Murphy. Houstoun complied with the request to remove O'Hannan's licence.[135] Moreover, the attorney general, Frederick Browne, summoned the recalcitrant priest before the magistrates and charged him with breaching the peace in refusing to turn over his chapel.[136] At this juncture O'Hannan complained to the chief justice about his treatment. Bent, sidetracking the lower bench, called the ecclesiastical visitors before him and dressed them down for being on the island without legal authority. Using provocative language, he described the priests as 'vagabonds' – in effect foreigners not entitled to be within the jurisdiction.[137] The judge and the attorney general, Frederick Browne, representing the clerics, engaged in an unseemly contretemps in open court, as Mr Attorney sought to make arguments and supply documents to the court (especially the letter of consent by Houstoun to their being on the island), which Bent was not prepared to receive.[138]

Houstoun, palpably seething at this challenge to his authority, ordered Bent to desist from further action against the church's representatives.[139] He added that if the jurist failed to comply, he 'might be under the disagreeable necessity of taking steps to prevent [the visitors] from being again subjected to the indignities they consider themselves to have suffered Saturday last.' Not one to take kindly to executive interference through the illegitimate use of power, Bent rejected the instruction and instead lectured the administrator on the obligations of a judge to administer justice impartially:[140] 'Your Honour may be aware that I am, by my oath of office, to do my duty without fear, favour or affection; and I have to state that your Honour's favour or protection of any one, or the implied threat in your Honour's letter to myself, will never induce me to swerve from the impartial exercise of the judicial functions. Does your Honour mean to contend that the numerous persons under your special protection … are not amenable to me in my judicial office?'

The chief justice was making an unambiguous and powerful statement of his belief that the rule of law on the island, with the judiciary as its protector, transcended the special interests of anyone subject to the jurisdiction of its courts, even if the executive had intervened to insulate those interests from scrutiny. On the law he was equally clear, that the visiting clerics had no special right to be on the island to do what they had been instructed to do by ecclesiastical authority, nor were their 'ecclesiastical dignities' in the Roman church known to English law. Moreover, he said, the issue of removing a licence to serve as a priest was not a matter of executive discretion, but of judicial determination. O'Hannan was, he concluded, still the legitimate incumbent of his parish.

It was at this point in the summer of 1829 that Houstoun, with the approval of the Legislative Council, suspended Bent from office for the first time, citing his alleged partiality and unbecoming conduct in the O'Hannan affair.[141] The first accusation was that he had acted extrajudicially in dealing with the O'Hannan case, in support of 'a person of dangerous character likely to excite a civil commotion,' who was resisting constituted secular and ecclesiastical authority and was under a charge of riot. The chief justice's actions were 'calculated to disturb the tranquility of the Country, and to be productive of dangerous consequences.' Secondly, he had acted improperly in sitting as a magistrate, and issuing a Warrant of Summons to the visitors without an oath as its basis. His third sin was that he had purposely stifled the magistrates' inquiry into O'Hannan's conduct, by withdrawing the principal sources of evidence and intimidating the priest's prosecutors. Fourthly, the judge by his actions at the hearing, especially refusing to listen to the attorney general, had effectively prejudged the case. Finally, Bent's behaviour was insulting to the president.

The chief justice responded to Houstoun's letter and the litany of accusations against him, asserting that the president had no legal authority to suspend him. That power, he argued, lay exclusively with His Majesty.[142] In putting his case against his suspension to the Colonial Office, Bent took care to point to the incestuous character of the relationship between both government officials, including the law officers and magistrates, and planters in the colony, and those serving on the council and assembly, and his low opinion of all of them.[143] The secretary of state's response to Houston's actions was swift and critical of him and the council for an ill-considered decision.[144] Sir George Murray indicated that 'the charges are insufficient to justify suspension,' and added that even if the charges had been substantiated 'by the most conclusive evidence, [that] would not have justified his suspension from office ... It would be subversive of every principle of justice to sanction a sentence of degradation passed on a Judge who was not even afforded the opportunity of being heard in his own defence.'[145] The minister ordered Houston to reinstate Bent immediately as chief justice.

The colonial government and its supporters in Grenada and England did not accept London's decision with good grace. Both law officers resigned in protest.[146] Houstoun expressed his profound disappointment at the result, and the Legislative Council, the assembly, and the planters' man in London, William Manning, pressed the imperial authorities to reverse their decision.[147] They all laid stress on the claim that Bent by his actions had forfeited the support and trust of the 'respectable' members of the community.

Further oil was added to the fires of conflict in legal sparring over the fate of O'Hannan. Under legislation passed hastily by the legislatures during Bent's suspension, Houstoun removed the priest's licence, and local magistrates committed the latter to jail for refusing to give up his charge and breaching the peace in February 1830.[148] Bent reacted swiftly by releasing the cleric on a writ of habeas corpus.[149] The judge also continued with the trial of one of the 'visitors,' Father Sanchez, for being in the colony without legal sanction.[150]

Most troubling to his enemies was that the chief justice now spoke out on slave mistreatment and undertook to do something about it through the administration of justice on the island. Bent had already made his concerns known to the Colonial Office about the insensitivity of the existing system to slave complaints of abuse, and advocated the establishment of a summary tribunal established 'of persons who are not themselves slaveholders' or their minions.[151] Early in February, during an address from the bench, the chief justice outraged the plantocracy by dramatically connecting the lack of respect shown to him to the injustices experienced by slaves. 'In this country,' he complained, 'little respect is shewn to a Chief Justice, or to any but those possessing large estates.' If he could be so unfairly attacked by the government, he continued, 'he would leave it to the people of England to Judge, what justice could be expected for a slave, or those who protected them.'[152] Bent then added insult to injury by announcing his intention to set up special court sessions on Saturdays to hear complaints from slaves, and hearings on Tuesdays for people who had received summonses as a result of the Saturday hearings.[153]

Further defections from the justice system occurred at this time, the complainants attacking the chief justice for poisoning the atmosphere in and seeking to destabilize the colony. For example, Assistant Judge Hoyes of the Supreme Court responded to Bent's outburst in court in February 1830, saying that he would 'leave it to the people of Grenada to judge, of the injustice of the accusation' made by Bent about his treatment and that of the slaves. He then resigned in protest as a result of his stated 'anxious desire to preserve the peace and tranquility of the Island, which ... have been endangered by the pernicious and inflammatory doctrine promulgated by the Chief Justice from the Bench.'[154] Hoyes had no doubts about where the jurist's sympathies lay, charging Bent 'with selling the Colony to Messrs Wilberforce, Macaulay and Stephen.'[155] Late in March three magistrates followed Hoyes's lead, informing the president, 'From the manner in which the proceedings of the Magistrates are now set aside, we have determined not to act longer in a capacity where our services cannot be useful to the public.'[156]

By the end of March 1830 the colonial elite had become so vexed that they were willing to try to dislodge Bent again.[157] This time the president informed him that his suspension was pending and requested him respond within a day to the resolutions from the assembly to that effect. The judge was cited for bringing the community into disrepute by his allegations of injustice towards and oppression of the slave population; his actions in causing a crisis of confidence in the justice system that threatened 'the peace, good government and well being of the Colony'; perverting the law and especially legislation in his favourable treatment of a dangerous character such as O'Hannan; and tending to encourage insubordination, and even sedition and rebellion and the overthrow of the government by the slave population, in inducing them to bring their complaints to him.[158] Bent responded with a terse reply dismissing all the charges as unfounded. When the president then suspended him, his riposte was that he enjoyed 'the confidence of the greater part of the community, (viz. those who need protection, and an impartial and disinterested Judge on the Bench),' a matter of more importance to him than the opinions of the majority of the House of Assembly.[159]

Secretary of State Murray was unwilling to make a departmental decision on Bent's future this time, as the judge seemed to him to have lost the confidence of the influential section of the community. He advised the chief justice to appeal to the Privy Council.[160] James Stephen Jr, legal counsel to the Colonial Office, in a report to Murray, had opined that Bent's application of the law in relation to the O'Hannan episode had on the whole been unimpeachable, if involving elements of overreaction in dealing with the visiting priests and their counsel, but that his rhetoric had been intemperate and irresponsible.[161] Bent's conduct left Stephen in two minds about whether the judge was taking a principled stand against the oppression to which slaves were subjected in this fundamentally unequal society, or his indignation reflected rather more egocentric motivations or 'a misguided desire to uphold the dignity of the Bench.' As had been the case with Willis, he observed, it was difficult to judge the jurist's conduct and its motivations, given the larger context and multiple meanings that were attributable to certain behaviours or gestures in late 1820s British culture. Counsel concluded by wondering whether 'Bent believed he was expressing a collective rage in and through his own subordination.'

Stephen was at the same time critical of Houstoun's undue deference to Bishop Macdonnell, for his seeking to enforce diktats of the Roman Catholic church, and for threatening Bent with dire consequences if he did not comply with his orders. He also faulted Attorney General Browne for misusing the law at every turn, employing the threat of resignation to force the government to get rid of the chief justice, and voting on resolutions of council directed against Bent.

On more immediate matters, the Colonial Office ordered the governor to release O'Hannan from jail, instructed that the legislation under which he was imprisoned to be held in abeyance (it was later disallowed), and announced that in future steps would be taken to ensure that an impartial party would be appointed to the acting governorship.[162] Murray was clearly of the view that, whatever the sins of Jeffrey Hart Bent, the colonial executive had acted with partiality, irresponsibly, and at times illegally, in this case.

In his brief to the Privy Council, Bent stressed a number of important points about the difficulties faced by an impartial judge in seeking to do justice in slave colonies.[163] He pointed again to the interpenetration of the elite among the colonial institutions, not least those administering justice. 'The Appellant feels deeply the arduous task on every judge of a West Indian Colony, unconnected with property therein, to preserve himself from continual attacks. The very circumstance of being almost the only Magistrate unconnected with Slaves, operates to excite a prejudice against him; and in the common course of his duty he must not hope for the confidence of the few influential persons, (who in this small colony have almost everyone under their control), and whose views a Judge's decision, when they are before him as suitors, must frequently thwart.'[164]

In his case, he argued, that he had suffered the additional misfortune of being subject to the attacks of detractors, including his own inferiors in the justice system, who were all part of a provisional government enjoying power in the absence of the governor. On a more optimistic note, Bent observed that he was not without his supporters, evident in the fact that the newly enfranchised free coloured residents nominated and elected him to be a member of the Legislative Assembly for the parishes of St George and St John in October 1830. He had declined this position, citing its incompatibility with judicial office.[165] In the judge's opinion the legal reasons for suspending him a second time amounted to two: his action in hearing slave complaints as a single magistrate, and in releasing O'Hannan on a writ of habeas corpus.[166] The first, he argued, was allowed by the colony's Slave Act. On the second, he was either right, or, if wrong, not open to censure for a mistake. His contention was that he had ample grounds for his decision, as the magistrates in committing the priest had been acting outside their powers.

The response of the House of Assembly rehearsed the indictments of the judge already made in earlier resolutions. The brief emphasized that there was a friendship between Bent and O'Hannan that caused the judge to be partial to the priest in every respect.[167] Although no proof was adduced to support the contention, the assembly claimed that the jurist had been a problem from the date of his appointment.[168] All his actions in the O'Hannan case and thereafter had encouraged dissension and unrest among those lower down the socio-economic ladder. His election to the House of Assembly, which, they suggested, the chief justice, assisted by O'Hannan, had engineered, was another example of this calculated and subversive attitude. The man was, in short, a menace to the community.[169]

There was a long delay in hearing the case, during which the mutual nastiness continued unabated, including charges of moral laxity against Houstoun and some of his officials by Bent, and a suggestion of moral turpitude on the part of Bent by his enemies.[170] Finally in 1832, the council in a typically terse opinion concluded that there was insufficient basis in the evidence to support removal of the chief justice from office. Accordingly it advised that Bent be restored to office.[171]

Bent's Survival: An Assessment

In the diametrically opposed views of Bent and his detractors in the assembly and council, we see clearly two very different interpretations of the rule of law in conflict. On the one hand, the chief justice believed that the law against which the actions of the colonial executive was to be evaluated in their legitimacy or otherwise, was the law of England. In that system all subjects (including slaves) had a right to equal access to the courts, and to be judged fairly and impartially, objectives lacking in the local system of slave courts and slave law. It was, accordingly, legitimate for an impartial Superior Court judge to intervene to see that justice was done, whether by invoking venerable institutions such as habeas corpus, or by holding special hearings to consider complaints from those barred from the normal processes of justice.

On the other, the planters, their political representatives, and friends in the legal system believed that it was local law and private discipline that should govern the fate of slaves, and even free coloureds. The rule of law, despite the exaggerated seventeenth-century rhetoric embracing it and constant references to 'the liberty of the subject,' was for this group of narrow compass in terms of who was entitled to its protections – exclusively the minority white population in a justice system designed and controlled by them. To espouse the broad and 'heretical' reading given to the concept by Bent had irresponsibly raised expectations, inciting dissension and even rebellion among the subject majority of the population, on whose servility social peace and economic wealth depended. At a time when the planters could see the writing on the wall pointing towards total abolition in British government policy, they were particularly sensitive on this issue and willing to go to extremes to protect what they could of the local administration of justice from the meddling of 'reformist' jurists.

It seems likely that at a time when Great Britain was in the throes of preparing to abolish slavery throughout the empire, the imperial authorities were reticent about disciplining a judge who, despite his prickly personality and acid tongue, had employed a liberal interpretation of the rule of law and acted in an anti-slavery spirit. An ad hoc committee of the Privy Council on which both the current secretary of state, Viscount Goderich, and his predecessor, Sir George Murray, sat, along with the lord chancellor and the lord chief justice, heard the case under the old system of appeals.[172] The opinion of the council was in large measure that of the Colonial Office, and reflective of the views of James Stephen Jr, earlier expressed to Murray.

Not surprisingly, given the hostility towards him in Grenada by the elite, Bent did not return to the island but was moved on in sequence to further judicial appointments in Trinidad as puisne judge, and in succession St Lucia and British Guiana as chief justice. He fell out with the governor and legislature in the second of these postings, but finally seems to have mellowed in his final posting on the South American mainland.[173] One can only assume that his Colonial Office masters were sufficiently impressed with his legal acumen and his principled espousal of the rule of law that these qualities outweighed his capacity for invective on the bench. Whether Bent's championing of the underdog was the result of a principled dislike of slavery, his friendship with O'Hannan, an inflated sense of judicial dignity, or even a dyspeptic nature is hard to fathom. From the record and the unlikely association of a chief justice and a radical Roman Catholic priest, there may well have been a sympathetic heart beating in the breast of this judge and a capacity to reach out to the oppressed. What is clear is that the tenor of imperial policy at the time meant that he was not going to be made a scapegoat to appease planter sentiment.

As time would tell, the abolition of slavery removed the fundamental social and economic inequalities in Britain's Caribbean colonies to only a limited extent. Imperial policy on trade in these colonies, and the retention and invention of various forms of exploitative labour regimes in them, was to preserve much of the economic power and political authority of the planter class in emancipation's wake. Bent was not the last jurist to challenge and incur the enmity of these well-entrenched and manipulative interests in the West Indian colonies, when acting in support of the oppressed in those societies. It is to two judges who ran into trouble in the second half of the nineteenth century that we now turn.

10

The Perils of the Colonial Judiciary: The Indelible Stain of Slavery in the West Indian Colonies, 1834–1900

The Abolition of Slavery, 1834 and Its Aftermath

The formal end to slavery in the British Empire at midnight on 31 July 1834, celebrated by the 750,000 slaves and their anti-slavery supporters, was a compromise – a sure sign that London, while taking the moral high ground on abolition, was not willing to sacrifice the plantation economies of former slave colonies.[1] In the first place, the planters in these possessions received £20 million collectively in compensation. Secondly, London substituted a temporary apprenticeship system for the former regime to induce most former slaves to continue working on the plantations.[2] Mary Turner notes that the British government in beginning to dismantle the slave laws in the pre-abolition period and by its directives on slave labour, in 1824 and 1831, had sought to alleviate the oppressive working regimes in place and remove the more extreme forms of punishment to which slaves had been subject, while preserving certain customs that slaves had managed to wrest from their masters. However, planters, especially in the colonies with representative government, griped bitterly about these concessions and sought to neutralize them. Once the British government had committed to abolition, it entered all too readily into an alliance with those local interests to try to ensure that the former slaves would constitute a closely ordered and compliant 'free' workforce on the estates.[3] A consequence was that after the mid-1830s the regulatory regimes applied to labour locally in the West Indies and elsewhere in the multiracial empire had features reminiscent of those of slavery.

The apprenticeship system quickly broke down for a variety of reasons.[4] The first was former slave resistance to what seemed to them like a new form of servitude, manipulated by planters. In British Guiana in 1834, for example, apprentices protested en mass, arguing that the King had made them free. The governor quickly quelled the outburst by sending in the militia and prosecuting the alleged ringleaders.[5] Secondly, the system of magistrates' courts with jurisdiction over the system lacked sufficient resources to make it viable. Moreover, although under Stephen's guidance, the Colonial Office dispatched stipendiary magistrates from England to inject an impartial element into the local administration of justice, and some proved equal to the challenge, others demonstrated decidedly pro-planter attitudes. Thirdly, anti-slavery activists were increasingly critical of the system, which they felt little removed from what it had replaced. Finally, planters in some colonies with representative assemblies became fearful that Parliament, under pressure from the anti-slavery lobby, would abrogate their constitutional right to legislate for themselves on labour matters, and they mobilized to get rid of the system.[6] This complex of forces combined to ensure the early demise of apprenticeship in 1838.[7]

The planters in colonies with assemblies, believing that they would now be free to craft their own work regimes, felt frustrated and resentful when the Colonial Office, under the ever-watchful eye of Stephen, now permanent undersecretary of state for the colonies, advised disallowance or sent back for reconsideration legislation that unduly favoured the planters, and dictated model Orders in Council to govern labour on the islands.[8] Stephen's attempts to be more proactive in reforming the administration of justice in the West Indies proved less availing. Implementation of the West Indian Judicature Act of 1836, designed to introduce more professional judges into the smaller colonies, had already run aground on the shoals of refusal of local assemblies and the Treasury to provide the cash for salaries, and the small number of qualified and respectable colonial barristers available for preferment.[9] Moreover, Stephen's proposal in the late 1830s to keep in place the system of stipendiary magistrates established under the apprenticeship experiment was rejected. These men would have replaced or at least controlled locally appointed justices of the peace, to ensure greater impartiality in the dispensing of colonial justice. The plan came up against the spirited objections of Sir Charles Metcalfe, governor of

Jamaica, where the pressure for preservation of local control of courts was at its strongest, as well as an emerging tendency among influential British politicians, such as Lord John Russell and Lord Stanley, to conciliate planter opinion.[10]

The planters sought to tie former slaves to the estates by one stratagem or another, while the latter (often with the support of black or coloured politicians and Baptist missionaries) opted to till their own plots, either individually or in 'free villages.'[11] There was particular resistance to calculated attempts by planters to demand rent from estate workers for their residences and provision grounds, that under slavery they had enjoyed at no cost. Employers deducted the money owed from the wages the labourers earned (the rent-wages system).[12] The resulting outflow of labour from the plantations was most significant in Trinidad and British Guiana, in which land outside the estates was plentiful. Depression in the sugar industry, assisted in part by imperial free trade legislation passed in the mid-1840s, exacerbated the outflow of workers and its unfavourable financial impact on plantations.[13] During that decade, with the humanitarian influence of Stephen now on the wane in its counsels, and economic expediency in the ascendant, London's policy priority had become the survival of the plantations.

The Introduction of Indentured Labour in the Sugar Colonies

The imperial government began to encourage the importing of indentured labour into former slave possessions.[14] After disappointing results with European, Sierra Leonean, and even American free black migrants, London opened the door to immigrants from India, and later China through Hong Kong.[15] This state initiative predictably achieved greatest success in Trinidad and British Guiana.[16] The formal regimes set up to regulate this new labour force, while placing duties on planters to house, sustain, and protect their workers from disease, primarily emphasized control and work discipline.[17] A combination of indenture for a number of years with long work hours, a rigid pass system, and a litany of fines and imprisonment for non-compliance made sure of that. Little consideration was directed towards the workers' interests, with the administration of work regulation firmly in the hands of estate managers and their often harsh overseers or drivers, and a magistracy who administered the criminal law and master and servant legislation and were inherently sympathetic to the planter cause.[18]

Guiana as a British Colony and Dependence on Indentured Labour

The Caribbean possession that imported the largest number of indentured workers from Asia was British Guiana, predominantly a sugar colony, to which 60,000 Indians and Chinese had migrated by 1871.[19] This territory on the South American mainland was ceded by the Dutch to Great Britain at the Peace of Paris in 1814. Although nominally a Crown colony, the planters had its governance in their pockets. In conjunction with the governor they made the laws governing the colony, through a body dating from its years as a Dutch possession, the Court of Policy.[20] This was a legislative council with official and nominated, unofficial members.[21] In the event of a vacancy in the latter's ranks, the Court of Policy selected the replacement from a list produced by an elected College of Electors (*Keizers*), who were substantial landowners and held their positions for life. In addition the British had established a Combined Court, embracing the members of the former body and elected financial representatives, thereby producing a majority of unofficial members, to determine the means for raising revenue. This body possessed clout lacking in other Crown colonies in the region, as it could refuse supply.

Magistrates who were themselves planters, or beholden to them, administered the law relating to indentured labour, a regime adapted from English master and servant legislation. Already punitive enough, they skewed it further against the workers. [22] The problem of unequal justice was magnified by the migrants' poor knowledge of English, and the use of interpreters, some of whom were dishonest. Members of the colonial bar served the needs and shared the values of the estate owners. By 1862 the period of indenture had been extended from three to five years for most indentured labourers, at a fixed rate of pay. The pass system severely limited the workers in their freedom of movement outside the estates.[23]

Enter Chief Justice Beaumont

It was into this fraught environment that English Equity barrister Joseph Beaumont, a protégé of Sir Roundell Palmer, solicitor general of England at that time, arrived as chief justice in 1863.[24] He was described as 'a gentleman of some eminence at the English Bar' whose credentials rested on 'very high authority.'[25] Beaumont was the son of a noted

Wesleyan minister, the Reverend Doctor Joseph Beaumont, who was, by his son's account, a vigorous opponent of slavery in all its forms.[26] The Supreme Court had two assistant judges, one of whom, Edward Beete, had knowledge of Dutch civil law, which to a significant extent obtained in the colony. The laws on crimes and master and servant relations were based on English law.

Beaumont's appointment was not popular with the local legal fraternity, who felt that one of their own, the serving attorney general, John Lucie Smith, should have been appointed, a position that Governor Francis Hincks had advocated.[27] Hincks stressed Lucie Smith's record of loyal service and experience and his knowledge of Roman Dutch Law. But the Colonial Office made it clear to the chief executive that it had a policy of not appointing chief justices from the local profession, because of its concern about partiality among colonial lawyers towards interests that they had served, or with which they identified.[28]

There was already an alliance between most of the planters and the governor. Hincks, a mercurial Northern Irishman, had led a reform government in the early 1850s in the province of Canada.[29] However, he left the country and its politics under a cloud, involving charges of fiscal manipulation of railway construction for his own benefit.[30] London, as part of an attempt to reward 'successful' colonial politicians, ignored this aura of peculation and blithely appointed him in succession as governor of Barbados and Guiana.[31] In Barbados Hincks had quickly learnt not to rock the boat and threaten the status quo on the island. He opposed the importation of indentured labour to the Windward Islands where Creole estate labour had declined, engaging in a lively argument with the governor of British Guiana on the issue.[32] In Guiana the new governor was well received by the planters, but not by a group of merchants, the 'Bermuda clique.' One of these men, a Newfoundlander, Frederick Winter, had exposed Hinck's murky record in railway development in Canada in the local opposition press, the *Creole*.[33] Early in his tenure Hincks made disparaging remarks about the group and their legal representative, J. Trounsell Gilbert, who was also solicitor general for the colony. Hincks suspected that Gilbert was out to undermine his authority and embarrass him.[34] The spat came to a head when Hincks recommended Attorney General Lucie Smith for the chief justiceship, a clear snub to his rival. This resulted in Gilbert's resignation in anticipation of his firing by Hincks, who had no desire to continue the former as a law officer.

The chief justice arrived in the colony in early September 1863, as

Mangru suggests, 'to a mixed reception; some regretting the non-appointment of Lucie Smith, others like the *Creole*, organ of the black population, rejoicing that the Colonial Office had selected an official "free from local ties and influences."'[35] Hincks treated the judge cordially, and at first blush they were capable of collaboration. This was the case on the matter of impressing on the indentured population in cases of murder, in particular of women, English law's strictures on the sanctity of life and firm application of the death penalty in such instances.[36] After some months, however, the spirit of harmony became increasingly strained.

Hincks did not appreciate Beaumont's announcement that he would act independently as an official member of the Court of Policy, even to the point of dissenting publicly from legislative initiatives of the governor and his executive council. This stance by Beaumont, Hincks argued, ran counter to imperial policy set out in a letter from the Duke of Newcastle, secretary of state for the colonies, to Governor Keate of Trinidad, in 1862.[37] That communication strongly suggested that the chief justice or any official member should explain his adverse views in private conference with the governor and avoid a contrary vote in council. When Chief Justice Beaumont openly opposed legislation relating to the disposal of land in the capital, Georgetown, the governor complained to Edward Cardwell, the secretary of state, seeking approval to dismiss the jurist from the Court of Policy.[38] The latter agreed with Hincks that his predecessor's letter to Keate in Trinidad applied to British Guiana as well.[39] Cardwell emphasized that the chief justice was not expected 'to take an active part in local politics or in the general financial business of the Legislature, both because judicial functions are best exercised by a person holding himself aloof from political discussions and conflicts, and because his proper and peculiar duties are arduous.' The threat of removal from the legislative body was not pursued.

The temperature rose when the chief justice also sought to establish dominant control over the administration of justice in the colony, in a series of moves that the governor resisted vigorously. Conflict occurred over who had the power to appoint and set out the conditions of employment for court officials, another point on which the Colonial Office supported the executive's position.[40] London's response was similarly sympathetic to Hincks's position when Beaumont moved to take a leave of absence without seeking the consent of the governor.[41]

These disagreements, however, proved minor by comparison to the extended battle with the executive over the operation of commutations of sentences in the colony. The chief justice, suspicious about the magistracy's administration of justice and the executive exercise of clemency, acted independently by proposing to hold general gaol delivery at the distant penal settlement of Mazuruni in Essequibo.[42] He questioned as improper commutations of death sentences and the holding of such prisoners in the establishment without proper judicial scrutiny. Beaumont had enquired about the process of commutation early in July 1864, noting that the normal practice of the Court issuing an order in the wake of the governor's expression of the royal intention had not been followed for some time. This oversight might, the judge warned, provide the basis for releasing inmates on writs of habeas corpus.[43] Hincks referred the matter to Attorney General Lucie Smith, who reported that the gaol delivery provisions did not apply to a penal settlement to which those already sentenced had been dispatched. Lucie Smith also stressed that the validity of a royal pardon was not dependent on any final judicial order. The lawyer described the proposed action of the judges as extrajudicial.[44] This opinion formed the basis of Hincks's representations to the Colonial Office, where Cardwell referred the matter to the English law officers.[45] The secretary of state cautioned the governor, meanwhile, against publicizing the views of the chief justice.

Beaumont, on leave in England at this juncture, discussed his views in person at the Colonial Office, although he communicated at length in writing with Permanent Undersecretary Frederic Rogers, setting out his reservations about gaol delivery and commutation in the colony.[46] At the time the impression at the Office seems to have been that the jurist had a valid point, and that Hincks would be well advised to take it seriously.[47] The issue of gaol delivery and commutation had also given rise to a dispute between the executive and the judiciary in the case of William Harris, who had had been convicted of manslaughter in 1851 and sentenced to fourteen years in prison.[48] On reviewing the record, Beaumont considered that an injustice might have been done in incarcerating the man for this length of time, and he questioned the governor on why this was so. Predictably, Hincks reacted unfavourably to the judge, seeking out cases for criticism in which penalties had already been imposed, a matter that was, in his mind, for the aggrieved party and counsel to take up on appeal, or by petition to the executive.[49]

Early in 1865 Cardwell mildly censured Beaumont for his stand on gaol delivery and commutation.[50] Gaol delivery related to those sent for trial, not those who had been tried and sentenced, and commutation was a preserve of the executive, said the secretary of state. Moreover, although a judge might visit a prison and relay evidence of abuse to the governor, the management of prisons and convicts also lay in the executive sphere. Cardwell chided the chief justice for searching out cases where a party felt aggrieved by a sentence passed and carried out, rather than leaving the matter to the justice system's normal processes. He described this as 'extrajudicial activism.' To the extent that there might be technical flaws in the process, they could be easily cleared up by legislation. Hincks quickly took the hint and introduced legislation to limit the role of the senior judge and his associates conducting gaol deliveries – an initiative that drew a sharp attack from Beaumont, who had his speeches on the issue published.[51] When the English law officers, who included the judge's sponsor, Roundell Palmer, approved the governor's position, the Colonial Office gave the ordinance the green light.[52] Beaumont – who had reluctantly concluded that the Court of Policy was not a legislative forum in which he could influence policy, given its membership and proclivities – had already decided to resign from his seat in that body and made his decision official in February 1865.[53] In accepting his resignation, Cardwell was careful to impress upon Hincks the need to refrain from attaching any stigma to the jurist's action.[54]

Beaumont's Stand on the Oppression of Indenture Workers

Less evident from Colonial Office records but equally charged was the tension resulting from Beaumont's attempts to combat the partiality of the stipendiary magistrates to the planters when disciplining indentured workers. He did this by overriding their decisions on appeal. His antagonists claimed that this was typically on technical grounds.[55] The chief justice's stand coincided with the views and actions of two other officials in the justice system, both of whom were to suffer for their initiatives in providing protection and equal justice to the immigrants.[56] George William Des Voeux, a stipendiary magistrate from England who had qualified as a lawyer and practised briefly in Toronto, took seriously and followed in his judgments the injunctions of the senior judge against partial and unjust application of the penal and master and servant laws.[57] He approved of the chief justice's 'disregard of what had apparently come to be accepted by the courts as a settled principle, viz. that when the evidence of "white" and "coloured" was opposed that of the "white" must necessarily prevail.'[58] This judge also applauded Beaumont's efforts to 'condemn with severity the irregularities of trustees and executors which,' he mused, 'must have been unusually prevalent in a colony where it was a familiar saying: "Don't make me your heir, make me your executor."'[59] Des Voeux noted that European men of prominence were often trustees of estates of any value, including those where the *cestui que trust* were coloured people. The magistrate's open sympathy for the chief justice, whom he felt both the local executive and the Colonial Office had treated shabbily, as well as his own criticism of government policy, landed him in hot water with Hincks too.[60] The governor moved him from the area in East Demerara where he and his family had settled and were well received, to the coast of West Demerara, where the more extreme planters had their estates and made their displeasure at his attitudes and actions known to him.

James Crosby, also a lawyer, had been in the colony longer than Beaumont and Des Voeux. London appointed him immigration agent general for the colony in 1858, with wide powers of supervision over the indenture system. His energy and the fairness of his administration of the system made him popular among the immigrants. When he took legal action on behalf of his charges against employers for illegal stoppage of wages or for any ill-usage, and to appeal convictions of indentured labourers, action that pointed to defects in the system, the result was a clash with the planters and Hincks.[61] By an administrative subterfuge Hincks stripped Crosby of his powers of independent action, by requiring all his recommendations to be vetted in the governor's office and denying him the money to travel to the estates to investigate complaints.[62]

Support for the chief justice was not limited to these officials. He enjoyed considerable respect among the oppressed, Creole members of the colonial community and among the Baptist preachers who ministered to them, and was lauded by the sympathetic reformist wing of the local press, especially the *Creole* and the *Guiana Times* for his impartiality and integrity.[63]

Despite London's definitive opinion on gaol delivery and commutation, the matter was to become the basis for new conflict between the governor and chief justice. On Beaumont's return from furlough in England he committed the clerk of the Supreme Court, William Campbell, to trial for tampering with judicial records of commutations.[64] During the jurist's absence, the clerk had completed the pardon records relating to five cases in 1863 and 1864 in which the chief justice had imposed the death penalty on immigrants convicted of murder, whose convictions were later commuted. Campbell post-dated them under the name of the senior judge, and also altered an entry on the instructions of Attorney General Lucie Smith.[65] Beaumont discovered the changed entries and demanded an explanation. Campbell argued that he had a duty to record commutations as the governor granted them, and had not by his actions shown any lack of respect for the judges, let alone done anything wrong. He also denied that he acted 'under pressure.'[66] When late in July 2009 Campbell appeared before the chief justice and Justice Beete, the matter was deferred so that a full bench of three judges might hear the matter, but not before Beaumont had stated that in his opinion the executive government was complicit in Campbell's actions.[67]

Hincks, beside himself with anger at this attack that he felt was directed at him, peremptorily suspended Beaumont from office.[68] The stated grounds were five: culpable indiscretion in publishing his speeches made in the Court of Policy; culpable neglect of duty in not making up the pardon records; unfounded imputations against the executive, calculated to bring it into disrepute by alleging its negligence in not observing the 'proper' formalities in completing pardon forms, and illegality in ordering their completion by Campbell; improper interference with public records and official documents; and judicial misconduct, in particular in searching extrajudicially to extend the supervision of the judges in matters, such as commutation, where the proper process was appeal, or petition to the government.[69] The governor was at pains to stress that the chief justice was continuing a conflict the Colonial Office had already resolved by indicating that commutations were exclusively within the executive's power, and that, as a consequence, neither William Campbell nor the attorney general had done anything amiss in completing the pardon forms. For Beaumont to have made an issue of this and to have stressed a sinister design by the colonial government showed his complete lack of discretion and wrongheadedness. The judge, Hincks asserted, had caused public scandals and made the colony more difficult to govern.[70]

Hincks's actions and reasons produced a scathing and lengthy judicial attack from the chief justice on the governor's 'unconstitutional and illegal procedures.'[71] Beaumont asserted that the governor had acted illegally in suspending him. Parliamentary privilege or freedom of speech protected any provocative statements he made, and the government, not he, was delinquent in failing to abide by the proper procedures for registering commutations. If he had erred, his decisions were open to appeal to the full court or the Privy Council. His suspicions remained strong that the government had directed the completion of the pardon forms and changes to one of them to circumvent judicial scrutiny, which was illegal. He also entertained no doubt that, if he as a judge was convinced that prisoners were in illegal custody, he was bound as a matter of law to free them.

Beyond this reworking of his position, the document is remarkable in alleging a conspiracy against him by the governor, Attorney General Lucie Smith, and William Campbell (Lucie Smith's close friend).[72] He based this allegation on a speech by John Trounsell Gilbert, Hincks's erstwhile enemy, to the Court of Policy. The speech, it was reported to him, revealed that, while the governor was castigating the chief justice for his unwarranted attacks on the executive prior to suspending him, he had dispatched Campbell, under judicial investigation for contempt, to open negotiations with Gilbert in order to bury the hatchet between them. Campbell and Gilbert were also close friends. The purpose of the meeting was to placate the Bermuda clique, but more precisely to offer the post of acting attorney general to Gilbert, should Beaumont be suspended. He would replace John Lucie Smith, who would become acting chief justice. The timing was such that Gilbert knew of this offer when he sought an adjournment of the investigation of Campbell's conduct by the chief justice and Justice Beete.

This 'gathering of eagles,' as the jurist branded the stratagem, leaves one with the sense that Hincks was determined to ensure that the colony's elite to a man were on side, as he moved decisively to end Beaumont's tenure as senior judge, and at the same time to protect Campbell from further legal proceedings. Even if it is argued that, as the chief executive, he was entitled to plan for the consequences of suspending the chief justice for what he considered cause, it seems particularly ill-judged if not outright devious, that he would use as his agent a man facing contempt allegations before the Supreme Court on such a matter of state.

If there was a conspiracy, it quickly fell apart when the Colonial Office reviewed the charges and countercharges. Beaumont repaired to London, where he made his representations to officials in person. Cardwell roundly criticized the governor for his unwarranted conduct in suspending the judge, without giving him any opportunity to defend himself prior to the suspension directive.[73] This was, the minister asserted, contrary both to the terms of his commission and royal instructions. The allegations against the judge 'taken in and of themselves and irrespective of Mr Beaumont's replies, [were] insufficient to sustain such a proceeding as the suspension of a judge.' Hincks had lost sight of the necessity of upholding the honour and legitimacy of the judiciary in the eyes of the community. The secretary of state did criticize Beaumont for his public allegations against the colony's executive, although he observed the judge was entitled to notice the irregularities in the new entries of pardons. In conclusion, Cardwell recommended that, if the governor thought a judge unfit to sit, the approach taken should be an address by the legislature to the Judicial Committee of the Privy Council.[74] He ordered the chief justice's reinstatement.

Hincks did as he was ordered and restored Beaumont as chief justice, to the exaggerated applause of the opposition press.[75] However, in a speech to the Court of Policy the governor unrepentantly painted himself as the protector of peace and order in the colony, and the enemy of the sort of political agitation that had recently plagued Jamaica under Governor Eyre.[76] The antagonism between the executive and judiciary in British Guiana had been troubling to the planters and merchants and the stability of the possession. He acted as he had, he claimed disingenuously, because to have continued to battle or even debate with the chief justice would have created a risk of encouraging conditions of revolt among the jurists' excitable, unreasoning Creole supporters.[77]

In his letter to Cardwell on his reinstatement and in response to Hincks's speech, Beaumont stressed his policy of remaining aloof from party politics, and his less than flattering opinion of black people:

> I have had frequent occasion to comment severely in their disregard of truth; to repudiate the popular colonial creed that a Negro was to be believed rather than an Asiatic; to censure their gross and shameless defiance of the law of marriage, their insolent, disrespectful demeanour, their cruelty to their children, their laziness and extortions and their shams of religion. I have had occasion to point out the fallacy of flattering them with their comparative immunity from crime, merely because the gaols are filled with Asiatic immigrants confined under the 'labour laws'; and that, taking true account of the graver offences, they are found not only to be sadly lawless, but that under aggravating circumstances, in defiance of Christianity and the most studious care for their education and well-being.[78]

If this was more than an attempt by the chief justice to ingratiate himself with the minister, it suggests that any anti-slavery sentiments he harboured were complex and reflected a mind that discriminated between the characteristics of other 'races' on the basis of stereotyping, with African Caribbeans labelled as less civilized and reliable than Asians.

There is no evidence that this message ever came to the notice of the Creole population or its leaders. In their book, Beaumont was solicitous of their interests and was ready to use the law where he could to protect their rights. The crucial example of his concern in their eyes was the stand he took against the Village Ordinance enacted by Hincks in an attempt to improve several large Creole villages on the East Coast of Demerara. These were considered disaster areas in terms of their physical condition and health hazards.[79] The locals demonstrated considerable resentment at the imposition of improvement taxes on them, and then the seizure of properties when they failed to pay them. The chief justice quashed the conviction of a dispossessed owner for trespass to property, when he forcibly repossessed his residence on the ground that the ordinance was legally defective. This made the new occupant a trespasser. The judge's action was interpreted as providing relief to all those removed from their properties, cast Beaumont as a 'brother' in the struggle against the governor, and impressed the Wesleyan and Baptist missionaries who supported the freed population.[80] To Hincks and his supporters it represented another example of a gratuitous attack on executive authority and one likely to stir up the Creole population and destabilize the colony.

The governor, who considered but rejected resigning, continued to draw support from the conservative press in the colony and favourable testimonials from members of the elite. Despite Cardwell's hope that the earlier differences between the two men and their supporters would be forgotten, tensions continued. For his part, the chief justice continued to rile his antagonists. He pressed forward with the Campbell prosecution. This resulted in a Supreme Court judgment that the clerk had falsified the commutation records.[81] The governor labelled this as 'vituperative' and designed to cast a stigma on both him and the attorney general, as well as Campbell. Hincks announced that he had refused to accept Campbell's attempted resignation, which the judges were pressing for as well as a public apology. However, in the absence of the latter and continued demands from the Supreme Court for the clerk's admission of wrongdoing, the governor ultimately felt it necessary to let him resign.[82] Sentiment among officials in the Colonial Office, tiring of this squabble, was that a reprimand of Campbell would have been the appropriate response to his misfeasance in the circumstances.[83]

But there was more to come. The determination by the Court in the Campbell case prompted the *Colonist* newspaper to attack Acting Judge James Crosby's presence on the bench in that case as a 'farce.' He was labelled an 'eccentric gentleman' who should return to his position of obscurity.[84] When the judges called editor Laurence McDermott before them on a charge of contempt, the paper thundered about the trampling on the rights of colonists to trial by jury – an act of judicial usurpation that 'will perhaps open the eyes of Mr Secretary Cardwell to the dangerous character of the gentleman [Beaumont] who he has taken under his protection.'[85] The judges found the editor guilty of contempt and consigned him to the common jail for six months for his pains.[86] Moreover, they complained bitterly when they discovered that McDermott's quarters had received a facelift and that he was being treated substantially better than other prisoners.[87]

However, despite these seemingly confident moves, the sense is strong that the judges were now developing a garrison mentality. The evidence lies in a letter from the judges pleading with both the colonial government and the Colonial Office to protect the Court from unwarranted, libellous attacks on its members.[88] Based on comments scribbled on the letter by Undersecretary Rogers, London's response was unsympathetic. The scrawl suggests Colonial Office officialdom's frustration with the whole mess, an acceptance that the squabble over legal issues had become a running political battle, and a tendency to lay primary blame for its continuation at the chief justice's door. The Colonial Office official criticized Campbell for his stubbornness in not taking his error seriously enough, but found Beaumont's treatment of him unjustifiably mean-spirited – 'exceedingly offensive and injurious' were the words Rogers chose. Most revealing is his observation that the judge and the governor were attacking each other through Campbell, both using him as a pawn.[89] The Colonial Office was not convinced that it should intervene to protect the reputation of the court in this instance.

McDermott's imprisonment provided the rallying point for a renewed attempt by the planter and merchant elite to rid the colony of Beaumont. In May 1866 the Court of Policy submitted a series of memorials through Hincks to the secretary of state, moving for the chief justice's dismissal.[90] The charges against the jurist focused on his 'constantly and evinced tendencies to unsettle the practice as previously established; to decry and discredit our system of law … to introduce innovations unwarranted by his own dicta; and to depart as widely as possible from the paths pursued by his able and learned and experienced predecessors.' The chief justice, it was alleged, had tampered with official court records in several cases, and his conduct and demeanour in both the *Campbell* and *McDermott* cases were attacked. The memorial concluded, 'We must affirm our earnest belief – a belief founded not only on the instances of judicial indiscretion, error and misconduct which we have specified, but on our observation of Mr Beaumont's entire career as Chief Justice – that the success of this movement on our part is absolutely necessary to the reestablishment of that general confidence in the administration of justice in this Colony, without which no man can feel that his dearest interests are safe, or can carry on securely and satisfactorily, even the most ordinary transactions of life.'

Beaumont's supporters, led by a Baptist missionary, the editor of the *Creole*, and a Creole lawyer, responded with two memorials of their own, praising the judges for their 'ability, independence, integrity and discretion.'[91] The documents stressed the elite's distaste for Beaumont, the sympathy for that position in 'high places,' the desire of the executive to prefer local candidates in the judiciary, and the influence of Gilbert and the Bermuda clique on official policy. Beaumont dismissed the charges against him as groundless and forwarded in an incompetent manner.

The initial view in the Colonial Office, as expressed by Henry Taylor, senior clerk for the West Indies, was that Beaumont should be censured and admonished for his indiscretions – such as on the gaol delivery issue and his overreaction to Campbell's and McDermott's errancy – but not dismissed.[92] The judge's concern to expose defects in local legislation and the way in which he had administered justice had merit. Despite this modest in-house disciplinary proposal, by the end of June the Office had decided to forward the memorial from the Court of Policy to the Privy Council, for the Judicial Committee's consideration. In the following month Hincks, who was in London on leave, in commenting on his difficulties with his senior judge remarked on the problems created in a colony when a jurist was asked to combine political or executive duties with his judicial functions.[93] He also drew upon his Canadian experience in suggesting that the practice of excluding judges from legislative bodies had improved matters for all the parties involved.

There followed a long period in which the recriminations between Beaumont, still in office pending the outcome of the address by the Court of Policy to the Judicial Committee, and Hincks (who remained in England until August 1867) and his other detractors continued. The correspondence was long and tedious and the attacks overblown. Two examples will suffice. Firstly, correspondence revealed that communications had broken down within the Supreme Court, and the legal community was shunning the chief justice. Beaumont and court officials were apparently unable to talk to each other, and, when on circuit, members of the bar excluded him from their mess.[94] Secondly, his judgments in favour of indentured workers were capable of producing dramatic reaction from his enemies. In December 1867 Beaumont on appeal struck down the conviction of an Indian worker for 'insufficient work' on the complaint of his employer, and upheld the dismissal of a charge by Des Voeux in a similar case, on the ground that the relevant ordinance failed to define the word *task* and to provide any measuring rod for adjudging whether the offence had occurred. In retaliation the Court of Policy refused to include the chief justice's salary in the civil list.[95]

The case for the Court of Policy before the Judicial Committee rehearsed the familiar complaints about Beaumont:[96] vexatiously embarrassing and injuring the authority of the executive government; holding up the governor and officials 'to hatred and obloquy and charging them with arbitrary and unfair conduct'; publicly censuring, punishing vindictively, and humiliating an official of the Court; and using the bench to make intemperate remarks about influential inhabitants who were not before the Court or represented by counsel there. Two other charges were added, presumably to make the point that, while the chief justice had used the bench to play politics, he had at the same time erred badly in his purely judicial role. In the first place he was charged very specifically with 'hastily and irregularly annulling a marriage without any formal proceedings or declaring [the] marriage void.' Secondly, the charges alleged the judge's tampering with Court records to screen his own mistakes, and otherwise being guilty in several instances of haste and careless, negligent and irregular conduct in office.

Beaumont, whose case Sir Roundell Palmer, acting pro bono, argued in part, focused not on the 'political' charges, which were dismissed as vague, generalized, and lacking in substance, but concentrated on answering the allegations of impropriety in the judge's application of the law and legal procedures. The arguments here were crafted to demonstrate that his decisions (including those in *Campbell* and *McDermott*) were supported by the law applicable, and that alleged procedural errors were neither typical of his court nor intentional, and had been remedied.

After hearing both lines of argument, the Judicial Committee recommended to the Queen that Joseph Beaumont be relieved of his position as chief justice of British Guiana.[97]

The committee was of the opinion that the major charge, 'judicial misconduct,' had not been made out. However, the judge was found guilty of 'proofs of indiscretion and a want of judicial temper.' His conduct was characterized as tending 'to embarrass the Executive Government rather than to promote the ends of justice.' The strategy of the Court of Policy and its legal advisers in stressing the political difficulties created by the jurist's conduct had paid off.

Beaumont's Performance and the Changes in Imperial Policy towards the Multiracial Colonies: An Assessment

The case raised the same sort of tension as that in Bent's thirty-six years earlier. Here was a judge with a strong sense of legality, a commitment to English law and its values, and to the rule of law, who demanded equality before the law, and had a profound distrust of local customs and practices that reflected the narrow desires and vision of an entrenched white elite. Allied against him were planters and merchants motivated by a desire to preserve the status quo in the management of labour and labour discipline, and the local law that compliant judges and magistrates had willingly applied in the past. In the middle was a governor concerned about not rocking the boat and alienating the economic movers and shakers in the colony, and unduly concerned about the breakdown of peace and order among the non-white majority. He was also a man deeply unhappy about having his position undermined by competitors, and probably uncomfortable with the less than subtle dynamics of politics in Britain's Caribbean possessions.

Unlike Bent, who had the fortune to have his case heard by imperial authorities sympathetic to his stand against abuse of power by the plantocracy, Beaumont's case was not. He fell victim to London's fundamental reappraisal during the 1860s of how imperial power should be deployed in multiracial colonies with European minority populations. This reassessment occurred in the wake of the Indian Mutiny of the late 1850s, but more especially as a result of Governor Eyre's bloody actions in1865 in invoking and maintaining martial law to quell dissent in one parish in Jamaica.[98] The lesson taken from the rebellion or resistance of the 'coloured' subjects of the Crown against oppression and injustice was not to initiate ways of bringing them into the legislative process in the colonies they inhabited. It was rather to clip the wings of the planter elite by closing down local legislative power entirely, and substituting direct rule by a governor working with councils dominated by officials.[99] This move reflected indirectly the influence of a powerful imperialist lobby in Britain, men such as Thomas Carlyle, A.J. Froude, and John Ruskin, who believed that the 'coloured races' were not to be trusted, that they required close control, and that violence against them or the threat of it was legitimate if the colonial authorities believed them to be engaged in or threatening riot or rebellion.[100]

With the exception of Barbados, all Britain's West Indian colonies became Crown colonies by the mid-1870s. In this new colonial order, the notion of a reforming chief justice who would challenge the colonial executive, as he pressed vigorously his own legal and constitutional agenda, was plainly not acceptable. To condone such behaviour was to jeopardize peace, order, and good government, and to give the subject peoples dangerous ideas about rights and full political participation. Conciliation maybe, but single-minded dedication to reformist change, no! Like Smith and Bent, Beaumont believed strongly in the virtue of his cause and had a jaundiced opinion of officials in colonial government. As his friend Des Voeux observed, he also allowed himself 'to be goaded into indiscretions which laid open his guard and gave the opportunity for a fatal thrust.'[101] Whether a more moderate approach would have produced a result more favourable to a liberal notion of the rule of law in the colony, given the tenor of the times, is unlikely, although it might have saved him his job. The clash of personalities and the new imperial priorities in the non-white empire made it inevitable that Beaumont would be dismissed from office in Guiana and would be unlikely to secure further preferment.[102]

Beaumont returned to England and practice, embittered by his treatment. He set out his frustrations in a book, *The New Slavery*.[103] In it he described the abuses committed against the indentured workers, from the inadequate information supplied to them in their places of origin about that labour system, to the unreasonable and often harsh demands made of them as workers on the estates, the injustices of the pass system, the inadequate health facilities available to them, the squalor and unhealthy nature of their lodgings, and the parody of justice received from the magistrates when their employers considered them to have erred. He detailed too the difficulties he had faced in securing fair and decent treatment for them. He made a searing indictment of the system: 'This is not a question of more or less, of this or that safeguard, of an occasional defect there, or excess there. But it is that of a monstrous, rotten system, rooted in slavery, grown in its stale soil, emulating its worst abuses, and only the more dangerous because it presents itself under false colours, whereas slavery bore the brand of infamy on its forehead.'[104]

If there were any consolations for the former judge, they lay in the support from the Creole population of the colony who held him a hero and, indeed, made a place for him in the folklore of the later independence movement, and the report of a commission of inquiry into the indenture system in British Guiana in the early 1870s.[105] The inquiry was a consequence of complaints made to Earl Granville, secretary of state for the colonies, by the former stipendiary magistrate William Des Voeux, who had survived Hincks's displeasure and been appointed administrator in St Lucia. As we have seen, he shared Beaumont's view of the injustices being done in Guiana.[106] The Commissioners' Report substantiated several of the two men's complaints, and, as a result, some beneficial changes were made to the system by restoring the former status of the immigration agent-general for immigration and improving health services to the migrants.[107]

The Wandering Jurist: Sir John Gorrie

The colonial judicial career of John Gorrie in multiracial possessions during the late nineteenth century, which stretched over twenty two years, in some respects belies the trend towards greater control of judges, including chief justices, by executive authority in the Caribbean and elsewhere in the non-white empire, from the 1860s on. This remarkable individual manifested well-developed progressive political views on a range of issues in the jurisdictions that he served, which he was not afraid to use as the basis for both judgments and policy pronouncements. He was in sequence puisne judge in Mauritius and chief justice of Fiji, the Leeward Islands, and Trinidad and Tobago between 1870 and 1892.[108] Gorrie, a lawyer trained in Scotland, came by his political beliefs honestly. He had been a member of the radical wing of the Liberal Party under William Gladstone in the late 1860s. As a lawyer and activist he had gone to Jamaica in the wake of Governor Eyre's invocation of martial law. He was there both as a journalist for the liberal daily, the *Morning Star*, and as counsel on behalf of the anti-Eyre Jamaica Committee, to report on and participate in the hearings of the royal commission established to investigate those events.[109]

As a judge in the various jurisdictions, all of which had multiracial populations, Gorrie made no bones about his concern at settler elites' oppression of the most disadvantaged members of local populations. His attitudes and actions reflected liberal reformist, if paternalistic, notions about responsible trusteeship of the subject peoples, and a romantic, humanitarian vision of what the empire could be.[110] Through his judicial decisions, the legislation he drafted, and the commissions he undertook, he sought to provide them with the protection of the law and British ideals of equal justice.

In Mauritius, Gorrie worked hand in glove with the governor, Arthur Gordon, who relied heavily on the judge's political and legal counsel.[111] The island, conquered by the British from France in 1810, had remained essentially French thereafter.[112] The Roman Catholic faith was dominant, the language was French and French Creole, the law was that of the *Code Napoleon*, and the court procedures French. French Creole settlers, organized in several landowning families, who formerly held slaves, dominated the society. With the abolition of slavery, these owners, predominantly sugar planters, introduced indentured labour from India in a system that in some ways constituted a new form of slavery.[113] The jurist used both the courtroom and his dominant role on the Police Inquiry Committee to criticize the policing of and attitudes of the magistracy towards indentured labour, and in particular the 'old immigrants,' former estate workers who had served out the five-year indenture period. The local police, who were notoriously corrupt, harassed and treated as vagabonds these workers who were nominally free but had no effective means of repatriation.[114] Gorrie's policy of activism on the matter, together with his attempts to simplify legal procedures and slash legal costs, created an unfavourable reaction against him (as well as the governor) among the Creole planter elite, officials drawn from that class, members of the bar, and the conservative press.[115] The judge's combative, interventionist style in court, especially his tendency to browbeat juries and counsel, and his capacity for what Gordon described as impetuosity and exaggeration, drew criticism from those sources about his fitness for the bench and his 'impartiality.'

Despite his propensity for combining law with reformist politics and an acerbic tongue, Gorrie enjoyed protection through his association with Gordon, something of a poster boy for colonial governors at the time. Moreover, his reforms of the legal system and his strictures on the treatment of serving or former Indian 'coolies,' substantiated by a royal commission dispatched from London to the island, drew praise in the Colonial Office.[116] There was no resistance in 1874 when Gordon, recently appointed the first governor of the newly ceded colony of Fiji, requested that Gorrie join him as the possession's first chief justice.

The judge arrived in 1876 in the capital, Levuka. The British had annexed Fiji only in 1874. This move was a result of concerns about the character of the white settler population, the kidnapping of islanders ('black birding') to labour on plantations elsewhere, most notably Queensland, and a desire to protect traditional Fijian landholding, while encouraging agricultural settlement and production (cotton, sugar, and coconuts) by newcomers.[117]

Sir John again worked closely with Gordon in establishing the judicial and governmental structures for the infant colony, and regulating the roles of its multiracial population.[118] He drafted legislation, including devising a civil code, and sat on the Legislative Council, which in a Crown colony 'of a severe type' was entirely nominated and official.[119] The governor's 'native policy' involved leaving and protecting native Fijians, who been largely Christianized by Methodist missionaries, on their traditional lands and governed by their communal property regimes, and, to a degree, by their own law. Indentured Pacific Islanders and Indians were to provide labour in the developing sugar and coconut estates, but subject to fair and just regulation, including protection against mistreatment. A land commission would control the granting of land to white settlers and entrepreneurs, considered essential to the economic welfare of the islands, by vetting transfers already made by Fijian communities to whites, and regulating future transactions to ensure consent and fair dealing.[120]

True to form, Gorrie criticized officials he considered incompetent and came down heavily on magistrates who closed their eyes to the mistreatment of estate labourers.[121] Moreover, when he could, through Supreme Court proceedings, he protected workers from dishonest labour practices and physical abuse, earning him the reputation of being pro-native, especially in the press.[122]

The regulation of the Polynesian labour trade also made enemies for Gordon and Gorrie, with the chief justice as a particular lightning rod. They found that controlling the labour practices of elements of the white population in Fiji was one thing, but trying to deal with the practice of estate owners in that territory and elsewhere in the Western Pacific of commissioning masters and vessels to kidnap Polynesians for work on plantations on the islands or in Queensland was quite another.[123] This nefarious trade was widespread in the region, where the jurisdiction of competing or would-be colonial powers was fragmentary and most of the source territories under Polynesian rule. The practice, resented in indigenous communities, had resulted in violent retaliation against some of the perpetrators, and in several instances innocent parties.[124] As the solution, London established a Western Pacific High Commission with powers to control British subjects' lawless activities in Pacific Islands that were not in the hands of 'civilized states.'[125] Under this regime a judicial commissioner, the chief justice of Fiji, working under the governor of the colony as high commissioner, had jurisdiction over British subjects engaging in the trade who had committed the felony of kidnapping or decoying Polynesians into forced labour. A number of successes were recorded in bringing the culprits to book before the commission's court, but a variety of jurisdictional problems frustrated other attempts at prosecution.[126]

Gorrie's activism led him to consider ill-judged proactive measures to control the trade and to stymie attempts by Australasians to extend their authority in the region. This was particularly problematic in the late 1870s when he was acting high commissioner in the absence of Gordon, on leave.[127] Relations with the Royal Navy, which had a roving mandate to preserve order in the region, also became strained, especially on the issue of whether and to what extent the commission court had jurisdiction over naval reprisals against indigenous individuals or groups who had retaliated against Europeans for offences against them.[128] Gorrie's role in the work of the commission opened him to searing criticism in the Queensland press from the supporters of imported plantation labour. One American journalist, Stanley James, writing under the pseudonym of 'The Vagabond' in a flight of emotional rhetoric, accused the jurist of allowing 'the noble savage' without exception 'to slaughter and plunder England's pioneers.'[129] He also highlighted the judge's close connections with the Aborigines' Protection Society and Exeter Hall, the colloquial term for the anti-slavery movement in Britain.[130] However, the judge's straight-talking manner and fearlessness in standing up to free-booting Europeans in this unstable area of colonial encounter earned him praise in London.[131]

Gorrie's tenure as chief justice of Fiji ended because of his fraught relations with Gordon's successor as governor. The new man was none other than William Des Voeux, loyal supporter of Joseph Beaumont in British Guiana, whose complaints about the injustices of the indenture system in that colony had led to a major investigation of it.[132] Caribbean historian Bridget Brereton sees the friction between the two men as the product of a profound personality clash. On the one side was the governor, who was 'a quick tempered, insecure, impulsive man, often ill, and prone to fits of petulance; he saw slights everywhere and could react almost irrationally at times.'[133] Bad chemistry with the chief justice, who was also quick-tempered and impulsive, self-confident and devoted to Gordon, was, she suggests, inevitable. Despite the fact that they had much in common in their values, they were capable of amazing pettiness in disagreements over less than vital issues. This was true, for example, of a squabble over the pace of the movement of the capital of the colony and its institutions from Levuka to Suva.[134] The cutting rhetoric began to fly. However, it was their falling out on the more substantial subject of who should provide legal representation to Fijians, when a European claimed that the land they possessed was his by right, that persuaded the Colonial Office that the only solution was the chief justice's promotion out of the colony.[135]

London offered Gorrie the chief justiceship of the Leeward Islands, which he accepted after some hard bargaining. Despite his truculence towards those he despised, he still had the firm support of Gordon and a solid record of achievement, as the Colonial Office saw it, in establishing law, order, and good government in Fiji, and in taking on the sinister forces of trade and commerce in the Western Pacific. A gregarious and social creature who took a full part in the educational and recreational life of the colony, he had earned a place in the hearts of some members of the white community, including members of the bar.[136] Moreover, his attempts to use the law to protect the vulnerable brought him respect from both native Fijians and Indian migrants. In a very real sense his rough and tough approach to law and justice was appropriate to this oceanic frontier of the late-nineteenth-century empire.

If Fiji represented the new frontier of British colonialism, the Leeward Islands (Antigua, St Kitts and Nevis, Dominica, Monserrat, and the British Virgin Islands) were examples of an older colonial system in economic decline.[137] Their sugar plantations were in financial trouble. Steps has been taken to rationalize the government and administration of justice in these micro possessions, with a single governor and chief justice based in Antigua, and a federated council drawing representatives from each of the local island councils.[138] Gorrie's attempts at further reform and his criticisms of the justice system were to earn him the enmity of some.[139] Planters, the associate justices, and most members of the bar vigorously opposed his advocacy of greater centralization of the court system, and a reduction in the number of circuits.[140] The judge's characteristic attacks on the magistracy for indifference to the poor and partiality in their treatment of petty offenders, his activism in affording protection to sharecroppers (*metayers*), securing to them compensation from estate owners for improvements they made, and dishing out severe penalties to riotous young whites, all produced bitter criticism among the elite and their conservative mouthpieces in the colonial press.[141] Moreover, his uncomplimentary remarks on the performance of lawyers including the attorney general, Stephen Gatty, did nothing to endear him to the legal fraternity.

Gorrie added to these negative perceptions, while dealing with the tragedy of his wife's illness and death, by his unpredictable behaviour from the bench on circuit in 1884 and part of 1885. This had drawn an abortive motion in council to have him impeached.[142] However, he weathered the storm, recovered his equilibrium, and rendered very helpful service in drafting legislation introducing the Torrens system of land registration and extending the Supreme Court's jurisdiction to preserve local interests in land when mortgage complications arose.[143] Less successful were his attempts to establish a system of state-sponsored mortgage guarantees in which he faced Gatty's opposition.[144] As in his previous postings, the judge immersed himself and members of his family in the civic, social, religious, and recreational life of the islands. Once again, notwithstanding his garrulousness, London promoted him to the chief justiceship of Trinidad in 1886, a sign that the Colonial Office still had faith in him and his legal and law reform skills.[145] Gorrie became chief justice of Tobago in 1889 when the two island colonies were joined. It was in these territories that his reputation for taking the part of the underdog, his short temper, overactive tongue, and restless activism caught up with him.

Trinidad and Tobago in the Late Nineteenth Century

Trinidad had continued its status as Crown colony through the nineteenth century, although the imperial government had granted it a nominated legislative council in 1831.[146] The other major change was that English law had replaced earlier Spanish civil law by 1850.[147] Most of the men appointed to the judiciary after the tumultuous tenure of George Smith kept their heads down, did what was expected of them, avoided reformist colonial politics, and maintained their seats. The one exception, who managed to survive the 'slings and arrows of outrageous misfortune' directed at him, was George Scotland, chief justice from 1832 to 1849. Hailing from a family that had settled in Antigua, Scotland was sympathetic to the abolition of slavery.[148] He incurred the wrath of the planters when he sought to enforce new legislation passed by London in 1831, establishing offences designed to protect slaves from ill-treatment by their owners, and was openly critical of the *alcades*, hostile to these changes, who refused to sit with him to hear their prosecution.[149] Possibly because of Scotland's more diplomatic approach to criticizing the power structure, and the fact that he was acting, as far as London was concerned, in a perfectly judicious way, disciplinary action or threats of it were never entertained.

Like British Guiana, Trinidad faced a labour shortage in the decades after abolition, solved too by the importation of indentured labourers, primarily from India.[150] As a consequence, the colony, in addition to planters of both French and British heritage, and an emerging black and mixed-race middle class, possessed a segmented underclass of Afro-Caribbeans and South Asians. By the time Gorrie reached the island, the sugar industry was well organized and capitalized, and cocoa was set fair to match it in exports.[151] Tobago, a smaller, less-productive island with a predominantly former slave population, but with a legislative assembly, had faced an increasing economic crisis during the century because of the vagaries of the sugar trade. London joined the territory with Trinidad in 1889, so that its fortunes might improve by making it part of a larger, more viable economic unit.[152]

J. Gorrie Takes on the Plantocracy

Soon after his appointment, Gorrie antagonized the settler elite, who formed a majority in the Legislative Council of the recently merged colonies (the nominated 'unofficials').[153] In both possessions he changed procedures to provide access for poor people to the Supreme Court by granting suits *in forma pauperis*, and by summonses to defendant planters – processes that the planters complained clogged the system and allowed the judge to victimize them unfairly.[154] On Tobago he challenged the control of the *metayage* system of sharecropping, and from the bench revised the system to provide rights to labourers against planters, inter alia affording a form of fixed tenure to the former.[155] Gorrie added to his negative halo among the elite by attacking, often in intemperate and injudicious language, members of both the medical and legal professions who he felt did not live up the obligations and ethics required of them.[156] In some cases he treated jurors to similarly abusive conduct.[157] The police objected to his criticisms of partiality and protectiveness of their own. The judge's active involvement in political roles, such as chairing the Trade and Taxes Commission, to which he brought his strong free trade proclivities, also raised the ire of his detractors.[158] Among his many foes he could count the new attorney general, Stephen Gatty, an antagonist from his days in the Leeward Islands, because Gorrie cast aspersions on how he handled his office.[159] Another sworn enemy was R.B. Anderson, a doctor, planter, and merchant on Tobago who felt particularly aggrieved by the judge's treatment of him in several lawsuits.[160] In the case of *Franks v. Anderson* Gorrie had set out his controversial views on the obligations of planters and the rights of *metayers* (sharecroppers) in the *metayage* system. He denied the defendant's claim that he was entitled to terminate the contract and evict the plaintiff at will. Anderson was also outraged at the way in which the court had dealt with two actions relating to his medical practice. In *Anderson v. Marshall*, an action against a patient for his fees that went against him, Anderson delayed paying damages and costs. Associate Justice Cook cited him for contempt and ordered him imprisoned for failing to provide surety and bail in the amount of £500, a decision upheld by the Court of Appeal on which all three judges, including Gorrie, sat.[161] A right of appeal to the Privy Council had been denied Anderson in both the *Franks* and *Marshall* cases.[162]

Gorrie's enemies pressed vigorously for the amoval of this 'tyrannical' and even 'socialist' judge. The Creole and mixed-race population's lionizing of Gorrie (the 'Ah We Judge' or 'Papa Gorrie') was cast by his antagonists as evidence of the subversive and dangerous character of the man and his motives.[163] For several years the Colonial Office resisted such pressure and supported the judge's stance on a number of legal and political issues, although expressing frustration at his garrulousness and confrontational tactics.[164] Unphased by criticism, the judge took a strong unsuccessful stand against legislation that, as he saw it, skewed contracts between planters of cocoa and coconuts, and small holders who did the groundwork.[165]

The pressure for the jurist's removal built up late in 1891, and both the minister and officials in London began to tire of the ongoing saga of conflict, not to mention growing concern about his involvement in promoting a peoples' banking venture in the islands.[166] As a consequence the secretary of state, Lord Knutsford, appointed a blue ribbon commission of inquiry into the administration of justice in the twin colonies.[167] The commissioners, the eminent former Indian judge and Reader in

Indian Law at Oxford, William Markby, and Frederick Pollock, Regius Professor of Jurisprudence at the same university and an eminent English barrister, found against the chief justice.[168] They concluded that the judge had abused his powers to satisfy his own visions of justice and accessibility to the courts, albeit from worthy motives, by allowing actions *in forma pauperis* outside the rules; that he had mismanaged funds lodged by suitors with the court; that he was guilty of 'intemperate conduct and language' from the bench; and that there were serious irregularities in the handling of some elements of the Anderson litigation in Tobago. Change in the system was essential, said the commissioners, if confidence in it was to be restored. With the report in hand, Governor Broome endeavoured to get Gorrie to resign and leave quietly. The judge refused and Broome 'interdicted' him from carrying out his judicial duties, pending what the chief executive predicted would be a decision of the Executive Council in a 'trial,' confirming the jurist's suspension.[169]

Gorrie took a sick leave to go to England to present his case to the Colonial Office and, if necessary, the Privy Council. He died shortly after arriving, before he could present his case.[170] The judge's rough-hewn approach to the administration of justice and calling a spade a spade that had essentially served him well in the frontier conditions of Fiji and the Western Pacific had proven problematic in the long-standing and hypersensitive planter societies in the Caribbean. Moreover, unlike his situation in Mauritius and Fiji, in the West Indies he no longer had a powerful patron on hand to afford him protection.

J. Gorrie's Career Assessed

Of the judicial careers canvassed here, that of Gorrie draws the greatest sympathy, although, like several others, he proved too aggressive in some instances in his political stances and demeanour. As his biographer suggests, he was perhaps better suited for a career in politics, which had eluded him as a young man, or in colonial administration, which he sought shortly before he left Fiji, than for service in the colonial judiciary.[171] Gorrie stands out as one having deep and principled concerns about the fate of the downtrodden throughout the multiracial empire. His departure from office and his death were deeply regretted by those whose interests he had tried to serve and who publicly voiced their regret, and his memory lived on in reformist circles on the islands for many decades.[172]

Beaumont's and Gorrie's treatment indicate that subservience of the judicial arm of the colonial state to the executive was a sine qua non of law and politics in the Caribbean, and other multiracial colonial possessions during the late nineteenth century. Judges were meant to comply with a governor's vision of what was good for the colony, even if it meant compromising the deployment of the rule of law to protect the disenfranchised and oppressed. Although the swing to Crown colony government could and sometimes did have the beneficial result of providing political will in some territories that had been lacking before, it also meant that executive decisions could be and were made that were insensitive to local conditions, and more committed to preserving order than to promoting political and social change. Not surprisingly, local people who had the ear of the colonial executive were all too often planters, merchants, or their minions. As a consequence the system could and did preserve the social and economic status quo in these grossly unequal societies. It delayed the growth of democratic government.[173] To the extent that the political balance of power in these possessions was set in favour of elite local economic interests to the cost of the majority of the population, the colonies continued to be haunted by slavery and its seemingly indelible stain.[174]

11

Judges, Courts, and Empire in the Nineteenth Century and Beyond

The Significance of These Stories

What of the significance of these stories? It might be tempting to treat them as a series of ripping yarns of empire, the tales of a parade of eccentrics, malcontents, mavericks, and egomaniacs that have nothing useful to tell us about the roles of judges in colonial society. I argue vigorously that it is wrong to commit them to the ashcan of historical ephemera. In the first place, several of them had important thoughts on the constitutional relationship between Great Britain and its colonies, and the need to change and further liberalize it. Although those opinions and reservations were dismissed as improper for a colonial judge to hold and were not typically pursued, or even recognized, at the time the men were active as jurists, they did feed into later debate on changes to the constitutional arrangements between the colonies and the metropolis. In that sense, their pronouncements and reflections were part of a pattern of reformist opinion woven from various sources that is important in understanding the trajectories of imperial and colonial histories in the nineteenth century and beyond. The stories of the more conservative judges in the sample are instructive, too, in that they demonstrate the constitutional system and mindset to which reform-minded colleagues were reacting. They also reveal strains of thinking that, while they were in many ways eclipsed by the pressures for liberalization of the imperial–colonial relationship, underwent refinement and continued to bring a more conservative vision to discussion and debate on colonial governance and law, and their future. It is unlikely that one gets as sharp an image of the place of judges in colonial constitutional and legal orders by looking at the journeymen jurists with their heads down, attending to their judicial business, and not rocking the boat. Finally, it is important not to fall into the mistake of concluding that law was somehow a sideshow in the cultural development of empire, and was either irrelevant or of marginal importance to the political, social, economic, or intellectual history of the era under examination.[1] Law was an important instrument in the extension of imperial authority to the expanding range of territories that it encompassed, for the exercise of power and the establishment of British conceptions of order in those possessions, for facilitating their economic and social development, and for ordering relations and rights and responsibilities within them. Moreover, the discourse deployed to support or deny political change within the empire during the nineteenth century was infused with and supported by constitutional and legal values, rhetoric and imagery from the English-speaking world of the two previous centuries.

How do the accounts of the careers addressed in this book enlighten us about the realities and significance of judicial service in British colonies during the nineteenth century?

The Nineteenth-Century Empire and the Judiciary

In the course of the nineteenth century, the judges in the United Kingdom settled into the limited but more or less comfortable role of dispute resolution, involving the application of the Common Law and determining the effects of a burgeoning body of statutory and regulatory law.[2] To the extent that the legal system countenanced superior courts second-guessing executive or administrative action through judicial review, its ambit was limited and imprecise.[3] Ironically, just as the royal courts were crowding out the last of the traditional local and special jurisdictions and seemed to have an open field in which to operate, they faced a new set of competitors associated with the awakening of the regulatory state that had the effect of limiting the range of their decision-making responsibilities.[4]

True, disputes could and did raise issues of rights and liberties associated with the rule of law and the kaleidoscope of principles and meanings that the notion embodied, as well as fundamental issues of constitutional importance, such as the extent of parliamentary privilege and freedom of thought.[5] Accordingly, some litigation inevitably reflected and refracted political values more directly. Moreover, few of these men were free of prior political involvement and connections. Indeed, it was often a factor in their appointments.[6] However, the lord chancellor, who was a political appointee, and the law lords, who were entitled to sit and participate in the House of Lords as a legislative body apart, the combined effects of the crystallizing of parliamentary sovereignty, the emergence of a separation of powers in British constitutional practice, and a gradual movement to democracy was to insulate, as well as to discourage, the judiciary from direct involvement in politics and political life.[7] This is not to suggest that judges were political empty vessels or that they were free of biases in their judgments, as political activists, such as Chartists and union organizers, would have readily attested.[8] However, the formal commitment to judicial independence embodied in the Act of Settlement largely ruled out their being active players in the politics of the nation. As Lord Ellenborough's experience as a member of Cabinet in 1807 suggests, such involvement was frowned upon.[9] Where assumptions were made by those outside the law that British judges could be appealed to do justice as political saviours – the strategy of the Jamaica Committee in the Governor Eyre controversy, for example – the results were disappointing.[10] In Britain, then, the tensions of the seventeenth century over judicial accountability became a faded memory, although rhetorically effective when circumstances seemed to demand it. Judges there occupied a relatively safe middle ground between the competing ideals associated with Sir Edward Coke and Lord Francis Bacon.

The field of conflict over the state's relationship to the judiciary had not, however, disappeared by the nineteenth century, but had shifted from the metropolis to the colonies. It was in those territories that tensions between the executive and judges – and, where they existed, legislative assemblies – over the proper role of the judiciary and the nature of judicial tenure pulsated and seemed to those involved to replicate those under the Stuart monarchs. The discourse and rhetoric surrounding those tensions was often suffused with language reminiscent of seventeenth-century disputes. At the dawning of the nineteenth century – reflecting both a messy and often reactive process of managing the colonial judiciary and anxieties about the survival of the empire and internal security – the British government's position was clear, that judges appointed to the colonies would hew to a Baconian model.[11] This position manifested itself in the retention of the prerogative as the instrument for selecting candidates and appointing them, and in large part for their firing, the continuation of appointments at pleasure, and a dogged refusal to countenance the extension of the Act of Settlement or anything like it to the empire. To the limited extent that legislation may have related to judicial discipline, Burke's Act, it reflected in large part confirmation of the existing authority of colonial executives embodied in their instructions.

As the nineteenth century progressed, the sorts of conflicts about judicial tenure and independence that marked seventeenth-century England were replicated in the empire. Some judges challenged what they considered the irresponsible exercise of executive power by and abuses of the rule of law by colonial governors and their local supporters.[12] Other judges made it clear that their allegiances were firmly with the colonial state and the Crown's exercise of prerogative power.[13] In some possessions in which legislative assemblies existed, representative bodies that reformist forces controlled or influenced challenged the claims of executives to supervise and discipline the judiciary.[14] In others the alliances between traditional powerful local elites in assemblies and conservative governors resulted in attacks on judges who had the temerity to try to import liberal and inclusive rule-of-law thinking into – and to question the validity of – local law in the territories they served.[15] Several judges were at the centre of tensions over a widespread trend towards English substantive and procedural law and its underlying values in the colonies, and the reach of that process of legal change.[16]

The pattern of imperial control was in time to break down but not disappear. In fact two distinct policy trajectories developed on the issue of judicial independence within the empire during the century. After the 1830s the British government realized grudgingly that it faced real trouble if it continued to ignore the voices in the white settler colonies arguing for a new constitutional relationship between the metropolis and its possessions based on self-government. As part of London's reassessment, it progressively released its control over the appointment and conditions of service of judges, and in large part over their disciplining, by acceding to their appointment during good behaviour, denying them membership of executive or legislative bodies, and emulating the process in the Act of Settlement for removing judges from office.[17]

The second trajectory reflected a much more traditional and conservative imperial posture that applied to the multiracial empire where small European or mixed-race elites exercised and maintained close control over indigenous or imported majorities. In these territories the imperial government's desire was at one and the same time to prevent elites from exercising untrammelled authority (a concession to the anti-slavery movement and its successors), while conceding limited political and social rights to their non-white and mixed-race populations. Moreover, London wanted to ensure that colonial officials, including judges, avoided rocking the boat in challenging or otherwise embarrassing colonial governments. By accidents of history some of these possessions had representative assemblies that, unlike their counterparts in the white settler empire, were not reformist but intensely reactionary. Others, more recently acquired, had Crown colony status and executive government with plenary powers. In all these territories the imperial government considered it important to appoint judges, particularly chief justices, who would support the executive, except where it clearly mistook the law and palpably abused the rule of law, and work at conciliating the local elite.[18]

Ironically, at about the time that the imperial government was loosening its control over governance and justice (including disciplining of the judges) in the white settler empire, it ramped up control within the multiracial empire. Increasingly worried about dissension and, worse still, rebellion in these possessions, it got rid of most of the legislative assemblies, substituting direct rule through Crown colony government, and tried to foster more openly a climate of loyalty within the colonial service, including the judges.[19]

By 1900 the role and status of judges within the British Empire depended on which territories and histories the observer was considering.

Judges and the Challenges of the Colonial Experience

The Realpolitik of Empire

A central feature of the British imperial project was the fragility of the enterprise. Lauren Benton has recently exposed the degree to which claims of absolute sovereignty by imperial powers – even in the nineteenth century, thought to be the period when the colonial state reached its full development – over the territories they administered were belied by the realities of the colonial experience locally.[20] Control over the colonial land mass was not invariably uniformly secure, nor were territories subject to the full authority of the colonial government. The imperial frontier was a reality in many colonial territories: 'We ... know that sovereignty is often more myth than real, more a story that polities tell about their own power than a definite quality they possess. Most boundaries are porous and many are contested, and states cannot consistently enforce laws to regulate activities across and within borders.'[21]

Sovereignty could be and was shared, if not de jure then de facto, with other groups occupying the same territory. Assertions that British rule was firmly established throughout the length and breadth of possessions were often just that – assertions. Colonies often embraced several sovereigns and more than a single legal system, and were subject to both internal and external threats to their existence as outposts of British rule and culture. Dangers from within, actual or imagined, might come from within the colonial population itself, inherited former subjects of other European powers, or indigenous or migrant non-white communities.[22] The sources of external threat were typically other imperial powers that were seeking to expand their own colonial reach in the same region – the French in the Antipodes and the West Indies, the United States in North America in the early decades of the century, and later on a combination of German, French, and American expansive designs in Oceania, for instance.[23]

The reality was, of course, that the colonial state was incompletely formed, often sparsely and inexpertly staffed, stretched in exerting consistent authority, inadequately provided with the military or naval clout to protect itself, and subject to ongoing and sometimes visceral competition among government officials, settlers of wealth and status, and common folk over who should exercise political authority and social leadership, or share in the political process. Together, these factors made for political units that were immature and unstable. In such an environment, it was perhaps inevitable that the imperial government, without the control it might have wished, to one degree or another emphasized strong executive government, reminiscent of that in seventeenth-century England, and downplayed the separation of powers within the colonial state in the interests of loyalty and of furthering the common cause. Given the realpolitik of colonial governance, it was not considered wise to treat colonial officials, including judges, as warranting the sort of respect and freedom of thought that may have been acceptable at home, especially with the absence of cultural and professional constraints that existed in Britain. Political judges were expected to be, but it was the politics of the imperial cause, of strong colonial government, and of maintaining a compliant polity that they were called to support.

It should be no surprise that the earlier strong manifestation of this imperial attitude to colonial governance existed during the long counter-revolutionary period following the loss of the thirteen colonies and encompassing the French Wars, in which anxieties about domestic security and the fate of the empire were foremost.[24] By the same token, we should not wonder that it was during the decades after the Indian Mutiny that London reacted to doubts about the loyalty of its 'coloured subjects' and turmoil in other possessions, and its ability to maintain its much extended empire and its world power and influence, by tightening its control over multiracial colonies and stressing cooperation and discouraging rivalry within the ranks of colonial regimes.[25] It was during the intervening period, when external threats had diminished in the 'white' empire, colonial confidence was strong, indeed overbearing, and effective social and economic infrastructures seem to have developed, that imperial control was significantly relinquished and with it the full constraints of political and legal, if not emotional, loyalty.[26]

For jurists brought up to believe in the independence of the judiciary as an article of faith in the British constitution, the requirement of loyalty to the colonial state above all else could be a bitter pill to swallow, especially when the conditions they found in the possessions to which they were assigned proved offensive to their notions of legality and constitutional values. At the same time, for those who were comfortable with and benefited from the old verities, the fading of the ties demanded by loyalty and the emergence of a more liberal constitutional relationship between the metropolis and the colonies were difficult for them to stomach.

It was, however, not the substance of their judicial decisions that typically got colonial jurists into trouble. In most instances the Colonial Office or English law officers would vindicate those decisions as consonant with accepted law, or they could be appealed. Where they did get into trouble for their judgments was when they used the bench as a platform for strong political stances, or engaged in thoroughly injudicious conduct and statements. Outside the courtroom, it was for involvement in political action and their actual or imagined political connections that they were typically to attract criticism and discipline. Depending on time and place, disloyalty, or attraction to radical or even reform politics were frowned on, and if seriously pursued, likely to get a judge into hot water and removed from office. Deciding against the government in a judicial decision was one thing (even that could be dangerous in certain circumstances, as a level-headed judge, such as Francis Forbes, found), but taking open and public issue with government policy, especially if voiced intemperately, was another, as Robert Thorpe and John Walpole Willis, in Upper Canada,[27] Joseph Beaumont in Guiana, and John Gorrie in Trinidad and Tobago[28] found to their cost. This was in certain executive circles viewed as tantamount to 'rule by judge.'[29] In some instances 'disloyalty' also meant getting on the wrong side of powerful groups in colonies, typically allied with colonial executives, including settlers in legislative assemblies. As the empire had both inherited or spawned colonies with representative legislatures, judges could run into trouble with those bodies, as their counterparts had with Parliament in seventeenth-century England, either because – like Jeffery Hart Bent in Grenada and Beaumont – they rejected the perversely self-interested policies and grossly inequitable law that emanated from them,[30] or because, as conservatives, they offended reformist sentiment in white settler colonies, typically represented in assemblies – the problem of Jonathan Sewell and James Monk in Lower Canada and Henry John Boulton in Newfoundland.[31]

The Contested Colonial Legal Domain

As we have seen, there was a decisive move from amateurism to professionalism in the superior court colonial judiciary during the nineteenth century (replicated only to a very limited extent within the magistracy). This important trend produced a clearly definable sense of the value of embedding legal cultures with their roots firmly in English jurisprudence and the rule of law, and of lawyer-judges as the agents of that process. This was especially true of judges whose experience as lawyers was in the English and Irish courts. Jurists who came up through local colonial bars and had worked therefore for local interests, were not always as enthusiastic about English legal culture, or, as in some slave or post-slavery colonies, were more selective in their views about who should benefit from the rights and protections of that tradition.[32]

Judges who had served as lawyers in the British Isles possessed an attachment to both the historical and contemporary significance of English law, and generally believed in its doctrinal and practical superiority to locally devised law and custom, not to mention other European systems of law. It is this attitude that explains the conflicts, on the one hand, in Australia (from the Bents to Boothby),[33] and on the other those in the slave and former slave colonies (from Smith to Gorrie),[34] between professional judges and local interests over which and whose law applied, and what legal institutions were appropriate in doing justice. The tension was one that reached back to the first empire.[35] The cultural bias helps to explain why English and Irish colonial judges struggled with the principles, rules, and procedures of other legal systems that they were required to administer. Rare were the examples of men like George Smith with earlier experience in a mixed law jurisdiction, Grenada,[36] and Jonathan Sewell who as chief justice of Lower Canada read and grew to admire French civil law,[37] who did not assume or came to doubt that English law was inherently superior in quality and its prescriptions.

As we have observed, English judges in the seventeenth century differed in how they related to executive government and legislative bodies – the extent to which they tended towards a Baconian conception of loyalty to the Crown as their prime motivation, or towards a Cokeian view of a primary obligation of stewardship of the Common Law that transcended loyalty to the Crown where the royal prerogative and that body of jurisprudence were in conflict.[38] This tension was complicated by the fact that forces in Parliament had challenged attempts by the Crown to dictate to the judges where their loyalties properly lay, and claimed their own right to call judges to account.

Although resolved in Britain by the Act of Settlement and its aftermath, these stresses continued in the colonies, in which executive power and governance were maintained through the exercise of the royal prerogative, rather than by any significant parliamentary control.[39] Relations between the viceroy and his officials, the judiciary, and, where they existed, legislative bodies either reproduced or were seen as reproducing the tensions of England's constitutional and legal history during that earlier century. This explains the often emotional and long-winded justifications by judges, colonial governors, and legislatures of their positions in cases of disagreement on constitutional issues and matters of legality that consume page after page of Colonial Office records during certain periods in the nineteenth century and tried the patience of imperial officials. The rhetoric reflects that of seventeenth-century England and the strongly held positions during those earlier struggles between the advocates of dominant executive government, the constraints of the Common Law, controlled by the judiciary, on arbitrary state action, and incipient notions of parliamentary sovereignty – rhetoric that in one form or another was couched in the language of legality.[40]

In the case of the remaining colonies of the Old Empire, particularly those in the Caribbean, those struggles reflected part of their own actual or fabricated constitutional history.[41] In newer colonies, they were the product of the transference of a sense of historical identity and commitment to an external legal culture to territories with which the newcomers had no previous historical ties.[42]

That colonial judges should have entertained different views on their roles should not surprise us, given that earlier history and the contested loyalties it created, the peculiarities of the transference of constitutional and legal culture, and the realities of governance and the administration of justice in these insecure and immature territories. Judges steeped in Common Law culture and its values naturally turned to the rule of law as providing a standard for evaluating clashes between the colonial state and individuals and social groups over rights. An inherently tensile concept, it embraced a range of meanings that reflected not only a received body of practice and process from the metropolis, but also the pressure of local colonial realities, as well as the underlying political and social views of the men in question.[43] Where they took their stand depended very much on whether they gave the rule a broad and liberal interpretation that inspired them to resist arbitrary or abusive state action, on the one hand, such as Robert Thorpe, Forbes, Beaumont, and Gorrie, or accorded it a limited meaning that focused on its formal demands, such as Sewell and Boulton. Between these poles, there was room for movement, for jurists to shift positions as circumstances and their own predilections changed, as with Bent and Willis. Despite occasional suspicions about the motivations of some colonial jurists – apparent in Lieutenant Governor Francis Gore's belief that Robert Thorpe was a closet United Irishman,[44] and in Francis Forbes' enemies trying to brand him a 'Yankee republican'[45] – all these characters were committed to the British Empire and its rule. They could and did differ in their vision of empire, what it meant and could mean, and the role of law and the administration of justice within it. None of them harboured the radical and subversive belief that imperial rule should be dismantled.

Among other legal tensions related to authority and legitimacy in these politico-legal conditions was whether colonial executives, legislatures, or the judiciary had the prime responsibility for how the administration of justice was ordered and ran day to day. Imperial or local legislation might provide the framework, which might itself give rise to different interpretations, as it did in Upper Canada in 1828, when Willis took on the executive over the sittings of the Court of King's Bench.[46] The crafting of rules of court was generally accepted as within the purview of the judges, especially the chief justices. Executives, however, might balk at this concession, especially where the result was to bestow 'undue' authority on the judiciary, such as George Smith securing multiple judicial roles in Trinidad,[47] or judges extending their jurisdiction, as Bent in Grenada and Gorrie in Trinidad had sought to do in order to provide greater access to justice to the poor in those territories.[48] Legislatures, however, were not always happy with this bilateral relationship and sought to make their own claims to control of the process, as was true of the House of Assembly in Lower Canada in its determination to bring to heel Chief Justices Jonathan Sewell and James Monk, and that in Newfoundland in seeking to rid the possession of Boulton.[49]

Conflicts would also arise where the issue was whether the executive in exercising the royal prerogative was seen by the judiciary as trenching upon its powers in the administration of justice and rule of law sensibilities. As Chief Justice Joseph Beaumont of British Guiana found to his cost, London's position, following domestic practice, was that governors and other viceroys possessed prerogative powers over aspects of the administration of justice, not least in remitting sentences, and that the judges had no right to exercise an independent power of review in these matters.[50]

Also deprecated in some colonial executive and legislative circles was what was viewed as subversion of the administration of justice by judges undercutting or manipulating the system for their own ends. In some instances this conduct involved the importation of a strain of legal fundamentalism that viewed English law as supreme and treated as odious any attempt to inject discretion and accommodate local needs – the sort of conduct that was viewed in certain quarters as reflecting badly on Willis in Upper Canada,[51] and damning Benjamin Boothby in South Australia.[52] In others it was judicial attempts to depart from accepted procedures in the cause of a personal desire to improve the system and its appeal to victims of oppression – one of the charges laid against Bent in Grenada and a cardinal factor in the downfall of Gorrie in Trinidad and Tobago.[53]

It is likely that, if the political status of colonies was tenuous and uncertain, so was the law that applied. English law, it may be argued, was no more sovereign than British governance in these territories. Like it not, colonial judges were not complete masters in their own house. Like their counterparts in England they had to struggle with the place of custom in English law – although in colonies, as often as not, the customs and law-ways of peoples from fundamentally different cultures.[54]

Unlike those English judges, with the exception of law lords in the case of Scots law, they often grappled too with the place and significance of other European systems of law in the possession to which they went.[55] Finally, as Peter Karsten has demonstrated, there were a multitude of situations in which colonists chose to order their relationships and resolve their differences according to 'low law' – modalities developed at a personal or communal level, rather than imposed from on high.[56] Appointment as colonial judges undoubtedly gave men a feeling of power and authority. Most of the jurists whose careers have been traced in this book, by their conduct and rhetoric, certainly lived the part. One wonders, however, whether, apart entirely from the constitutional constraints that affected them, they also felt a certain professional insecurity that reflected the reality of the limited sovereignty of law in the societies where they laboured.

Societal Realities

These histories also reveal important insights about social views of the place of the judiciary, and the administration of justice in these fragile and often disputatious micro-communities. These were men who were big fish in small ponds. On one hand this meant a sense of achievement and satisfaction in the very fact of judicial preferment. However, it also meant that judges worked in full public view in societies in which perceptions about them and their positions could be and were negative, particularly if they consciously or even unconsciously offended key social and economic players, or the values of an important segment of the community.

Although impelled by a desire to administer law impartially, and in a spirit of equal justice for all, some liberally minded jurists found that the exclusive expectations of powerful social and economic groups in the colonies made achieving those aims a daunting task. When judges tried to do justice in that broader sense, they sometimes became marked men within the communities that they served. Smith, Thorpe, Forbes, Beaumont, and Gorrie all provide examples. Those jurists who hewed to a conservative line and saw support for the executive or law and order as the dominant elements in their mission – for example, Bent and Field in New South Wales, Sewell and Monk in Lower Canada, and Boulton in Newfoundland – could also face branding, resistance, and excoriation from radical and reformist groups in the societies in which they served.

The presence of a legal fraternity in the colonial possession served did not by any means ensure unqualified support and camaraderie for a new judge in a colony, although in some instances it could and did. If appointed from the English or Irish bars, his very presence might be resented, if a local boy had been overlooked for the appointment. Both Willis in Upper Canada and Beaumont in Guiana ran into this problem of professional jealousy and resentment.[57] Moreover, if a jurist took issue with the way in which the administration of justice had been conducted or the law was being practised, as being offensive to English law, his conception of the rule of law, and legal ethics, he could well be branded as a troublemaker, and in some instances found not only the bar at odds with him, but also his fellow judges. Bent's problems in Grenada provides a signal example.[58]

There seems to have been no obvious correlation between the lifestyle that a judge chose and the presence or absence of antipathy to him. Highly social characters, like John Gorrie, and those like Montagu and Boothby who seemed intent on keeping their judicial and private lives separate could equally run afoul of powerful segments of the community who deprecated their political and legal philosophies, and records. Associations did matter, and the fact that a judge had connections, real or imagined, with groups whose ideology or motivations were suspect could make him the target of criticism and punitive responses from those who opposed them. Group connections ranged from those with the common folk, radicals and reformers, and nonconformist missionaries at one end of the spectrum to powerful merchants, landowners, ranchers, planters, and prelates and ministers of the established church at the other. Thorpe's connection with Irish oppositionists, Willis's with reformers, Bent's with a 'rogue' Roman Catholic priest, Boulton's with powerful merchants and a conservative pressman, and Beaumont's and Gorrie's with the downtrodden, made them lightning rods for criticism, and ultimately attempts at discipline.

The cultural life of colonial communities also attracted the interest of some colonial judges, especially those who had literary and either sacred or secular educational interests, such as Barron Field, Francis Forbes, Willis, and Gorrie. The last two, in particular, dedicated part of their time to the promotion of religious education and Sunday school.[59] In principle, these volunteer initiatives were expected and applauded. But even in the realm of charitable activity, judges could run into criticism. This is true of the gregarious Gorrie, who took an active part in the social and recreational life of a colony, even outside the charmed walls of official receptions, balls, and dinner parties. As the Scottish judge was to find, some of these connections could be a mixed blessing when political and social opponents read these associations as fraternization with radicals, reformers, and other 'agents of disorder,' not least the gullible common folk only too ready, it was feared, to rally to 'demagogic' cries for change and even violence in its cause.[60]

An important variant in how 'troublesome' judges were treated in the societies in which they moved was the attitude of the colonial press. The decades after the end of the Napoleonic Wars saw an efflorescence of newspapers (daily and weekly) and newspaper journalism in British colonies.[61] Politics and law provided good and often controversial fare for editors and their newshound readers. The letters to the editor columns also constituted a rolling forum for a lively exchange of opinion from the community on public issues, including those involving the law. These were often penned under pseudonyms. In some instances, judges were suspected with some justification of themselves having joined the anonymous letter-writing fray – Willis in the Port Phillip District providing a good example.[62] In the absence of official reporter systems, the publication of criminal trials and civil actions in the columns of the press meant that the law, courts, and judges were continuously in the public gaze and consciousness. Moreover, in the absence of other frequent diversions, such as the theatre and music hall, courts could, sometimes at least, provide a forum for entertainment as well as information.

As we have seen in the case of Willis's encounters with his bêtes noires in Melbourne, such drawing power did not always add to the dignity and stature of the Courts.[63] For a controversial judge or one forced to make controversial decisions, whether on the liberal or conservative side of the ideological divide, he could expect excoriation from newspapers representing the opposite position, and at the same time support from those in his camp.[64] The interest of the press in the conduct and ideas of judges meant that issues sometime took on a life of their own, deflecting attention from other matters, including much other, uncontroversial work that the jurist and his colleagues were doing. As evident in the stories of men like Boulton, Willis, and Boothby, turbulent jurists could become lightning rods for and points of fission, related on the one hand to the ills of colonial governance in general in a colony, and on the other to the more particular ills that afflicted those societies.

A major issue for colonial judges was what to do about defamatory attacks on them, predominantly by or through the press. A few were willing to let matters pass, on the premise that one had to do so to respect a degree of press freedom. Others such as Willis sought to persuade the executive through the law officers to launch prosecutions for criminal or defamatory libel. Such moves could be problematic if the latter was incompetent, or, as in that case, the justice in question was the only professional judge in town. Although a firm pattern of practice against being judge in one's own suit had yet to develop in the colonies, while fast developing in England, the Colonial Office, and especially the English law officers, were inclined to frown on such situations. Some governors had their reservations, too, as was true of George Gipps's doubts about Willis's proceedings against newspaper editor George Arden.[65] Most problematic of all was judges' use of the contempt power to indict, try, and sentence newspapermen. This step that was and is offensive to the rules of natural justice, got judges, including George Smith, Boulton, and Beaumont into official hot water, and, on occasion, left their detractors – hypercritical pressmen of the ilk of Matthew Gallagher, Robert Parsons, and Laurence McDermott – looking like martyrs to the cause of press freedom. In some instances, such as that of Justice Willis in Port Phillip, there were clearly other options, including defamation prosecution before a fellow judge or at a different level of court.[66] However, in the absence of any final and definitive guidance on these matters, and in light of the anxieties caused to the men who felt, with some justification, personally and professionally exposed, these conflicts continued to be a source of contention throughout the century.

Religious Divisions

In some colonial settings religious differences could be a complicating factor for the assertive jurist. Despite the pretensions of the Church of England to be recognized and favoured as the established church in British colonies, religious demographics, the often-languid pace of Anglican missionary work, the aspirations of non-Anglican Christians to freedom of religion, and a developing tolerance for other Christian faith groups among some Anglicans (evidenced in emancipation steps in Britain itself), worked against them.[67] Religious tensions were perhaps most marked in colonies with a majority or sizeable minority of Roman Catholics in the European and/or the non-white population, such as Lower Canada and Grenada. They wanted full recognition of their freedom of religion and the same rights to support for education, for instance, as their Anglican neighbours. In some colonies, too, large assemblies of dissenting Protestants added to the pressure on the imperial and colonial governments to treat Christian faith groups equally and fairly.[68] Most colonial judges were Anglicans out of conviction or convenience, with varying views on the wisdom of granting religious rights and civil rights to Catholics and Protestant dissenters, not to mention non-Christians. Chief Justice Forbes and Chief Justice William a'Beckett of Victoria, for example, demonstrated a tolerance for diverse Christian belief.[69] By contrast, others like Chief Justice Sewell in Lower Canada,[70] Chief Justice John Pedder of Van Dieman's Land,[71] and Justices Willis and Burton in New South Wales[72] were unashamedly biased in favour of Anglicanism as the established faith. Where colonial judges wore their Anglican beliefs on their sleeves in both their judicial decisions and public statements, they could expect and received strong criticism from the representatives of other Christian denominations.

But, as we have seen, issues of religious identity and the colonial judiciary could be more complex, where a judge took a stand on a matter that divided a particular faith group, as, for example, Bent in Grenada[73] and Boulton in Newfoundland.[74] This was especially true where the population in question was Roman Catholic. In these situations a desire in London to avoid antagonism leading perhaps to disorder had to be balanced by consideration of the legal reality that official direct diplomatic relations between London and the Vatican were non-existent, and by consideration of the actual or imagined sensibilities of Protestants, whether in the British Isles or the colonies.[75]

The dynamics of these conflicts did not necessarily follow any consistent pattern, given the nature of the dispute, its imperial and local significance to the political and social evolution of colonies, the quality of church–state relations within them, and the personalities involved. Assessed on the basis of its reactions to cases in the first half of the century, the British government was consistent in its view that it did not want troublesome Catholic prelates or priests stirring up dissent, whether in Ireland or in its colonies. London used the Byzantine system of corresponding with Rome to make that clear, while fighting shy of giving official diplomatic recognition to the Vatican.[76]

As early as the 1770s it had given recognition to freedom of religion and worship to Roman Catholics in Quebec, as well as engaging in sub rosa representations to the Vatican on its preferences in episcopal appointments.[77] This move was followed by opening Catholic access to offices of state, including the judiciary, and after the establishment of

Lower Canada in 1791, the grant of a limited franchise and representation by co-religionists in the House of Assembly.[78] Upper Canada inherited these concessions. Legal recognition of freedom of religion was slower in coming in other British colonies. In the remaining British North American and the Caribbean possessions, apostolic vicars and then bishops were permitted to establish themselves to minister to their flocks, and by 1830 there was provision in some colonies for state subventions of the salaries of Catholic as well as dissenting clergy.[79] The Catholic Emancipation Act of 1829 in the United Kingdom opened the way for the extension of the franchise to Roman Catholic subjects of colonies with elective legislative bodies.[80] This had its greater impact on assemblies, although Bishop Alexander Macdonnell of Upper Canada, who had sought to ensure the loyalty of his people to the Crown, was invited to become a member of the Legislative Council of the province in 1831.[81] The conflicts involving Jeffery Hart Bent in Grenada and Henry John Boulton in Newfoundland both occurred during the period of transition to fuller recognition of Catholic rights. The different outcomes for the two judges are explained by the more liberal political and religious winds swirling through Westminster, with Bent benefiting from his apparent empathy with the ascendant anti-slavery movement,[82] and Boulton suffering for his seeming insensitivity to Roman Catholics at a time of imperial crisis.[83]

In the stories from the Caribbean in the latter half of the century, the concern of colonial executives and planter assemblies about religion and the administration of justice was more related to the missionary activities, not of the Roman Catholic Church, but of 'troublesome' nonconformist Protestants, primarily Baptists or Methodists (Wesleyans).[84] These were men who were close to the poor and downtrodden whose spiritual needs they sought to serve, and who, given the conditions of living of their charges that they found, had little or no compunction about speaking out against injustice and oppression under which their congregants laboured. The missionaries were at times accused by the plantocracy and their allies in government of engaging in the sort of subversion that led to disaffection and rebellion. Beaumont, who came from a devout Wesleyan family, and Gorrie, who was a practising Presbyterian, and thus both religious outsiders and considered unsound in official and local, predominantly Anglican, elite circles, clearly attracted a negative halo for their sympathy for the impoverished majority.[85] Their 'sins' were magnified when nonconformist ministers and their charges lionized or came to the defence of the jurists. Support from these segments of the population was by its very nature to be discounted in official and elite rhetoric, in the face of complaints from respectable members of the community about judicial misbehaviour.

Economic Challenges

Colonial judges, like other colonial officials, often had personal interests in the economies of the colonies in which they served. There was a widespread practice, particularly during the first three decades of the nineteenth century, for imperial and colonial authorities to provide judges with land grants, to allow them not only to build residences, but also to use the land productively. Indeed, apart from viewing this practice in terms of the rewards of office, it may very well have been considered desirable for colonial officials, including judges, to exercise some leadership in investing in the economic future of colonial possessions.[86] Even later, although land grants were not usual, there was no policy against judges acquiring capital and investing it in land or other economic enterprises.[87]

The economic activities of judges could, as we have noted, be perilous, where the value of investments, particularly in land, declined dramatically during recession and depression. In some instances, as in the case of Montagu, the result was seriously increased indebtedness.[88] The institutional problem was that judicial involvement in economic activity could compromise or at least raise questions about the impartiality of particular judges. This was an issue for Montagu with his chronic indebtedness and strange views on repayment,[89] and for Chief Justice Richard Temple in British Honduras for moonlighting with legal advice to resource companies operating in the possession.[90] Ongoing economic embarrassment may also have played a part in the complex distempers that afflicted Benjamin Boothby.[91] The financial connections of judges such as their providing mortgage loans could also come back to haunt them, if they were otherwise the butt of criticism, as Willis found to his annoyance in the Port Phillip District.[92]

Personality Problems

That most of the men whose judicial careers have been examined in this book had difficult and contentious personalities would be an understatement. On the basis of the accounts of their tenure in this book, the Colonial Office could hardly claim any finesse in its appointments process. What is puzzling about these stories is the extent to which judges who openly exhibited independent ideological stances or personality quirks or both received appointments to other colonial judgeships after amoval or recall. Why was this?

One might suppose that, on the basis of his previous record, a judge like Thorpe, Smith, Bent, Willis, or Gorrie was unlikely to 'change his spots,' and might cause problems elsewhere. So why reappoint him? Is the answer to the question simply reducible to Peter Howell's observation that the Colonial Office was unduly genial in looking after its own?[93]

The answer is, I would suggest, more complex, although necessarily tentative. In the first place, these jurists were men who had experience in colonial judicial work and were generally agreed to be talented lawyers, if sometimes perverse in their views and volatile in character. A man like Gorrie who had remarkable staying power was, for all his faults, seen to be a hardworking, principled, and creative servant of the empire.[94] Even those who lasted for much shorter periods, such as Willis and Smith, were recognized as able legal professionals when they were deciding cases and providing legal advice.[95] Viewed in that light, they might well have seemed a better investment than neophytes without colonial experience.

Secondly, they were or were accounted gentlemen. The officials in the Colonial Office and some colonial executives, naively as it turned out, seem to have been of the belief that a change of colony, climate, and professional challenges might work wonders in changing the demeanour and behaviour of their problem children, and that the latter, as gentlemen, would somehow mature and learn from their mistakes. These sentiments seem to have been operative in the cases of Smith, Thorpe, Bent, and Willis. Given the changing character of a 'gentleman' from a person of aristocratic breeding and leisure to a middle-class standard-bearer of 'entrepreneurial morality,' well represented among the ranks of Colonial Office officials, there may well have been a tendency to assume that others of that ilk would find the way to moderation.[96]

Thirdly, one senses that, although there was a steady stream of new aspirants to the colonial judiciary among the legal professions in England and Ireland in particular, it is not at all clear that the pools were of equal size for individual colonies. We know, for instance, that the Indian judiciary was considered the plum in status and financial rewards, attracting many aspirants, few of whom were chosen.[97] From there, choice would have reflected considerations of geographic distance, salaries offered, available information on the political, social, and economic circumstances of the colony, concerns about contracting terminal and painful diseases, as well as the economic circumstances of a man and his family. Where pools were small, as one suspects was the case with colonies such as Sierra Leone and several of the Caribbean colonies, such as British Guiana, in which tropical diseases were a menace, transferring a former judge, even one with an attitude, must have been tempting.[98]

Fourthly, it is not fanciful to suggest that, despite the Colonial Office's and Judicial Committee's reservations about particular individuals and their past problems, there was also a sense that what they represented in ideology had value in balancing the executive or legislative predilections in certain colonies. Even though the imperial government wanted stability in its colonies, it was not necessarily willing to have it at any cost, and would have been willing to take a gamble on a judge who had been ready to counter worrying autocratic proclivities in executive government. A Smith, Thorpe, Willis, or Gorrie might have further uses in carrying their message, hopefully better modulated, elsewhere in empire. By the same token, in a colony that was being blessed with representative government of a reformist bent, it might have seemed politic, if unwise, to appoint a hard-nosed conservative to lead the judiciary in that possession. This is surely the only explanation for the appointment of Boulton to Newfoundland.[99]

Finally, lurking in the background was the reality of patronage. Where influential patrons had appointed or supported the appointment of colonial jurists, the fact that the latter had erred in one colony was not seen as a reason for denying him further preferment. Lord Castlereagh had little compunction about appointing Thorpe to Sierra Leone after his demise in Upper Canada,[100] and may have assisted Smith in securing his later appointment in Mauritius. Lord Goderich, who had appointed Willis to Upper Canada and later questioned his judgment in that regard, ultimately went to bat for the jurist by appointing him to British Guiana, citing his integrity in his work in the Canadian province.[101] Gorrie clearly benefited in his progress round the empire by his friendship with and mentorship by Arthur Gordon, a son of the former prime minister, the Earl of Aberdeen, and one of the most peripatetic colonial governors of the later nineteenth century.[102] These were the factors that individually or collectively may explain this phenomenon of repeat colonial judicial appointments, even of individuals who had already suffered dismissal as judges in other possessions.

Networks of Empire and the Colonial Judiciary

An issue that also merits examination is that of the relationship of colonial judges to the sort of networks that historians of empire have noted in recent decades as sources of inspiration for colonial officials more generally, the character of those networks in both relations with the metropolis and across the colonies, and the allied question of the extent to which colonial judges were influenced by and exercised influence through their own travels within the imperial system.[103]

In several of the narratives in this book we have observed correspondence between judges and sponsors, patrons, or friends. One notable example is the collection of letters from Francis Forbes in New South Wales to R. Wilmot Horton, the parliamentary undersecretary at the Colonial Office.[104] This connection flowed from similar political views, and the fact that Forbes spent close to two years, from 1822 to 1824, as an honorary adviser to the Colonial Office on legal and constitutional matters as they related to the Antipodean colony.[105] A recommendation by Horton to Lord Bathurst helped Forbes secure the position of chief justice in New South Wales, and the Westminster politician was anxious that the jurist keep in correspondence with him from Sydney. As John Bennett puts it, 'Forbes left England charged with Wilmot Horton's desire that he write on what he observed in Australia – of the country, the people, the politics and anything else worthy of notice.'[106] Forbes did not disappoint his mentor and wrote at length on his experiences in the colony. It is from this remarkable collection that we have a strong sense of Forbes's progressive imperialism and commitment to a liberal conception of the rule of law, including an independent judiciary, the recognition of constitutional liberties under the law (to be enjoyed even by convicts), and the need for reform of the law. Although we lack responses from Horton, we do know that he considered the content of some of Forbes's missives important enough to be shared with other members of the government in Westminster and to be lodged in Colonial Office files.[107] Here we see, in measured prose, evidence of the constitutional and legal thinking of the man and of his contribution to embedding of the rule of law in Australia and his reflections on its place in a dynamic, developing, and more open empire.

The fact that other judges, Thorpe and Smith being good examples, assumed that they had some mission to report their evaluations of the state of colonies, not only in the context of the administration of justice, but of governance more generally, suggests that they may have thought, rightly or wrongly, they had been enlisted as London's eyes and ears in the colonies in which they served. Given that the Colonial Office more generally did not always have faith that it was getting the true state of affairs from the governor and his administrative officers, this possibility is not entirely fanciful. As several narratives suggest, however, especially those of Thorpe, Bent in New South Wales, and Field, the Colonial Office could tire of these sources of information and opinion, particularly if they became coloured by disputes involving the jurist in question. The Office may well have wanted information and informed opinion, but not whining, or worse still, invective, snide backbiting, or bombast.

Another significant example of colonial correspondence involving the judiciary is presented by the letters between John Gorrie and his political mentor, Arthur Gordon, on the one hand, and his close contact in the humanitarian and anti-slavery world of the late nineteenth century, Frederick Chesson, on the other.[108] The correspondence with Gordon shows the close bond between the men, dating from their first encounter in Mauritius, and the interesting chemistry between the cultured, self-possessed, aristocratic servant of empire, with progressive, if strongly imperialist, inclinations, and the rougher, tougher judge, with equally strong feelings for the imperial mission, but with an impatience to give equal justice meaning in highly unequal British possessions.[109] The spark produced was capable of producing common cause on projects on which they agreed, and tension when Gordon felt that the judge's wilder enthusiasms had got the better of him. Until the judge's last posting, the support of Gordon seems to have been important in assisting his advancement. Gorrie's correspondence with Chesson, a Wesleyan who was a leading member of the Aborigines' Protection Society (popularly known at 'Exeter Hall'), a part-time journalist for the liberal *Daily News* and an advocate of 'responsible imperialism,' extended over more than twenty years. These private letters reflect the emotional as well as the institutional and informational support that Chesson provided to those doing good humanitarian work in the far-flung corners of empire, and on Gorrie's side a means of validating and seeking support in the United Kingdom for his initiatives in both elevating and protecting the interests of the downtrodden and impoverished in the colonies in which he served.[110]

The peregrinations of several colonial judges mentioned in this book – Thorpe, Forbes, Burton, Willis, and Gorrie – raise the interesting issue of the transference of ideas and experience round the empire. One can see this in the judicial careers of Forbes and Gorrie, who had developed early on in their careers a liberal vision of imperial constitutionalism, if not as a 'living tree,' then as an organism capable of further beneficial development. Both men were willing to take risks, Forbes in Newfoundland and New South Wales,[111] and Gorrie in the four colonial settings in which he was judge,[112] in promoting their progressive vision of empire and how it should affect particular colonies. Although there were differences between the two men born of place, time, and personality – Forbes was more of a gradualist, while Gorrie was impatient to initiate change immediately – they both unashamedly carried their opinions with them from one colony to another, and, on the basis of their experiences, strengthened their resolve to make a difference. Although not invariably vindicated by events, they both left a legacy of liberal constitutionalism and rule-of-law thinking that was picked up and furthered by others in later decades. A degree of consistency in attitude is also evident in the peregrinations of a conservative judge, like William Burton, who tended to wear his conservatism in legal, political, and religious matters on his sleeve.[113] However, that branding as conservative or liberal can sometimes be misleading is evident in Burton's career. Despite his normal conservative mien, he took a decidedly liberal approach towards bankruptcy and insolvency. In these fields he initiated progressive reform in the Cape Colony designed to enable bankrupts to return to productive enterprise, erecting a legislative model that he then carried with him to New South Wales.[114]

With several other judges whose careers have been examined, it is more difficult to associate a consistent ideology with their moves. This is because of the difficult personalities of the men in question – Thorpe and Willis are the clearest examples. In their Upper Canadian incarnations they both produced principled arguments in favour of reform in the administration of justice, and in Thorpe's case, government more generally.[115] But their subsequent careers, Thorpe in Sierra Leone and Willis in New South Wales,[116] were so dominated by angst, disputatious conduct, petulance, and personal frustration that it is difficult to get a clear sense of their political and legal values except in the vaguest sense. As a consequence one is left with the feeling that self-absorption was all too often their guiding light.

That a judge could undergo a change in perspective produced by his experience in a particular colony is demonstrated by Jeffery Hart Bent's reaction to what he considered the abuse of the rule of law in the victimization of a radical Roman Catholic priest, during his sojourn in Grenada.[117] Bent's career in New South Wales gives the impression of that of an intensely conservative, vain, and prickly personality who closely identified with the cause of the exclusives in that territory.[118] He had no time for the convicts – the local serf class, as it were. His battle with the plantocracy in Grenada does not gainsay all of these characteristics, particularly the personal crustiness, but it does show him in a very different light on the issue of exploitation of those without or possessing only minimal rights under local law. If there is an explanation outside orneriness or concerns about personal or institutional status, it lies in a distaste for the practices of slavery that may have developed during the Grenada years, as well as the perception that the elite in the colony were quite happy to avoid or manipulate English law when it was likely to inconvenience them.

The peregrinations of some of these judges, and no doubt others serving in the colonies, point to the need for much more work on the impact of the judiciary in and across the British colonial world. Together with the lawyers who chose a life of practice outside the United Kingdom, these were the standard-bearers and agents of English law in the furthest reaches of empire. They were, in short, the transmitters of a legal culture, an imperium, that has had and continues to have global significance.

The Independence of the Colonial Judiciary and the Mechanics of Discipline beyond 1900

In 1900, outside the white settler empire, judges in British colonies continued to be appointed at pleasure. This situation continued until the effective break-up of the imperial system after the Second World War. So in 1962 T. Olawale Elias, in *British Colonial Law*, was able to report on discussions that continued to rage over whether or not colonial judges were as independent as their English counterparts.[119] At a formal level at least, the answer was 'No,' because they were appointed at pleasure. Official statements, however, sought to suggest that de facto they were just as independent.[120]

Despite the late-nineteenth-century moves towards closer imperial control of multiracial colonies and its corollary that colonial officialdom must stick together, currents and forces in a colonial world in which voices were increasingly raised in support of equality of treatment, and even more dramatically in favour of independence from colonial rule, rendered the experiment ultimately a transitional one. This is not the place to expose the often tortuous journey to independence of British colonies, and the blood, sweat, and tears that were often shed en route.

What is clear is, as Martin Wiener has recently shown, that in the first third of the twentieth century, the rule of law became more clearly a rallying point for those imperial and colonial politicians and officials, judges, lawyers, and, not least the 'subject peoples' who argued with ever greater vigour that, if British rule meant anything, it should mean equality of treatment before and under the law.[121] In Wiener's study he examines how this increasing pressure for equal justice in territories in which there were great political, social, and economic disparities and strong racist sentiment among European minorities, played out in the courts administering criminal justice.

He points to several British jurists who played important roles in this trend. One notable example was the first chief justice of Kenya, Robert Hamilton, who went out of his way to try to see that Africans received justice in the courts, even from white settler juries, and received the predictable vindictive attacks from a white elite minority who assumed that English law was there exclusively to protect them and their interests, and not the mass of the colonial population.[122] He survived these barbs and on his retirement was elected a Liberal MP in Westminster, where he made it his business to oppose the self-interested and the racial supremacist attitudes of Kenya's settlers.[123]

However, far more effective in the long run were the remonstrations of the non-European colonials who argued with increasing effectiveness that the vaunted virtues of British justice were for them a cruel joke if it meant that they were to be shut out of its protections.[124] As Lauren Benton has noted, 'subject peoples' were astute practitioners in negotiating across legal cultural borders, and in turning the arguments of Britons about the civilized quality of their institutions against them.[125] Independence of the judiciary featured in these campaigns for greater equality, and later in independence negotiations.

By 1900 the system for disciplining judges in the empire had developed into a complex set of procedures that differed, depending on whether the jurisdiction was self-governing (that is, part of the white empire) or not. This rather messy structure reflected developments before and during the late eighteenth century and in the nineteenth century, which have been traced above. In part it also grew out of the uncertainties surrounding what to do about Benjamin Boothby in South Australia, and an attempt in a memorandum on the matter produced by the Judicial Committee of the Privy Council in 1870 in the wake of the Boothby Affair to rationalize disciplinary practices.[126]

In the case of non-self-governing colonies, the normal procedure for relieving a colony of a troublesome jurist was by amoval under Burke's Act of 1782, with a right of appeal by the judge to the Judicial Committee of the Privy Council. According to the memo, it was considered desirable that both the lord president and secretary of state for the colonies sit with the Judicial Committee on such cases.[127] What looks like a practice amounting to a conflict of interest – and probably was – was justified on the ground that the suit was between the judge disciplined and the colonial executive, not the Colonial Office, let alone the Crown. It provided the Office with considerable influence on the outcome of appeals.

A disciplinary power available to a colonial viceroy, falling short of outright amoval, was suspension of a judge from the bench. This expedient that was not covered by Burke's Act called for either the reference of the case by the secretary of state to the Judicial Committee or determination by the secretary of state himself, confirming or disallowing the suspension.[128] One assumes that if he confirmed it, then the matter would need to be referred to the committee for final consideration. In the case of both amoval and suspension, the legal obligations of the colonial executive were clear. He was 'bound to give to the accused person full notice of all the charges brought against him, to call upon him for his answer and to hear it.'[129]

The memo indicated that amoval was the preferable way to proceed in these cases, as it cast the Judicial Committee in its appropriate role as an appellate body.[130] It was also thought that it would ensure that appropriate pressure was on the governor to provide a credible basis on the evidence for taking the action he had.

At the same time, it was recognized that in colonies with legislative bodies it was open, under long-standing imperial practice, to them to petition the Privy Council directly to remove a troublesome judge.[131] From the Judicial Committee's vantage point, this was not as comfortable a process as an appeal from an amoval, for here the committee was cast in the role of a trial court, with a lack of established pleadings and procedures, problems with securing reliable evidence from afar, and inevitable delay. This process also meant that a judge under attack continued serving until the committee disposed of the case. Yet the practice was there, and was, the committee concluded, undeniably part of the imperial constitution.[132]

Nowhere in the memorandum is the option of recall by the secretary of state mentioned, although in the cases of Thorpe in Sierra Leone and Bent in New South Wales we have seen examples of the use of this expedient.[133] By 1870 this method of dismissal would have become inoperative in possessions with responsible government, in which the constitutional system for judicial discipline was initiated by the local government. Presumably it was still an option in cases elsewhere in the empire where the royal prerogative continued to govern imperial–colonial relations, and, in the circumstances, the Colonial Office felt the need for resolute action at the centre. The three options of amoval, petition, and recall continued to be available in the British Empire of 1900, although not consistently, and lasted until the era of progressive independence in the non-white empire. However, unlike in the nineteenth century, there were few if any cases of colonial judges being dismissed by these formal methods. Indeed the leading case from English twentieth-century jurisprudence on independence of the judiciary in the colonies had nothing to do with judicial discipline.[134] It addressed the issue of whether the secretary of state had the power to remove a judge from office earlier than the compulsory retirement age.[135] The British Parliament repealed Burke's Act in 1964 in a general house-cleaning statute.[136]

The situation with colonies enjoying responsible government was more hazy and was not addressed specifically in the memorandum of 1870. True, the statutes establishing these colonies as self-governing from the late 1840s had adopted a removal process, similar to that in the Act of Settlement, which required a joint address of both houses of the colonial legislature.[137] However, as we have seen in the Boothby case, the secretary of state, the Duke of Newcastle, opined in 1862 that the final word on removal was entrusted to 'Her Majesty acting on the advice of Her Ministers in Great Britain.'[138] This approach contemplated a colonial system for removal equivalent to that in the Act of Settlement that, however, left the final word with the British government. It reflected a clear concern about judges in these territories being held hostage to the unreasonable sentiments of powerful local interests or 'irresponsible' democratic forces.[139] Lord Carnarvon for the Colonial Office took a similar position when the two legislative bodies in South Australia sought to achieve Boothby's removal a second time in 1867 by a joint address. Citing the need to have certain legal questions determined by the Privy Council, he prevaricated. In this instance, however, the secretary of state held out another option, the invocation of Burke's

Act, to amove the judge, if his behaviour made the matter urgent.[140] This is exactly the process that Governor Daly employed.

The situation in the self-governing colonies was theoretically then that the local legislatures could initiate removal by a joint address, but the outcome of that process, if unfavourable to the judge, was subject to review in Westminster. After the Boothby farrago the condition of review of local decisions on the dismissal of a judge in London was effectively dropped. In the Dominion of Canada this seems to have already been the effect of section 99(1) of the British North America Act of 1867, which provided that superior court judges 'shall hold office during good behaviour, but *shall* be removable by the Governor General on Address of the Senate and House of Commons.'[141] This wording precluded any reference to Westminster in the matter. A similar provision was contained in the Commonwealth Australia Act of 1901 at section 72 (ii) and had the same effect.[142] During the late nineteenth or twentieth century Burke's Act was repealed or otherwise rendered ineffective in the dominions, as they moved to full independence.[143]

There is an absence of cases of formal dismissal of and appeal by British colonial judges during the twentieth century in territories still subject to the memorandum of 1870. Undoubtedly there existed other less formal methods of putting pressure on colonial judges to resign or retire that would have appealed to the local government or the Colonial Office or both, if not to the jurist himself. The lack of evidence of the invocation of the formal processes needs to be addressed. One assumes that sources of friction between judges and colonial executives did not magically evaporate. Indeed, we do have evidence of one such spat, that between the high commissioner for the Palestinian Mandated Territory, General Arthur Wauchope, and its chief justice, Sir Michael McDonnell, in the late 1930s.[144] This case and how it was handled gives a clue to the lack of official dismissals and the attraction of informal strategies for resolving these conflicts.

During an Arab uprising in 1936, the British military wanted to raze an old congested area of Tel Aviv for strategic purposes. The excuse dreamed up to justify this action was that the demolition was required for sanitary reasons. A resident of the neighbourhood refused to fall for this line and took the administration to the High Court. There the chief justice made no bones over his outrage at the fraudulent and cowardly behaviour of the colonial government in the circumstances, a position that caused Wauchope apoplexy and induced him to call for McDonnell's firing or transfer to another colony. The jurist refused to budge and made his view known to London in insulting terms. The legal adviser to the Colonial Office, Sir Henry Bushe, took the judge's part, blocking any attempt to fire him, on the ground that such action would be an unwarranted interference with McDonnell's judicial independence. The issue was resolved quietly by a retirement deal for the judge, who desired to retire early anyway. The Colonial Office effectively bought him off for a pension of £2,000 per annum for the seven years until compulsory retirement age.

The position of Bushe in this story is vital, because it reflects an attitude that harkens back to the positions of the Duke of Newcastle and Lord Carnarvon in the 1860s in not being seen to compromise judicial independence in the Boothby case.[145] It was a sentiment that the Colonial Office had reaffirmed and generalized in 1929 in a circular that came close to recognizing that colonial judges enjoyed the same independence as their English counterparts, without saying so openly. Again the setting was Britain's troubled mandate in Palestine. Frustration in officialdom in that territory about the administration's inability to get rid of a Jewish local judge who was suspected of corruption in land deals, because London would not accept that the evidence of wrongdoing was adequate, caused the Colonial Office to seek the advice of Lord Chancellor Hailsham on the matter. Hailsham produced a letter to the secretary of state ruling on the process for disciplining colonial judges, described as a Declaration of Independence.[146] Among his strictures he made it clear that a colonial supreme court justice could be removed from office only through a decision of the Privy Council. This ruling was subsequently embodied in a 'circular dispatch' by Lord Passfield, the secretary of state, to all colonies, the stated aim of which was to safeguard the judicial branch from the executive branch.[147]

Given what we know about the history of disciplining colonial judges, Hailsham's opinion and Passfield's directive were hardly earth-shattering. However, they did make it clear that colonial executives were not empowered to act on their own in these matters, if there was any doubt about that, and underlined the overarching authority of the Privy Council over dismissal or suspension proceedings. My guess, and it is only that, is that the psychological effect of the initiative taken in London would have deterred most, if not all colonial executives from contemplating engaging the process, except in the most outrageous instances of judicial misbehaviour. Its likely effect was, as in the McDonnell case, to encourage a search for less formal methods of dispute resolution – either get the antagonists to bury the hatchet, or make it possible for one or the other or both to save face, and to retire or move the jurist on. As to motives, the likelihood is that changes in Britain's policy towards its colonies and their future during a period of developing pressure for self-government or outright independence across the empire and growing doubts at home, whether economic or moral, about the worth of the imperial mission, induced London to counsel executive restraint when tension developed with the colonial judiciary.

None of this is to suggest that the task of navigating the risky boundary between law and politics has become easier in the former colonies of the British Empire. In several countries that gained independence from the British Crown, with constitutions embodying a grave and abiding commitment to the independence of the judiciary, the onset of dictatorial rule has put that principle into jeopardy and judges have suffered removal and more dramatic penalties 'at the pleasure' of the ruler. Zimbabwe and Pakistan provide two examples.[148] On a more positive note, the principle of independence of the judiciary enjoys a central and fundamental place in modern conceptions of the rule of law in the British world and beyond, and is a reality in many states.[149]

However, the difficulties of navigating the line between law and politics are not confined to dramatic cases like those of Zimbabwe and Pakistan. They continue to present a challenge to systems of judicial appointment and discipline, as well as to judges personally, in the former dominions, as well as elsewhere in the world.[150] In recent decades the Canadian Judicial Council has taken to task individual jurists for expressing political concerns in public. They rapped Thomas Berger, formerly of the British Columbia Supreme Court, over the knuckles for advocating Aboriginal rights in the discussion and negotiations leading up to the Constitution Act of 1982 and the Charter of Rights and Freedoms.[151] A panel of the council cited Ted Matlow of the Ontario Superior Court in 2008 for misconduct for failing to recognize the conflict of interest in being a vocal member of a municipally based protest organization campaigning against a real estate development in the neighbourhood, and sitting on a case involving one of the interested stakeholders. It recommended his dismissal. The council by a majority declined to follow the panel's recommendation, while criticizing the judge for acting as a legal representative to his neighbours, and his intemperate language directed towards the developers.[152] The challenge is no doubt a perennial one and may have taken on a new life in jurisdictions such as Canada in which judges are now challenged to decide cases involving major political, social, and economic issues. On the one hand they have a more clearly defined role in the formation of policy, but on the other need to be vigilant not to use their new role to further personal political agendas.

It is hoped that this book has demonstrated that the struggle for judicial independence in England itself and then the English and British empires was a long and chequered one. Furthermore, it demonstrates that, after the formal recognition of independence of the judiciary in England in 1701, with the exception of the United States, it took another 130 years before its absence elsewhere in the British Empire was challenged, and the principle was accepted in the white empire. In the non-white empire it continued to be a contested matter until dusk settled on colonial rule. The rather motley crew of jurists whose stories are told here illustrate the tensions embodied in and the political and legal values that were at stake in that struggle – the liberal, conservative, or even opportunist voices that were heard – and the fates that they suffered for taking a stand on one side of the issue or another. Their stories, as well as being intriguing tales, are important in filling an important gap in the history of judicial independence in the British world, and point the way to other studies of jurisdictions not covered here, as well as the comparative status of judges in both the British and other European empires.

Notes

1: Colonial Judges in Trouble

1 Robert Hett, 'Judge Willis and the Court of King's Bench in Upper Canada,' *Ontario Historical Society* (1973): 19–30; Leo A. Johnson, 'John Walpole Willis's Judicial Career in Upper Canada, 1827–28: The Research Impact of Computerized Documentation on a Non-Controversial Theme,' *Ontario History* 85 (1993): 141–66; G.H. Patterson, 'John Walpole Willis,' *Dictionary of Canadian Biography Online* (*DCBOL*), http://www.biographi.ca/009004-119.01-e.php?&id_nbr=5321&&PHPSESSID=bsehpbc4lt07bknod67.

2 John V. Barry, 'John Walpole Willis,' *Australian Dictionary of Biography On Line* (*ADBOL*), http://adbonline.anu.edu.au/biogs/A020546b.htm; B.H. Keon-Cohen, 'John Walpole Willis: First Resident Judge in Victoria,' *Melbourne University Law Review* 8 (1972): 703–14; Janine Rizzetti, 'Judging Boundaries: John Walpole Willis, Local Politics and Imperial Justice,' *Australian Historical Studies* 40 (2009): 362–75; Janine Rizzetti, 'Sifting to the Bottom of Financial Impropriety: Judge Willis and Insolvency in Port Phillip, 1841–1843,' *Journal of Historical and European History* 2 (2009): 97–109.

3 India has a unique colonial history with the co-existence of private, public, and indigenous jurisdictions, and was outside the control and supervision of the Colonial Office.

4 In settler colonies in North America and the Antipodes that gained responsible government in the 1840s and 1850s, responsibility for judicial appointments and discipline devolved on local governments. The appoint-

ment of judges in those possessions was 'during good behaviour,' not, as elsewhere in the empire, 'at pleasure.'

5 See, for example, William Cornish, Stuart Anderson, Raymond Cocks, Michael Lobban, Patrick Polden, and Keith Smith, *The Oxford History of the Laws of England* (*OHLE*), vol. 11, *1820–1914: English Legal System* (Oxford: Oxford University Press, 2010), 32–5; Daniel Duman, *The Judicial Bench in England, 1727–1875: The Reshaping of a Professional Elite* (London: Royal Historical Society, 1982); W.J. Jones, *Politics and the Bench: The Judges and the Origins of the English Civil War* (London: George Allen & Unwin, 1971); W.R. Lederman, 'The Independence of the Judiciary,' *Canadian Bar Review* 34 (1956): 769–809, 1139–79; David Lemmings, 'The Independence of the Judiciary in Eighteenth-Century England,' in *The Life of the Law: Proceedings of the Tenth British Legal History Conference*, ed. Peter Birks, 125–49 (London: Hambledon, 1993); C.H. McIlwain, 'The Tenure of English Judges,' *American Political Science Review* 7 (1913): 217–29, at 217–18; Wilfred Prest, 'Judicial Corruption in Early Modern England,' *Past and Present* 133 (1991): 67–95; Shimon Shetreet, *Judges on Trial: A Study of the Appointment and Accountability of the English Judiciary* (New York: North-Holland Publishing, 1976); Robert Stevens, *The English Judges: Their Role in the Changing Constitution* (Portland, OR: Hart Publishing, 2002), chap. 1; Ralph V. Turner, *The English Judiciary in the Age of Glanvill and Bracton* (Cambridge: Cambridge University Press, 1985).

6 See, for example, J.M. Bennett, *Sir Francis Forbes: First Chief Justice of New South Wales 1824–1837*, The Lives of the Australian Chief Justices (Sydney: Federation, 2001); Bridget Brereton, *Law, Justice and Empire: The Colonial Career of John Gorrie 1829–1892* (Kingston, Jamaica: University of the West Indies Press, 1997); C.H. Currey, *The Brothers Bent: Judge-Advocate Ellis Bent and Judge Jeffery Hart Bent* (Sydney: Sydney University Press, 1968); C.H. Currey, *Sir Francis Forbes: The First Chief Justice of the Supreme Court of New South Wales* (Sydney: Angus & Robertson, 1968); Basedo Mangru, 'The Hincks–Beaumont Imbroglio: Partisan Politics in British Guiana in the 1860s,' *Boletín de Estudios Latinoamericanos y del Caribe* 43 (1987): 99–114; John McLaren, 'The King, the People, the Law … and the Constitution: Justice Robert Thorpe and the Roots of Irish Whig Ideology in Early Upper Canada,' in *People and Place: Historical Influences on Legal Culture*, ed. Jonathan Swainger and Constance Backhouse, 11–24 (Vancouver: UBC Press, 2003); David R. Williams, '… *The Man for a New Country': Sir Matthew Baillie Begbie* (Sidney, BC: Gray's Publishing, 1977).

7 Barry Cahill and Jim Phillips, 'The Supreme Court of Nova Scotia: Origins to Confederation,' in *The Supreme Court of Nova Scotia, 1754–2004: From*

Imperial Bastion to Provincial Oracle, ed. Philip Girard, Jim Phillips, and Barry Cahill, 53–139 (Toronto: University of Toronto Press for Osgoode Society for Canadian Legal History, 2004); P.A. Howell, 'The Van Diemen's Land Judge Storm,' *University of Tasmania Law Review* 2 (1966): 253–69; Luc Huppé, *Histoire des Institutions Judiciaires du Canada* (Montreal: Wilson & Lafleur, 2007); Evelyn Kolish and James Lambert, 'The Attempted Impeachment of the Lower Canadian Chief Justices, 1814–1815,' in *Canadian State Trials*, vol. 1, *Law, Politics, and Security Measures, 1608–1837*, ed. F. Murray Greenwood and Barry Wright, 450–86 (Toronto: University of Toronto Press for Osgoode Society for Canadian Legal History, 1996); Peter Oliver, 'Power, Politics and the Law: The Place of the Judiciary in the Historiography of Upper Canada,' in *Essays in the History of Canadian Law*, vol. 8, *In Honour of R.C.B. Risk*, ed. G. Blaine Baker and Jim Phillips, 441–68 (Toronto: University of Toronto Press for Osgoode Society for Canadian Legal History, 1999); Stefan Petrow, 'Moving in an "Eccentric Orbit": The Independence of Judge Algernon Sidney Montagu in Van Diemen's Land, 1833–47,' in *The Grand Experiment: Law and Settler Culture in British Settler Society*, ed. Hamar Foster, Benjamin L. Berger, and A.R. Buck, 156–75 (Vancouver: UBC Press for Osgoode Society for Canadian Legal History, 2008); John Williams, 'Justice Boothby: A Disaster That Happened,' in *State Constitutional Landmarks*, ed. George Winterton, 21–52 (Sydney: Federation, 2006).

8 Lauren Benton, *Law and Colonial Cultures: Legal Regimes in World History, 1400–1900* (Cambridge: Cambridge University Press, 2002); Lauren Benton, *A Search for Sovereignty: Law and Geography in European Empires, 1400–1900* (Cambridge: Cambridge University Press, 2010); Foster, Berger, and Buck, *Grand Experiment*, chaps. 1, 2, 5, 10, 11, and Afterword; Peter Karsten, *Between Law and Custom: 'High' and 'Low' Legal Cultures in the Lands of the British Diaspora: The United States, Canada, Australia and New Zealand* (Cambridge; Cambridge University Press, 2002); Paul D. Halliday, *Habeas Corpus from England to Empire* (Cambridge, MA: Belknap, 2010); Diane Kirkby and Catharine Coleborne, eds., *Law, History and Colonialism: The Reach of Empire* (Manchester: Manchester University Press, 2001); B.H. McPherson, *The Reception of English Law Abroad* (Brisbane: Supreme Court of Queensland Library, 2007; John Weaver, *The Great Land Rush and the Making of the Modern World, 1650–1900* (Montreal and Kingston: McGill-Queen's University Press, 2003); Martin Wiener, *An Empire on Trial: Race, Murder, and Justice under British Rule 1870–1935* (Cambridge: Cambridge University Press, 2009).

9 See Catherine Hall, *Civilizing Subjects: Metropole and Colony in the English Imagination 1830–1867* (Cambridge: Polity, 2002); Zoe Laidlaw, *Colonial*

Connections 1815–45: Patronage, the Information Revolution and Colonial Government (Manchester: Manchester University Press, 2005); David Lambert and Alan Lester, eds., *Colonial Lives across the British Empire: Imperial Careering in the Long Nineteenth Century* (Cambridge: Cambridge University Press, 2006). For works that refer specifically to judicial movements and connections, see Brereton, *Law, Justice and Empire*; Kirsten McKenzie, *Scandal in the Colonies: Sydney and Capetown* (Melbourne: Melbourne University Publishing, 2004), 17–45, and several of John Bennett's judicial studies.

10 Philip Girard, 'Judging Lives: Judicial Biography from Hale to Holmes,' *Australian Journal of Legal History* 7 (2003): 87–106.

11 Anthony Musson, 'Lawyers' Lands in Late Medieval and Early Tudor England' (unpublished paper, Australian and New Zealand Legal History Conference, Wellington, NZ, 11–13 Dec. 2009); Mary Jane Mossman, *The First Women Lawyers: A Comparative Study of Gender, Law and the Legal Professions* (Oxford: Hart Publishing, 2006); Tony Earls, 'Who Stuffed Up? Drafting Duffy's Land Act of 1862' (unpublished paper, Australian and New Zealand Legal History Conference Conference, Wellington NZ, 11–13 Dec. 2008).

12 (1701) 12 & 13 Will. III, c. 2, s. 2.

2: Judicial Tenure, Accountability, and Independence

1 See John Baker, *English Legal History*, 4th ed. (London: Butterworths, 1990), 165–9; Stevens, *English Judges*, chap. 1; Lederman, 'Independence of the Judiciary,' 769–809; McIlwain, 'Tenure of English Judges,'; Wilfred Prest, 'Judicial Corruption in Early Modern England,' 67–95, 779–85.

2 Enid Campbell, 'Oaths and Affirmations of Public Office under English Law: An Historical Retrospective,' *Legal History* 21 (2000): 1–31, at 2–5.

3 Baker, *English Legal History*, 166.

4 Ibid., 168.

5 On Chief Justices Robert Tresilian and John Cavendish in the reign of Richard II, see Anthony Musson and W.M. Ormrod, *The Evolution of English Justice: Law, Politics and Society in the Fourteenth Century* (London: Macmillan, 1999), 39, 98, and on Chief Justice John Fortescue in the reigns of Henry VI and Edward IV, see Thomas G. Barnes, introduction, *De Laudibus (In Praise of the Laws of England)* (Birmingham, AL: Legal Classics Library, 1984), 3–11.

6 John Baker, *Oxford History of the Laws of England*, vol. 6, *1483–1558* (Oxford: Oxford University Press, 2003), 416–18.

7 See Stevens, *English Judges*, 1–7.
8 On the changes to the oath, see Campbell, 'Oaths and Affirmations,' 5–7.
9 On Coke's judicial career, see A.W.B. Simpson, *Biographical Dictionary of the Common Law* (London: Butterworths, 1984), 117–19.
10 Jones, *Politics and the Bench*, 141–3.
11 Stephen Black, 'The Courts and the Judges of Westminster Hall during the Great Rebellion, 1640–1660,' *Journal of Legal History* 7 (1986): 23–52, at 24.
12 See Simpson, *Biographical Dictionary*, 26–7, for Bacon's legal career.
13 Jones, *Politics and the Bench*, 123–31; D.X. Powell, 'Sir James Whitlocke's Extra-Judicial Advice to the Crown in 1627,' *Historical Journal* 39 (1996): 737–41. Like all typologies, this one on the obligations of the royal judges oversimplifies the true nature of their roles. As Halliday in *Habeas Corpus* avers, the royal justices were the guardians of elements of the prerogative, as well as the Common Law, and quite capable of using it in the case of illegal imprisonment or detention against not only subordinate and parallel jurisdictions but also the executive.
14 Stephen F. Black, '*Coram Protectore:* The Judges of Westminster Hall under the Protectorate of Oliver Cromwell,' *American Journal of Legal History* 20 (1976): 32–64; Alfred F. Havighurst, 'James II and the Twelve Men in Scarlet,' *Law Quarterly Review* 69 (1953): 522–46; Alfred F. Havinghurst, 'The Judiciary and Politics in the Reign of Charles II,' *Law Quarterly Review* 66 (1950): 62–78, 229–52.
15 Jones, *Politics and the Bench*, Document 28, 199–208.
16 On Scroggs and Jeffreys, see Lois Schwoerer, 'William Scroggs,' *Oxford Dictionary of National Biography*, http://www.oxforddnb.com/view/article/24950?docPos=2; and Paul D. Halliday, 'George Jeffreys,' *Oxford Dictionary of National Biography* (*ODNB*), http://www.oxforddnb.com/view/article/14702?docPos=7.
17 Havighurst, 'James II,' 545–6.
18 Act of Settlement, (1701) 12 & 13 Will. III, c. 2, s. 3. See also Stevens, *English Judges*, 5–10. The practice of new monarchs reviewing the tenure of existing judges continued until 1760, when the practice was abolished by an Act for rendering more effectual section 3 of 12 & 13 Will. III, (1760) I Geo. III, c. 2. On this development, see Shetreet, *A Study of the Appointment and Accountability of the English Judiciary*, 10–11.
19 On eighteenth-century appointments, see Lemmings, 'Independence of the Judiciary, 125–49; and H.J. Laski, 'The Techniques of Judicial Appointments,' *Studies in Law and Politics* (1932): 168, referenced in Brian Abel-Smith and Robert Stevens, *Lawyers and the Courts: A Sociological Study of*

the English Legal System 1750–1965 (London: Heinemann, 1967), 129, for nineteenth-century preferments.

20 See, for example, *Entick v. Carrington* (1765), 19 State Trials 1045 C.P.; and comment by E.N. Williams, *The Eighteenth Century Constitution: Documents and Commentary* (Cambridge: Cambridge University Press, 1960), 385–6.

21 John Manning Ward, *Colonial Self-Government: The British Experience 1759–1856* (Toronto: University of Toronto Press, 1976), 4–19.

22 Elizabeth Mancke, 'Colonial and Imperial Contexts,' in Girard, Phillips, and Cahill, *Supreme Court of Nova Scotia*, 30–50.

23 Mary Sarah Bilder, 'English Settlement and Local Governance,' in *Cambridge History of Law in America*, vol. 1, *Early America (1580–1815)*, ed. Christopher Tomlins and Michael Grossberg (Cambridge: Cambridge University Press, 2007), 63–103, at 65–83; Kermit Hall, *The Magic Mirror: Law in American History* (New York: Oxford University Press, 1989), 13–14.

24 Jack P. Greene, 'Metropolis and Colonies: Changing Patterns of Constitutional Conflict in the Early Modern British Empire, 1607–1763,' in *Negotiated Authorities: Essays in Colonial Political and Constitutional History*, ed. Jack P. Greene (Charlottesville: University Press of Virginia, 1984), 43–77, at 43–5; Edwin Surrency, 'The Courts in the American Colonies,' *American Journal of Legal History* 11 (1967): 253–76, at 262.

25 Hall, *Magic Mirror*, 16–17.

26 James A. Henretta, 'Magistrates, Common Law Lawyers, Legislators: The Three Legal Systems of British America,' in *Cambridge History of Law in* America, 1:555–92, at 556–61.

27 Hall, *Magic Mirror*, 17–18, notes the tendency of the colonists to rely on their memory of local courts in England. See also Lawrence Friedman, *A History of American Law*, 3rd ed. (Toronto: Simon & Schuster, 2005), 4–5, who emphasizes folk laws, norms and practices of law, environment, and the colonists' beliefs.

28 Bilder, 'English Settlement,' 91–3; Surrency, 'Courts in the American Colonies,' 262–9.

29 Surrency, 'Courts in the American Colonies,' 268–9.

30 Friedman, *History of American Law*, 8.

31 Hall, *Magic Mirror*, 19. The author notes, 'Sentencing patterns suggests the discretionary role of these courts as agencies of social control and as safety valves for individuals in society.' Friedman, *History of American Law*, 13–14, talks about suspicion of lawyers and formal law. He notes the inclination to use mediation and arbitration and refers to 'the persistent dream of doing without lawyers: and there is a related dream about simple, clear, natural justice, stripped clean of obfuscation and jargon.'

32 Bilder, 'English Settlement,' 92–3.

33 Helen Taft Manning, *British Colonial Government after the American Revolution 1782–1820* (1933; repr., Hamden, CT: Archon Books, 1966), 151–3.

34 On the hierarchy of planter rule in seventeenth-century Barbados, see Richard S. Dunn, *Sugar and Slaves: The Rise of the Planter Class in the English West Indies 1624–1713* (Chapel Hill, NC / Barbados: University of North Carolina Press / University of the West Indies Press, 1972), 98–100.

35 Hilary Beckles, *A History of Barbados: From Amerindian Settlement to Nation-State* (Cambridge: Cambridge University Press, 1990), 33–5. The 1661 version was applied, with a few amendments to Jamaica, and the 1688 legislation copied in Antigua, South Carolina, and later Georgia. For the process of borrowing both from English law on vagabonds ('innovative borrowing') and then between the colonial jurisdictions ('code borrowing'), see Bradley J. Nicholson, 'Legal Borrowing and the Origins of Slave Law in the British Colonies,' *American Journal of Legal History* 38 (1994): 38–54; and David Barry Gaspar, '"Rigid and Inclement": Origins of the Jamaica Slave Laws of the Seventeenth Century,' in *The Many Legalities of Early America*, ed. Christopher L. Tomlins and Bruce H. Mann, 78–96 (Chapel Hill, NC: University of North Carolina Press, 2001).

36 See E.V. Goveia, *The West Indian Slave Laws of the 18th Century* (Lodge Hill, Barbados: Caribbean Universities Press, 1970).

37 For insight into the Caribbean slaves courts and laws of the seventeenth and eighteenth centuries, see Dunn, *Sugar and* Slaves, 227–46; Howard Fergus, 'The Early Laws of Monserrat (1668–1680): The Schema of a Slave Society,' *Caribbean Quarterly* 24 (1978): 34–43; D. Barry Gaspar, '"To Bring Their Offending Slaves to Justice": Compensation and Slave Resistance in Antigua 1669–1763,' *Caribbean Quarterly* 30 (1984): 45–59; Orlando Patterson, *The Sociology of Slavery: An Analysis of the Origins, Development and Structure of Negro Slave Society in Jamaica* (London: Associated Universities Press, 1967), 70–93; Diana Paton, 'Punishment, Crime and the Bodies of Slaves in Eighteenth-Century Jamaica,' *Journal of Social History* 34 (2001): 923–54.

38 Daniel R. Coquillette, 'Radical Lawmakers in Colonial Massachusetts: The "Countenance of Authoritie" and the *Lawes and Libertyes*,' *New England Quarterly* 67 (1994): 179–211, at 186.

39 George Haskins, 'Law and Colonial Society,' *American Quarterly* 9 (1957): 354–64, at 361.

40 Friedman, *History of American Law*, 19; Hall, *Magic Mirror*, 19–20. On the broader political and constitutional context, see Greene, 'Metropolis and Colonies,' 46–61.

41 Bilder, 'English Settlement,' 88–9; Mancke, 'Colonial and Imperial Contexts,' 37–8. For a more extensive discussion of the tools of imperial control and direction, see Leonard Woods Labaree, *Royal Government in America: A Study of the British Colonial System before 1783* (New Haven; Yale University Press, 1930), 1–36.
42 Mary Sarah Bilder, *The Transatlantic Constitution: Colonial Legal Custom and the Empire* (Cambridge, MA: Harvard University Press, 2004).
43 Ibid., 2.
44 Ibid., 39. Bilder notes that, although in his first edition Blackstone's words ignored the claims of local lawmakers to pay attention to the needs and circumstances of the community, he had revised that position by the time of the second edition in 1775.
45 Bilder, 'English Settlement,' 92.
46 Ibid., 116–22; Henretta, 'Magistrates,' 561–9.
47 Labaree, *Royal Government in America*, 382.
48 Ibid., 383. The judges in Barbados would have been laymen at that time and continued to be so for long thereafter.
49 Ibid., 388–9. Labaree suggests that a power of removal was implicit in the negatively worded instruction noted in the text.
50 Leonard Woods Labaree, *Royal Instructions to British Colonial Governors, 1670–1776* (New York: Octagon Books, 1967), 1:369 (#516: Officers Not To Be Displaced without Good Cause).
51 Joseph H. Smith, 'Administrative Control of the Courts of the American Plantations,' in *Essay in the History of American Law*, ed. David H. Flaherty (Chapel Hill: University of North Carolina Press, 1969), 281–335, at 309.
52 Lederman, 'Independence of the Judiciary,' 1139–41.
53 Smith, 'Administrative Control,' 307–8. The author mentions Antigua (1728), Nevis (1704), South Carolina (1733, 1754, and 1768), and North Carolina (1761).
54 Labaree, *Royal Government in America*, 390–1.
55 Ibid. The author refers to the 1753 opinion of Attorney General Dudley Ryder and Solicitor General William Murray, at n21.
56 Labaree, *Royal Instructions to British Colonial Governors*, 1:567–568 (#514: Judges' Commissions during Pleasure Only).
57 John D. Cushing, 'The Judiciary and Public Opinion in Revolutionary Massachusetts,' in *Law and Authority in Revolutionary America*, ed. George Athan Billias (Barre, MA: Barre Publishers, 1965), 168–86, at 168, 173; Henretta, 'Magistrates,' 577–82; Labaree, *Royal Government in America*, 400–1.
58 The details are rehearsed in Labaree, *Royal Government in America*, 391–8.
59 Ibid., 394.

60 In New Jersey in the 1750s, through the connivance of the governor and chief justice, the latter's appointment was made during good behaviour. When the Assembly sought to renew the appointment on the same terms on the accession of George III, London remonstrated and the terms of tenure were altered. See ibid., 398–9.
61 Peter Charles Hoffer and N.E. Hull, *Impeachment in America 1635–1805* (New Haven: Yale University Press, 1984), 21–3.
62 Ibid., 11. Earlier two colonial chief justices, Nicholas Trott of South Carolina in 1719, and William Smith of North Carolina in the late 1730s, both formerly English barristers, who got on the wrong side of proprietors, survived attempts to remove them by impeachment, by working their English contacts and manipulating Assembly members respectively; see ibid., 35–8.
63 Ibid., 42–6.
64 Ibid., 45.
65 Ibid., 49–56. See also Bernard Bailyn, *The Ordeal of Thomas Hutchinson: Loyalism and the Destruction of the First British Empire* (London: Allen Lane, 1974), 265–6.
66 Bailyn identifies Oliver as Hutchinson's kinsman (son-in-law) and as younger brother of Lieutenant Governor Andrew Oliver; see ibid., 277.
67 Hoffer and Hull, *Impeachment in America*, 56.
68 Andrew Jackson O'Shaughnessy, *An Empire Divided: The American Revolution and the British Caribbean* (Philadelphia: University of Pennsylvania Press, 2000), 117–19.
69 Mancke, 'Colonial and Imperial Contexts,' 30–50.
70 On the political and strategic significance of the establishment of the colony of Nova Scotia, see W.S. McNutt, *The Atlantic Provinces: The Emergence of Colonial Society* (Toronto: McClelland & Stewart, 1965), 36–7.
71 Cahill and Phillips, 'Supreme Court of Nova Scotia,' 54–7.
72 Mancke, 'Colonial and Imperial Contexts,' 40.
73 D.G. Bell, 'Maritime Legal Institutions and the *Ancien Regime,* 1710–1850,' in *Canada's Legal Inheritances*, ed. De Lloyd J. Guth and W. Wesley Pue (Winnipeg: Canada Legal History Project, University of Manitoba, 2001), 103–31, at 103–4 (also in *Manitoba Law Journal* 25 [1996]: 101–31).
74 Ibid., 104.
75 Ibid.
76 Ibid., 119–21.
77 The 'Judges Affair' is outlined in Cahill and Phillips, 'Supreme Court of Nova Scotia,' 53–139, at 67–71. For a more detailed discussion, see Jim Phillips, 'The Impeachment of the Judges of the Nova Scotia Supreme Court' (unpublished paper, 2006).

78 Ralph Greenlee Lounsbury, 'Jonathan Belcher Jnr, Chief Justice and Lieutenant Governor of Nova Scotia,' in *Essays Presented to Charles McLean Andrews by His Students*, 170–97 (repr., New York: Books for Libraries Press, 1966).

79 Barry Cahill, '"*Fide et Fortitudine Vivo*": The Career of Chief Justice Bryan Finucane,' *Collections of the Royal Nova Scotia Historical Society* 42 (1986): 53–169.

80 J.A. Chisholm, 'Three Chief Justices of Nova Scotia,' *Collections of the Royal Nova Scotia Historical Society* 78 (1949): 148–58, at 150–3.

81 It took London three years to replace Finucane with Pemberton, and another two years was to elapse between the premature retirement of Pemberton and the arrival of Thomas Strange, his successor.

82 Phillips, 'Impeachment of the Judges,' 10, notes that 'for most of the period between early 1782 and mid-1790 … the court was staffed only by the two assistant judges.'

83 Allan C. Dunlop, 'James Brenton,' *DCBOL*, http://www.biographi.ca/009004-119.01-e.php?&id_nbr=2287&&PHPSESSID=kelf6kl1lefr1a07kdns9b2501; and Grace M. Tratt, 'Isaac Deschamps,' *DCBOL*, http://www.biographi.ca/009004-119.01-e.php?&id_nbr=2366&&PHPSESSID=kelf6kl1lefr1a07kdns9b2501.

84 Cahill and Phillips, 'The Supreme Court of Nova Scotia,' 67–8; Phillips, 'Impeachment of the Judges,' 5–7.

85 See Parr to Nepean, 8 Mar. 1788, Colonial Office (CO) 217, vol. 60, 173; and Parr to Nepean, 18 Apr. 1788, CO 217, vol. 60, 177–177v.

86 See Phillips, 'Impeachment of the Judges,' 14–16.

87 Phillips, ibid., 19, comments that it is not surprising that the Council backed Parr, given that the majority were 'men thoroughly connected to the indigenous establishment,' and the two Loyalist members were Sampson Salter Blowers, the attorney general, and John Halliburton, a high Tory averse to criticism of established institutions, and a friend of both Blowers and Judge Brenton.

88 Phillips, 'Impeachment of the Judges,' 20–1. The two lawyers repaired to London to seek reinstatement – a quest in which they were unsuccessful.

89 Ibid., 22.

90 Ibid., 30–3.

91 Ibid., 33; National Archives of the United Kingdom (NAUK), PC 1, 63, 24.

92 On the career of Strange, see Donald F. Chard, 'Sir Thomas Andrew Lumsden Strange,' *DCBOL*, http://www.biographi.ca/009004-119.01-e.php?&id_nbr=3679&&PHPSESSID=kelf6kl1lefr1a07kdns9b2501.

93 Phillips, 'Impeachment of the Judges,' 34.

94 Supra, 17–18.
95 Infra, 28.
96 An Act to Provide for the Support of the Puisne Judges of His Majesty's Supreme Court, (1782), Stat. N.S., c. 14.
97 An Act to Provide for the Support of the Puisne Judges of His Majesty's Supreme Court (1789) SNS, c. 12. As either process required the consent of the Legislative Council, it arguably contained nothing that worried London. The basic purpose of the statute was to provide for permanent salaries for the assistant judges as a fixed charge on the colony's budget.
98 Phillips, 'Impeachment of the Judges,' 28–9.
99 Alpheus Todd, *Parliamentary Government in the British Colonies*, 2nd ed. (London: Longman, Green, 1894), 835.
100 Phillips, 'Impeachment of the Judges,' 27–8. The author notes the irony of the enthusiasm of the Assembly for impeachment just as the Hastings proceedings were causing sober second thoughts about the legitimacy of its use in Westminster (at 29).
101 See chapter 5, 92–8.
102 F. Murray Greenwood, *Legacies of Fear: Law and Politics in Quebec in the Era of the French Revolution* (Toronto: University of Toronto Press for Osgoode Society for Canadian Legal History, 1993), 28; L.F.S. Upton, 'Peter Livius,' *DCBOL*, http://www.biographi.ca/009004-119.01-e.php?&id_nbr=2029&interval=25&&PHPSESSID=43l80e45ltoiid4a3d749flej3.
103 J. Grant, *Acts of the Privy Council of England*, Colonial Series: vol. 5, *1766–1784* (Hereford, 1912), 463–71 (March 1779).
104 See R.J. Morgan, 'Richard Gibbons,' *DCBOL*, http://www.biographi.ca/009004-119.01-e.php?&id_nbr=1904&interval=25&&PHPSESSID=mf7ac6kfj6k9219tjv5bhtvvs6.
105 Ibid., and NAUK, PC 1, 63, 22, Report of Committee of Council on the case of *Re Richard Gibbons*, 9 Mar. 1791. Gibbons never returned to Cape Breton Island. When he tried three years later, the ship on which he and his family were travelling was captured by a French vessel. The judge died in prison before the family was released.
106 J.M. Bumsted, 'Peter Stewart,' *DCBOL*, http://www.biographi.ca/009004-119.01-e.php?&id_nbr=1904&interval=25&&PHPSESSID=mf7ac6kfj6k9219tjv5bhtvvs6.
107 J.M. Bumsted, 'Politics and the Administration of Justice in Early Prince Edward Island,' in *Essays in the History of Canadian Law*, vol. 9, *Two Islands: Newfoundland and Prince Edward Island*, ed. Christopher English (Toronto: University of Toronto Press for Osgoode Society for Canadian Legal History, 2005), 49–78, at 49.

108 At ibid., 56, the author indicates that Patterson's seduction of Sarah Stewart was common knowledge in the colony.
109 Bumsted, 'Peter Stewart.'
110 Ibid.
111 Ibid., and Privy Council, *Report ... of Complaints against Lieutenant Governor Fanning and Other Officers of His Majesty's Government in the Island of St John* (London, 1792). See also NAUK, PC 4, 4, Minutes of George Chetwynd, 1772–1795 (Memorial from Stewart's enemies).
112 Ibid.
113 Labaree, *Royal Government in America*, 388–9, and see text supra, 17–18.
114 An Act to Prevent in Future Any Patent Office to Be Exercised in Any Plantation or Colony, Now, or at Any Time hereafter, Belonging to the Crown of Great Britain, for Any Longer Term Than during Such Time as the Grantee thereof, or Person Appointed to, Shall Discharge the Duty thereof in Person, and Behave Well Therein (1782) 22 Geo. III, c. 75. Under s. 3 of the Act the official had a right of appeal to the Privy Council.
115 Ibid., s. 4.
116 Burke's Act was not used in the Gibbons and Stewart cases, as both judges were suspended, not 'amoved.' The Livius case clearly predated the legislation of 1782. Express recognition of the statute's application dates from the mid-nineteenth century – see chapter 7, 167.
117 Manning Ward, *Colonial Self-Government*, 1–3; Robert Fraser, '"All the Privileges Which Englishmen Possess": Orders, Rights and Constitutionalism in Upper Canada,' in *Provincial Justice: Upper Canadian Legal Portraits*, ed. Robert Fraser (Toronto: University of Toronto Press for Osgoode Society for Legal History, 1992), xxi–xcii, xxv–xl, xlvii–xlviii.
118 A mixed message may have been given by the first lieutenant governor of Upper Canada, John Simcoe, who referred to the Constitution Act as 'the Magna Carta of the Colony,' adding, 'It was my duty to render the Province as nearly as may be "a perfect Image and Transcript of the British Government and Constitution."' See J.M. Bliss, *Canadian History in Documents 1763–1966* (Toronto: Ryerson Press, 1966), 34–5.
119 The Constitutional Act, (1791) 30 Geo. III, c. 31 , ss III, XIII, XXVI.
120 Greenwood, *Legacies of Fear*, 27–34.
121 See Paul Romney, *Mr Attorney: The Attorney General for Ontario in Court, Cabinet and Legislature 1791–1899* (Toronto: University of Toronto Press for Osgoode Society for Canadian Legal History, 1986), 18–19; Oliver, 'Power, Politics and the Law,' 450–1.
122 Barry Cahill, 'Henry Dundas' Plan for Reforming the Judicature of British North America, 1792,' *University of New Brunswick Law Journal* 39 (1990): 158–70.

123 An Act for the Division of the Province Lower Canada for Amending the Judicature thereof and for Repealing Certain Laws therein Mentioned (1794) 34 Geo. III, c. 6.
124 An Act to Establish a Superior Court of Civil and Criminal Jurisdiction and to Regulate the Court of Appeal (1794) 34 Geo. III, c. 2 (UC).
125 Cahill and Phillips, 'Supreme Court of Nova Scotia,' 61. Loyalist lawyers with practice experience in the thirteen colonies had been appointed to the bench in New Brunswick (Chief Justice George Ludlow in 1784) and in Lower Canada (Chief Justice William Smith, 1786, who had been a short-lived chief justice of New York, 1779–82). The first Loyalist lawyer to be appointed chief justice in Nova Scotia was Sampson Salter Blowers in 1797.
126 Mancke, 'Colonial and Imperial Contexts,' 44–5.
127 Manning, *British Colonial Government*, 127–65.
128 See, for example, *The Commission of Inquiry into the Administration of Justice in the West Indies: First Report (Jamaica)* (London: Joseph Butterworth, 1827), 96.
129 Neville Hall, 'Law and Society in Barbados at the Turn of the Nineteenth Century,' *Journal of Caribbean History* 5 (1972): 20–45. Barbados boasted a plethora of courts and no less than fifty judges, a remarkable number, considering that in the main the judiciary serviced a white population of 20,000 souls.
130 Manning Ward addresses the issue in *Colonial Self-Government*, 84–123. See, in particular, the agonizing decisions on West Indian colonies, especially Trinidad.
131 Manning, *British Colonial Government*, 415–17.
132 See chapters 9 and 10.
133 The Gibraltar connection with the administration of justice in early New South Wales is mentioned in Alan Atkinson, *The Europeans in Australia: A History*, vol. 1, *The Beginnings* (Melbourne: Oxford University Press, 1999), 90–1.
134 On the early legal system of New South Wales, see Bruce Kercher, *An Unruly Child: A History of Law in Australia* (Sydney: Allen & Unwin, 1995), 22–64; and David Neal, *The Rule of Law in a Penal Colony: Law and Power in Early New South Wales* (Cambridge: Cambridge University Press, 1991).
135 Gerry Bannister, *The Rule of Admirals: Law, Custom and Naval Government in Newfoundland 1699–1832* (Toronto: University of Toronto Press for Osgoode Society for Canadian Legal History, 2003). See also Christopher English, 'Newfoundland's Early Law and Legal Institutions: From Fish-

ing Admirals to the Supreme Court of Judicature in 1791–1792,' in Guth and Pue, *Canada's Legal Inheritances*, 55–78.

136 Bannister, *Rule of Admirals*, 178. The Supreme Court of Newfoundland was set up in 1792.

137 See William Blackstone, *Commentaries on the Laws of England* (1765: repr., Birmingham, AL: Legal Classics Library, 1983), 1:104–5, for the distinction between territories acquired by occupancy (found as 'desart' and uncultivated) in which British settlers took their institutions and law with them, and those acquired by conquest or cession (inhabited and cultivated) in which the previous law in force subsisted until changed by the action of the British Crown.

3: Administration of Colonial Justice and Law

1 Martin Wight, *The Development of the Legislative Council 1606–1945* (London: Faber & Faber, 1947), 53–4.

2 Paul Knapland, *James Stephen and the British Colonial System, 1813–1847* (Madison: University of Wisconsin Press, 1953). For his role in amelioration of the slave laws, see Russell Smandych, '"To Soften the Extreme Rigor of Their Bondage": James Stephen's Attempt to Reform the Criminal Slaves Laws of the West Indies,' *Law and History Review* 23 (2005): 537–88.

3 Wight, *Development of the Legislative Council*, 55–6.

4 J. Ll. J. Edwards, *The Law Officers of the Crown* (London: Sweet & Maxwell, 1964), 1–11.

5 P.A. Howell, *The Judicial Committee of the Privy Council 1833–1876* (Cambridge: Cambridge University Press, 1979), 14–48; D.B. Swinfen, *Imperial Appeal: The Debate on the Appeal to the Privy Council, 1833–1986* (Manchester: Manchester University Press, 1987), 4–8; and An Act for the Better Administration of Justice in His Majesty's Privy Council (1833) 3 & 4 Will. III, c. 41.

6 Memorandum of the Lords of the Council on the Removal of Colonial Judges, (1870) 6 Moore P.C. (N.S.) 551, Appendix II; 20 E.R. 447.

7 Peter Burroughs, 'Imperial Institutions and the Government of Empire,' in *The Oxford History of the British Empire: The Nineteenth Century*, ed. Andrew Porter (Oxford: Oxford University Press, 1999), 176–7.

8 C.A. Bayly, *Imperial Meridian: The British Empire and the World 1780–1830* (London: Longman, 1989), 109–16, 194–5.

9 Thomas Tremlett, chief justice of Newfoundland from 1808 to 1815, was a layman. It is, perhaps, a mark of the casual nature of British interest in

these colonies and their management at the time that Tremlett, who was unpopular among the merchants in St John's, was switched with Caesar Colclough, the legally trained chief justice of Prince Edward Island, who had many detractors there. See chapter 5, 104.

10 Hall, 'Law and Society in Barbados'; and Manning, *British Colonial Government after the American Revolution*, 150–65, 186–90.

11 Fortunatus Dwarris, *The Substance of the Commission of the Three Reports of the Commissioner of Inquiry into the Administration of Civil and Criminal Justice in the West Indies* (London: Joseph Butterworth, 1827), 436–7, 445–6. This set of reports covered the Leeward and Windward Islands, as well as Barbados.

12 See also *The Commission of Inquiry into the Administration of Justice in the West Indies: First Report (Jamaica)* (London: Joseph Butterworth, 1827) (hereinafter *Jamaica Report*), 96.

13 Dwarris, *Substance of the Three Reports*, 446; *Jamaica Report*, 196.

14 Hall, 'Law and Society in Barbados,' 31.

15 Dwarris, *Substance of the Three Reports*, 447; *Jamaica Report*, 100. There were local apologists for lay justice, such as Dr Lucas, a surgeon who became chief justice of Barbados, on the grounds that the system dispensed justice 'without legal foppery and forensic technicality.' Others, such as Chief Justice Adams of the same colony, were less sanguine, confessing to discomfort when acting in a role that required legal knowledge and skill; see Hall, 'Law and Society in Barbados,' 22, 24.

16 Dwarris, *Substance of Three Reports*, 434.

17 Ibid., 167–8. This was a less daunting task in Grenada than in the older colonies. It had been added to the empire only in the early 1760s.

18 Ibid., 436–7, 445–6, 459–66; *Jamaica Report*, 96, 99–101, 111, 113.

19 See Kercher, *Unruly Child*, 22–123; Neal, *Rule of Law*.

20 On the administration of justice in these territories, see Manning, *British Colonial Government*, 365–7 (St Lucia); 367–75 (Demerera/Berbice – British Guiana); 385–9 (Trinidad); 346–63, 401–8 (Cape Colony); 453–5 (Ceylon); 469–73 (Mauritius).

21 Ibid., 364–5. Manning notes the statement made by Henry Goulburn, undersecretary for the colonies, to the House of Commons in 1816, 'that through the efforts of the Colonial Office the conquered colonies were gradually being prepared for the introduction of British institutions.' Robert Wilmot Horton, Goulburn's successor, voiced similar sentiments. Peter Burroughs, 'Imperial Institutions and the Government of Empire,' in Porter, *Oxford History of the British Empire: Nineteenth Century*, 175.

22 Shetreet, *Judges on Trial*, 14–15.

23 Thomas Erskine May, *The Constitutional History of England since the Accession of George the Third 1760–1860*, 2nd ed. (London: Longmans, 1863), 1:317.
24 On the case of Lord Westbury, see R.C.J. Cocks, 'Richard Bethell,' *ODNB*, http://www.oxforddnb.com.ezproxy.library.uvic.ca/view/article/2305. Shetreet, *Judges on Trial*, 141–8, canvasses the questions raised.
25 This was so, even though as Harold Laski pointed out, 'Of 139 appointments made to the High and Appeal Courts between 1832 and 1906, 80 had been M.Ps., of whom 63 had been appointed by the party they supported.' Abel-Smith and Stevens, *Lawyers and the Courts*, 129, text and n7. On the character of judicial independence in England in the nineteenth century, see Cornish et al., *OHLE*, 11:32–5.
26 Shetreet, *Judges on Trial*, 140–1.
27 Ibid., 157–8.
28 *R. v. Johnson* (1805) 29 State Trials 81 et. seq. at 499 (K.B.).
29 An Irish Vice-Admiralty judge, Jonah Barrington, suffered removal on a joint address in 1830 for embezzlement of funds. Shetreet, *Judges on Trial*, 143–5.
30 Cahill and Phillips, 'The Supreme Court,' 84–5; Huppé, *Histoire des Institutions Judiciaires*, 234–6.
31 Greenwood, *Legacies of Fear*, 27–32; Oliver, 'Power, Politics and the Law,' 450.
32 Bell, 'Maritime Legal Institutions,' 120.
33 Greenwood, *Legacies of Fear*, 32–34; Oliver, 'Power, Politics and the Law,' 451.
34 Barry Wright, 'The Gourlay Affair: Seditious Libel and the Sedition Act in Upper Canada, 1818–1819,' in Greenwood and Wright, *Canadian State Trials*, 1:487–504, 697–702; Oliver, 'Power, Politics and the Law,' 451–3.
35 The Canada Committee of the British House of Commons in its 1828 report had advocated the removal of judges from Executive Councils, and all but chief justices from Legislative Councils. Arthur G. Doughty and Nora Story, *Documents Relating to the Constitutional History of Canada 1819–1828* (Ottawa: J.G. Patenaude, 1935), 466–77, at 471–2.
36 Huppé, *Histoire des Institutions Judiciaire*, 346–8; Lederman, 'Independence of the Judiciary,' 1149–52. For the Maritimes, see Bell, 'Maritime Legal Institutions,' 119–21; Cahill and Phillips, *Supreme Court*, 84–6; Lederman, 'Independence of the Judiciary,' 1152–7.
37 See, for example, Rainer Baehre, 'Trying the Rebels: Emergency Legislation and the Colonial Executive's Overall Legal Strategy in the Upper Canadian Rebellion,' in Greenwood and Wright, *Canadian State Trials*, vol. 2,

Rebellion and Invasion in the Canadas 1837–1839 (Toronto: University of Toronto Press for Osgoode Society for Canadian Legal History, 2002), 41–61, at 42–3, 48–9, 53–5.

38 Bennett, *Sir Francis Forbes*, 66–72; Kercher, *Unruly Child*, 69–74.

39 Hamar Foster, 'British Columbia: Legal Institutions in the Far West, from Contact to 1871,' in Guth and Pue, *Canada's Legal Inheritances*, 293–340, at 307–10, 321–4.

40 Kercher, *Unruly Child*, 61–2, 80; Enid Russell, *A History of Law in Western Australia and Its Development from 1829–1979* (Perth: University of Western Australia Press, 1980), 1–232.

41 Manning, *British Colonial Government*, 161–3.

42 Ibid., 155.

43 See Kercher, *Unruly Child*, xi–xxi, for a helpful account of the confused and confusing state of English law at the close of the eighteenth century. The extent to which colonial communities and their members resorted to informal methods of resolving disputes and seeking certainty in their relations is canvassed extensively in Karsten, *Between Law and Custom*.

44 Dwarris, *Substance of the Three Reports*, 430–5.

45 Bannister, *Rule of the Admirals*; Kercher, *Unruly Child*, 22–75.

46 See, for example, Patrick Atiyah, *The Rise and Fall of Freedom of Contract* (Oxford: Oxford University Press, 1979).

47 W.R. Cornish and G. de N. Clarke, *Law and Society in England 1750–1950* (London: Sweet & Maxwell, 1989), 38–43.

48 See, for example, Paul McHugh, *Aboriginal Societies and the Common Law: A History of Sovereignty, Status and Self-Determination* (Oxford: Oxford University Press, 2004), 178–214.

49 Ibid., 130–5.

50 Roy Porter, *English Society in the Eighteenth Century* (Harmondsworth, UK: Penguin, 1982), 149.

51 John McLaren, 'The Uses of the Rule of Law in British Colonial Societies in the 19th Century,' in *Law and Politics in British Colonial Thought: Transpositions of Empire*, ed. Shaunnagh Dorsett and Ian Hunter, 71–90 (New York: Palgrave Macmillan, 2010).

52 See Yvonne Cramer, *This Beauteous, Wicked Place: Letters and Journals of John Grant, Gentleman Convict* (Canberra: National Library of Australia, 2000); Neal, *Rule of Law*, 61–83; Romney, *Mr Attorney*, 62–157; Greg Marquis, 'In Defence of Liberty: 17th Century England and 19th Century Maritimes Political Culture,' *University of New Brunswick Law Journal* 42 (1993): 69.

53 John McLaren, 'Reflections on the Rule of Law: The Georgian Colonies

of New South Wales and Upper Canada, 1788–1837,' in Kirkby and Coleborne, *Law, History, Colonialism*, 46–64, at 46–9.

54 O'Shaughnessy, *Empire Divided*, 116–21.

55 See Neal, *Rule of Law*; Paul Romney, 'Very Late Loyalist Fantasies: Nostalgic Tory History and the Rule of Law in Upper Canada,' in *Perspectives on Law and Society: Issues in Canadian Legal History*, ed. W. Wesley Pue and Barry Wright, 119–48 (Ottawa: Carleton University Press, 1988).

56 Daniel Duman, *The English and Colonial Bars in the 19th Century* (London: Croom Helm, 1983), 94–104; Duman, *Judicial Bench in England*, 72–104; Patrick Polden, 'The Legal Professions,' in Cornish et al., *Oxford History of the Laws of England*, 11:959–91.

57 See J.M. Bennett, *Sir James Dowling: Second Chief Justice of New South Wales 1837–1844* (Sydney: Federation, 2001), 5–6, for James Dowling's involvement in reporting and publishing King's Bench and Nisi Prius decisions. Bennett, *Sir Charles Cooper, First Chief Justice of South Australia, 1856–1861* (Sydney: Federation, 2002), 2, notes that Cooper authored a minor practice book on municipal corporations in 1835. Matthew Baillie Begbie, the first chief justice of British Columbia, had supplemented his income as a Chancery barrister by acting as a law reporter to the *Times*. Williams, *'Man for a New Country,'* 21–3.

58 Bennett, *Sir James Dowling*, 5.

59 See R.M. Hague, *Sir John Jeffcott: Portrait of a Colonial Judge* (Melbourne: Melbourne University Press, 1963), 4, 7, 57–60, for a particularly notorious example. Jeffcott was in sequence chief justice of Sierra Leone and the first professional judge in South Australia.

60 Abel-Smith and Stevens, *Lawyers and the Courts*, 38. The chief justices of King's Bench and Common Pleas received £8,000, the master of the rolls £7,000, and the vice-chancellor £6,000.

61 Duman, *English and Colonial Bars*, 136–7. The author notes that two rising stars at the English Bar, Roundell Palmer and John Rolt, declined service in India as advocate general.

62 Cahill and Phillips, 'Supreme Court of Nova Scotia,' 86; Clara Greco, 'The Superior Court Judiciary of Nova Scotia, 1754–1900: A Collective Biography,' in Philip Girard and Jim Phillips, *Essays in the History of Canadian Law*, vol. 3, *Nova Scotia* (Toronto: University of Toronto Press for Osgoode Society for Canadian Legal History, 1990), 42–79, at 62. The figures are expressed in sterling value, which was worth 1.5 in the local currency.

63 Cahill and Phillips, 'Supreme Court of Nova Scotia,' 85. The stalemate was resolved when Secretary of State Glenelg persuaded the judges to accept

a commutation of fees, in a return for an increase in judicial salaries – to £1,000 for the chief and to £650 for the puisnes.

64 Bennett, *Sir Francis Forbes*, 46.

65 Hague, *Sir John Jeffcott*, 56–7. The figure was increased to £800 in 1842 and £1000 in 1847 after pressure from the first long-serving justice, Charles Cooper. By the time he retired in 1859, Cooper was earning £1,500 *per annum*. Interestingly, his predecessor Jeffcott is reputed to have had a salary of £2,000 in his previous posting in Sierra Leone (a product, maybe, of 'danger pay,' four of his five predecessors having died in office), ibid., 6–7. Hague comments, 'The Chief Justice's salary was high for a colonial judge – so also were his prospects of death.'

66 Dwarris, *Substance of the Three Reports*, 142.

67 Bennett, *Sir Charles Cooper*, 10.

68 The turn of the eighteenth century marked the beginning of transition in the meaning of *gentleman* from a one who was a person of leisure, drawn from the aristocracy or gentry, free to pursue any interest, including government, and whose honour was often protected by the duel, to the Victorian notion of the gentleman of 'entrepreneurial morality,' one who made himself by his conduct, work, and moral character, and who shunned duelling as a means of restoring his honour. Included would have been many professional men. See Harold Perkin, *The Origins of Modern English Society 1780–1880* (London: Routledge, Kegan, Paul, 169), 55–6, 273–5, 278.

69 No judges were appointed directly from Britain to the benches of Nova Scotia and New Brunswick after 1800, and the last appointment from Britain to Upper Canada was the ill-fated John Walpole Willis in 1827. In Lower Canada, while men trained at the English bar were appointed after 1800, they had, like Chief Justice Emsley and Alcock, already held judicial appointments in Upper Canada, or like James Kerr practised at the Lower Canadian Bar.

70 Bell, 'Maritime Legal Institutions,' 123.

71 Perhaps the most importunate applicant for colonial preferment was John Jeffcott, the rakish Irishman who quickly decided after his call that he was not willing to struggle to make it at the English or Irish bars. His biographer R.M. Hague, *Sir John Jeffcott*, 4–5, reveals that in succession he badgered the Colonial Office to appoint him attorney general of Grenada, attorney general of St Kitts, chief justice of Dominica, puisne justice in Lower Canada (he claimed to be fluent in French), a judgeship in Ceylon, and chief justice of Tobago. His persistence paid off, as he was offered the chief justiceship of Sierra Leone and the Gambia in 18 Jan. 1830. No doubt

delighted with the salary offered of £2,000, he was to find very quickly that the salary reflected London's concerns about duration of tenure, rather than any thought that this was a pinnacle of judicial preferment.

72 McLaren, 'The King, the People, the Law,' 13.

73 See chapter 4, 68–9, and chapter 9, 227.

74 Bennett, *Sir James Dowling*, 6–9.

75 Ibid., 7.

76 Bennett, *Sir Charles Cooper*, 2–7.

77 Ibid., 4.

78 Williams, *'Man for a New Country,'* 29–30. Begbie was initially being considered for the position of stipendiary magistrate in the colony, but when it occurred to Colonial Office officials that a judge in the territory would need 'original jurisdiction' he was appointed a superior court judge (Williams, 33).

79 Ibid., 31.

80 Ibid.

81 Bennett, *Sir James Dowling*, 98–109.

82 Ibid., 102–5.

83 Ibid., 105–7.

84 Ibid., 107–8.

85 Ibid., 108–9.

86 Duman, *Judicial Bench in England*, 22–5. Duman points out that the judiciary were not subject to such respect from those to whom the law, as they interpreted it, had little to offer in way of protection, and often was used vigorously against them. This was particularly true of the 'working classes,' particularly those that sought to organize themselves into unions (102–4).

87 See Atiyah, *Rise and Fall of Freedom of Contract*, 293–4, 369, 374.

88 Bennett, *Sir Francis Forbes*, 38–9, notes that by 1820 Forbes, who as chief justice of Newfoundland (the only professional judge in the colony) 'wearied of the constant battles with naval officers [including Governor Hamilton] and the lack of professional legal support or even company in dispensing the law, sought leave of absence for the summer.'

89 The more one reads about life in most British colonies during the nineteenth century, the more one is struck by the viciousness of local politics that obtained, and the crassness of the competitive ploys and posturing that went on. This seems to have been true whether the colony was a settler, conquered, or special purpose colony. The amount of malevolence seems to have been in inverse proportion to the size of the colonial community. For just one example of the overheated political and social condi-

tions in colonial life, see Brendan O'Brien, *Speedy Justice: The Tragic Last Voyage of His Majesty's Vessel Speedy* (Toronto: University of Toronto Press for Osgoode Society for Canadian Legal History, 1991), 20–8.

90 See B.H. MacPherson, *Reception of English Law Abroad* (Brisbane: State of Queensland Supreme Court Library, 2007), at 470–1: 'Lacking the constraints inherent in larger and more collegiate institutions, while at the same time combining all the status and powers of the Court and judges at Westminster Hall, sole judges in far-off places sometimes fell victim to delusions of their own grandeur.'

91 For examples of press criticism of colonial judges, see J.M. Bennett, *Sir William a'Beckett: First Chief Justice of Victoria 1852–1857* (Sydney: Federation, 2001), 30–5, 53–4, 66–7, 76, 78, 104–5 (attacks on the chief justice for partiality, insensitivity, and 'incompetence' in handling cases); Gertrude Gunn, *The Political History of Newfoundland 1832–1864* (Toronto: University of Toronto Press, 1966), 25, 45 (attacks on Chief Justice Boulton for his harsh administration of criminal justice, insensitive reform of civil law, and his angst towards reformers); Williams, *'Man for a New Country,'* 182–201 (attacks on Chief Justice Begbie for anti-democratic proclivities, hauteur, and partiality to interests he approved of). One should add that in some colonies there were also segments of the press sympathetic to judges, even the more difficult characters.

92 Bennett in *Sir James Dowling*, 15, describes New South Wales as 'a settlement notorious for its inflated cost of living.'

93 A classic case of salary arrears is that of Robert Thorpe as chief justice of Prince Edward Island, who felt the need to travel to London in 1804 to get action on his back pay. See Graeme Patterson, 'Robert Thorpe,' *DCBOL*, http://www.biographi.ca/009004-119.01-e.php?&id_nbr=3696&&PHPSESSID=t7ad88eud22rmhmiki8ockdma7. See also Williams, *'Man for a New Country,'* 59–61, for Judge Begbie's battles with officialdom over his claims for circuit accommodation and travel expenses in British Columbia.

94 Bennett, *Sir James Dowling*, 14–15, refers to Dowling as a puisne judge in New South Wales benefiting from the grant of 2,500 acres of rural land. Although, comments the author, the judge had to deal with an inflated cost of living and the demands of his dependents, 'all things considered he was well-placed. His standing as a landed gentleman far exceeded expectations he could ever have attained had he stayed in England.'

95 An example is Algernon Montagu, associate justice of the Supreme Court of Van Dieman's Land. See P.A. Howell, 'Of Ships and Sealing Wax: The Montagus, the Navy and the Law,' Tasmanian Historical Research Papers, *Papers and Proceedings* (1964): 101–28, at 119–21, and chap. 7 this volume.

Another instance was Sir Francis Forbes. The value of the land that he held in New South Wales fell dramatically as a result of a prolonged drought in the late 1830s. Governor George Gipps reported that his widow and two sons, 'during the late period of pecuniary distress lost everything they possessed; and Lady Forbes is, I am assured, at this moment in state of destitution.' Currey, *Sir Francis Forbes*, 521–3.

96 See, for the original less-than-ideal facilities in Adelaide, Bennett, *Sir Charles Cooper*, 14, 29, 30–1, 35–6.

97 This was major complaint of Robert Thorpe's during his sojourn in Prince Edward Island. See Patterson, 'Robert Thorpe,' *DCBOL*.

98 See Hague, *Sir John Jeffcott*, 7, who reports, 'It was said of officials sent out to Sierra Leone: "They arrived flushed with hope and expectation: one by one they dropped into an untimely grave, or perhaps lingered out an existence, stamped in their sallow, pallid or jaundiced looks, emaciated limbs, and tottering gait."'

99 We know of at least one judge who died by misadventure on circuit. That was Thomas Cochran, puisne judge of the Upper Canada Court of King's Bench, who died in the wreck of HMS *Speedy* in a storm on the north shore of Lake Ontario in 1804. See O'Brien, *Speedy Justice*, 97–110. For complaints about the rigours of travel on circuits, see Jim Phillips and Philip Girard, 'The Nova Scotia Supreme Court on Circuit, 1816–1850,' in Foster, Berger, and Buck, *Grand Experiment*, 117–34, at 129–31.

100 Williams, *'Man for a New Country,'* 44–59.

4: Perils of the Colonial Judiciary: Courting Reform

1 Graeme Patterson, 'Whiggery, Nationality and the Upper Canadian Reform Tradition,' *Canadian Historical Review* 41 (2000): 24–44, at 31–2; McLaren, 'The King, the People, the Law,' 12–13.

2 Gough to the electors of York, Durham, and Simcoe (undated, but before January 1807), in *Report on Canadian Archives, 1892: Political State of Upper Canada in 1806–7*, ed. Douglas Brymner (Ottawa: Public Archives of Canada, 1893), 68.

3 On Weekes's mercurial rise and fall as a lawyer, see G.H. Patterson, 'William Weekes,' *DCBOL*, http://www.biographi.ca/009004-119.01-e.php?&id_nbr=2707&&PHPSESSID=heu3liib202mck0j9s2mgu4pj0.

4 Gore suspended Thorpe from office and sought authority from the Colonial Office to remove him. Gore to William Windham, secretary of state for the Colonies, 13 March 1807, in Brymner, *Report on Canadian Archives*, 61–4. The latter's successor, Lord Castlereagh, removed him. CO 43, vol. 40/3, 49–50, 19 June 1807.

5 Manning Ward, *Colonial Self-Government*, 19–28.
6 Jane Errington, *The Lion, the Eagle and Upper Canada: A Developing Colonial Ideology* (Montreal and Kingston: McGill-Queen's University Press, 1987), 20–54.
7 Patterson, 'Robert Thorpe.'
8 John McLaren, 'The Rule of Law and Irish Whig Constitutionalism in Upper Canada: William Warren Baldwin, the "Irish Opposition" and the Volunteer Connection,' in *Essays in the History of Canadian Law*, vol. 10, *In Memory of Peter Oliver*, ed. Jim Phillips and John Saywell (Toronto: University of Toronto Press for Osgoode Society for Legal History, 2008), 320–52, at 321–8.
9 CO 226, vol. 17/2, 81, Lord Hobart, secretary of state for the Colonies, to Lieutenant Governor Fanning, 3 June 1802.
10 Supra, chap. 2, 26–7.
11 J.M. Bumsted, *Land, Settlement and Politics on Eighteenth-Century Prince Edward Island* (Montreal and Kingston: McGill-Queen's University Press, 1987).
12 CO 226, vol. 19, 202–3, Thorpe to Sir George Shee, undersecretary of state, Colonial Office, 10 Jan. 1803.
13 CO 226, vol. 19, 242–50, Thorpe to Lord Hobart, secretary of state for war and the colonies, 26 Apr. 1803.
14 CO 226, vol. 19, 202–3, Thorpe to Shee, 10 Jan. 1803.
15 CO 226, vol. 19, 242–50, 243–6, Thorpe to Hobart, 26 Apr. 1803.
16 CO 226, vol. 19, 289–94, addendum in Thorpe to undersecretary of state, Colonial Office (unnamed), 16 Oct. 1803.
17 Thorpe indicated that, although he would not be interested in being the judge, he would be ready on a voluntary basis to review every grant on the island. Ibid., 292.
18 CO 226, vol. 20, 160–6, at 160–2, Thorpe to Edward Cooke, undersecretary of state, Colonial Office, 6 Mar. 1804.
19 CO 226, vol. 19, 311–17, at 313, Thorpe to undersecretary (unnamed), 2 Dec. 1803.
20 CO 226, vol. 19, 242–50, at 247–8, Thorpe to Hobart, 26 Apr. 1803.
21 CO 226, vol. 20, 215–16, at 215, Thorpe to Adam Gordon, 14 Oct. 1804.
22 CO 226, vol. 19, 311–17, Thorpe to undersecretary (unnamed), 2 Dec. 1803.
23 Ibid., 313–14. One option the judge suggested was a position as adviser to the secretary of state on the affairs of the colony. This would, he claimed, counter the information the latter was receiving from 'ignorant, interested persons, speculating in land and jobbers in money.'
24 On Magowan's career, see J.M. Bumsted, 'Peter Magowan,' *DCBOL*,

http://www.biographi.ca/009004-119.01-e.php?&id_nbr=2524&interval=25&&PHPSESSID=qvsk4fdfope5tn6ts501ilmb22.

25 Magowan's perspectives are contained in a communication from him to Secretary of State Lord Camden, CO 226, vol. 20, 26–50, at 28, 3 Aug. 1804.

26 Ibid., 35–7, Magowan to Thorpe, 21 Feb. 1804.

27 Ibid, 38–9, Thorpe to Magowan, 21 Feb. 1804.

28 Ibid., 39–50, Magowan to Fanning, 7 Aug. 1804. Magowan refers to a letter from the chief justice to Mr Cormack, a Newfoundland merchant, which Cormack's family thought should be shared with its contacts in Prince Edward Island.

29 CO 226, vol. 19, 283–8, at 283–5, Thorpe to undersecretary of state (unnamed), 16 Oct. 1803,

30 Thorpe noted that Protestant dissenters who were 'evident republicans' were represented in both the Assembly and the magistracy, and unlike Roman Catholics, had not been pressed to conform to the law on public worship. Ibid., 284–5.

31 CO 226, vol. 20, 160–6, at 164–6, Thorpe to Cooke, 6 Mar. 1804.

32 Ibid., 165. Thorpe claimed that Holland had been booted out of Quebec, Halifax, and the 7th Regiment.

33 Ibid.

34 Ibid.

35 CO 226, vol. 19, 202–3, Thorpe to Shee, 10 Jan. 1803; CO 226, vol. 20, 160–6, Thorpe to Cooke, 6 Mar. 1804.

36 CO 226, vol. 20, 160–6, at 163, Thorpe to Cooke, 6 Mar. 1804.

37 See, for example, CO 226, vol. 19, 199–201, at 200–201, Thorpe to undersecretary of state (unnamed), 19 Apr. 1803; and CO 226, vol. 20, 160–6, at 160–1, Thorpe to Cooke, 6 Mar. 1804.

38 Thorpe to Shee, CO 226, vol. 19, 202–3, at 202, 10 Jan. 1803. He contrasted himself with Lieutenant Governor Fanning who, claimed the judge, had an allowance for expenses in addition to salary 'which he pockets,' fees from tenants on his land, and had 'married his cook' so that he could nearly do without servants.

39 The journey back to England was eventful, to say the least. A French naval vessel captured the vessel on which Thorpe was travelling off the coast of Ireland, and put into a Spanish port. The judge escaped and found passage back to England. See CO 226, vol. 20, 223–4, Thorpe to Camden, 7 Nov. 1804.

40 The correspondence about Thorpe's salary arrears related to his claim that he was owed salary for the time of his appointment to the position of chief justice in July 1802 and his actual arrival on the island in November of that

year. See CO 226, vol. 20, 223–4, Thorpe to Camden, 7 Nov. 1804; 225–6, Thorpe to Cooke, 15 Nov. 1804; 245–52, Thomas Cook, Treasury, to Cooke, 24 Jan. 1805.

41 CO 226, vol. 20, 223–4, Thorpe to Camden, 7 Nov. 1804.

42 CO 226, vol. 20, 278–80, Thorpe to Cooke, 22 Apr. 1805, indicating that he was ready to embark for Upper Canada. He replaced Thomas Cochran, his predecessor as chief justice of Prince Edward Island, who had perished in a shipwreck while on circuit along the north shore of Lake Ontario. See O'Brien, *Speedy Justice*.

43 An example is Chief Justice Francis Forbes of New South Wales, who had a vigorous and candid correspondence with his friend Robert Wilmot-Horton, undersecretary of state at the Colonial Office between 1822 and 1828. See John Bennett ed., *Some Papers of Sir Francis Forbes, First Chief Justice in Australia* (Sydney: Parliament of New South Wales, 1998), 12–182, 184–90, and chap. 11, 293.

44 CO 226, vol. 19, 240–1, Thorpe to Hobart, 4 May 1803.

45 Supra, 60.

46 On Fanning's career and views on the settlement of Prince Edward Island, see J.M. Bumsted, 'Edmund Fanning,' *DCBOL*, http://www.biographi.ca/009004-119.01-e.php?&id_nbr=2399&interval=25&&PHPSESSID=dti7rokq7nhftpm871ioavtjh5.

47 Fraser, '"All the Privileges,"' xxv–xxiii. See also 'A Loyalist Petition, 1784,' in J.M. Bliss, *Canadian History in Documents, 1763–1966* (Toronto: Ryerson Press, 1966), 11–13.

48 William N.T. Wylie, 'Instruments of Commerce and Authority: The Civil Courts in Upper Canada 1789–1812,' in *Essays in the History of Canadian Law*, ed. David Flaherty (Toronto: University of Toronto Press for Osgoode Society for Canadian Legal History, 1983), 2:3–48.

49 See the Constitutional Act (1791) 31 Geo. III, c. 31, ss 13 and 26.

50 Oliver, 'Power, Politics and the Law,' 450–1.

51 Errington, *Lion, Eagle and Upper Canada*, 35–54.

52 Fraser, '"All the Privileges,"' xlvii–xlix.

53 The case was *Bliss v. Street*, and the statute, An Act for the Recovery of Debts in His Majesty's Plantations and Colonies in America (1732) 5 Geo. II, c. 7.

54 Romney, *Mr Attorney*, 77–8.

55 On the law and indebtedness in Upper Canada, see Karen Pearlston, 'For the More Easy Recovery of Debts in His Majesty's Plantations: Credit and Conflict in Upper Canada, 1788–1809' (LLM thesis, University of British Columbia, 1999).

56 See David Wilson, *United Irishmen, United States: Immigrants in the Early Republic* (Ithaca NY: Cornell University Press, 1998).
57 McLaren, 'Upper Canada and Irish Whig Constitutionalism,' 320–8.
58 On the effects of the war on Irish Whig thinking, see R.B. MacDowell, *Irish Public Opinion, 1750–1800* (1944; repr., Westport, CT: Greenwood, 1975), 43–8; Maurice O'Connell, *Irish Politics and Social Conflict in the Age of the American Revolution* (Philadelphia: University of Philadelphia Press, 1965), 25–9.
59 See Alan J. Ward, *The Irish Constitutional Tradition: Responsible Government and Modern Ireland, 1782–1992* (Washington DC: Catholic University of America Press, 1994), 15–29.
60 W.W. Baldwin, 'Account of the Life of His Father, Robert Baldwin,' 1816, 13–16, Metro Toronto Reference Library, Baldwin Room, William Warren Baldwin Papers, L12.
61 Patterson, 'Whiggery, Nationality and the Upper Canadian Reform Tradition,' 32–5.
62 Carol Whitefield, 'Alexander Grant,' *DCBOL*, http://www.biographi.ca/009004-119.01-e.php?&id_nbr=2427&&PHPSESSID=orh26jhoko35c6ugld48gucjq2.
63 Edith Firth, 'Peter Russell,' *DCBOL*, http://www.biographi.ca/009004-119.01-e.php?&id_nbr=2643&&PHPSESSID=orh26jhoko35c6ugld48gucjq2.
64 G.H. Patterson, 'William Weekes,' *DCBOL*, http://www.biographi.ca/009004-119.01-e.php?&id_nbr=2707&&PHPSESSID=kv3r38ns43hemupvoojan415uo.
65 On Hunter's land policy, see In Collaboration, 'Peter Hunter,' *DCBOL*, http://www.biographi.ca/009004-119.01-e.php?&id_nbr=2471&&PHPSESSID=744b7rid3u4n2romjrinik4g67.
66 (1804) 44 Geo. III, c. 1 (UC). See Upper Canada, House of Assembly and Legislative Council, *Journals*, Feb.–Mar. 1804, from *Sixth Report of the Bureau of Archives for the Province of Ontario* (Toronto: Bureau of Archives, 1911); and Barry Wright, 'Migration, Radicalism and State Security: Legislative Initiatives in the Canadas and United States,' *Studies in American Political Development* 16 (2002): 48–60.
67 *Upper Canada Gazette*, 25 Jan. 1805. The legislation was not used until the War of 1812. Infra.
68 Whitefield, 'Alexander Grant.'
69 Ibid.
70 Fraser, '"All the Privileges,"' xlvii–lx, especially the story of Benjamin Mallory. See also Brymner, *Report on Canadian Archives*, 52, address to Lieutenant Governor Gore by 301 inhabitants of the Home District presented by William Weekes, MLA, 27 Aug. 1806.

71 Fraser, '"All the Privileges,"' lv. The author notes that Weekes dealt mainly with civil cases involving debt and land.
72 Ibid. The case ultimately reached the Privy Council in London, which affirmed the *Bliss* decision.
73 For several fascinating examples of this symbiosis between Thorpe and juries in southwest Upper Canada (the Home District), see Brymner, *Report on Canadian Archives*, 48, petition from Petit Jury, Home District, to Thorpe, 27 Mar. 1806, and response, 29 Mar. 1806; 53–8, Grand Jury, London District, to Thorpe and response, 17 Sept. 1806; Grand Jury, Western District, to Thorpe and response, 4 Sept. 1806; Petit Jury, Western District, to Thorpe and response, 6 Sept. 1806; and Petit Jury, Niagara District, to Thorpe and response, 6 Oct. 1806.
74 Patterson, 'Whiggery, Nationality and the Upper Canadian Reform Tradition,' 30–2.
75 Brymner, *Report on Canadian Archives*, 39, Thorpe to Cooke, 24 Jan. 1806; and 46–7, Thorpe to Cooke, 1 Apr. 1806.
76 Ibid., 39–40, Thorpe to Castlereagh, 4 Mar. 1806.
77 Ibid., 41, Thorpe to Cooke, 5 Mar. 1806.
78 Ibid., 49, Thorpe to Adam Gordon, 14 July 1806; and 50, Thorpe to Shee, 22 Oct. 1806. The British had finally wrested the Cape of Good Hope from the Dutch in 1806 and established it as the Cape Colony.
79 Ibid., 57, Thorpe to Shee, 1 Dec. 1806. See also S.R. Mealing, 'Francis Gore,' *DCBOL*, http://www.biographi.ca/009004-119.01-e.php?&id_nbr=3941&&PHPSESSID=70icum03ttil4bdci420d05554. Like his predecessor, Gore had served in Ireland during the 1798 uprising.
80 Ibid., 56–7, requisition to Thorpe from a meeting of the freeholders of the counties of York, Durham, and Simcoe that the judge be requested to represent them in Parliament, 20 Oct. 1806, and positive response from him.
81 Patterson, 'William Weekes,' 845.
82 Brymner, *Report of Canadian Archives*, 67, Robert Hamilton and Joseph Edwards, magistrates, to Lieutenant Governor Gore, n.d.
83 Ibid., 59–60, D'Arcy Boulton, solicitor general of Upper Canada to Gore, 26 Dec. 1806.
84 Ibid., 51, 59, Gore to William Windham, secretary of state for the colonies, 29 Oct. 1806; Gore to Windham, 27 Feb. 1807.
85 Ibid., 61–4, Gore to Windham, 13 Mar. 1807. Documents relating to Thorpe's impropriety accompanied this missive. Attached was an account of a meeting between Gore and Thorpe on 31 Oct. 1806. In his remarks on the conversation with the judge, who addressed a litany of complaints to him, Gore commented, '*I, the People*, though not the only language is in reality the motto of Mr Thorpe and every other factious Demagogue.'

86 Ibid., 81, Gore to Castlereagh, 21 Aug. 1807.
87 Ibid., 100–1, Thorpe to Shee, 22 Apr. 1807.
88 For examples, see ibid., 60, Quetton St George to Gore about the intemperate tone of Thorpe's views on the government, 22 Dec. 1806; and 85–6, anonymous letter from New York to McGill about Thorpe stirring up trouble in the colony, 17 June 1807.
89 CO 43, vol. 40/3, 49–50, Castlereagh to Gore, 19 June 1807.
90 Patterson, 'Robert Thorpe,' *DCBOL*.
91 Patterson, 'Whiggery, Nationality and the Upper Canadian Reform Tradition.'
92 See Shetreet, *Judges on Trial*, 140–1, 157–8, and chapter 3, 40. This was not necessarily an Irish judicial quirk. In his note in the *DCB* on Henry Allcock, an Englishman, Frederick Armstrong notes that his letters as chief justice of Lower Canada were similar in tone and content to those of Thorpe. Armstrong, 'Henry Allcock,' *DCBOL*, http://www.biographi.ca/009004-119.01-e.php?&id_nbr=2234&interval=25&&PHPSESSID=mjrtittkc667ek91unv7c5k986.
93 Thorpe certainly believed this. See Brymner, *Report on Canadian Archives*, 11–112, Thorpe to Cooke, 18 Sept. 1807.
94 K.D. McRae, 'An Upper Canada Letter of 1829 on Responsible Government,' *Canadian Historical Review* 31 (1950): 288–96, at 291–6 (text of tract).
95 See Michael Bliss, *Canadian History in Documents*, 34–6.
96 Errington, *Lion, Eagle and Upper Canada*, 34–54.
97 Gore did not state expressly that Thorpe was a United Irishman, but the accusation is implicit. See Brymner, *Report on Canadian Archives*, 61–4, Gore to Windham, 13 Mar. 1807. Thorpe's friend and confidant Joseph Willcocks, the sheriff of York, also fired by Gore, was labelled a United Irishman in an anonymous note to the lieutenant governor under the signature 'Fidelitas.' Brymner, 85–6, to Gore, 17 June 1807.
98 Justice Alcock had stood for election in 1802 in Upper Canada, only to be robbed of his win because of the importuning of his agent, one William Weekes (Patterson, 'William Weekes,' *DCBOL*). Judges sat in the Lower Canadian and several Maritime colonies during the first ten years of the nineteenth century. Irish judges were not excluded from Parliament until 1821, and the master of the rolls sat in the British Commons until 1871. Erskine May, *Parliamentary Practice*, 17th ed. (London: Butterworths, 1964), 212–13.
99 McLaren, 'Rule of Law and Irish Whig Constitutionalism in Upper Canada,' 334–8.

100 Fraser, 'William Warren Baldwin,' *DCBOL*, http://www.biographi.ca/009004-119.01-e.php?&id_nbr=3226&interval=25&&PHPSESSID=2aiepdmqrhmo187kcvbo7lnan5.
101 McRae, 'An Upper Canada Letter.'
102 Hett, 'Judge Willis,' 19–31; Johnson, 'John Walpole Willis's Judicial Career'; Alan Wilson, 'John Walpole Willis,' *DCBOL*, http://www.biographi.ca/009004-119.01-e.php?&id_nbr=5321&&PHPSESSID=n6o15qi049g3fv7e4ae9di7dc7.
103 See Elwood H. Jones, 'Joseph Willcocks,' *DCBOL*, http://www.biographi.ca/009004-119.01-e.php?&id_nbr=2713&interval=25&&PHPSESSID=84ocibqun8spk9l2n8ijnfbik4; and F. Murray Greenwood and Barry Wright, 'Parliamentary Privilege and Repression of Dissent in the Canadas,' in Greenwood and Wright, *Canadian State Trials*, 1:409–49, at 418–23.
104 Paul Romney and Barry Wright, 'State Trials and Security Proceedings in Upper Canada during the War of 1812,' in Greenwood and Wright, *Canadian State Trials*, 1:379–408.
105 The most notable series being at the community of Ancaster (near present-day Hamilton) during 1814 and 1815.
106 Ibid., 397.
107 Errington, *Lion, Eagle and Upper Canada*, 89–96; David Mills, *The Idea of Loyalty in Upper Canada 1784–1850* (Montreal and Kingston: McGill-Queen's University Press, 1988), 25–9; Romney, *Mr Attorney*, 62–5.
108 Errington, *Lion, Eagle and Upper Canada*, 92–6. A number of the young men who formed the nucleus of the local Tory elite had been educated at the grammar school in Cornwall run by the arch-conservative Anglican divine, the Reverend (later Bishop) John Strachan.
109 Ibid., 112–15, 117–18.
110 Mills, *Idea of Loyalty*, 34–51; Romney, *Mr Attorney*, 82–104. The issue of naturalization was finally put to rest in 1827. Meanwhile, the machinations of Maitland's government in preventing Barnabas Bidwell and his son, Marshall, both born in the United States, from taking their seats in the Assembly, to which they had been duly elected, had further poisoned the political climate.
111 Barry Wright, 'The Gourlay Affair: Seditious Libel and the Sedition Act in Upper Canada, 1818–1819,' in Greenwood and Wright, *Canadian State Trials*, 1:487–504.
112 Ibid., 491–6. For the reference by the law officers to the judges of the Court of King's Bench, see ibid., 701–2, Supporting Documents N 2.
113 See Barry Wright, 'Libel and the Colonial Administration of Justice in Upper Canada and New South Wales,' in Foster, Berger and Buck, *Grand*

Experiment, 15–29, 35–7. This was the crime deployed to convict Bartimus Ferguson, Gourlay's publisher.

114 See Leo Johnson, 'The Gore District "Outrages," 1826–1829: A Case Study of Violence, Justice and Political Propaganda,' *Ontario History* 88 (1991): 109–26; Carol Wilton, '"Lawless Law": Conservative Political Violence in Upper Canada, 1818–1841,' *Law and History* 13 (1995): 111–36, 117.

115 See Barry, 'John Walpole Willis,' *ADBOL*. The fullest account of his childhood years is contained in H.F. Behan, *Mr H.F. Willis: First Resident Judge in Port Phillip* (Glen Iris, VICT: printed by the author, 1979), 1–5. However, as the author did not use footnotes, and no original sources have been found in the obvious places, the narrative there must be viewed with caution.

116 Alan Wilson, 'John Walpole Willis,' *DCBOL*, http://www.biographi.ca/009004-119.01-e.php?&id_nbr=5321&&PHPSESSID=lc0e3p55s1dfcd2asa7gip3q03.

117 John C. Weaver, 'While Equity Slumbered: Creditor Advantage, A Capitalist Land Market, and Upper Canada's Missing Court,' *Osgoode Hall Law Journal* 28 (1990): 871–914.

118 Ibid., 877–81.

119 CO 42, vol. 386, 260–3, Earl Bathurst, secretary of state for the colonies to Lieutenant Governor Peregrine Maitland, 9 Apr. 1827.

120 CO 42, vol. 385, Goderich to Maitland, 19 July 1827, introducing Willis and expressing the desire of His Majesty's Government that an equitable jurisdiction be established in the province. The wording, although not entirely clear, is such that it gives the impression that a court of chancery is contemplated. Reprinted in Doughty and Story, *Documents Relating to the Constitutional History of Canada*, 369.

121 Wilson, 'Willis,' *DCBOL*.

122 Johnson, 'John Walpole Willis's Judicial Career,' 142–5.

123 Ibid., 143–4.

124 Johnson notes that Willis developed a friendship with William Galt, superintendent of the Canada Company, the largest land company in the colony, whom Maitland detested. On Willis's association with reformers, see infra, 76–7.

125 Romney, *Mr Attorney*, 144, claims that James Macaulay was disappointed in his expectations that he would succeed to the vacancy left by the retiring judge, D'Arcy Boulton.

126 Wilson, 'Willis,' *DCBOL*, notes that Lady Willis was considered a threat in terms of relative social status by the wife of the governor, Sir Peregrine Maitland, Lady Sarah, the daughter of a duke.

127 Weaver, 'While Equity Slumbered,' 884–6.
128 CO 42, vol. 385, 416–17, Huskisson to Maitland, received 25 Nov. 1827. Huskisson encouraged Maitland to have the local legislative bodies consider the matter, as well as seeking the opinion of the judges and local law officers.
129 CO 42, vol. 382, 72–4, J. Scarlett and N.C. Tindal to Huskisson, 25 Sept. 1827.
130 *Colonial Advocate*, 28 Feb. 1828.
131 Upper Canada, *Journal of the House of Assembly*, 10 Feb. 1828, 4th Sess., 9th Parl. 8th Geo. IV, 57.
132 CO 42, vol. 385, 'Report Bolton' to Major Hillier, secretary to the lieutenant governor, 12 Jan., in *Papers relating to the Removal of the Honourable John Walpole Willis from the Office of One of His Majesty's Judges of the Court of King's Bench of Upper Canada, 1829*, 146–7, favouring extending the powers of King's Bench. Boulton was later reported as arguing for a separate court of Equity. *Colonial Advocate*, 6 Mar. 1828.
133 *Colonial Advocate*, 28 Feb. and 6 Mar. 1828. On his likely motivations, see Weaver, 'When Equity Slumbered,' 888–90.
134 CO 42, vol. 385, 416–17, Huskisson to Maitland, 25 Nov. 1827.
135 CO 42, vol. 385, Robinson to Hillier, 19 Feb. 1828, in *Papers re Willis*, 144–5.
136 Fraser, '"All the Privileges,"' 335–7.
137 Patrick Brode, *Sir John Beverley Robinson: Bone and Sinew of the Compact* (Toronto: Osgoode Society for Canadian Legal History, 1984), 147.
138 Romney, *Mr Attorney*, 144. The Colonial Office, through James Stephen Jr, concluded that both Forsyth's and the Assembly's concerns about the use of military force in this instance were justified and that the normal processes of law, i.e., an ejectment action against Forsyth, should have been pursued.
139 Wilson, 'Willis,' avers that the reformers 'were anxious to bargain with the government by log-rolling – an equity court for a more independent judiciary.' They succeeded in getting a resolution on judicial independence and the inadvisability of the chief justice in the Executive Council passed by the Assembly. Upper Canada, *Journal of the House of Assembly*, 15 Mar. 1828, 102, 4th Sess., 9th Parl. The Legislative Council rejected the resolution.
140 Johnson, 'John Walpole Willis' Judicial Career,' 146–7.
141 Weaver, 'While Equity Slumbered,' 889.
142 Romney, *Mr Attorney*, 65–82.
143 *Colonial Advocate*, 10 Apr. 1828.
144 CO 42, vol. 386, 5–7, Willis to Huskisson, 21 Apr. 1828.

145 Hett, 'Judge Willis,' referencing CO 42, vol. 385, Maitland to Huskisson, 15 Apr. 1828.

146 CO 42, vol. 384, pt 2, 27–30, Maitland to Huskisson, 14 May 1828. Willis's bid had come to the attention of the lieutenant governor when the judge requested its forwarding to the Colonial Office. CO 42, vol. 386, 18, Willis to Undersecretary Robert Wilmot Horton, 8 May 1828.

147 It is possible that the plaudits Francis Collins, the radical editor of the *Canadian Freeman*, directed at Willis, beguiled the judge. See *Canadian Freeman*, 11 Dec. 1827 ('a man of enlightened and liberal mind' appointed by 'an enlightened and liberal ministry' of whom 'much good to the colony is expected').

148 Fraser, '"All the Privileges,"' lxv–lxxiv; Romney, *Mr Attorney*, 62–157.

149 Paul Romney, 'Upper Canada in the 1820s: Criminal Prosecution and the Case of Francis Collins,' in Greenwood and Wright, *Canadian State Trials*, 1:505–21.

150 *Canadian Freeman*, 17 Apr. 1828.

151 Ibid. McKenzie, distrustful of the criminal law process, had opted to sue the rioters civilly.

152 Ibid. CO 42, vol. 385, 24–5, Willis to Maitland, 12 and 14 Apr. 1828; CO 42, vol. 385, 178–9, Robinson to Maitland, 20 May 1828, reaffirming his views on the attorney general's prosecutorial discretion, which was not subject to judicial supervision. This position was upheld by the Colonial Office. Hett, 'Judge Willis,' referring to CO 42, vol. 386, James Stephen Jr to Maitland, 5 June 1828.

153 *Canadian Freeman*, 17 Apr. 1828.

154 Ibid. Judge Willis is said to have shed tears at this point.

155 Fraser, '"All the Privileges,"' lxix–lxx.

156 CO 42, vol. 386, 24–5, Willis to Maitland, 12 and 14 Apr. 1828. The issue of whether the colonial law officers were accountable for their actions to the judges, which he believed firmly they were, should, he suggested, be cleared up by London.

157 CO 42, vol. 385, 178–9, Robinson to Maitland, 20 May 1828.

158 Romney, *Mr Attorney*, 104–41.

159 As Carol Wilton has shown, this episode of violence was only one of a series of vigilante acts by supporters of the Tory establishment. Wilton, 'Lawless Law,' 111.

160 W.W. Baldwin Papers, MTL, Baldwin Room, L16, draft letter, 31 May 1828.

161 For an account of this application to King's Bench to have a new trial – which was unsuccessful because, while Willis said 'Yes,' his colleague

Levius Sherwood said 'No' – see *Colonial Freeman*, 15 May, 22 May, 29 May, 5 June 1828. Johnson, 'John Walpole Willis' Judicial Career,' 155, notes that the Tory press openly attacked Willis, and that he and his wife were insulted in the street.

162 He mentioned this in his letter of 21 Apr. 1828, seeking the position of chief justice. CO 42, vol. 386, 5–7. The title of the proposed publication, *A View of the Present System of Jurisprudence in Upper Canada, by an English Barrister, Now One of His Majesty's Judges of the Province*, was reported in the *Colonial Advocate*, 12 May 1828.

163 Johnson, 'John Walpole Willis' Judicial Career,' 145, quoting Maitland to Huskisson, 15 Dec. 1827, CO 42, vol. 381, 399–405. The lieutenant governor was, it seems, reacting to the news that, earlier that year, judges appointed to the Cape Colony had been granted tenure 'during good behaviour.'

164 Ibid., 151, for an account of the falling out of Willis and Levius Sherwood and his son Henry, over Willis's refusal to take Henry on the Eastern circuit with him as court clerk, where he would be hearing an action in the ongoing battle between Robert Randal and the senior Sherwood. There was further bad blood when the younger Sherwood threatened and insulted Willis on the street in Toronto.

165 CO 42, vol. 386, 20, Willis to James Stephen Jr, 31 May 1828.

166 (1794) 34 Geo. III, c. 2, s. 19.

167 CO 42, vol. 386, 31, Willis to Hillier, 3 June 1828.

168 Ibid., Maitland to Huskisson, 6 June 1828; *Papers re Willis*, 5–7.

169 Hett, 'Judge Willis,' referencing CO 42, vol. 386, Stephen to Colonial Office, 5 June 1828.

170 See *Upper Canada Herald*, 1 July and 8 July 1828. Sherwood, left behind to adjourn the court, reported to Maitland concerning the bizarre behaviour of Willis. CO 42, vol. 385, Sherwood to Maitland, 16 June 1828; *Papers re Willis*, 64–5.

171 Judicature Act (1794) 34 Geo. III, c. 2 (UC). Willis read the words 'His Majesty's Chief Justice of this Province, together with two Puisne Justices, shall preside in said Court' in section 19 to mean 'with all three judges in attendance' rather than as 'and.'

172 Johnson, 'John Walpole Willis' Judicial Career,' 155. Willis's solution to this conundrum was for Maitland to appoint a third judge. As Chief Justice Campbell had been granted leave by the lieutenant governor illegally, the judge had vacated his office, he argued. Accordingly, all that Maitland needed to do was to appoint a replacement to the senior position. This sounds very much like a case of special pleading for Willis's

campaign for further preferment. Moreover, it did not deal with the question mark hanging over cases decided by the Court in the past.

173 Hett, 'Judge Willis,' 26.

174 *Gore Gazette*, 2 Aug. and 9 Aug. 1828; *Kingston Chronicle*, 2 Aug. 1828.

175 CO 42, vol. 385, 142–7, Robinson to Maitland, 17 June 1828.

176 Hett, 'Judge Willis,' 27–8.

177 For the reference to Lady Mary's attempted intervention, see Johnson, 'John Walpole Willis' Judicial Career,' 155.

178 Ibid., 156.

179 Ibid.

180 CO 42, vol. 386, 410–14, Hillier to Willis, 27 June 1828.

181 Ibid., Willis to Hillier, 28 June 1828.

182 Ibid., Hillier to Willis, 2 July, 1828.

183 CO 42, vol. 386, 377–410, 6 July 1828.

184 Willis wrote to Huskisson contesting his removal. CO 42, vol. 386, 71, 93–8, 1 July 1828.

185 CO 42, vol. 386, 203–6, 7 Aug. 1828; *Papers re Willis*, 203–6, petition in favour of Willis and political and legal reform.

186 Gerald M. Craig, *Upper Canada 1784–1841: The Formative Years* (Toronto: McClelland & Stewart, 1963), 192–3. See also Powell Papers, MTL, L16, B82, Samuel P. Jarvis to William Dummer Powell, 12 July 1828.

187 Ibid., 195–6. The author attributes the failure of the reformers to capitalize on their majority to the Legislative Council's opposition, and their relative lack of control of the purse strings in the province.

188 Ibid., 193–5. The report of the Select Committee of the British House of Commons in 1828, which had criticized certain features of government in Upper Canada, including the composition of the Legislative Council, had encouraged the reformers. By the time the petition reached London, the Duke of Wellington was in office. His administration was of the view that preserving the status quo in Upper Canada was essential to its security and British interests, given its frontier status and the proximity of the United States. Craig notes that the secretary of state for the colonies, Sir George Murray, considered a replication of the British constitution in the colony as impossible, given the lack of a local aristocracy.

189 Romney, *Mr Attorney*, 151. An Act to Render the Judges of the Court of King's Bench in the Province Independent of the Crown (1834) 4 Will. IV, c. 2, s. 1 (UC).

190 See CO 42, vol. 386, 203–6, 7 Aug 1828; *Papers re Willis*, 203–6.

191 CO 42, vol. 386, 71, 93–8, Willis to Huskisson, 1 July 1828. Willis also sought to pressure the colonial government in Upper Canada to launch

a libel prosecution against the *Gore Gazette* for criticizing his handling of both the Collins prosecution and his refusal to sit with fewer than three judges on the bench. CO 42, vol. 385, Hillier to Willis, 4 July 1828, rejecting the request.

192 After Willis's persistent badgering about the injustice done to him, the Colonial Office referred his dismissal to the Privy Council. One has the impression that the Willis case in Upper Canada and the Forbes-Darling contretemps in New South Wales over press legislation, which were contemporaneous, had produced jaded sentiments about strong-minded colonial judges in the Colonial Office, especially in the mind of James Stephen Jr. See supra, 81, note 169, and chapter 6, 152–5.

193 CO 42, vol. 386, 260–3, Willis to Colonial Office, 22 Nov. 1828. For the reference to 'little insects,' see CO 42, vol. 386, 293–9, Willis to Colonial Office, 5 Dec. 1828.

194 CO 42, vol. 386, 164–97, Willis appeal to the Colonial Office, 23 Sept. 1828. He followed this up with a revised version: CO 42, vol. 386, 293–9, 5 Dec. 1828. Interestingly, Willis did not at this stage raise specifically the objection that he had been denied natural justice in not being allowed to answer the charges against him. This he raised later after the Privy Council had spoken. One wonders whether he had been apprised of the Colonial Office's negative reaction to the suspension of Jeffery Hart Bent in Grenada on this ground, during the summer of 1829. See chapter 9, 238.

195 CO 42, vol. 386, 325–44, advice of the Privy Council in the Willis case, 11 Feb. 1829, taking its cue from a report of the committee that heard the appeal, dated 30 Jan. 1829.

196 Wilson, 'Willis,' *DCBOL*.

197 Romney, *Mr Attorney*, 141.

198 Ibid.

199 *Canadian Freeman*, 11 Dec. 1827.

200 Johnson, 'John Walpole Willis's Judicial Career,' 143–4, quoting from the segment in the manuscript contained in CO 42, vol. 386, 500–6 at 503. The author also makes the point that Willis was shocked to find that the range of capital offences in the colony was extensive, compared with reformed English criminal law. Ibid., 148–9.

201 See Rainer Baehre, 'Trying the Rebels: Emergency Legislation and the Colonial Executive's Overall Legal Strategy in the Upper Canadian Rebellion,' in Greenwood and Wright, *Canadian State Trials*, 2:41–61, at 41–3, and 53–5.

202 Oliver, 'Power, Politics and the Law,' 456.

5: Perils of the Colonial Judiciary: Ultra-Conservative Judges

1 For the general history of Quebec during the period 1769 to 1791, see Hilda Neatby, *Quebec: The Revolutionary Age, 1760–1791* (Toronto: McClelland & Stewart, 1966); Fernand Ouellet, *Economic and Social History of Quebec 1760–1850* (Toronto: Carleton Library, 1980, translation of French original, 1966).

2 Manning Ward, *Colonial Self-Government*, 4–13.

3 Neatby, *Revolutionary Age*, 156–89.

4 Greenwood, *Legacies of Fear*, 9–27.

5 A prime judicial example was William Smith, short-lived chief justice of New York, appointed chief justice of Quebec in 1785. See L.F.S. Upton, 'Introduction,' in *The Diary and Selected Papers of Chief Justice William Smith 1784–1793*, ed. L.F.S. Upton (Toronto: Champlain Society, 1963), xiii–xl.

6 Neatby, *Quebec*, 124–41.

7 See Lord Mansfield C.J. in *Campbell v. Hall* (1774) 1 Cowp. 204; 98 E.R. 1045 (K.B). Mansfield asserted that, once the Crown had exercised its prerogative in changing the pre-existing laws of a conquered or ceded colony, it had exhausted that power, and that further changes to the constitution and law of the colony required parliamentary legislation.

8 See chapter 2, 28–9. For insights into British policy on Lower Canada, embodied in the Constitution Act, (1791) 30 Geo. III, c. 31, see Greenwood, *Legacies of Fear*, 43–9; and Fernand Ouellet, *Lower Canada 1791–1840: Social Change and Nationalism* (Toronto: McClelland & Stewart, 1980), 21–7.

9 Greenwood, *Legacies of Fear*, 27–34, 56–170.

10 F. Murray Greenwood, 'Judges and Treason Law in Lower Canada, England and the United States during the French Revolution,' in Greenwood and Wright, *Canadian State Trials*, 1:241–95, at 264–6.

11 Ouellet, *Lower Canada*, 52–76.

12 Greenwood, *Legacies of Fear*, 177–84.

13 Ibid., 202–12.

14 See Jean-Marie Fecteau, F. Murray Greenwood, and Jean-Pierre Wallot, 'Sir James Craig's "Reign of Terror" and Its Impact on Emergency Powers in Lower Canada,' in Greenwood and Wright, *Canadian State Trials*, 1:323–78; Ouellet, *Lower Canada*, 77–94.

15 Fecteau, Greenwood, and Wallot, 'Sir James Craig's "Reign of Terror,"' 327–8; Greenwood, *Legacies of Fear*, 223–6, 230–1; Evelyn Kolish and James Lambert, 'The Attempted Impeachment of the Lower Canadian Chief Justices, 1814–1815,' in Greenwood and Wright, *Canadian State Trials* 1:462; Ouellet, *Lower Canada*, 88–90.

16 Ouellet, *Lower Canada*, 80–2.
17 Greenwood, *Legacies of Fear*, 213–16.
18 Ibid., 218. In the legislative session earlier that year, the House of Assembly passed a bill, proposed by the *parti Canadien*, to exclude the Superior Court judges from sitting in that body. The governor accepted this with equanimity. The issue became explosive only when the Legislative Council vetoed the bill.
19 Fecteau, Greenwood, and Wallot, 'Sir James Craig's "Reign of Terror,"' 337–8.
20 Ibid., 338–9; Greenwood, *Legacies of Fear*, 233–7.
21 Greenwood, *Legacies of* Fear, 237, where the author describes Sewell as Craig's 'prime minister' and notes his report to Craig on the security issues; and Kolish and Lambert, 'Attempted Impeachment,' 460–1.
22 F. Murray Greenwood and James H. Lambert, 'Jonathan Sewell,' *DCBOL*, http://www.biographi.ca/009004-119.01-e.php?&id_nbr=3655&&PHPSESSID=bqlmeojeilog4q3nvu2e5g8sm3.
23 Kolish and Lambert, 'Attempted Impeachment,' 463.
24 Ibid., 455–9.
25 Fecteau, Greenwood, and Wallot, 'Sir James Craig's "Reign of Terror,"' 34, and for the text of the address, see Library and Archives of Canada (LAC), Sewell Papers, MG23, GII 10, vol. 12, 5592–600.
26 Fecteau, Greenwood, and Wallot., 'Sir James Craig's "Reign of Terror,"' 342–4.
27 Ibid., 344–5.
28 Ibid., 349–50. On Prevost's career, see Peter Burroughs, 'George Prevost,' *DCBOL*, http://www.biographi.ca/009004-119.01-e.php?&id_nbr=2620&&PHPSESSID=bqlmeojeilog4q3nvu2e5g8sm3.
29 Ibid., 351. Two members of the *parti* were named to the Legislative Council.
30 Ibid., 351–64.
31 Kolish and Lambert, 'Attempted Impeachment,' 450–86.
32 Ibid., 453–5. On the serpentine career of Andrew Stuart who would in time become chief justice of Lower Canada, see Ginette Bernatchez, 'Andrew Stuart,' *DCBOL*, http://www.biographi.ca/009004-119.01-e.php?&id_nbr=3681&&PHPSESSID=k1rofb3ansoaubarvhvt67h4d4.
33 Supra, 92n18.
34 For the heads of impeachment against Sewell, as set out in the *Proceedings in the Assembly of Lower Canada on the Rules and Practice of the Courts of Justice and the Impeachments of Jonathan Sewell and James Monk, Esquires* (1814), see Greenwood and Wright, *Canadian State Trials*, 1:688–94.

35 For the charges against Monk, see ibid., 694–6.
36 Kolish and Lambert, 'Attempted Impeachment,' 457.
37 Ibid., 457–9.
38 Ibid., 464–5. Ironically, this was the only time in his career that Stuart steadfastly espoused the cause of French civil law. Ibid., 459.
39 Ibid., 469–71.
40 Monk had sensed pending trouble as early as January 1813, when the Assembly determined to consider the issue of rules of court. See Sewell Papers, vol. 5, 2040–51, Monk to Sewell, 22 Jan. 1813. He noted that if the judges were incorrect in applying rules that ran contrary to positive law, then the solution was correction on appeal, and if they had misconstrued a statute, then the necessary response was an act declaring the law or restricting its interpretation. Judges, he averred, could not be impeached for an error of judgment.
41 See Sewell Papers, vol. 5, 2041–51, Monk to Sewell, 22 Jan. 1813, for the elaboration of this strategy.
42 Ibid., 2184–8, Monk to Sewell, 10 Feb. 1814. The Assembly designated Stuart to present its case in London.
43 Ibid. This argument had been elaborated in Monk's letter of 22 Jan. 1813. Sewell Papers, vol. 5, 2041–51.
44 Ibid., 2041–51, Monk to Sewell, 22 Jan.; and 2175–8, Monk to Sewell, 7 Feb. 1814.
45 Monk was careful to secure information about the abortive Nova Scotia impeachment attempt towards the end of the previous century. See chapter 2, 21–5.
46 Sewell Papers, vol. 5, 2220–2, Monk to Sewell, 28 Feb. 1814.
47 The executive councillors were brought in as members of the final colonial Court of Appeal, the governor's Court.
48 See also notebook beginning 'Journal of my proceedings in consequence of the Impeachment preferred against me by the Assembly of Lower Canada' [June 1814], Sewell Papers, vol. 1, Journals and Notebooks, 1(a); and notebook beginning 'Agenda London, September 29, 1814,' Sewell Papers, vol. 1, Journal and Notebooks 1(b).
49 Sewell Papers, vol. 1(a), notebook, journal, 17 July 1814.
50 Ibid., 25 July 1814.
51 For the reference to the report of the English law officers, see Sewell Papers, vol. 16, 8077–119, at 8016–17, 20 May 1815.
52 For the advice of the committee, see ibid., 8071–3, at 8072–3, *Order of His Royal Highness the Prince Regent in Council*, 29 June 1815.
53 Ibid., 8075, Lord Chetwynd to Sewell, 17 Aug. 1815. The list included the

lord president; Lord Bathurst, the secretary of state for the colonies; Lord Chief Justice Ellenborough; the lord chief justice of common pleas; the lord chief baron of exchequer, and the master of the rolls.

54 Sewell Papers, vol. 5, 2521–5, at 2524–5, Bathurst to Drummond, 12 July 1815.

55 Kolish and Lambert, 'Attempted Impeachment,' 477–9.

56 Brian Young, *The Politics of Codification: The Lower Canadian Civil Code of 1866* (Toronto: McGill-Queen's University Press for Osgoode Society for Canadian Legal History, 1994), 25–8. This position was not shared among the Anglophone Chateau Clique judges of the period. For example, King's Bench Justice James Kerr asserted provocatively that Canadian law 'was unworthy of an English judge,' and that in any case 'he did not know what the law of Lower Canada might be' (ibid., 31).

57 Ibid.

58 The two abortive attempts at impeachment were against Louis-Charles Foucher by an Assembly dominated by the *parti* and against Pierre-Stanislas Bédard by their conservative opponents in 1819. See Doughty and Story, *Documents relating to the Constitutional History of Canada*, 19–21, Resolutions of the Assembly, Lower Canada on the Impeachment of Judge Bédard, 5 Feb. 1819; and Ouellet, *Lower Canada*, 255. Ouellet suggests that the latter campaign may have been in reprisal for the attacks by the *parti* on Sewell, Monk, and Foucher.

59 See Evelyn Kolish, 'The Impact of the Change in Legal Metropolis on the Development of Lower Canada's Legal System: Judicial Chaos and Legislative Paralysis in the Civil Law, 1791–1838,' *Canadian Journal of Law and Society* 3 (1988): 1–26, at 15–17. The secretary of state for the colonies, without inquiry, removed from office the most unyielding of the Anglo judges, James Kerr, against whom the Assembly inveighed for his alleged incompetence, malversation, partiality, bad temper, and for amending his judgments. See Huppé, *Histoire des Institutions*, 368–9.

60 See Jean-Marie Fecteau, '"This Ultimate Resource": Martial Law and State Repression in Lower Canada, 1837–38,' and F. Murray Greenwood, 'The Montreal Court Martial, 1838–39: Legal and Constitutional Reflections,' in Greenwood and Wright, *Canadian State Trials*, 2:207–47, at 225–30; 2:325–52, at 326–9; Halliday, *Habeas Corpus*, 279–81. For the establishment of the Special Council and its impact on the justice system, see the same volume, Steven Watt, 'State Trial by Legislature: The Special Council of Lower Canada, 1838–41,' 2:248–78. All three judges were restored to office before the Union of the Canadas.

61 See An Act for the Better Administration of Justice in Lower Canada (1843) 7 Vict., c. 16, s. 5 (Can.); An Act to Render Independent of the Crown the Judges of the Court of Queen's Bench of Lower Canada (1843) 7 Vict., c. 15 (Can.).; and Huppé, *Histoire des Institutions Judiciaires*, 340–2.
62 See J.M. Bumsted, 'The Consolidation of British North America, 1783–1860,' in *Canada and the British Empire*, ed. Phillip Buckner (Oxford: Oxford University Press, 2008), 43–65, at 57–8.
63 See chapter 4, 72–4, 77, 78–80.
64 Gertrude Gunn, *The Political History of Newfoundland 1832–1864* (Toronto: University of Toronto Press, 1966), 19.
65 Romney, *Mr Attorney*, 155.
66 Hereward and Elinor Senior, 'Henry John Boulton,' *DCBOL*, http://www.biographi.ca/009004-119.01-e.php?&id_nbr=4311&interval=25&&PHPSESSID=ubb40f0de0au93qs8c7ldb86u7.
67 On the career of the father, see John Lownsbrough, 'D'Arcy Boulton,' *DCBOL*, http://www.biographi.ca/009004-119.01-e.php?&id_nbr=2765&interval=25&&PHPSESSID=q2c0guumj102lngklbnr8blh76.
68 Hereward and Senior, 'Henry John Boulton,' *DCBOL*.
69 Ibid.
70 Lownsbrough, 'D'Arcy Boulton,' *DCBOL*.
71 Douglas Leighton and Robert J. Burns, 'Samuel Peters Jarvis,' *DCBOL*, http://www.biographi.ca/009004-119.01-e.php?&id_nbr=3988&&PHPSESSID=n7n00agg2533pgcrnuuk8n7qv6.
72 Francis Gore, the lieutenant governor, was one such sceptic. See MTL, Baldwin Room, Powell Papers, L16, A93, 239–42, Gore to Chief Justice William Dummer Powell, 17 Jan. 1818.
73 Romney, *Mr Attorney*, 10. The author describes Boulton as 'intellectually competent ... but perhaps also intellectually arrogant in a politically damaging way,' at 165.
74 Ibid., 65–82.
75 Wright, 'Gourlay Affair,' 489–91.
76 *Colonial Advocate*, 6 Dec. 1827.
77 Romney, *Mr Attorney*, 126–7.
78 Ibid., 109–15.
79 *Colonial Advocate*, 6 Sept. and 7 Sept. 1827. The defendants claimed that they had acted to protect the honour of a woman taken into Rolph's household and allegedly compromised by him. Boulton argued that the plaintiff could appeal the denial of a contempt hearing to the Court of King's Bench.
80 *Canadian Freeman*, 22 May 1828.

81 Baldwin Papers, L11, B104, Correspondence, 127–74, 28 May 1828, Bidwell to W.W. Baldwin.
82 CO 42, vol. 389, 61–5, at 62, Colborne to Sir George Murray, secretary of state for the colonies, 19 Aug. 1829.
83 Although the Tories in the Assembly were in the ascendant, their effectiveness was hampered by leadership squabbles between Boulton and Solicitor General Christopher Hagerman. See Craig, *Upper Canada*, 196–7.
84 F. Murray Greenwood and Barry Wright, 'Parliamentary Privilege and the Repression of Dissent in the Canadas,' in Greenwood and Wright, *Canadian State Trials*, 1:424–9.
85 Phillip A. Buckner, *The Transition to Responsible Government: British Policy in British North America, 1815–1850* (Westport, CT: Greenwood, 1985), 163–4.
86 *Upper Canadian Herald*, 8 May 1833.
87 Hereward and Senior, 'Henry John Boulton,' *DCBOL*.
88 Gunn, *Political History of Newfoundland*, 19. Parliamentary Undersecretary Howick was infuriated by this move, labelling it as the resurgence of Toryism 'in directing the policy of this country towards her North American colonies.' See Buckner, *Transition to Responsible Government*, 180.
89 For the history of Newfoundland's governing and legal institutions, see Bannister, *Rule of the Admirals*; Christopher English, 'The Development of the Newfoundland Legal System to 1815,' *Acadiensis* 20 (1990): 89–119; Christopher English, 'Newfoundland's Early Laws and Legal Institutions: From Fishing Admirals to the Supreme Court of Judicature in 1791–92,' in Guth and Pue, *Canada's Legal Inheritances*, 55–78; Patrick O'Flaherty, *Old Newfoundland: A History to 1843* (St John's: Long Beach, 1999).
90 (1699) 10 & 11 William III, c. 25; Bannister, *Rule of the Admirals*, 26–32; English, 'Newfoundland's Early Laws,' 56–63.
91 English, 'Newfoundland's Legal System,' 100–3.
92 Ibid., 103. King Williams's Act had contemplated capital offences being tried in England, but this did not happen.
93 Bannister, *Rule of the Admirals*, 280–8.
94 English, 'Newfoundland's Early Laws,' 67–8.
95 Newfoundland Judicature Act (1792) 32 Geo. III, c. 46. On Reeves's career, see Peter Neary, 'John Reeves,' *DCBOL*, http://www.biographi.ca/009004-119.01-e.php?&id_nbr=3094&&PHPSESSID=utrqgcq7eauue39k20a9708ng5.
96 Ibid., s. 1.
97 J.M. Bumsted and K. Matthews, 'Thomas Tremlett,' *DCBOL*, http://www.biographi.ca/009004-119.01-e.php?&id_nbr=3176&interval=25&&PHPSESSID=ngmtu2p9dn8lgmjbl52f3mdqq2.

98 See Sean T. Cadigan, *Hope and Deception in Conception Bay: Merchant–Settler Relations in Newfoundland* (Toronto: University of Toronto Press, 1995), 88–90.

99 J.M. Bumsted, 'Caesar Colclough,' *DCBOL*, http://www.biographi.ca/009004-119.01-e.php?&id_nbr=2812&interval=25&&PHPSESSID=3vn9q2hfo6o1rgpuo1bcmrr834.

100 Bennett, *Sir Francis Forbes*, 19–43; Patrick O'Flaherty, 'Francis Forbes,' *DCBOL*, http://www.biographi.ca/009004-119.01-e.php?&id_nbr=3386&interval=25&&PHPSESSID=g5vq5vc6lt32d83mmro3usclb6.

101 Bruce Kercher and Jodie Young, 'Formal and Informal Law in Two New Lands: Land Law in Newfoundland and New South Wales under Francis Forbes,' in English, *Essays in the History of Canadian Law*, 9:147–91.

102 Cadigan, *Hope and Deception*, 93–5. The author refers to Forbes's decision in *Crawford v. Cunningham, Bell & Co.* as embodying the views of the jurist on this matter. He also notes that the resistance of naval judges in the surrogate courts undermined the chief justice's position.

103 Leslie Harris and P.G. Cornell, 'Richard Alexander Tucker,' *DCBOL*, http://www.biographi.ca/009004-119.01-e.php?&id_nbr=4750&interval=25&&PHPSESSID=1lereboidvaj1ocu6aviu207ao. Forbes in due course became the first chief justice of New South Wales. See chapter 6, 149–56.

104 An Act for the Better Administration of Justice in Newfoundland and for Other Purposes (1824) 5 Geo. IV, c. 67.

105 Joseph Smallwood and Robert Pitts, eds., *Encyclopedia of Newfoundland and Labrador*, vol. 3 (St John's: Newfoundland Book Publishers, 1967), s.v. 'John William Molloy.'

106 Bannister, *Rule of the Admirals*, 256–79.

107 John Fitzgerald, 'Conflict and Culture in Irish Newfoundland Catholicism' (PhD diss., University of Ottawa, 1997), ii–iii; Raymond J. Lahey, 'Michael Anthony Fleming,' *DCBOL*, http://www.biographi.ca/009004-119.01-e.php?&id_nbr=3384&interval=25&&PHPSESSID=3d889s6ubo6p63pedj4b4ms7m3; O'Flaherty, *Old Newfoundland*, 144–5. Full Catholic emancipation on the island came with the grant of representative government in Newfoundland in August 1832.

108 The Colonial Office was actually in favour of one legislative body combining appointed and elected members, but concluded that London should not impose this. The Council and Assembly should be encouraged to do this through a joint initiative. For the communication announcing the British government's intention to grant representative government, see CO 195, vol. 18, 37–9, Howick to Cochrane, 14 Jan. 1832. For the legislation, see The Newfoundland Act (1832) 2 & 3 Will. IV, c. 78.

109 Frederic F. Thompson, 'Thomas John Cochrane,' *DCBOL*, http://www.biographi.ca/009004-119.01-e.php?&id_nbr=4903&&PHPSESSID=gurics78u5mcnso6kpc3r34043.
110 Harris and Cornell, 'Richard Alexander Tucker,' *DCBOL*; O'Flaherty, *Old Newfoundland*, 153–4; and see CO 194, vol. 85, 109, reproduction of Tucker's speech in the Assembly on the Council's rejection of the bill, Cochrane to Goderich, 11 Mar. 1833.
111 CO 195, vol. 86, 259–61, Tucker to Cochrane, 5 Mar. 1833. For the governor's rejection, CO 195, vol. 86, 261–2, James Crowdy, secretary to Governor Cochrane, to Tucker, 6 Mar. 1833.
112 Ibid., 264–5, Tucker to Cochrane, 8 and 11 Mar. 1833. In 1833 Tucker's resignation was confirmed. See Gunn, *Political History*, 17.
113 Cadigan, *Hope and Deception*, 143–4. See Extract from Report of Chief Justice Tucker, and Des Barres and Brenton, Aug. 1831, *Re Boulton* (1838), 28 P.C.I.C.A., *Petitioners' Case*, Appendix, 11 et seq.
114 Gunn, *Political History*, 18–19. Stanley advised Boulton of his appointment, CO 195, vol. 86, 111–12, 20 June 1833.
115 CO 194, vol. 85, 64–8, Cochrane to Goderich, 13 Feb. 1833.
116 On Fleming's conscious commitment to making a political difference, as well as a spiritual one, see O'Flaherty, *Old Newfoundland*, 156–8.
117 Fitzgerald, *Conflict and Culture*, 146.
118 On the very different religious conditions in Upper Canada, as they related to the Roman Catholic church, see Craig, *Upper Canada*, 168–9.
119 Vatican Archives/Library, Archives of Propagation of the Faith, *Scritture riferite nei Congressi*, 1831–6, vol. 3, fols 338r–343, Eliza Boulton to cardinal prefect, 10 Sept. 1834.
120 Cadigan, *Hope and Deception*, 146.
121 Gunn, *Political History*, 20–1; O'Flaherty, *Old Newfoundland*, 154–5.
122 See address to grand jurors, early Jan. 1834 in *Re Boulton*, Appendix, document #7, 3, remarking on the number of serious crimes committed in the colony recently, and changes to the jury system.
123 CO 363/1, 112, Cochrane to Stanley, 23 May 1834, enclosing the Rules of the Supreme Court; *Journal of the House of Assembly* (*JHA*) 1837, *Report of the Committee on the Administration of Justice*, 246, 10 Oct. 1837.
124 Gunn, *Political History*, 22; An Act to Provide for the Banishment of Person Convicted of Certain Offence and Also to Provide Certain Modes of Punishment in Divers Criminal Cases (1834) 4 Will. IV, c. 5 (New'fld).
125 Ibid., referencing CO 43, vol. 78, Permanent Undersecretary R.W. Hay to O'Connell, 13 Mar. 1834.
126 On the *Downing and Malone* case, see The Rooms, Newfoundland and

Labrador Archives, GN 2/2, Governor's Correspondence, 1834, box 12, 55, Boulton to Cochrane, 14 Jan. 1834; on the *Hackett* case, see ibid., 296 et seq., Attorney General Simms to colonial secretary, 29 Mar. 1834.

127 Elizabeth A. Wells, 'John Valentine Nugent,' *DCBOL*, http://www.biographi.ca/009004-119.01-e.php?&id_nbr=5191&interval=25&&PHPSESSID=eh1qqnckbciupq6tebons91ie5. Wells indicates that Nugent had studied law for four years (one assumes that he was not a member of an Inn, or that he was qualified as a barrister).

128 Gunn, *Political History*, 22–3. See also An Act to Declare the Qualifications and Character of Persons Admitted to Practice as Barristers and Attorneys in the Supreme Court of Newfoundland (1833) 3 Will. IV, c. 6 (New'fld).

129 Fitzgerald, *Conflict and Culture*, 172, reveals that the British government was making representations to the Vatican about the difficulties with Bishop Fleming and his priests. Although there were initial indications that the Propaganda would chide Fleming, nothing happened immediately.

130 John P. Greene, *Between Damnation and Starvation: Priests and Merchants in Newfoundland Politics, 1745–1855* (Montreal and Kingston: McGill-Queen's University Press, 1999), 94, 96.

131 Fitzgerald, *Conflict and Culture*, 175.

132 O'Flaherty, *Old Newfoundland*, 160–1. The author notes that to add insult to injury Snow's body was dissected. See also F. Murray Greenwood and Beverley Boissery, *Uncertain Justice: Canadian Women and Capital Punishment 1754–1953* (Toronto: Durndurn Press for Osgoode Society for Canadian Legal History, 2000), 104–7.

133 Fitzgerald, *Conflict and Culture*, 193, citing CO 194, vol. 93, fols 200r–210v, Fleming to O'Connell, 5 June 1835, and an enclosed address to His Majesty on behalf of Snow's children.

134 Gunn, *Political History*, 25.

135 Ibid.

136 See *Colbert v. Howley* and Boulton's explanation of his decision in Cadigan, *Hope and Deception*, 147–9; and CO 194, vol. 99, 146–65, Boulton to Prescott, 27 Sept. 1837.

137 Supra, 105, and 106.

138 Cadigan, *Hope and Deception*, 149–51.

139 See 'Anonymous Letter to Chief Justice Boulton,' *Public Ledger*, 19 Sept. 1834, in CO 195, vol. 68, 267.

140 Gunn, *Political History*, 25, citing CO 194, vol. 93, Boulton to Hay, 7 Jan. 1835, enclosing Cochrane to Boulton, Nov. 10, 1834.

141 Ibid., 24–5. Prescott sought to follow a rule of entire impartiality and in that spirit ordered an action against a Catholic priest, the Reverend Edward Troy, for libel launched under the authority of his predecessor, discontinued. He also claimed to be on good terms with Bishop Fleming.

142 GN 2/2, box 13, 107–8, Simms's comments on a request by House of Assembly to the colonial secretary for documents and papers relating to Boulton, 20 Jan. 1835.

143 GN 2/2, box 14, 57–9, report by John Stark, 19 Apr. 1835. The attack only strengthened Winton's resolve to support the merchant interest.

144 See GN 2/2, box, 13, 22–3, Boulton to the colonial secretary, 29 Jan. 1835, recommending mercy for John Flood, convicted of the capital offence of robbery and the substitution of seven years' transportation. Also consider his remonstrance at the removal of a lunatic from the hospital to the jail by executive order, arguing that the Court alone had the authority to do this and that the man should be in safe custody at the hospital rather than consigned to the common jail. Ibid., 141–5, Boulton to the colonial secretary, 31 Jan. 1835.

145 'Newfoundland, In the Central Circuit Court' Regarding an Affidavit for David Rogers in connection with Robert J. Parsons, Printer for Contempt of Court in *Re Boulton, Petitioner's Case*, Supplementary Appendix to Assembly's Petition, xii et seq.

146 Ibid. See O'Flaherty, *Old Newfoundland*, 162–4.

147 CO 194, vol. 90, 278–81, Lord Glenelg, secretary of state for the colonies, 14 Aug. 1835, responding to CO 194, vol. 91, 2, Prescott to Glenelg, 1 July 1835, forwarding the petition.

148 Gunn, *Political History*, 26, citing CO 194, vol. 93, Boulton to Sir George Grey, parliamentary undersecretary, Colonial Office, 20 Aug. 1835. Interestingly, Viscount Ripon, formerly Lord Goderich, who had removed Boulton from his position as attorney general of Upper Canada, demonstrated sympathy with the chief justice's situation in Newfoundland and implied that a transfer would be appropriate. An anonymous placard signed 'Red Indian' had been attached to the courthouse in St John's threatening the chief justice with the fate of Winton unless Parsons was immediately released. See CO 363, vol. 1, 242–3, Prescott to Earl of Aberdeen, secretary of state for the colonies, 30 May 1835.

149 Ibid., 122, Prescott to T. Spring Rice, secretary of state for the colonies, 29 May 1835.

150 CO 194, vol. 90, 62–6, Lord Aberdeen, secretary of state for the colonies, to Prescott, 15 Apr. 1835.

151 Gunn, *Political History*, 25.
152 CO 194, vol. 93, 200–10, Fleming to O'Connell, 5 June 1835.
153 Fitzgerald, *Conflict and Culture*, 194–5.
154 CO 363, vol. 1, 124, Prescott to Glenelg, 30 June 1835.
155 Gunn, *Political History*, 28.
156 Ibid. See also Fitzgerald, *Conflict and Culture*, 204, in which the author refers to a letter from Cardinal Capaccini apologizing to Fleming for have reproved him, although he did include 'a brief warning against using the chapel as a "place of political assembly."'
157 O' Flaherty, *Old Newfoundland*, 167–8. The report on this episode is to be found in CO 194, vol. 94, 3–9, Prescott to Glenelg, 4 Jan. 1836.
158 Ibid. See Simms to Crowdy, 12 Nov. 1836, CO 194, vol. 95, 184–90, taking on himself the responsibility for moving the trial.
159 The governor was to complain to London that 'it is with infinite regret that I see the flames of discord again breaking out in various directions, and defeating all my hopes.' CO 194, vol. 94, 45–6, 11 Jan. 1836.
160 On death sentences, see letter to Prescott, GN 2/2, 1836, box 15, 44–6, advocating clemency and banishment for Maurice Deady and Lawrence Rielley, and the Report of Chief Justice Boulton to the Governor on Prison Discipline, *Re Boulton, Respondent's Case*, Appendix, 21–2. An extract from the secretary of state's letter may be found in the same source.
161 See CO 194, vol. 94, 3–9, Prescott to Glenelg, 4 Jan. 1836 seeking naval and military assistance; and CO 195, vol. 18, 438–9, Glenelg to Prescott, 5 Feb. 1836, responding positively.
162 CO 194, vol. 94, 47–9, James Stephen Jr to Prescott, 7 Feb. 1836.
163 CO 194, vol. 90, Prescott to Glenelg, 29 May 1836, referenced in Gunn, *Political History*, 25, n99.
164 GN 2/2, 1836, box 16, 274–7, Nugent to governor, 12 July 1836, attaching a petition with 8,864 signatures, forwarded to London; CO 194, vol. 95, 50–60, Prescott to Colonial Office, 16 July 1836. Boulton responded to Prescott, describing 'the various allegations it contains [as] so devoid of truth and are at the same time so impertinently expressed, that I cannot condescend to regard them as entitled to the smallest notice.' GN 2/2, 1836, box 16, 293–5, 19 July 1836. O'Flaherty, *Old Newfoundland*, 170, notes that during another Boulton visit to London in the summer of 1836 looking for a new job, the Colonial Office snubbed him and ordered him back to St Johns.
165 CO 194, vol. 95, 46–9, Glenelg to Prescott, 21 Aug. 1836.
166 CO 194, vol. 94, 136, Prescott to Glenelg, 21 May 1836, in response to a

proclamation by the governor calling on the accused to surrender. CO 363, 1836, 136, 7 May 1836.

167 GN 9/1, Minutes of Executive Council, 291–2, 12 Sept. 1836.

168 Gunn, *Political History*, 30–1.

169 See CO 363, vol. 2, 141 and enclosures, Prescott to Glenelg, 9 Dec. 1836, for a detailed report on the election violence and intimidation.

170 GN 2/2, 1836, box 17, 335–6, Boulton to Prescott, 10 Nov. 1836; GN 9/1, 294, 10 Nov. 1836.

171 GN 9/1, Minutes of Evidence, 295–8, 10 Nov. 1936

172 On the Willis-Boulton encounter, see chapter 4, 80–2.

173 CO 194, vol. 95, 159–63, Prescott to Glenelg, 11 Nov. 1836.

174 CO 194, vol. 95, 175–6, Glenelg to Prescott, 15 Dec. 1836. The letter suggested that it would have been preferable had 'the Chief Justice acquiesced publicly in an informality to which so substantial importance belongs and had communicated to you in private and confidential manner the error which had occurred.'

175 See petition organized by John Nugent in February 1837 and transmitted to the Colonial Office by Prescott, CO 194, vol. 96, 146, 7 Feb. 1837.

176 See Judges' Chambers. H.J. Boulton, E.B. Brenton, and George Lilly to governor, *Re Boulton, Respondent's Case*, Appendix 19–20, giving their opinion on the pre-election related trials of 1836. See CO 194, vol. 96, 80–96, report by Boulton to Prescott, 25 Jan. 1837, responding to a request from the governor for observations on the Supreme Court and the state of society in the colony and party feeling.

177 CO 194, vol. 96, 133–4, Stephen's note on Prescott's dispatch, 22 Mar., dated 24 Apr. 1837. The permanent undersecretary advocated sending copies of the rules of procedure devised by the judges in New South Wales as a possible model for Newfoundland. See also CO 195, vol. 19, 54–6, Glenelg to Prescott, 15 May 1837. Cadigan, *Hope and Deception*, 145–7, sees the Liberal reformers as the instigators of this view of the judge.

178 There is no hard evidence to suggest that there was in fact any conspiracy. The Colonial Office, having reviewed the file, concluded that there had been a bona fide mistake. CO 195, vol. 19, 39–40, Glenelg to Prescott, 7 Mar. 1837. By this time, however, the main combatants invariably thought the worst of each other. Prescott was not impressed with the new House, as it was composed of 'violent leaders under the influence of the Catholic priesthood and individuals of the humblest class.'

179 *Re Boulton*, Petitioners Case, Appendix, xii.

180 CO 195, vol. 19, 67–70, Glenelg to Prescott, 31 May 1837.

181 O'Flaherty, *Old Newfoundland*, referencing *Public Ledger*, 19 May 1837.

182 See CO 194, vol. 98, 389–92, Boulton to Stephen, 11 Jan. 1837, seeking an appointment to King's Bench. He followed this up with another dated 2 Feb. 1837, CO 194, vol. 98, 393–4, in which he suggested himself as a worthy candidate for a court of Equity.
183 CO 194, vol. 98, 392, Stephen's note on Boulton's letter of 11 Jan., dated 16 Feb. 1837. In a later note attached to Boulton's letter of 2 Feb., Stephen refers to an appointment in Upper Canada as involving 'many embarrassing considerations,' advising that Lord Glenelg should merely respond that there are no vacancies at present.
184 CO 194, vol. 96, 131–3, Prescott to Glenelg, with Simms's letter, 22 Mar. 1837. Boulton and his brethren has expressed their displeasure at the fees charged by Simms and the solicitor general in the prosecutions arising out of the election of 1836. Prescott was not pleased at this spat, as he reported to Glenelg. CO 194, vol. 96, 76–7, 2 Mar. 1837.
185 CO 194, vol. 96, 76–7, Prescott to Glenelg, 2 Mar. 1837.
186 Ibid., 77, note by Stephen on dispatch of Prescott, 2 Mar., dated 19 Apr. 1837.
187 Ibid., 133–4, Stephen's note on Prescott's dispatch, 22 Mar., dated 24 Apr.1837.
188 See Gunn, *Political History*, 39–42.
189 CO 194, vol. 98, 172, House of Assembly's address to Prescott, 6 Nov. 1837, including printed version of Morris's speech, 25 Aug. 1837.
190 Cadigan, *Hope and Deception*, 148, citing CO 194, vol. 99, fols 146–52, Boulton to Prescott, 27 Sept. 1837.
191 John V. Nugent, chairman, *Report of Committee of Whole House on the Present State of the Administration of Justice in Newfoundland, Journal of the House of Assembly* (*JHA*), 12 Oct. 1837, 244–52.
192 CO 194, vol. 103, 6B, Instructions to Delegates Passed in the House of Assembly, 14 Oct. to 11 Nov. 1837; and CO 194, vol. 98, 213–14, Memorial of House of Assembly to Queen Victoria, 18 Oct. 1837.
193 Gunn, *Political History*, 42.
194 *Re Boulton, Petitioners' Case*, 11.
195 George Grey, parliamentary undersecretary at the Colonial Office, advised Boulton that the matter was proceeding to the Privy Council, ibid., 1.
196 Howell, *Judicial Committee of the Privy Council*, 32–5.
197 Ibid., 34, n46. The committee hearing the petition comprised Lord Chief Justice Denman, Lord Holland (chancellor of the Duchy of Lancaster), and C.E. Poulett Thompson (president of the Board of Trade).
198 Glenelg had already decided, at the suggestion of Prescott, that Boulton should be removed from his seat on the Council, because of the

confounding of politics and law that it had produced. CO 194, vol. 100, 39–43, Prescott to Glenelg, 5 Jan. 1838; CO 195, vol. 19, 142–3, Glenelg to Prescott, 5 Mar. 1838. By May 1838, Glenelg was intimating 'that it was quite possible that Boulton would not return to Newfoundland.' See Fitzgerald, *Conflict and Culture*, 270, citing CO 195, vol. 19, 149, 153–6, Glenelg to Prescott, 18 May 1838. A practice of including the secretary of state in the deliberations of the Judicial Committee on cases of judicial discipline may date from this time.

199 *Re Boulton, Petitioner's Case*, 1–12.

200 *Re Boulton, Respondent's Case*, 1–23.

201 Ibid., Advice of the Privy Council to Her Majesty, 5 July 1838.

202 Ibid.

203 Ibid.

204 Bourne was granted preferment on the recommendation of Lord Chief Justice Denman, who had sat on the committee that advised Boulton's removal. While leaning towards the Liberal reformers politically and Roman Catholic rights (his wife was also Catholic), he did not impress either constituency on the island when he upheld Boulton's decision in *Colbert v. Howley*. Drawn into contention with one of his colleagues and some members of the legal profession, the secretary of state dismissed him from office in 1844 for the unsubstantiated charges he levelled at Governor John Harvey. See Phillip Buckner, 'John Gervas Hutchinson Bourne,' *DBOL*, http://www.biographi.ca/009004-119.01-e.php?&id_nbr=3261&interval=25&&PHPSESSID=tr93iosb53seob5q7klqnvj274.

205 Hereward and Senior, 'Henry John Boulton,' *DCBOL*.

206 See supra, 107n115, for Cochrane's advice, and chapter 4, 83–4, on changes to the relationship between judges and the executive arm in Upper Canada.

207 Gunn, *Political History*, 11–12, for reference to the Colonial Office's ruminations on a blended Council of representative government and noting memorandum from Stephen. CO 194, vol. 82, no. 21, 19 Dec. 1831.

208 Lord Glenelg, in reflecting on the problems caused by the conjunction of religious and political differences on the island, could do no better in suggesting a cure than 'the diffusion of sound knowledge and in the prevalence of a better understanding of the real principles and obligations of Christianity.' Ibid., 35, referencing CO 195, vol. 19, Glenelg to Prescott, 15 Jan. 1837.

209 Cadigan, *Hope and Deception*, 160–1.

210 Gunn, *Political History*, 43–4.

211 Boyd Hilton, *A Mad, Bad and Dangerous People? England, 1783–1846* (Oxford: Oxford University Press, 2006), 566–7.

6: Perils of the Colonial Judiciary: Guarding Common Law

1 Kercher, Unruly Child, 31–2; C.H. Currey, 'Barron Field, Judge of the Supreme Court of New South Wales 1817–1824' (unpublished manuscript on Law Library, University of Sydney, n.d.), 62–6.
2 See chapter 2.
3 See chapter 2, 14–17.
4 See chapter 9, 218–19, and chapter 5, 104.
5 For Western Australia, see Russell, *History of Law in Western Australia*, 8–232; Rupert's Land, see Dale Gibson, 'Company Justice: Origins of Legal Institutions in Pre-Confederation Manitoba,' in Guth and Pue, *Canada's Legal Inheritances*, 247–71; Vancouver Island, see Tina Loo, *Making Law, Order, and Authority in British Columbia, 1821–1871* (Toronto: University of Toronto Press, 1994), 21–53; and British Columbia, Loo, *Making Law, Order and Authority*, 54–72.
6 Alex C. Castles and Michael Harris, *Lawmakers and Wayward Whigs: Government and Law in South Australia 1836–1986* (Adelaide: Wakefield, 1987), 94–134; Williams, 'Justice Boothby,' 31–51.
7 J.B. Hirst, *Convict Society and Its Enemies: A History of New South Wales* (Sydney: George Allen & Unwin, 1983), 78, notes the parallels between New South Wales and the eighteenth-century English jail. Its military character was evident in the forms of justice, as well as in the corporal nature of punishment.
8 Atkinson, *The Europeans in Australia*, 1:37–58. Atkinson notes the influence on the colonizing imagination of, on the one hand, earlier unconventional British settlements such as Georgia, Nova Scotia, and Honduras, and on the other, the fictitious account of the moulding of a group of former pirates into a civil society in Daniel Defoe's *Robinson Crusoe*.
9 An Act to Enable His Majesty to Establish a Court of Criminal Judicature on the Eastern Coast of New South Wales, and the Parts Adjacent (1787) 27 Geo. III, c. 2, and the First Charter of Justice for New South Wales, Letter Patent, 2 April 1787, in J.M. Bennett and Alex C. Castles, *A Source Book of Australian Legal History: Source Materials from the Eighteenth to the Twentieth Centuries* (Sydney: Law Book Company, 1979), 18–22. The letters patent describe the court as the Court of Criminal Jurisdiction.
10 Kercher, *Unruly Child*, 20–9.
11 Ibid., 29–30.
12 The First Charter of Justice for New South Wales, Letters Patent, 2 April 1787, in Bennett and Castles, *Source Book of Australian Legal History*, 19–22.
13 Neal, *Rule of Law*, 1–7.

14 Kercher, *Unruly Child*, 46 et seq.
15 Ibid., 46–7.
16 Hirst, *Convict Society and Its Enemies*, 9–27.
17 On the rebellion, the classic work is H.V. Evatt, *Rum Rebellion: A Study of the Overthrow of Governor Bligh by John Macarthur and the New South Wales Corps* (Sydney: Angus & Robertson, 1943).
18 N.D. McLachlan, 'Lachlan Macquarie,' *Australian Dictionary of Biography Online* (*ADBOL*), http://adbonline.anu.edu.au/biogs/A020162b.htm. For the appointment, see *Historical Records of Australia* (*HRA*), ser. 1, vol. 7, 80–3, Lord Castlereagh, secretary of state for the colonies, to Lachlan Macquarie, 14 May 1809.
19 For Ellis Bent's short career, see C.H. Currey, 'Ellis Bent,' *ADBOL*, http://adbonline.anu.edu.au/biogs/A010086b.htm. Bent's commission is mentioned in the letter in n18.
20 On Atkin's unhappy career, see J.M. Bennett, 'Richard Atkins,' *ADBOL*, http://www.adb.online.anu.edu.au/biogs/A010036b.htm. Bruce Kercher is kinder to Atkins, noting, for instance, his humane attitude towards debtors in debts actions. See Kercher, *Debt, Seduction and Other Disasters: The Birth of Civil Law in Convict New South Wales* (Sydney: Federation, 1996), 29–35.
21 Currey, *Brothers Bent*, 42.
22 See David Pope, 'The Wealth and Social Aspirations of Liverpool's Slave Merchants of the Second Half of the Eighteenth Century,' in *Liverpool and Transatlantic Slavery*, ed. David Richardson, Suzanne Schwarz, and Anthony Tibbles (Liverpool: Liverpool University Press, 2007), 166–226, at 179, 219.
23 Ibid.
24 *HRA*, ser. 1, vol. 7, 80–3, at 81, Secretary of State Lord Castlereagh to Governor Macquarie, 14 May 1809.
25 See ibid., 245 et seq., at 266, Macquarie to Castlereagh, 30 Apr. 1810, for a laudatory assessment by the governor of the services provided by Bent.
26 *HRA*, ser. 1, vol. 7, 525–33, at 530, 9 Nov. 1812.
27 Currey, *Brothers Bent*, 51–2.
28 Judge-Advocate E. Bent on Defects of the First Charter to Under-Secretary Cooke, 7 May 1810, in Bennett and Castles, *Source Book of Australian Legal History*, 27–9; *HRA*, ser. 4, vol. 1, 57–9, 19 Oct. 1811, E. Bent to Liverpool.
29 Bennett and Castles, *Source Book of Australian Legal History*, 27–9.
30 *HRA*, ser. 4, vol. 1, 57–9, 19 Oct. 1811, Bent to Liverpool. Former secretary of state Castlereagh had asked Bent to advise on whether he thought trial by jury in criminal cases was feasible in the colony. Macquarie supported

Bent's recommendations. See *HRA*, series 1, vol. 7, 378 et seq., at 395, 18 Oct. 1811.

31 Currey, *Brothers Bent*, 60.

32 See ibid., 62–3, reference to *Report of the Committee on Transportation* (the Eden Committee) 1812, 7. The changes were incorporated in 'The Second Charter of Justice for New South Wales' (1814). Bennett and Castles, *Source Book of Australian Legal History*, 31–8.

33 *HRA*, ser. 4, vol. 1, 100–8, E. Bent to Bathurst, 14 Oct. 1814. Bathurst's curt response is found at ibid., 170–3, Bathurst to E. Bent, 11 Dec. 1815.

34 *HRA*, ser. 1, vol. 7, 777, Macquarie to Bathurst, 23 June 1813.

35 Currey, *Brothers Bent*, 69.

36 *HRA*, ser. 1, vol. 8, 389–99, at 391–2, Macquarie to Bathurst, 24 Feb. 1815.

37 Currey, *Brothers Bent*, 74–5.

38 *HRA*, ser. 1, vol. 8, 400–9, at 408–9, 31 Dec. 1814, and the governor's testy reply, 409–10, 9 Jan. 1815.

39 Currey, *Brothers Bent*, 77–78

40 *HRA*, ser. 1, vol. 8, 422–4, E. Bent to Macquarie, 11 Jan. 1815.

41 *HRA*, ser. 1, vol. 9, 110–11, Bathurst to E. Bent, 12 Apr. 1816; responding to the latter, *HRA*, ser. 4, vol. 1, 122–42, 1 July 1815.

42 Ibid., 107–10, at 108, Bathurst to Macquarie, 18 Apr. 1816.

43 *HRA*, ser. 4, vol. 1, 94, commission for Judge Jeffrey Hart Bent, 7 Feb. 1814.

44 Ibid., 95–6, J.H. Bent to Bathurst, 21 Feb. 1814.

45 Ibid., 96–7.

46 *HRA*, ser. 4, vol. 1, 95, Bathurst to Macquarie, 13 Feb. 1814. Their individual salaries were £300 per annum.

47 Currey, *Brothers Bent*, 100.

48 *HRA*, ser. 1, vol. 7, 300–1, Macquarie to Bathurst, 7 Oct. 1814.

49 *HRA*, ser. 4, vol. 1, 108–10, J.H. Bent to Goulburn, 15 Oct. 1814.

50 Ibid., 94–5, J.H. Bent to Goulburn, 7 Feb. 1814.

51 Ibid., 108–10, J.H. Bent to Goulburn, 15 Oct. 1814.

52 Currey, *Brothers Bent*, 72.

53 *HRA*, ser. 4, vol. 1, 114–17, J.H. Bent to Macquarie, 5 Dec. 1814,.

54 *HRA*, ser. 4, vol. 1, 117, Macquarie to Bathurst, 6 Dec. 1814. Earlier Macquarie had reported to Bathurst on Bent's less than honourable motives, as he saw it, on the courtroom issue. *HRA*, ser. 1, vol. 7, 380–1, 30 Nov. 1814.

55 *HRA*, ser. 4, vol. 1, 112–13, J.H. Bent to Goulburn, 16 Dec. 1814.

56 See *HRA*, ser. 1, vol. 8, 481–9, Macquarie to Bathurst, 22 June 1815,.

57 McLachlan, 'Lachlan Macquarie,' *ADBOL*.

58 Bruce Kercher, 'A Convict Conservative: George Crossley and the English Legal Tradition,' in *Misplaced Traditions: British Lawyers, Colonial Peoples*, ed. Rob McQueen and W. Wesley Pue (Sydney: Federation, 1999), 17–30.
59 Supra, 127–8.
60 *HRA*, ser. 4, vol. 1, 114–17, Bent to Macquarie, 5 Dec. 1814.
61 See *HRA*, ser. 1, vol. 7, 466, Macquarie to Bathurst, 24 Mar. 1815, describing the judge's reasons for delaying the opening of the court as 'frivolous and ridiculous,' and observing that, as Garling might never turn up, the court could be closed indefinitely.
62 *HRA*, ser. 1, vol. 8, 495–500, J.H. Bent to Macquarie, 20 Apr. 1815.
63 An Act to Prevent Frivolous and Vexatious Arrests (1726) 12 Geo. I, c. 29, s. 4.
64 *Ex Parte Boonsell* (1778, K.B., 27 June – unreported).
65 *HRA*, ser. 1, vol. 8, 497, J.H. Bent to Macquarie, 20 Apr. 1815.
66 Ibid., 496, in response to letter from the governor, *HRA*, ser. 1, vol. 8, 489–91, 18 Apr. 1815. Two of the former convict attorneys, George Crossley and Edward Eagar, had petitioned Macquarie to be allowed to plead in court.
67 Currey, *Brothers Bent*, 106–7.
68 *HRA*, ser. 1, vol. 8, 510–16, General Minutes of the Proceedings of the Supreme Court, 1–11 May 1815.
69 *HRA*, ser. 4, vol. 1, 159–60, Address of Judge Bent in Supreme Court, 11 May 1815
70 *HRA*, ser. 1, vol. 8, 516–17, 517–20, J.H. Bent to Riley and Broughton, 15 May 1815.
71 Under its charter of 1814, if the Court split with the two magistrates in the majority in a case, there was a right of appeal by the chief judge to the governor, whose decision on the matter of contention was final. Bent avoided a decision of the magistrates against him by refusing to appear in person at further court sessions. See *HRA*, ser. 1, vol. 8, 528–9, Minutes of Proceeding of the Supreme Court, 25 May 1815; ibid., 531–2, J.H. Bent to Broughton and Riley, 26 May 1815; *HRA*, ser. 4, vol. 1, 154–8, statement by Mr Justice Bent, 1 July 1815.
72 *HRA*, ser. 1, vol. 8, 534–6, Macquarie to J.H. Bent, 29 May 1815. The governor also pointed out that Bent had selected court officers without consulting him, in contravention of the Patent for the Court. For Bent's strong separation of powers response, see *HRA*, ser. 1, vol. 8, 536–40, 31 May 1815.
73 *HRA*, ser. 1, vol. 8, 540–1, Macquarie to J.H. Bent, 2 June 1815.

74 *HRA*, ser. 1, vol. 8, 479 et seq., Macquarie to Bathurst, 22 June 1815.
75 Ibid., 484.
76 Ibid., 487.
77 *HRA*, ser. 1, vol. 8, 620–2, Macquarie to Bathurst, 1 July 1815.
78 *HRA*, ser. 1, vol. 9, 11–12, J.H. Bent to Macquarie, 18 Aug. 1815.
79 *HRA*, ser. 1, vol. 9, 13–4, J.H. Bent to Macquarie, 25 Aug. 1815.
80 Currey, *Brothers Bent*, 120–2. The remonstrations of Justice Bent to the attempts of a toll-keeper to make him pay were peppered with language such as 'you damned scoundrel' and 'rascal.' He threatened, moreover, to 'commit [the man] to jail for his natural life.' See also *HRA*, ser. 1, vol. 9, 19–20, J.H. Bent to Police Magistrate D'Arcy Wentworth, 8 Sept. 1815.
81 For the gubernatorial pronouncement, see *HRA*, ser. 1, vol. 9, 20–2, Government and General Orders, Civil Department, 9 Sept. 1815, and for J.H. Bent's response to Macquarie, ibid., 22–5, 2 Oct. 1815.
82 Ibid., 25–6, J.H. Bent to Macquarie, 24 Oct. 1815, and for the governor's reply, ibid., 26.
83 *HRA*, ser. 4, vol. 1, 162–70, J.H. Bent to Bathurst, 4 Nov. 1815.
84 The death was reported to London by a letter from J.H. Bent to Bathurst, 25 Feb. 1816, ibid., 180 et seq. Jeffery could not resist associating his brother's death with the labours and anxieties of his office, and the unhealthy courtroom in which he was compelled to sit.
85 Ibid., 170–3, Bathurst to E. Bent, 11 Dec. 1815.
86 Ibid., 173–4, 11 Dec. 1815, Goulburn to J.H. Bent., responding to the latter's of 16 Dec. 1814.
87 Ibid., 174, commission of J. Wylde as deputy judge advocate, 1 Jan. 1816. On Wylde's career, see R.K. McKay, 'John Wylde,' *ADBOL*, http://www.adb.online.anu.edu.au/biogs/A020574b.htm?hilite=wylde.
88 *HRA*, ser. 4, vol. 1, 177–8, Robert Bent to Bathurst, 29 Jan. 1816.
89 *HRA*, ser. 4, vol. 1, 178–9, Goulburn to R. Bent, 31 Jan. 1816.
90 *HRA*, ser. 1, vol. 9, 110–11, Bathurst to E. Bent, 12 Apr. 1816.
91 Currey, *Brothers Bent*, 95.
92 *HRA*, ser. 1, vol. 9, 112–13, Bathurst to J.H. Bent, 12 Apr. 1816.
93 *HRA*, ser. 4, vol. 1, 201, Bathurst to Macquarie, 18 Apr. 1816.
94 *HRA*, ser. 4, vol. 9, 3–11, at 11, Macquarie to Bathurst, 20 Feb. 1916.
95 Currey, *Brothers Bent*, 96–7.
96 Ibid., 126–31.
97 *HRA*, ser. 1, vol. 9, 206–7, Bathurst to Macquarie, 6 Feb. 1817. The secretary of state had referred the matter to the English law officers.
98 Currey, *Brothers Bent*, 128–9, 131–2.
99 See *HRA*, ser. 4, vol. 1, 198, J.H. Bent to Bathurst, 22 Mar. 1816.

100 *HRA*, ser. 1, vol. 9, 385, Bathurst to Macquarie, 22 Apr. 1817, and for Macquarie's less than cooperative rejoinder, see ibid., 493–5, 24 Nov. 1817.
101 Ibid., 495–500, 1 Dec. 1817.
102 Currey, *Brothers Bent*, 133–4.
103 *HRA*, ser. 4, vol. 1, 205–8, J.H. Bent to Macquarie, 21 May 1816.
104 Ibid., 208, Macquarie to Bent, 22 May 1816; and ibid,, 204–5, J.H. Bent to Bathurst, 12 June 1816.
105 Ibid., 205, J.H. Bent to Bathurst, 12 June 1816.
106 Currey, *Brothers Bent*, 135–7.
107 Elements of the story appear in *HRA*, ser. 1, vol. 9, 163–7, Proceedings of Meeting of Magistrates, 29 June 1816.
108 *HRA*, ser. 1, vol. 9, 160–3, Macquarie to Bathurst, 31 Aug. 1816.
109 Wylde arrived in the colony on 5 Oct. 1815.
110 Currey, *Brothers Bent*, 147–2.
111 *HRA*, ser. 4, vol. 1, 240–3, J.H. Bent to Bathurst, 5 Apr. 1817, acknowledging the latter's letter of 12 Apr. 1816 recalling him. To add weight to his annoyance, he noted that his successor, Justice Field, was forced to sit with lay justices, including 'a transported Felon, and … a notorious Highwayman … to the astonishment, the ridicule and the Dismay of the whole Colony.'
112 Ibid., 302–7, Bent to Goulburn, 25 June 1818.
113 Currey, *Brothers Bent*, 153–7.
114 *HRA*, ser. 4, vol. 1, 302, Goulburn to J.H. Bent, 18 June 1818. The irrepressible former judge, having got wind of possible changes in the governance of New South Wales, offered himself as the new governor of the colony. Ibid., 313–14, J.H. Bent to Goulburn, 3 Aug. 1818.
115 See infra, 142–3.
116 Supra, 126–9.
117 John Ritchie, *Punishment and Profit: The Reports of Commissioner John Bigge on the Colonies of New South Wales and Van Diemen's Land, 1822–1823; Their Origins, Nature and Significance* (Melbourne: Heinemann, 1970), 1–30.
118 Ibid., 23–4, 27–8.
119 See J.M. Bennett, 'John Thomas Bigge,' *DABL*, http://adbonline.anu.edu.au/biogs/A010093b.htm?hilite=john%3Bbigge.
120 On Bigge's association with Woodford and his career in Trinidad, see Ritchie, *Punishment and Profit*, 41–51.
121 Ibid., 63.
122 Ibid., 101.
123 Ibid., 124–5. Macquarie who had desisted in 1814 from appointing any more emancipists to the magistracy, decided to appoint the emancipist

doctor and his own physician, William Redfern, to the bench in 1819. Bigge remonstrated at what he considered an undesirable policy and an undeserving candidate, but Macquarie refused to budge.

124 Bennett, 'John Thomas Bigge,' *ADBOL*.
125 C.H. Currey, 'Barron Field,' *ADBOL*, http://adbonline.anu.edu.au/biogs/A010355b.htm?hilite=barron%3Bfield.
126 Ibid. See also Atkinson, *The Europeans in Australia*, 2:35.
127 *HRA*, ser. 4, vol. 1, 201, Goulburn to the new judge advocate, 3 May 1816. For Field's acceptance of the position offered, see *HRA*, ser. 4, vol. 1, 202, his letter to Goulburn, 14 May 1816.
128 Currey, 'Barron Field,' *ADBOL*.
129 See *HRA* ser. 1, vol. 9, 381, Macquarie to Goulburn, 8 Apr. 1817.
130 *HRA*, ser. 4, vol. 1, 322–3, Opinion of Mr Justice Field on Validity of Duties Imposed by Governor Macquarie, 23 Feb. 1818.
131 Ibid., 331–3, Field to Bathurst, 17 Feb. 1819.
132 Ibid., Field to Bathurst, 1 Aug. 1821, 389–90; and 4 Feb. 1822, 404. See also ibid., 415–17, 1822, James Stephen Jr, 'Jurisdiction of Lt Governor of New South Wales in Governor's Absence.'
133 See *HRA*, ser. 4, vol. 1, 254–7, Wylde to Goulburn, 14 Dec. 1817.
134 See *HRA*, ser. 1, vol. 9, 695–7, Field to Wylde, 18 Sept. 1817; and ibid., 678–81, Wylde to Macquarie, 26 Nov. 1817, together with Field's rejoinder to Wyld's position, ibid., 702–3.
135 Manning Clark, *A Short History of Australia* (Ringwood, VIC: Penguin Australia, 1986), 59–60. See also John Ritchie, ed., *The Evidence to the Bigge Reports: New South Wales under Governor Macquarie*, vol. 2, *The Written Evidence* (Melbourne: William Heinemann, 1971), 225–6 (Eagar Evidence).
136 Clark, *A Short History*, 60–3.
137 Ibid., 59–60.
138 *HRA*, ser. 1, vol. 10, 625–6, Wylde and Field to Brisbane, 19 Jan. 1822. Their opposition was not well received by Lord Bathurst. See Currey, 'Barron Field,' 103–4.
139 *HRA*, ser. 4, vol. 1, 770–3, 'Judicial Evidence Taken by Mr Commissioner Bigge, No. 5, Mr William Henry Moore,' Nov.–Dec. 1819.
140 Ibid., 760–6, 'Judicial Evidence Taken by Mr Commissioner Bigge, No. 2, Mr Samuel Terry,' Nov.–Dec., 1819. See also Currey, 'Barron Field,' 38–47, for account of the contretemps and its aftermath.
141 Ibid., 767–8.
142 Ritchie, *Punishment and Profit*, 230.
143 The irony of the situation was lost on Amos's brother. See *HRA*, ser. 4, vol. 1, 339–43, letter to Bathurst, 20 July 1820. In striking Amos off the list

of those entitled to practise, Field had cited as a reason the former's association with Crossley.

144 Ritchie, *Punishment and Profit*, 161.

145 *HRA*, ser. 1, vol. 10, 351–64, at 354, Macquarie to Bathurst, 1 Sept. 1820.

146 Ritchie, *Evidence to the Bigge Reports*, 2:200–259 (Eagar Evidence), 201–6. See Currey, 'Barron Field,' 62–71, for the case and its background and fallout.

147 *HRA*, ser. 1, vol. 10, 351–64, Macquarie to Bathurst, 1 Sept. 1820, with Enclosure No. 3, 27 Mar. 1820, 'Affidavit of Mr Justice Field,' 356–7. See also *Bullock v. Dodds* (1819) 2 B. & Ald. 258; 106 E.R. 361 K.B.

148 *HRA*, ser. 1, vol. 10, 549–56, Macquarie to Bathurst, 22 Oct. 1821.

149 Ritchie, *Punishment and Profit*, 228. Legislation to cure the effects of felony attaint on those who had received pardons came relatively quickly – An Act for the Transportation of Offenders from Great Britain (1825) 4 Geo. IV, c. 84, s. 26. However, it was not until much later that the right to sue was restored to those on tickets of leave – An Act to Amend the Law as Affects Transported Convicts with Respect to Pardons and Tickets of Leave (1843) 6 Vict., c. 7, ss 2, 3.

150 Ritchie, *Evidence to the Bigge Reports*, 2:171.

151 Ibid.

152 Ibid.

153 *HRA*, ser. 4, vol. 1, 423–9, Field to Bathurst, 15 Jan. 1823. Also ibid., 483–4, 12 June 1823, Francis Forbes, 'Remarks upon Mr. Justice Field's letter to Earl Bathurst touching certain parts of Commissioner Bigge's Report, 1823.'

154 For the allegation by surgeon James Hall to the Reverend Samuel Marsden, 14 Aug. 1822, see *HRA*, ser. 1, vol. 10, 764–5. Hall reported the same to Brisbane, 16 Aug. 1822, *HRA*, ibid., 765–6. On the episode, see also Curry, 'Barron Field,' 78–82.

155 Ibid., 759–61, Brisbane to Bathurst, 6 Sept. 1822. There was conflicting evidence as to whether Rumsby volunteered the charge against Douglass or was pressured by Hall into making it. Currey, *Sir Francis Forbes*, 52–4.

156 Ibid., 748–50, Brisbane to Bathurst, 6 Sept. 1822, on the governor's actions against the magistrates.

157 Act for the Administration of Justice in New South Wales and Van Diemen's Land (1823) 4 Geo. IV, c. 96, s. 2.

158 John Wylde, recognized as a capable lawyer, had developed a reputation for long-windedness in his advice to the executive. He had crossed swords with Governor Brisbane on a number of matters, including the Douglass case, wage-fixing regulations, his role on the 'Court of Appeal'

(Governor's Council), and reprieves in capital cases (McKay, 'John Wylde,' *ADBOL*). He was in due course to be appointed chief justice of the Cape Colony. While in that post, he fell under suspicion of an incestuous relationship with his single daughter, who had become pregnant under mysterious circumstances. Despite dismay in London at these allegations, nothing was proved, and Wylde ultimately settled back into judicial life, until retiring in 1855. His relations with his wife had deteriorated in New South Wales. She declined to follow him to Capetown and he divorced her in 1836. See McKenzie, *Scandal in the Colonies*, 1–47.

159 Currey, 'Barron Field,' *ADBOL*.

160 See, for example, a bitter Brisbane to Bathurst, 21 Jan. 1824, *HRA*, ser. 1, vol. 11, 199. The former governor also suspected Field of being the author of an injurious attack on him in the *Morning Chronicle*. *HRA*, ser. 4, vol. 1, 519, Brisbane to Bathurst, 9 Feb. 1825.

161 Currey, 'Barron Field,' *ADBOL*.

162 The announcement of Forbes's appointment is contained in a dispatch from Bathurst to Brisbane, *HRA*, ser. 4, vol. 11, 492, 4 Aug. 1823. On Forbes's career, see Bennett, *Sir Francis Forbes*; Currey, *Sir Francis Forbes*.

163 New South Wales and Van Diemen's Land Act (1823) 4 Geo. IV, c. 96, s. 24.

164 Ibid., s. 29. For the background to this provision, see Enid Campbell, 'Colonial Legislation and the Laws of England,' *University of Tasmania Law Review* 2 (1964–7): 149–75, at 155–7. Forbes foresaw the provision as giving rise to tension with the executive.

165 D.B. Swinfen, *Imperial Control of Colonial Legislation 1813–1865: A Study of British Policy towards Colonial Legislative Powers* (Oxford: Clarendon: 1970), 54–8.

166 Bennett, *Sir Francis Forbes*, 63. The author reveals that Forbes was not comfortable about assuming this role, especially in light of his membership on the Legislative Council and power of vetoing proposed legislation. Bennett refers to the chief justice having become the equivalent of a chief minister (the medieval justiciar). Ibid., 67–8.

167 New South Wales Act, ss 1–3, 9–10.

168 Ibid., ss 4, 6. A petit jury could be substituted where both parties agreed.

169 Bennett, *Sir Francis Forbes*, 9–21.

170 Ibid., 21–41.

171 Kercher, *Unruly Child*, 82–3. The third chief justice of New South Wales, Alfred Stephen, described Forbes as 'a liberal, in advance of the age.' See Bennett, *Some Papers of Sir Francis Forbes*, xii.

172 Bennett, *Sir Francis Forbes*, 44–56.

173 Forbes to R. Wilmot-Horton, parliamentary undersecretary, Colonial Office, 6 Mar. 1827, in Bennett, *Forbes Papers*, 123–33, esp. 123–7.

174 Ibid., 117–22, and see letters to Wilmot Horton, 7 Nov. 1824, and 26 Nov. 1825, ibid., 45 and 92–93, respectively. An initiative to make the legislative changes in Westminster allowing for juries in criminal trials was stonewalled by pressure from exclusive interests (including Barron Field) and had to await the arrival of a change in government policy in Britain and the arrival of Governor Richard Bourke in the early 1830s. See A.C.V. Melbourne, *Early Constitutional Development in Australia* (St Lucia: University of Queensland Press, 1963), 192–8.

175 Currey, *Sir Francis Forbes*, 299–300.

176 Bennett, *Forbes Papers*, 80–6, Forbes to Wilmot-Horton, 30 Oct. 1825.

177 *HRA*, ser. 4, vol. 1, 731–43, at 741, Forbes to Wilmot Horton, 20 Sept. 1827.

178 J.D. Heydon, 'Sir Thomas Makdougall Brisbane,' *ADBOL*, http://www.adb.online.anu.edu.au/biogs/A010141b.htm?hilite=Thomas;brisbane.

179 See Hirst, *Convict Society and Its Enemies*, 162–3, 178–9, on the motivations of these reformist press men.

180 On the historical background to the British and colonial states' use of defamation prosecutions against newspapers, and the growth of arguments in favour of public space for debate and dissent, see Brendan Edgeworth, 'Defamation Law and the Emergence of a Critical Press in Colonial New South Wales, 1824–1831,' *Australian Journal of Law and Society* 6 (1990–1): 50–82, at 52–60; Wright, 'Libel and the Colonial Administration of Justice,' 15–24.

181 Bennett, *Forbes Papers*, 47–8, Forbes to Wilmot-Horton, 17 Nov. 1824.

182 Bennett, *Sir Francis Forbes*, 80. To be fair to the governor, he did take steps to improve the operation of the colonial civil service.

183 C.H. Currey, 'Saxe Bannister,' *ADBOL*, http://www.adb.online.anu.edu.au/biogs/A010052b.htm?hilite=saxe;bannister. For a more complete and sympathetic portrayal of Saxe Bannister as a reformer and man of faith, see Atkinson, *The Europeans in Australia*, 2:38–44.

184 Bennett, *Forbes Papers*, 115–16, Forbes to Wilmot-Horton, 15 Dec. 1826.

185 Currey, *Sir Francis Forbes*, 192–9.

186 Bennett, *Sir Francis Forbes*, 80–2.

187 Currey, *Sir Francis Forbes*, 172–3.

188 J.J. Spigelman, 'Foundations of Freedom of the Press in Australia,' *Australian Bar Review* 23 (2002–3): 89–109.

189 Bennett, *Forbes Papers*, 119–20, Forbes to Wilmot-Horton, 6 Feb. 1827.

190 Edgeworth, 'Defamation Law,' 62–6. Darling has refused to lend support to Bannister's desire to prosecute his detractors.

191 Bennett, *Sir Francis Forbes*, 85–6.
192 Forbes was inclined to think that Arthur rather than the Colonial Office was the originator of the licensing approach. See Bennett, *Forbes Papers*, 88–94, at 91, Forbes to Wilmot-Horton, 26 Nov. 1825.
193 J.M. Bennett, *Sir John Pedder: First Chief Justice of Tasmania, 1824–1854* (Sydney: Federation, 2003), 55–8. For Forbes's less than favourable reaction to Pedder's certification of the Van Diemen's legislation, see Bennett, *Forbes Papers*, 117–23, at 120, letter to Wilmot-Horton, 6 Feb. 1827.
194 See the Newspaper Regulating Act, (1828) 8 Geo. IV, No. 2 (NSW).
195 Newspaper Acts Opinion [1827] NSWSC 23 (1 May 1827). http://www.austlii.edu.au/au/other/NSWSupC/1827/23.html.
196 Bennett, *Sir Francis Forbes*, 84.
197 See, for example, Brian H. Fletcher, *Ralph Darling: A Governor Maligned* (Oxford: Oxford University Press, 1984), 252–6, 259–60, 262.
198 Kercher, *Unruly Child*, 85–6. The political dimension of disallowance for repugnancy are canvassed in Damen Ward, 'Legislation, Repugnancy and the Disallowance of Colonial Laws: The Legal Structures of Empire and *Lloyd's Case*,' *Victoria University of Wellington Law Review* 41 (2010): 381–402.
199 Edgeworth, 'Defamation Law,' 72–6. Hall spent significant periods of time in jail, where he was prone to writing material that led to further prosecutions and convictions. Edgeworth suggests that the court, led by the new judge, James Dowling, was likely showing less patience with newspaper editors during this period.
200 Currey, *Sir Francis Forbes*, 235–6.
201 Ibid., 341–51.
202 See *Hall v. Hely* [1830] NSWSC 18 (22 October 1830) http://www.austlii.edu.au/au/other/NSWSupC/1830/18.html.
203 Currey, *Sir Francis Forbes*, 329–31.
204 Ibid., 331–2.
205 Bennett, *Sir Francis Forbes*, 78.
206 *HRA*, ser. 1, vol. 14, 356–65, secretary of state for the colonies, Sir George Murray, to Darling, 1 Sept. 1828. This missive was accompanied by another 'confidential' dispatch addressed to Forbes and Justice John Stephen, under the same date. Murray's letter reflected in large part a memorandum undertaken by James Stephen Jr, in which he had been very critical of Forbes's conduct. See Bennett, *Sir Frances Forbes*, 97, quoting from CO 201, vol. 195, fols 418a–21 (n.d.). What explains the coolness between the two men, who shared some liberal sentiments about empire? The answer may lie in the description of Forbes by Stephen as 'one

inflated with Benthamite ideas of men and society' (the wording is that of Manning Ward, *Colonial Self-Government*, 146). For an evangelical paternalist like Stephen, Benthamism may have seemed all too calculating and possibly too democratic, in matters of colonial politics – traits that he believed he detected in Forbes's conduct during this conflict in not cooperating with the governor, and arguing for press freedom.

207 Currey, *Sir Francis Forbes*, 377–8. Edgeworth, 'Defamation Law,' 77–80, suggests that, by 1829, the Colonial Office was cooling to Darling's campaign against the press, and with the election of the Whigs in Westminster, his approach to colonial rule seemed increasingly anachronistic.

208 See Ian Holloway, 'Sir Francis Forbes and the Earliest Australian Public Law Cases,' *Law and History Review* 22 (2004): 209–42; Ian Holloway, Simon Bronitt, and John Williams, 'Rhetoric, Reason and the Rule of Law in Early Colonial New South Wales,' in Foster, Berger, and Buck, *The Grand Experiment*, 78–100, at 87–7.

209 See chapter 3, 41–2. Forbes was required to relinquish his membership of the Executive Council after the contretemps with Darling over the Press Acts. See Currey, *Sir Francis Forbes*, 340.

210 Australian Courts Act (1828) 9 Geo. IV, c. 83, s. 23.

211 See Kercher, *Unruly Child*, 32–4, at 36–8 (on the felony attaint issue), 105–8 (on bush ranging), and 87–91 (on usury).

212 See Australian Court Act (1828) 6 Geo. IV, c. 83, s. 24.

213 Bennett, *Sir Francis Forbes*, 117–22.

214 Currey, *Sir Francis Forbes*, 399–405. Halliday in *Habeas Corpus*, 294–6, notes that Forbes was a colonial judge who tended towards an activist view on the use of the 'Great Writ.'

7: Perils of the Colonial Judiciary: English Legal Culture

1 See Howell, 'Van Diemen's Land Judge Storm'; Howell, 'Ships and Sealing Wax,' 101–28, at 121–2; and Petrow, 'Moving in an "Eccentric Orbit,"' 156–75, at 171. On Denison's career, see C.H. Currey, 'William Thomas Denison,' *ADBOL*, http://adbonline.anu.edu.au/biogs/A040048b.htm.

2 (1828) 9 Geo. IV, c. 83, s. 25.

3 Petrow, 'Moving in an "Eccentric Orbit,"' at 171, indicates that Montagu 'converted' Pedder to his way of thinking.

4 Howell, 'Van Diemen's Land Judge Storm,' 254–5.

5 Ibid., 258. According to Howell, the solicitor general estimated that four-fifths of the colony's revenue was at risk.

6 (1828) 9 Geo. IV, c. 83, s. 22. For this evolution and its relationship to the

Morgan case, see Campbell, 'Colonial Legislation and the Laws of England,' 161–4.

7 Swinfen, *Imperial Control of Colonial Legislation*, 47–50. In Canada, interestingly, the extent of repugnancy had been reduced in the Province of Canada (Upper and Lower Canada joined) by the Canada Act of Union (1840) 3 & 4 Vict., c. 35, s. 3, to legislation or law that that was repugnant to imperial legislation 'by express words or necessary intendment.'

8 Alex C. Castles, *Lawless Harvests or God Save the Judges: Van Diemen's Land 1893–55; A Legal History* (Melbourne: Australian Scholarly Publishing, 2007).

9 Ibid., 9–11.

10 Ibid., 19–58. The colony was in a particularly disorderly state under Lieutenant Governor Thomas Davey ('Mad Tom' Davey) from 1813 to 1816.

11 Ibid., 46–7, 85–6.

12 'Commentary and Recommendation of Commissioner J.T. Bigge,' from *Report on the Judicial Establishment of New South Wales and Van Diemen's Land*, House of Commons, 1823, in J.M. Bennett and Alex C. Castles, eds., *A Sourcebook of Australian Legal History* (Sydney: Law Book, 1979), 39–42, at 40–2.

13 Ibid., 39–40; and Castles, *Lawless Harvest*, 65–71.

14 See Act for the Administration of Justice in New South Wales and Van Diemen's Land (1823) 4 Geo. IV, c. 96, s. 24.

15 Ibid., s. 1 et seq. For the establishment of the new court, and for the appointment of the chief justice, see The First Charter of Justice for Van Diemen's Land, excerpted in Bennett and Castles, *Source Book*, 112–15.

16 A.G.L. Shaw, 'George Arthur,' *ADBOL*, http://www.adb.online.anu.edu.au/biogs/A010034b.htm?hilite=Arthur.

17 Bennett, *Sir John Pedder*, 6–10; P.A. Howell, 'John Lewes Pedder,' *ADBOL*, http://www.adb.online.anu.edu.au/biogs/A020285b.htm?hilite=Pedder.

18 R.W. Baker, 'The Early Judges in Tasmania,' *Tasmanian Historical Research Association Paper and Proceedings* 8 (1960): 71–84, at 72–5; Bennett, *Sir John Pedder*, 17–44. Note, however, that Halliday in *Habeas Corpus*, 294–5, suggests that Pedder was even more of an activist than Forbes when it came to using the writ.

19 Petrow, 'Moving in an "Eccentric Orbit,"' 163–4.

20 Howell, 'Of Ships and Sealing Wax,' 105–8.

21 Ibid., 108–12.

22 Ibid., 113. Howell indicates that Algernon, 'struggling to build a practice, ... became deeply indebted.' In his application he named the vice-chancel-

lor and attorney general of England as sponsors, and it was probably his acquaintance with James Stephen Jr that tipped him off to the opening in the Antipodes.

23 Baker, 'Early Judges in Tasmania,' 76–8. On the short, inglorious career of Baxter and how preferment sometimes reflected family pressure on politicians (in this instance, Baxter's father's entreaties to Sir George Murray), see Anonymous, 'Alexander Macduff Baxter,' *ADBOL*, http://www.adb.online.anu.edu.au/biogs/A010070b.htm?hilite=Baxter.

24 Howell, 'Of Ships and Sealing Wax,' 118–19.

25 Petrow, 'Moving in an "Eccentric Orbit,"' 159.

26 Ibid., 159–60, quoting from the *Courier*, 11 June 1841.

27 Ibid., 160–2.

28 The reference to Judge Jeffreys was to George Jeffreys, chief justice of King's Bench in the reign of James II. That judge is forever associated with the excesses of the so-called Bloody Assize for the trial of rebels in southwest England, in the wake of the abortive rising of the Duke of Monmouth in 1885.

29 CO 280, vol. 50, 301, D. 63, Smith Stanley, secretary of state for the colonies, to Arthur, 10 July 1835; and Archives of Tasmania (AOT), Governor's Office GO 1, vol. 26, 483, Law Officers to Glenelg, 17 Jan. 1837.

30 GO 1/33, at 341, D. 36, Lord Normanby, secretary of state for the colonies, to Lieutenant Governor John Franklin, 30 Mar. 1839. The amount was £2068 6s. 8d.

31 *Colonist*, 27 May 1834; *Independent*, 17 May 1834; and *Colonial Times*, 29 Dec. 1835, and 24 July 1838.

32 Petrow, 'Moving in "Eccentric Circles,"' 162. Sidney Stephen was the son of the first puisne judge in New South Wales, John Stephen, and nephew of James Stephen Jr.

33 Ibid.

34 *In Re Stephen*, (1847) 42 P.C.I.C.A. (JCPC, VDL) http://www.law.mq.edu.au/pc/InreStephen,1847.htm.

35 Ibid., 163–4.

36 Ibid., 164.

37 Ibid. Montagu, when asked his opinion, had stated that there was not enough work for three judges. Moreover, a survey of decisions of the Supreme Court between 1833 and 1840 revealed that out of hundreds of cases they had disagreed only six times, and between 1840 and 1844 on five occasions. See GO 1, vol. 17, 49, D. 159, Lord Stanley, secretary of state, to Lieutenant Governor Eardley-Wilmot, 5 May 1845.

38 Ibid., 162–3.

39 Ibid., 165–8. The source of the details of this running feud is AOT, Executive Council Records (EC) 2, vol. 3.
40 EC 2, vol. 3, Stephen to Arthur, 9 July, and 5 and 30 Sept. 1836.
41 Ibid.
42 Ibid., Stephen to Arthur, 11 Aug. 1836.
43 Ibid., vol. 3, Montagu to Arthur, 29 Aug. 1836.
44 Petrow, 'In an "Eccentric Orbit,"' 167, EC 2. vol. 3, ibid. Montagu was of the opinion that the roots of the animosity between the two men went back to the time when he, as attorney general, had threatened a prosecution of Stephen for compounding a felony, and the latter had vowed to 'crush' him (ibid., Montagu to Arthur, 19 Sept. 1836).
45 CO 280, col. 74, 3, D. 100, Arthur to Glenelg, 26 Oct. 1836. Arthur was lieutenant governor of Upper Canada in the midst of the Rebellion and patriot invasion crisis of 1838.
46 GO 1, vol. 26, 627, D. 171, Glenelg to Franklin, 7 Aug. 1837.
47 Ibid., 168. Petrow notes that the *Launceston Advertiser* (25 Jan. 1838, and 1 Feb. 1838) quickly concluded that the decision in London reflected pressure brought by Montagu's father, with the result, the paper claimed, that the colony would continue to be lumbered with an 'incompetent' jurist, whose 'distinction ... rests upon his freaks and eccentricities.'
48 Ibid., 164.
49 In this respect, Montagu may have shared the views of Henry Chapman, the first puisne judge of the Supreme Court of New Zealand and an open advocate of philosophical radicalism. See Peter Spiller, *The Chapman Legal Family* (Wellington: Victoria University Press, 1992), 120–1.
50 Petrow, 'Moving in an "Eccentric Orbit,"' 164. The author notes that the *Austral-Asiatic Review*, 18 Dec. 1838, and 8 Jan. 1839, praised the judge as 'a watchful guardian' against laws that could be applied oppressively.
51 Ibid., 164–5.
52 Ibid.
53 Ibid., 165.
54 GO 1, vol. 47, 569, D. 159, Stanley to Franklin, 27 Sept. 1842.
55 Petrow, 'Moving in an "Eccentric Orbit,"' 168–9.
56 *Hobart Town Courier*, 28 June 1844; and *True Colonist*, 10 July 1844.
57 Howell, 'Of Ships and Sealing Wax,' 119, notes that, in addition to his agricultural pursuits, Montagu engaged in yachting.
58 Howell, 'Of Ships and Sealing Wax,' 118–19. Montagu had married a free settler, Maria Ann Adams, in 1832, who gave birth to two children. He purchased a large home on the Derwent estuary, and, assisted by a legacy

from his maternal grandfather, added to his estate so that it increased to 800 acres.

59 Ibid., 119–21.
60 Ibid., 120–1.
61 Ibid., 113.
62 GO 1, vol. 51, 123, D. 57, Stanley to Eardley-Wilmot, 17 July 1843.
63 GO 1, vol. 54, 414, D. 225, Stanley to Eardley-Wilmot, 26 June 1844.
64 Eardley-Wilmot reported the judge's compliance with the order related to the specific debts in question. CO 280, vol. 173, 437, D. 265, Eardley-Wilmot to Stanley, 18 Dec. 1844.
65 CO 280, vol. 223, 405, D. 119, Denison to Lord Grey, secretary of state for the colonies, 17 Jan. 1848.
66 Text supra, at 1.
67 Petrow, 'Moving in an "Eccentric Orbit,"' 171.
68 CO 280, vol. 223, 405, D. 19, Denison to Grey, 17 Jan. 1848, enclosing Young to Bicheno, colonial secretary, 3 Dec. 1847, and Minute by Denison, 6 Dec. 1847.
69 Ibid., enclosing minute by Denison, 6 Dec. 1847, and letter to Bicheno, 3 Dec. 1847.
70 CO 280, Vol. 223, 501, Montagu to Denison, 28 December 1847.
71 Ibid., 405, D. 19, Denison to Grey. There was one dissenting voice, that of the colonial treasurer, Dr Adam Turnbull, who felt that the substitution of amoval for suspension, without allowing the judge an opportunity of answering, was improper.
72 (1782) 22 Geo. III, c. 75.
73 CO 280, vol. 223, 617, Denison to Gray, 23 Jan. 1848.
74 See Minutes by Merivale, CO 280, vol. 223, 622, 2 June 1848; CO 280, vol. 224, 261, 50, 141, 16 June 1848.
75 *Courier*, 8 Jan. 1848, and 15 Jan. 1848.
76 *Examiner*, 8 Jan. 1848.
77 Petrow, 'Moving in an "Eccentric Orbit,"' 173–4; *Courier*, 19 Jan. 1848; and *Colonial Times*, 1 Feb. 1848.
78 *Montagu v. Denison*, (1849) 45 P.C.I.C.A., *Appellant's Brief*, 1–9.
79 The arguments on the inapplicability of Burke's Act and on the dictates of natural justice are set out in the oral arguments of Montague's counsel, Messrs Teed and Wood QC in *Montagu v. Lieutenant Governor of Van Diemen's Land* (1849) 6 Moore 489, at 495–7; 13 E.R. 773, at 775–6.
80 *Montagu v. Denison*, 508–18, *Appellant's Brief*.
81 *Montagu v. Van Diemen's Land*, 499–500; 778, report pronounced by Lord Brougham, on behalf of himself and Lord Langdale, Dr Lushington and

the Rt Hon. T. Pemberton Leigh. Both Brougham and Pemberton Leigh had sat on *Willis v. Gipps*.

82 This conclusion is not surprising, given that the JCPC had already reached that conclusion earlier in *Willis v. Gipps* (1846) 5 Moo. P.C. 379; 13 E.R. 536, in which John Walpole Willis had appealed his amoval by Governor George Gipps of New South Wales from the Supreme Court of that colony. See text infra, 184–5.

83 Essentially the arguments put forward on behalf of Denison and the Executive Council by Sir Frederick Thesiger QC and Dr Fillimore, ibid., 497–9; 776–7.

84 Ibid., 499; 777.

85 Ibid., 489–500; 777.

86 See Howell, 'Van Diemen's Land Judge Storm,' 259–63.

87 Text, supra, 165.

88 Bennett, *Sir John Pedder*, 96–102. Petrow, 'Moving in an "Eccentric Orbit,"' at 174n117, notes that in the Colonial Office records there is a draft letter marked 'cancelled,' exhibiting anxiety about Horne's 'pecuniary difficulties,' which might affect 'his independence,' further compromising 'public confidence' in the judiciary.

89 Howell, 'Van Diemen's Land Judge Storm,' 260–2.

90 Bennett, *Sir John Pedder*, 101–2, referring to CO 280, vol. 224, fol. 147, at fols 150a, 152a. Howell, 'Van Diemen's Land Judge Storm,' 269, notes that Grey, presumably in an attempt to mitigate the thrust of what had gone before, added a sentence indicating to Denison that, in the circumstances, his 'mistake of judgment' had not lowered him in his lordship's estimation and that the lieutenant governor could expect his continued support.

91 *Willis v. Gipps* (1846) 5 Moo. P.C. 379; 13 E.R. 536.

92 Lloyd Robson, *A History of Tasmania*, vol. 1, *Van Diemen's Land from the Earliest Times to 1855* (Melbourne: Oxford University Press, 1983), 317–437.

93 Manning Ward, *Colonial Self-Government*, 291–6.

94 *Courier*, 5 Jan. 1848.

95 *Launceston Examiner*, 16 Aug. 1844.

96 Howell, 'Of Ships and Sealing Wax,' 112–25, at 122.

97 Ibid., 125–7. Montague's spats with Governors Blackall and Kortright both related to their alleged responsibility for smells wafting into the lawyer's residence.

98 He also rationalized and published the Laws or both Lagos (Southern Nigeria) and the Gold Coast (Ghana).

99 Chapter 4, 84–5.

100 See, for example, CO 43, vol. 74, 176, Hay to Willis, 30 Oct. 1830; and 197, 14 Nov. 1830.

101 Sir George Murray, in response to a petition on Willis's behalf by Lord Milton, (1830) 24 *Hansard Parliamentary Debates* coll. 554, 555.

102 CO 111, vol. 119, 459–63, Goderich to Willis, 9 Mar. 1831. This puts paid to claims by various historians that the Privy Council somehow reversed itself in favour of Willis – an error that William Renwick Riddell exposed in *The Bar and the Courts of the Province of Upper Canada or Ontario* (Toronto: Macmillan of Canada, 1928), 'The Courts,' at 147–8, and 159n12.

103 CO 111, vol. 119, 441, Willis to Goderich, 15 Mar. 1831.

104 See CO 111, vol. 130, Willis to Governor D'Urban, 12 Apr. 1833.

105 Ibid., Willis to D'Urban, 15 Apr. 1833.

106 This diary is contained in the Willis Family Papers, A2, held in Special Collections, University of Canterbury, Christchurch, New Zealand. The diary and others that mention John Walpole Willis are erroneously attributed to Willis, but are the work of his sister, Jane Willis.

107 See *Willis v. Bernard* (1832) 5 C. & P. 342; 172 E.R. 1003 (C.P.); 8 Bing. 376; 131 E.R. 439 (C.P.).

108 For Willis's appointment, see CO 112, vol. 20, secretary of state, Lord Glenelg, to Smyth, 10 Sept. 1835.

109 See CO 111, vol. 143, 338–47, for correspondence relating to the contretemps between Smyth and Willis during late 1835.

110 CO 112, vol. 20, 85, Glenelg to Smyth, 10 Dec. 1835.

111 CO 111, vol. 143, 346–7, Willis to Colonial Office, 9 Dec. 1835, worrying that someone else might be appointed chief justice. An annotation by Henry Taylor, the clerk responsible for the West Indies, indicates that, in his opinion, Willis would not be a good choice for the position. For Bent's appointment, see announcement in CO 112, vol. 20, 116–17, Glenelg to Smyth, 20 Jan. 1836.

112 CO 111, vol. 147, 619, certificate from Dr Stewart Crawford, 3 July 1836, and another from Dr Holland, 5 July 1836, indicating that Willis was suffering the effects of the 'dysentery of that Country' and that a return to that climate could be attended by 'fatal effects.' The more up-to-date diagnosis may be found in Keon-Cohen, 'John Walpole Willis,' 707–8n46, based on reference to modern physicians. Keon-Cohen notes that earlier doctors' reports from British Guiana on Willis refer to 'a functional derangement of the liver.'

113 CO 111, vol. 157, 609–10, Rev. Willis, brother of the judge, to Glenelg, 13 Apr. 1836.

114 Wilson, 'John Walpole Willis,' *DCBOL.*
115 See Stephen to Willis transmitting Glenelg's offer in *Willis v. Gipps* (1846) 38 P.C.I.C.A., *Appellant's Case*, 79.
116 Stephen H. Roberts, *The Squatting Age in Australia 1835–1847* (Melbourne: Melbourne University Press, 1964), 1–185.
117 J.S. Gregory, *Church and State: Changing Government Policies towards Religion in Australia; With Particular Reference to Victoria since Separation* (North Melbourne: Cassell Australia, 1973), 13–25.
118 Hirst, *Convict Society and Its Enemies*, 163–9.
119 Melbourne, *Early Constitutional Development in Australia*, 194–201.
120 On the 'velocity' phenomenon on this and other imperial frontiers, see Weaver, *Great Land Rush*, 119–25.
121 Roger Milliss, *Waterloo Creek: The Australia Day Massacre of 1838, George Gipps and the British conquest of New South Wales* (Sydney: University of New South Wales Press, 1992).
122 Bennett, *Sir James Dowling*, 111, quoting from Dowling Correspondence 1831–9 (M.L., A 486), letter to J.S. Dowling, 20 Apr. 1838.
123 Ibid., 111–12.
124 See Gregory, *Church and State*, 13–26, for background to this event.
125 Bennett, *Sir James Dowling*, 112. Burton had drawn criticism from Catholic sources for his less than charitable views in court on witnesses of that faith group making the sign of the cross when taking the oath.
126 Ibid., quoting from the report of the meeting in the *Australian*, 31 July 1838. Gipps reported these events to London. See *HRA*, ser. 1, vol. 19, 586–8, Gipps to Glenelg, 17 Sept. 1838.
127 Ibid. See also John N. Molony, *An Architect of Freedom: John Hubert Plunkett in New South Wales 1832–1869* (Canberra: Australian National University Press, 1973), 198.
128 *Australian*, 31 July 1838.
129 Bennett, *Sir James Dowling*, 112.
130 The question raised by Willis was forwarded to London for the consideration of the Colonial Office. *HRA*, ser. 1, vol. 20, 117–18. Neither Dowling nor his predecessor Forbes had demanded any money for these additional duties. The relevant section of The Third Charter of Justice is found in Bennett and Castles, *Source Book*, 54.
131 Bennett, *Sir James Dowling*, 114–15.
132 *HRA*, ser. 1, vol. 20, 395, Law Officers' Report, 9 Nov. 1839.
133 Ibid., 629–30, Willis to Gipps, 30 Apr. 1840 and 6 May 1840, which the governor forwarded to Russell. Ibid., 629, 13 May 1840.
134 *Walker v. Hughes* [1839] NSW Sup. Ct. 71 (24 Sept. 1839) http://www

.austlii.edu.au/au/other/NSWSupC/1839/71.html, referring to the report in the *Australian*, 25 June 1839, Willis J. dissenting.

135 Ibid., 116–18. Nicholls claimed that he had a statement from Forbes C.J. to the effect that the barrister/attorney distinction did not apply at Sessions, or at least that he would not be adversely affected by such a division of roles. Dowling agreed to formalize the understanding, joined by Willis. When Justice Alfred Stephen, opposed to the concession, reported that Forbes disclaimed any knowledge of such a pledge and advised the chief justice of this denial, he changed his mind. Willis took this as a personal affront. Gipps sought to bring the parties together, without attributing blame to Willis, and induced them to shake hands. *HRA*, ser. 1, vol. 21, 160–5, Gipps to secretary of state for the colonies, Lord John Russell, 16 Mar. 1840.

136 Ibid., 120–1. Dowling wrote to Gipps bitterly complaining of Willis's practice of making disparaging comments about him behind his back, especially relating to his 'character, habits, manner and feelings.' CO 201, vol. 306, fols 391–391a, 17 Dec. 1840.

137 Ibid., 122–8.

138 The Administration of Justice Act, (1840) 4 Vict., No. 22, s. 20 (NSW) provided that the governor was empowered to appoint either the chief justice, or, if he should decline, one of the puisnes to sit alone on Equity cases. Willis, expecting that his colleagues and Gipps would automatically defer to him, played coy, and Dowling, at the suggestion of his colleague Stephen, did not decline the appointment. Gipps, recognizing Willis's expertise in the field, was uncomfortable with the result. See *HRA*, ser. 1, vol. 21, 155–7, 1 Jan. 1841, letter to Russell.

139 Bennett, *Sir James Dowling*, 128. Note appended by Gairdner, the colonial officer responsible for New South Wales matters.

140 CO 201, vol. 306, fol. 340, Dowling to Gipps, 4 Dec. 1840.

141 The Administration of Justice Act, s. 4, gave the power to appoint one of the Supreme Court as a puisne justice to Port Phillip or New Zealand, with the same jurisdiction as the NSW Court. See A.G.L. Shaw, ed., *Gipps–La Trobe Correspondence 1839–1846* (Melbourne: Melbourne University Press, 1989), 53–54, letter 38, Gipps to Superintendent La Trobe, 20 Dec., advising him of the appointment; and *HRA*, ser. 1, vol. 21, 160–5, Gipps to Russell, 3 Jan. 1841.

142 Gipps to La Trobe, 11 June 1842, in Shaw, *Gipps–La Trobe Correspondence*, 133–4, letter 112, re proposed incorporation of Sydney and Melbourne. Willis's objections flowed from his belief that only a royal charter could establish a municipal corporation (despite the Colonial Office's view to

the contrary), and that taxation contemplated by the incorporation legislation was outside the powers of a nominated legislature (even though the NSW legislature had already passed such legislation, without demur in London).

143 From *Ex Parte Lyons*, (1896) Legge, *A Selection of Supreme Court Cases in N.S.W.*, 149.

144 *HRA*, ser. 1, vol. 21, 160–5, 3 Jan. 1841.

145 See the pretentious and rambling 'Notes on the Acquisition of New Zealand as a Dependency of New South Wales with Reference to Parts Obtained by British Subjects from the Aborigines,' Willis to Gipps, May 1840, the Mitchell Library, ML A857 (CY reel 746). I am indebted to Ned Fletcher of the University of Auckland School of Law for this lead.

146 The secretary of state approved Gipps's actions in moving Willis. *HRA*, ser. 1, vol. 21, 406, Russell to Gipps, 22 June 1841.

147 Russell's Tory successor at the Colonial Office, Lord Stanley, had a more grounded view of Willis. See letter to Gipps, 17 Jan. 1842, rejecting Willis's claim for removal expenses to Port Phillip, *HRA*, ser. 1, vol. 21, 635, because the judge's transfer was due in large part to his own misbehaviour.

148 See Rizzetti, 'Sifting to the Bottom of Financial Impropriety,' 97–109, at 98. See also, on the general historical context of the District, A.G.L. Shaw, *A History of the Port Phillip District: Victoria before Separation* (Melbourne: Miegunyah, 1996), 32–86.

149 Shaw, *History of the Port Phillip District*, 170–7.

150 Ibid., 111–43.

151 George Augustus Robinson came highly recommended by Lieutenant Governor Arthur of Van Diemen's Land. See Jan Crichett, *A 'distant field of murder': Western District Frontiers 1834–148* (Melbourne: Melbourne University Press, 1990), 4–18.

152 On the jockeying for status among gentlemen by birth and those who felt that they had achieved that status by merit, and the central role of the Melbourne Club to a gentlemanly existence, see Paul de Serville, *Port Phillip Gentlemen and Good Society in Melbourne before the Gold Rushes* (Melbourne: Oxford University Press, 1980). On the squatting phenomenon, see Shaw, *History of the Port Phillip District*, 87–110.

153 Rizzetti, 'Sifting to the Bottom,' 100, for a helpful account of the chains of credit, the use by banks of merchants as 'middlemen and credit checkers,' and the resulting exposure of the latter in hard times. On the general slide to Depression, see Shaw, *History of the Port Phillip District*, 144–69.

154 Keon-Cohen, 'John Walpole Willis,' 706–7.

155 Rizzetti, 'Sifting to the Bottom,' 100–1.
156 R. Therry, *Reminiscences of Thirty Years' Residence in New South Wales and Victoria* (1863; repr., Sydney: Royal Australian Historical Society and Sydney University Press, 1974), 342.
157 Paul R. Mullally, *Crime in the Port Phillip District 1835–51* (Melbourne: Hybrid Publishers, 2008), 23.
158 *Willis v .Gipps* (1846) 38 P.C.I.C.A., *Respondent's Case*, 7, Willis's address to the common jury at the opening of the Criminal Sessions, 15 Oct. 1842, published by the *Port Phillip Patriot* as a pamphlet.
159 Kercher, *Unruly Child*, 112–18. See also Rizzetti, 'Sifting to the Bottom,' 103–4.
160 This accords with his position stated from the bench in Sydney, supra, text, at 176.
161 See *Willis v. Gipps* (1846) 38 P.C.I.C.A., *Appellant's Case*, Appendix, 83–4, 85, letters Willis to Gipps, 20 Jan. 1843, Willis to La Trobe, 27 Feb. 1843.
162 Ibid., *Respondent's Case*, 19–20, letter of the judges of the Supreme Court of New South Wales to Gipps, 4 Nov. 1842. It is ironic that it was Burton who took the lead on pushing this legislation, as he was on most issues, if anything, more conservative and English law–bound than Willis. On debt reform, however, he was progressive and borrowed from legislation that he had already drafted in the Cape Colony. Kercher, *Unruly Child*, 116–18.
163 *R. v. Bonjon* [1841] NTSWSC 92 (18 Apr.), *Decisions of the Superior Courts of New South Wales 1788–1899*, http://www.law.mq.edu.au/scnsw/cases1840-41/cases1841/R%20v%20Bonjon,%201841.htm.
164 Kercher, *Unruly Child*, 10–11, and Willis's notes on Aboriginal title in New Zealand, supra, note 145.
165 See *R. v. Murrell and Bummaree*, [1836] NSWSC 35 (11 Apr.), http://www.law.mq.edu.au/scnsw/cases1835-36/html/r_v_murrell_and_bummaree__1836.htm; and Gipps to Stanley, reporting on Willis's judgment and the reaction to it, *HRA*, ser. 1, vol. 21, 653–4, 24 Jan. 1842; and *HRA*, ser. 1, vol. 22, 133, Stanley to Gipps, 2 July 1842.
166 This is certainly how Willis saw himself, and his friends in the local press imagined him. See Keon-Cohen, 'John Walpole Willis,' 711–12, referring to an address delivered by the judge on 16 Aug. 1841, that invoked the ghost of Lord Mansfield, reprinted in the *Port Phillip Patriot*, 21 Aug. 1841.
167 The judge quickly balled out a solicitor, a Mr Sewell, for appearing in his court with a 'fiercely voluminous moustache.' When he rose to address the bench, Willis is reported to have shouted that this was not a place for '[a] Whiskered Pandour or a fierce Hussar!' Edmund Finn ('Garryowen'),

Chronicles of Early Melbourne, 1835 to 1852 (Melbourne: Ferguson & Mitchell, 1888), 71.

168 In the Royal Victoria Historical Association Archives in Melbourne there is an undated letter (possibly a draft, which may or may not have been sent) that reads like a code of ethics for attorneys, and no doubt reflected Willis's beliefs in this matter. See Gipps to La Trobe for the reference to Willis's lecturing magistrates, in Shaw, *Gipps–La Trobe Correspondence*, letter 57, 15 May 1841.

169 Rizzetti, 'Sifting to the Bottom,' 104.

170 *Willis v. Gipps, Respondent's Case*, Supplement to the Appendix, 1, Willis to La Trobe, 3 Apr. 1843.

171 Ibid., 78–9, Court Record Extract from *Batman et al. v. Lonsdale et al.*, as published in the *Port Phillip Gazette*, 28 Apr. 1843. Gipps, in reporting to the Colonial Office, considered Lonsdale's actions over the shares ill-considered, but otherwise did not consider his financial transactions dishonest.

172 La Trobe later raised questions about his own temerity in not taking on Willis and dealing firmly with him. *Willis v. Gipps, Appellant's Case*, Appendix, 30–4, La Trobe's remarks on correspondence from Willis, 28 Feb. 1843.

173 Ibid., *Respondent's Case*, 15, reference to comments of Judge Willis in Court, 8 June 1841. See also Mullally, *Crime in the Port Phillip District*, 365–9, *R. v. Jenkins, Remington, Martin, Collins and Morris*, 18 May 1841; 369–75, *R. v. Sandford George Bolden*, 2 Dec. 1841.

174 *Willis v. Gipps, Respondent's Case*, ibid. Shaw, *History of the Port Phillip District*, 137, notes that, in his decision in *Bolden*, Willis pointedly criticized the Crown prosecutor for acting 'solely on the evidence of a savage boy ... who but partially understood English,' and made no bones about his view that squatters had a right to turn Aboriginal people off 'their' land, whether the latter were aggressive or not.

175 *Willis v. Gipps*, ibid., Appendix, 87–8, Edward S. Parker, assistant protector, to Chief Protector G.A. Robinson, 9 June 1842.

176 Ibid., Supplementary Documents, 2–3, Memorial of Carrington to Gipps, 20 May 1842.

177 Ibid., *Appellants Case*, Appendix, 51, judges of the Supreme Court to Willis, reported in the *Port Phillip Herald*, 24 June 1842. Presumably the Sydney justices considered that location appropriate, because the will was made there.

178 Ibid., *Respondent's Case*, 4, refers to the 'indecorous and improper comments' about the Supreme Court judges. See also ibid., *Appellant's Case*, Appendix, 55, Law Report excerpt from *Bragg and Askew v. Williams*.

179 Ibid., *Appellant's Case*, Appendix, 50. Public Papers, from *Port Phillip Herald*, 24 June 1842; and *Respondent's Case*, Appendix, excerpt from *Port Phillip Patriot*, 30 June 1842.
180 Ibid., *Respondent's Case*, Appendix, 2–3, extract from *Port Phillip Patriot*, 23 June 1842.
181 Ibid., *Appellant's Case*, Appendix, 50, Supreme Court Justices to Willis, 7 July 1842, and Willis's reply, 19 July 1842.
182 Peter Ryan, 'Redmond Barry,' *ADBOL* http://adbonline.anu.edu.au/biogs/A030104b.htm?hilite=John%3BWalpole%3BWillis.
183 *Willis v. Gipps, Respondent's Case*, Appendix, 80, Croke to La Trobe, 4 May 1843. Croke received the full support of his colleagues in this complaint at his treatment. Ibid., 81, Edward Eyre Williams, Archibald Cunninghame, S. Raymond, Redmond Barry, Robert W. Pohlman, and W. Foster Stawell to Croke, 1 May 1843.
184 *Willis v. Gipps, Respondent's Case*, 16–17, and *Appendix to Respondent's Case*, 72–3, Were to La Trobe, 3 June 1843, from Melbourne Jail.
185 De Serville, *Port Phillip Gentlemen*, 21. When Arden became bankrupt, the ownership of the paper changed hands, and it thereafter took a more moderate course, including in its attitude towards Willis.
186 Finn, *Chronicles of Early Melbourne*, 75–7.
187 *HRA*, ser. 1, vol. 22, 56 et seq., Gipps to Stanley, 18 May 1842; 56, 108, Gipps to Stanley, 8 June 1842, enclosing two letters from the judge justifying his actions; and 434–5, Stanley to Gipps, 19 Dec. 1842, approving of the governor's actions, but making it clear that he did not consider the latter as being impelled by dishonourable motives.
188 De Serville, *Port Phillip Gentlemen*, 21.
189 See *Willis v. Gipps, Respondent's Case*, 4. There is no doubt that a letter complaining about Willis from Edward Curr to La Trobe, which La Trobe sent, as a courtesy, to the judge was forwarded to Kerr, who published extracts, together with attacks against Curr's character. *Willis v. Gipps, Appellant's Case*, 5.
190 Ibid., and *Appellant's Case*, Appendix, 53–4, judges to Stanley, 2 Oct. 1842; and extract from *Port Phillip Patriot*, 18 Aug. 1842.
191 Barry, 'John Walpole Willis,' *ADBOL*.
192 See *Willis v. Gipps, Appellant's Case*, Appendix 29, Willis to Henry Watson Parker, private secretary to Governor Gipps.
193 Ibid., *Respondent's Case*, 7. Gipps had no doubt that Willis was at all times aware of what was going on in his cause. Clearly the judge was reading the newspapers, as he endeavoured to get Croke to launch a libel suit for a calumny against him in one of them. Willis ultimately requested Kerr to abandon the plans for the meeting.

194 The governor's misgivings about the state of affairs in Melbourne are set out in letters to Stanley, *HRA*, ser. 1, vol. 22, 320–3, 351–3, 13 Oct. and 14 Nov. 1842.
195 *Willis v. Gipps, Respondent's Case*, 7, and Appendix, 43, letter from James Simpson, C.H. Ebden, Edward Curr, and G. Ward Cole with forty-three signatures, 21 Nov. 1842.
196 Gipps mentioned in a letter to Stanley, 27 Aug. 1842, that he had provisionally granted a request from Willis to go on leave. *HRA*, ser. 1, vol. 22, 226.
197 *Willis v. Gipps, Appellant's Case*, 2–9, Minutes of Executive Council, 20 Jan. 1843; and 9–19, Willis's rejoinder to Stanley, 8 Feb. 1843.
198 Willis had been drawn into expressing support publicly for Kerr's candidacy in an altercation in a store with Edward Curr, a leading Roman Catholic, who was running in the same ward. Ibid., *Respondent's Case*, 17.
199 See Rizzetti, 'Sifting the Bottom,' 101–2, for an account of the meltdown in 1843, and its impact on institution, families, and individuals.
200 See remarks by La Trobe on Willis's letter of 8 Feb., dated 20 Feb. 1843, *Willis v. Gipps, Appellant's Case*, Appendix 60–4.
201 *HRA*, ser. 1, vol. 22, 796–7, Gipps to Stanley, 26 June 1843.
202 *Willis v. Gipps, Appellant's Case*, 62, two undated addresses of support for Willis, the first with approximately 1,500 signatures, and a second with 300.
203 *HRA*, ser. 1, vol. 23, 47–52, Gipps to Stanley, 19 July 1843.
204 Rizzetti, 'Judging Boundaries,' 369. In *Manuel*, Willis had convicted the accused of a capital felony for being at large while under a sentence of transportation. The offence was a misdemeanour. On the advice of the justices in Sydney, Gipps pardoned the man. See *Willis v. Gipps, Respondent's Case*, 16; and *Appendix to Respondent's Case*, 82–5.
205 *Willis v. Gipps, Appellant's Case*, 1–5.
206 Ibid., 5–13.
207 *Willis v. Gipps, Respondent's Case*, 1–22.
208 See Howell, *Judicial Committee of the Privy Council*, 32–4.
209 Ibid., 33.
210 Sitting on the hearing were Lord President, the Duke of Buccleuch; Lord Chancellor Lyndhurst; Lord Brougham (ironically one of Willis's original patrons); Chief Justice Tindal; Baron Parke; Rt Hon. Pemberton Leigh; and the Rt Hon. William Gladstone. *Willis v. Gipps* (1846) 5 Moo. P.C. 379; 13 E.R. 536.
211 Ibid., at 392; 541.

212 *HRA*, ser. 1, vol. 25, 206–8, Colonial Office to Willis, 25 Aug. 1846, responding to letter from him, ibid., 206.
213 *HRA*, ser. 1, vol. 25, 209, Colonial Office to Willis, 15 Sept. 1846, responding to letter from Willis, 4 Sept. 1846.
214 John Walpole Willis, *On the Government of the British Colonies* (London: Trelawney Saunders, 1850). Barry, 'John Walpole Willis,' *ADBOL*, refers to the tract, which propounded 'a completely unacceptable scheme of colonial government.'
215 Howell, *Judicial Committee*, 34n46. Rizzetti notes wryly that even in retirement Willis, who had problems with boundaries, was complaining to his neighbour about his servant exercising horses too close to his property. Rizzetti, 'Judging Boundaries,' 375.
216 See Bennett, *Sir John Pedder*, 94, concerning correspondence between the two men about contempt of court (in the context of the *Arden* case).
217 Finn, *Chronicles of Early Melbourne*, 67.
218 Therry, *Reminiscences*, 342–3.
219 *Willis v. Gipps, Respondent's Case*, 16. Section 7 of the Act, (1840) 4 Vict., No. 22, gave the resident judge the same powers and jurisdiction as the Supreme Court, whether exercised individually or collectively by its judges.
220 Bennett, *Sir James Dowling*, 116.
221 *Sydney Herald*, 16 Oct. 1841.
222 *HRA*, ser. 1, vol. 20, 118–24, Willis to Gipps, 30 Mar. 1839.
223 Keon-Cohen, 'John Walpole Willis,' 78.
224 On this stance by Gipps, see text above 184, and Rizzetti, 'Judging Boundaries,' 369.
225 Finn, *Chronicles of Early Melbourne*, 67.
226 Finn, ibid., was to give an inspired, if unsettling, Antipodean perspective to Willis's reactions to enemies: 'Willis was not unlike a kangaroo perched upon the stump of a tree surrounded by a pack or yelping, biting dogs, at which he used to snarl and snap in return, and when one would approach too near, the "old man" would give him a claw or a hug which he would have reason to remember.'
227 See chapter 4, 74–83.
228 Two immediate successors as resident judge in Port Phillip District, William Jeffcott and Roger Therry, were applauded for their equable and conciliatory characters. See R.M. Hague, 'Sir William Jeffcott,' *ADBOL*, http://www.adb.online.anu.edu.au/biogs/A020015b.htm?hilite=jeffcott; and Finn, *Chronicles of Early Melbourne*, 85.
229 Rizzetti, 'Sifting the Bottom,' 104–6.

8: Repugnancy in Australia after 1850

1 Colonial Laws Validity Act (1865) 28 & 29 Vict., c. 63.

2 Ibid., s. 7.

3 See Alex C. Castles, 'Benjamin Boothby,' *ADBOL*, http://adbonline.anu.edu.au/biogs/A030185b.htm; Castles and Harris, *Lawmakers and Wayward Whigs*, 126–34, 196–203; R.M. Hague, 'The Judicial Career of Benjamin Boothby' (unpublished, ca. 1991); Ralph M. Hague, *Hague's History of the Law in South Australia 1837–1867* (Adelaide: University of Adelaide Press, 2005) 1:219–474; Peter S. Howell, 'The Boothby Case' (MA thesis, University of Tasmania, 1965); Williams, 'Justice Boothby,' 21–51.

4 The key piece of legislation was the Australian Constitutions Act (1850) 13 & 14 Vict., c. 59, s. 14, which enabled Legislative Councils to make laws as long as they were not repugnant to the Laws of England, but dropped reference to the judicial privilege.

5 South Australia Act, (1834) 4 & 5 Will. IV, c. 95, s. 2. On the practice of disallowance in imperial practice, see D.B. Swinfen, *Imperial Control of Imperial Legislation*.

6 (1855–56) 19 & 20 Vict., No. 2, ss 31–2 (SA). These provisions accorded with imperial legislation establishing the constitutions of the other Australian colonies. The wording in s. 32 and its counterparts contemplates other ways of moving against troublesome judges, although, unlike earlier Canadian legislation, there was no stated right of appeal in these statutes by a dismissed judge. See chapter 4, 83–4, and chapter 5, 99.

7 For South Australia's constitution and its legislative system, see Douglas Pike, *A Paradise of Dissent: South Australia 1829–1857*, 2nd ed. (Melbourne: Melbourne University Press, 1967), 461–94; and the South Australia Constitution Act (1855–6) 20 Vict., No. 2 (SA).

8 Swinfen, *Imperial Legislation*, 61–3, quoting from Sir Frederic Rogers, CO 323, vol. 87, Rogers to Herman Merivale, Undersecretary, Colonial Office, 5 May 1858. Rogers does mention the possibility of the Crown intervening by disallowance or otherwise to prevent the enactment of laws 'manifestly at variance with the fundamental principles of English legislation,' such as acts denying the Queen's sovereignty, prohibiting Christianity, or allowing slavery, polygamy, or punishment without trial. He seems, however, to have had in mind initiatives by the imperial authorities, not the colonial courts (ibid., 58–9).

9 Pike, *Paradise of Dissent*, 3–28.

10 South Australia Act, (1834) 4 & 5 Will. IV, c. 95, ss 2–4.

11 Pike, *Paradise of Dissent*, 52–83.

12 Castles and Harris, *Lawmakers and Wayward Whigs*, 29.
13 Ibid., 35–6.
14 Pike, *Paradise of Dissent*, 221–42.
15 Ibid., 242–8.
16 Castles and Harris, *Lawyers and Wayward Whigs*, 38.
17 Ibid., 55–73.
18 Hague, *Sir John Jeffcott*, 51–127.
19 Bennett, *Sir Charles Cooper*; Castles and Harris, *Lawmakers and Wayward Whigs*, 73–7.
20 Supreme Court Act (1837) 7 Will. iv, No. 5, ss 7–9 (SA).
21 Anonymous, 'Charles Cooper,' *ADBOL*, http://www.adb.online.anu.edu.au/biogs/A010232b.htm?hilite=charles;cooper; Castles and Harris, *Lawmakers and Wayward Whigs*, 74–7.
22 Castles, 'Benjamin Boothby,' *ADBOL*. In Hague, *Hague's History of the Law*, 1:399, there is a family tree entitled 'The Pedigree of Boothby' suggesting noble ancestors, but this looks like a Victorian vanity tree.
23 (1839) 5 Ad. & E. 1; 111 E.R. 1067 (K.B.). The case dealt with the issue of whether parliamentary privilege extended to publications authorized by Parliament.
24 Castles, 'Benjamin Boothby,' *ADBOL*.
25 B. Boothby (1844), *Local Courts Not the Remedy for the Defects of the Law, with Suggestions of a Plan for Adapting the Superior Courts of Common Law at Westminster, the Circuit Courts of Assize, and the Sessions of the Peace, to the Increased Demands of the Country, Arising from Its Extended Population and Commerce* (London: Saunders & Benning, 1844).
26 John M. Ward, 'Fifth Duke of Newcastle-under-Lyme,' *ADBOL*, http://www.adb.online.anu.edu.au/biogs/A050379b.htm?hilite=Newcastle.
27 See Letters Patent appointing Benjamin Boothby, 25 Feb. 1833; Parliament of South Australia, *Correspondence with Mr Justice Boothby*, Parl. Paper No. 128, (1861), vol. 3, p. 3.
28 Hague, *Hague's History of the Law*, 219, quoting from a column in the *South Australian Register*, 24 May 1853.
29 Williams, 'Justice Boothby,' 23.
30 On the salary issue, see Castles, 'Benjamin Boothby,' *ADBOL*.
31 On Boothby's chequered financial affairs, I am indebted to legal historian Peter Moore for his insights, reflecting ongoing research into the records of the South Australian Banking Company.
32 Hague, 'Judicial Career of Benjamin Boothby,' 6–8. The political position of the two newspapers is discussed in Pike, *Paradise of Dissent*, 394–5.
33 See Greg Taylor, 'The Grand Jury of South Australia,' *American Journal of*

Legal History 45 (2001): 468–516, at 469. For the repealing legislation, see An Act to Provide for the Trial of Offenders without the Intervention of Grand Juries (1852) 15 & 16 Vict., No. 5 (SA).

34 Williams, 'Justice Boothby,' 25.

35 South Australia Act (1855–6) 20 Vict., No. 2 (SA).

36 Schedule A of the South Australian Constitution Act (1855–6) 20 Vict., No. 2 (SA), that set the salary of the second judge at £1,300.

37 Hague, 'Judicial Career of Benjamin Boothby,' 10–11, quoting the *Times*, 26–7 Sept. 1855; Williams, 'Justice Boothby,' 26.

38 Cooper had only recently been designated chief justice of the colony, recognition that, as Bennett asserts, was 'long overdue.' Boothby undoubtedly saw this as improving his chances of becoming chief in due course. At a dinner in his honour, Cooper was complimentary about his colleague and their relationship at that point. Bennett, *Sir Charles Cooper*, 100.

39 Williams, 'Justice Boothby,' 26–7. Howell sees this case as causing the first real division of opinion about Boothby's approach to justice. Howell, 'Boothby Case,' 9–10.

40 Boothby posed the question to the jury: 'Gentlemen are you dissatisfied with this woman's evidence? Do you wish the case to go on?' Several jurors responded 'No.' There was shock among some of them when the judge concluded as he did, and one earned a stiff rebuke when he tried to explain that the word 'No' related to the first part of Boothby's question.

41 Supreme Court Act (1852) 15 Vict., No. 5, s. 182 (SA).

42 Williams, 'Justice Boothby,' 27.

43 Hague, 'Judicial Career of Benjamin Boothby,' 25, quoting the *Register*, 29 Sept. 1857.

44 Ibid., 27, quoting the *Register*, 20 Feb. 1858.

45 Williams, 'Justice Boothby,' 27–8. Williams notes that there was venerable authority in Blackstone's *Commentaries*, 3:375, for sequestering a jury in this way, but that the advisability of this approach was raising questions in judicial circles at roughly this time. See comments of Mellor J. in *Winsor v. The Queen* (1866) LR 1 QB 289, at 320–1.

46 Bennett, *Sir Charles Cooper*, 101.

47 Real Property Act, (1858) 22 Vict. 15 (SA). See also Greg Taylor, *The Law of the Land: The Advent of the Torrens System in Canada* (Toronto: University of Toronto Press for Osgoode Society for Canadian Legal History, 2008), 5–27.

48 D. Pike, 'Introduction of the Real Property Act in South Australia,' *University of Adelaide Law Review* 1 (1960–2): 169–89, at 180–1.

49 Taylor, *Law of the Land*, 25. Taylor also mentions other motivations, such

as emotional attachment to the old order, and scepticism about a system devised by a non-lawyer.

50 Gwynne had earlier sought to describe himself exclusively as a solicitor, in order to insulate himself from appearance in court before Boothby. Williams, 'Justice Boothby,' 28–9, referring to a notice to that effect in the *Register*, 20 Nov. 1858.

51 David St Leger Kelly, 'Edward Castres Gwynne,' *ADBOL*, http://www.adb.online.anu.edu.au/biogs/A040354b.htm.

52 *Johnson v. Torrens*, Hague, 'Judicial Career of Benjamin Boothby,' 38; *Hutchison v. Torrens*, Williams, 'Justice Boothby,' 30; *Hutchison v. Leeworthy*, Hague, 'Judicial Career of Benjamin Boothby,' 46.

53 Hague, 'Judicial Career of Benjamin Boothby,' 43.

54 Real Property Amendment Act (1860) 24 Vict., Nos. 11 and 22 (SA).

55 See the Supreme Court Act, (1837) 7 Will. IV, No. 5, s. 16 (SA), renacted (1855–6) 19 Vict., No. 31, and confirmed (1865–6) 29 Vict., No. 12.

56 *Payne v. Dench*, South Australia, Parl. Paper No. 142 (1861), 22–5.

57 English law officers to Newcastle, South Australia, *Minutes of the Proceedings of the Executive Council Relating to the Conduct of Mr Justice Boothby*, Parl. Paper No. 22 (1867), 15 Apr., xi. The legislation confirming the existence of the Court of Appeals was An Act Confirming the Existence of the Court of Appeals (1861) 24 & 25 Vict., No. 5 (SA).

58 *McEllister v. Fenn*, South Australia, *Report of Select Committee re Judge Boothby*, Parl. Paper No. 141 (1861), 15–23. Hague, 'Judicial Career of Benjamin Boothby,' 64.

59 Williams, 'Justice Boothby,' 32.

60 Hague, 'Judicial Career of Benjamin Boothby,' 67. Under the South Australia law it was not necessary, as it was in England, for the coroner to take depositions, let alone reduce to writing everything said during a hearing.

61 Ibid., 68.

62 See Swinfen, *Imperial Control*, 78–92. The author's view on this allied issue of the validity of colonial legislation that so exercised Boothby is that the Colonial Office did not consider instructions as legally binding on colonial executives, except in several special cases. Accordingly, in general terms, if governors gave their assent to legislation that should have been reserved, this did not per se invalidate the legislation in question.

63 Williams, 'Justice Boothby,' 34–5. The quote is from the *Register*, 20 June 1861. Boothby claimed that he had been thrown out of the 'dog cart' that he used to get to Court, because he could not afford a better ride.

64 See ANZ Group Archives, South Australian Banking Co., Local Board Minute Book, 1858–60. SA4/1/11, 19 Sept. 1858, and 11 Mar. 1859. Once again

I am indebted to Peter Moore for bringing these records and other insights about Boothby's finances and financial connections to my attention.

65 Hughes finally settled out of court with the other claimants, and had his lease validated by legislation in the late 1860s.

66 The complete saga of the Moonta Mines affair is addressed by Patricia Jane Sumerling in 'Walter Watson Hughes and Moonta and Wallaroo Mines' (MA thesis, Flinders University, 2001). On the circumstances of George Boothby's involvement, see 35–8.

67 Peter Moore to the author, email 19 Dec. 2010.

68 Williams, 'Justice Boothby,' 32.

69 South Australia, *Correspondence with Judge Boothby*, Parl. Paper No. 128 (1861), vol. 3, 2–3.

70 Williams, 'Justice Boothby,' 33.

71 Hague, 'Judicial Career of Benjamin Boothby,' 73.

72 South Australia, *Report of the Select Committee of the Legislative Council upon Recent Decisions and Conduct of Mr Justice Boothby*, Parl. Paper No. 141 (1861), v.

73 Hague, 'Judicial Career of Benjamin Boothby,' 79.

74 South Australia, *Report of the Select Committee of the House of Assembly Appointed to Inquire into the Recent Judgments of Justice Boothby*, Parl. Paper No. 154 (1861).

75 Williams, 'Justice Boothby,' 34.

76 Hague, 'Judicial Career of Benjamin Boothby,' 85–6.

77 South Australia, *Mr Justice Boothby's Decisions*, Parl. Paper No. 48 (1862), 22–7.

78 Hague, 'Judicial Career of Benjamin Boothby,' 88–9.

79 South Australia, *Despatches on the Appointment of Chief Justice Hanson*, Parl. Paper No. 86 (1862), MacDonnell to Newcastle, 22 Nov. 1862, 1. On Hanson's career, see Anonymous, 'Richard Davies Hanson,' *ADBOL*, http://www.adb.online.anu.edu.au/biogs/A040384b.htm?hilite=richard;hanson.

80 Castles, 'Benjamin Boothby,' *ADBOL*.

81 South Australia, *Despatches on the Appointment of Chief Justice Hanson*, Parl. Paper No. 86 (1862), Boothby to Newcastle, 26 Nov. 1861, 3.

82 Hague, 'Judicial Career of Benjamin Boothby,' 92–3.

83 Williams, 'Justice Boothby,' 37.

84 An Act to Explain an Act Intituled an Act for the Better Government of Her Majesty's Australian Colonies (1862) 25 & 26 Vict., c. 11.

85 South Australia, *Despatch on Addresses for the Removal of Judge Boothby*, Parl. Paper No. 68 (1862), 2–4, Law Officers to Newcastle, 12 Apr. 1862.

86 Ibid., at 4.

87 Ibid., Newcastle to Daly, 24 Apr. 1862, 1–2.

88 It is difficult to understand how Newcastle manages to circumvent the effect of section 32 of the South Australia Constitution Act, allowing removal of a judge on a joint address of the local Parliament. It is true that the wording of that provision leaves open other means of dealing with a troublesome jurist, but his lordship gave no hint of what the process would be. A possibility would be the invocation of Burke's Act of 1782, but the engagement of the imperial authority in that instance was contingent on the judge appealing. There was no appeal provision in the Australian constitutive acts like that in the earlier Canadian legislation. See chapter 4, 83–4, and chapter 5, 99. One can only assume that as the Crown appointed colonial judges under the royal prerogative, even if the power were locally exercised, it could claim the ultimate right to determine whether a judge was dismissed.

89 South Australia, *Minutes of the Proceedings of the Executive Council relating to the Conduct of Mr Justice Boothby*, Parl. Paper No. 22 (1867), LXVIII–LXXIII.

90 An Act to Remove Doubts as to the Appointments and Dismissal from Offices of Certain Persons (1862) 26 Vict., No. 2 (SA).

91 Williams, 'Justice Boothby,' 39–40.

92 An Act to Confirm Acts of a Colonial Legislature (1863) 26 & 27 Vict., c. 84.

93 Secretary of state to Daly, 25 July 1863, cited in Hague, 'Judicial Career of Benjamin Boothby,' 124–5.

94 For an account of *Auld v. Murray*, see South Australia, *Report of the Select Committee of the House of Assembly Appointed to Prepare an Address to the Queen on Validity Laws*, Parl. Paper No. 142 (1864), 37–40.

95 Ibid.

96 ANZ Group Archives, South Australian Banking Company, Letter Book: SA4/19/23, London Board to SA manager, 24 Oct. 1864.

97 Williams, 'Justice Boothby,' 41.

98 Hague, 'Judicial Career of Benjamin Boothby,' 139.

99 The history of judicial ethics in the colonies is one that merits study. We have seen some evidence in this book of judges in trouble because of conflict of interests – Richard Temple of British Honduras moonlighting as a legal adviser to a resource company; Montagu for his irresponsible approach to his indebtedness; Willis criticized for his financial dealings with the owner of a newspaper, whose editor was his friend. It is difficult from these random cases to get a clear sense of the ethical culture in which such judges operated, and whether Boothby would have traversed an ethical line in judicial practice at that time. It is interesting, however, to note that

in 1852 Lord Chancellor Cottenham (Charles Pepys) suffered the indignity of the House of Lords on appeal finding him guilty of a conflict of interest in sitting on litigation involving a company in which he owned shares. See Gareth H. Jones, 'Charles Christopher Pepys,' *ODNB*, http://www.oxforddnb.com.ezproxy.library.uvic.ca/view/article/21902; and Frank Sharman, 'Feudal Copyholder and Industrial Shareholder: The *Dimes* case,' *Journal of Legal History* 10 (1989): 71–90. The decision, in which their lordships consulted all the judges, was unanimous, leaving no doubt about the English law position at the time.

100 Williams, 'Justice Boothby,' 41–2, quoting from the Law Officer's Report, 28 Sept. 1864, reprinted in E.G. Blackmore, *The Law of the Constitution of South Australia* (Adelaide: Government Printer, 1894), 68.

101 Daly to secretary of state for the colonies, Edward Cardwell, 26 Jan. 1865, quoted in Hague, 'Judicial Career of Benjamin Boothby,' 68.

102 Local Courts Act (1861) 25 Vict., No. 15 (SA). The repugnancy related to the courts being able to operate without juries.

103 See *Dawes v. Quarrel* (1865) Pelham Reports 1, excerpted in Bennett and Castles, *Source Book on Australian Legal History*, 183–5.

104 Williams, 'Justice Boothby,' 42.

105 Ibid., 43.

106 *Register*, 25 Sept. 1865.

107 South Australia, 'The Crown Solicitor's Report on Acts and Dicta of His Honor Mr Justice Boothby during May Criminal Sittings, 1866,' in *Proceedings in Supreme Court*, Parl. Paper No. 4 (1866).

108 South Australia, 'Report of the Attorney General to His Excellency the Governor-in-Chief, concerning the Conduct and Proceedings of His Honor Mr Justice Boothby, 26 May 1866,' *Proceedings of Mr Justice Boothby*, Parl. Paper No. 3 (1866).

109 South Australia, *Hansard*, 26 June 1866, 47.

110 South Australia, *Minutes of Proceedings of the Executive Council Relating to the Conduct of Mr Justice Boothby*, Parl. Paper No. 22 (1867), XXX–XXXI, XLIX–XL.

111 Ibid., XXX, LI.

112 South Australia, *Minutes of Proceedings of the Executive Council relating to the Conduct of Mr Justice Boothby*, Parl. Paper No. 22 (1867), LVI–LVII, Carnarvon to Daly, 26 Feb. 1867, referring back to Newcastle's letter of 24 Apr. 1862. Supra text at 202–3, and note 87.

113 Ibid., Sir Frederic Rogers, permanent undersecretary, Colonial Office, to Henry Reeve, Privy Council registrar, 19 Oct. 1866.

114 Williams, 'Justice Boothby,' 45.

115 *Advertiser*, 11 Mar. 1867. In similar vein was a satirical letter sent to the newspaper by 'Spectator' describing Boothby as the 'Quasher General.' Williams, 'Justice Boothby,' 45.
116 South Australia, *Minutes of the Proceedings of the Executive Council relating to the Conduct of Mr Justice Boothby*, Parl. Paper No. 22 (1867), CLXII.
117 Ibid., IV–V, Hanson and Gwynne to Daly, 24 Apr. 1867.
118 Ibid., III–IV, Boucaut to Chief Secretary Ayers, 5 June 1867.
119 Ibid., IV, Ayers to Boothby, 6 June 1867.
120 Williams, 'Justice Boothby,' 47.
121 Ibid., 48.
122 South Australia, *Minutes of Proceedings of the Executive Council relating to the Conduct of Mr Justice Boothby*, Parl. Paper No. 22 (1867), 35.
123 Ibid., CCXXXVIII.
124 Ibid., 68.
125 Ibid., 69. Williams notes that the order was published in a *Gazette Extraordinary* that evening, and that Jason Brook, clerk to Inquiry Counsel Samuel Way, went to Boothby's home to deliver a certified minute of Council and a copy of the order. 'Justice Boothby,' 50.
126 See John B. Hughes in the *South Australian Satirist*, 17 Aug. 1867, 2.
127 *Advertiser*, 22 June 1868, 2. Even the *Register*, 22 June 1868, called for the Boothbyites and anti-Boothbyites to bury the hatchet and 'foreswear their animosities over the corpse of their champion and bugbear.' *Dropsy* was the contemporary term used for what would now be considered *congestive heart failure*.
128 Williams, 'Justice Boothby,' 50.
129 P.A. Howell, 'Saints or Scoundrels? A Reappraisal of Some Notable South Australians with Reflections on Related Issues,' *Journal of Historical Society of South Australia* 7 (1980): 3, at 12.
130 Castles and Harris, *Lawyers and Wayward Whigs*, 126.
131 Text, supra, 201–2. The statement of the law officers had been prefaced by a statement of Frederic Rogers for the Colonial Office in May 1858, pointing to the difficulty of making any more than a 'vague statement' about the extent of repugnancy. Supra, note 8.
132 Castles, 'Benjamin Boothby,' *ADBOL*.
133 Kelley, 'Edward Castres Gwynne,' *ADBOL*.
134 See H.W. Arthurs, *'Without the Law': Administrative Justice and Legal Pluralism in Nineteenth Century England* (Toronto: University of Toronto Press, 1985), 158–60, 200.
135 A good example is John Beverley Robinson, chief justice of Upper Canada, 1829–64. See Brode, *Sir John Beverley Robinson*.

136 Castles and Harris, *Lawmakers and Wayward Whigs*, 118–19.

137 At least four of his nine sons gave him cause to feel proud. William Robinson Boothby was sheriff for a large part of his career; Josiah Boothby served for many years as chief clerk in the Colonial Secretary's Office (essentially the Cabinet office); Benjamin Junior was a public surveyor and engineer; and Thomas was a pastoralist. As we have seen, a fifth, George, may have assisted the family finances by trying to pay off his father's debts.

138 Castles, 'Benjamin Boothby,' *ADBOL*.

139 Elizabeth Olsson, 'The Justice Gone Wrong or the Justice Wronged? The Trials of Mr Justice Boothby' (LL.M. thesis, University of Adelaide, 1998), 34.

140 See chapter 7, 185.

141 Shetreet, *Judges on Trial*, 129–51.

142 See *Memorandum of the Lords of the Council on the Removal of Colonial Judges* (1870) 12 Moo. Indian Appeals, Appendix, 551; 20 E.R. 447. This document sought to clarify the issue of disciplining colonial judges in the wake of the Boothby experience. See chapter 11, 297–9.

143 The odd jurisdictions out were those in southern Africa, such as Cape Colony, that enjoyed responsible government, despite a minority European population.

9: Perils of the Colonial Judiciary: Incubus of Slavery

1 Bridget Brereton, *A History of Modern Trinidad 1783–1962* (London: Heinemann, 1981), 32–51; and James Millette, *Society and Politics in Colonial Trinidad* (London: Zed Books, 1985), 230–66.

2 O'Shaughnessy, *Empire Divided*, 117.

3 For a comprehensive study of a slave regime, see Patterson, *Sociology of Slavery*; and for perspective on the lives of slaves, see Elizabeth Abbott, *Sugar: A Bittersweet History* (Toronto: Penguin Canada, 2008), 75–120. Also Beckles, *A History of Barbados*, 33–5; and Hilary McD. Beckles, 'The "Hub of Empire": The Caribbean and Britain in the Seventeenth Century,' in *The Oxford History of the British Empire: The Origins of Empire: British Overseas Enterprise to the Close of the Seventeenth Century*, ed. Nicholas Canny (Oxford: Oxford University Press, 2001), 218–40, at 231–3.

4 Dunn, *Sugar and Slaves*, 248, and see more generally on the slave laws, ibid., 238–46; and Goveia, *The West Indian Slave Laws of the 18th Century*, 18–36, at 38.

5 See Edward L. Cox, *Free Coloreds in the Slave Societies of St Kitts and Grenada, 1763–1833* (Knoxville, TN: University of Tennessee Press, 1984), 92–110.
6 See chapter 3, 37–8, and Fortunatus Dwarris, *The Substance of the Three Reports* , 436–7, 445–6.
7 See Gad Heuman, 'The British West Indies,' in Porter, *Oxford History of the British Empire: Nineteenth Century*, 470–94, at 474–7.
8 CO 253, vol. 41, 3–5, Lieutenant Governor Farquharson to Lord Goderich, secretary of state for the colonies, 5 Nov. 1832, with proceedings of an investigation into charges against the chief justice, and report of the Colonial Office on the case, 14 Nov. 1832 (5–12).
9 CO 253, vol. 90, no. 2, Report of Court of Inquiry into Charges by Lieutenant Arthur Torrens against Chief Justice Reddie, 1847. As the inquiry found the charges substantiated, Governor Reid, who was based in Barbados, suspended Reddie. CO 253, vol. 95, 178, Reid to Earl Grey, secretary of state for the colonies, 20 Dec. 1847. Grey referred that decision to a committee of the Privy Council, which confirmed the conclusions of the Court of Inquiry. CO 253, vol. 90, no. 2, Grey to Reid, 14 July 1848.
10 See CO 124, vols. 9 and 10, 1855–62, for this developing saga from the Colonial Office end. The Colonial Office first considered that the charges against Temple by the superintendent of British Honduras, Frederick Seymour, should be referred to the Judicial Committee of the Privy Council. However, for reasons that are not entirely clear, the Office itself reviewed the matter. As a result, the charges were considered substantiated (CO 124, vol. 10, 215–45, C. Fortescue, Colonial Office, to Temple, 13 July 1861). Accordingly, the Duke of Newcastle, secretary of state for the colonies, instructed Governor Darling to revoke Temple's appointment (CO 124, vol. 9, 413–15, Newcastle to Darling, 15 Aug. 1861).
11 Articles of Capitulation for the Surrender of the Island of Trinidad 1796, from Papers relating to the Island of Trinidad; CO 295, vol. 26/2, 1811, 94. Some estate development had taken place on the island, after legislation of the Spanish monarch in 1783 offering tracts of land to those of the Roman Catholic faith willing to pledge allegiance to the Spanish Crown. This produced an influx of French planters with their slaves from neighbouring islands. See Brereton, *History of Modern Trinidad*, 13–15.
12 Brereton, *History of Modern Trinidad*, 11–51; and Millette, *Society and Politics*.
13 Manning Ward, *Colonial Self-Government*, 82–123, esp. 82–91; and Brereton, *History of Modern Trinidad*, 40–2. The latter author notes the cautionary effect of the decision of Lord Mansfield in the case of *Campbell v. Hall* (1774) 1 Cowp. 204; 98 E.R. 1045 (KB), that decreed that, once the King had instructed a colonial governor to establish a legislative assembly in a

conquered or ceded territory, the Crown forfeited any further power to legislate for the new colony.

14 Stephen's ideas were set out in *The Crisis of the Sugar Colonies* (London: J. Hatchard, 1802).

15 Brereton, *History of Modern Trinidad*, 34–8.

16 Ibid., 40–7.

17 See chapter 3, 38. Lord Castlereagh had appointed Smith to Grenada in 1805. Millette, *Society and Politics*, 230.

18 CO 295, vol. 20/2, 120–6, Smith to Castlereagh, 28 Mar. 1808.

19 Ibid., 191–2, Smith to Castlereagh, 20 Oct. 1808.

20 Lillian Estelle Fisher, *Viceregal Administration in the Spanish-American Colonies* (Berkeley: University of California Press, 1926), 1–94, 130–81.

21 On 3 Nov. 1808 Smith sent a draft commission to Edward Cooke, undersecretary, Colonial Office. CO 295, vol. 20/2, 201–19.

22 Ibid., 221, V. Gibbs, attorney general, and Thomas Plummer, solicitor general, to Castlereagh, 16 Nov. 1808. The final instructions excluded a role for the chief justice as acting governor. Smith had argued that he should be appointed president of the Governor's Advisory Council. This was conceded subsequently. Millette, *Society and Politics*, 233. Smith's salary was set at £2,000, plus fees on a regulated scale.

23 Millette, *Society and Politics*, 234.

24 CO 295, vol. 21/1, 70, Hislop to Castlereagh, 28 May 1809; and ibid., 110, Hislop to Castlereagh, 1 July 1809. In approving Smith's appointment as chief justice, the Colonial Office had directed Hislop to undertake reforms to facilitate religious education, provide adequate provisions to slaves, secure to slaves all the rights and privileges available to them under Spanish law (by enacting a liberal set of slave laws), and improve the condition of the free people of colour. This agenda of reform was ignored as the governor and chief justice fell out with each other, and Castlereagh was replaced by Lord Liverpool. Millette, *Society and Politics*, 236.

25 Millette, *Society and Politics*, 237.

26 CO 295, vol. 21/1, 74–6, Nihell to Hislop, 27 May 1809; and ibid., Nihell to Castlereagh, 27 May 1809. He was allowed to retain his seat on Council, and appointed an *alcade*.

27 CO 295, vol. 24, 140–6, Smith to Cecil Jenkinson, undersecretary, Colonial Office, 2 Mar. 1810.

28 CO 295, vol. 22/2, 117–24, Smith to Edward Cooke, 28 Oct. 1809.

29 Ibid.

30 Ibid. A group of planters and merchants on the island had moved in a public meeting to send an Address and agent to London requesting that

'the British Constitution' be extended to them. Ibid., 104–7, Alexander Williams, chair, Implementation Committee, to Castlereagh, 12 Sept. 1809.

31 Ibid., 113–16, Smith to Castlereagh, 4 Oct. 1809.

32 Ibid., 117–24, Smith to Edward Cooke, 28 Oct. 1809.

33 Millette, *Society and Politics*, 240.

34 Ibid., 244–9.

35 CO 295, vol. 24, 1810, 128, Acting Governor P.J. Tolley and Smith to secretary of state, Lord Liverpool, 28 Feb. 1810.

36 Ibid., 140–6, Smith to Jenkinson, 2 Mar. 1810.

37 Ibid.

38 See, for example, ibid., 112, Smith to Liverpool, 14 Feb. 1810.

39 Ibid., 140–6, Smith to Jenkinson, 2 Mar. 1810; and 189–96, Smith to Jenkinson, 13 May 1810.

40 Millette, *Society and Politics*, 249–51.

41 The disagreement started civilly enough. See CO 295, vol. 24, 179, Smith to Hislop, 30 Mar. 1810; and ibid., Hislop to Smith, 3 Apr. 1810. The governor made it clear to London that he favoured the introduction of English law into the colony. CO 295, vol. 23/1, 48–9, Hislop to Liverpool, 9 Apr. 1810, and 63–6, 19 Apr.

42 CO 295, vol. 24/2, 209–14, Smith to Hislop, 1 May 1810, 'Letters and Other Documents Relative to the Imprisonment and Discharge of Mathew Gallagher, Printer and Publisher of the Trinidad Courant.' On the Lockhead complaint, see CO 295, vol. 23/1, 279–80, Hislop to Liverpool, 11 May 1810.

43 CO 295, vol. 25/3, 29–34, Extract of Minutes of His Majesty's Council, 27 June 1810.

44 CO 295, vol. 23, 94–7, Extract of Minutes of His Majesty's Council Held by Summons at the Government House, 18 May 1810, with speech of Smith in dissent. On the lobbying of merchants, see CO 295, vol. 24, 123 (Minutes of Meeting of the Merchants Trading to the Island of Trinidad and Others Interested in That Colony Held at the City of London on 8 February, 1810), John Inglis to Liverpool, 16 Feb. 1810.

45 Reference in the *Trinidad Courant* for 12 May 1810 to a meeting of William Knox and Lord Liverpool, see CO 295, vol. 24, 217.

46 Marryat was a successful London merchant. Although not born in the West Indies, he had spent his youth in Grenada, and his sympathies lay with the merchants and planters who operated in the region. Millette, *Society and Politics*, 227.

47 The battle between the two men had evolved into one about who had the overarching authority over and the final word in the administration of

justice. See CO 295, vol. 25/3, 132–3, Smith to Hislop, 4 Sept. 1810; and at 133–4, the governor's response, 22 Sept. 1810.

48 Ibid., 23–7, 28 June 1810; CO 295, vol. 24, Smith to Jenkinson, 16 May 1810, complaining about gubernatorial pressure on him in the Gallagher case; CO 295, vol. 25/3, 23–7, Smith to Jenkinson, 28 June 1810, complaining of the governor and Council's treatment of him as a judge. CO 295, vol. 23/1, 230–2.

49 CO 295, vol. 25/3, 96–106, report of Stephen to Liverpool, 1 Sept. 1810.

50 CO 295, vol. 24, 1810, Hislop to Liverpool, 6 Dec. 1810.

51 CO 295, vol. 27/1, 37–44, extract from the Minutes of His Majesty's Council, 5 Mar. 1811.

52 CO 295, vol. 26, 1811/2, 3–4, Smith to Liverpool, 3 Mar. 1811.

53 CO 295, vol. 27, 232 et seq., including Sanderson's inflammatory letter to Liverpool, 3 Jan. 1811, 243–6.

54 For Hislop's order, see CO 295, vol. 27/1, 340, 19 Mar. 1811.

55 That Smith has decided to leave the island in secret seems evident from reports to the governor and Council by witnesses about his sighting in rural Trinidad and then Grenada. See CO 295, vol. 27/1, 99–100, Extract from the Minutes of His Majesty's Council Held by Adjournment at the Government House, 17 April 1811.

56 Petition of John Sanderson in response to charges made against him by Smith, see CO 295, vol. 27, 243–6, Sanderson to Liverpool, 3 Jan. 1811. For biographical detail on James Stephen Sr, see Patrick C. Lipscomb III, 'James Stephen,' *ODNB*, http://www.oxforddnb.com.ezproxy.library.uvic.ca/view/article/26373?dicPos=1.

57 Brereton, *History of Modern Trinidad*, 40–2.

58 CO 295, vol. 23/1, 26–7, 15 Mar. 1810, Liverpool to Hislop, requesting the governor's views and those of other respectable members of the community.

59 See CO 295, vol. 23, 94–7, Liverpool to Hislop, 27 Nov. 1810. For Smith's sympathetic attitude to the free coloured population of the island, see, for example, CO 295, vol. 24, 189–96, Smith to Jenkinson, 13 May 1810.

60 Smandych, '"To Soften the Extreme Rigour of Their Bondage."'

61 The initial response of the Colonial Office that he be fully reinstated to office (this was not possible, as he had already left the island) was contained in a letter of 25 May 1811 from Liverpool to the governor, referred to in CO 295, vol. 27/1, 181, Governor William Monroe to Liverpool, 4 Aug. 1811

62 The failure of Smith's appeal against his treatment by Hislop to the Privy Council is mentioned in CO 295, vol. 30/2, 8–9, Governor Ralph Woodford

to Lord Bathurst, secretary of state for the colonies, 3 Aug. 1813. See also Manning, *British Colonial Government after the American Revolution*, 389, quoting from the Privy Council Register, CXCIV, 363.

63 Manning, *British Colonial Government*, 471.

64 CO 43, vol. 40/3, 51–3, Cooke to Thorpe, 18 June 1807.

65 See ibid., 52–3, Castlereagh to Gore; ibid., 49–50, 19 June 1810, stressing that Thorpe should be seen only as having blotted his copybook in Upper Canada.

66 CO 267, vol. 24, Sierra Leone, Thorpe to Castlereagh, 16 Feb. 1808.

67 Christopher Fyfe, *A History of Sierra Leone* (Oxford: Oxford University Press, 1962), 13–104; and John Peterson, *Province of Freedom: A History of Sierra Leone 1787–1970* (Evanston, IL: Northwestern University Press, 1969), 17–44.

68 On the Nova Scotian story, see Simon Schama, *Rough Crossings: Britain, the Slaves and the American Revolution* (Toronto: Viking Canada, 2006); and James St G. Walker, *The Black Loyalists: The Search for a Promised Land in Nova Scotia and Sierra Leone* (New York: Africana Publishing, 1976).

69 Macaulay, a campaigner against slavery after witnessing it first hand as an overseer on an estate in Jamaica, arrived in Sierra Leone in 1793 as a councillor, became acting governor in 1794, and was governor between 1796 and 1799. Fyfe, *History of Sierra Leone*, 48–77.

70 Peterson, *Province of Freedom*, 27–33. When Macaulay as governor undertook to carry through on the promise, his intention of imposing quit rents on the land prompted a new round of resistance. Ibid., 31–2.

71 Ibid., 33–5.

72 Ibid., 35–6.

73 Act for the Abolition of the Slave Trade (1807) 48 Geo. III, 1st Session, c. 36.

74 Wayne Ackerson, *The African Institution (1807–1827) and the Anti-Slavery Movement in Great Britain* (Lewiston: Edwin Mellen, 2005), 5–26.

75 Ibid., 55–67.

76 Ibid., 67.

77 Peterson, *Province of Freedom*, 54–61.

78 See, for example, CO 267, vol. 28, n.p., Thorpe to Robert Peel, parliamentary undersecretary, Colonial Office, 19 Mar. 1810, in which he notes that he understands that he is waiting until the Charter of Justice is finalized.

79 Ackerson, *African Institution*, 121, referencing Zachary Macaulay, *A Letter to His Royal Highness the Duke of Gloucester, President of the African Institution, from Zachary Macaulay* (London: Ellerton and Henderson, 1815), 1–5.

80 Macaulay, *Letter to His Royal Highness*, 4–5.

81 Fyfe, *History of Sierra Leone*, 116.

82 Ibid.
83 Slave Felony Act (1811) 51 Geo. III, c. 23.
84 Ackerson, *African Institution*, 89, referring to the *Seventh Report of the Directors of the African Institution*, 23–4.
85 Fyfe, *History of Sierra Leone*, 120.
86 Ibid.
87 CO 267, vol. 34, no. 12, Governor Charles Maxwell to Bathurst, 29 May 1812; ibid., 25, Maxwell to Bathurst, 25 Nov. 1812.
88 CO 267, vol. 35, n.p., Thorpe to Colonial Office, 8 May 1812.
89 CO 268, vol. 19, 1, Bathurst to Maxwell, 11 May 1813.
90 CO 268, vol. 19, 16, Henry Goulburn, undersecretary, Colonial Office, to Thorpe, 18 Jan. 1814.
91 Goulburn had written Thorpe, July 1814, enjoining him to return to Sierra Leone with all haste, CO 268. vol. 19, 18.
92 Fyfe, *History of Sierra Leone*, 121.
93 CO 268, vol. 19, n.p., Goulburn to Thorpe, 22 Mar. 1815.
94 Ibid.
95 Ibid.
96 Robert Thorpe, *Letter to William Wilberforce ... Containing Remarks on the Reports of Sierra Leone Company and African Institution with Hints Respecting the Means by Which a Universal Abolition of the Slave Trade Might Be Carried into Effect* (London: F.C. and J. Rivington, 1815).
97 Ibid., 1–6.
98 Ibid., 40–5, 60–5.
99 Ibid., 27–33.
100 Ibid., 46–7.
101 Ibid., 49–51.
102 Ibid., 53, 18–20.
103 Macaulay, *Letter to the Duke of Gloucester*.
104 Ibid., 17, 27–9.
105 *Special Report of the Directors of the African Institution Made at the Annual General Meeting on 12th April, 1815 Respecting the Allegations Made in a Pamphlet Entitled 'A Letter to William Wilberforce, Esq. & Etc. by R. Thorpe Esq.'* (London: J. Hatchard, 1815).
106 Robert Thorpe, *Preface to the Fourth Edition of a Letter to William Wilberforce, Esq., M.P. Containing a Reply to a Letter from Zachary Macaulay Esq., to the Duke of Gloucester* (London: F.C. and J. Rivington, 1815).
107 Ibid., liii.
108 Ibid., lv.
109 Robert Thorpe, *A Reply 'Point by Point' to the Special Report of the Directors of the African Institution* (London: F.C. and J. Rivington, 1815).

110 Ibid., 49–54.
111 Ackerson, *African Institution*, 124–5; and Knapland, *James Stephen and the British Colonial System*, 96–7.
112 See, for example, Gilbert Mathison, *A Short Review of the Reports of the African Institution and of the Controversy with Dr Thorpe Etc* (London: William Stockdale, 1816). Fyfe, *History of Sierra Leone*, 122, reveals that James Marryat, the English MP, active in the planter lobby for Trinidad, supra 224, wrote several tracts in which he relied in part on the critiques by Thorpe. There is nothing to suggest in all of this that Thorpe's sympathies lay with slavery interests.
113 Fyfe, *History of Sierra Leone*, 121.
114 Ibid., 122.
115 Ackerson, *African Institution*, 154–5.
116 Ibid., 122–3. See also ibid., 194–230, on the demise of the organization in the 1820s and his conclusions on its mixed record.
117 Patterson, 'Robert Thorpe,' *DCBOL*.
118 Hague, *Sir John Jeffcott*, 1–50.
119 George Brizan, *Grenada: Island of Conflict; From Amerindians to People's Revolution 1498–1979* (London: Zed Books, 1984), 59–78.
120 Ibid., 104–5.
121 Ibid., 104.
122 Ibid., 83.
123 Ibid., 104.
124 Chapter 6, 130–7.
125 Currey, *Brothers Bent*, 151–57. See also CO 101, vol. 59, Bent to Goulburn, 1 Sept. 1819, accepting position as chief justice of Grenada.
126 On the British government's earlier disapproval of this practice in Grenada, see CO 101, vol. 18, 1814, 208, Bathurst to Governor Sir Charles Shepley, 25 July 1814. Despite the instructions of the minister that the latter reinstate the then chief justice to the Council, the practice seems to have continued until the early 1830s. See CO 101, vol. 61, 5, Governor Riale to Bathurst, 11 Apr. 1821, raising a question about the legitimacy of excluding Bent from the Council.
127 *Re Bent*, (1832) 18 Privy Council Indian and Colonial Appeals (P.C.I.C.A.).
128 Brizan, *Grenada, Island of Conflict*, 105.
129 CO 101, vol. 68, 102–3, An Act for Granting a Salary to the Reverend Anthony O'Hannan, Roman Catholic Clergyman in This Government, 18 Nov. 1828 (Gren.).
130 Edward L. Cox, *Free Coloureds in the Slave Societies of St Kitts and Grenada, 1763–1833* (Knoxville, TN: University of Tennessee Press, 1984), 117–18, 125.

131 Brizan, *Grenada Island of Conflict*, 106.

132 See CO 101, vol. 72, 32, O'Hannan to Right Rev. Bishop Macdonnell, 3 July 1829, announcing intention to resign; and ibid., 33, Macdonell to President Andrew Houstoun, acting governor of Grenada, 3 July 1829, indicating that he has accepted the resignation.

133 See *Re Bent, Respondent's Brief*, Appendix, No. IV, 1, Macdonnell to Houstoun, 6 July 1829, outlining his plan.

134 Ibid., 2, which reveals that the delegation arrived in Grenada on 17 July. The governor, Sir James Campbell, was at this time on leave in Britain.

135 CO 101, vol. 72, Vicar General Le Goff to Houstoun, 18 July 1829. On the removal of the licence, see *Re Bent, Respondent's Brief*, Appendix, No. VIII, 4, J.B. Gaff, government secretary to O'Hannan, 20 July 1829.

136 *Re Bent, Respondent's Brief*, 2, request of Attorney General Browne for a General Meeting of Magistrates to investigate O'Hannan's 'outrageous conduct,' 24 July 1829.

137 *Re Bent, Respondent's Brief*, Appendix, No. IX, 4, Bent's order to Provost Marshall General, 24 July 1829, summoning the priests to appear before him. The implication of Bent's characterization of the trio was that they were in breach of the Vagabond's Act of the island.

138 Bent alleged that Browne had assaulted him, although there are conflicting accounts of what happened from the supporters of the two men. For the indictment brought by Bent, see *Re Bent, Respondent Brief*, Additional Appendix, No. II, 2–3. The grand jury, drawn from the island's elite, refused to issue a bill.

139 CO 101, vol. 68, 181, Houstoun to Bent, 26 July 1829.

140 *Re Bent, Respondent's Brief*, Appendix, No. IV, 6, Bent to Houstoun, 26 July 1829.

141 Ibid., No. XV, 7, Houstoun to Bent, 27 July 1829.

142 Ibid., No. XVI, 8, Bent to Houstoun, 28 July 1829.

143 CO 101, vol. 68, 179–80, Bent to Sir George Murray, secretary of state for the colonies, 31 July 1829.

144 Houstoun had advised the Colonial Office of his actions by a letter dated 1 Aug. 1829 to Murray, CO 101, vol. 72, 1–8. Murray's response is contained in *Re Bent, Appellant's Brief*, Murray to Houstoun, 30 Sept. 1829.

145 This is an interesting assertion, given the treatment accorded to John Walpole Willis earlier the same year.

146 *Re Bent, Respondent's Brief*, Appendix, No. VI, 5, Browne to Houstoun, 20 Nov. 1829; for that of the solicitor general, see ibid., Additional Appendix, No. VII, 6, Henry Otway to Houstoun, 21 Nov. 1829.

147 Houstoun to Murray, 3 Dec. 1829, ibid., Additional Appendix, No. I, 1; for Resolutions of the Legislative Council and the House of Assembly, see ibid., 5–7, 18 Dec. 1829. For an example of Manning's lobbying, see his letter to Murray, 15 Mar. 1830, CO 101, vol. 72, 551–66.
148 An Act to Prevent Persons Officiating as Roman Catholic Priests in This Colony, without Due Authority for That Purpose (19 Dec. 1829) (Gren.), subsequently disallowed by London. The commitment was made 15 Feb. 1830, *Re Bent, Respondent's Brief*, Appendix, No. XIX, 9, and the recalcitrant cleric imprisoned, 26 Feb. 1830.
149 Bent issued a writ of habeas corpus 27 Feb. 1830 for the release of O'Hannan from jail. O. Rowley's Secretarial Minute, ibid., Appendix, No. XX, 11.
150 Bent issued a fresh warrant to apprehend Father Sanchez on 1 Dec. 1829, ibid., Appendix, No. XVII.
151 Ibid., Additional Appendix, No. V, 4–6, Bent to Murray, 2 Jan. 1830.
152 Ibid., 7–8, 2 Feb. 1830.
153 Contained in speech of government secretary in the House of Assembly, 20 Mar. 1830, referencing the statement of the chief justice in court on 2 Feb. 1830, *Re Bent, Appellant's Brief*, 5.
154 Ibid., Appendix, No. XVIII, 8, Senior Assistant Judge Hoyes to Houstoun, 3 Feb. 1830. Tension had developed between the chief justice and his associates over their failure to call together a grand jury to consider possible criminal prosecutions in cases that were piling up, the assistants claiming that this was the job of the attorney general who had resigned and Houstoun had not replaced.
155 Bent to Houstoun, 15 Feb. 1830, complaining of this attack on him, reproduced in ibid., 8.
156 Ibid., Appendix, No. XXI, 11, Magistrates Stephenson, Todd, and MacEwan to Houstoun, 27 Mar. 1830.
157 Murray had written to Houstoun on 4 Mar. 1830 reasserting the tenor of his letter of 30 Sept. 1829, and stressing that he had to assume that the conduct of a colonial judge 'is regulated by upright motives and by a correct view of his duty, unless the contrary be proved.' *Re Bent, Appellant's Brief*, 3–4.
158 CO 101, vol. 68, 144, Houstoun to Bent, 1 Apr. 1830.
159 Ibid., 145, Bent to Houstoun, 1 Apr. 1830.
160 Referred to in *Re Bent, Appellant's Brief*, 6, Murray to Sir James Campbell, governor of Grenada, 21 June 1830.
161 CO 101, vol. 72, 1830, 499–550, report by James Stephen to Horace Twiss, undersecretary, Colonial Office, 2 Feb. 1830. Secretary of State Murray

sent a letter to Campbell, 30 Apr. 1830, inter alia stressing that Bent was right on the law in his actions, although deprecating his intemperate language and lack of discretion on the bench, and expressing his chagrin that the jurist had lost the confidence of the influential members of Grenadan society. *Re Bent, Respondent's Brief,* Additional Appendix, No. X, 9–10.

162 CO 101, vol. 74, 1830, 442–52, Murray to Campbell, 21 June 1830.

163 Bent applauded the policy of appointing independent men from outside the colonial bars, to be judges in the West Indian colonies. *Re Bent, Appellant's Brief,* 1.

164 Ibid., 6.

165 Ibid., 7.

166 Ibid., 7–8.

167 *Re Bent, Respondent's Brief,* 2.

168 Ibid., 6.

169 Ibid., 11–12.

170 Ibid., 13.

171 Ibid., Report of the Privy Council in the Case of Chief Justice Jeffery Hart Bent, 15 Feb. 1832. Grenada was to prove the scene of another attempt by the island's elite to rid itself of an uncooperative jurist, Chief Justice John Sanderson, previously the scourge of George Smith. In this instance the Privy Council received a petition from the island's House of Assembly for the judge's amoval in 1847 and exercised its original jurisdiction in the matter (see *In the Matter of the Representatives of the Island and Grenada and Chief Justice John Sanderson* (1847) 6 Moore P.C. 38; 13 E.R. 596). The evidence heard suggested to their lordships that the judge had indeed engaged in intemperate and in several instances illegal conduct while on the bench (see (1847) 42 P.C.I.C.A.). The Judicial Committee, however, concluded that the judge should not be removed from office. Apart from the mistreatment of the magistrates, all the other incidents were of some years' vintage. The Council asserted that, as Sanderson's slate had, with the exception of the magistrates' complaints, been clean ever since, and as the action on the magistrates fell within his judicial duties, there was not a sufficient basis for dismissing him from office.

172 Annotation at the head of the *Re Bent, Appellant's Brief,* 1.

173 Currey, *Brothers Bent,* 163–4. In St Lucia, says Currey, 'once more that restless and wounding pen was busy. On 5 January 1835, the Governor forwarded to the Colonial Office "a quite uncalled for" memorandum from Mr Bent accusing the Legislative Council of "having acted interestedly."'

10: Perils of the Colonial Judiciary: Stain of Slavery

1 Heuman, 'British West Indies,' 470–93, at 476–7. The operative legislation was An Act for the Abolition of Slavery throughout the British Colonies; for Promoting the Industry of the Manumitted Slaves; and for Compensating the Persons Hitherto Entitled to the Services of such Slaves (1833) 3 & 4 Will. IV, c. 73. Although sentiment among Colonial Office officials, especially James Stephen Jr, was against both compensation and apprenticeship, the secretary of state at the operative time, E.G. Smith Stanley, was a strong proponent of placating the planters. William A. Green, *British Slave Emancipation: The Sugar Colonies and the Great Experiment 1830–1865* (Oxford: Clarendon, 1976), 118–21. It was the compensation decision that induced Thomas Macaulay, Zachary's son, to resign his parliamentary seat and head for India.

2 Heuman, 'British West Indies,' 476–7.

3 Mary Turner, 'The British Caribbean, 1823–1838: The Transition from Slave to Free Legal Status,' in *Masters, Servants and Magistrates in Britain & the Empire, 1562–1955*, ed. Douglas Hay and Paul Craven (Durham: University of North Carolina Press, 2004), 303–22, at 305–13; Mary Turner, 'Modernizing Slavery: Investigating the Legal Dimension,' *New West Indian Guide / Nieuwe West Indische Gids* 73 (1999): 5–26, at 17–25.

4 Green, *British Slave Emancipation*, 129–61.

5 Philip J. McLewin, *Power and Economic Change: The Response to Emancipation in Jamaica and British Guiana, 1840–1865* (New York: Garland Publishing, 1987), 146.

6 Turner, 'Modernizing Slavery,' 23–5.

7 By an Act to Amend the Act for the Abolition of Slavery in the British Colonies (1838) I Vict., c. 19 for Crown colonies and local legislation in the representative possessions.

8 Heuman, 'British West Indies,' 478–9.

9 An Act to Make Provision for the Better Administration of Justice in Certain of His Majesty's West Indian Colonies (1836) 7 Will. IV, c. 17. See also William Green, 'James Stephen and British West Indian Policy,' *Caribbean Studies* 13 (1974): 33–56 at 42–3.

10 Ibid., 44–6.

11 Heuman, 'British West Indies, 480–2.

12 Green, *British Slave Emancipation*, 297–8, 300.

13 Ibid., 229–44.

14 Heuman, 'British West Indies,' 482–5.

15 Green, *British Slave Emancipation*, 261–94. Indian immigration had been

introduced in British Guiana in 1838 to satisfy the need of John Gladstone (William's father) and several of his planter colleagues. London quickly abandoned it in the face of anti-slavery outrage. Lord Stanley revived it in 1844.

16 Walton Look Lai, *Indentured Labour, Caribbean Sugar: Chinese and Immigrants to the British West Indies, 1838–1918* (Baltimore: John Hopkins University Press, 1993), 4–7; Ron Ramdin, *Arising from Bondage: A History of the Indo-Caribbean People* (London: I.B. Tauris, 2000), 1–131.

17 Look Lai, *Indentured Labour*, 50–86.

18 Ibid., 87–153; Basdeo Mangru, *A History of East Indian Resistance on the Guyana Sugar Estates* (Lewiston: Edward Mellon, 1996), 66–100; and Mangru, *Indenture and Abolition: Sacrifice and Survival on the Guyanese Sugar Plantations* (Toronto: TSAR Publications, 1993), 17–42.

19 See Look Lai, *Indentured Labour*, 302, table 33.

20 Green, *British Slave Emancipation*, 77–9.

21 Mangru, *Indenture and Abolition*, 16. For a sense of how pervasive the political and economic control of the plantocracy was, see Brian L. Moore, *Race, Power and Social Segmentation in Colonial Society: Guyana after Slavery, 1838–1891* (New York: Gordon & Beach, 1987), 61.

22 Look Lai, *Indentured Labour*, 126–9.

23 Ibid., 52.

24 Mangru, 'The Hincks–Beaumont Imbroglio,' 99–114.

25 CO 112, vol. 37, Duke of Newcastle, secretary of state for the colonies, to Governor Hincks, 20 Mar. 1863. Beaumont's experience and credentials as a lawyer are obscure. He does not merit an entry in the *Oxford Dictionary of National Biography*. Apart from a book on bills of sale, he had published two pamphlets during the 1850s, referring to himself as a barrister of Lincoln's Inn, one advocating the repeal of law preventing marriage with a deceased's wife's sister and the other in support of British policy and action in China during the second Opium War: *Marriage with a Deceased Wife's Sister Considered in a Letter Addressed to the Right Hon. Lord Ellesmere D.C.L.* (London: Houston & Stoneman, 1851); *What Is Lord Elgin to Do? The Canton Dispute and Our Relations with China Considered* (London: Longman Brown, 1857).

26 Joseph Beaumont, *The Life of the Rev. Joseph Beaumont* (London, 1856), 113–14.

27 Ronald Stewart Longley, *Sir Francis Hincks: A Study of Canadian Politics, Railways and Finance in the Nineteenth Century* (Toronto: University of Toronto Press, 1943), 332–3.

28 Ibid. See CO 112, vol. 37, 142, Frederick Rogers, permanent undersecre-

tary, Colonial Office, to Hincks, 30 Mar. 1863. The incestuous relationship between the magistracy in British Guiana is seen in an undated survey of their political and commercial connections in the 1860s (in the Rhodes House Library, Oxford, MSS Empire, 1, G 38).

29 William G. Ormsby, 'Sir Francis Hincks,' *DCBOL*, http://www.biographi.ca/009004-119.01-e.php?&id_nbr=5583&&PHPSESSID=akoigii6oq92vol3aet1fvdino. See also Paul Romney, '"The Ten Thousand Pound Job": Political Corruption, Equitable Jurisdiction and the Public Interest in Upper Canada 1852–6,' in Flaherty, *Essays in the History of Canadian Law*, 2:143–99.

30 Longley, *Sir Francis Hincks*, 214–41.

31 Mangru, 'Hincks–Beaumont Imbroglio,' 101. Hincks's reputation as 'the most able and powerful man in the country at present,' in the view of the governor of Canada, Lord Elgin, may have submerged any doubts created by his fiscal manipulations (Longley, *Sir Francis Hincks*, 306).

32 See Longley, *Sir Francis Hincks*, 308–6 for the Barbados period.

33 Ibid., 330, referencing CO 111, vol. 337, Winter to Newcastle, 6 Oct. 1862.

34 Ibid., 100–1.

35 Ibid.

36 CO 111, vol. 342, no.199, Hincks to Newcastle, 17 Dec. 1863.

37 Newcastle to Governor Keate of Trinidad, 7 Oct. 1862, In the Matter of the Address and Memorial to Her Majesty of the Court of Policy of British Guiana, Praying Her Majesty to Remove His Honour Chief Justice Beaumont from the bench of That Colony (*Re Beaumont*), *Petitioners' Case*, Evidence in Support, No. XCI, (1868) 68 Privy Council Indian and Colonial Appeals (P.C.I.C.A) 100–1.

38 CO 111, vol. 345, no. 80, Hincks to Cardwell, 21 Apr. 1864.

39 CO 112, vol. 38, no. 30, 29, Cardwell to Hincks, 26 May 1864.

40 CO 111, vol. 346, no. 109, Hincks to Cardwell, 23 June 1864, reporting on the dispute; and ibid., vol. 347, no. 122, Hincks to Cardwell, 20 July 1864, enclosing an Order in Council on the matter dated 3 Apr. 1864, confirming the power of the governor and Court of Policy to regulate the offices of government, including that of court registrar. For London's favourable response, see CO 112, vol. 38, no. 101, 57, Cardwell to Hincks, 31 Oct. 1864.

41 CO 111, vol. 347, no. 125, Hincks to Cardwell, 23 July 1864; and CO 112, vol. 38, no. 94, Cardwell to Hincks, 10 Oct. 1864.

42 Mangru, 'Hincks–Beaumont Imbroglio,' 102.

43 CO 111, vol. 347, 1864, no. 126, Hincks to Cardwell, 23 July 1864, enclosing letter to him from Beaumont of 2 July 1864.

44 Ibid., Lucie Smith to Hincks, 21 July 1864.

45 CO 112, vol. 38, no. 81, 48, Cardwell to Hincks, 31 Aug. 1864.
46 CO 112, vol. 38, no. 109, Beaumont to Rogers, 3 Oct. 1864.
47 See CO 112, vol. 38, no. 96, 110–11, Cardwell to Hincks, 13 Oct. 1864.
48 Mangru, 'Hincks–Beaumont Imbroglio' 102, referencing CO 111, vol. 347, Rogers to Beaumont, 29 Sept. 1864.
49 CO 111, vol. 348, no. 182, Hincks to Cardwell, 22 Nov. 1864.
50 CO 112, vol. 36, no. 138, 93, Cardwell to Hincks, 3 Jan. 1865.
51 Hincks transmitted the Ordinance, No. 3 of 1865, An Ordinance to Explain and Amend the Law relating to Gaol Delivery and for Other Purposes (BG), to Cardwell, CO 111, vol. 50, no. 40, 7 Mar. 1865.
52 *Re Beaumont, Respondent's Brief*, Appendix, No. XVII, 53–5, Roundell Palmer and R.P. Collier to Cardwell, 7 June 1865. Cardwell indicated approval of the Ordinance: ibid., 14 June 1865.
53 CO 111, vol. 348, no. 196, Hincks to Cardwell, 22 Dec. 1864, with enclosed letter to him from Beaumont, 8 Dec. 1864; CO 111, vol. 350, no. 91, Beaumont to Hincks, 11 Feb. 1865.
54 CO 112, vol. 38. no. 145, 17, Cardwell to Hincks, 18 Jan. 1865.
55 Mangru, 'Hincks–Beaumont Imbroglio,' 103–4.
56 Ramdin, *Arising from Bondage*, 58–61.
57 G. William Des Voeux, *My Colonial Service in British Guiana, St Lucia, Trinidad, Fiji, Australia, Newfoundland and Hong Kong with Interludes* (London: John Murray, 1903), 1:122.
58 Ibid.
59 Ibid.
60 Ibid., 1:124–6.
61 See Mangru, 'Hincks–Beaumont Imbroglio,' 104.
62 Ibid.
63 Ibid., 105.
64 *Re Beaumont, Petitioner's Case*, Evidence in Support, No. L, 51–4, Beaumont to Cardwell, 26 July 1865.
65 Mangru, 'Hincks–Beaumont Imbroglio,' 104.
66 CO 111, vol. 352, no. 7, 10–11, Campbell to Beaumont, 25 July 1865.
67 Ibid., no. 13, 13, statement of chief justice in the Supreme Court of Justice, Demerara, 28 July 1865.
68 CO 111, vol. 352, no. 128, n.p., Hincks to Colonial Office, 5 Aug. 1865.
69 CO 111, vol. 353, no. 243, 1–10, acting government secretary to Beaumont, 9 Aug. 1865.
70 CO 111, vol. 352, no. 129, 1–53, Hincks to Cardwell, 21 Aug.1865.
71 CO 111, vol. 353, no. 243, 131–6, Beaumont's answer to charges against him, 9 Aug. 1865.

72 Mangru, 'Hincks–Beaumont Imbroglio,' 106–7.
73 CO 112, vol. 38, no. 297, 320–36, Cardwell to Hincks, 17 Nov. 1865. Beaumont had argued his case to Cardwell in a missive dated 21 Aug. 1865, CO 111, vol. 352, no. 130, 1–43.
74 Here Cardwell referred to the case of Chief Justice John Sanderson of Grenada in 1845, as providing a precedent. See chapter 9, note 171.
75 *Creole*, 25 Dec. 1865; *Guiana Times*, 26 Dec. 1865. The latter actually demanded Hincks's resignation.
76 *Re Beaumont, Petitioners' Case*, Appendix, No. XXII. Excerpt from *Creole*, 27 Dec. 1865, 'Speech of the Governor in the Court of Policy to-day.'
77 Hincks admitted that Beaumont enjoyed the support of over half of the population.
78 *Re Beaumont, Respondent's Case*, Appendix, No. XXIII, 69–72, Beaumont to Cardwell, 29 Dec. 1865.
79 Longley, *Sir Francis Hincks*, 336–9. Hincks had received praise from the Duke of Newcastle for his important and well-conceived initiative.
80 Mangru, 'Hincks–Beaumont Imbroglio,' 108, referencing *Creole*, 4 Dec. 1865.
81 See CO 111, vol. 356, no. 55, 1–41, Hincks to Cardwell, 22 Mar. 1866.
82 *Re Beaumont, Respondent's Case*, Appendix, No. XXIX, 76–7, Hincks to Cardwell, 5 Apr. 1866.
83 An annotation to the original of this communication (probably penned by Permanent Undersecretary Frederic Rogers) reflects this feeling.
84 *Re Beaumont, Petitioners' Case*, Appendix, No. XVIII, A, 25–6, 29 Mar. 1866, Articles in the 'Colonist' Newspaper.
85 Article in *Colonist*, 2 Apr. 1866.
86 McDermott was unsuccessful in an appeal to the Judicial Committee on the procedural grounds that the Supreme Court, a court of record, had confined him for contempt. As the exercise of the power was discretionary, it was not the subject of an appeal. *McDermott v. Judges of British Guiana* (1868) L.R. 2 P.C. 341 (BG), per Lord Chelmsford at 359–64. Interestingly, that same year another panel of the JCPC, in reviewing an order by the chief justice of Hong Kong fining a barrister for contempt for alleged disrespect to the court, 'reported' rather giving a judgment, that an order for contempt was legitimate only when the grounds were precisely stated and he was given a chance to defend himself. As those elements had been lacking on the facts, the order was set aside and the fine remitted. *Re Pollard* (1868) L.R. 2 P.C. 106 (HK) per the Court at 120–1.
87 *Re Beaumont, Petitioners' Case*, Evidence in Support, No. LXXX, 82–3, Beaumont to acting government secretary, 21 Apr. 1866.

88 CO 111, vol. 357, no. 72, 1–24, Hincks to Cardwell, 7 Apr. 1866, enclosing the letter from the judges, ibid., 27–34, 4 Apr. 1866, including *inter alia* a complaint of failure by the governor to order the prosecution of the publishers of libels against the Supreme Court.

89 Ibid., 24 et seq., comment of Rogers on this correspondence and enclosed materials.

90 On 5 May 1866, Hincks forwarded the lead memorial to the Colonial Office. CO 111, vol. 357, no. 99, n.p.

91 Memorials of 12 and 16 May 1866, included with letter Hincks to Cardwell, 23 May 1866, CO 111, vol. 358, no. 121.

92 Mangru, 'Hincks–Beaumont Imbroglio,' 110, referencing CO 111, vol. 358, Taylor's minute, 18 June 1866.

93 CO 111, vol. 359, no. 115, Hincks to Cardwell, 7 July 1866.

94 CO 111, vol. 364, no. 126, n.p., Lieutenant Governor Mundy to the Duke of Buckingham and Chandos, secretary of state for the colonies, 11 Sept. 1867.

95 Mangru, 'Hincks–Beaumont Imbroglio,' 110. The cases were *Seewootahul v. Menzies* and *Field v. Sohun* respectively.

96 *Re Beaumont, Petitioner's Case.*

97 CO 112, vol. 40, no. 237, Duke of Buckingham and Chandos, to Hincks, 16 July 1868, and 'Government Notice,' Official Gazette [Extraordinary] of British Guiana, vol. 4, 6 Aug. 1868, quoting from the advice of the Council.

98 See Julie Evans, *Edward Eyre: Race and Colonial Government* (Dunedin, NZ: University of Otago Press, 2005), esp. 99–150; Rande Kostal, *A Jurisprudence of Power: Victorian Empire and the Rule of Law* (Oxford: Oxford University Press, 2005).

99 Heuman, 'British West Indies,' 487–8.

100 Ibid., 491–2. There were, of course, counter-narratives. See, for example, the remarkable J.J. Thomas, *Froudacity: West Indian Fables by James Anthony Froude* (1889; repr., London: New Beacon Books, 1969).

101 Des Voeux, *My Colonial Service*, 123.

102 Beaumont's major antagonist, Hincks, did not have his governorship renewed at the end of his term in 1868 but returned to an active political life in Canada as a member of Sir John A. Macdonald's Dominion Conservative government as minister of finance. Longley, *Sir Francis Hincks*, 347–82.

103 Joseph Beaumont, *The New Slavery: An Account of the Indian and Chinese Immigration to British Guiana* (London: W. Ridgeway, 1871).

104 Ibid., 14.

105 Mangru, 'Hincks–Beaumont Imbroglio,' 111–12.
106 British Guiana, *The Inquiry as to the Treatment of Immigrants* and *The Dispatch of the Secretary of State and Mr Des Voeux's Letter* (Demerara: The Colonist Office, Georgetown, 1870), MSS Empire, 18, G 38, held in the Rhodes House Library, University of Oxford.
107 Isaac Dookhan, 'The Elusive Nirvana: Indian Immigrants in Guyana and the Des Voeux Commission 1870–1871,' *Revista/Review Interamericana* 17 (1988): 54–89, at 85–9. In the main, however, the system of labour regulation, and planters' control of it, continued.
108 The life of Gorrie in these far-flung colonies is the subject of a fine biography: Brereton, *Law, Justice and Empire.* I have drawn heavily on that work in dealing with his story, prior to and during his sojourn in Trinidad and Tobago.
109 Ibid., 32–65.
110 Ibid., 318–26.
111 Ibid., 83–5. On Gordon's career, see Mark Francis, 'Arthur Charles Hamilton Gordon' *ODNB,* http://www.oxforddnb.com.ezproxy.library.uvic.ca/view/article/33459.
112 Brereton, *Law, Justice and Empire,* 69–71. On Mauritius in the nineteenth century, see also J.K. Chapman, *The Career of A.H. Gordon, First Lord Stanmore* (Toronto: University of Toronto Press, 1964), 102–54.
113 Brereton, *Law, Justice and Empire,* 71.
114 Ibid., 71, 89–90. For the Report of the Police Inquiry Committee (1872), penned by Gorrie, see CO 167, vol. 543, no. 147 (enclosure), Gordon to Lord Kimberley, secretary of state for the colonies, 5 Feb. 1872.
115 Brereton, *Law, Justice and Empire,* 74–8.
116 Ibid., 88–98. The Report of the Mauritius Commission (modelled on the Des Voeux Commission in British Guiana) is at (1875) Brit. Parl. Papers, col. 1115.
117 Ibid., 105–11. See also Deryk Scarr, *Fiji: A Short History* (Sydney: Allen & Unwin, 1984).
118 Ibid., 104–5.
119 Ibid., 115–20.
120 Ibid., 121.
121 Ibid., 127–30.
122 Ibid., 131–2. An example is *Aromasi v. G.B. Evans and J. Rannie, Fiji Argus,* 27 July 1877. In this case he found in favour of Fijian labourers, tricked into a work contract with a planter, and asserted that Fijian evidence was as valid and reliable as that of whites.
123 Ibid., 159–92.

124 Ibid., 159–61. See, for a detailed discussion of this matter as both a legal and political issue in Queensland, Wiener, *Empire on Trial*, 39–60.

125 Brereton, *Law, Justice and Empire*, 161–3. On the Western Pacific Commission, see Deryk Scarr, *Fragments of Empire: A History of the Western Pacific High Commission, 1877–1914* (Canberra: Australian National University Press, 1967).

126 See, for example, the attempt to prosecute successfully W.J. Hunt, an Englishman in Samoa, charged with murder by lynching of an American citizen. In the opinion of the British government, Samoa had an 'organized' government, and treaties with 'civilized' powers, namely Germany and the United States. Brereton, *Law, Justice and Empire*, 164–7.

127 Ibid., 168–83.

128 Ibid., 181–2. On the regulatory and humanitarian motivations of Royal Navy officers in the Pacific, see Jane Samson, *Imperial Benevolence: Making British Authority in the Pacific Islands* (Honolulu: University of Hawaii Press, 1998).

129 See Stanley James ('Vagabond'), *Vox Populi: British Despotism in the South Sea Islands* (Wellington, 1883), 12–17.

130 'Vagabond's' views were given some currency at the Inter-Colonial Conference of the Australasian Colonies in 1881, when several of his newspaper articles were copied in an appendix to the conference report. The latter contained a resolution that appeals in capital cases from the High Commission's Court should lie to the Supreme Court of one of the Australian colonies, rather than to that of Fiji. Brereton, *Law, Justice and Empire*, 189.

131 Ibid., 190–1.

132 See text supra, 252–3, 262–3. E.F. im Thurn, rev. Lynn Milne, 'George William Des Voeux,' *ODNB*, http://www.oxforddnb.com.ezproxy.library.uvic.ca/view/article/32795.

133 Brereton, *Law, Justice and Empire*, 142.

134 Ibid., 144.

135 Ibid., 148–9.

136 Ibid., 149–58. In 1881 Gorrie had received a knighthood.

137 Ibid., 193–8.

138 See H. Wrong, *Government of the West Indies* (New York: Greenwood, 1969), 145–55.

139 Brereton reveals that Gorrie's enemies in Fiji and the South Pacific made sure that his reputation preceded him to the Caribbean, not least the attacks against him by the 'Vagabond.' Brereton *Law, Justice and Empire*, 198.

140 Ibid., 199–201. The other two judges on the Leeward Islands' bench, Semper and Pemberton, were opposed to centralization of the justice system.
141 Ibid., 202–5. For an example of Gorrie's felt need to protect the poor and uneducated blacks, see *Queen v. Mary Donaldson*, *Antigua Observer*, 21 May 1884, excerpted at ibid, 205–6. This involved a trial of the accused for the murder of her infant.
142 Ibid., 205–11. As the local press on the various islands had it, Gorrie was guilty of invariably casting Europeans as oppressors in their dealings with members of the black and coloured communities, rushing through cases, inconsistency in judgments, and bullying both counsel and court officials.
143 Ibid., 211–18.
144 Ibid., 218–20.
145 Ibid., 226. He was sent off with the predictable ungenerous comments of his enemies in the press, and a petition in his favour, praising his administration of justice in the islands, signed by 600 souls.
146 Brereton, *History of Modern Trinidad*, 52–75, 136–56. On the composition of the Council, including both government officials and nominated 'unofficials,' and subsequent changes to the mix, see ibid., 136–42.
147 Ibid., 138.
148 The chief justice does not receive an entry in the *ODNB*, although his journalist brother, James Scotland, who was also opposed to slavery, does.
149 Documents relating to these incidents may be found in Lionel Mordaunt Fraser, *A History of Trinidad*, vol. 2, *From 1814 to 1839* (Port-of-Spain, TRIN: Government Printing Office, 1896), 276–85. In his comments it is clear that Fraser was sympathetic to the planters. See also CO 295, vol. 93/2, 1832.
150 Brereton, *History of Trinidad*, 100–6; and Look Lai, *Indentured Labour*, 87–141.
151 Brereton, *Law, Justice and Empire*, 227–8.
152 Brereton, *History of Modern Trinidad*, 153–6.
153 On the Trinidad and Tobago phase of Gorrie's career, see Brereton, *Law, Justice and Empire*, 227–314.
154 Ibid., 229–31, 262–3. An action *in forma pauperis* allowed an indigent person to proceed with a claim, though lacking the normal fiscal resources to press it. There were widespread complaints that under Gorrie's predecessor, Joseph Needham, a man more drawn to his cocoa estate than his judicial duties, there was no room in the Supreme Court system for ordinary people, and little justice from the magistrates exercising civil jurisdiction.
155 Ibid., 259–63.

156 Ibid., 235–8. The minister was not pleased by the judge's attack on the competence of the police surgeon and even mused about his removal. CO 295, vol. 315, no. 256, secretary of state, Sir Henry Holland, to Governor William Robinson, 8 Dec. 1887. The Bar was sufficiently exercised by Gorrie's antics in court, especially his rudeness, that they pressed for the appointment of third judge.

157 Ibid., 238. The judge was capable of berating a jury when they reached what he considered perverse verdicts, not least in cases where he suspected them of racial discrimination.

158 Ibid., 240–2.

159 Ibid., 239–40.

160 Ibid., 267–70, 275–8.

161 His treatment in this case induced Anderson to launch an action against the three Trinidad judges before the Court of Queen's Bench in England. See infra, note 179.

162 An account of Anderson's battles with the judges is set out in Patrick Polden, 'Doctor in Trouble: *Anderson v. Gorrie* and the Extension of Judicial Immunity from Suite in the 1890s,' *Journal of Legal History* 22 (2001): 37–68, at 40–4.

163 Brereton, *Law, Justice and Empire*, 244–5, 284–5, 296–9, for the reverence in which he was held in the black Creole and mixed-race communities. On the views and tactics of the judge's detractors, see ibid., 240–58, 267–78.

164 Ibid., 274–5.

165 Ibid., 289–93. The legislation was the Agricultural Contracts Ordinance (1889) 50 Vict., No. 9. Gorrie did not like the fact that local magistrates had jurisdiction over disputes between planters and small holders.

166 On the banking venture, see Brereton, *History of Modern Trinidad*, 294–6.

167 Ibid., 286–96.

168 For the process of the commission, from which Gorrie largely absented himself, see ibid., 300–6, and for the conclusions of the commissioners, ibid., 306–10, and Judicial Inquiry Commission, *Trinidad Royal Gazette*, 27 June 1892.

169 The denouement is described in ibid., 310–14.

170 Gorrie and his judicial colleagues in the Supreme Court of the colony were the subjects of a lawsuit brought by doctor/planter, R.A. Anderson, alleging judicial misfeasance in requiring him to put up bail that was much larger than the debt he owed and in imprisoning him when he failed to comply. The decision of the Court of Queen's Bench, affirmed on appeal, was that the action of the judges was oppressive and malicious to the

prejudice of the plaintiff and to the justice system, but that as judges they were immune from suit for their conduct in a judicial capacity. *Anderson v. Gorrie* [1895] 1 Q.B. 668 (C.A.). See Polden, 'Doctor in Trouble,' 37–68.

171 Brereton, *Law, Justice and Empire*, 69, 191–2.

172 Ibid., 311–14, 319–25.

173 See, for example, Bridget Brereton, *Race Relations in Colonial Trinidad 1870–1900* (Cambridge: Cambridge University Press, 1979). Brereton does point out that, even under these conditions, subject populations were able by self-advancement through education to lay the basis for challenging 'the divine right of colonial whites to rule.'

174 Ibid. Even judges who were viewed as rocking the colonial boat on more prosaic issues were not immune to executive pressure to comply or forfeit office. See the story of the two successive chief justices of the Bahamas who were forced out of office in the 1890s after spats with the colonial executive and through the influence of Joseph Chamberlain, secretary of state for the colonies in the second half of the decade. Wiener, *Empire on Trial*, 115–27.

11: Judges, Courts, and Empire

1 It is noticeable, for instance, that in Porter, *Oxford History of the British Empire: Nineteenth Century*, although there is perfunctory reference to constitutionalism, law, and the administration of justice in the empire, there is no single chapter or even a long passage that seeks to address these issues more generically.

2 William Cornish et al., *Oxford History of the Laws of England*, 11:32–3.

3 Ibid., 486–522.

4 Arthurs, '*Without the Law*.'

5 Cornish et al., *Oxford History of the Laws of England*, 11:495 (the issue of whether parliamentary privilege extended to libel outside the Commons); 11:387–8 (the efforts of atheist Charles Bradlaugh to take a seat in the Commons).

6 Ibid., 11:971–4; Duman, *Judicial Bench in England*, 96–104.

7 R.B. Stevens, *Law and Politics: The House of Lords as a Political Body, 1800–1976* (Chapel Hill, NC: University of North Carolina Press, 1979), 84. Stevens has argued elsewhere (*English Judges*, 9) that a more apt description of the British constitution is a balance of powers, rather than their separation. Given the overlap between the judiciary and the Upper House, not to mention that between the executive and Parliament, the point is well taken.

8 Duman, *Judicial Bench in England*, 102–4; Shetreet, *Judges on Trial*, 145.
9 Shetreet, *Judges on Trial*, 14–15.
10 Kostal, *Jurisprudence of Power*.
11 Supra chapter 2, and chapter 3.
12 Chapter 4, chapter 6, chapter 9, and chapter 10.
13 Chapter 5.
14 Ibid.
15 Chapter 9, and chapter 10.
16 Chapter 6, chapter 7, and chapter 8.
17 Chapter 4, 83–4, 86–7.
18 Chapter 3, 39–42, chapter 9, and chapter 10.
19 Chapter 10, 261–2.
20 Benton, *Search for Sovereignty*, 279.
21 Ibid.
22 Radicals and reformers in Upper Canada; convicts in Australia; *Patriotes* and Creoles in former French territories, Quebec and Grenada; the subject peoples of India and Africa, slaves in the West Indies and Indian Ocean colonies, indentured workers there and in Oceania; and Aboriginal communities wherever they existed.
23 Porter, 'Introduction,' 10–15.
24 Greenwood, *Legacies of Fear*, 27–34.
25 Chapter 10, 261–2.
26 Porter, 'Introduction,' 20–2.
27 Chapter 4.
28 Chapter 10.
29 B.H. McPherson, *Reception of English Law Abroad* (Brisbane: Supreme Court of Queensland Library, 2007), 470–1.
30 Chapter 9, 234–44, and chapter 10, 248–63.
31 Chapter 5.
32 See, for example, chapter 9, 239–40, for the dissension between Jeffery Hart Bent and his associate justices.
33 Chapter 6, chapter 7, and chapter 8.
34 Chapter 9 and chapter 10.
35 Bilder, *Transatlantic Constitution*, 2, 39, 116–22.
36 Chapter 9, 220.
37 Chapter 5, 98.
38 Chapter 2, 11.
39 Manning, *British Colonial Government after the American Revolution*, 100–26.
40 See Marquis, 'In Defence of Liberty,' 69; Neal, *Rule of Law in a Penal Colony*, 61–83.

41 O'Shaughnessy, *Empire Divided*, 116–21.
42 Marquis, 'In Defence of Liberty,' 69; Neal, *Rule of Law*, 6–83.
43 McLaren, 'Uses of the Rule of Law,' 71–90.
44 Brymner, *Report on Canadian Archives*, 61–4, Gore to William Windham, undersecretary Colonial Office, 13 Mar. 1807.
45 Bennett, *Sir Francis Forbes*, 74–5.
46 Chapter 4, 80–2.
47 Chapter 9, 220–2.
48 Ibid., 239, and chapter 10, 269. The concentration of too much power in the judiciary was something that worried James Stephen Jr. See his testimony before the Canada Committee of the British House of Commons in 1828. Knapland, *James Stephen and the British Colonial System*, 60–1.
49 Chapter 5.
50 Chapter 10, 250–2. Governors were also often seen as having the final say in who was appointed to the colonial bureaucracy, including court officials, despite the claims of the judges that this function fell exclusively to them.
51 Chapter 4, 79–83.
52 Chapter 8.
53 Chapter 9, 240, and chapter 10, 270–1.
54 See, for example, Sidney J. Harring, *White Man's Law: Native People in Canadian Jurisprudence* (Toronto: University of Toronto Press for Osgoode Society for Canadian Legal History, 1998); Kercher, *Unruly Child*, 3–21.
55 See chapter 5, 92–8, and chapter 9, 220–5.
56 Karsten, *Between Law and Custom*.
57 Chapter 4, 75, and chapter 10, 249–50.
58 Chapter 9, 239–40. Willis's problems in the Port Phillip District reflect in part his lack of patience with what he saw as the slovenly practices and lack of etiquette of some lawyers who appeared before him. Chapter 7, 179.
59 Chapter 4, 75, and chapter 10, 268.
60 Chapter 10, 270.
61 See, for example, for Upper Canada, Craig, *Upper Canada*, 200; and Neal, *Rule of Law*, 20–1, for the rather more modest pace in New South Wales.
62 *Willis v. Gipps, Respondent's Case*, 4, and *Appellant's Case*, Appendix, 53–4, letter from the Sydney Supreme Court judges to Lord Stanley, secretary of state for the colonies, 2 Oct. 1842, and extract from *Port Phillip Patriot*, 18 Aug. 1842.
63 Finn, *Chronicles of Early Melbourne*, 67.
64 See, for example, Boulton in Newfoundland, chapter 5, 110–11, and Beaumont in British Guiana, chapter 10, 257–9.

65 Chapter 7.

66 Ibid., 182.

67 Andrew Porter, 'Religion, Missionary Enthusiasm, and Empire,' in Porter, *Oxford History of the British Empire: The Nineteenth Century*, 222–46, at 225–9.

68 See, for instance, the influence of the Presbyterians in New South Wales under the leadership of Andrew Dunmore Lang, in Gregory, *Church and State*, 5–43, and of the Methodists led by Egerton Ryerson in Upper Canada, in William Westfall, *Two Worlds: The Protestant Culture of Nineteenth Century Ontario* (Montreal and Kingston: McGill-Queen's University Press, 1989), 3–49.

69 Bennett, *Sir William a'Becket*, 41–2; Currey, *Sir Francis Forbes*, 427–36.

70 Chapter 5, 93.

71 Bennett, *Sir John Pedder*, 110.

72 Bennett, *Sir James Dowling*, 112; Gregory, *Church and State*, 30.

73 Chapter 9, 236–7.

74 Chapter 5, 107.

75 Gary Mooney S.J., 'Diplomatic Relations with the Holy See 1793–1830,' *Recusant History* 14 (1978): 193–210, at 204–5.

76 On the two-centuries-old reasons for the lack of official channels between the British government and the Vatican, see Mooney, 'Diplomatic Relations,' 194, and for the tortuous process of communication between the two, Matthias Buschkuhl, *Great Britain and the Holy See 1746–1870* (Dublin: Irish Academic, 1982), 15–82.

77 Neatby, *Quebec*, 125–41.

78 Ouellet, *Lower Canada*, 29–51.

79 Colonial governments provided support for priests, such as in New South Wales – Gregory, *Church and State*, 8 – and in Grenada – CO 101, vol. 68, 1828, 102–3, An Act for Granting a Salary to the Reverend Anthony O'Hannan, Roman Catholic Clergyman in This Government, 18 Nov. 1828 (Gren.).

80 Fitzgerald, 'Conflict and Culture,' ii–iii. In Newfoundland full Catholic emancipation came with the grant of representative government in August 1832.

81 Craig, *Upper Canada*, 169.

82 Chapter 9, 243.

83 Chapter 5, 120.

84 See, for example, Heuman, 'British West Indies' 480–1; Madhavi Kale, '"When the Saints Come Marching In": The Anti-Slavery Society and Indian Indentured Migration to the British Caribbean,' in *Empire and Others: British Encounters with Indigenous Peoples, 1600–1850*, ed. Martin Daunton

and Rick Halpern, 125–45 (Philadelphia: University of Pennsylvania Press, 1999).

85 Chapter 10, 257, 270.

86 This is a point made in Rizzetti, 'Sifting to the Bottom,' 98.

87 This was true, for example, of Chief Justice Joseph Needham in Trinidad, and the man who had replaced him as chief justice of the combined colonies of British Columbia and Vancouver Island, Matthew Baillie Begbie. Both of them seem to have prospered as a result. See Brereton, *Law, Justice and Empire*, 229; David R. Williams, *'Man for a New Country,'* 185.

88 Chapter 7, 164–5.

89 Ibid.

90 Chapter 9, 219, note 10.

91 Chapter 8, 194, 198–9, 204–6.

92 Barry, 'John Walpole Willis,' *ADBOL*. See also chapter 7.

93 Howell, 'Van Diemen's Land Judge Storm,' 253.

94 Chapter 10.

95 Chapter 7, 176, 178, 187, and chapter 9, 221.

96 On changing notions of the 'gentleman,' see Perkin, *Origins of Modern English Society*, 273–5, 278, 298.

97 Chapter 9, 235. Craving an appointment to an Indian judgeship was to cause Jeffery Hart Bent to delay departing for Grenada in 1819, where he had been appointed chief justice. Currey, *Brothers Bent*, 156.

98 A further incentive may have been the fact that in some of these territories, the salary for the chief justice was high, perhaps reflecting an element of danger pay. John Jeffcott, the sixth chief justice of Sierra Leone, was paid £2,000 per annum in the 1830s, the same as Chief Justice Forbes in New South Wales. See Hague, *Sir John Jeffcott*, 7.

99 Chapter 5, 106–7.

100 Chapter 9, 227.

101 Chapter 7, 171.

102 Chapter 10, 263–5.

103 For examples of the literature, see Hall, *Civilizing Subjects*; Laidlaw, *Colonial Connections 1815–45*; Lambert and Lester, *Colonial Lives across the British Empire*.

104 Many of these letters are collected in Bennett, *Some Papers of Sir Francis Forbes*.

105 Ibid., 'Editor's Introduction,' ix.

106 Ibid.

107 Ibid., x–xii.

108 Brereton, *Law, Justice and Empire*.

109 Ibid., 83–5, 104–5.
110 Of many references, see, for example, ibid., 187–8, on Gorrie's work with the Western Pacific Commission. There were other less prosaic and helpful connections between colonial judges and important patrons. John Walpole Willis, for instance, was both a hunter and amateur naturalist. He had an ongoing correspondence on the natural world with several people, including Edward Smith Stanley (later the Thirteenth Earl of Derby), sometime Whig member of Parliament, and passionate naturalist. Laidlaw, *Colonial Connections*, 33–4. The Thirteenth Earl was the father of Smith Stanley, later Lord Stanley, secretary of state for the colonies, and later still, Lord Derby, Tory prime minister. This connection did nothing to further the Willis career as a colonial judge.
111 Chapter 5, 105, and chapter 6, 150–5.
112 Chapter 10, 263–71.
113 K.J. Allars, 'William Westbrooke Burton,' *ADBOL*, http://www.adb.online.anu.edu.au/biogs/A010171b.htm?hilite=william;burton.
114 Kercher, *Unruly Child*, 116–17. In another context, in the draconian bushranging legislation introduced in New South Wales, Burton dissented from his brethren, including Forbes, on the ground that the statute was repugnant to the Law of England – a sign that a conservative stance could result in greater protection of individual rights (ibid., 106–7).
115 Chapter 4, 69–70.
116 Chapter 10, 229–31, and chapter 7, 172–85.
117 Chapter 9, 235–42.
118 Chapter 6, 130–40.
119 T. Oalawale Elias, *British Colonial Law: A Comparative Study of the Interaction between English and Local Laws in British Dependencies* (London: Stevens & Sons, 1962), 59–69. See also Kenneth Roberts-Wray, *Commonwealth and Colonial Law* (London: Stevens & Sons, 1966), 495–8.
120 Elias, *British Colonial Law*, 59–60.
121 Wiener, *Empire on Trial*, 1–19.
122 Ibid., 197–9, 203, 210.
123 Ibid., 209.
124 Ibid., 232–3.
125 Benton, *Law and Colonial Cultures*, 253–65.
126 *Memorandum of the Lords of the Council on the Removal of Colonial Judges* (1870) 12 Moore's Indian Appeals 551 (Appendix); 20 E.R. 447 (Appendix). The Appendix is numbered 9–16.
127 Ibid., 10–11.
128 Ibid., 10.

129 Ibid., 12–13.
130 Ibid., 13.
131 Ibid., 12–13.
132 Ibid., 15.
133 Chapter 9, 231, and chapter 6, 136.
134 *Terrell v. Secretary of State for the Colonies* [1953] 2 Q.B. 482. Because of the exigencies of warfare, the plaintiff, a member of the Supreme Court of Malaya, who had been on holiday in Australia when the Japanese army invaded the peninsula, lost his position. Rather than reassign him for the relatively short period before compulsory retirement, the secretary of state determined that he should be removed from office immediately.
135 Lord Chief Justice Goddard concluded that the Act of Settlement did not apply to colonial judges who, like Terrell, were appointed at pleasure.
136 An Act to Revise the Statute Law by Repealing Obsolete, Spent, Unnecessary and Superseded Enactments (1964) 12 & 13 Eliz. II, c. 79.
137 In the case of the Canadian colonies, the power had been subject to an appeal by the jurist to the Privy Council. Lederman, 'Independence of the Judiciary,' 1150–6.
138 Chapter 8, 202–3.
139 Reference was made to this position of the imperial government in the *Memorandum* of 1870. Mention was made of the need 'to protect Judges against the party and personal feelings that sometimes sway Colonial Legislatures' (at 10).
140 Chapter 8, 209.
141 British North America Act (1867) 30 & 31 Vict., c. 3.
142 Commonwealth of Australia Constitution Act (1900) 63 & 64 Vict., c. 12.
143 Lederman, 'Independence of the Judiciary,' 1163; Bennett and Castles, *Sourcebook of Australian Legal History*, 342. Castles notes that Burke's Act was never used again in Australia after the Boothby case.
144 Nathan Brun, 'It Was Not Easy for the British Empire to Fire a Judge from Haifa (Palestine, 1925–1930)' (unpublished paper, British Legal History Conference, Oxford, 2–5 July 2007). I am indebted to Professor Brun for sending me a copy of his paper.
145 Chapter 8, 202–3, 209.
146 Brun, 'It Was Not Easy,' 6–7, referencing NAUK, Lord Chancellor's Records (LCO) 2/3229.
147 Ibid., 7, referencing CO 854/73/60/180.
148 In Zimbabwe, President Mugabe has reduced the judiciary to the status of ciphers for government policies, first through intimidation, and then, when he had rid himself of independent judges, by appointing his sup-

porters. See Derek Maytsak, 'Creating a Compliant Judiciary in Zimbabwe, 2000–2003,' in *Appointing Judges in an Age of Judicial Power*, ed. Kate Malleson and Peter H. Russell, 331–54 (Toronto: University of Toronto Press, 2006); and 'Mugabe Unilaterally Appoints Judges as MDC Cries Foul,' *SW Radio Africa*, 21 May 2010. In Pakistan, former president Musharaff fired Chief Justice Chaudry in 2007 for decisions uncomfortable for his military government. In 2009 the new democratically elected government reinstated the jurist. See 'Pakistan Reinstates Sacked Judge,' *BBC News*, 16 Mar. 2009.

149 Brian Z. Tamanaha, *On the Rule of Law: History, Politics, Theory* (Cambridge: Cambridge University Press, 2004), 122–6.

150 See, for example, Peter H. Russell and David M. O'Brien, eds., *Judicial Independence in an Age of Democracy: Critical Perspectives from around the World* (Charlottesville: University Press of Virginia, 2001), esp. Robert Stevens, 'Judicial Independence in England: A Loss of Innocence,' 155–72; and John Williams, 'Judicial Independence in Australia,' 173–93.

151 See Philip Girard, *Bora Laskin: Bringing Law to Life* (Toronto: University of Toronto Press for Osgoode Society for Canadian Legal History, 2005), 516–27, for discussion of the 'Berger Affair.'

152 See Philip Slayton, 'The Professional Death Penalty,' *Canadian Lawyer* (Sept. 2008): 33–5, for the panel's decision, and the *Toronto Star*, 3 Dec. 2008, for news of the reprieve.

Index

PUBLICATIONS OF THE OSGOODE SOCIETY FOR CANADIAN LEGAL HISTORY

2011 Robert J. Sharpe, *The Lazier Murder: Prince Edward County, 1884*
Philip Girard, *Lawyers and Legal Culture in British North America: Beamish Murdoch of Halifax*
John McLaren, *Dewigged, Bothered, and Bewildered: British Colonial Judges on Trial, 1800–1900*
Lesley Erickson, *Westward Bound: Sex, Violence, the Law, and the Making of a Settler Society*

2010 Judy Fudge and Eric Tucker, eds., *Work on Trial: Canadian Labour Law Struggles*
Christopher Moore, *The British Columbia Court of Appeal: The First Hundred Years*
Frederick Vaughan, *Viscount Haldane: 'The Wicked Step-father of the Canadian Constitution'*
Barrington Walker, *Race on Trial: Black Defendants in Ontario's Criminal Courts, 1858–1958*

2009 William Kaplan, *Canadian Maverick: The Life and Times of Ivan C. Rand*
R. Blake Brown, *A Trying Question: The Jury in Nineteenth-Century Canada*
Barry Wright and Susan Binnie, eds., *Canadian State Trials, Volume III: Political Trials and Security Measures, 1840–1914*
Robert J. Sharpe, *The Last Day, the Last Hour: The Currie Libel Trial* (paperback edition with a new preface)

2008 Constance Backhouse, *Carnal Crimes: Sexual Assault Law in Canada, 1900–1975*
Jim Phillips, R. Roy McMurtry, and John T. Saywell, eds., *Essays in the History of Canadian Law, Volume X: A Tribute to Peter N. Oliver*
Greg Taylor, *The Law of the Land: The Advent of the Torrens System in Canada*
Hamar Foster, Benjamin Berger, and A.R. Buck, eds., *The Grand Experiment: Law and Legal Culture in British Settler Societies*

2007 Robert Sharpe and Patricia McMahon, *The Persons Case: The Origins and Legacy of the Fight for Legal Personhood*
Lori Chambers, *Misconceptions: Unmarried Motherhood and the Ontario Children of Unmarried Parents Act, 1921–1969*
Jonathan Swainger, ed., *A History of the Supreme Court of Alberta*
Martin Friedland, *My Life in Crime and Other Academic Adventures*

2006 Donald Fyson, *Magistrates, Police, and People: Everyday Criminal Justice in Quebec and Lower Canada, 1764–1837*

Dale Brawn, *The Court of Queen's Bench of Manitoba, 1870–1950: A Biographical History*
R.C.B. Risk, *A History of Canadian Legal Thought: Collected Essays*, edited and introduced by G. Blaine Baker and Jim Phillips

2005 Philip Girard, *Bora Laskin: Bringing Law to Life*
Christopher English, ed., *Essays in the History of Canadian Law: Volume IX – Two Islands: Newfoundland and Prince Edward Island*
Fred Kaufman, *Searching for Justice: An Autobiography*

2004 Philip Girard, Jim Phillips, and Barry Cahill, eds., *The Supreme Court of Nova Scotia, 1754–2004: From Imperial Bastion to Provincial Oracle*
Frederick Vaughan, *Aggressive in Pursuit: The Life of Justice Emmett Hall*
John D. Honsberger, *Osgoode Hall: An Illustrated History*
Constance Backhouse and Nancy Backhouse, *The Heiress versus the Establishment: Mrs Campbell's Campaign for Legal Justice*

2003 Robert Sharpe and Kent Roach, *Brian Dickson: A Judge's Journey*
Jerry Bannister, *The Rule of the Admirals: Law, Custom, and Naval Government in Newfoundland, 1699–1832*
George Finlayson, *John J. Robinette, Peerless Mentor: An Appreciation*
Peter Oliver, *The Conventional Man: The Diaries of Ontario Chief Justice Robert A. Harrison, 1856–1878*

2002 John T. Saywell, *The Lawmakers: Judicial Power and the Shaping of Canadian Federalism*
Patrick Brode, *Courted and Abandoned: Seduction in Canadian Law*
David Murray, *Colonial Justice: Justice, Morality, and Crime in the Niagara District, 1791–1849*
F. Murray Greenwood and Barry Wright, eds., *Canadian State Trials, Volume II: Rebellion and Invasion in the Canadas, 1837–1839*

2001 Ellen Anderson, *Judging Bertha Wilson: Law as Large as Life*
Judy Fudge and Eric Tucker, *Labour before the Law: The Regulation of Workers' Collective Action in Canada, 1900–1948*
Laurel Sefton MacDowell, *Renegade Lawyer: The Life of J.L. Cohen*

2000 Barry Cahill, *'The Thousandth Man': A Biography of James McGregor Stewart*
A.B. McKillop, *The Spinster and the Prophet: Florence Deeks, H.G. Wells, and the Mystery of the Purloined Past*
Beverley Boissery and F. Murray Greenwood, *Uncertain Justice: Canadian Women and Capital Punishment*
Bruce Ziff, *Unforeseen Legacies: Reuben Wells Leonard and the Leonard Foundation Trust*

1999 Constance Backhouse, *Colour-Coded: A Legal History of Racism in Canada, 1900–1950*
G. Blaine Baker and Jim Phillips, eds., *Essays in the History of Canadian Law: Volume VIII – In Honour of R.C.B. Risk*
Richard W. Pound, *Chief Justice W.R. Jackett: By the Law of the Land*
David Vanek, *Fulfilment: Memoirs of a Criminal Court Judge*
1998 Sidney Harring, *White Man's Law: Native People in Nineteenth-Century Canadian Jurisprudence*
Peter Oliver, *'Terror to Evil-Doers': Prisons and Punishments in Nineteenth-Century Ontario*
1997 James W.St.G. Walker, *'Race,' Rights and the Law in the Supreme Court of Canada: Historical Case Studies*
Lori Chambers, *Married Women and Property Law in Victorian Ontario*
Patrick Brode, *Casual Slaughters and Accidental Judgments: Canadian War Crimes and Prosecutions, 1944–1948*
Ian Bushnell, *The Federal Court of Canada: A History, 1875–1992*
1996 Carol Wilton, ed., *Essays in the History of Canadian Law: Volume VII – Inside the Law: Canadian Law Firms in Historical Perspective*
William Kaplan, *Bad Judgment: The Case of Mr Justice Leo A. Landreville*
Murray Greenwood and Barry Wright, eds., *Canadian State Trials: Volume I – Law, Politics, and Security Measures, 1608–1837*
1995 David Williams, *Just Lawyers: Seven Portraits*
Hamar Foster and John McLaren, eds., *Essays in the History of Canadian Law: Volume VI – British Columbia and the Yukon*
W.H. Morrow, ed., *Northern Justice: The Memoirs of Mr Justice William G. Morrow*
Beverley Boissery, *A Deep Sense of Wrong: The Treason, Trials, and Transportation to New South Wales of Lower Canadian Rebels after the 1838 Rebellion*
1994 Patrick Boyer, *A Passion for Justice: The Legacy of James Chalmers McRuer*
Charles Pullen, *The Life and Times of Arthur Maloney: The Last of the Tribunes*
Jim Phillips, Tina Loo, and Susan Lewthwaite, eds., *Essays in the History of Canadian Law: Volume V – Crime and Criminal Justice*
Brian Young, *The Politics of Codification: The Lower Canadian Civil Code of 1866*
1993 Greg Marquis, *Policing Canada's Century: A History of the Canadian Association of Chiefs of Police*
Murray Greenwood, *Legacies of Fear: Law and Politics in Quebec in the Era of the French Revolution*

1992 Brendan O'Brien, *Speedy Justice: The Tragic Last Voyage of His Majesty's Vessel Speedy*
Robert Fraser, ed., *Provincial Justice: Upper Canadian Legal Portraits from the Dictionary of Canadian Biography*
1991 Constance Backhouse, *Petticoats and Prejudice: Women and Law in Nineteenth-Century Canada*
1990 Philip Girard and Jim Phillips, eds., *Essays in the History of Canadian Law: Volume III – Nova Scotia*
Carol Wilton, ed., *Essays in the History of Canadian Law: Volume IV – Beyond the Law: Lawyers and Business in Canada, 1830–1930*
1989 Desmond Brown, *The Genesis of the Canadian Criminal Code of 1892*
Patrick Brode, *The Odyssey of John Anderson*
1988 Robert Sharpe, *The Last Day, the Last Hour: The Currie Libel Trial*
John D. Arnup, *Middleton: The Beloved Judge*
1987 C. Ian Kyer and Jerome Bickenbach, *The Fiercest Debate: Cecil A. Wright, the Benchers, and Legal Education in Ontario, 1923–1957*
1986 Paul Romney, *Mr Attorney: The Attorney General for Ontario in Court, Cabinet, and Legislature, 1791–1899*
Martin Friedland, *The Case of Valentine Shortis: A True Story of Crime and Politics in Canada*
1985 James Snell and Frederick Vaughan, *The Supreme Court of Canada: History of the Institution*
1984 Patrick Brode, *Sir John Beverley Robinson: Bone and Sinew of the Compact*
David Williams, *Duff: A Life in the Law*
1983 David H. Flaherty, ed., *Essays in the History of Canadian Law: Volume II*
1982 Marion MacRae and Anthony Adamson, *Cornerstones of Order: Courthouses and Town Halls of Ontario, 1784–1914*
1981 David H. Flaherty, ed., *Essays in the History of Canadian Law: Volume I*

PUBLICATIONS OF THE FRANCIS FORBES SOCIETY FOR AUSTRALIAN LEGAL HISTORY

2011 John McLaren, *Dewigged, Bothered, and Bewildered: British Colonial Judges on Trial, 1800–1900*

2009 Bruce Kercher and Brent Salter, *The Kercher Reports: Decisions of the New South Wales Superior Courts, 1788 to 1827*

2005 T.D. Castle and Bruce Kercher, *The Dowling Legacy: Foundations of an Australian Legal Culture, 1828–1844* (Forbes Lecture)
T.D. Castle and Bruce Kercher, eds., *Dowling's Select Cases, 1828 to 1844: Decisions of the Supreme Court of New South Wales*
J.M. Bennett, ed., *Callaghan's Diary: The 1840s Sydney Diary of Thomas Callaghan, BA of the King's Inns, Dublin, Barrister-at-Law*

2004 Hon. P.E. Powell, AM, QC, *The Origins and Development of the Protective Jurisdiction of the Supreme Court of New South Wales* (Forbes Lecture)

2003 Ian Barker, QC, *Sorely Tried: Democracy and Trial by Jury in New South Wales* (Forbes Lecture)

Publications may be obtained from the Society's agent: The Federation Press, PO Box 45, Annandale, NSW, 2038, Australia. Email: info@federationpress.com.au. Website: http://www.federationpress.com.au.

www.ingramcontent.com/pod-product-compliance
Lightning Source LLC
LaVergne TN
LVHW090758070826
844660LV00022B/1025

* 9 7 8 1 4 8 7 5 4 8 8 8 9 *